VOLUME 1

COMPUTER ARCHITECTURE

Software and Hardware

RICHARD Y. KAIN

Department of Electrical Engineering
University of Minnesota

PRENTICE HALL, Englewood Cliffs, New Jersey 07632

Library of Congress Cataloging-in-Publication Data

KAIN, RICHARD Y.
Computer architecture.

Includes bibliographies and indexes.
1. Computer architecture. 2. System design.
3. Ada (Computer program language) 4. Motorola 68020
(Microprocessor) I. Title.
QA76.9.A73K34 1989 004.2′2 87-35708
ISBN 0-13-166752-1 (v. 1)

Editorial/production supervision
and interior design: John Fleming
Cover design: Wanda Lubelska Design
Manufacturing buyer: Mary Noonan

A Division of Simon & Schuster
Englewood Cliffs, New Jersey 07632

Printed in the United States of America
10 9 8 7 6 5 4 3 2 1

ISBN 0-13-166752-1

Prentice-Hall International (UK) Limited, *London*
Prentice-Hall of Australia Pty. Limited, *Sydney*
Prentice-Hall Canada Inc., *Toronto*
Prentice-Hall Hispanoamericana, S.A., *Mexico*
Prentice-Hall of India Private Limited, *New Delhi*
Prentice-Hall of Japan, Inc., *Tokyo*
Simon & Schuster Asia Pte. Ltd., *Singapore*
Editora Prentice-Hall do Brasil, Ltda., *Rio de Janeiro*

TRADEMARK INFORMATION

To

my parents,

Louise and Richard Kain,

my wife,

Katherine,

and our children,

Helen Louise,

Karen,

Susan,

Matthew, and

Rachel.

CONTENTS

PREFACE

The man who sees two or three generations
is like one who sits in the conjurer's booth at a fair,
and sees the tricks two or three times.
They are meant to be seen only once.
— Schopenhauer

Schopenhauer suggested that tricks are repeated over generations and are meant to surprise the audience. Viewed from the other side, however, the magician must learn basic techniques before performing and astounding an audience. These techniques change little from one generation to the next. Computer design has progressed through several "generations;" the designers of successive generations have faced similar basic issues. Like the conjurer, the architect can choose from basic techniques developed in response to basic questions.

A recent book ([KLAP86], p. 112) suggests that one reason for the current "lag in meaning" is that people do not have enough time to ponder recent ideas. Despite the fact that time for "wondering" is time for finding new connections and relationships, the rapid introduction of new computer systems has kept designers busy meeting pressing deadlines, leaving them little time to wonder. The structure of this book has evolved over a number of years as I have wondered and developed ways to piece the design puzzle together. My belief that system design involves a combination of software and hardware has influenced the way I organized the material.

I hope that as designers ponder questions and devise solutions they will consider issues from all levels of design (such as software issues that affect hardware design). I have tried to illustrate such connections to motivate the specifications that might be dictated by software considerations. It would be a shame to have a processor design fail due to omissions relating to the true nature of the problem. I believe that a successful contemporary computer designer must be aware of many facets of programming languages, operating systems, and firmware considerations, in addition to the opportunities and limitations of the currently available hardware technology.

This book brings together in a common framework several levels of computer system design. Within this framework I collect issues and approaches from different levels if a common thread exists. My goal is to show the connectedness between the various design levels and, at the same time, to show how approaches from one level both limit and open new opportunities at other levels. The levels arise from the traditional compartmentalization that human beings impose upon computer system design problems. According to this view, a contemporary computer system is constructed from many interacting parts, including:

An application program
A compiler for a programming language
An operating system program managing the computer system
A system architecture
A processor architecture
A microprogrammed host machine

One reason for compartmentalizing the system is the enormous complexity of a contemporary computer system. It has become almost impossible for a single human being to be expert in the design issues and approaches that are faced at all system levels.

Yet I believe that by restructuring one's approach to the problem, one can regroup for a rational attack on the design problem. In particular, I believe that if one could focus on a single portion of the problem at several system levels one would see the common features of the design issues and approaches and be in a position to accumulate a set of solutions appropriate to the specific situation. Therefore, each of Chapters 3 through 7 of Volume 1 and 1 through 4 of Volume 2 focuses on a limited aspect of the system design problem. Chapters 1 and 2 of Volume 1 set the stage for the remainder of the book; Chapter 1 introduces the design problem along with some basic structural and quantitative notions. Chapter 2 introduces several processor designs, including a RISC (Reduced Instruction Set Computer) and the Motorola MC68020. In each of the remaining chapters I focus on a related set of issues, such as memory issues (Chapters 3 through 5, Volume 1), control issues (Chapter 6, Volume 1), object manipulation (Chapter 7, Volume 1), parallelism (Chapter 1, Volume 2), message passing (Chapter 2, Volume 2), object sharing (Chapter 3, Volume 2), and computer security (Chapter 4, Volume 2). Each of these discussions starts with a description of the types of problems faced by designers working in a particular niche, followed by a collection of approaches, described in reasonably general terms. I believe that this collection illustrates the common approaches and the interrelationships between the choices made at different levels. Following the collection of common approaches, I discuss the design issue at different system levels, starting with the requirements imposed by programming languages and ending with the host architecture.

I do not move to the gate level of design, since numerous books adequately cover that level. At the end of some chapters there is a section describing some interesting features of a particular nonstandard design. In this fashion, I cover the implementation of associative memories (Section 5.7, Volume 1), Prolog's unique control structure (Section 6.5, Volume 1), list-processing architectures (Section 7.5, Volume 1), data flow architectures (Section 2.6, Volume 2), and secure system design (Section 4.4, Volume 2). The design of more conventional systems is covered in a distributed manner throughout the topic-oriented chapters.

Because of its length, the book has been divided into two volumes. It was written with the expectation that the reader would start at the beginning and progress toward the end without too much interruption in the flow. Uniprocessor designs are found in the first volume, and designs using multiple execution streams and multiple processors in the second. The chapter covering computer security is placed in the second volume (Chapter 4) because it covers topics that arise from the resource-sharing models presented in Chapter 3 of Volume 2. Volume 1 contains the Appendices (which cover details of Ada and the Motorola MC68020). Volume 2 contains the chapters about designs with multiple control streams and designs of secure computer systems. These areas are the focus of recent innovations in computer architecture.

What background do you, the reader, need? I believe that a person familiar with any aspect of computers should be able to read portions of this book and gain valuable information. Previous experience with a high-level programming language may not be necessary but would be helpful (I introduce their features and designs, albeit piecemeal, in the text). Similarly, previous experience with operating systems issues is not necessary, but knowing some operating systems problems and approaches would be helpful.

I developed this material as I taught a graduate course to electrical engineering and computer science students interested in computer system architecture. I believe that this material can be taught to computer science students at the senior level, since knowing electronics, logic design, or VLSI design is not necessary to understand this book.

I believe that Volume 1 can be covered comfortably in one semester by skipping some of the specialized sections at the end of Chapters 5, 6, and 7 if readers already know something about high-level language programming. Volume 2 plus the specialized sections could be covered in another semester. Either volume could be supplemented with material concerning the design of a machine to which the students have access.

Throughout the book I use examples taken from various programming languages, processor designs, and system architectures. I believe that by showing diverse examples I can convince the reader of common features and show that certain design alternatives are realistic (because they have been used in a real system). If you, the reader, are actually asked to create a design, do not take an arbitrarily selected option from the book and apply it with the expectation that it will necessarily satisfy all your needs. After all, your environment is probably not the same as the one faced by the design team that devised the option. If it is, then perhaps you, the designer, should consider purchasing a solution for your problem. If you have to design a system, you will need to know the benefits and costs involved with each design approach. I have directly mentioned some benefits and costs, and others are hinted at, sometimes in an example or in a problem at the end of the chapter.

The majority of the examples I use to illustrate points and to show how the general approaches have been applied in "real" designs come from computers designed in the United States. This bias arose simply because detailed information about American computer designs is more readily available to me. I have chosen to use Ada as the principal programming language for examples of language features because Ada is a contemporary language design that incorporates many features which illustrate design issues that may affect other levels of the system design. I do not expect that every reader knows Ada. I have included a summary of many Ada features in Appendix A, so that you can read and understand that Ada programs included in the text. Other Ada features are introduced in examples throughout the text. I have chosen the Motorola MC68020 processor as the principal source of processor examples because this contemporary processor design includes many features that directly support the operating system and the implementation of features taken from high-level programming languages. Many features of the MC68020 are described in Chapter 2 of Volume 1 along with features of the Berkeley Reduced Instruction Set Computers (RISCs). The Berkeley RISC designs include a number of performance-enhancement features found previously only in more complex processors. Other processor examples illustrate machine features from many American computer companies, including some obsolete, but historically important, designs.

By not choosing a particular single design, a single language, or a single application area, I have tried to make the book relatively independent of the implementation technology. The design choices presented in the text cover a spectrum of situations. If you are a designer, I think that you can find something that applies to your situation. If you are an instructor, I think that you can appreciate the commonalities illustrated by the book's structure, and that you can enhance the student's understanding of these points by illustrating them with features taken from computer systems familiar to your students. If you are a student, I think you will learn to appreciate the problems faced by designers at all levels and their solutions. I hope that all readers will see the connections between different aspects of the complex issues related to computer system design.

Richard Y. Kain
Minneapolis, Minnesota

ACKNOWLEDGMENTS

I thank my students and colleagues, some of whom have acted as my teachers, for their thoughts, support, and encouragement while this project was in the works. I thank the many students in my computer architecture classes over the years this book has been in the making; they have tolerated many incomplete and sketchy drafts of this text as it evolved to its present form.

I would like to extend special thanks to Earl Boebert, Rich Enbody, Tom Haigh, Magdy Hanna, and Sami Saydjari, who gave me detailed comments that impacted the presentation or approach in one or more chapters. The book's presentation has improved as a result of many contributions from them as well as from numerous unnamed individuals.

I thank the University of Minnesota for permitting me to teach the evolving computer architecture courses on which this book is based and for their support during a sabbatical year during which I was able to improve the draft markedly.

I thank the staff at Prentice Hall, especially John McCanna and Jim Fegen, who had the courage to sign me up and the patience to wait for me to finally finish this project. Their help and the help of John Fleming lightened my shoulders.

I thank my family, who have endured as I spent inordinate time on this project. They have put up with my repeated deferrals—the phrase "when the book is finished" is all too familiar to them.

I thank Matthew Frank for special emergency help in copying the disks holding the manuscript into a format that could be used by the typesetters; without this help, production might have been delayed, proofreading would have been more arduous, and there might have been more errors.

I especially thank my wife, Katherine Simon Frank, for her continuing support and encouragement as I have worked to put the finishing touches on the draft. Without her help and encouragement, this book would not have been completed this quickly.

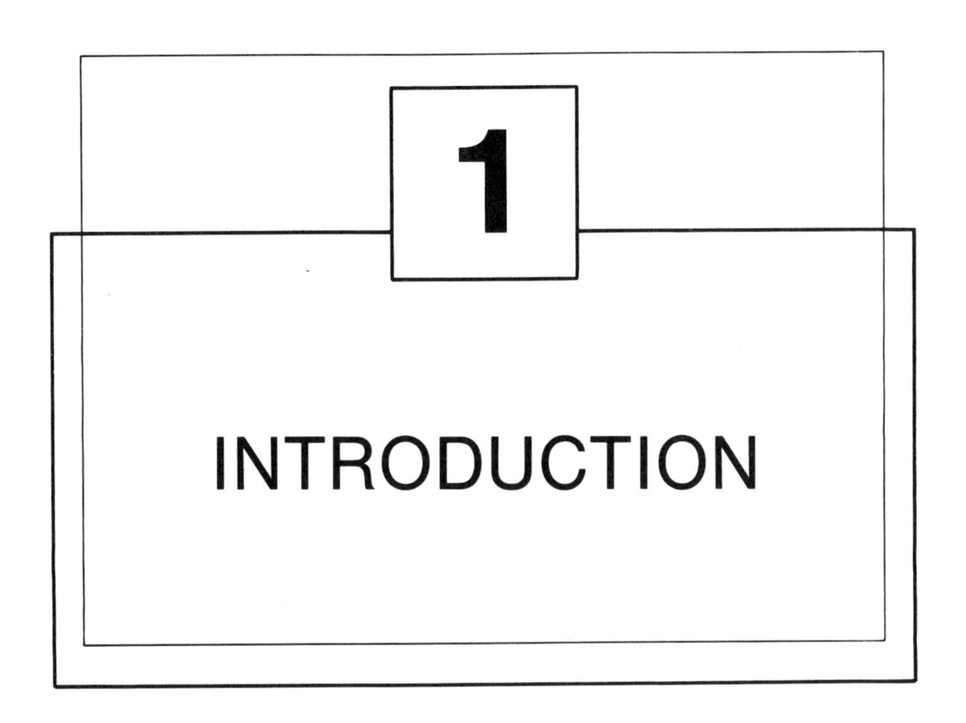

All architecture is what you do to it
when you look upon it.
— Walt Whitman

Computers command an increasing role in our daily lives; they support diverse applications, including production-line control, word processing, and weather forecasting. Technological improvements have made the "personal" computer economically possible; these computers have operational capabilities exceeding those of the most advanced computers of the 1950s, yet cost less by a factor of over 10,000! Computers have even replaced people as the most significant occurrence of the year [TIME83].

Computer systems are implemented using hardware, software, and firmware, orchestrated to perform the system's function. In this book we describe techniques used to structure and interrelate hardware, firmware, and software, paying particular attention to designs that have played important roles. Two major theses structure our views and explain many developments in computer system design.

The first thesis holds that the system's functions can be implemented at any level of this implementation hierarchy, and that an implementation pushed closer to the hardware will often perform more efficiently than one that implements the functionality in software alone. If one believes this thesis, one tries to move support for commonly performed functions closer to the hardware level to increase system performance. At the same time, this move may increase the cost of the system.

Our second thesis holds that certain basic design and implementation strategies can be useful at different levels of the implementation hierarchy. Historically, some designs were initially developed at the hardware level and moved toward the software level. It is more common, however, for designs developed at the software level to move toward the hardware level. We shall see many instances of this pattern in the book.

A significant consequence of these two theses is that an intelligent system design results from having an understanding of many design options from the different levels and from knowing how to select a design for each level such that the levels are compatible with each other. Our presentation is biased toward showing many interrelationships and common design features among the system implementation levels so that the reader can come to understand the traditional design options and the interrelationships among the hierarchical design levels.

In this chapter we present an approach to structuring systems using modules as the basic building blocks. We show how some representative system designs function. We discuss some criteria that are used to compare designs; among these the performance criterion often influences system design. We show different approaches to system modularization.

After reading this chapter, you should understand why certain design decisions are made. You should know the basic ideas behind virtual machines. In short, you should be prepared for the remainder of the book. And you will briefly meet the chief players in our examples—the languages and systems that we use to illustrate our points.

In the remainder of the book we study computer system design spanning the range from software to hardware, showing the relationships among the design issues and options from software to hardware. We do this in the following order. In Chapters 2 through 7 we explore the design of nonparallel systems, first their instruction sets (Chapter 2), then their memories (covering naming in Chapter 3, allocation in Chapter 4, and accessing in Chapter 5), their control sections (Chapter 6), and their object manipulation units (Chapter 7). In Chapters 1 through 3 of Volume 2 we explore the use of parallelism to enhance system performance, first by synchronous parallelism (Chapter 1), then by passing messages among cooperating entities (Chapter 2), and finally, by sharing resources (Chapter 3). We complete the study with an overview of secure computer systems, which are designed to prohibit illegal accesses in accordance with a specified security policy (Chapter 4 of Volume 2); some of these designs are biased to enhance understandability and to ease proofs that the system does meet its design specifications.

1.1 STRUCTURE

A realistic computer system design requires a combination of hardware and software. Software implements high-level functions, such as applications software and system programs. On the other hand, basic hardware implements simple logical functions such as AND, OR, and NOT. Firmware—between software and hardware—assists in the implementation of the software functions by providing an intermediate-level "virtual" machine which is neither the application nor the hardwired structure. There is an enormous gap between the complexity of the application and the complexity of the hardware elements. The architect's challenge is to bridge that gap effectively. To overcome the gap, the architect divides the system's functions into modules, each performing a "simple" function that will contribute to the system's usefulness. These modules are then combined to form larger modules whose functions are even closer to the end functions.

In a good system architecture the entire system will be divided into modules. Each module will interact with other modules in simple ways. Each module will have a clearly defined function—it may utilize other (simpler) modules to realize its function; that detail is hidden in the next level of the design. The architect's job is to work intelligently from the desired system characteristics and the characteristics of available components to develop a modular realization of the system. In this book we describe modularizations at many levels of system architecture, showing how the requirements imposed by applications, operating system functions, and programming language functions affect system structure. Design options are presented and contrasted. We will see that some basic design options are useful across the entire software–hardware spectrum, and that others are usable with minor adaptations and variations across the spectrum.

Let's examine several examples of modularized system descriptions. First we look at systems with bus-connected modules—the design of most home computer systems. Then we discuss an enhanced personal computer with a separate display buffer. Our third example shows how format-based categorizations can form the basis for a modular decomposition. We look next at a pipelined adder and a functional subdivision of conventional processor functions. Based on these examples, we make several generalizations about the system design process. Details of these examples and further explanations of these designs follow in succeeding chapters or problems.

Example 1-1

The four basic components in the von Neumann division of computer system functions are:

1. Processing
2. Memory
3. Control
4. Input/output

In the basic design separate physical modules support processing, memory, and input/output. Many control functions are distributed among those modules, but some centralized system control is provided from the processor module. The modules are interconnected (Figure 1-1) using a bus, which communicates control information, addresses, and data among the attached modules. All information passing on the bus is observed by all modules connected to the bus; interface logic in each module decides whether the passing information should be seen inside the module. Further, any module can place information onto the bus.

The system performs programs, themselves composed from basic processor instructions. Each processor instruction is executed by performing a simple algorithm; the

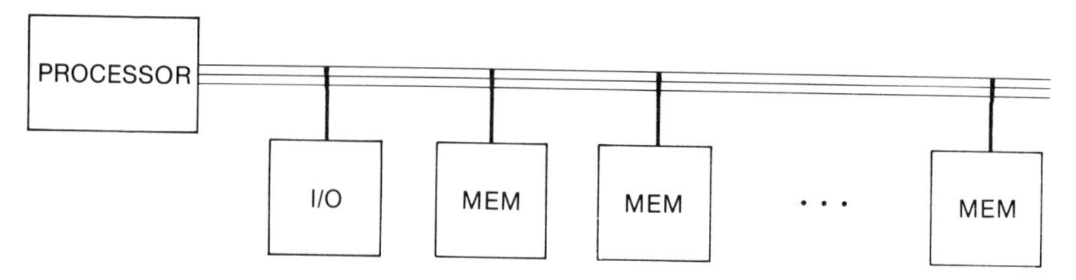

Figure 1-1 A bus-connected system

following steps emulate the instruction whose address is held in a processor register called the program counter (PC):

1. Fetch the next instruction from the memory location whose address is held in PC;
2. Compute its operand addresses and update PC;
3. Decode the operation;
4. Perform the operation;

At one level, the system's behavior can be described by the sequence of its intermodule bus transactions. Consider the execution of an ADD instruction that adds together the contents of a processor register and a memory location, placing the sum in the processor register. Suppose that the instruction itself and the operand value each occupy a single memory word, and suppose that a memory word is identical in size to the amount of information accessed during a single memory cycle. For this simple case two bus cycles are required to perform the instruction, one to fetch the instruction and one to fetch the operand value. Steps 2 and 3 of the instruction execution algorithm are performed within the processor module and do not initiate visible bus activity. Let us examine the steps in more detail.

In the *first step* the instruction is accessed; the processor initiates a READ bus cycle directed to the memory module that contains the instruction (the contents of the program counter determine which module is required and which location within the module should be read). The memory module reads the contents of the addressed location and sends those data back (along the bus's data lines) to the processor, which stores the instruction in its instruction register IR.

In the *second step* the processor examines IR to find the operand address contained therein. If the instruction specified indexing or some other address calculation, the processor performs the specified address arithmetic; the result is the effective address of the instruction's operand. Finally, the program counter is updated to point to the program's next instruction.

In the *third step* the processor's control logic examines IR to determine which operation is specified in the instruction held there.

In the *fourth step* the appropriate sequence of control steps to effect the instruction is performed. For the addition instruction of our example, the step sequence involves reading the operand value, selecting the designated processor register, and adding the value read from memory to the register's contents. To read the memory location holding the operand value, the processor initiates a READ bus cycle directed to the module containing the operand value. The memory address is sent along the bus from the processor to the memory, which replies with the data contained in the selected location. After it receives these data, the processor adds the two operand values and stores the result in the register.

Example 1-2

The speed of a bus-based system is limited by the bus bandwidth. Some functions require high bandwidth. Consider maintaining a raster-scan display with only 250 × 300 points, which need to be refreshed 30 times per second. Even if there are only two possible intensities at each point in the display, just to read the display data requires an average bandwidth of 2.25 megabits per second; if the word size is 16 bits, a word must be accessed every 7 microseconds (μs). If color is used, and 16 colors were possible in any image, each pixel (picture element) requires a 4-bit color specification, and the memory must read and provide a 16-bit word to the display controller every 1.75 μs. Higher image resolution requires higher bandwidth.

In a single bus design, all data passing between the memory and the display controller would be communicated along the single bus. These display transactions contend with processor-initiated bus transactions supporting instruction execution. This contention may reduce the instruction execution rate to an unacceptable slow rate. To relieve this bus contention, consider a design with a dedicated display memory and a dedicated data path from the display memory directly to the video generator (Figure 1-2). The control logic in the display memory controller must be designed to accept requests from either the system bus or the video generator, with priority given to access requests from the video generator.

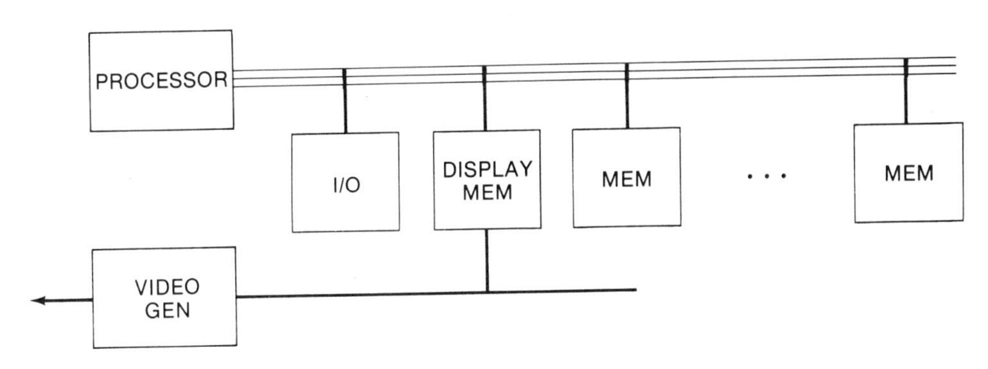

Figure 1-2 A bus-connected system with a dual-port display memory

Example 1-3

Figure 1-3 illustrates the structure of the Honeywell DPS 6/47 minicomputer. Within the processor complex there are three processing modules: the CPU, which executes conventional processor instructions having word operands; a Scientific Instruction Processor (SIP), which executes operations on floating-point and double-precision operands; and a Commercial Instruction Processor (CIP), which executes operations on character string operands. All instructions are fetched and decoded within the CPU module; those that can be performed by the CIP or the SIP are dispatched by the CPU's control logic to the proper module for execution. The CIP module's operands and results are character strings stored in main memory. Therefore, the CIP will generate

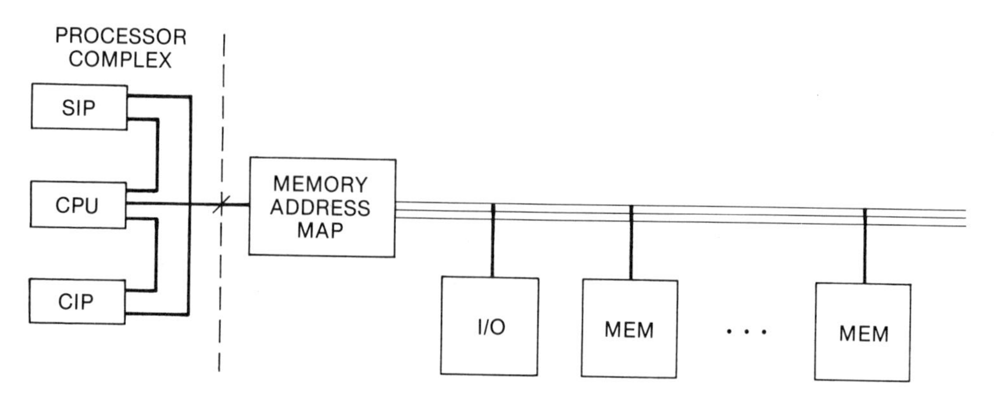

Figure 1-3 The Honeywell DPS 6/47 computer

memory access requests, which are sent along the system bus to the memory. The SIP does not require the capability to access memory during its operation, since its instructions are register based.

Example 1-4

Any processor implementation requires several quite different internal functions. Register contents must be stored, their contents must be manipulated, instructions must be fetched and held during execution, data operands must be fetched and stored, and the entire system must be controlled. To keep all these diverse functions in mind at the same time is confusing; with a modular decomposition of the processor itself, these diverse functions can be compartmentalized.

Figure 1-4 illustrates one decomposition of processor functions for the Motorola MC68020 processor (which we describe more fully in Chapter 2). The processor's modules are assigned separate parts of the processor's function, as follows. The sequencer module contains a clock that defines operation cycle timing; it is connected to the control module, which knows the command sequences necessary to perform the processor

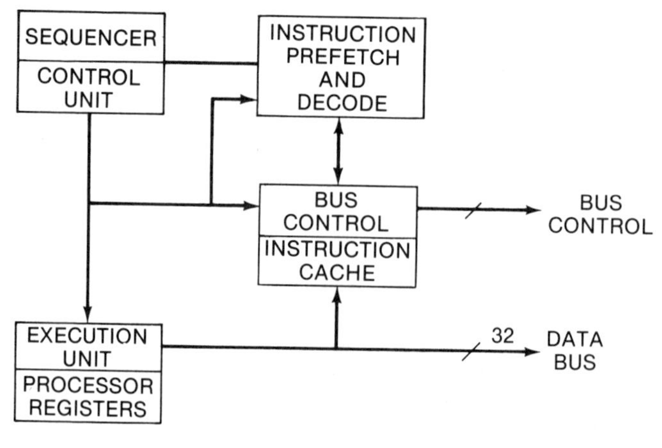

Figure 1-4 Inside the MC68020 processor (from [MOTO84]; courtesy of Motorola, Inc.)

instructions and issues control signals to the other modules to effect correct operation. The bus controller module determines which module (among those connected to the bus) may emit bus requests. The bus controller also serves as the interface between the processor logic and the bus signals. The execution unit actually performs the data manipulation instructions and contains the processor registers that can be programmed to hold intermediate results. All the functions noted above are required in processors designed for bus-connected systems such as that shown in Figure 1-1.

The additional modules in the MC68020 processor are included to speed up its instruction execution by reducing the need to fetch instructions across the bus from memory and by reducing the time spent in such fetches whenever possible. Two strategies are used. Under the first strategy, *prefetching*, the processor attempts to fetch the next instruction even though the present instruction may not be completed. The instruction fetch is attempted if the bus is not busy in the execution of the present instruction. If the prefetch succeeds, the program execution time will be reduced by the saved instruction fetch time. Under the second strategy, *instruction caching*, the processor keeps copies of recently executed instructions in the processor, gambling that the program is executing a short loop. If that gamble succeeds, the next instruction will already be in the processor's instruction cache, and an instruction fetch from memory will be saved.

Example 1-5

A pipelined implementation can speed arithmetic operations. From logic design we know that an arithmetic operation can, in principle, be implemented as a combinational circuit, and that such a circuit can always be realized with two levels of logic. For complex operations or for large data objects, this strategy is not attractive, because of the fan-in to the logic gates that will be required. Common implementations of integer adders use a full adder for each bit position; they are interconnected through carry propagation logic. Two carry propagation strategies are the ripple carry and the carry tree. In either structure the data remain in the result register, waiting while the carries propagate to their proper bit positions. The addition speed is bounded by the carry propagation delay.

In a pipeline design the data and the preliminary results are propagated through a sequence of computational stages designed so that the proper result is produced at the end of the sequence. Buffer registers are placed in between the computational stages, as shown in Figure 1-5. Not all useful operations are amenable to pipelining, since for pipelining the subdivision of the operation into a sequence of stages must make sense and be nontrivial. For example, the logical OR operation cannot be usefully subdivided into a sequence of suboperations. Floating-point addition, on the other hand, can be

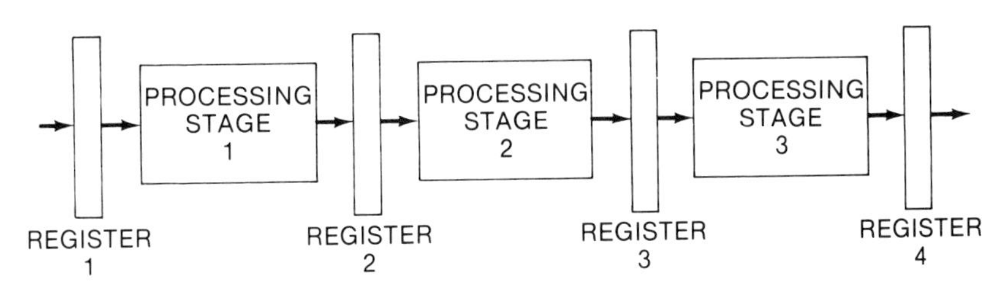

Figure 1-5 A three-stage pipeline

divided into four suboperations which do have to be performed sequentially, since the result of each step is an operand for the next step. These four substeps are:

1. Compare exponent values;
2. Shift mantissas to align them;
3. Add mantissas;
4. Normalize the result;

A floating-point adder could be realized by building a module for each of these substeps and wiring the outputs from one stage directly to the inputs of the next stage. For this design, the network delay will be the sum of the delays through the stages. The pipelined realization contains a register between each pair of modules; these registers hold the data flowing through the pipeline. One function of the registers is to ensure that proper signal propagation across successive stages is not affected by differences among signal delays through the stages. We shall see another function of the registers presently.

A little thought should convince the reader that the pipeline structure for floating-point addition (or any other operation) will entail more logic gates than will the non-pipelined implementation of the operation, at the very least because the interstage registers are in addition to the logic that actually performs addition. Why consider this structure, then? In the pipeline the interstage registers buffer the operands and results for one addition from those for another addition. This means that with the pipeline it is possible to perform several additions at the same time! All that is required for simultaneous operation is that every pair of separate data sets pass through two different stages during one time interval. The addition pipeline could simultaneously perform the following additions:

```
a:=b + c;
d:=e + f;
g:=h + i;
```

Now, of course, this parallelism is not possible if the sum from one addition is an operand for the succeeding addition. This situation occurs in the following sequence of additions, which therefore cannot be processed simultaneously in a pipeline:

```
a:=b + c;
d:=b + a;
e:=d + a;
```

In the fortunate case where additions in a sequence are "unrelated," they can all be in process in the same pipeline at the same time. The system's speed will be increased by the addition of the pipeline. The benefit will accrue, however, only if programs perform many unrelated additions in rapid sequence. Both the system's speed and its cost will be increased by the addition of the pipeline.

These examples illustrate different strategies for modularizing system functions and system implementations. Is any one better than any other? Is there a clear reason to prefer one over another? Some modularizations, such as using modules connected to a bus to implement processing functions (Figure 1-1), are noncontroversial, since all can easily see why the division has been chosen and can see that there is a cogent reason for that choice. In this case it was based on the category of the function performed by each module. Other modularizations, such as adding special modules to perform character string manipulations (Figure 1-3) and adding pipelines to perform additions, give performance improvement with certain program structures, but either degrade or do not improve the speed of other programs. Other strategies, such as implementing instruction prefetch and caching, result in statistical performance improvement, because the actual benefit depends on program behavior. Most designs giving statistical performance improvement require more complex control than the simpler designs on which they are based, so their implementations will be more expensive than those of the base designs.

The previous examples illustrated some hardware design modularization and structuring options. Similar design issues and options arise in software system design. One method for structuring a software system uses modularization based on function. Under this paradigm, the system is built from many subroutines. In fact, there is a separate subroutine for each complex function.

Example 1-6

The following Ada[1] program uses the procedure/function modularization technique:

```
procedure main() is
  type int_matrix is
  ..  --definition of the representation of int_matrix
  z : int_matrix;
  ..  --other declarations
   function matrix_mpy(x, y : int_matrix)
     return int_matrix is
     ..
  begin
     ..  --body of matrix_mpy
  end;
begin
  ..      --body of main
end;
```

There are two (nested) modules: main and matrix_mpy. From the position of the declaration of z, we conclude that the object z is visible within both main and matrix_mpy.[2] Furthermore, its representation is visible within both of these blocks. Therefore, a single component of z can be accessed from a statement within either program block by using a name like z(i, j).

[1]Ada is a registered trademark of the U.S. government (Ada Joint Program Office).

[2]We do not show an explicit declaration of the dimensions of z, which could have been specified within the declaration of the type int_matrix; the dimensioning detail has been omitted to reveal the essence of our example without excess clutter.

Another method for structuring software systems uses the type of object being manipulated, such as whether the operands are reals or character strings.[3] The following example illustrates the skeleton of this technique applied in an Ada program.

Example 1-7

Using Ada's **package** modularization technique, the programmer can collect a group of declarations, objects, and procedures (or functions) which, when lumped together, present a clean interface to the remainder of the program. The "header" of the package contains declarations of the information that can be "seen" outside the package; this information may include names of objects, procedures, and types. Any one of these objects, procedures, or types can be declared *private*, which means that even though its existence may be visible outside the package, the details of its representation and/or implementation cannot be seen from outside the package.

Here is a sketch of the declaration of the interface to a package hiding the realization of objects of type int_matrix:

```
package int_matrix_type is
  type int_matrix is private;
  function matrix_mpy(x, y : int_matrix)
      return int_matrix;
  .. --other declarations
private
  type int_matrix is
  .. --definition of the representation of int_matrix
end int_matrix_type;
```

This package structure defines the representation and implementation of a new object type. Everything declared in the header before the separator line **private** is public, being visible wherever the package itself is visible. Things declared after the **private** separator line or within the package body (which is declared in a separate program region) are not publicly visible. Thus in our example the existence of the type int_matrix is declared public, but the implementation of the type is declared private, so that the details of the type's representation cannot be seen outside the package. Therefore, another program could declare an object of type int_matrix, yet not be able to access its component parts. Outside the package the programmer may declare an object z of type int_matrix, but its representation is not available, so that it is not legal to write "z(i, j)" outside the package, since such a reference implies access to the representation of the object z. It is legal to pass z as a parameter to a procedure declared within the int_matrix package. The components of z will be individually accessible inside the package, since the representation of objects of type int_matrix is visible within the package.

Although one might think that reference restrictions like those in the preceding example make programs less efficient, one must realize that the emphasis is on structure and modularization; the advantage of this structure is that it restricts the

[3]Notice the similarity of this approach to the Honeywell (DPS) 6/47 architectural modularization discussed in Example 1-3.

information that must or can be known outside the module. In other words, the programmer can use the module without having to worry about implementation details. Furthermore, the implementer of the package can change the details of its implementation without affecting any programs using the package, *provided* that the changes preserve the external semantics (note that even the representations need not remain fixed).

The Ada package visibility restrictions are enforced during compilation; an executing program does not have to make any validity checks to enforce the visibility restrictions. Comparing the speeds of two functionally identical programs, one written using the package construct and the other not, we might find that the version using packages will be slower. One contributor to the speed difference is the overhead for the extra calls to procedures that perform operations on objects with hidden representations. Therefore, building a system with fast procedure call and return operations will certainly reduce the speed differential incurred by using packages in the programs. This example shows how it can be worthwhile to design a processor with a view to the software likely to be executed on that processor.

Generalizing, we could state that some software design options require some hardware support for efficient system operation. If there is no hope of hardware support, a software design option may impose too much time delay in program execution and therefore may have to be discarded even though it provides attractive modularity for the programmer. This potential conflict between the desires of the software modularizer and designer and the support provided by the hardware must affect the system architect. We see how the computer architecture problem spans both hardware and software design issues. In this book we show these interactions by illustrating how desirable software modularizations could be supported by hardware or firmware modules or functions. We also point out similarities and commonalities between design options usable at hardware, firmware, and software implementation levels.

1.2 THE BASIS FOR MODULARIZATION

We have seen that the grouping of module functions can be based on various factors, including processing functions and object types. Hierarchical decompositions of system functions can be created by decomposing operations, objects, or types. Operational decomposition was illustrated in Example 1-6 by the traditional decomposition of programs into procedures and functions. In contrast, object-based or type-based decomposition is based on the identity or type of the object. The specification of an object's type implies (1) the operations that may be performed on the object, (2) the encoding used to represent the object, and (3) the algorithms that implement the defined operations. The specification of a type defines these three aspects of all objects of that type. A type specification module was illustrated by the Ada package structure in Example 1-7. Every primitive operation (one whose implementation requires knowledge of the representation scheme) that may be performed on objects of the given type must be defined within the type specification module. Additional operations may be defined outside the package, provided that they can be constructed from the operations defined inside the type definition. For example, one can implement operations on complex numbers using operations on real numbers without having to know the representations of the real numbers or the implementations of operations on real numbers. In Chapter 7 we explore the relationships between object-oriented programming, type-based decompositions, and object transformations, such as those performed by arithmetic units and numeric coprocessors.

Example 1-8

Here are two different ways to implement operations on real numbers:

```
procedure p(..) is
  type realt is
    record
      exponent : integer;
      mantissa : integer;
    end record;
  function addrealt(x, y : realt) return realt is
    ..                      --addition of realts
  end addrealt;
  function subrealt(x, y : realt) return realt is
    ..                      --subtraction of realts
  end subrealt;
  procedure shift_align(x, y : in out realt) is
    ..
  end shift_align;
  ..                        --other procedures and objects
begin
  ..                        --p's procedure body (using realts)
end p;

procedure q(..) is
  package realt_pack is
    type realt is private;
    function addrealt(x, y : realt) return realt;
    function subrealt(x, y : realt) return realt;
  private
    type realt is
      record
        exponent : integer;
        mantissa : integer;
      end record;
  end realt_pack;
  package body realt_pack is
    function addrealt(x, y : realt) return realt is
      ..
    end addrealt;
    function subrealt(x, y : realt) return realt is
      ..
    end subrealt;
```

```
        procedure shift_align(x, y : in out realt) is
          ..
        end shift_align;
        ..                  --other procedures here
      end realt_pack;
      ..                    --declarations for q
    begin
      ..                    --body of q
    end q;
```

Inside procedure p the representation of objects of type realt is visible to the entire program. The procedures addrealt and subrealt, which add and subtract realt objects, respectively, are callable from all points within the program. The procedure shift_align, used in both addrealt and subrealt, is also defined such that it is visible to the entire program within p. This structure may seem unwieldy, but it is the only way to follow the nesting rules and avoid duplicating the shift_align procedure.

In contrast, inside procedure q the type realt is known and objects can be declared to have that type. The two procedures that manipulate these types are callable from everywhere in the program. But the representation of objects of type realt is not visible outside the package realt_pack. Furthermore, the procedure shift_align is "hidden" inside the package, where it can be shared between addrealt and subrealt without making it visible to all of q.

"What difference does this make?" one might ask. One problem arises because within p any program can examine the exponent component of a realt object without considering the mantissa component of the representation. Therefore, one can perform representation-dependent operations on the objects of type realt, and a reader of the program would have a difficult time, to say the least, to understand the program. Notice that an unwary reader might assume (quite naturally) that the procedures addrealt and subrealt are the only ways that objects of type realt are, in fact, manipulated. This assumption is not valid and could confuse the reader's reasoning about the program and its properties. On the other hand, the implementation of the package construct, known to be correct if the Ada compiler is correct, is known to assure that the functions defined within the package are the only ones that can manipulate objects of type realt. This limitation should simplify one's understanding of the program and reasoning about its properties.

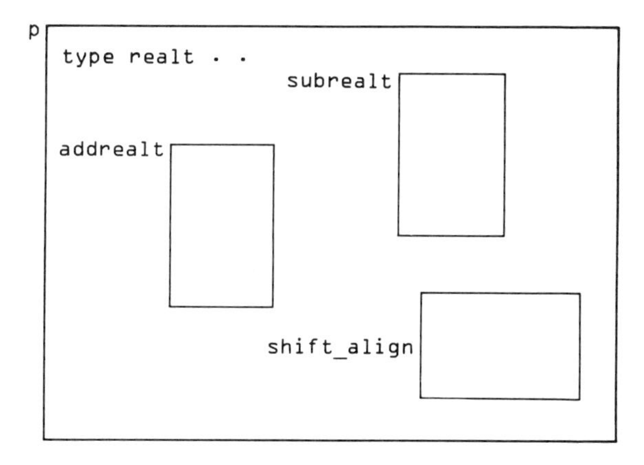

Figure 1-6 Module nesting in Procedure p (Example 1-8)

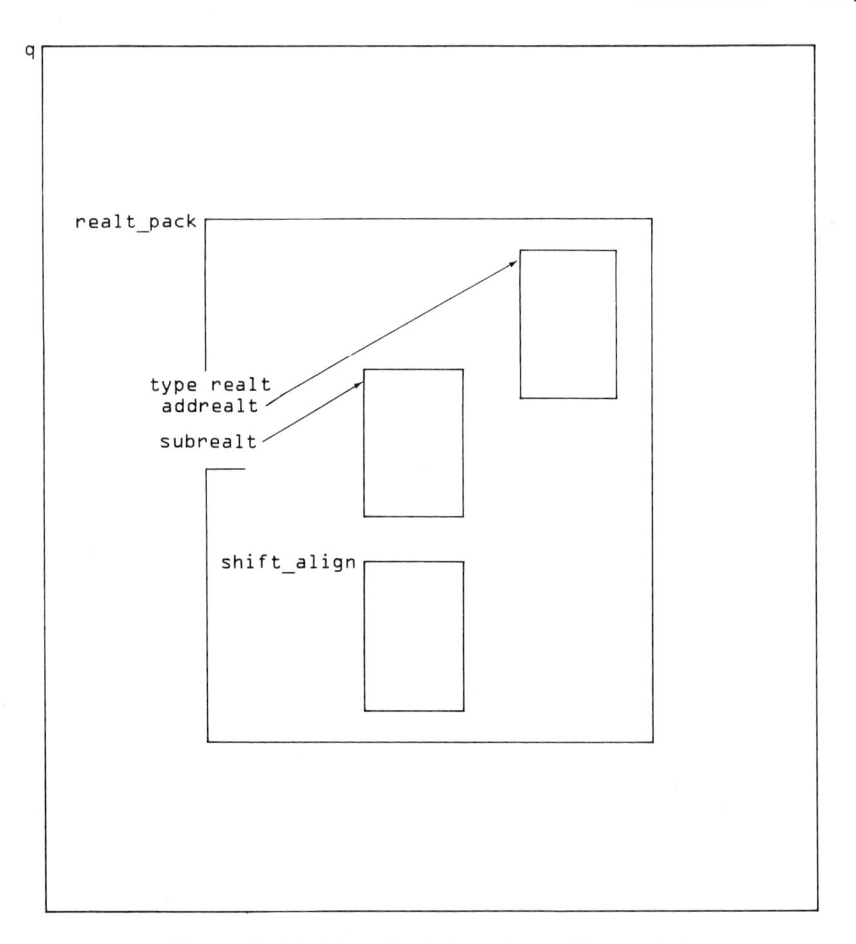

Figure 1-7 Module nesting in Procedure q (Example 1-8)

These modular structures can be pictured in terms of a nested set of boxes. Figure 1-6 depicts the module nesting of procedure p. The nested structure is quite obvious in the picture. Figure 1-7 depicts the module structure of procedure q. We have to modify the traditional way that nested modules are shown to reflect the more complex interface that makes more things available to the environment around the package. The list in the "doorway" to the module shows the types, functions, and procedures that are visible outside the module. Other procedures or types could be defined within the module, but in a way such that they are not visible to the outside. The procedure shift_align is one such procedure.

A modular system description can be arranged as a hierarchical structure based on the relationship "the implementation of the module at the higher level uses the module at the lower level." For example, a processor contains an arithmetic unit, which itself contains an adder. Therefore, the implementation of the processor uses an arithmetic unit, whose implementation uses an adder. This "implementation uses" relationship is important in structuring and understanding many parts of

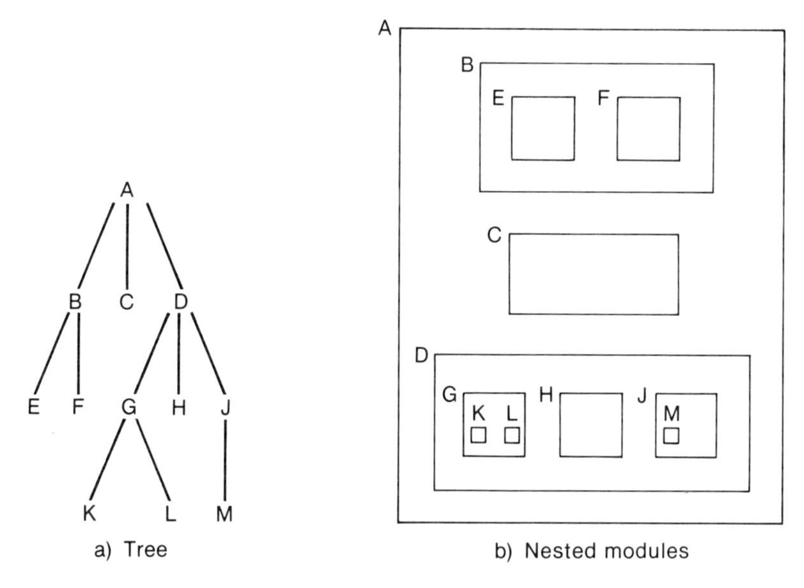

Figure 1-8 Two representations of a hierarchical implementation

computer systems. Its hierarchical structure can be depicted as a nested set of blocks or as a tree structure (Figure 1-8).

There are two approaches to using a hierarchically structured description. *First*, one could expand the description so that the entire system is described in terms of its lowest-level description elements. Many logic simulation systems work in this manner, reducing the entire system to a network of logic gates before simulating any actions. For hardware the lowest level of abstraction is the gate; for software, it might be the machine instruction. For sequential machine design, the lowest level might be the states used to describe the machine's behavior. We know from logic design that the state description technique is completely general, in the sense that any sequential machine can be described as a state machine. The expansion of any complete computer system in this manner produces a description of ridiculously great complexity, and it should be obvious that one would not wish to construct such a state machine description of a complete computer system. Just consider a memory containing a megabyte of information; it contains more than 8 million elements, each holding a single bit of information. If we adopted the traditional state-machine view, we would have a machine with over $2^{8,000,000}$ states and an incredible state transition description. The appeal of this "expansion" technique is that it is guaranteed always to work. Thus any structure in the description is not important. On the other hand, if the description has a lot of structure, a description in terms of that structure is better for human beings than a description in terms of states. We certainly want to view the megabyte memory in terms of bytes and read/write operations.

The *second* approach to using a hierarchically structured description describes the machine's behavior in terms of sequences of the simpler functions performed by the modules within its implementation. And at the module level we generate a simple description in terms of the functions of the submodules. This view of the system structure and description is preferred, since it emphasizes the hierarchical reason for the modular description. With this approach to hierarchical description, the description's structure is important, since that structure reflects the observer's view of the system. This hierarchical description approach will be especially effective *if* each module's role and function can be concisely defined.

How do we characterize a "good" hierarchical decomposition? Clearly, it is not useful to decompose a processor directly to flip-flops, half-adders, and multiplexers. Why not? Because the processor contains too many of these elements. Its decomposition in these terms would be very large and difficult to understand. The von Neumann decomposition of the processor into two pieces (control and arithmetic) is more appropriate, but it does not give much information beyond the starting description—"processor."

In an attempt to quantify these preferences, computer architects have introduced an important measure of a hierarchical structure: the *distance* between two adjacent levels of the hierarchy. How could we measure the "distance" between levels? Think of the implementation of the hierarchically described system. The realization of a function at one level uses copies of the modules from the next lower level. If n module copies are required for this realization, we define n to be the distance between the levels. Clearly, this "definition" is not precise, but it does give substance to the intuitive notion of distance. A "good" hierarchy has a "reasonable" distance between its adjacent levels—if the distance is too small, the realization results in too many levels; if the distance is too large, the realization requires a complicated implementation of the higher level, and the correctness of the realization will be less apparent. One cannot help but introduce the software complexity guideline here—it has been suggested that a good-sized software module's description will fit on a single page (without photo reduction!).

1.3 SYSTEM DESIGN PROCESSES

At each level of the hierarchy, the system architect must move from requirements to implementation. She may use the following steps:

1. Determine how the system will be used.
2. Determine functional specifications.
3. Determine nonfunctional specifications.
4. Collect alternative designs.
5. Evaluate candidate designs.
6. Select a design.
7. Simulate the chosen design.
8. Build a prototype version of the design.
9. Test and modify the design.
10. Produce the system.

Now consider these steps in a little more detail.

How will the system be used? There may be little specific information. Potential customers may describe how they anticipate using the system. But this information may not really define the system's characteristics. For example, the customer might state, "I want a system to operate in a multilevel secure environment." Although this specification rules out many possible designs, it certainly does not specify a unique design.[4] Or the customer may want to use integrated spreadsheet–graphics–word processing software. The software market illustrates the fact that many options can provide substantially identical functionality using quite different hardware.

Determine specifications which state what criteria a design must meet in order that it be considered satisfactory. Specifications fall into two groups:

1. Functional specifications
2. Nonfunctional specifications

Functional specifications describe logical system properties. For example, the fact that a system must satisfy multilevel security constraints regarding who can see and modify each data item is a functional system constraint. Nonfunctional specifications describe other characteristics of acceptable system designs, such as power dissipation and speed. The speed might be specified in terms of an instruction execution rate or in terms of the maximum acceptable delay between the occurrence of a keyed input and a visible response on a display.

The next step is to *collect alternative designs* which seem reasonably efficient in meeting the specifications. To generate options, the designer should consider the implementation of each system function in hardware, firmware, software, or combinations of the preceding. The architect must have an open mind as she identifies options, although she might reject some out-of-hand as too costly or too inefficient. Watch out here! Although the functional constraints may seem to imply an expensive solution, there may exist an efficient implementation that does not happen to cross the designer's mind. Thus it may be wise to include some "wild" ideas among the design options.

The architect must *evaluate* both good and bad features of those options that remain to determine the consequences of their selection. These deliberations involve both the implementation complexity and the performance of the system under each design.

The architect may be able to *select* a design after she has culled the options; it is, however, also possible that she will have to start the next level of design to be able to determine sufficient information to choose intelligently from among the options.

The architect may *simulate* a system design, choosing a level of detail that covers the features to be analyzed during the simulation. Simulations may be used to evaluate the system's performance or to verify the correctness of the design. If performance is to be determined, simulator inputs must be chosen to reflect actual usage in the anticipated environment. If design correctness is to be verified, the simulator's

[4]In Chapter 4 of Volume 2 we discuss this design problem in detail.

inputs must include a sufficient mix of stimuli so that all important design features are checked during the simulation.[5]

After simulation has convinced the design team that the design is correct and that the system will perform to specifications, a *prototype* implementation is built and checked out. Timing and other nitty-gritty details can be verified in a prototype system. The goal of prototyping is to show that all design details do correlate and harmonize to effect a correct system. In addition, prototyping can uncover any manufacturing problems inherent in the design and its implementation.

Producing the system entails *manufacturing*, marketing, and service. Replicating the system's hardware requires much detail, and the products must be tested carefully. Although marketing is far beyond the scope of this book, servicing is not. Clever modularization and packaging can greatly reduce servicing costs.

In this book we describe many design options, including important ones used in contemporary systems. We discuss their advantages and disadvantages. We emphasize similarities among the design options at all levels of system design, ranging from software to hardware. We present simple performance models and estimates for some design options, especially for designs introduced for performance enhancement. We do not detail designs to the level of logic gates, although that level of detail could easily be provided by the reader familiar with computer system design. Our emphasis, then, includes design problems and design options that are commonly used or that are extensions of reasonable designs. Often, we demonstrate the feasibility of an option by citing a system that incorporates the option, showing, in some cases, just how the option is used in a real system.

1.4 SYSTEM DESIGN APPROACHES

Our preceding discussion presented an approach to system design and implementation without concern for the level of detail at which the design is being developed. Just as a system cannot be described efficiently at one level, a system cannot be designed at a single level. The designer must remain aware of both the implementation details and the consequences for software design. Thus interactions between adjacent levels of the system modular hierarchy can strongly affect system design. In this section we discuss three aspects of the design process:

1. Starting out
2. Using generic designs
3. Designing for test

1.4.1 Starting Out

Just as we divide functions into modules with well-defined interfaces and implement each separately, so, too, we divide the enormous task of making decisions as the

[5]Selecting test inputs can be a difficult task, especially because the testing process should be somewhat independent of the actual design; but at the same time, testing should exercise all of the logic in the design.

system structure develops during the design process. Such *refinement by decomposition* is extremely useful; in this book we use this modular decision structure and show how it is related to the modular functional structure.

Where in the decomposition hierarchy might the designer start? The two extremes and the middle are obvious options. One may start the design process at the top (*top-down*) or from the bottom (*bottom-up*). With these options it can be difficult to keep perspective because the other end is so distant. To keep perspective without overloading the designer, an *inside-out* approach, starting in the middle of the range, is preferred.

1.4.2 Using Generic Designs

Although one may consider a module design to be a specific implementation for a specific purpose (an adder for 16-bit integers, for example), one could work with *generic modules*, which define the common structure for a set of related designs. One could use generic modules to specify a family of "compatible" systems (i.e., that have identical functional characteristics). For example, one can define the structure of an integer adder without knowing the widths of the operands (leaving the width as a design parameter). A particular adder can then be specified by using the generic adder description with the parameter value that defines operand the width for the particular adder. The generic module specification approach provides structure and has some advantages and some disadvantages. One major advantage is that correct behavior of the realization can be guaranteed based on a proof or argument concerning the correctness of the generic specification. Such proofs or arguments must not depend on the parameters having particular values. Such a general argument guarantees correctness for all combinations of the parameter values.

How can one know that any design, generic or otherwise, will exhibit correct behavior? One is tempted to answer this question by stating that testing will demonstrate correctness. Although this sounds ample, it is an inadequate answer, since testing a complex system is difficult. Other arguments can be based on proofs; one tries to argue that the implementation is structured in such a manner that certain functional properties can be shown to hold, and that these properties guarantee correct behavior.

Hierarchical modularization, especially using generic module specifications, is useful if the component modules are not very "far" from the functions required for the implementation. In this case, the entire system can be described simply by using a few component modules. The decreased complexity of the description, it is also argued, can make the system description more comprehensible; this comprehensibility improves the chances that errors will be apparent. This observation reinforces our desire for small distances between the descriptive levels.

If we believe that generic descriptions are useful to simplify the system design problem, and if we believe that it is difficult to obtain a correct implementation of system functions, shouldn't we use the same implementation all the time, once we show that it is functionally correct? The problem is that the effectiveness of a design's implementation may be based on a particular logic technology, such as CMOS, a particular implementation strategy, such as microprogramming, or a particular packaging strategy, such as fin-cooled integrated modules. Once the technology is changed, say to bipolar ECL logic to improve system speed, the performance bottlenecks inherent in the original design may reduce system speed below the level that could be obtained from the new technology. In other words, while a particular implementation may be attractive when using one underlying technology, it may not be optimum with another technology. We see that functionally equivalent designs may have quite different cost and performance characteristics when implemented atop different underlying technologies or lower-level mechanisms.

1.4.3 Designing for Test

We mentioned that system complexity can defeat testing attempts. In the absence of information about the structure of the implementation, the tester must try all possible input combinations. Conceptually, this testing approach is valid for any combinational circuit. Many practical combinational circuits cannot be checked this way, for the number of input combinations grows exponentially with the number of input signals. Just presenting all input combinations to a 32-bit adder would require hundreds of years.[6] Clearly, to reduce the number of test stimuli and still be complete, the test input selection must reflect the implementation structures.

Testing a system that may exhibit time-dependent behavior is even more difficult than testing a combinational system. First, the number of input sequences is much greater than the unmanageable number of input combinations. In addition, it may be difficult to set or observe the system's internal state. In particular, the system under test may not be *controllable*, which means that by using the external inputs the tester may not be able to place the system in an arbitrary desired state before applying test inputs. Also, the system may not be *observable*, which means that by using the external outputs the tester may not be able to observe the system's state. One way to provide both controllability and observability is to add external access paths both to and from all memory elements in the implementation, thereby allowing examination and control of their contents. The *scan-path* approach connects all flip-flops in a module as a serial shift register (controlled by a separate testing clock). In each part of the test, the tester first uses the scan shift register and the testing clock to load all memory elements with a test pattern. Then the tester uses the system clock to cause the system to execute a few steps of the algorithm. Finally the shift register is pulsed to read the resulting state of the memory elements; this state is compared against the "correct" result to reveal any errors that may have occurred. The selection of the tests to be made rests on knowledge of the system's implementation structure.

Even if the system is thoroughly tested, it can still make mistakes when components or connections fail. It is desirable to confine the errors that do occur after failures. If we could completely confine the effects of an error to the single module where it originated, testing and maintenance would be greatly simplified. Unfortunately complete confinement is difficult, if not impossible. Suppose that an adder module fails and produces a "5" when asked to perform "2 + 2." The "5" result

[6] With 64 inputs (the bits in the two 32-bit operand values) we have 2^{64} input combinations. Even at the high speed of one input combination per nanosecond, the test requires 585 years!

cannot be rejected immediately because "5" would have been correct if the problem had been "2 + 3." We see that we cannot simply examine the module's outputs to detect errors. One might add redundancy to the module's implementation to check the module's computations before "releasing" the result(s). But the redundancy cannot be a perfect checker, either, for there is some chance that the redundant mechanism itself fails in such a way that it verifies an incorrect result as correct. Adding redundancy does reduce module error probabilities, but can never get them to zero.

1.5 VIRTUAL MACHINES

One method for hierarchical decomposition views the computer system as a collection of *virtual machines*, each having many characteristics of a simple computer executing a single sequence of instructions. The virtual machine concept is useful for programmers. A programmer writing an Ada program can think that her program is executed on a private (virtual) machine that directly executes Ada programs. Although this view may seem strange, it is useful for several reasons. First, the programmer need not worry about how the machine implements Ada's semantics. Second, the programmer knows that the implementation guarantees that there will be no interaction between her program and any transactions the actual computer might have with other users. Third, the details of how these properties are achieved do not have to concern the programmer. A system design providing this type of logical separation of every user from others supports a separate virtual machine for each user. In this section we explore several different methods by which the system could be designed to support separated virtual machines.

A virtual machine may be implemented by providing a physical machine for the private use of the virtual machine. Often, however, it is effective to provide the virtual machine's functionality and separation through a combination of firmware, software, and hardware designed so that a single host (physical) machine may provide logically different virtual machines for different users.

1.5.1 Virtual Machine Separation

The programmer's view of a virtual machine's independence must be supported by the underlying implementation. Some means must be provided to separate virtual machines from each other, including both those that support the implementation of a virtual machine and those that happen to share, in their implementation, the same physical resources.

A designer may have to restrict the virtual machine's capabilities if several virtual machines are to share some physical resources. To uncover necessary restrictions, we look for machine operations that could violate the machine's boundary even if executed with "legal" operand values. The potential problem areas include:

1. Address generation
2. Communication control
3. Logical boundary control

Address generation must be controlled if memory is shared. The restriction ensures that a program cannot access memory space allocated to another virtual machine. Suppose that this restriction were not imposed and virtual machine V_1 were allowed to write into a memory location M within the space allocated for another virtual machine V_2. Then if V_1 did write to M, the actions of V_2 might be affected; the interference of V_2 by V_1's write to M violates the required separation between V_1 and V_2. A similar interference argument can be made if V_1 were permitted to read from memory locations allocated for V_2.

Communication control must be limited if communications devices are shared among different virtual machines. Suppose that device D has been allocated to virtual machine V_1 for a specific time interval. During this interval, virtual machine V_2 should not be able to change that allocation; in fact, it should not be allowed to communicate with D in any manner whatsoever.

Logical boundary control must be reserved for the supervisory program which allocates system resources to virtual machines. A violation of this rule will subvert the entire separation of virtual machines. If the boundary could be changed by a machine V, V could change its boundaries and thereby encroach on other virtual machines. One typical design for a host processor includes limit registers that define the boundaries imposed upon an executing virtual machine. In this design, the boundary control restriction states that a program should not be allowed to change the contents of any register defining memory address limits.

1.5.2 A Taxonomy

We construct a taxonomy of techniques for separating virtual machines, using two dichotomies: spatial versus temporal separation, and static versus dynamic separation. The four classes thus defined suggest classes of enforcement mechanisms, presented in general terms in Section 1.5.3. Detailed mechanisms actually used for virtual machine separation are discussed in appropriate sections throughout the book. The taxonomy serves to categorize these techniques and to suggest the advantages and disadvantages of the options. We may also obtain clues leading toward sensitive portions of each design.

1.5.2.1 Spatial or temporal separation? One dimension of our taxonomy concerns whether virtual machines are separated by time or space.

Definition. A virtual machine is *spatially separated* from another virtual machine if each machine is assigned a separate set of physical resources.

The separation can be made at the granularity of physical modules. However, if a physical module can be logically subdivided without interference between the separated parts (as with a memory module), spatial separation can be achieved by assigning different parts of the same physical module to different virtual machines.

We will not include any passive interconnections as modules when we consider separations among virtual machines. In particular, two machines might share an interconnection bus and not share any active modules. In this case we would say that the two machines were physically separated. This seemingly awkward rule does not have a direct effect on any design, but it does clarify the nature of the separations.

Example 1-9

Consider an office network of personal workstations. When these are performing text editing, they are operating as physically separated virtual machines. Communications with central servers for filing documents or making hard copies may be provided in the network. When using the printer, a workstation's virtual machine extends to the physically shared printer, and thus is not physically separated from the other virtual machines. A physical structural diagram of such a system is shown in Figure 1-9.

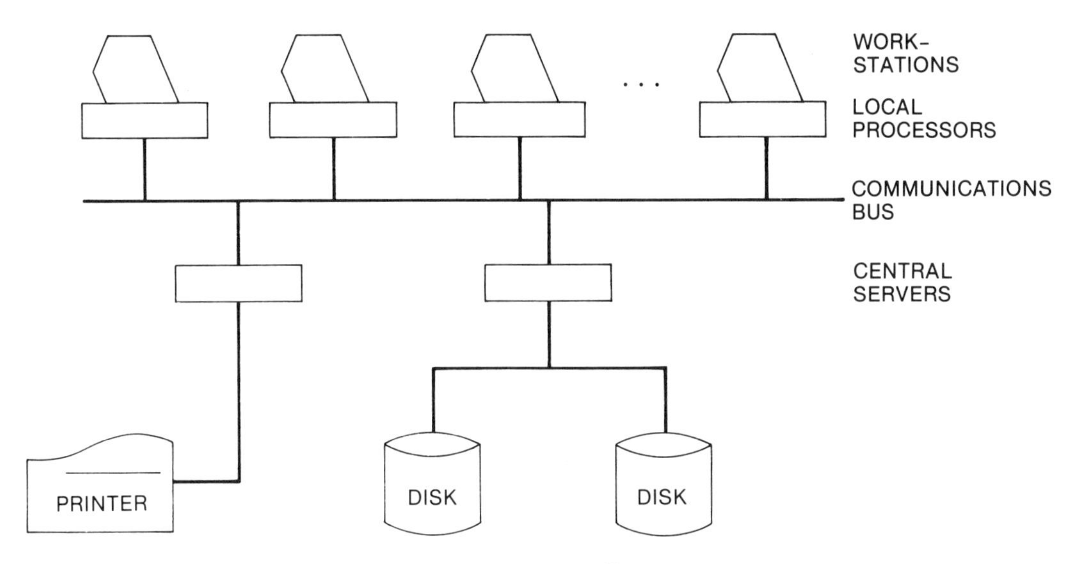

Figure 1-9 An office network

Definition. A pair of virtual machines is *temporally separated* if they are separated by scheduling them on the same physical module during different, nonoverlapping time segments.

To switch virtual machines, the shared module must be switched from one virtual machine to the next. The machine's controller must manage this switching so that the machines do not interact through any status information that may be retained in the physically shared module. For example, processor registers must be saved and restored during a transition so that the contents of the registers left by the departing virtual machine cannot be inspected by the arriving virtual machine.

Example 1-10

In time-shared computing, a process, which is the execution of a program on behalf of a user, plays the role of a virtual machine. One simple allocation policy schedules each process on the processor for an equal time interval. A scheduling module in the operating system manages this timing; it gains control after an interrupt, and then may

> schedule another process for execution during the next interval. Before control can be passed, however, the state associated with the dismissed process must be saved, and the saved state describing the scheduled process must be restored. Proper state management and control over other logical boundary enforcement mechanisms is necessary to provide the desired isolation among the virtual machines sharing the physical machine.

Generally, temporal separation is harder to implement but more flexible than spatial separation.

1.5.2.2 Static or dynamic boundaries?

Boundaries between virtual machines may be forever fixed, or may be varied to reflect changing needs or a new management policy. This option suggests a taxonomic question: Are the virtual machine boundaries fixed or variable? Variable boundaries are clearly more flexible, but they may be more expensive to implement. A related taxonomic question concerns the length of time during which virtual machine boundaries remain unchanged.

A virtual machine implemented on a host machine may have two different boundaries. One boundary describes limits imposed on the logical actions requested from within the machine. The second boundary describes limits imposed by the host machine on the effects of the virtual machine's activities. There may be a difference between these boundaries if the host machine actually limits the reach of each virtual machine by restricting it to a *compartment*. The compartment is significant from the host's view.

These definitions reflect these possibilities.

Definition. A boundary enclosing a virtual machine is *static to the virtual machine* if it remains unchanged for the lifetime of the virtual machine.

Definition. A boundary enclosing a virtual machine compartment is *static to the host machine* if it remains unchanged for the lifetime of the host machine.

Definition. A boundary enclosing a virtual machine is *dynamic to the virtual machine* if it may change during the lifetime of the virtual machine.

Definition. A boundary enclosing a virtual machine compartment is *dynamic to the host machine* if it may change during the lifetime of the host machine.

The relationship between the lifetime of a machine and the duration of the boundary affects the structure of the implementation. For example, if the host system uses physical separation which is static with respect to the host, the host is effectively divided permanently into a fixed set of virtual machine compartments. This static division might be implemented by physically disconnecting the ties crossing the virtual machine boundaries. Clearly, this static policy is not as flexible as a dynamic policy, which could permit a single virtual machine to be allocated almost all of the host's resources. However, we expect that the static policy would be easier to enforce. We return to the enforcement issue after we examine a simple example of dynamic boundaries from a time-shared system.

Example 1-11

In a time-sharing system, memory allocation modules within the operating system allocate physical memory to executing processes. The allocation is enforced by hardware that checks every memory address generated by an executing program by comparing it against the contents of certain bounds registers or allocation tables accessible to the processor. If these registers or tables always contain the same values while virtual machine V is scheduled for execution, the memory boundary imposed on machine V is static from V; this situation would apply if the allocation of Table 1-1 were used at all times.

Alternatively, the memory allocation module may change the table entries between V's execution intervals. This situation would apply if during one execution interval Table 1-1 were used, while during another execution interval Table 1-2 were used. In

TABLE 1-1 MEMORY ALLOCATION TO TWO VIRTUAL MACHINES

Virtual Machine Number	Physical Memory Addresses Allocated
1	0–32,767
2	32,768–65,535

TABLE 1-2 ANOTHER MEMORY ALLOCATION TO TWO VIRTUAL MACHINES

Virtual Machine Number	Physical Memory Addresses Allocated
1	32,768–65,535
2	0–32,767

TABLE 1-3 A THIRD MEMORY ALLOCATION TO TWO VIRTUAL MACHINES

Virtual Machine Number	Physical Memory Addresses Allocated
1	4,096–32,863
2	36,864–69,632

this case the boundaries are dynamic from the viewpoint of a virtual machine that can see physical addresses. On the other hand, if the virtual machine sees memory as a block of virtually addressed locations, it still sees 32,768 available locations, and the boundaries appear to be static.

Even if each virtual machine sees static boundaries, it is not necessarily the case that the host sees static boundaries. For example, the host could use Table 1-2 and Table 1-3 at different times. In this case each virtual machine sees the same amount of virtual memory, but the physical boundary is changed when the table is changed.

There are four combinations of the answers to the issues concerning virtual machine boundaries. These combinations correspond to the "leaves" of a taxonomic tree (Figure 1-10). Let us enumerate the combinations:

1. (*Spatial, Static*) separation is illustrated by a system with physically separate processors, sharing nothing but a communications medium (Figure 1-11).
2. (*Spatial, Dynamic*) separation is illustrated by a multiprocessor system with shared memory using changeable bounds registers to limit the memory region accessible from each processor, as explained in Example 1-11.
3. (*Temporal, Static*) separation is used in a system with a single processor cycled in a fixed manner among a set of virtual machines. It must be understood that the schedule, illustrated in Figure 1-12, does not change, for otherwise the separation is not static.
4. (*Temporal, Dynamic*) separation is illustrated by the same scheduling mechanism, but with time slots assigned dynamically to virtual machines. This scheduling is illustrated in Figure 1-13.

A little reflection on these distinctions reveals that they do not provide clear criteria for assigning each possible design to a single category. Nevertheless, we will use the classifications to describe some designs, because the categories do reflect design decisions and may suggest some consequences of those decisions.

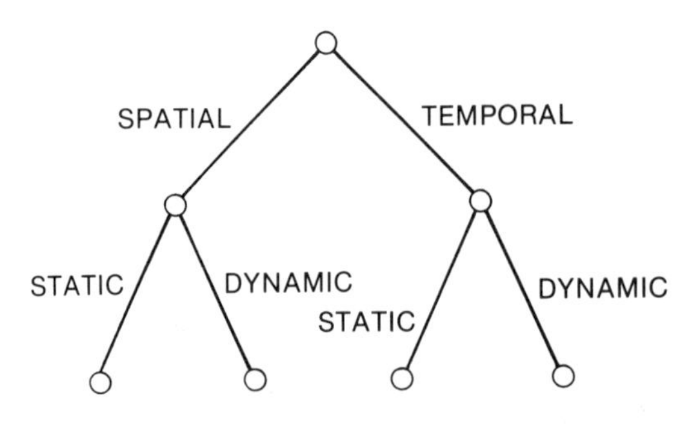

Figure 1-10 The taxonomy of separation techniques

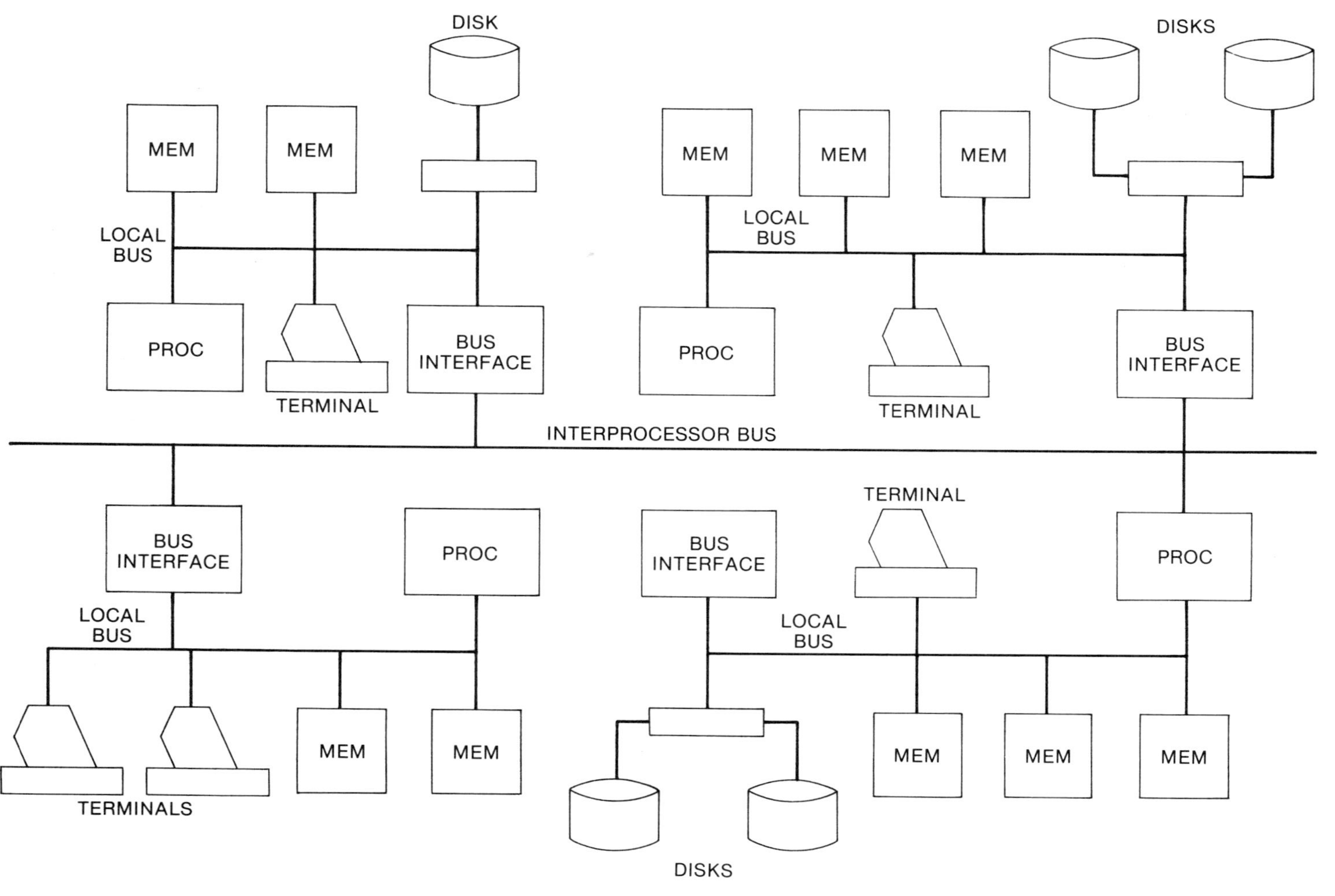

Figure 1-11 Physical separation in a multiprocessor system

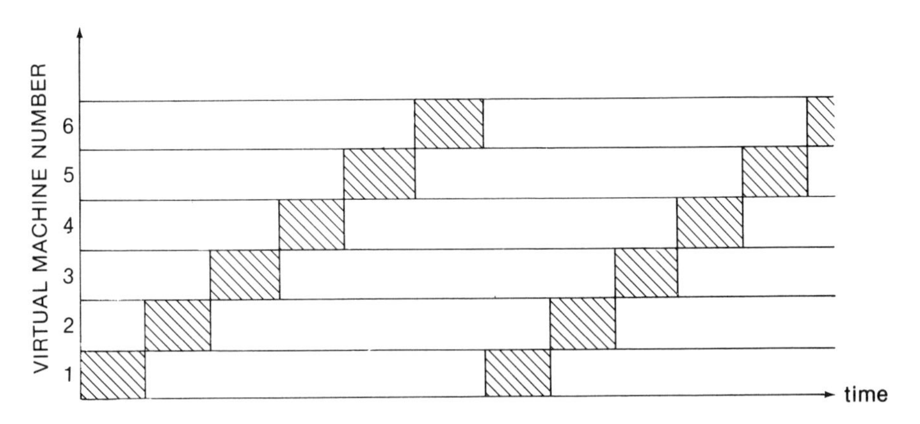

Figure 1-12 A static, temporal separation schedule. (Shading indicates time when machine runs.)

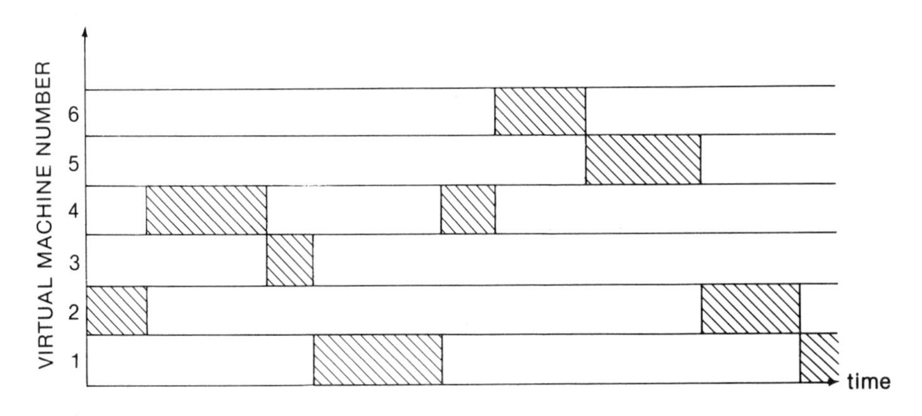

Figure 1-13 A dynamic, temporal separation schedule

1.5.3 Enforcement

A proper enforcement mechanism must separate the virtual machines sharing physical resources and must ensure that each virtual machine operates only within its defined boundaries. The enforcement mechanism should be reasonably efficient, in the sense that its presence not slow system operation, and should be flexible, in the sense that the mechanism design should not restrict the choice of management policies.

Three basic approaches to confining virtual machines differ with respect to the time that checks are made to ensure that boundaries are not violated:

1. Any process can be executed; anything that a virtual machine might do is legal within the boundary. We say that an enforcement mechanism that permits this flexibility is an *anything goes* mechanism. Under this scheme an action of a virtual machine need not be checked for legality.

2. Any process can be executed; everything that a virtual machine tries to do is checked to see that it is within limits. We say that an enforcement mechanism that makes these checks is an *everything checked* mechanism. Under this scheme every action of a virtual machine must be checked during program execution (i.e., dynamically).
3. Only certain programs can be executed; in these "safe" programs nothing illegal is ever attempted. We say that an enforcement mechanism that uses this constraint supports the *nothing illegal* approach. Under this scheme every virtual machine is statically verified not to violate the restrictions before it is presented for execution; therefore, there is no need for dynamic legality checks.

Under the "anything goes" design, anything that an executing process can generate, such as an address or an instruction, has a legal interpretation within its context.

Example 1-12

Consider the enforcement of memory allocation policies. A simple mapping from virtual machine V's memory space to the physical machine's memory space could be defined by the address translation relation

$$p = v + R \tag{1-1}$$

where p and v are the physical and virtual addresses, respectively, and R is a "relocation constant." Suppose that the host system's memory allocator guarantees that sufficient space is allocated such that every value of p that can result from applying the translation of V's virtual addresses does access space allocated for V. Then the system supports an "anything goes" memory-accessing policy.

Under the "everything checked" design, a constituent virtual machine is not trusted to do things correctly, and there exist requests that it can generate but should not be allowed to execute. For example, it might be able to create virtual memory addresses that translate to physical memory locations which have been assigned to another virtual machine. Clearly, under this design the enforcement mechanism must check every memory address against the address limits before the access can be allowed.

Example 1-13

Suppose that a memory address mapping is defined by a pair of registers specifying the origin of the (single) physical memory block and the address bound. The checking mechanism must verify that each address is within the specified limit. If the limit is violated, the checking mechanism should interrupt the machine's operation and pass control to the system.

A simple machine emulator can be augmented to check memory addresses and verify the legality of each access attempt. For a simple case, assume that each instruction contains a single operand address and that each instruction occupies a single addressable memory location. If any address check fails, the program raises (or causes) an exception called "error." After the error exception is raised, the system regains control and prevents the program from proceeding; these details are not shown in the program fragment that follows. The memory limit held in the variable address_limit defines the range of memory addresses allocated to the virtual machine. The calculation required to map the virtual address to the allocated physical block is not shown.

```
    error : exception; --declare the error object
    ..                 --declare other objects
begin
    loop
        ..
        if program_counter > address_limit then
            raise error; --instruction out of bounds
        end if;
        fetch_next_instruction;
        ..                                  --decode it
        eff_addr:=effective_address(instruction);
                        --compute the operand's address
        if eff_addr > address_limit then
            raise error; --operand out of bounds
        end if;
        ..         --execute the rest of the instruction
    end loop;
end;
```

Under the "nothing illegal" design, the virtual machine's instruction stream is guaranteed to abide by the boundary constraints. Although an arbitrary virtual machine operating in the same context might violate the boundaries, such "illegal" machines will not be allowed to execute. Guarantees may be provided by a compiler, which has been verified to produce only "proper" object programs. Since the compiler cannot be expected to know (before execution) when the system might change boundaries, the virtual machine must be confined within static boundaries (as seen from the virtual machine). The boundary enforcement mechanism for such a system must ensure that every executed program was created by an approved compiler. The compiler or the system must mark all program files that every approved compiler produces and the system must guarantee that others cannot spoof such files. If these restrictions are violated, the system integrity might be compromised.

The three design philosophies can be depicted diagrammatically; see Figure 1-14. The outer box in the drawings represents the host's capabilities. The solid box inside represents the virtual machine's compartment within the host's space. The dashed box represents the scope of what the virtual machine may ask to be done. The shaded area within the dashed box indicates the range of the virtual machine's actual requests. Under the "anything goes" option, the shaded box must not extend outside the VM's solid box inside the host's (compartment) box (see Figure 1-14a). Under the "everything checked" option, the checking process prohibits any request that lies in the dashed box but is outside the solid VM box; thus this design option leads to a situation in which the shaded area extends into disallowed territory (see Figure 1-14b). Under the "nothing illegal" design, the shaded area automatically lies within the solid VM box (Figure 1-14c).

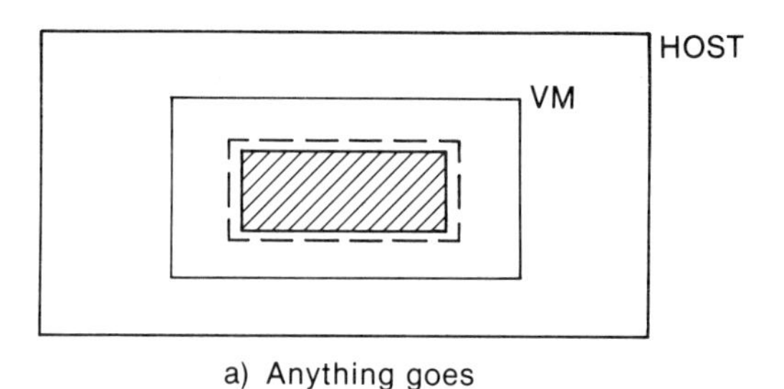

a) Anything goes

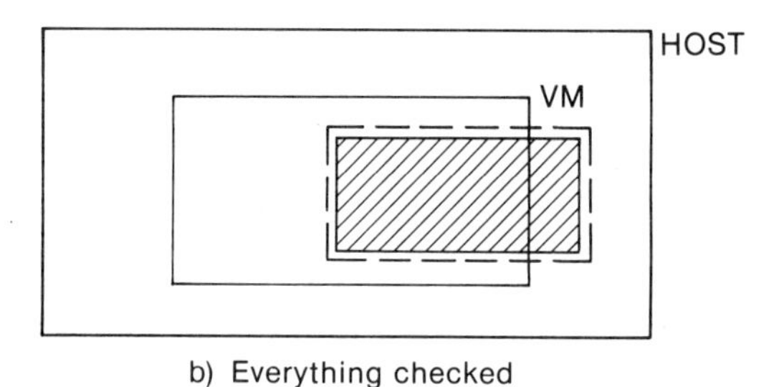

b) Everything checked

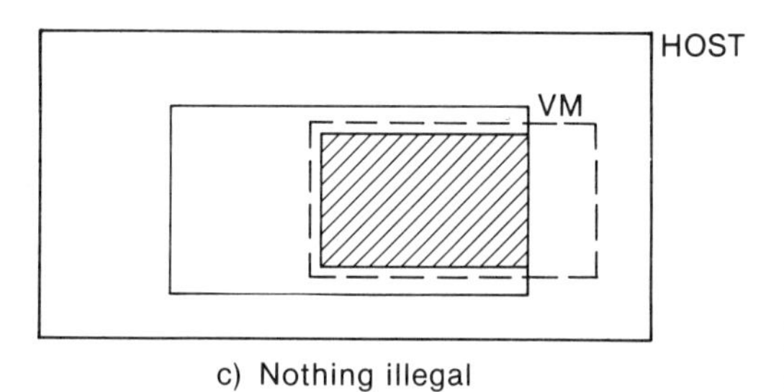

c) Nothing illegal

Figure 1-14 Illustrating virtual machine confinement techniques

1.6 SYSTEM PERFORMANCE

Many design options have been developed and implemented to improve system performance. Therefore, to evaluate a design option, one must be able to estimate the performance of a design utilizing that option. Unfortunately, the precise determination of system performance can be difficult, possibly requiring a detailed simulation of the complete system.

Three performance determination techniques span the spectrum of possibilities:

1. Actual measurement
2. Approximate measurement
3. Statistical estimation

In *actual measurement* we implement the system and its application software and then run the system and time its operation. For *approximate measurement*, we implement both the system and "important" portions of the application software and then execute and time that part of the software. By examining the structure of the complete software suite, we extrapolate the measured performance of the partial system to estimate the performance of the system executing the complete software. For *statistical estimation*, we build a statistical model of the programs to be executed, we determine the execution times of small elements, such as individual instructions, and then we combine the usage statistics with the actual execution times to estimate the system's speed. This method is limited, however, since simple performance models provide only rough performance comparisons between similar system designs. If two designs diverge greatly, they cannot be compared while using the simplifying assumptions that lie behind statistical estimates.

The advantage of actual measurement is that the experimenter learns exactly how the application will perform on the system. The disadvantage, of course, is that the system must exist, either in hardware or in a timed simulator. The cost of implementing the system to this degree of fidelity may be too high. The value of the increased timing accuracy may not be worth the price.

The advantage of executing important portions of the application (often called "kernels") and then estimating the speed of the complete system is that the cost of the measurement will be greatly reduced compared to the cost of a complete system implementation. However, the accuracy suffers. It may be necessary to implement significant portions of the application to obtain sufficient accuracy.

Simple statistical performance estimation models are based on statistical characterizations of the behavior of programs to be executed on the system. One simple characterization often used for this purpose describes each program in terms of its use of processor instructions. In the first-order statistical model, a program is characterized by the probabilities $\{p_i\}$, $1 \leqslant i \leqslant N$, where p_i is the probability that an instruction randomly chosen from the program is an instruction whose function code corresponds to the ith processor instruction. To obtain a better estimate, similar statistics concerning the use of addressing modes can be collected and incorporated in the model. Still better fidelity can be obtained by gathering statistics about the use of special system features that have a significant impact on system performance. Note that this selection of the level of detail at which statistics are gathered is somewhat arbitrary. One major advantage of working at this low level of detail is that for many simple processor implementations, accurate data concerning the actual execution time for each function code and addressing mode can be obtained. When we discuss parallelism within implementations, we will find that such simple speed estimates may not be realistic—for example, system speed might depend on second-order statistics regarding program behavior.

An important question related to statistical performance estimation concerns the method of collecting the statistics. We could collect statistics about *static* program behavior by examining the memory locations containing instructions to count the number of occurrences of each feature (such as a function code). Real programs do not execute all of their instructions an equal number of times; instructions within repetitive loops will be performed a larger proportion of the time than it would appear from a static examination of the program. So *dynamic* statistics, which show the proportions of the instructions in execution, are required. But to obtain dynamic statistics, one needs to know the path of execution; finding this may require implementing the system.

One must be careful when mathematically combining the statistics; execution times can be probabilistically combined, but rates cannot be so combined. To illustrate the method, take processor instructions as the basic elements. Suppose that we have timed each instruction type and determined the execution probabilities of all instruction types. Let t_i and p_i denote the execution time and the execution probability, respectively, for instruction type *i*. Then the average instruction execution time (AIET) for a processor instruction is given by

$$\text{AIET} = \sum t_i p_i \quad (1\text{-}2)$$

This time can be converted into an execution rate by inversion; the reciprocal of the average instruction execution time will be the average instruction execution rate, often expressed in units of millions of instructions per second (MIPS).

We expect that the execution times of frequently executed instructions are important factors in system speed. We also expect that instructions that are almost never executed have little effect on the AIET, since their weights are so small. But in the intermediate probability range, the execution time of a long instruction will affect the system speed. For example, subroutine calling and return require state saving, which does take a number of memory cycles. It is important to have speedy subroutine entry and exit in a computer system if structured programming and hierarchical designs are to be used in the software, since these structuring techniques imply frequent subroutine calling. We explore designs for subroutine call and return in Chapter 6.

Example 1-14

To illustrate the effect of varying the execution probability and the basic speed of a processor instruction on the system's speed, we consider an artificial situation. Suppose

TABLE 1-4 SYSTEM PERFORMANCE IMPROVEMENT BY HALVING THE EXECUTION TIME OF AN INSTRUCTION WITH EXECUTION PROBABILITY *P* AND INITIAL EXECUTION TIME *T*

	T		
P	10	5	2.5
0.0	0.0	0.0	0.0
0.01	4.8	2.5	1.2
0.02	9.3	4.9	2.5
0.05	20.8	11.6	6.2
0.10	35.7	21.7	12.2
0.20	55.6	38.5	23.8
0.50	83.3	71.4	55.6
1.00	100.0	100.0	100.0

that all instructions except one require an identical amount of time, which we normalize to unity. The lone exception is one instruction I, whose speed we will improve by modifying the design. In the first design we suppose that I requires a normalized time T. Suppose that its execution time will be improved by redesign to $T/2$. Let P denote I's execution probability. Table 1-4 lists the percentage improvement in system performance as a function of P and T.

Even with the execution probability as low as 5%, a performance improvement of over 20% can be achieved by the assumed 50% reduction in I's execution time. On the other hand, when the instruction already performs well (having a small T, that is), the 50% reduction is achieved only when the execution probability is much higher.

A speed computed from instruction execution probabilities does not take into account realistic program structures. Program patterns show up in higher-order statistics about instruction type usage. Some program patterns have an important influence on computer design; these include loop structures and repetitive operations on related data. A very simple pattern, such as computing an indexed address and then loading the addressed object, can be implemented as a single processor instruction. Even if the two operations did remain separated (for compatibility), the processor designer can include logic to detect this pattern and then to execute the pair as a single operation. Looping structures make instruction caching worthwhile (as in Example 1-4). Repetitive patterns, such as repeated additions for adding two vectors, make a pipeline structure attractive (as in Example 1-5). In later chapters and in Volume 2 we discuss other patterns and some strategies to make their implementations more efficient.

It is important to note that comparisons among quite different architectures based on the raw MIP rate alone can be deceptive, since a single instruction in one machine might perform an operation that comprises a larger fraction of the function required for a particular application. The following simple example illustrates this point.

Example 1-15

Suppose that an application frequently copies large blocks of contiguous memory locations. With a simple processor architecture having no support for block copying, a program loop would have to be written to copy each individual object in the block from the source space to the destination space. Suppose that this basic object copy can be performed by a memory-to-memory move instruction, and suppose that the move requires two memory accesses to read the instruction and two memory accesses to copy the object. The loop also requires a count-and-test operation and an operation to modify the memory addresses used as the program progresses through the block. If the counter is kept in an index register, the loop test-and-count function could be performed by a single instruction, requiring a single memory fetch. We counted five memory accesses within the loop, which means that $5n$ memory accesses are required to copy n objects.

Now consider another processor design with a block move instruction; that instruction can be read in five memory accesses (more than the two for the copy because it requires more operand specifications) and thereafter the system copies the block of information using two memory accesses per object. In this design the entire block of n objects will be copied in $5 + 2n$ memory cycles. Despite this speedup, the raw MIP rate of the second design is much lower than that of the first design (see Problem 1-5).

In summary, system performance is an important design criterion. Crude estimates of a design's speed can be obtained from first-order statistics of instruction usage, but higher-order statistics are required to estimate the performance obtainable from sophisticated designs. Even high-order statistical models cannot be used to compare the speeds of two systems that have significantly different architectures. Nevertheless, knowing instruction execution probabilities helps the designer prioritize her design efforts when system performance is an important goal.

1.7 OUR EXAMPLE LANGUAGES

Throughout the book we use program fragments to illustrate linguistic features and to write algorithms. We primarily use Ada [ANSI83], a contemporary programming language based upon Pascal, since Ada contains many interesting features, including many supporting structured programming. Other programming languages will be used from time to time to illustrate linguistic features not present in Ada or to show the pervasiveness of the points under discussion.

The brief overview of Ada in Appendix A is designed to give the reader a reading knowledge of the language. We do not expect the reader to become a proficient Ada programmer before proceeding. In problems we may ask for an algorithm; an answer written in any language familiar to the reader should be adequate unless the problem is exploring the aspects of a particular linguistic feature, in which case the language to be used will be specified in the problem. When a language choice is permitted, a correct step-by-step algorithm will constitute a sufficient answer.

1.8 OUR EXAMPLE SYSTEMS

Throughout the book we pick out processor features that illustrate how processor designers have chosen to support features of programming languages, operating systems, and simple object manipulation and accessing. We use the Motorola MC68020 [MOTO84] processor as a source of many of these examples; many features of this processor are introduced in Chapter 2. We use other processors, as appropriate, to illustrate interesting or historically important designs.

As with the Ada language, we do not expect the reader to become proficient with all details of any single processr design. We expect an appreciation of the details of the implementations of these processors and the implications of the design features on other aspects of the complete computer system. In some problems we ask about features from "a familiar machine," in which case, choose any machine with which you are familiar.

1.9 SUMMARY

In this chapter we have seen how computer systems can be designed using varied approaches to modular structuring. We have seen the importance of such modular structures, both for conciseness of description and for increased probability of correct implementation. We have seen how virtual machine constructs can be used to implement modular structures and how the virtual machine abstraction can be implemented under different options. We have seen how system performance can be estimated using statistical characterizations of execution patterns. We have briefly surveyed the machines and languages that we use for examples in the remainder of the book. In later chapters we explore the space of design options for different system components.

1.10 PROBLEMS

1-1. Draw a block diagram of a familiar machine (choose any machine whose implementation is familiar to you) and write a description of the bus transactions required to implement a simple ADD instruction with an operand from memory. Be sure to account for all bus transactions required to access the instruction and its data operand. Check whether READ requires a second bus transaction during which the memory sends to the processor the data it has read. Explain the sequence of operations in your answer.

1-2. Consider the display memory from Example 1-2. The memory's controller must arbitrate among (potentially) conflicting requests to access the memory. In this problem we consider the average rates of access to the memory and the display. We do not distinguish

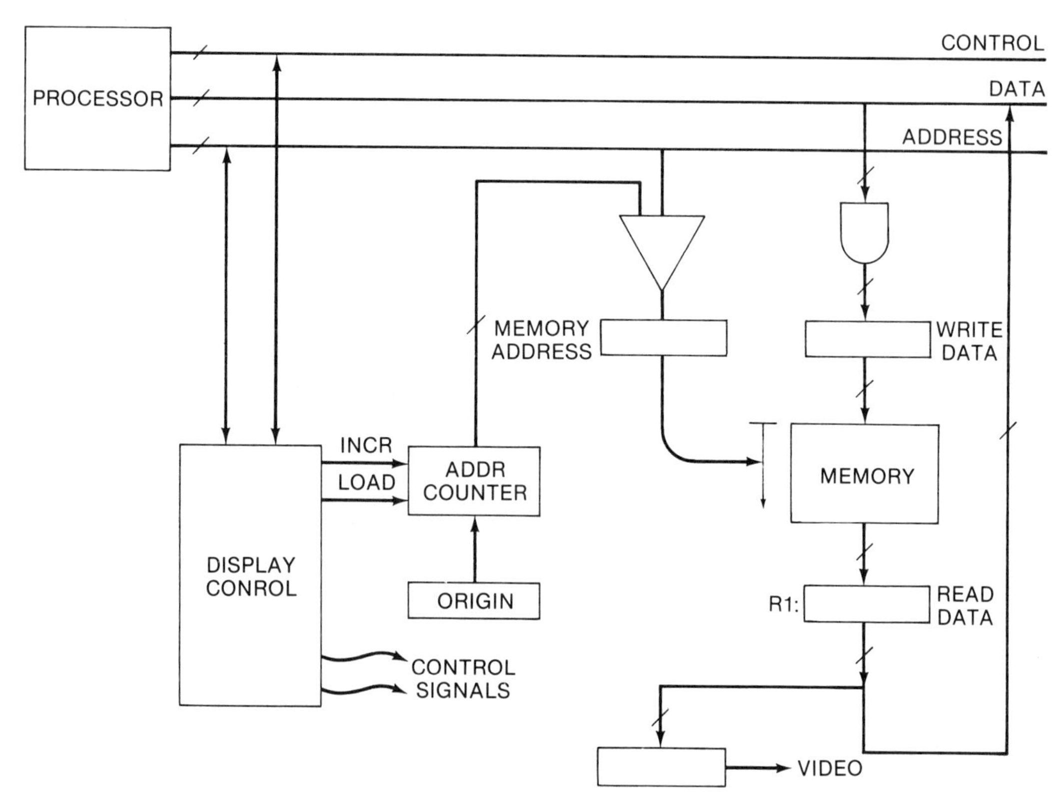

Figure 1-15 A display memory/controller system

between the line and blanking intervals. Since the performance constraint imposed on the memory's speed comes from the pixel rate of the display, priority must be given to requests for data to be presented on the display, but when time permits, requests from the processor to update the display must be serviced. In this problem use the data rates from the example for black/white pixels at conventional scan rates.

Suppose that the display generation logic looks like the structure in Figure 1-15. The memory is designed so that a new memory cycle cannot be initiated while another memory cycle is in progress. Any word read from memory is not available until the end of the memory cycle. Any word read from the memory for display purposes can be stored in register R1 until it is required for the next piece of the display line. As long as there are display data in R1 which have not yet been displayed, the memory cannot initiate another read cycle that would overwrite R1. However, a write cycle could be initiated to store information from the processor.

Here are three optional rules governing the priorities between memory requests from the display controller and from the processor:

1. A display request has priority and is initiated immediately after the previous word of display data is taken from R1.
2. A display request can be deferred until the last moment consistent with providing the data in time for use by the display generation logic. Processor requests can be handled as long as servicing them does not cause violation of this timing constraint. If a processor request arrives late in the cycle, such that initiating service for the processor request would force the display logic to miss data, service for that processor request will be deferred until after the display data have been retrieved.
3. Processor requests have priority, so they are serviced immediately after they arrive, provided that the memory is not busy. If the memory is busy when a processor request arrives, that request will be handled as soon as the memory becomes free.

Suppose that the display memory cycle time is 500 nanoseconds (ns), and that the processor requests access to the display memory on the average every 500 milliseconds (ms),[7] at times uncorrelated with the cycling of the memory for display generation. Each processor request requires a burst of 10 memory cycles to satisfy the request; the processor can be interrupted between these memory cycles, but these interruptions occur only if the display generator has priority for access to the display memory.

(a) For each of the three priority rules, draw a diagram illustrating the intervals between consecutive times that the display generation logic takes the word from R1. On the diagram show the times when service for a display read request could be initiated and the times when service for a processor-initiated request could be initiated.

(b) For each of the three priority rules, compute the probability that a processor request will actually disrupt the display due to data not being available when needed. In other words, compute the probability that a particular randomly arriving processor request will cause a disruption in the display.

(c) For each rule, compute the average amount of time that a processor-initiated read request will have to wait to be completed. Define the wait time as the interval between the time that the first request is made to the time that the last memory cycle satisfying that request is completed. Assume that every request accesses exactly 10 memory words.

[7]This is an average rate and is not meant to imply a regular pattern correlated with the display's cycling.

1-3. We described three techniques for the separation of virtual machines: "anything goes," "everything checked," and "nothing illegal." For each technique, describe an example of its use and clearly identify the module(s) responsible for the integrity of the virtual machine boundaries in the system.

1-4. In Example 1-14 the assumption was made that the details of the execution probabilities of the instructions not being speeded up were irrelevant in the determination of the entries in Table 1-4. Show that this assumption is valid.

1-5. This problem will make you aware of the difficulties inherent in specifying system performance in terms of raw instruction speeds, such as MIPs. To illustrate the problem, consider the block move instruction mentioned in Example 1-15. We consider two machine designs (A and B) which are identical except that machine A has the block move instruction and machine B does not. Machine B executes instructions at a rate of 0.75 MIPs. Machine A executes all of its instructions (except the block move) at the same rate as machine B. On the average machine B initiates a block move every 20 ms. Let the average block size be 300 objects, each object being accessible in a single memory cycle; this means that it will take two memory cycles to copy a single element of the block within the block move instruction. Use the timings of the block move instruction and the equivalent loop specified in the example. Each memory cycle lasts for 750 ns in both machines.

(a) Determine how long it would take machine A to perform the average block move.

(b) Determine how long it would take machine B to perform the same block move. Assume that machine B must execute a copying loop to copy all elements of the block, as described in the example. Use the loop timing parameters from the example.

(c) Determine how long it would take machine A to perform the functions executed by machine B in 1 second.

(d) Determine how many instructions would be executed by machine A to perform the same functions as machine B performs in 1 second. Remember that a single instruction performs the block copy.

(e) What is the MIP rate for design A?

(f) Compare the answers to parts c and e against the performance of machine B.

2

INSTRUCTION SET DESIGN

It is not enough to have a good mind.
The main thing is to use it well.
— Descartes

Methods are habits of the mind
and economies of the memory.
— A. Rivarol

The design of the processor's instruction set is an important architectural issue. We must provide ways to use the computer well. This is best accomplished by encapsulating frequent (or habitual) sequences into processor operations, thereby speeding execution while saving program space. In this chapter we present some important options in the design of a processor instruction set, and introduce the instruction sets of three computers.

The instruction set defines the system at the processor level. The instruction set simultaneously reflects the programmer's view of the system's state, the primitive operand types (that are manipulated by the system), and the operations that can be performed on those operands. Finally, the instructions specify how memory operands are accessed—specifically, how operand addresses are determined from the instruction and the contents of processor registers and memory locations.

In this chapter we present several examples of processor instruction set design. We start with a "minimum" machine, move forward to a RISC (Reduced Instruction Set Computer) machine, and then discuss a contemporary sophisticated microprocessor—the Motorola MC68020. The MC68020 will be a major source of examples of processor design in this book. We present the basic features of the

MC68020's instruction set and its operand addressing modes in this chapter. Further details of the MC68020 design are presented in subsequent chapters. We also discuss the notion of "orthogonality" between a processor's instruction set and its addressing modes.

After reading this chapter the reader should have a feeling for processor design, for what is essential in processor operation, and for the basic components of a complete computer system. The reader will learn about the representations and functions of some processor instructions, will learn the fundamentals of the MC68020, and will be prepared for the processor-level discussions that follow in succeeding chapters.

2.1 A MINIMAL INSTRUCTION SET

We start with a processor design which is minimum in the sense that a minimum set of logic gates would be required to implement a processor that matches the design. We call this design the MIN computer. There are many reasons why one would not actually want to implement this MIN design, including software complexity and slow operation. Nevertheless, our MIN discussion will introduce basic processor design concepts and our approach to discussing these concepts.

A processor design comprises several major aspects, all of which must be understood to write effective programs for the machine. These aspects must be specified completely and must be implemented properly in any realization of the machine. Four major aspects are:

1. Processor state
2. Memory system
3. Program control instructions
4. Object manipulation instructions

The *processor state* describes programmer-visible information which conceptually is stored within the processor; this state includes the contents of processor registers and control registers, such as the program counter. The *memory system* describes both the information stored in memory and the addressing techniques used to select information from memory during program execution. The *program control instructions* specify instruction sequencing for correct program execution. Finally, the *object manipulation* instructions specify how values can be manipulated by the processor. We discuss instruction formats as we discuss the processor's instructions.

2.1.1 MIN Processor State

MIN has two programmer-visible processor registers—a data register, called the accumulator (abbreviated ACC), and a control register, called the program counter (PC). The ACC contains 8 bits, designated by ACC_7 .. ACC_0 (with ACC_7 being the most significant bit). In figures the most significant bits will be drawn on the left side of the value. The PC contains 14 bits. These registers are depicted in Figure 2-1.

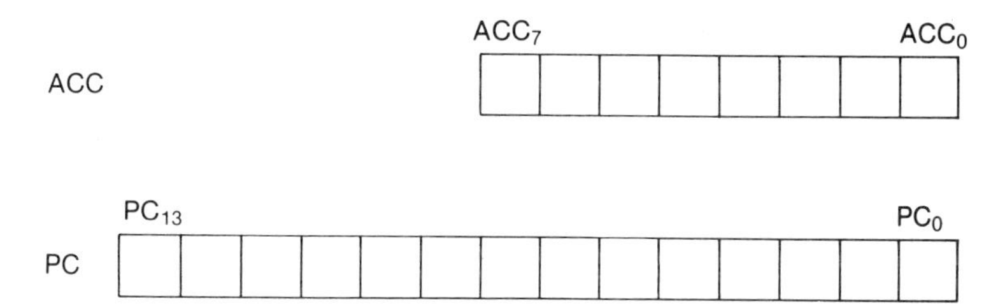

Figure 2-1 Programmer-visible MIN registers

Other registers we use to describe MIN include a memory address register (MAR), which contains 14 bits, a memory data register (MDR), which contains 8 bits, and an instruction register (IR), which contains 16 bits. Figure 2-2 shows these registers with some data paths connecting them to each other and to the processor and the memory. A curious reader may enjoy speculating about whether these other registers are used in the actual processor implementation; we show such registers

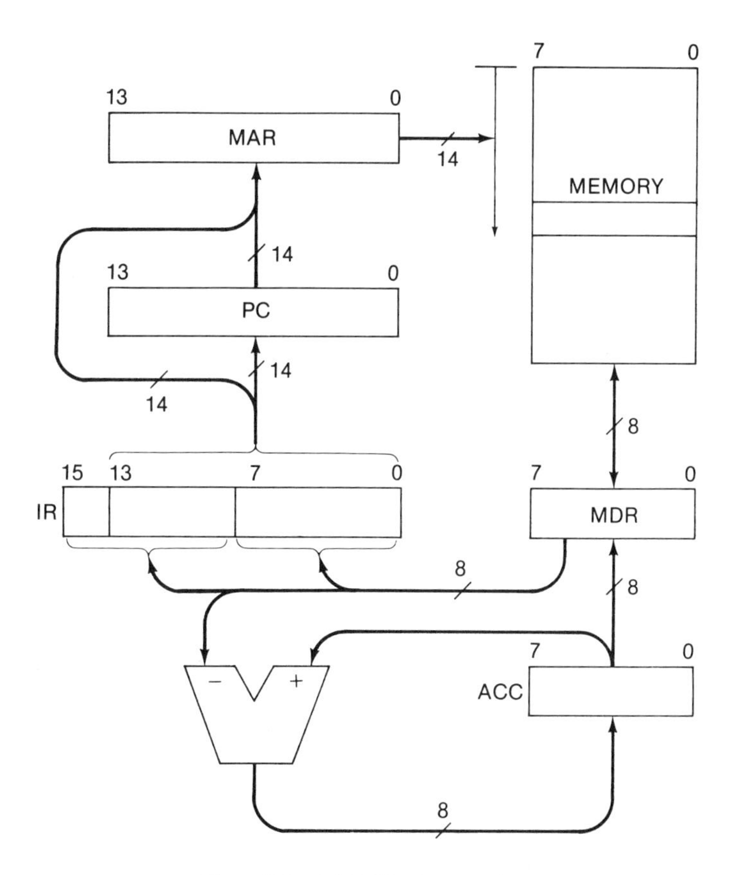

Figure 2-2 A MIN implementation

when they help explain the processor's behavior. Although we use these other registers, the reader should not conclude that all registers shown in these descriptions are necessarily present in a particular implementation of the described processor.

The symbolism introduced in Figure 2-2 is used consistently throughout the book. The basic figure elements are:

1. Horizontal rectangles
2. Braces
3. Directed branches
4. Large rectangles
5. Arrows
6. Stylized "V"

A horizontal rectangle symbolizes a register; a brace next to the rectangle indicates a portion of the register which may be transferred as a unit during some operation. Decimal integers that indicate bit positions may be placed above a register's rectangle to specify the positions of field boundaries within the register. To reduce clutter, we often mark these field boundaries only on one side.

A directed branch indicates a path along which data may flow, subject to control by the control unit (which may not be explicitly shown). If the path is a single bit wide, it is designated by a single line; otherwise, its width (in bits) is indicated by an integer next to a slash across the path.

A larger, usually vertical rectangle denotes a memory array, and an arrow along its side (usually the left) denotes the selection of the object in the memory array whose address matches the value arriving along a path that ends at the arrow. The data path to and from the memory usually ends in a register,[1] shown at the bottom of the array.

Finally, a stylized "V" module denotes an arithmetic unit, with the operand values arriving at the open ends of the "V" and the result delivered at the base of the "V."

2.1.2 MIN Memory Structure

The MIN memory contains 2^{14} bytes. A memory address designates an individual byte and therefore contains 14 bits. The basic memory operations are READ and WRITE.[2] During READ the memory system accesses the location designated in MAR and copies the byte found there into MDR. During WRITE the memory system copies the byte found in MDR into the memory location designated in MAR. To store a byte of information in MIN's memory, a program must first load the byte into the ACC and then execute a store (STO) instruction to copy it from the ACC to the memory location.

[1]Even though the memory may be implemented using a technology for which this data register is not electrically required, we will show the register in many drawings.

[2]READ and WRITE are not processor instructions but basic memory system operations; they are used to implement processor instructions.

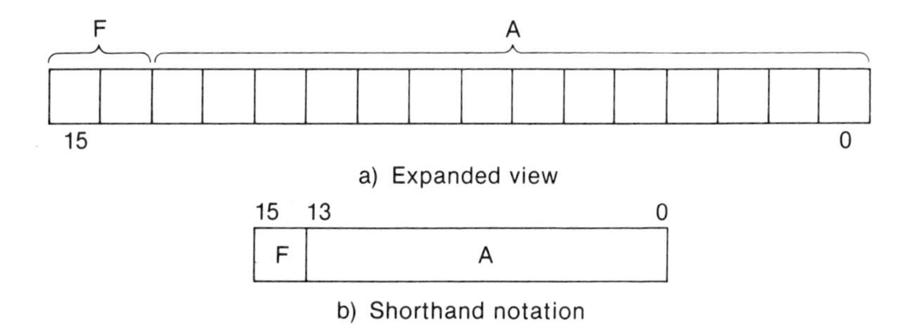

Figure 2-3 MIN instruction format

Every MIN instruction is two bytes long and is formatted into a 2-bit function code field (F) and a 14-bit address field (A), as shown in Figure 2-3. The division of an instruction into these fixed fields is reflected in the data path structure shown in Figure 2-2. The MIN function codes are listed in Table 2-1.

TABLE 2-1 MIN FUNCTION CODE ENCODING

Operation	Function Code
STO	0
SUB	1
JNG	2

To execute an instruction a processor must perform the following generic steps:

G1. Fetch the instruction;
G2. Advance PC;
G3. Decode the instruction;
G4. Perform the instruction.

A processor implementation of the MIN STO instruction could use the following detail steps to implement these generic steps:

D1. Copy PC into MAR;
D2. Read memory;
D3. Copy MDR into the left half of IR;
D4. Increment PC (add one to PC);
D5. Copy PC into MAR;
D6. Read memory;
D7. Copy MDR into the right half of IR;
D8. Increment PC;

D9. If bit $IR_{15} \neq 0$ or $IR_{14} \neq 0$, go elsewhere;

D10. Copy IR_{13} .. IR_0 to MAR;

D11. Copy ACC to MDR;

D12. Write memory;

D13. Go to step D1;

Here step G1 is implemented by steps D1 .. D7, step G2 by D8, step G3 by D9,[3] and step G4 by D10 .. D12. Step D13 completes the loop so that the processor will initiate the execution of its next instruction when the STO instruction is completed.

Now we will write the same semantics in a register-transfer form—a form more amenable to machine processing. We introduce some notation. Let IRH and IRL designate the high-order and low-order halves of IR, respectively, and let F and A designate the two instruction-field portions of IR. Let the assignment operator ":=" denote the act of placing a copy of the value of the expression on the right side into the location named on the left side. The register-transfer steps that implement STO are:

```
 D1. MAR:=PC;
 D2. READ;
 D3. IRH:=MDR;
 D4. PC:=PC + 1;
 D5. MAR:=PC;
 D6. READ;
 D7. IRL:=MDR;
 D8. PC:=PC + 1;
 D9. if F ≠ 0 then goto elsewhere;
D10. MAR:=A;
D11. MDR:=ACC;
D12. WRITE;
D13. go to step D1;
```

Since steps G1 and G2 are the same for all instructions, steps D1 .. D8 are identical for all MIN instructions.

2.1.3 MIN Control Instructions

MIN's control instructions and the PC advance rules embedded in its other instructions together determine the flow of execution through a processor's program. In MIN, any instruction not in the control instruction class changes PC by advancing it to the byte following the instruction being executed. This rule has the effect that instructions are performed in the same order that they are stored in memory. Of course, this sequencing rule is not adequate to perform general algorithms, so we need program control instructions to allow exceptions to the otherwise rigid sequential control flow.

[3]Actually, as written it simply verifies the function code, which is adequate here since we are not showing the execution of the other MIN processor instructions.

There is a single MIN control instruction, jump on negative (JNG). While executing JNG the processor tests the contents of ACC and either advances PC to the next instruction (like a noncontrol instruction) or loads PC with the address contained in the JNG instruction. The test, based on the value in the accumulator's most significant bit (ACC_7), causes the jump to occur when that bit is a 1.[4] Problem 2-4 asks for the detail steps necessary to execute this instruction.

2.1.4 Object Manipulation in MIN

In MIN all object manipulation is performed by a two-operand subtract instruction (SUB) whose operands are the contents of a memory location and the contents of the accumulator. It may seem surprising, but the system is functionally complete even though it supports only one object manipulation operation—integer subtraction.

After executing a SUB instruction, MIN's ACC will contain the difference between its previous contents and the contents of the memory location specified in the instruction. The data paths connected to the subtract module in Figure 2-2 are used to implement this instruction.

If we use a primed name to designate a value before the operation and a nonprimed name to designate a value after the operation, the SUB operation can be described by the relation

$$ACC = ACC' - M(A) \tag{2-1}$$

Here $M(x)$ denotes the contents of the memory location whose address is x, and A denotes the address specified in the SUB instruction. We use the equality operator rather than the assignment operator in this equation since the equation states a relationship among values rather than an action performed by a computer system.

2.1.5 More Complex Operations in MIN

Our claim that MIN is sufficient to perform any computer algorithm may seem farfetched, so in this section we present a few programs that perform simple functions. These programs are written in assembly language format using alphabetic names for memory locations and the three-letter mnemonics described in Table 2-1 to denote MIN function codes.

Example 2-1

This MIN program loads the accumulator with the contents of memory location X; it uses a temporary memory location, called T:

```
STO T;
SUB T;
SUB X;
STO T;
SUB T;
SUB T;
```

[4]In a complement representation for negative values, a 1 in the most significant bit denotes a negative value.

To illustrate the operation of this program, the reader can take initial values and follow the operation by emulating the behavior of the computer, tracking the contents of ACC, X, and T.

Another way to illustrate the function of the program is to perform a *symbolic execution* of the program. Before starting the symbolic execution, mathematical symbols are defined to denote the initial values in significant locations. During symbolic execution one develops mathematical formulas that express the values held in each location after each program instruction is executed. For the preceding program, the contents of ACC after executing the third instruction is $-x$, where x denotes the initial contents of memory location X. Problem 2-3 reveals more details concerning symbolic program execution.

Example 2-2

This MIN program adds the contents of X to the contents of the accumulator:

```
STO T;
SUB T;
SUB T;
SUB X;
STO T;
SUB T;
SUB T;
```

These example programs should be adequate to convince the reader that MIN can perform any object manipulation, if only because they show how functions that are primitive in other processors can be performed on MIN. More complex functions and programs can be constructed using these simple programs as building blocks. Using ADD, we can construct SHIFT LEFT, and that can be used with ADD to construct MULTIPLY. Continuing in this manner, we can build more complex functionality. In building the modular structure for complex functions, we may need more complex control structures than the simple JNG, however.

In generalizing the control structures, we must attend to the fact that the only way that control can be transferred is by first having a negative byte in ACC, so it is not possible to write a program to make an arbitrary control transfer and at the same time preserve the contents of ACC.

Example 2-3

As a simple illustration, consider the following attempt to implement an unconditional jump to location Y:

```
JNG Y;
STO T;
SUB T;
SUB T;
JNG Y;
```

It is easy to see that the contents of ACC will always be negative when Y is reached. It is also easy to see that this program does not work properly if the initial contents of ACC were zero. Problem 2-1 asks the reader to fix this "bug."

Since the ACC is modified during a control transfer, all program state information must be placed in memory prior to executing a program control function. Other information affecting program state might have to be treated as program constants. For example, subroutine calling in MIN requires that the return point location be a program constant and that it be stored in a designated memory location before control is transferred to the subroutine. The generic steps for subroutine calling in MIN are:

S1. Copy the return address to location R;
S2. Jump to location E;

Here R is the location reserved for holding the return address, and E is the location containing the first instruction of the subroutine. The generic steps for subroutine calling can be implemented in a MIN program by concatenating a copying program fragment with the jump program fragment given above.

2.1.6 Comments

There are several obvious reasons why the MIN design is not desirable, including:

1. Programs that perform "simple" functions are long and awkward.
2. Program execution will be slow.
3. The single accumulator implies lots of copying between the processor and memory.

On the other hand, there is one obvious reason why the MIN design might be desirable—it requires little logic to implement its functionality.

2.2 REDUCED INSTRUCTION SETS

Minimum processor instruction set designs (such as MIN) have an inherent speed disadvantage. A program to perform even a simple function will have many steps, since each instruction can perform only a small portion of the algorithm. On the other hand, a processor with a complex instruction set has a speed disadvantage due to the complexity of instruction decoding, the size of its control unit, and additional logic delays due to the number of sequencing decisions which must be made in the control unit. Reduced instruction set computers (RISCs[5]) have been proposed because, by providing a carefully selected small (but not minimum) instruction set, the instruction execution process can be made efficient and fast. The instruction set can provide some instructions outside the logically minimum set (MIN's set is close to the absolute minimum), so that practical programs do not grow too long. For example, a commercial implementation of the VAX architecture [SUPN84] on a single chip

[5] A computer with a complex instruction set (this includes most designs) is sometimes called a complex instruction set computer (CISC, pronounced "cisk").

relies on internal microcode to implement commonly executed instructions and supports other operations through a floating-point chip and through operating system software invoked after the processor logic causes an interrupt upon detecting an unimplemented operation code. In a sense, this microVAX is also a RISC design, even though it directly supports 175 function codes (out of 304 in the complete VAX architecture).

Practical implementations of RISC designs use a number of architectural techniques discussed in later chapters; here we present the essential features of the RISC architecture seen from the programmer's viewpoint. Several different RISC designs have been specified and constructed; here we discuss the Berkeley RISC systems which are well documented in the literature. There are two Berkeley RISC designs, RISC I [PATT82] and RISC II [SHER84], which implement the same instruction set but differ in implementation details (which we discuss later). To discriminate between the general RISC approach and the Berkeley processor design, we call the latter the BRISC design. Two other early RISC designs are the IBM 801 [RADI82] and the Stanford MIPS [HENN82].

2.2.1 BRISC Processor State

A BRISC processor handles 32-bit integers. From the programmer's viewpoint, there are 32 operand registers in the processor; each can hold one 32-bit value. In fact, however, the operand register numbered zero always contains zero, so 31 writable operand registers are available during a computation. We denote the ith operand register by $R(i)$.

The remaining programmer-visible registers are the 32-bit program counter (PC) and the 4-bit condition code register (CCR). There are four condition bits in the BRISC CCR:

1. N (negative)
2. Z (zero)
3. C (carry)
4. V (overflow)

The values in CCR reflect the result of an operation or the state of a copied value; the programmer has explicit control over when CCR will be modified, as discussed later. All of these condition bits have obvious interpretations, except V, which is set if an arithmetic operation results in sign inconsistencies that signal arithmetic overflow. On addition, for example, V is set if the operand signs are the same and the result sign has the opposite value.

2.2.2 BRISC Memory Structure

BRISC memory addresses are 32 bits long, and these memory addresses designate individual bytes.

BRISC memory access instructions have the format illustrated in Figure 2-4a. There is only one addressing mode, with an address specified by the values in the

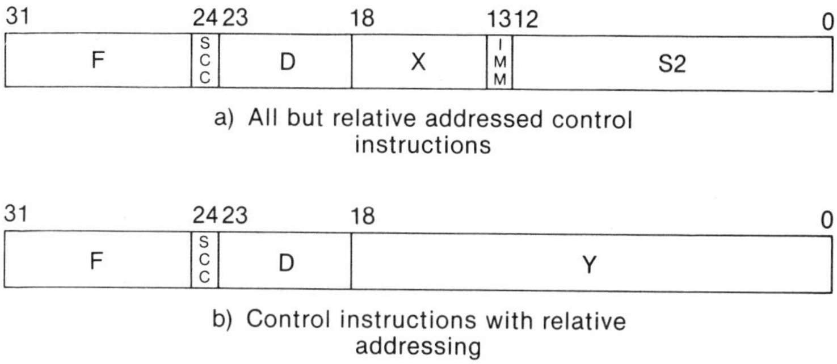

31 — 24	23	— 18	— 13	12	— 0
F	SCC	D	X	IMM	S2

a) All but relative addressed control instructions

31 — 24	23	— 18	— 0
F	SCC	D	Y

b) Control instructions with relative addressing

Figure 2-4 BRISC instruction formats (from [PATT82]; © 1982 IEEE)

instruction fields X,[6] IMM, and S2. The memory address A is computed as follows:

1. **If** IMM = 0 **then** OFF := R(S2) **else** OFF := sign_ext(S2);
2. A := R(X) + OFF;

In the first step the offset is determined; either the contents of the S2 field[7] or the contents of the register specified in that field are used, with the immediate bit IMM denoting which option is used. In the second step the offset is added to the "index" value, taken from the register specified in the X field. A simple address computation is specified by choosing R(0), which always contains zero.

To express memory addresses in BRISC assembly programs, we use the notation (Rx)OFF, where OFF is the offset value and x is the index register number [SHER84]. If OFF is a constant, the OFF field contains that integer. On the other hand, if the offset is to be taken from register Ri, we write the symbol "R" in the OFF field, followed by the register number.

Example 2-4

Suppose that register *i* contains 3*i*, for all *i*. Table 2-2 illustrates several address specifications and the corresponding memory addresses. The names often used to describe the corresponding addressing modes are also given.

TABLE 2-2 ILLUSTRATING BRISC ADDRESS CALCULATIONS[a]

Address Specification in Program Text	Instruction Field Contents			Actual Address	Addressing Mode
	IMM	S2	X		
(R0)3	1	3	0	3	Absolute
(R0)R3	0	3	0	9	Base
(R6)0	1	0	6	12	Register indirect
(R3)3	1	3	3	C	Indexed
(R3)R3	0	3	3	12	Base and index
(R5)R3	0	3	5	18	Base and index

[a]All values are represented in hexadecimal notation.

[6]Later we discuss the use of this field to specify the source of an operand; at that time, we refer to this field by the name "S1."

[7]With its sign extended, which means that $OFF_{31} = OFF_{30} = OFF_{29} = .. = OFF_{12} = S2_{12}$.

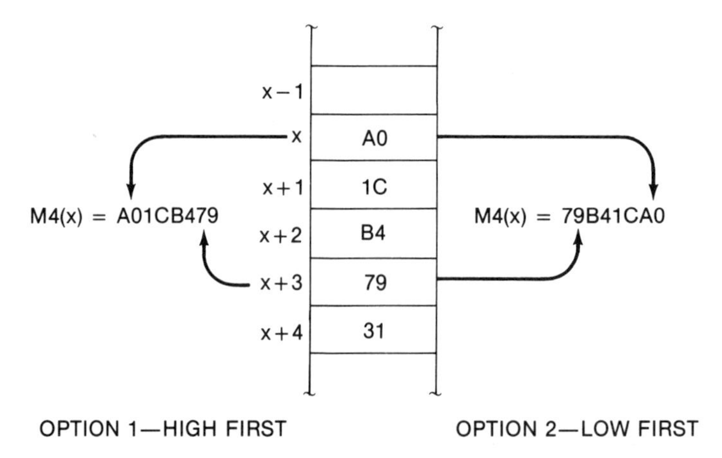

Figure 2-5 Byte ordering options

BRISC processors access memory for operands only in LOAD and STORE class instructions. These operations support byte (b—8-bit), half (h—16-bit), and word (w—32-bit) operand widths. On copying word operands, the complete destination is filled with the designated value. On copying byte or half operands to memory, the right portion of the designated register is copied to the specified memory locations. The leftmost byte selected from the register is always copied into the address specified in the instruction and any additional bytes are stored in succeeding locations. This rule states that a multiple-byte value is stored with the first byte holding the most significant portion of the value; this rule is used in BRISC, the VAX machines, and the MC68020, and is illustrated in Figure 2-5.[8] When copying half or byte operands to a register, the bytes from memory are placed at the right end of the destination register, and the programmer must specify whether the leftmost register bits are to be copies of the sign (leftmost) bit from memory or are all to be cleared (in which case the operand is considered to be *unsigned*).

Table 2-3 lists all the BRISC LOAD and STORE class instructions. In the

TABLE 2-3 BRISC LOAD AND STORE INSTRUCTIONS

Mnemonic	Operands	Name	Effect
ldw	Rd, (Rx)OFF	load word	Rd := M4(A)
ldhu	Rd, (Rx)OFF	load half	Rd := M2(A)
ldhs	Rd, (Rx)OFF	load half signed	Rd := sign_ext(M2(A))
ldbu	Rd, (Rx)OFF	load byte	Rd := M1(A)
ldbs	Rd, (Rx)OFF	load byte signed	Rd := sign_ext(M1(A))
stw	Rd, (Rx)OFF	store word	M4(A) := Rd
sth	Rd, (Rx)OFF	store half	M2(A) := Rd
stb	Rd, (Rx)OFF	store byte	M1(A) := Rd

Source: After [SHER84] © 1984 IEEE.

[8]The opposite rule, illustrated in Figure 2-5b, states that the lowest location holds the lowest portion of the value; this rule is used in the IBM 370 series, in the 6502, and in the Intel 8086 series (used in IBM PCs).

	BEFORE			AFTER	
	LOCATION	CONTENTS		LOCATION	CONTENTS
MEMORY:	A	A B		A	A B
	A + 1	3 4	1dw R1, (R0)A →	A + 1	3 4
	A + 2	5 6		A + 2	5 6
	A + 3	7 8		A + 3	7 8
PROCESSOR:					
R1:	C D E F A 1 B 2		R1:	A B 3 4 5 6 7 8	

	LOCATION	CONTENTS		LOCATION	CONTENTS
MEMORY:	A	A B		A	A B
	A + 1	3 4	1dhu R1, (R0)A →	A + 1	3 4
	A + 2	5 6		A + 2	5 6
	A + 3	7 8		A + 3	7 8
PROCESSOR:					
R1:	C D E F A 1 B 2		R1:	0 0 0 0 A B 3 4	

	LOCATION	CONTENTS		LOCATION	CONTENTS
MEMORY:	A	A B		A	A B
	A + 1	3 4	1dhs R1, (R0)A →	A + 1	3 4
	A + 2	5 6		A + 2	5 6
	A + 3	7 8		A + 3	7 8
PROCESSOR:					
R1:	C D E F A 1 B 2		R1:	F F F F A B 3 4	

	LOCATION	CONTENTS		LOCATION	CONTENTS
MEMORY:	A	A B		A	A B
	A + 1	3 4	1dbu R1, (R0)A →	A + 1	3 4
	A + 2	5 6		A + 2	5 6
	A + 3	7 8		A + 3	7 8
PROCESSOR:					
R1:	C D E F A 1 B 2		R1:	0 0 0 0 0 0 A B	

	LOCATION	CONTENTS		LOCATION	CONTENTS
MEMORY:	A	A B		A	A B
	A + 1	3 4	1dbs R1, (R0)A →	A + 1	3 4
	A + 2	5 6		A + 2	5 6
	A + 3	7 8		A + 3	7 8
PROCESSOR:					
R1:	C D E F A 1 B 2		R1:	F F F F F F A B	

	LOCATION	CONTENTS		LOCATION	CONTENTS
MEMORY:	A	A B		A	C D
	A + 1	3 4	stw R1, (R0)A →	A + 1	E F
	A + 2	5 6		A + 2	A 1
	A + 3	7 8		A + 3	B 2
PROCESSOR:					
R1:	C D E F A 1 B 2		R1:	C D E F A 1 B 2	

	LOCATION	CONTENTS		LOCATION	CONTENTS
MEMORY:	A	A B		A	A 1
	A + 1	3 4	sth R1, (R0)A →	A + 1	B 2
	A + 2	5 6		A + 2	5 6
	A + 3	7 8		A + 3	7 8
PROCESSOR:					
R1:	C D E F A 1 B 2		R1:	C D E F A 1 B 2	

	LOCATION	CONTENTS		LOCATION	CONTENTS
MEMORY:	A	A B		A	B 2
	A + 1	3 4	stb R1, (R0)A →	A + 1	3 4
	A + 2	5 6		A + 2	5 6
	A + 3	7 8		A + 3	7 8
PROCESSOR:					
R1:	C D E F A 1 B 2		R1:	C D E F A 1 B 2	

Figure 2-6 Illustrating BRISC load and store operations

effect column the arrays M1, M2, and M4 all refer to the same memory, the difference being the width of the data accessed. All three are indexed by the byte address of the most significant byte of an item. The number in the name indicates the number of bytes accessed. When the lengths of the operands on the two sides of an assignment operation do not match, a zero-filled right-adjusted operation is assumed to have been used to make the widths compatible. Figure 2-6 illustrates the effects of the different cases.

2.2.3 BRISC Control Instructions

BRISC load, store, and arithmetic instructions advance the PC to the next word, which contains the next instruction. In this manner, sequential instruction execution is supported by BRISC processors. Control instructions provide exceptions to "normal" sequencing.

The BRISC control instruction set in user mode contains five instructions, comprising two jump instructions, two call instructions, and one return instruction. Table 2-4 lists these instructions. There are two different methods by which BRISC jump and call instructions compute the destination address. First, the absolute memory address can be specified in the instruction (using the operand addressing methods discussed in the preceding section). Second, the PC value can be modified by adding a signed 19-bit displacement Y (see the format in Figure 2-4b) to the previous (incremented) PC value.

TABLE 2-4 BRISC USER CONTROL INSTRUCTIONS[a]

Mnemonic	Operands	Name	Effect
jmpx	COND, (Rx)OFF	conditional jump (indexed)	if COND then PC:=A
jmpr	COND, Y	conditional jump (relative)	if COND then PC:=PC + sign_ext(Y)
callx	Rd, (Rx)OFF	call indexed	Rd:=PC; PC:=A
callr	Rd, Y	call relative	Rd:=PC; PC:=PC + sign_ext(Y)
ret	(Rx)OFF	return	PC:=A

Source: After [SHER84] © 1984 IEEE.
[a]Register changes during call and return not shown.

All JUMP instructions are conditionally executed; the D instruction field's contents are decoded to determine which condition must be true for the JUMP to be taken. If the value in the CCR meets the condition, the processor loads the PC with the specified address, to be effective for fetching the instruction *after* the one that follows the JUMP instruction. This timing produces a *delayed jump*, which is discussed further in Section 1.6 of Volume 2.

Example 2-5

Consider a program executing sequentially which starts at location A0. The consecutive instructions will be taken from locations A0, A4, A8, AC, B0, B4, B8, BC, ... If the instruction in location A8 contains a jump to location BC, and the other instructions contain no control transfers, then the consecutive instructions are taken from locations A0, A4, A8, AC, BC, C0, C4, ... The effect of the delayed branching is that the instruction after the branch (the one at location AC) is executed after the branch instruction and before the branch is taken. This sequencing is counterintuitive, because when the branch is taken, the next instruction does not come from the location specified in its destination. In some algorithms, it may be possible to rearrange the program to place a useful instruction immediately after the branch, but if that is not possible, a no-operation (NOP) instruction will have to be placed there.

Subroutines, an important modularization tool, are supported in the control structure of every practical machine. Separate instructions assist subroutine initiation (call) and subroutine completion (return). In BRISC machines, the two call instructions store the incremented program counter (which points to the instruction two locations following the call instruction) in the register designated by the D field. In addition, the processor registers are adjusted, as will be described in Section 6.3. The return instruction generates its address using the general operand addressing mode described in Section 2.2.2. The offset should be zero and the register in which the saved PC value is stored should be selected.[9]

2.2.4 Object Manipulation in BRISC

The BRISC processors support operand manipulations between values in registers only. Every operand comes from a register, and the result is always placed in a register. Figure 2-7 depicts the operand flow. This type of operation is usually called an RR instruction since the information flow is from Register to Register. In BRISC the three roles (two operands and one result) may be assumed by three different

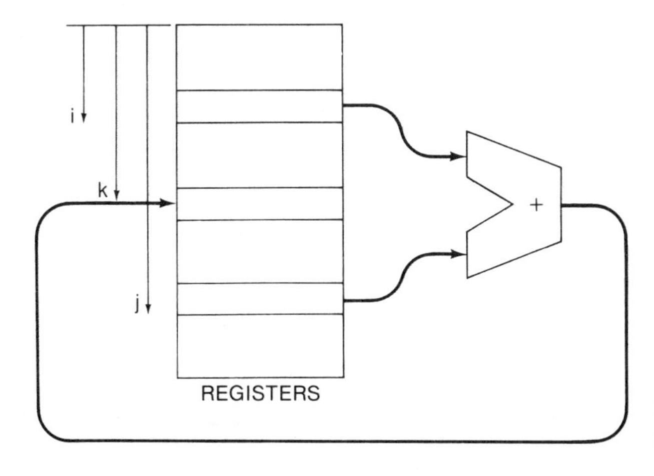

Figure 2-7 Operand flow for the BRISC instruction; Add Rk, Ri, Rj

[9]Due to register adjustment, this, in fact, requires using a register number in the return instruction greater by 16 than the register number used in the matching call instruction; see Section 6.3.

registers; the S1[10] and S2 instruction fields designate the register numbers of the two source operands, while the D field designates the register number of the destination of the result. However, if the IMM bit is 1, the S2 operand is the constant value found in the S2 instruction field. Since the S2 operand value is determined just like an address offset would be determined during a memory address computation, we use OFF to denote that value in our descriptions.

Both integer and boolean operations are provided in BRISC. The integer operations are ADD and SUBTRACT, each having two variants, based on whether the carry bit C (from CCR) is used as an operand.[11] In addition, there is an inverse subtract operation in which the roles of the two operands are reversed (see Table 2-5).

TABLE 2-5 BRISC OPERAND MANIPULATION INSTRUCTIONS

Mnemonic	Operands	Name	Effect
add	Rd, Rs, OFF	integer add	Rd := Rs + OFF
addc	Rd, Rs, OFF	add with carry	Rd := Rs + OFF + C
sub	Rd, Rs, OFF	integer subtract	Rd := Rs − OFF
subc	Rd, Rs, OFF	sub with borrow	Rd := Rs − OFF − C
subi	Rd, Rs, OFF	inverse subtract	Rd := OFF − Rs
subci	Rd, Rs, OFF	subi with borrow	Rd := OFF − Rs − C
and	Rd, Rs, OFF	logical AND (bits)	Rd := Rs and OFF
or	Rd, Rs, OFF	logical Or (bits)	Rd := Rs or OFF
xor	Rd, Rs, OFF	exclusive OR (bits)	Rd := Rs xor OFF
sll	Rd, Rs, OFF	shift left by OFF	Rd := shleft (Rs, OFF)
srl	Rd, Rs, OFF	shift right by OFF	Rd := shrlog (Rs, OFF)
sra	Rd, Rs, OFF	shift right by OFF	Rd := shrtar (Rs, OFF)

Source: After [SHER84] © 1984 IEEE.

The BRISC boolean operations are AND, OR, and EXCLUSIVE OR. Finally, there are three shift operations that take the shift count from S2 and shift the S1 operand to the left, logically to the right, or arithmetically to the right. Logical and arithmetic shifts differ in the manner in which the end bits of the result value are determined; this is a problem only at the end away from which the information is moving during the shift. In a left shift, zeros are always used to fill the right bit position, regardless of the previous value of that bit. In a right shift, zeros are filled in if the shift is *logical*, whereas the sign bit is retained if the shift is *arithmetic*. The latter rule is compatible with the interpretation of a right shift as a division by 2, if negative values are encoded using a complement representation. In the table we use shift functions to specify the effects of the operations; these functions shift the left operand by the number of bit positions given by the right operand.

The condition codes contained in CCR can be modified during the execution of any processor instruction. Whether CCR will be written is specified by the bit in the

[10]This is the instruction field that we called "X" while discussing the processor's addressing modes; it is labeled X in Figure 2-4.

[11]The carry is used as an operand to implement multiple-precision arithmetic operations.

SCC field in the instruction; if this field contains 1, CCR will be updated during the instruction's execution. In assembly programs a "(C)" after an instruction's operand specifications denotes setting the SCC bit in that instruction, so that the processor will leave new status information in CCR when the instruction is completed.

2.2.5 More Complex Operations in BRISC

BRISC does not support integer multiplication, integer division, or floating-point operations of any kind. The omission of floating-point operations can seriously degrade performance in scientific applications.

Example 2-6

Here is a program for double-precision integer addition. Each value is located in a pair of consecutive words, with the first location containing the most significant bits. With the operand locations specified in registers 2 and 3, and the result location specified in register 4, the program is

```
ldw R6,(R2)4        --load least significant part of operands
ldw R7,(R3)4
add R8,R6,R7(C)     --perform the least significant addition
stw R8,(R4)4        --store least significant part of result
ldw R6,(R2)0        --repeat above for most significant parts
ldw R7,(R3)0
addc R8,R6,R7(C)    --note use of C bit left from other part
stw R8,(R4)0
```

After this program fragment completes execution, the value in the Z condition code bit will not reflect the nature of the result, but the other condition code bits will be correct.

2.2.6 Orthogonality in BRISC

Computer architects use the term "orthogonal" to indicate that two design features can be specified independently. In BRISC, for example, the addressing modes are orthogonal to the instruction set, since the function code does not limit the selection of addressing modes, provided that the instruction does require an address.

The BRISC condition-code-setting options are orthogonal to the instruction set. In addition, the instruction field formats for the F, D, and SCC fields are identical for all instructions.

Orthogonality not only simplifies the assembly programmer's task of remembering constraints, but also simplifies compiler code generation logic, especially if operand addressing and location options are independent of the operation being performed.

At the hardware design level, orthogonality decreases delays and simplifies implementation logic, since every orthogonal aspect removes a need to check one portion of the instruction to decide how to handle other portions of the instruction.

Many CISC architectures have far less orthogonality in their processor instruction sets than does BRISC. We will see a lot of interaction between the function code and the instruction format in the MC68020; these interactions arise partly due to compatibility design constraints.

2.3 THE MOTOROLA MC68020 INSTRUCTION SET

The Motorola MC68020 processor contains several sophisticated features that support the implementation of high-level languages and complex intermodule control structures; for this reason we have selected this processor as the primary processor for our descriptions of processor architectures. In this section we present some simpler features of the MC68020; most of these features were inherited from the earlier MC68000 and MC68010 processor designs. Although it is interesting to observe such similarities and to root out the changes, we discuss only the MC68020 processor here to keep the presentation simple.

This section is designed to give the reader an appreciation for the instruction set and certain instruction representations used in the MC68020. We also observe the complexity of the instruction representations and the consequent impact on the design's orthogonality. We assume that assembly language programming for at least one processor is familiar to the reader starting the section. The reader is not expected to become a proficient assembly language programmer by reading this section.

2.3.1 MC68020 Processor State

The MC68020 handles 32-bit operands and addresses, and its data and address registers contain 32 bits. Despite the processor registers containing 32 bits, historical evolution dictates that MC68020 documentation use the term "word" to denote a 16-bit quantity. The term "long word" is used to denote a 32-bit quantity. For consistency with the available documentation, we also use the foregoing terminology.

The processor contains eight data registers, called D0 .. D7, and eight address registers, called A0 .. A7. Register A7 has a special role as a stack pointer, so it should not be used wantonly. In addition, the user-mode[12] programmer sees a 32-bit program counter (PC) and a 16-bit condition code register (CCR), of which the leftmost 11 bits are always zero in user mode. Figure 2-8 depicts these user-visible registers.

The conditions indicated by CCR bits are listed in Table 2-6. The C, N, V, and

TABLE 2-6 CCR BITS IN THE MC68020

Bit Position	Mnemonic	Meaning
0	C	Carry
1	V	Overflow
2	Z	Zero
3	N	Negative
4	X	Extension

[12] In supervisor mode other status information is visible in CCR.

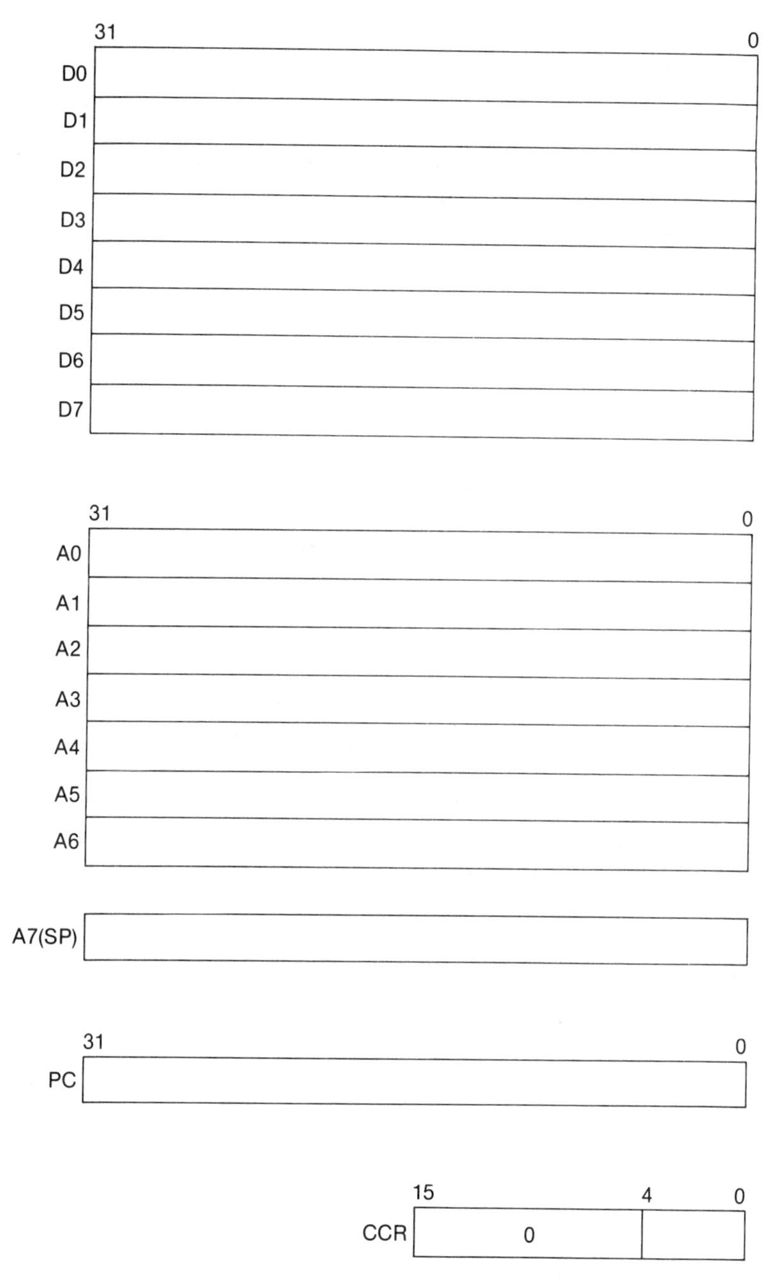

Figure 2-8 User-visible MC68020 registers (after [MOTO84]; courtesy of Motorola, Inc.)

Z bits are interpreted as in BRISC processors. The X bit supports extended-precision operations. The X bit is not modified during the execution of most instructions; in fact, it is modified only during addition, subtraction, negation, certain rotate, and certain shift instructions. The state of the X bit cannot be determined through conditional branching, but it can be used as an additional operand in specific addition, subtraction, negation, and rotate instructions.

Recall that in BRISC the programmer could selectively specify when CCR would be affected by instruction execution. In the MC68020, whether CCR is affected is determined by the function code of the instruction being executed; the programmer has no option to selectively override the built-in rules.

To describe the processor's operation, we introduce other registers which are not programmer visible and, in fact, may not actually exist in a particular implementation of the system. We use MAR, MDR, and IR registers (as we did with MIN); in this system all of them contain 32 bits.

2.3.2 MC68020 Memory Structure

The MC68020's memory is viewed as a set of bytes. Memory addresses select individual bytes. Conceptually, the memory may access a byte, a word, or a long word in a single memory cycle, and any of these items may begin at any (byte) address. To construct a word or long word, the constituent byte with the lowest address is placed in the leftmost result position, and the last byte is placed in the rightmost result position, just as in BRISC.[13]

We use three different data structures to describe the (identical) memory contents: M1(A), M2(A), and M4(A). The integer in the name indicates the number of bytes being accessed. The index (A) is the byte address of the constituent byte with the lowest address. Thus M4(7) denotes the bytes with addresses 7, 8, 9, and A formed into the long word depicted in Figure 2-9. In a similar manner we define the memory operations READ, READ2, READ4, WRITE, WRITE2, and WRITE4, where, as before, the integer denotes the number of bytes involved in the data transfer. All these operations use MAR and MDR and modify either MDR or the memory.[14]

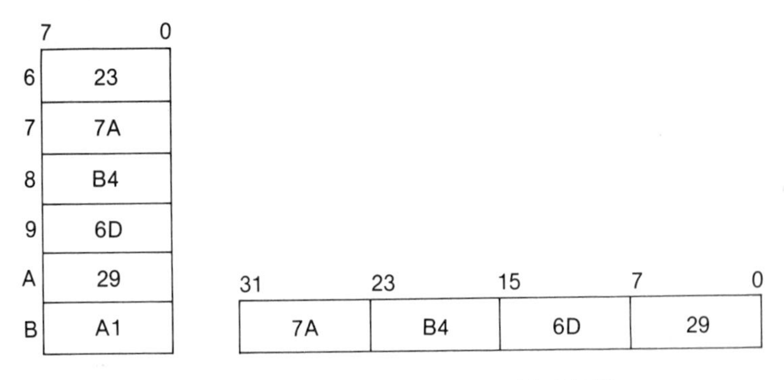

Figure 2-9 Illustrating the long word in M4(7)

[13]We noted before that this rule is not universal; there exist processor designs that do not follow the rule.

[14]Writing to memory will affect the perceived contents of all the arrays M1, M2, and M4.

The computation of an effective address can be described in several equivalent ways:

1. Giving an implementation
2. Drawing a figure showing information flows and computations
3. Writing an equation

In the following we use all three techniques.

In the MC68020, instructions are composed of one or more words. Each instruction word must be located on a word boundary; this means that its memory address is an even number. The information in the first word of an instruction determines whether a single word is adequate to specify the instruction. Instruction-length information may be derived from either addressing mode specifications or the contents of succeeding words of the instruction which may hold additional address information. For those instructions that require a memory operand, the rightmost 6 bits of the first instruction word specify the addressing mode (the way that the address is to be determined) and the register to be used, if any. For certain combinations of function code, addressing modes, and register numbers, the instruction may be extended to succeeding word(s). Figure 2-10 illustrates the instruction format of a simple word add instruction, which adds the contents of two words. This format is used in many MC68020 instructions that have a memory source plus a register serving as both source and destination (D(n) is the register holding the operand and receiving the result).

In describing the processor's addressing modes we assume that the address interpretation process is performed at the beginning of step G4 in the generic instruction execution sequence. As a consequence, PC points to the first program word beyond the last word of the instruction which has been interpreted when the address interpretation sequence is initiated. The address interpretation sequence should be written so that this property holds at the completion of the address interpretation process. A general statement of the property is:

PC State Property. The PC points to the next program word to be interpreted in the execution sequence.

This property is used in the descriptions of all processors with which the author is familiar. The implementation of the MC68020 actually maintains two program counters; the one called scanPC obeys the property stated above. The one simply called PC holds the address of the first byte of the instruction being executed; it is used in case the instruction must be retried.

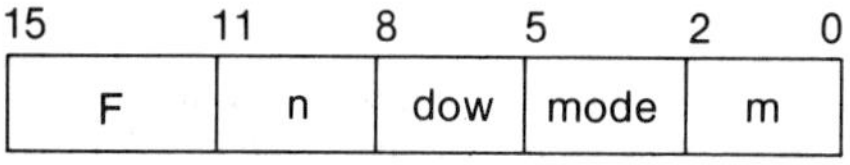

15 — 11	11 — 8	8 — 5	5 — 2	2 — 0
F	n	dow	mode	m

F—function
n—D register number
dow—direction or width
mode—addressing mode
m—register number

Figure 2-10 The format of an MC68020 add instruction

In MIN and BRISC, all instructions have the same length, so instruction fetch and PC advance (steps G1 and G2) are the same for all instructions. In the MC68020, instruction lengths are multiples of a single word; they vary from 1 to 10 words for a complete instruction. The actual length of an instruction is determined by its function code and (mostly) by the addressing modes used.[15] The MC68020 processor must advance its scanPC as a side effect of the effective address computations; this can easily be accomplished while any required extension words are interpreted.

The MC68020 addressing modes are divided into two classes: general addressing modes and branch addressing modes. The *general addressing modes* are used to access operand values and to determine destinations of JUMP class instructions. We will use the term "general operand" to denote an operand whose location or value is determined by a general addressing mode specification. A general operand might come from a "literal" included in the program, from a processor register, or from memory. The mode of address computation and the location of the operand together determine whether the operand location may be read or written, or may be used as the destination for a JUMP class instruction. A *branch addressing mode* can be used only to determine the destination for a branch class instruction. A complete listing of the MC68020 addressing modes is given in Appendix B. The listing also specifies the ways in which the operand location can be accessed.

In the following subsection we present register operand addressing techniques. Then in the next four subsections we discuss these four general operand addressing modes:

1. Absolute addressing
2. Long absolute addressing
3. Simple indexed addressing
4. Double indexing

In the sixth subsection we discuss one branch addressing mode.

2.3.2.1 Direct register addressing.

Addressing modes 0 and 1 are used to specify that the operand is the contents of a processor register. The mode number determines the class of register selected; mode 0 selects a D register, while mode 1 selects an A register.

2.3.2.2 Absolute addressing.

Absolute addressing with a 16-bit address is specified in assembly language by "⟨loc⟩.W" (here ".W" indicates that the address is one word long[16]). In the encoded MC68020 instruction, this mode is specified by

[15]The major mode selections are specified in the first word of each instruction that accesses memory—whether for an operand or result or to branch to the destination instruction (which is not executed immediately afterward).

[16]This specification technique is described in [MOTO84] and is clearly not necessary, since a smart assembler could determine the length required to represent the address.

15	13	11	8	5	2 0
0	2	5	0	7	0
4	A	3	F		

Figure 2-11 A MOV instruction that performs D5: = M4($4A3F_{16}$). (The memory operand specification is outlined.)

mode 7 and register 0,[17] and uses one extension word for the address; the contents of that word are sign extended to fill the 32-bit MAR. This addressing mode is similar to that achieved in BRISC[18] with S1 the address, S2 zero, and IMM = 1. Figure 2-11 illustrates a move instruction using this addressing mode to load register D5 with the contents of the long word at location 4A3F. The address specification fields are emphasized in the figure.

For this mode, the address generation process can be implemented by the following steps:

```
MAR:=PC;
READ2;        --read the extension word
PC:=PC+2;  --move beyond the extension word
A:=sign_ext(MDR2);
```

Here the reference REGn denotes the *n* rightmost bytes of register REG. A second description of this addressing mode is given by the flows shown in Figure 2-12.

Finally, the address computation can be described by an equation. We have to define the names of the instruction parts in order to write the equation. Denoting the extension word's contents by ew1 ("1" for the first extension word), the address is given by the equation

```
A=sign_ext(ew1);                                        (2-2)
```

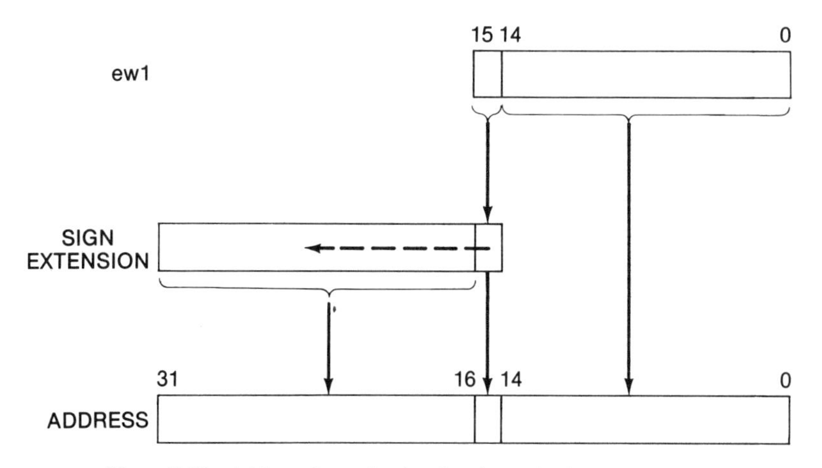

Figure 2-12 Address determination for short absolute addressing

[17]In mode 7 the register numbers serve as extensions of the mode specification.

[18]The widths of the address specification fields are different in the MC68020, however.

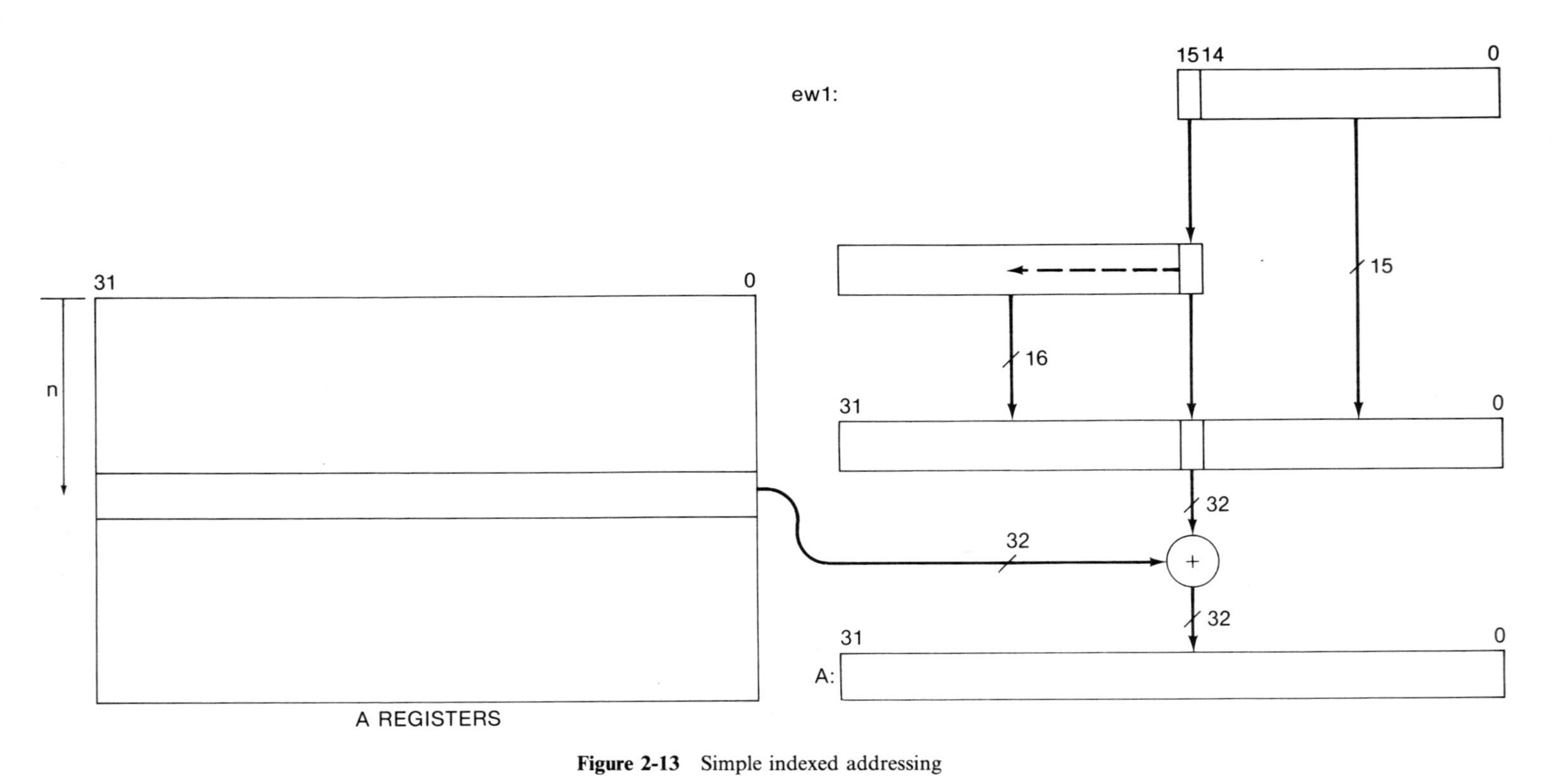

Figure 2-13 Simple indexed addressing

2.3.2.3 Long absolute addressing. Long absolute addressing with a 32-bit address is specified in a processor instruction by mode 7 and register 1, and uses a long word extension for the address. The computation of the operand address is:

```
MAR:=PC;
READ4;          --read the extension long word
PC:=PC+4;       --move PC beyond the extension data
A:=MDR4;
```

This mode is similar to the previous absolute address mode, but with a wider address. Here we have the equation

$$A = el1; \qquad (2\text{-}3)$$

where el denotes a long extension word.

2.3.2.4 Simple indexed addressing. Indexed addressing with a displacement (the displacement serves the same role as the "offset" in BRISC) is specified in assembly language by "(⟨disp⟩,A⟨n⟩)", where disp and n are the parameters of the address computation. The mode is specified in a processor instruction by mode 5 and a register number (n). The extension word contains the displacement, which is sign extended and added to A(n) to find the address. The address computation is

```
MAR:=PC;
READ2;          --read the extension word (the displacement)
PC:=PC+2;
A:=A(n)+sign_ext(MDR2); --add the index
```

Figure 2-13 depicts this computation.

2.3.2.5 Double indexing. Double indexing is specified in assembly language by "(⟨disp⟩,A⟨n⟩,D⟨m⟩)" and in a processor instruction by mode 6 and a register number (n) in the first instruction word.[19] This register number always specifies an A register. For double indexing, there is one instruction extension word

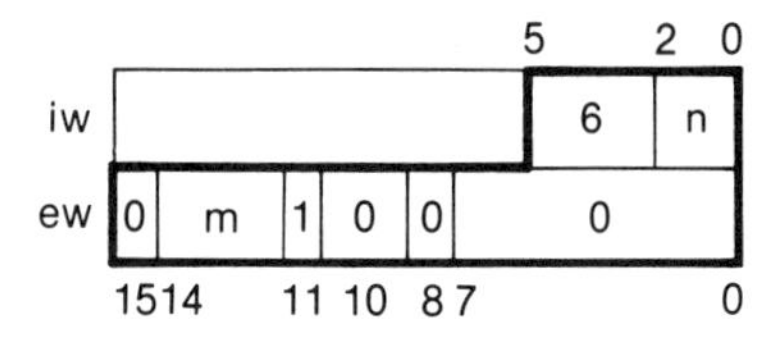

Key
iw <2..0> = A reg #
ew <7..0> = disp (= 0)
ew <8> = 0 (brief format)
ew <10..9> = 0 (scale = 1)
ew <11> = 1 (long word from Dreg)
ew <14..12> = reg #
ew <15> = 0 (for Dreg)

Figure 2-14 Double indexing specification

[19]The situation described here is only one of many cases included under mode 6; the others utilize other patterns in the extension word.

containing a zero in bit 8 (specifying the format of that word) and other register specifications. Bit 15 in the extension word selects the register set to be used for the index quantity (0 for a data register and 1 for an address register), and bits 14 .. 12 contain the number (m) of the second register to be used in the index calculation. Figure 2-14 shows the bit patterns for the address computation expressed by the equation

$$A = A(n) + D(m); \qquad (2\text{-}4)$$

2.3.2.6 Branch addressing. A distinct type of address computation, PC-relative addressing,[20] is used in BRANCH class instructions. For small displacements, the first instruction word contains a signed 8-bit displacement, which is added to the PC to determine the destination of the branch. A 16-bit signed displacement can be used—when the 8-bit displacement is zero, the next extension word is taken for the 16-bit displacement. Similarly, a 32-bit signed displacement can be placed in two extension words following the branch instruction; this case is indicated by the 8-bit displacement in the first instruction word being FF.

Example 2-7

Figure 2-15 illustrates the encoding of an unconditional branch to a location 12 bytes earlier in the program (measured from the origin of the jump instruction). The value of Y in the branch instruction is F2, the 1-byte two's complement representation for −14. Recall that the PC is modified by adding Y only after the PC has been advanced to the next word of the program.

15	11	7	0
6	0	F	2

Figure 2-15 Illustrating destination addressing in branch instructions

2.3.3 MC68020 Control Instructions

The MC68020 has a large variety of control instructions. Some of them support special features which we discuss later; here we concentrate on three simple types available in user mode:

1. Transfer instructions
2. Loop support instructions
3. Subroutine support instructions

2.3.3.1 Transfer instructions. There are two classes of control transfer instructions—branch and jump—which differ in how the destination address is

[20]This form of PC-relative addressing, used for branch instructions, is similar to certain PC-relative operand accessing modes in the general addressing modes (see Appendix B), but the details are different.

computed. The MC68020, like many processors, provides conditional control transfers in the branch instruction class, but not in the jump class. There are three simple combinations within the transfer instruction set:

1. Unconditional branch
2. Unconditional jump
3. Conditional branch

To execute an unconditional transfer instruction, the processor simply loads the destination address into PC. To execute a conditional branch instruction, the processor determines whether the branch condition is met and then loads PC with the destination address if the condition is met.

In assembly language, the condition to be tested is specified within the function code mnemonic, which is constructed from the letter "B" followed by the condition's mnemonic shown in the Table 2-7. Four bits in the branch instruction ("cond" in Figure 2-16) signify the condition to be tested, using the coding specified in Table 2-7. Note that the least significant bit of the condition code signifies testing the complementary condition. The false condition listed in the table is not available for conditional branching (since it causes the conditional branch never to be taken, and therefore the instruction has no effect); the bit combination corresponding to the false condition is used to specify the subroutine call instruction **BSR**, which uses branch addressing modes to find the entry address of the called subroutine.

The branch condition is evaluated from the bits in the CC register, which were set previously during the execution of another processor instruction.

TABLE 2-7 MC68020 CONDITIONAL BRANCH CONDITION CODES

Mnemonic	Condition	Code	Mnemonic	Condition	Code	Condition Code Logic
T	True	0	F	False	1	0
HI	High	2	LS	Low or same	3	$C + Z$
CC	Carry clear	4	CS	Carry set	5	C
NE	Not equal	6	EQ	Equal	7	Z
VC	Overflow clear	8	VS	Overflow set	9	V
PL	Plus	A	MI	Minus	B	N
GE	Greater or equal	C	LT	Less than	D	$NV' + N'V$
GT	Greater than	E	LE	Less than or equal	F	$Z + NV' + N'V$

Source: From [MOTO84]; courtesy of Motorola, Inc.

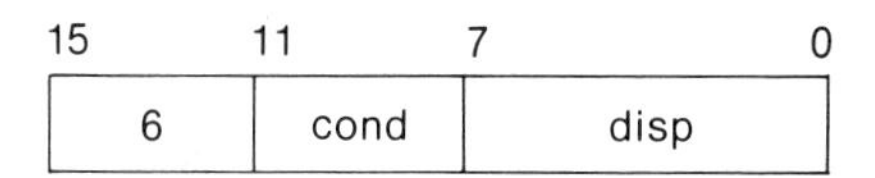

Figure 2-16 Instruction format for Bcc instructions

The following steps describe the semantics of BMI, but may not correspond to any actual implementation:

```
D1. IR:=M2(PC);   --instruction fetch
D2. PC:=PC+2;
D3. if N=0 start_next_instruction;
D4. compute A;     --the 32-bit signed relative address
D5. PC:=PC+A;
```

2.3.3.2 Loop support. A class of MC68020 control instructions supports counting loops in programs. The DBcc group of instructions uses a designated data register as a counter and the condition code specified by the function code as a completion condition. Executing the instruction does not change CCR. The codes specified in Table 2-7 are used to determine the condition to be checked. The execution of a DBcc instruction proceeds through these detail steps:

D1. Fetch the instruction to IR (IR:=M2(PC));
D2. Increment PC by 2 (to point to the next word of the program);
D3. Decode the instruction;
D4. If the condition is true, go to step D10;
D5. Decrement (subtract 1 from) the rightmost 16 bits of Rn;
D6. If the result of the decrementation is -1, go to step D10;
D7. Read the extension word (MDR2:=M2(PC));
D8. PC:=PC + sign_ext(MDR2);
D9. Start the next instruction;
D10. Increment PC by 2 and go to step D9;

The DBcc instruction is intended for use at the end of a loop body. The loop can terminate either because the condition was met (see step D4) or because the loop counter was exhausted (step D6). If the specified branch condition in a DBcc instruction is met, control flows from DBcc to the next sequential instruction (as occurs after going to step D10); this action corresponds to terminating the loop. Otherwise, the branch is taken, going back to the start of the loop to initiate another iteration.

Example 2-8

Here is the skeleton for a counting loop that exits only when the count value reaches its limit:

```
   MOVEQ #D,D6 --copy the constant D (hexadecimal) to register D6
L: ..          --loop body in here
   DBF D6,L
```

The false condition guarantees that the loop will terminate only when the count has reached -1, which occurs after the loop body has been executed 14 times.

A single DBcc instruction performs several functions which match the needs of the common looping program control structure. Correspondences like this are the deliberate consequence of good processor design, which takes into account the needs of the programs to be executed on the system. It is especially effective to move frequently used functions, such as loop count, test, and branch, to the processor's instruction set level of the system. In a similar manner, frequently used features of programming languages or operating systems might be supported at lower levels. In this way the designer can improve the execution speed of commonly used program structures by providing supporting processor instructions.

2.3.3.3 Subroutine support. Subroutine calling is an important processor control function. Recall that the MIN processor does not directly support routine calling; a MIN programmer has to explicitly place the return address in a reserved (by convention) memory location and then perform a jump. The BRISC processor saves PC in a processor register upon subroutine call.

Subroutine calling in the MC68020 uses a *memory stack* that grows toward lower memory addresses. The address in register A7 is the address of the byte most recently pushed on the stack, so register A7 is decremented (by the item size) before pushing an item on the stack. Similarly, to pop data from the stack, A7 must be increased (by the item size) after reading the data. Since stack structures are commonly used, the MC68020 processor's general addressing modes include some with automatic register incrementation and decrementation; these modes can be used to push and pop data on stack structures as the data are processed. The MC68020 supports subroutine calling with several call instructions in which the processor saves PC on the top of the stack before jumping to the specified entry point. Note the progression of increasing functional support for subroutine calls across our three designs (MIN, BRISC, and the MC68020).

Since the MC68020 PC contains a 4-byte address, a subroutine call instruction could be performed as the sequence

```
A7:=A7-4;
M4(A7):=PC; --save PC on the stack
PC:=dest_address;
```

The destination address (dest_address) is determined by using either a general addressing mode (if the instruction was JSR—Jump to subroutine) or the PC-relative computation discussed in Section 2.3.2.5 (if the instruction was BSR—branch to subroutine).

Example 2-9

Figure 2-17 illustrates the contents of memory in the region of the top of the stack along with the stack pointer and the PC. These are shown both before and after the execution of the instruction

```
JSR #AB6
```

located at byte D36 (the instruction is 4 bytes in length, since it uses absolute addressing).

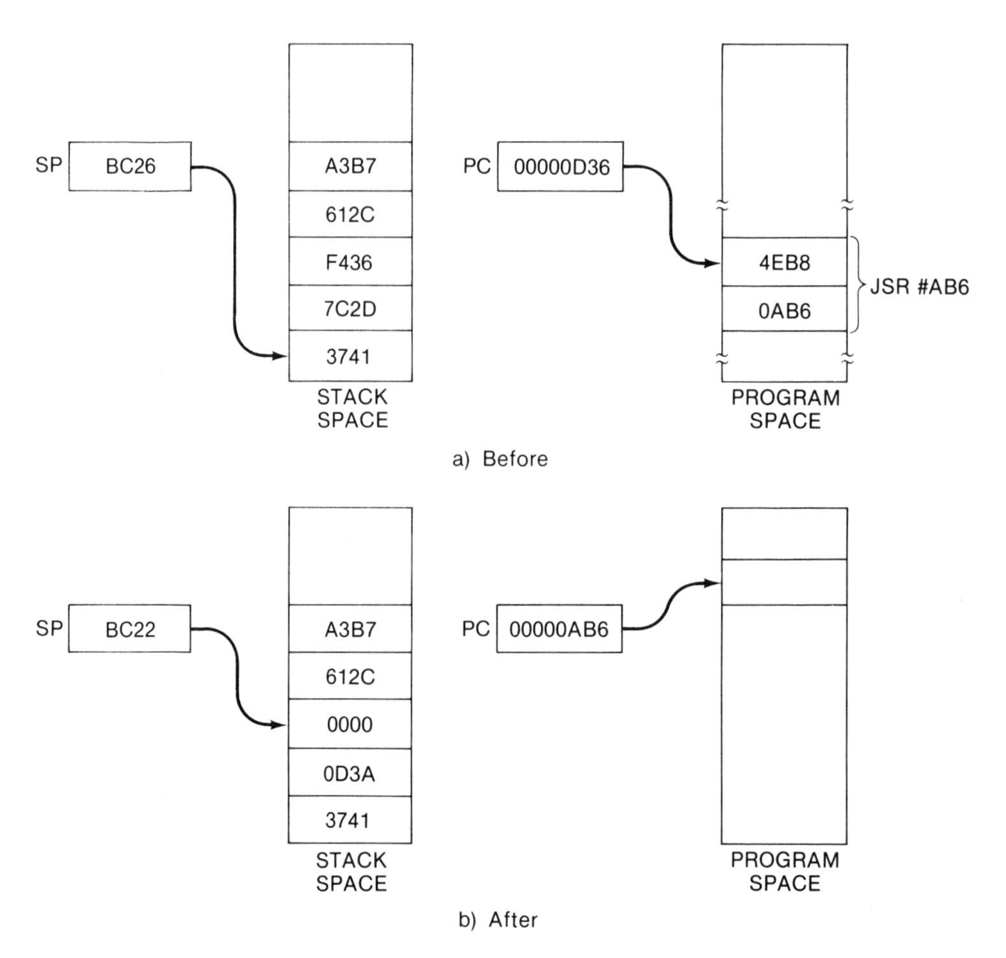

Figure 2-17 Illustrating the execution of the subroutine call instruction JSR #AB6

Upon subroutine completion the saved PC must be retrieved from the stack (where it was saved) and the stack status must be restored by incrementing register A7. In the MC68020, subroutine completion is supported by the return instruction (RTS), which pops the saved PC from the memory stack and adjusts A7 accordingly, as in the following:

```
PC := M4(A7);
A7 := A7 + 4;
```

2.3.3.4 Summary. The MC68020 control instructions discussed above provide basic program flow structures. Other MC68020 control instructions relate to specialized MC68020 features; some of these are described in Chapter 6, and all are tabulated in Appendix C.

2.3.4 Object Manipulation in the MC68020

The MC68020 operand manipulation set is richer than the BRISC operand manipulation set. While it is still the case that only integer arithmetic is supported, all four arithmetic operations are provided, and most are provided for several combinations of operand lengths. Logical and shifting operations are also supported. Compare operations test data values and set CCR but discard the difference computed to make the test.

2.3.4.1 Operand specifications. We discuss the ways that the operands of object manipulation instructions can be specified before we turn to the semantics of the operations themselves. The operand specification details are determined by the number of operands.

In the MC68020, *two operand instructions*, such as ADD, take one operand from a processor data register and the other from a general operand. The result may be placed in the data register, or if the result is the same size as the operand size, in the general operand's location (provided that this location is writable). The destination of the result is specified by the value in bit 8 of the instruction (see Table 2-8).

TABLE 2-8 DESTINATION ENCODING FOR SOME MC68020 TWO-OPERAND OPERATIONS

Value of Bit 8	Destination
0	Operand register
1	General operand location

Example 2-10

Figure 2-18 shows the encoding of two ADD instructions with different register specifications. Examining bit 8, which determines the direction, we see that in case (a) the

D	n	0	2	mode	m

a) Result to data register Dn

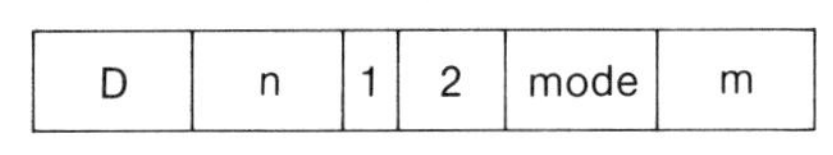

b) Result to general operand

Figure 2-18 Long add destination variation encoding

destination is the data register, whereas in case (b) the destination is the general operand's location. Both of the instructions add exactly the same data in exactly the same way. In this case long words are added, since bits ⟨7,6⟩ contain 2.

For many operations in the MC68020, the same operation code is used to specify the same operation applied to data of several different widths. The actual operand width is specified by bits 7 and 6 of the instruction, according to the codes listed in Table 2-9. The fourth code value is illegal for a width specification, so that bit combination can be used to specify another processor operation code. Note that while this coding scheme allows the processor to have more functions within a given instruction size, it does complicate the instruction decoding process in the control unit, and makes at least the instruction representation (and possibly the functionality) depend on the function being performed—compromising orthogonality.

TABLE 2-9 OPERAND WIDTH ENCODINGS FOR MANY MC68020 TWO-OPERAND INSTRUCTIONS

Value of Bits 7, 6	Width
0	byte
1	word
2	long

Example 2-11

Figure 2-19 contrasts the encoding of an ADD instruction with the encoding of the ADDA instruction. (The ADDA instruction adds the contents of a general operand to a specified A register, leaving the result in the A register.) Notice that the width code of 3 in the ADDA instruction distinguishes ADDA from ADD, the function code value being common. The value of bit 8 determines the operand width for ADDA: 0 specifies a word width and 1 specifies a long word width.

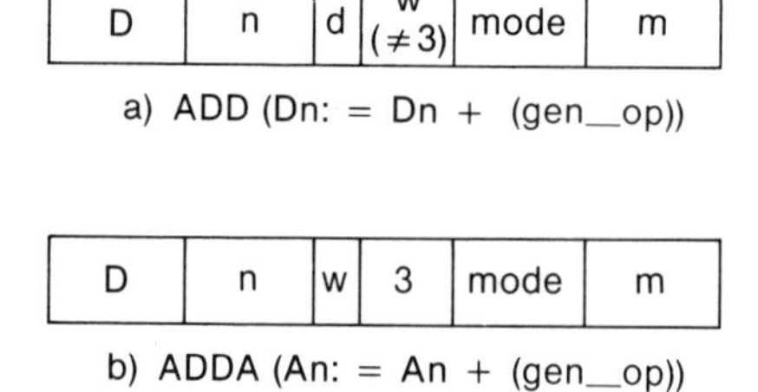

Figure 2-19 Illustrating the use of the illegal width codes to specify other functions

In the MC68020 *single operand operations* (such as negation) bits 7 .. 0 specify the operand width and addressing, using the same encoding as for two operand operations. The result of the operation always replaces the single operand, so the addressing mode must specify a writable location.

2.3.4.2 Data movement operations.

The MC68020, unlike BRISC and MIN, does not have specific load and store instructions. Rather, it has a general data movement operation, which permits the programmer to specify data copying between registers and memory in all combinations. In other words, a data value can be copied from one register to another, from a register to memory, from memory to a register, or from one memory location to another memory location. All of this generality is achieved within the single MOV instruction by using appropriate addressing mode selections for its two general operands. Of course, the destination must be a writable location.

15	13	11	8	5	2 0
		DESTINATION		SOURCE	
00	S	n	mode	mode	m

Figure 2-20 MOV (move) instruction format. (See Table 2-10 for s encoding.) Adapted from [MOTO84]; courtesy of Motorola, Inc.

Figure 2-20 shows the format of the MOV instruction. The size encoding in this instruction does not follow Table 2-9, but rather uses the codes shown in Table 2-10.[21] The size code 0 is used for other operations.

TABLE 2-10 OPERAND WIDTH ENCODINGS FOR MOV INSTRUCTIONS

Value of Bits 13, 12	Width
1	byte
2	long
3	word

Example 2-12

Table 2-11 gives hexadecimal and octal values of the representations of MOV instructions corresponding to a variety of data movements listed in the table. The octal interpretations of the instruction words are shown in the table since the MOV instruction fields specifying the operands are each 3 bits wide.

[21]There is an apparent violation of orthogonality between the function code and the width code here, but actually since the MOV width code is placed within the field usually considered as the function code field, one might consider that the MOV width codes are part of the function code. Taking the latter viewpoint, there is no orthogonality violation here, since there are three MOV class instructions with three different function codes. The fact that the assembler does not treat these three cases as three different instructions does not have to affect our view of orthogonality from the processor side.

TABLE 2-11 SOME MOV INSTRUCTION ENCODINGS

Instruction Word(s)		
Hexadecimal	Octal	Assignment
2A45	025105	Reg_A5:=Reg_D5;
2A0D	025015	Reg_D5:=Reg_A5;
3A74 0734	035170 003464	Reg_A5:=M(734_{16});
11CD 0734	010715 003464	M(734_{16}):=Reg_A5;
21C5 0734	020705 003464	M(734_{16}):=Reg_D5;

2.3.4.3 Two-operand operations. In the MC68020, many two-operand data manipulation operations share the common instruction format depicted in Figure 2-21. The common elements of these instruction representations serve the roles

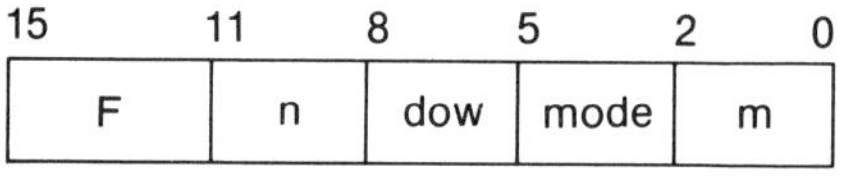

15–12	11–9	8–6	5–3	2–0
F	n	dow	mode	m

Figure 2-21 A two-operand instruction format. (See text for function set.)

listed in Table 2-12. The two operands are the contents of processor register Dn[22] and the general operand specified by the mode and m fields; the result may be directed to either operand location in many of the operations, as specified in Table 2-13.[23] The interpretation of the dow field also depends on the function code, as specified in

TABLE 2-12 COMMON FIELDS IN SOME TWO-OPERAND INSTRUCTIONS

Bit Positions	Mnemonic	Role
15 .. 12	F	Function code
11 .. 9	n	Register number
8 .. 6	dow	Direction/operation/width
5 .. 3	mode	Addressing mode
2 .. 0	m	Register number

[22]An A register is selected for the register operand if the function mnemonic ends in "A"; see the table for details.

[23]The addressing mode must designate a writable location.

TABLE 2-13 ENCODING SIMILARITIES AND DIFFERENCES AMONG SOME MC68020 TWO-OPERAND INSTRUCTIONS

		dow Bit Values[a]			
Mnemonic	F	8	7	6	Comments
ADD	D	d	w		Add operands; use Dn
ADDA	D	k	1	1	Add operands; use An
SUB	9	d	w		Source − destination; use Dn
SUBA	9	k	1	1	Source − destination; use An
MUL	C	s	1	1	Word operands and long result
DIV	8	s	1	1	Long operands and word results
AND	C	d	w		Bitwise AND
OR	8	d	w		Bitwise OR
EOR	B	1	w		Bitwise exclusive or, result to general operand only
CMP	B	0	w		Dn − ⟨gen_op⟩; set CCR
CMPA	B	k	1	1	An − ⟨gen_op⟩; set CCR

[a]The symbols in these columns are interpreted as follows: w is the width encoded according to Table 2-9; d is the direction—0⇒to Dn; 1⇒to general operand; s signifies sign interpretation—0⇒unsigned; 1⇒signed; k is the width for A-register operations—0⇒word; 1⇒long.

Table 2-13. From Table 2-13 one can observe the diversity of the MC68020 processor operations. Also note how common encodings have been used to make the implementation simpler. However, dow has to be interpreted to determine the function, which adds complexity to the implementation.

2.3.4.4 Single-operand operations. As with the two operand instructions, we show only a few single-operand instructions, to illustrate both the common features and the functional diversity provided in the MC68020 processor. These instructions can be fit into the format of two-operand instructions (Figure 2-20), with $F = 4$ and $d = 0$. The single operand is a writable general operand, specified by mod and m. The operand width is specified in the w field. Table 2-14 lists three useful instructions in this class.

TABLE 2-14 SOME MC68020 SINGLE-OPERAND INSTRUCTIONS

Mnemonic	n	Comment
CLR	1	Clear destination
NEG	2	Take the two's complement
NOT	3	Take the bitwise logical complement

2.3.4.5 Other operations. The MC68020 supports many other operations not outlined above. These can be classified in terms of the data types supported by the operation. In addition to integers, other data types that can be manipulated by MC68020 processor instructions are:

1. Binary-coded-decimal character strings
2. Bit fields
3. Indicator bits
4. Status words
5. Stack pointers

Still other operations support commonly used system programming functions. Some of these additional MC68020 operations are presented in succeeding chapters; the complete operation list is summarized in Appendix C.

2.3.5 Orthogonality in the MC68020

The MC68020 processor instruction set design represents a middle ground in orthogonality—there are many orthogonal features in the instruction set, such as the independence of the general operand addressing encodings from the function code. However, there are many dependencies between the other instruction fields and the function code. It seems that these dependencies arise from the limitation of instruction words to 16 bits and the need for compatibility with previous processor models.

2.3.6 Summary of the MC68020

We have reviewed many features of the basic operations and addressing modes in the Motorola MC68020. This processor contains many instructions useful in supporting operating systems, other functions, and system expansions. We do not discuss these extensions here; rather we introduce some of these additional features in later chapters to illustrate how a unified processor design can support a complete system architecture.

2.4 SUMMARY

In this chapter you have been exposed to all aspects of a minimum processor design, which, clearly, you would never want to program. You have seen an implementation of a reduced instruction set design targeted for efficient execution of high-level languages, and you have seen some aspects of the Motorola MC68020, the system we use for many examples. It is easy to see that the MC68020 provides a much richer set of options than the other designs, except in the number of processor registers. Whereas the MC68020 supports more complexity than BRISC, for a given implementation technology BRISC will certainly perform individual instructions more quickly. However, it does not follow that the MC68020 will execute an Ada program more slowly than will a BRISC machine, whose machine-level program would probably execute many more instructions than the MC68020 program to perform the same algorithm. Finally, you have seen several examples of the inclusion of or lack of orthogonality among different instruction set features in processors.

Many of these points will repeat with variations as we progress through design issues concerning single-process systems, starting with the memory system.

2.5 PROBLEMS

2-1. Modify the MIN program of Example 2-3 so that it will work properly even if the accumulator initially contains zero. It is possible to keep the number of instructions the same as in the program of the example. You may wish to specify some constant values to be stored in memory.

2-2. In this problem you will develop a MIN program to shift a byte of information one place to the right, clearing the sign bit of the result. The sources and destinations are both memory locations; let their names be "source" and "dest."

(a) Write a generic algorithm (i.e., not at the MIN assembler level of detail) using left shifting and sign testing to achieve the desired effect. You may wish to draw a flowchart to organize your thinking.

(b) Translate the generic algorithm into a MIN assembly language program. Indicate the correspondence between steps of the generic algorithm and sequences of MIN instructions.

2-3. In this problem you will detail the symbolic execution of the MIN program from Example 2-2. You will deal with the contents of memory locations and processor registers.

(a) Make a list of the memory locations whose contents must be referenced in the symbolic execution description. We will call the locations in this list the "significant locations."

(b) Examine the set of significant locations and determine which ones initially contain values that must be represented in the mathematical expressions. Also determine which locations will receive new values during program execution. (The two sets may overlap. Why?)

(c) Construct a symbolic execution table (SET) which has a column for each changeable location or register. An additional first column contains the instruction being executed (and its location, if that assists you). The first row of SET describes the initial contents of the locations and the registers, and has a null entry for the instruction being executed. Each of the remaining rows lists an instruction and describes the status *after* the execution of the listed instruction; these rows are entered in the order of program execution. Thus the ith row of the table contains machine (and memory) conditions after the execution of the $(i - 1)$st instruction (numbered in order of execution, not in order of position within the program). Fill in this table for the program being studied.

(d) Discuss how your symbolic execution "proves" the correctness of the program.

2-4. Write out the detail steps for a MIN processor's execution of its JNG instruction. The answer should be a register-transfer-level program similar to the one given in the text for the STO operation.

2-5. Write a MIN program that starts from an unknown state (of the accumulator) and finishes with $x + y$ in the accumulator. Here x and y are names of memory locations, but the addition is performed on their contents. Try for both functional correctness and speed of execution.

2-6. A MIN design is augmented to include two accumulators. What aspects of the instruction representation and interpretation would have to be changed to accommodate this augmentation? Explain briefly.

2-7. A modified MIN processor design has the added option of indexed addressing. Indexing can be used with any instruction, but in practice it is found that indexing is less frequently used with JNG instructions. Suppose that indexing is used 30% of the time with JNG instructions and 50% of the time with the other instructions. A memory cycle requires 500 ns, and indexing adds 250 ns to the memory cycle when it is used. If the instruction frequencies are (STO - 25%, SUB - 45%, JNG - 30%), what is the average instruction execution rate for the machine?

2-8. Repeat Problem 2-4 for the BRISC processor's execution of the ldw instruction.

2-9. Write a BRISC subroutine to multiply two positive half-integers initially found in registers R3 and R4. Leave the result in R5. Try to leave the CC bits set to reflect the conditions in the result.

2-10. Write a BRISC instruction sequence that performs each of the integer additions specified below:

(a) $R6 := R6 + M(38_{16})$ (32-bit words).

(b) $R12 := R3 + R5$ (8-bit values).

(c) $M(2C0E_{16}) := M(347_{16}) + M(214_{16})$ (16-bit values).

2-11. Write a register-transfer description of the computation of an effective address for the MC68020 simple case of double indexing, expressed in the brief format used in Figure 2-14. Consider only the case of zero displacement (the general format is given in Appendix B) used in the figure.

2-12. Consider the computation of the effective address of an MC68020 branch instruction. Recall that there are several possible displacement lengths.

(a) Write a register-transfer sequence that implements the effective address computation.

(b) Suppose that one could obtain a special hardware module that produces a one output if all its input bits are identical and a zero otherwise (ignore any fan-in limitations that this module may have). Discuss the possibility of using one of these modules to assist in the computation of the effective address using the algorithm of part (a). Rephrase the effective address algorithm to use this module.

2-13. In this problem you will explore several ways to decode the combination of the F and dow fields in the MC68020 instructions listed in Table 2-13. Your answer to each part of the question should outline the implementation and then discuss that implementation. Discuss both decoding time and the space required for any tables or instructions in your evaluations.

(a) A microcode program using a single **case** statement for completely decoding the two fields. (In other words, the single decoding level distinguishes all possible values of the (F, dow) pair.)

(b) A microcode program using a two-level tree of **case** statements, the first level decoding F and the second level the dow fields.

(c) A single programmed logic array[24] replacing the **case** decoding of part (a).

(d) A set of PLAs mimicking the nested **case** structure of part (b).

[24]A programmed logic array (PLA) is a hardware module that contains a two-level AND/OR circuit. The PLA can be "programmed" to connect any of the input signals or their complements to each AND gate, and to connect the outputs of any of the AND gates to the inputs to each OR gate. The connection flexibility allows partial decoding—in which some, but not all, input bits are used to select a combination—to save AND gates; furthermore, the same AND combination can be used as input to several OR gates.

2-14. Find the hexadecimal representations of the MC68020 instruction(s) required to implement the following manipulations.

(a) Add the contents of memory location $38A5_{16}$ to register D7, placing the result in the register. All operand values are single words.

(b) Add the contents of memory location $38A5_{16}$ to memory location 632_{16}, where the result should be placed. All operand values are long words.

(c) Add the contents of memory location $38A5_{16}$ and register A4, placing the result in register D2. Again, the operand sizes are long words.

2-15. Write programs for BRISC and the MC68020 that use an iterative loop to sum the integers from 1 to *n*, where *n* is the contents of register 3 (use D3 in the MC68020). Discuss any differences between the two programs with respect to both static and dynamic length. A program's dynamic length is the number of instructions it executes to perform the function (this will be a function of *n*).

2-16. This problem concerns operand width encodings in the MC68020.

(a) What operand widths are transferred for each of the instructions in Table 2-11?

(b) Expand Table 2-11 to include columns giving the instruction representations for move instructions for each of the three data widths supported by the processor.

2-17. A designer proposes the following technique for enforcing a separation among virtual machines that run on a MC68020 system. In this problem the separation of memory spaces is the only concern. A designer proposes restricting the formation of addresses by limiting the use of the addressing modes of the MC68020. The proposed limitation would be enforced by restricting the system so that it be able to run only programs produced by "certified" assemblers and compilers. The following two questions ask about two important parts of this argument.

(a) Assume that the proposed enforcement mechanism guarantees that the prohibited addressing modes are never used. Can you then certify that two programs will always be separated in memory? In other words, is it possible to select a few addressing modes, restrict address generation to these modes, and then guarantee that certain addresses cannot be generated? Remember that the assembler does know the address information that is placed in the program when it is written.

(b) Now ignore the question of whether the mode restriction really guarantees the desired separation and consider whether the assemblers and compilers can check for nonuse of the prohibited modes. Can this checking mechanism work properly? Explain.

2-18. A general orthogonality test can be performed by constructing a matrix showing the possible combinations of options and examining that matrix for certain patterns. Suppose that we wish to determine whether the contents of two fields, *F* and *G*, have orthogonal interpretations. Create a matrix whose rows correspond to the options in the *F* field, and whose columns correspond to the options in the *G* field. Place a "1" at position (i, j) if it is legal to use option F_i in conjunction with option G_j. Now examine the matrix for patterns, as follows. If every row is the same, *F* and *G* are orthogonal. If there are *n* different row patterns, divide the *F* set into *n* groups; within one *F* group the *G* field is orthogonal to *F*. By symmetry, a limited number of different column patterns suggests dividing the *G* set into groups.

Develop an orthogonality matrix to test the MC68020 design for orthogonality between the function code field (bits 15 .. 12) and the register number field (bits 2 .. 0). Discuss any difficulties you encounter and any patterns you find.

2-19. Discuss this proposition: The orthogonality test of Problem 2-18 can be generalized by creating a field dependency matrix (FDM) for comparing the contents of a single field

K against all other fields. The entry FDM(i, j) will contain one if the contents of field j are not orthogonal to field K when the value of K is i, and zero otherwise. If this matrix can be organized into a block form by permuting its rows and/or columns, there exists a simple test sequence to interpret all fields.

In your discussion point out whether the claim is correct, and also briefly cover the variations that can fruitfully be employed if the FDM is not block diagonal but does contain sets of identical rows.

2-20. Choose a familiar processor and make an orthogonality matrix to test the relationships between the function code and the memory addressing modes for the processor instructions in the following classes:

1. Arithmetic
2. Logical
3. Load/store
4. Program branching
5. Subroutine call

3

NAMING MEMORY OBJECTS

'Of course they answer to their names?'
the Gnat remarked carelessly.
'I never knew them to do it.'
'What's the use of their having names,'
the Gnat said, 'if they won't answer to them?'

— Lewis Carroll

What's in a name? That which we call a rose,
By any other name would smell as sweet.

— Shakespeare, Romeo and Juliet

Memory systems consist of places that hold objects and a scheme for naming those places. In addition, there must be an addressing mechanism which, when given a name, selects the corresponding place. The addressing mechanism is the link by which the memory contents are associated with their names. The names are arbitrary, as Shakespeare poetically points out. Used consistently, names do provide a basis for communications and understanding. Although none of us were alive when Shakespeare wrote his words, we all know exactly what he was talking about. I could show you a rose, and I believe that it would be the same type of object that Shakespeare was writing about. This understanding is possible because the name "rose" has been used consistently since Shakespeare's time. In this chapter we discuss naming issues.

Before we focus on naming issues, let us briefly review the scope of memory design issues. The policies and mechanisms that support memory systems include schemes for naming objects, schemes for allocating space to hold the objects, and schemes for accessing the objects stored in the memory system. These activities take place at many levels of the system's implementation, including the high-level language program, the compiler, the processor-level program, the operating system, and the system hardware. The design issues and options are similar at all these levels.

The actions leading from the definition of a name in an Ada program to an access to the corresponding memory location may be performed during different phases of system activity. We emphasize three phases of system activity that affect and influence the memory system design. The first activity is *translation*, the term we will use not only for the compilation of a high-level language program into a lower-level representation, but also for the translation of symbolic assembly language programs. Translation reduces a program containing symbolic names to a program without symbolic names. The second activity is *linking*, the act of combining several separately translated programs to form a single larger program for execution. The third activity is *execution*, the running of the linked program.

This scenario contains several actions related to the memory system:

1. The Ada programmer chooses a legal name.
2. The programmer places the object declaration within the Ada program so that the compiler will allocate space with an appropriate lifetime.
3. The compiler allocates space for the object.
4. The compiler produces processor instructions to access the object.
5. The operating system allocates space for the process.
6. The operating system establishes memory mapping data so that the processor will access the proper physical location.
7. The processor allocates space for a group of objects.
8. The processor computes the effective address of an instruction accessing the object.
9. The hardware translates the effective address to an absolute memory address.
10. The cache looks for the object within itself.
11. The cache allocates space for the object.
12. The cache asks the memory to access the object.
13. The cache accesses the object.

These activities can be fit into the matrix shown in Figure 3-1. The rows of the matrix correspond to the activity phases: the high-level language program, the compiler, the operating system, the processor, and the memory hardware. The columns of the matrix correspond to the types of activity: naming, allocation, and accessing, with the latter including name translation. The activity flow through the matrix runs on a row-by-row basis, starting at the upper left, and ending at the lower right corner with an access to the location holding the value contained within the object. Despite the fact that the flow follows the rows, we present memory systems on a column-by-column basis, to illustrate the common issues and solution techniques used to approach similar problems at different levels of the system hierarchy. Therefore, we cover naming issues in this chapter, allocation issues in the next chapter, and then turn to accessing issues in Chapter 5.

	NAMING	ALLOCATION	ACCESSING ALGORITHM
PROGRAM			
COMPILER			
OPERATING SYSTEM			
PROCESSOR			
MEMORY			

Figure 3-1 Activity matrix

Since there is a common row structure in the matrix, in each chapter the discussion follows the same pattern. First, we define the general problem and show some techniques for solving various important aspects of the design problem. Then we turn to the high-level language level. Continuing down the virtual machine hierarchy, we turn to processor-level memory issues. The operating system manages memory space for users; it comes next in the hierarchy, since it controls name mappings performed on addresses generated by a programmer at the processor level. Finally, we cover hardware-level memory issues, including techniques that may enhance the memory system's performance.

The selection of allocation and accessing methods is affected by the selection of naming methods, but naming design options and selection criteria are largely independent of the design decisions concerning allocation and accessing. In this chapter we discuss naming methods, thereby laying the groundwork for the allocation and accessing options discussed in Chapters 4 and 5. In this chapter you will learn the semantics of names and the structures of objects that can be named. You will learn Ada naming rules, you will learn how processor operand specifications can be treated as names and how they are interpreted, and you will see how useful data structures can be specified and their contents accessed using the naming structures that we discuss. You will see how some processor designs have incorporated support for and taken advantage of high-level features or requirements. You will learn some criteria used to compare naming schemes. In short, you will have a basis for the following discussion of allocation and accessing.

3.1 GENERAL CONCEPTS

After the computer's memory system is presented with a name, it should provide access to the location corresponding to the given name. A name might appear in a high-level language statement, a processor instruction, a memory location, or some other place where a location can be named. We want to design the memory system so that the access will be speedy, so that the system will efficiently utilize the memory that is available, and so that the memory system does not unduly limit the system's speed.

Four general issues related to naming are:

1. Name construction rules
2. Object declaration syntax
3. Aliasing
4. Names for components of data structures

The general naming issue concerns name construction and naming semantics. At most levels, a name is either a character string or an integer value. However, a name may also be represented as an algorithm that accesses the location of interest. Or, alternatively, a name may be a set of parameters for a system algorithm which will access the location. A final name option includes a selector specifying an addressing algorithm and the parameters of that algorithm. The latter description applies to the MC68020 processor's operand addressing, the address mode specification being the selector.

We divide the naming problem into two parts, based on the complexity of the name itself. A *simple* name denotes a single object whose internal representation is not visible. In contrast, a *component* name denotes a portion of a compound object; it is possible (or legal) to name a component only if that component is a visible internal portion of the compound object. We start with simple names that describe single objects.

The interpretation of the term "single object" depends on the level of abstraction; a matrix may be considered to be a single object when calling matrix manipulation routines, but when writing the routines themselves, a matrix is a compound object, its elements being simple objects. A matrix element might be viewed as a compound object at the level of the processor program that does manipulate the elements; an element could be a complex number, for example. And the real and imaginary parts of the complex number might themselves be floating-point numbers that are viewed as compound objects from the hardware level—if the processor directly manipulates floating-point numbers. Clearly, there is no precise definition of a "simple" object; we must be satisfied to use the term intuitively in a context-dependent manner.

Each simple name is constructed in a manner compatible with the level of abstraction—in a high-level language program, a single character string is a simple name, while in a processor-level program, a bit pattern in an instruction is a simple name. Whatever the form of the names themselves, we view the set of names as a name space:

Definition. A *name space* is a set containing all possible names of memory places.

Example 3-1

The name space of simple names visualized by a Fortran programmer contains names constructed from character strings—all sequences of up to six alphanumeric characters (the first being alphabetic) are legal names. A name such as SIGMA selects one of the places.

Ada declarations are collected at the beginning of a block; each declaration takes the form[1]

```
⟨name⟩ : ⟨type⟩;
```

The type declaration defines both how space should be allocated to hold the value for the object and how the object's contents may be manipulated. In Ada a simple name is constructed from alphanumeric characters and the underscore character, with an alphabetic character in the first position. Here are some Ada declarations of simple objects:

```
thing : integer;
value : real;
bit : boolean;
```

A component name is constructed from several simple names or from a simple name conjoined with an element selector. The structure of a component name depends on the organization of the compound object whose component is being named.

Example 3-2

In Ada a component of an array is named by the array name plus a vector of integer[2] object selectors having the same number of components as the array object's dimensions. The following are legal Ada names for array components.

```
vect(8);
r(x+3, 5, v);
```

In Ada an element of a record object can be named by a *qualified* name, constructed from two simple names with a period in between. The first simple name is the record's name; the second simple name is the internal name of the desired record component. Here are some component names that might be legal in an Ada program:

```
rec.first
second.first
first.second
```

The final general naming question concerns the evaluation criteria used to compare naming options. These include orthogonality (separation of naming

[1]A name in angle brackets denotes a syntactic element of the syntactic type named within the brackets.

[2]An enumerated type can also be specified for object indices in the array declaration, as in

```
type day is (mon, tues, wed, thur, fri, sat, sun);
type bed_time is array(day) of integer;
type long_weekend_wake_up is
  array(day range fri .. sun) of integer;
```

The sequence of types of the component selectors must match the sequence of types specified in the array's declaration.

constraints from the usage context), flexibility, the ease of naming components of useful data structures, closeness between naming conventions at adjacent levels of the hierarchy, and efficiency of access to the named object. We will use these criteria in comparative discussions of memory designs.

Another important evaluation criterion for naming schemes concerns the compatibility of the scheme with context separation in a program or a system. Blocks are the first-level contexts; blocks are collected to form programs; programs are collected to form processes; processes together use the same system. While we would like to separate contexts from each other, we would also like to permit controlled sharing among contexts, as sharing can speed execution and save space while avoiding needless copying.

With these criteria in mind, let us turn to the naming questions that are the subject of this chapter.

3.2 NAMING IN HIGH-LEVEL LANGUAGES

We start at the high-level language level and examine typical naming rules. In later sections we will see how processor-level designs can support the naming and visibility structures of high-level languages. When this connection is exploited, the processor's execution speed can be enhanced and the memory required to hold the program may also be reduced. As we cover the naming and visibility rules for high-level languages, we emphasize Ada and related block-structured languages. First, we discuss briefly the requirements for high-level object naming.

The general requirements regarding the programmer's name space are:

1. Ability to create arbitrary names
2. Ability to name components of data structures
3. Ability to name objects shared among modules

The *ability to create arbitrary names* allows the programmer to construct a mnemonic name for an object so that the name is suited to both the application and the use of the designated object. This flexibility makes it easier to write understandable programs. For readability, long names may be preferred. In Ada the underline symbol may be used to construct readable compound names.

The *ability to name components of data structures* permits the programmer to specify an algorithm which manipulates the internal representation of a compound object. The naming conventions should be related to the internal structure and should permit a programmer to use her own structures and symbols to construct these component names.

The *ability to name objects in other program modules* is important when connecting modules to form a federation of modules that will cooperate to realize the program's application. This area of design will occupy much of our time, since relationships among modules are important determiners of the program's structure. The programmer must both limit the visibility of the defined names and permit sharing of the names to complete connections between cooperating modules.

Now we show some common techniques for constructing simple and compound names. Then we consider the relationships of object names among modules that together form an application program.

3.2.1 Names within a Single Context

In a single context several names may be defined and used. A simple single context program (i.e., a program having only a single context) includes both the definition and all uses of each name that appears in the program. Every unique name refers to a single object, and for each object there is a single declaration defining all attributes of that object, such as its type. Note that this does not prohibit us from having two different names for the same object.

Within a single simple program a name has the same interpretation everywhere. The simple program is a simple example of a naming context; the general case of a context is given by this definition:

Definition. A region of a program within which the interpretation of names does not change is a *naming context.*

A large program may reference many objects, so naming can become confusing unless the programmer structures the name space. One way to structure the name space is to divide it into different naming contexts. By associating a naming context with a function or phase of the program, the programmer can structure naming according to function, thereby enhancing program understandability. In succeeding subsections we explore the interrelationships among contexts and the consequences of these interrelationships on programmers as they create object names. For the moment we continue discussing the single-context situation.

Four pieces of the name construction design are:

1. Name construction
2. Declaration syntax
3. Aliasing
4. Component naming

Name construction rules state how a programmer may combine printed symbols to form names. Common rules concerning alphanumeric symbols and their use to construct names were illustrated earlier. The detailed simple name construction rules for high-level languages do not influence system architecture.

The *declaration syntax* also does not affect system architecture. It is important to know that each declaration must state the type of the declared object and something about the existence of the corresponding storage entity. Features that may be added to the declaration to control a name's visibility are discussed later; these visibility issues do have architectural consequences.

Aliasing occurs when a single object has two different names. It is logically necessary that there be only a single declaration for each object, but there is no logical necessity for the rule that "there can be only one name that refers to a single object."

In other words, there is no logical reason to prohibit aliasing. However, at least two dangers arise from aliasing. First, the declarations of all aliases of a simple object must specify the same type for the object.[3] Second, a programmer could become confused by forgetting where aliasing has been introduced. Errors in program logic or reasoning about the program can arise more easily when aliasing is present.

Finally, *component naming* must be supported in a programming language. We discuss more details of component naming after we discuss some aliasing options and some consequences of using aliasing.

3.2.1.1 Aliasing. Special declarations are used for aliasing. Examples include the Fortran EQUIVALENCE statement and the Ada **renames** statement.

Example 3-3

In Fortran, the statement

```
EQUIVALENCE (X, Y)
```

states that the objects named X and Y are to be located at the same memory address. Therefore, X and Y are aliases for the same object.

In Ada, the renames statement

```
x : real renames y;
```

specifies aliasing between the names x and y. Since x is real, it must be the case that y was declared to be real else the program is in error. In Fortran there is no analogous type-matching restriction; this flexibility allows programmers to create programs whose results depend on the internal representations used for various object types.

Aliasing may also occur as a result of parameter passing. Furthermore, aliasing can complicate reasoning about program properties, as shown in the following example.

Example 3-4

Consider this sumdiff procedure:

```
type ai is access integer;
procedure sumdiff(x, y : in out ai) is
begin
   x.all := x.all + y.all;
   y.all := x.all - 2 * y.all;
end;
```

A name with the qualification "**.all**" denotes the value that the access variable designates, rather than the access variable itself.

Looking at the body of sumdiff, it would appear that the pointers x and y denote different objects. If x and y do indeed denote different objects, we can show that the

[3]Otherwise, the results of a computation using the object may depend on the representation conventions used in the system.

sumdiff procedure does leave the sum of the operands in x.**all** and their difference in y.**all**.

When sumdiff is called by this program fragment

```
A:=3;
sumdiff(A, A);
```

the formal parameter names x and y are actually aliases for the same object, and the result left in A is neither 6 (the correct sum) nor 0 (the correct difference), but rather -6! We see that any reasoning about sumdiff that relied on x and y denoting different objects could not be applied to an invocation of sumdiff that introduces aliasing through the actual parameter specifications.

Aliasing affects program readability and understandability, but does not have a serious impact on system architecture issues. Thus, without loss of generality, we avoid aliasing in the remainder of the book.

3.2.1.2 Component naming. The rules for naming a component of a compound object relate to the object's structure; we discuss these conventions in the remainder of this section.

The set of compound object structures can be divided into four categories, based on whether the structure is static and whether all components within the compound object are themselves of the same type. There are four interesting cases:

1. Static structure, homogeneous component types
2. Static structure, heterogeneous component types
3. Dynamic structure, homogeneous component types
4. Dynamic structure, heterogeneous component types

The archetypical static structure with homogeneous components is the array. Let *d* denote the number of dimensions of the array. A component within the array is designated by the array's name and a *d*-dimensional vector of index values. The array's declaration specifies the type and allowable range of the index value for each "dimension." The "space" occupied by the array is a *d*-dimensional rectangular volume, since any index value can vary through its complete range independent of the particular values of the other indices. In Ada an array is declared by

```
type array105 is array(1 .. 10, 2 .. 5) of integer;
a : array105;
```

A component of this array has a name like

```
a(4, 3)
```

Compound objects in the second class have a static structure with heterogeneous components. In Ada and Pascal this kind of structure is called a "record," whereas in PL/1 it is called a "structure." For program understandability and readability, each component of such a compound object is declared with a separate (internal) name. The component's declaration names the component and defines its type. The name of a particular component within a compound object consists of the object's name and the component's name, with a period separating the two names. In Ada the name of a record component looks like a.b. A sample Ada record declaration illustrates the important elements of these structured data objects:

```
type bool4 is array(1 .. 4) of boolean;
type rec is
  record
    a : integer;
    b : bool4;
  end record;
```

This declaration declares the type named rec. The lines between the reserved words **record** .. **end record** define the components of the record type; the components of all objects declared to have type rec must name their component parts using the names a and b. Each record declaration also declares the types and sizes of its components.[4]

In Ada a record must be declared as a type before an object can be declared to have that type.[5] Following the type declaration above, the Ada programmer could write

```
c : rec;
```

This statement declares the existence of object c; c has the structure defined for objects of type rec. Therefore, the components of c have names like c.a, c.b(1), and c.b(4).

Compound objects in the third type class have dynamic structures with homogeneous component types. In one simple case, the structure is an array whose dynamic feature is its dimension, which will not become known until run time. In one typical situation the dimension is dynamically determined when the procedure is called.

Example 3-5

In Algol the dimension of an array local to a procedure can be specified in terms of the procedure's parameter values. The following fragment exemplifies this capability:

```
function a(n, x);      --Algol, not Ada!
   integer y(n);       --an Algol vector declaration
```

Since n, the dimension specified for the array named y, is a parameter of the function a, the dimension of y cannot be known during compilation; it must be determined when the function is called and the actual value of the parameter a is available. Thus the y array is dynamically dimensioned.

Dynamic dimensioning is not directly supported in Ada.

[4]By using a discriminant (see below), the type and/or size specification can be deferred by specifying its value as a parameter of the type declaration and stating its actual value within the declaration of each specific object.

[5]This restriction does not apply in Pascal, where an object can be declared directly to have a record structure without defining the record structure in a previous type declaration.

Compound objects in the fourth type class have dynamic structures containing components of heterogeneous types. One example is an object whose type is a record with variant forms. A record with variants is similar to a procedure with parameters; the variant used in an instance of the record is selected by the value(s) of one or more *discriminants* (which have roles like parameters). As with a procedure declaration, a type declaration having discriminants includes the formal name and type of each discriminant. All discriminant objects must assume discrete values (e.g., a discriminant of type real is not allowed). The actual value of each discriminant is included in the representation of the record, but is not declared like a record component. All discriminant values are constant for the life of the record instance.

A discriminant value may determine a subscript range within a record or it may select alternative components for inclusion in the record. A discriminant-based subscript range specification is made by using the formal discriminant name in the range specification. A discriminant-based record structure selection is specified by a **case** structure in which the selector is the formal name of a single discriminant and the selected statement(s) are component declarations. The **case** statement must include every possible value that could be assigned to an object of the type of the discriminant. These points will be demonstrated in the next example.

The declaration of an object whose type has discriminants must specify the actual values of all its discriminants. The compiler knows then how to allocate space for the object and how to access the object's components. It is also possible to create object instances during program execution. In this case, the program asks for an entity to hold an object; the actual discriminant value(s) must be specified as parameter(s) of the allocation request. Once the allocation has been made, the record structure for this instance is fixed and cannot be changed. When the allocator creates the object, it inserts the actual discriminant values in the record. The allocator also places a pointer to the new record in an access variable which can be used to access the new record.

Example 3-6

This Ada program fragment contains a declaration of an object type with two variants and statements requesting space allocation to hold instances of this type:

```
type sex is (male, female);
type name is string(1 .. 30);
type married_person(p_sex : sex) is
  record
    first_name : name;
    middle_name : name;
    last_name : name;
    case p_sex is
      when female =>
        maiden_name : name;
      when male =>
        null;
    end case;
  end record;
```

```
type personpoint is access married_person;
ppoint, qpoint : personpoint;          --pointers to instances
                                       --of type married_person
..
ppoint := new married_person(female);
                           --allocate an instance of the record⁶
qpoint := new married_person(male);
                           --allocate a male instance
```

The amount of information in a record of type married_person depends on the sex of the person being described. When the married_person is a male, the record has only four[7] components. On the other hand, when the person is female, the record has five components (see Figure 3-2). The allocation made in the next-to-last statement of the program creates an instance of the "female" version with five components, placing the value "female" in the discriminant. The last statement allocates another instance of variant "male." The name qpoint.maiden_name is thus illegal, whereas the name ppoint.maiden_name is legal.

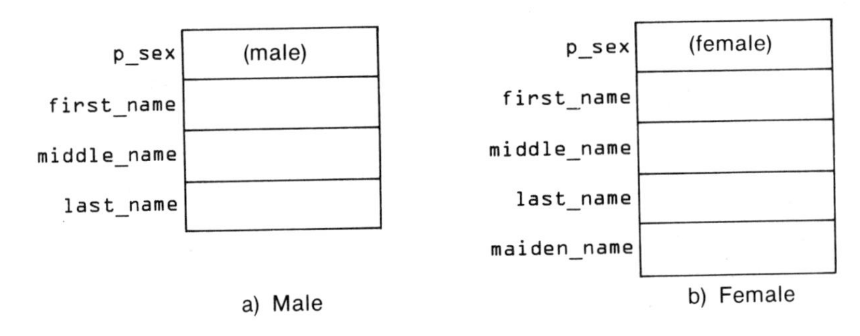

Figure 3-2 Forms of variant records for Example 3-6

3.2.2 Relationships among Naming Contexts

Suppose that a set of separately written program modules are being combined to constitute a larger program to perform a larger task. How are the modules combined? What naming environments are created? It is desirable to create separate naming contexts for separate modules so that programmers do not have to know about all names declared in every program. The naming contexts are created by limiting name visibility as the modules are combined. After discussing general visibility notions, we present alternative techniques for controlling name visibility and thus defining naming contexts.

Most programming languages support modular separation by providing visibility-limiting naming rules. A visibility-limited name declared in one module M_1 is

[6]The **new** operator is discussed in Section 4.3.

[7]We are counting the (hidden) discriminant value (named p_sex).

not visible in another module M_2. Thus visibility refers to the programmer's ability to use the object's M_1 name and thence to access the M_1 object. Formally, we have:

Definition. An object named N declared in module M_1, where it denotes entity E_1, is *visible* in module M_2 if N can be used within M_2 to refer to the object E_1.

If an object's name, when used in module M_2, causes access to the same object as declared in M_1, we say that the object's M_1 name is visible in M_2. This situation is depicted in Figure 3-3a, where N denotes the name and a dashed line indicates an access attempt. Suppose that an object E_1,[8] named N and declared in module M_1 is not to be visible in module M_2. If the name N were used in module M_2, either that use is illegal or it must denote an object E_2 different from E_1. Figure 3-3b depicts a forbidden attempt to access an invisible entity, which would occur if E_1 were not visible in M_2 and no other object named N were visible from N_2; the vertical dashed line depicts the visibility boundary. We see that the interpretation of a name must depend on the context of its use.

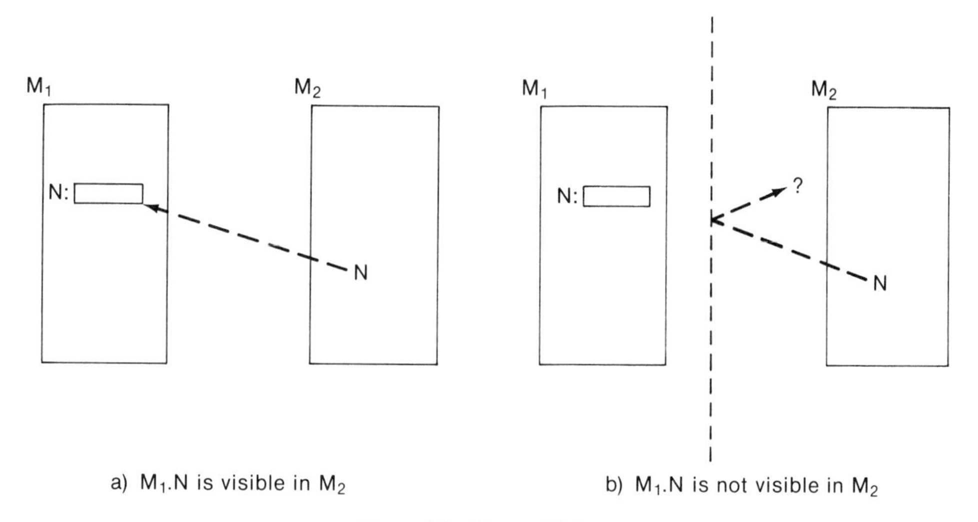

Figure 3-3 Name visibility

Name scope rules define name visibility in a program. Two features are desired: (1) It should be possible to declare that certain names shall remain *private* to a module, and (2) it should be possible to declare names that can be used to establish links among modules. A link may be made through procedure names, function names, or object names.

A program module that could be linked to other modules may contain three

[8]We use E (for Entity) since O (for Object) could be misinterpreted easily.

classes of name declarations:

1. Private (P)
2. Externally visible (EV), and internally defined
3. Externally defined (ED), yet internally used

An entity with a private name is not visible in a context other than the one that includes its declaration. Therefore, a module containing only P names cannot be linked, and P names can be ignored in this discussion of name sharing.

A link from module M_1 to another module M_2 can be established by declaring a name N in M_1 as an EV name and declaring N in M_2 as an ED name. The declaration inside M_2 defines both the name N and the attributes of the object named N. The compiler and the linker cooperate to associate the two declarations and to establish proper addressing information such that the linked interpretation is supported.

We will use two styles of figures to depict name space relationships. The first version, the *name space picture* shown in Figure 3-4a, depicts the space of names used in a program, subdivided according to visibility and usage. This version depicts the categorization of names actually used in a program module. The second version, the *entity set picture* shown in Figure 3-4b, depicts the set of entities declared in a program module (thus excluding ED names), separating the P and EV categories. This version depicts the set of entities (including both data objects and procedure objects) actually accessible to a set of program modules being combined to form the complete program.

Naming rules define how a name is associated with one of these categories. A related rule defines the relationships among object names and entities. We illustrate these rules in the next example.

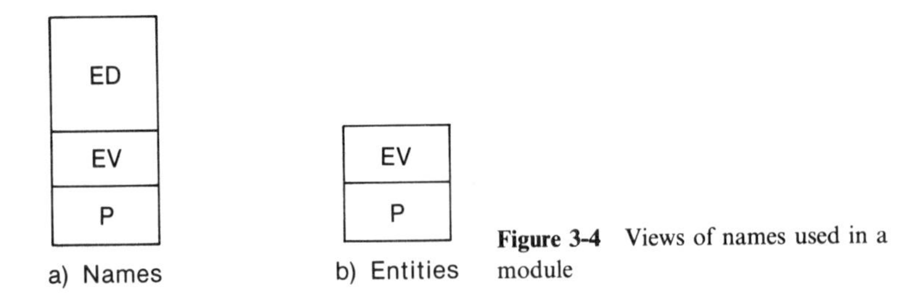

Figure 3-4 Views of names used in a module

Example 3-7

To free this example of any linguistic bias, we use a nonstandard declaration syntax. Explicit name category declarations are made.

```
procedure module1 is --None of this is Ada!!
  i : EV integer; --An externally visible entity
begin
  .. --module1's program
end module1;
```

```
procedure module2 is
  i : EV integer; --An externally visible entity
  b : P integer;  --An internally visible entity
begin
  ..
  b:=i;
  ..
end module2;

procedure module3 is
  i : ED integer; --A name of an externally defined entity
  b : P integer;  --An internally visible entity
begin
  ..
  b:=i;
  ..
end module3;
```

Four entities are declared in this program fragment; Table 3-1 defines the association between the entities and the declared names if the modules were combined to satisfy the name visibility requirements stated in the declarations. There is ambiguity regarding which EV declaration of i should be associated with the ED usage of i in module3, so the table entry lists both possibilities.

TABLE 3-1 NAME–ENTITY MAPPING FOR EXAMPLE 3-7

Module	Name	Entity
module1	i	E_1
module2	i	E_2
module2	b	E_3
module3	i	E_1 or E_2
module3	b	E_4

Module linkage rules or declarations must be used to resolve the ambiguous interpretation of the name module3.i. If the module linkage rules connect the i declarations in procedures module2 and module3, the name module3.i refers to entity E_2, and the entity named module3.b receives the contents of E_2 when the assignment statement in module3 is executed. On the other hand, if the linkages had connected the i declarations in procedures module3 and module1, the name module3.i would have referred to entity E_1, so the value that was assigned to module3.b by the assignment statement within module3 would have been obtained from E_1.

Requiring explicit declarations of name visibility along with name declarations permits great flexibility. However, the flexibility also allows a programmer to create arbitrary program structures that can be difficult to comprehend. Most languages use simple rules that define visibility implicitly and assign name types (e.g., P, ED, or EV) based on the program's syntactic structure.

A number of techniques can be used to relate name spaces and thus to create naming contexts. An isolated single context (or environment) has a single name space. A "flat" naming environment combines many program modules into a single naming context; in this environment every use of name N refers to the same object E(N). In a "globally flat" environment there are two classes of names: global and local, with all global names in the same name space; a global name is visible in all modules, whereas a local name is visible only in the module where it was declared. In a general structured naming environment there may be many classes of names; the same name may refer to different objects, depending on the context of the use of the name. In general, a nonlocal name N may refer to different global objects when used in different program modules.

3.2.2.1 A Single-level flat environment. The simplest visibility rule forms a single name space which contains all declared names; every named entity is accessible from every program module. This rule produces a simple "flat" environment, depicted in Figure 3-5. The dashed region in the figure encloses the set of global names. In this case the set includes every name declared in any program module. A programmer writing a program under this rule must remain aware of all names declared in all program modules; this rule makes programming difficult.

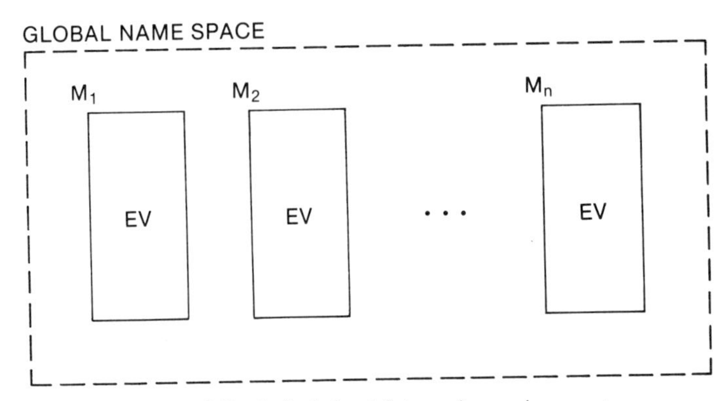

Figure 3-5 A single-level flat naming environment

3.2.2.2 A Two-level flat environment. Another simple visibility scheme permits explicit declarations of EV names in constituent modules, yet merges the sets of EV names from all constituent modules to form a single global name space. The *two-level flat* naming environment established by this rule is depicted in Figure 3-6. There is a single set of globally visible names. Within a module all P names declared within that module plus all EV names of all modules are visible. Under this scheme, a module programmer must be aware of all external declarations that appear in all modules collected to form the final program. This awareness rule is a slight improvement on the analogous rule for a single-level flat environment, but the programmer still has a lot to remember.

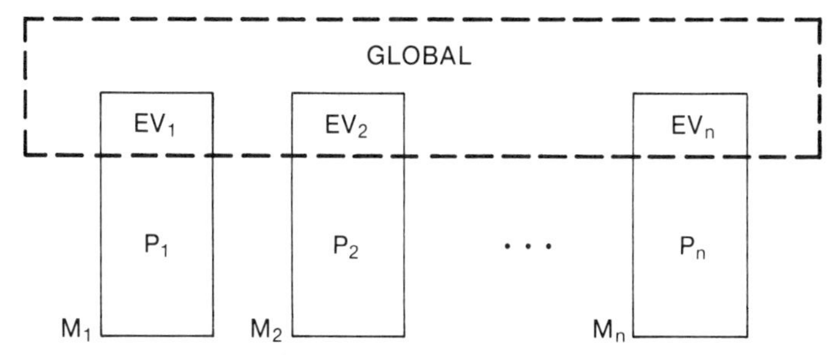

a) Constructing the higher naming context in a flat environment

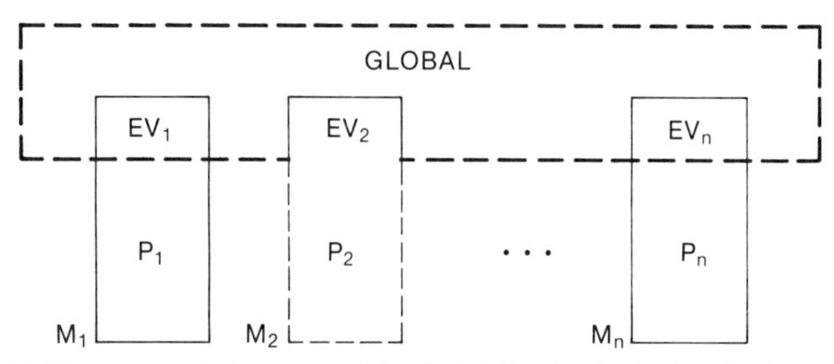

b) The names visible in module M_2 (within the dashed region)

Figure 3-6 Name visibility rules for a two-level flat environment

To complete the design of a two-level flat environment, we need a syntactic rule that distinguishes EV names from P names. One rule uses a name prefix in a declaration to state that the name must be an EV name. For example, an externally visible name could be prefaced with a dollar sign, as in

```
$this : integer; --Not Ada
```

The actual name declared here is "this", which is how the object will be referenced elsewhere in the program's text. Prefix rules to distinguish external visibility declarations are common at the assembly language level.

A name declared to be private in one module might be identical to a name declared to be externally visible in another module. What should happen in this case? To support module separation we want to allow private name declarations to be made without concern for name duplication. This means that the local private declaration must supersede any external declaration.

Example 3-8

Here is a program fragment in which the name i is declared to be globally visible in module1 and redeclared as a local name in module2. In module2 the name i refers to the local entity. In module3 the name i refers to the entity module1.i.

```
procedure module1 is --not Ada!!
  $i : integer;          --global declaration; entity E1
  ..
end module1;

procedure module2 is
  i : real;              --local declaration; entity E2
  ..
begin
  ..
  i:=2;                  --assignment to entity E2
  ..
end module2;

procedure module3 is
  ..
begin
  ..
  i :=4;                 --assignment to entity E1
  ..
end module3;
```

There are two ways to formulate the rule that defines the resolution of this potentially duplicate declaration. The first formulation defines the complete local name space, stating that the local name space is comprised of all locally declared names plus all EV names that were declared in other modules and that do not duplicate a local P name. The second formulation specifies a search strategy for determining the entity to be associated with a name. The search strategy statement for the two-level flat environment is:

Search Rule. To determine the entity corresponding to a name, the local name space containing the P names declared in the module is first searched for a declaration of the name. If this search succeeds, the local entity is the desired object. If this local search fails, a search of the global name space is made. If this search succeeds, the corresponding entity has been determined.

The two-level flat environment permits the local redefinition of a name that happens to be defined as globally visible within another program module, but the programmer still needs to be aware of the global declarations that appear in all other modules.

3.2.2.3 Structured naming environments. In a *structured naming environment* both the distinction between P and EV names and the linkage rules are implied either by the program's textual structure or by the program's execution sequence. The basic structural entity for these distinctions is a "context." As a basis for the rules, we must agree on the following points:

1. How a naming context is defined
2. How names are declared within a naming context
3. How contexts are related for naming purposes

Rather than describing all options for naming context definition, we first describe Ada naming rules and later introduce APL naming rules. In Ada a naming context is a block—which may be a procedure declaration, a package declaration, or a task declaration.

Name declarations within a block are gathered at the beginning of the block. A good programming practice can reduce confusion. The recommendation states that each name declared in a context should be different from all other names declared in that context.[9]

A program containing many blocks may, of course, contain many declarations with the same symbolic name. This is legal, provided that two definitions with the same symbolic name appear in different naming contexts. Each separate P or EV declaration defines a separate P or EV entity; in principle, every one of these entities could be declared with different attributes, although a program written with such syntactically similar, yet semantically diverse declarations would be very hard to read and understand.

In the next subsections we explore two ways that can be used to define the name–entity correspondences: nested naming rules and explicit export/import rules.

3.2.2.3.1 ***Nested Name Resolution.*** Nesting is a common basis for defining intercontext name visibility. With nesting, if a name is used in a block but not declared there, it is equivalent to having an implicit ED object declaration of that object in the block. The visibility rules are easily phrased in terms of the search strategy:

Nested Name Resolution Rule. To find the entity corresponding to the name N used in module A, first search A's local declarations for name N. If A does not contain a declaration of N, the declarations in the module within which A is nested are searched next. If this search fails, the search moves to the module within which that one was nested. The search continues in this manner through the module nest until either a declaration of N is found or the root module (one not nested within another) fails to have the desired declaration.

Figure 3-7 illustrates a module nest. The search for the entity corresponding to name N used in module F proceeds through the module sequence F, D, C, and A. The search terminates successfully when a declaration of N is found in one of

[9] Ada permits "overloading" by which the same name can be declared with different attributes to describe different entities in the same context. The compiler examines the usage context to resolve the ambiguity among the multiple declarations of the name. If some common property is shared among these objects, such overloading can enhance program readability. Overloading is more useful for names of functions and procedures than for names of data objects. For example, the same function name can be used to denote all procedures or functions that perform the same operation on different combinations of parameter types.

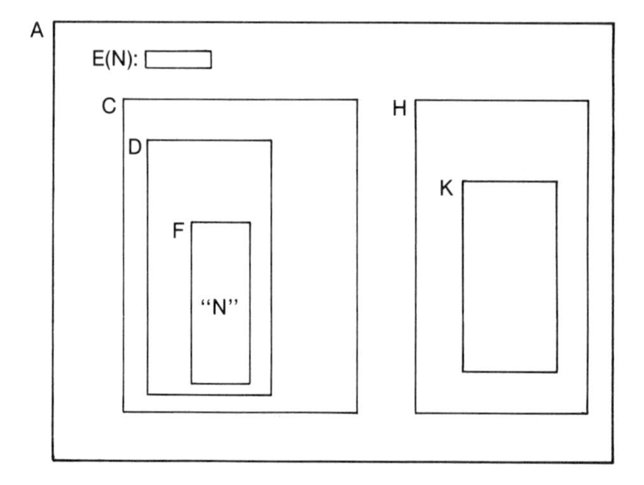

Figure 3-7 Module nesting

those blocks. The search terminates unsuccessfully if the nest is exhausted without finding a declaration of N. We can describe this search sequence as a sequence of questions:

```
--Algorithm execution illustrating the search
--for the entity named N
Is N declared in F? If yes, terminate;
Is N declared in D? If yes, terminate;
Is N declared in C? If yes, terminate;
Is N declared in A? If yes, terminate;
N has not been properly declared for this use.
```

The nested search may fail because the name was not declared in the nest. In this case the program may simply be in error. One could introduce a rule stating that a name not declared in the nest is actually an ED name to be resolved during linking. This rule is not entirely satisfactory, however, since the translator cannot produce instructions to access N correctly, as N's attributes are not known to the compiler. The uncertainty could either be resolved by postponing code generation until link time[10] or by requiring a declaration for each external object.[11]

The nested naming rule does not prohibit a programmer from using the same name for different objects in different modules within the same nested set of modules. Even if name N has multiple declarations in the nest, its meaning is always unambiguous because the entity first found during the nest scan will be taken to be the declaration of N. In fact, other declarations of N will not be uncovered during the nest search. Therefore, in effect, an entity E declared with name N in block A will not be visible in a block F nested within A if there is another declaration of name N in some intervening block (such as C or D in Figure 3-7). Even though name redeclaration has well-defined semantics, it is bad programming practice to use the same

[10]This delay is required by Ada semantics!

[11]This is also required in Ada.

name for different objects, as a person can become confused when writing, debugging, or reasoning about the program.

The general nested naming rule does not specify the meaning of module nesting. Two rules defining module nesting are the static and dynamic rules discussed in the following.

1. *Static nesting.* Static nesting defines module nesting based on the format of the program text.

Definition. *Static module nesting* is declared by textual inclusion; module B is nested within module A if and only if the text describing module B is included within the text describing module A.

The static nest structure is independent of program flow; in particular, the program's execution pattern never affects the static nest structure. Since program execution does not modify the static nesting structure, it follows that all names can be resolved during compilation or linking. Compile-time resolution of static nesting is used with Ada programs.

Example 3-9

```
procedure a is
  i, j : integer;
  procedure b is
    i, k : integer;
    procedure c is
      k, j : integer;
    begin
      .. --body of c;
    end c;
  begin
    .. --body of b;
  end b;
  procedure d is
    j, k : integer;
  begin
    .. --body of d;
  end d;
begin
  .. --body of a;
end a;
```

In this program only three different object names (i, j, and k) are used, but there are eight declared objects. The object names have different interpretations in different procedure blocks. Table 3-2 shows how each name that might be used in the program would be interpreted if it were used in each procedure body. To distinguish the different declarations from each other, we generate a unique name for each object by combining a simple object name (as a qualifier) with the block (procedure) name. The table shows which actual object would be designated by each possible name, if used in each procedure.

TABLE 3-2 NAME–OBJECT CORRESPONDENCES IN EXAMPLE 3-9

Name	Used in Procedure Block	Object Denoted
i	a	a.i
	b	b.i
	c	b.i
	d	a.i
j	a	a.j
	b	a.j
	c	c.j
	d	d.j
k	a	illegal
	b	b.k
	c	c.k
	d	d.k

TABLE 3-3 PROCEDURE NAME VISIBILITY IN EXAMPLE 3-9

Procedure Name	Visible in Blocks
a	a, b, c, d
b	a, b, c, d
c	b, c
d	a, b, c, d

Procedure names are resolved just like object names. Table 3-3 specifies the visibility of each procedure name in each block of this program.

Using static nesting for naming is equivalent to constructing a module tree, with the main (outer) module the root of the tree. The daughter(s) of a tree node P are the modules whose specifications are textually enclosed in the text of module P. Figure 3-8a illustrates the tree structure corresponding to the program in Example 3-9.

One way to visualize the name resolution search under static nesting is to construct a parenthesized string depicting module boundaries, name declarations, and textual inclusion. This character string is constructed by reading the program text, paying attention to module headers, name declarations, and module terminators. In particular, 1) change each module header into the module name followed by a left parenthesis, 2) change each module terminator into a right parenthesis, 3) make a list of all object declarations, and 4) keep the program statements. To find the interpretation of an instance of a name, start by placing a marker asterisk at the use

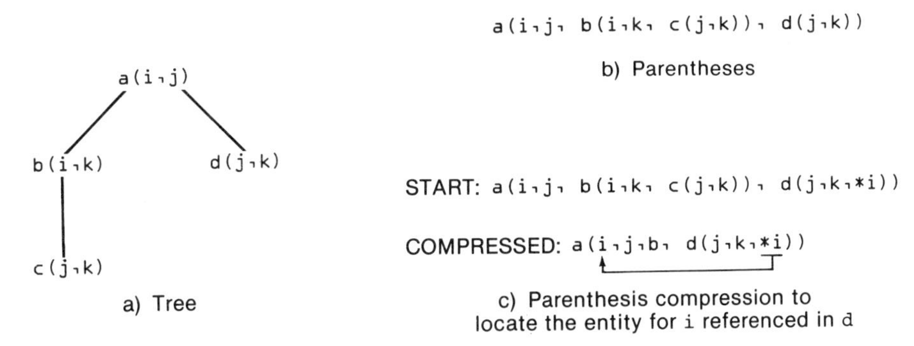

Figure 3-8 Representations of a statically nested naming environment

of the name. Delete all nondeclaration statements. Next, delete every balanced parenthesis pair which does not enclose the asterisk, along with everything enclosed between the parentheses. The string that remains includes all modules that may be scanned during the resolution of the marked name, along with their enclosed declarations. Looking to the left from the marker, the first declaration of the name corresponds to the entity to which the name refers. The name preceding the first left parenthesis to the left of that declaration is the name of the block within which the declaration was stated. Figure 3-8b shows the character string (without the nondeclaration statements) for the program of Example 3-9, and shows its compression for the resolution of the use of name i in module d. The left scan shows that this use of i corresponds to the declaration of i in module b.

Static nesting rules can be enforced by the translation program. In particular, the translator can fix the addressing algorithm that corresponds to each use of an object name. Thus the translator can be built to assure that the addressing algorithm accesses the proper entity. Since the algorithmic details and parameters may depend on the system's allocation and accessing policies and mechanisms, we will not detail the translator's name-address mapping here (see Chapter 5). Correct name interpretation is guaranteed by the correctness of the module's program generated by the translator (with respect to addressing, the translated program falls into the "nothing illegal" category described in Chapter 1).

2. *Dynamic nesting.* Dynamic module nesting is based on the actual program execution sequence; the nest structure is determined from the sequence of entries and exits to and from program contexts. In most languages contexts correspond to procedure and function bodies, so that context changes occur on calls and returns from procedures and functions. To make these notions precise, we introduce some definitions.

Definition. The *act of invoking a module* is the act of performing a call to the module.

Definition. The *act of completing a module* is the act of executing a return from that module.

Definition. A module is *alive* during the time interval between its invocation and its completion.

Definition. Module m is *dynamically nested within module n* at time t if modules m and n are alive at time t and if the act of invoking n preceded the act of invoking m.

This definition of dynamic nesting and the Nested Name Resolution Rule define the search process used to find the entity corresponding to a name.

Figure 3-9 illustrates one program's execution, showing the module activation intervals, from which one can easily determine the timing of module invocations and returns. The shaded interval opposite a module name indicates the time interval during which that module was alive. At time T_1 we see that module b is dynamically nested within module a. Similarly, at time T_2 module d is nested within module b, which is nested within module c, which in turn is nested within module a. The module enclosing b in the nest at time T_2 is different from the module enclosing b at time T_1.

The dynamic nest structure depends on the execution history up to the time the name is used, so the entity corresponding to a particular name N used in block B cannot be uniquely determined for all executions of block B. The compiler cannot create a static addressing path for the object program and cannot assure access to the proper dynamically nested entity, unless the space allocation for each entity is changed dynamically.

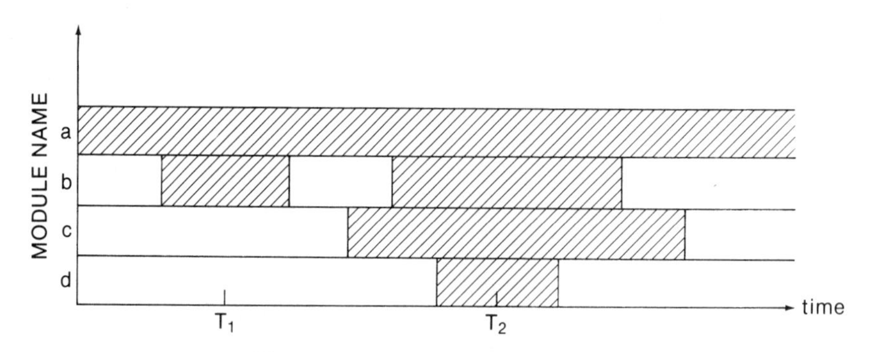

Figure 3-9 Module activation intervals

Example 3-10

```
procedure a is
  i, j : integer;
begin
  ..  --body of a
end a;
```

```
procedure b is
   i, k : integer;
begin
   ..  --body of b
end b;
procedure c is
   j, k : boolean;
begin
   ..  --body of c
end c;
procedure d is
   j, k : integer;
begin
   ..  --body of d
end d;
```

This program's flat textual structure does not affect name interpretation because that interpretation is dynamic. To interpret names, we must know the program's execution history of module changes. Suppose that the module call-return history was

```
call a;
call c;
call b;
return;
call d;
call a;
call b;
return;
return;
return;
return;
return;
```

Table 3-4 lists the entity corresponding to each possible name used within each procedure consistent with the given history.

TABLE 3-4 ACTUAL OBJECTS[a] REFERENCED IN A DYNAMIC NESTING EXAMPLE

	Corresponding Entity					
Name	First Call of a	c	First Call of b	d	Second Call of a	Second Call of b
i	a.i⟨1⟩	a.i⟨1⟩	b.i⟨1⟩	a.i⟨1⟩	a.i⟨2⟩	b.i⟨2⟩
j	a.j⟨1⟩	c.j	c.j	d.j	a.j⟨2⟩	a.j⟨2⟩
k	—	c.k	b.k⟨1⟩	d.k	d.k	b.k⟨2⟩

[a]Here x⟨j⟩ denotes the jth instance of the object named x. In this table qualified names based on block names are used to denote the allocated entities.

Although dynamic nesting appears complex, it can be implemented simply by copying values upon context changes. We digress from our naming discussion to turn briefly to a simple implementation of dynamic nesting, since it may help the reader understand the dynamic nesting semantics. In this implementation the translator allocates one visible entity corresponding to each distinct name appearing anywhere in the program. By properly managing the values held in the visible entities, things can be arranged so that in every context the entity denoted by name N is found at the visible location corresponding to the name N. Two activities are required to maintain this condition. First, when entering a new context, the value stored in each place that corresponds to a name redeclared in the new context is saved on a stack. Thus if N were redeclared in the new context, the value in the visible location corresponding to N would be saved. After stacking the old value, a new (initialized) value is assigned to a visible location whose redeclaration specifies initialization. Only after the stacking and reinitialization have been completed will the new context's program body be started. The second cluster of activities occurs on leaving a context. At this point, the values that were stacked on entry are restored to the visible locations. During execution of the nested context, the stacked values are not accessible and all locally declared entities can be accessed because their values are stored in the visible locations. Notice how the use of dynamic space allocation permits the use of static addressing paths.

Example 3-11

> Figure 3-10 shows both the contents of each visible named location and the contents of the stack holding their old values for the execution history of Example 3-10. The lifetimes of the activation records and the corresponding contexts are indicated in part (a) of the figure. Now let m denote the integer identifying the context (these numbers are shown in the figure). Figure 3-10b shows the current values stored in the common entities i, j, and k in each context. Figure 3-10c shows the contents of the stack if each saved set is stacked in alphabetical order (with i on top and k on the bottom).

One way to visualize the dynamic nesting semantics uses a parenthesized string reflecting the dynamic history of context entry and exit, along with information about name redeclarations. Construct the string starting with the dynamic history of calls and returns. Insert a left parenthesis for each entry and a right parenthesis for each exit. Before each left parenthesis, list the name of the context being entered. After each left parenthesis, list the objects declared in the context being entered. To find the entity that corresponds to a particular use of name N, insert an asterisk to denote the context where N was used. Remove all balanced pairs of parentheses that do not contain the asterisk, including everything enclosed between the parentheses. Then search to the left from the asterisk for a declaration of N; the first declaration found in this search corresponds to the declaration of the entity actually referenced from the marked location. Note the similarity between this parenthesis string reduction technique and the one used for static nesting; they are almost identical, but the static one started with the program's (static) text, whereas the dynamic one starts with the program's (dynamic) history.

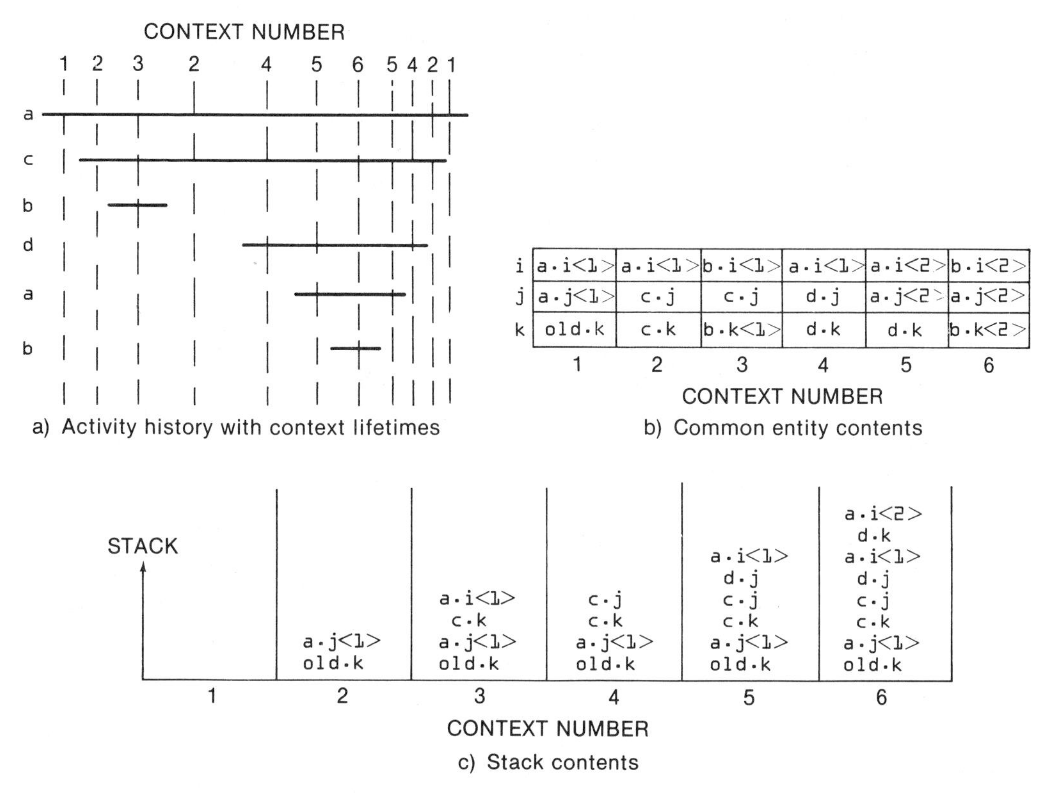

Figure 3-10 The dynamic stack for an execution history (Example 3-11)

Example 3-12

During the call to procedure d in the history of Example 3-10, the parenthesis structure for name resolution is

a(i, j, c(j, k, b(i, k), d(j, k

For resolution of the names from this context, we cancel out balanced parenthesis pairs, leaving this string:

a(i, j, c(j, k, b, d(j, k

So we see that the name i resolves to the leftmost context, which corresponds to the first call of a, and that the names j and k resolve to the current block, which is the call of d.

Dynamic nesting is used for all object names in a few languages, such as APL and Snobol. Ada and PL/1 use dynamic nesting rules to resolve exceptions; the Ada details in this regard are presented in Section A.5.7.

3.2.2.3.2 *Naming Objects Not in the Nest.* The nested visibility rules are simply understood rules determining the set of objects directly visible from any naming context. Occasionally, one may wish to reference objects not accessible according to the nesting rule. These exceptions are most important when static nesting is used; we concentrate on static nesting here. We consider two cases: 1) objects declared in the same translation unit, discussed in this section, and 2) objects declared outside the translation unit. The latter case can be used to create links between separate translation units, as discussed in the next section.

First, note that we can arrange things artificially so that every context in a single translation unit is in the same context tree. We achieve this arrangement by making each context be nested within the main context of the translation unit. The program structure may not correspond to this simple view, however, if the top-level structure of the translation unit contains a set of packages. In this situation, we just enclose the whole program in a (fictitious) outermost block which contains everything in the program. The outermost block (or context) serves as the *root* of the naming context tree.

Second, recall that the nested naming rule defines which objects can be named from a given naming context; all such objects were declared in some context along the path back to the root from the naming context.[12] The naming rule defines how we interpret names for procedures, objects, packages, records, and other entities.

We construct names for objects not directly visible by using the period naming operator. Just what role does the period assume in naming? It moves the name interpretation context to within the object named before the period. For example, if rec is a record, the name rec.b is interpreted as the object within rec whose name is b. In general, the period operator expands the space of nameable objects to include 1) the components of visible records or 2) the visible[13] components of visible package

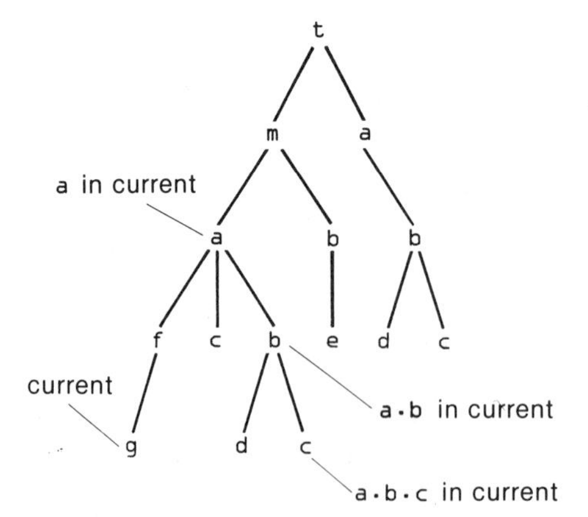

Figure 3-11 Cousin naming

[12]Some of objects declared in a context along the path may become invisible due to an intervening declaration, as we discussed earlier.

[13]This "visible" refers to the nonprivate parts of the package specification, while the previous and the following "visible" refer to the set of objects that can be named.

specifications. No other objects have components that are visible from above. If the visible component entities themselves are records or package names having visible components, those components can be named.

For example, under this view the name a.b.c is interpreted as a name for the object named c which lies within a module named b, which, in turn, lies within a directly visible module named a. Figure 3-11 illustrates this structure. The name a.b.c is a legitimate name within any naming context in which the name a is visible.

Example 3-13

Ada allows one to construct a qualified name to name an EV object declared within a visible package. Some of its components can be named in the same manner.

```
type t_record is
  record
    t_first : integer;
    t_second : real;
  end record;
package c is
  d : integer;
  e : t_record;
  ..
end c;
package body a is
  procedure e is
    i : integer;
  begin
    i := c.d; --here c.d refers to the d within
    ..        --package c
    i := c.e.t_first; --the first component of the
    ..                --record declared in package c
  end e;
end a;
```

These naming rules automatically make an object visible within a large context. Alternatively, an Ada programmer can completely hide an object by declaring it within a package body.

Example 3-14

```
package body c is
  d : integer; --an internal object declared within
  ..           --the package body
end c;
package body a is
  procedure e is
    i : integer;
```

```
    begin
      i:=c.d; --the name c.d is illegal since in
              --package c the name d is declared
              --in c's body and therefore is
              --invisible from outside c
      ..
    end e;
begin
  ..          --here is a's body
end a;
```

Qualified names with a lot of periods are tedious to read and type; Ada gives the programmer the option of making a whole set of components visible in another context while giving them simpler names. The **use** statement specifies this name simplification. The name of a record or package in the **use** statement specifies an entity whose internal names are to be made visible in the using environment, without any qualification by the record or package name. We conclude this topic with an example of the use of **use**. The use of **use** does not affect system functionality or architecture.

Example 3-15

```
package c is
  d : integer;
  ..
end c;
package body a is
  procedure e is
    use c;
    f : integer;
  begin
    f:=d; --here d refers to c.d
  end e;
begin
  ..        --a's body
end a;
```

The **renames** declaration provides a general way to rename Ada objects and thereby shorten their names. Consider the obvious declaration

```
x : integer renames M.p;
```

Since both the renaming statement and the declaration of the object being renamed contain a type specification for the same object, a programmer could err by making inconsistent type declarations. The consistency of the type declarations for a shared object can be checked from module specifications before execution.

Example 3-16

This simple Ada program makes the object a.c visible in module d, and renames it p:

```
package a is
  c : integer;
end a;
  ..  --body of a omitted
      --specification of d's interface omitted
package body d is
  p : integer renames a.c;
  ..
end d;
```

We have seen how the Ada programmer has some control over the visibility of the objects she declares. An object can be hidden within a package or procedure body or can be made globally visible within a package specification, but there is no way to confine the object's visibility to a specific naming context. In the remainder of the section we discuss some language design options that give the programmer finer control over object visibility.

Explicit visibility control permits a programmer either to hide a name or to make a name visible. Both forms of explicit visibility control relate to the visibility in a *using context* of an object that was declared in a *declaration context*.

We first explain the options using simple statements. Here are some statements related to some visibility control options:

S1: "I, the declarer, allow you, the user in context C, to know about object E which I have just declared."

S2: "I, the declarer, prohibit you, the user in context C, from knowing about object E which I have just declared."

S3: "I, the user, demand the use of object E which you, the declarer, have created."

S4: "I, the user, promise that I will not use object E which you, the declarer, have created."

S5: "I, the declarer, force you, the user in context C, to know about object E which I have just declared."

S6: "I, the user, wish to know about object E which you, the declarer, have created."

Some combinations of these declarer/user statements are incompatible; S2 and S3 do not make sense together, since the declarer prohibits something that the user demands. Other combinations make logical sense; S1 and S6 reflect a polite interchange which results in the user knowing about E with the permission of the declarer.

Let us leave the world of informal requests, permissions, and promises and return to the precise world of programming language design. To support fine-grained visibility control, we could design the language to allow the declarer, the user, or both to make statements regarding either visibility or denial of visibility. Table 3-5 summarizes six possible combinations of such statements. Some of these combinations do not make sense. It is pointless, for example, to make a promise at the receiving end. It seems pointless to impose externally a name into a using context from the declaration context. These two observations eliminate options 1 and 4. Furthermore, option 6 contains redundant statements about the invisibility of the object, so we eliminate it. Only options 2, 3, and 5 remain.

TABLE 3-5 COMBINATIONS OF VISIBILITY CONTROL STATEMENT LOCATION AND MODE

	Context Where Visibility Specified		
Type	Declaration	Using	Mode
1	x		Forced visibility
2	x		Prohibition
3		x	Permission
4		x	Promise
5	x	x	Permission
6	x	x	Prohibition

To illustrate a syntax for explicit visibility control, we choose option 3, in which the using context declares its desire to use a name declared elsewhere. We introduce the reserved word "**import**" to state this desire in a declaration, and use the **renames** syntax from Ada. Thus an importation request would be declared in a statement like

```
x : integer import m.x;      --not Ada
```

In a similar manner, we could introduce the reserved word **export** to state that a declared entity should be visible in (an)other module(s).

By combining renaming, exportation, and importation, a programmer can create an arbitrarily complex naming environment within each translation unit. These translation units can be combined to form the complete program.

3.2.2.3.3 ***Naming Objects Not in the Translation Unit.*** Two types of objects that are not created in a translation unit may nevertheless become visible within the unit: files, and objects declared externally (in another translation unit, that is). We need conventions such that the programmer can specify these objects and, where necessary, can specify their types. We consider files and externally declared objects separately.

An externally declared object has an object type describing its composition and size, and the program accessing the object must be aware of that type. Therefore, any externally declared object that is to be accessed in the translation unit must appear in a declaration, along with some indication that this particular declaration refers to an ED object. In Ada the reserved word **separate** indicates that a package body, task body, or procedure body is to be found in another compilation unit. Value-holding objects can be externally defined by collecting them into the body of a package, which is made separate. The following example illustrates the use of **separate** to refer to an ED object.

Example 3-17

```
package values is
  thing_1 : integer;
  thing_2 : real;
  thing_3 : integer;
end values;

package body values is separate

x : real renames values.thing_2;
```

The package specification is required to specify the types and local names of the entities visible within that package interface. This example happens to make only object names visible, but procedure and function names could have been made visible in an analogous manner.

With these declarations, the local name x can be used for the ED object values.thing_2. When the program is linked together, the instantiation of the values package will be linked into the program, and wherever the name x was used, the program will access the proper entity in the values package.

The second class of objects not within the naming nest includes files in the file system. A file name may appear within a program as a constant value that later will be a parameter within a request to the file system. The name interpretation rules that apply to file names are determined by the operating system. It is usually the case that the file system is structured as a tree structure. The leaf nodes of this structure are files and the internal nodes are directories and subdirectories. The tree structure is based on the relation "directory A is on the list of objects in directory B." When this relation holds, directory B is the parent of directory A. Figure 3-12 illustrates this relationship.

A user process is considered to be located at a particular internal node of this tree structure, known as the "working directory." The working directory has a special role in the file name resolution algorithm; the role is not unlike the role of the using context in a program. Let us recall the two parts of that role: First, the using context is the place where newly declared names will be inserted; and second, the path back toward the root defines the search path used to resolve names that cannot be locally resolved. With file names the definition context role carries over from object naming. The file name search rules do not use the ancestry structure, however. The directory structure can be used to construct file names by specifying a path through the tree structure.

First, let us examine the search rules for file name resolution. The usual convention associates a "search path" with each process. This path is specified as a list of file directories. The local context is implicitly at the head of the search path. Explicitly listed directories will be searched only if the local search fails to

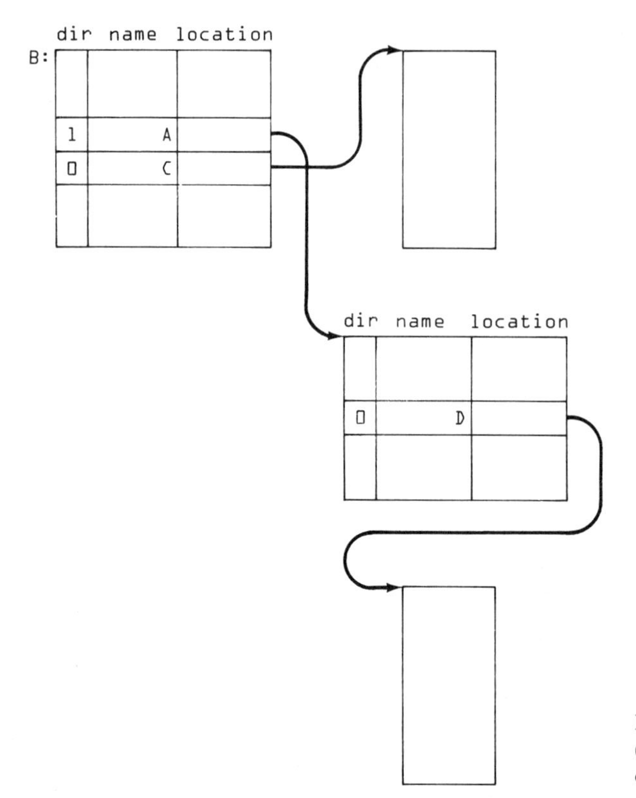

Figure 3-12 A file directory structure (dir = 1 if the described object is a directory)

obtain a match. The search continues in the order that the directories are listed in the path specification. Notice that this rule is a direct extension of the notion that the name resolution process can be considered as an algorithm. Here the search path can be constructed from any arbitrary sequence of directories, independent of the structure of the directory tree. As with object name resolution, if the directories along the path fail to provide a match, the search is unsuccessful.

The second role of the directory structure is to provide a naming structure. All systems provide some method for naming an arbitrary file or directory in terms of the path taken to the file from the tree's root. To construct a path specification, we require a means for specifying motion to a child directory; this operation is analogous to the operation specified by the period in an Ada name, except that here the search point moves through a directory structure, rather than through a naming context nest.

Example 3-18

In Multics the operator "〉" can be used in a file name to construct a qualified name; the operator denotes moving away from the tree's root. Consider the tree shown in Figure 3-13. A "complete" Multics path name starts the tree traversal from the tree's root; such a name starts with either the name "udd" or the "〉" operator. The complete path name of the node marked "2" in the figure is "〉a〉b〉r〉t", or "udd〉a〉b〉r〉t."

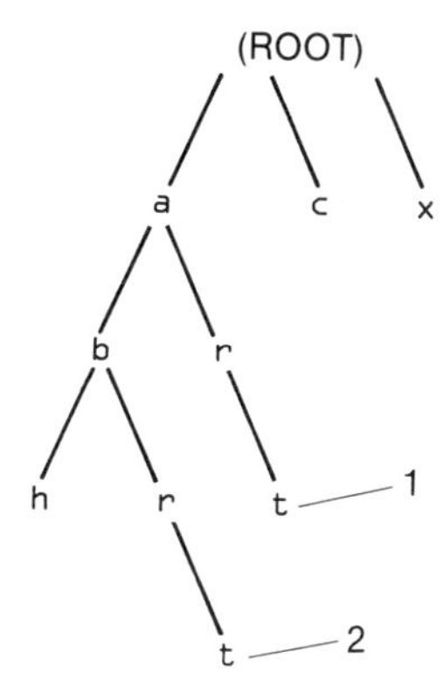

Figure 3-13 A Multics file tree (Example 3-18)

Example 3-19

The slash ("/") in a Unix file name serves the role of the ">" in Multics, forming a qualified file name and specifying motion down one level of the tree. The file tree's root is known as "root." Thus the file named "udd>a>b>r>t" in Multics would be named "root/a/b/r/t" in an analogous file tree under Unix.

The file tree structure is the basis for constructing path names relative to the working directory. In Multics the operator ">" is used to specify motion downward in the tree and the operator "<" specifies upward motion (along the path to the root from the current naming context).[14]

Example 3-20

Returning to Figure 3-13, suppose that my current (Multics) working directory is represented as the tree node named H. The node named "<<r>t" is my cousin; the node is marked in the figure with a "1." The node named "<r>t" is my niece; it is marked in the figure with a "2."

Many operating systems do not provide an analogous way to specify upward motion, with the effect that a complete file name must be used to name a file not in the directory subtree rooted at the working directory.

It is conceptually possible to combine the use of automatic path searching rules with the up-and-down operators, by, for example, defining the search for the first node in a path name to use the automatic search rules.

We have seen how objects not in the nest can be assigned names and referenced from within a program. The task of relating these uses to the appropriate declarations is handled by the linker, which is discussed in Section 3.3.

3.2.2.3.4 ***Procedure Parameters.*** A procedure parameter can be used to convey a name from one portion of the name space to another. The relationship between

[14]There is no need for an analogous naming rule in a programming language since the path back to the root will be traversed by the automatically invoked name resolution search.

naming considerations and the interpretation of procedure parameters has an important influence on the implementation of some systems, so we will examine the optional ways that a procedure parameter could be interpreted.

We start with the formal parameter, which is the name used to describe the parameter from within the procedure's body. The name of the formal parameter is included in the specification of the procedure. When the procedure is invoked from a program, both the procedure's name and the list of actual parameter values are specified. Usually, the order in which the actual parameters are listed in the program is the same as the order in which they will be associated with the formal parameters. In addition to the ordering, we have to define how the actual parameter is going to be interpreted within the procedure's body. Three options are listed in Table 3-6.

TABLE 3-6 PROCEDURE PARAMETER INTERPRETATION OPTIONS

Method of Parameter Interpretation	Conventional Name for the Option
Value	passed by value
Address	passed by reference
Addressing algorithm	passed by name

The programmer does not have explicit control over the interpretation option used with each passed parameter because implicit (usage-dependent) parameter interpretation rules are defined by the programming language. For example, an actual parameter written as an expression is passed as a value. This rule may seem obvious, since the result of evaluating an expression could not be anything but a value.

How is a parameter expressed as a name to be interpreted? Here programming languages differ. There is no semantic difference between interpreting the actual parameter "x" as an address or as a specification of an addressing algorithm. After all, interpreting the name "x" either as an address or as an addressing algorithm specification results in access to the object named x. The name of an array element, however, begins a different story. Consider the name "x(i)." To interpret this as an address, the program would read the value of i when the procedure call was being made, and the address of the corresponding entry within x would be passed as the actual parameter and used within the called procedure. On the other hand, if we were interpreting x(i) as an addressing algorithm, we would pass an algorithm to access the actual parameter. In this case the value of i would be read and interpreted as a component selector (in other words, the addressing algorithm would be executed) whenever p tries to access its formal parameter. The functional effect would be the same as if the parameter had been passed by reference, provided that the value of i had not been changed during the execution of p. On the other hand, if the value of i had been changed during p's execution, there is a significant difference between call by reference and call by name.

Example 3-21

Here is an Algol program using call by name, written in Ada syntax:

```
procedure f(a, b : integer) is
  c, d : integer;
  type ar10int is array(1 .. 10) of integer;
  e : ar10int;
  procedure g(x, y : integer) is
                    --the parameters are passed by name
                    --since there is no specification to
                    --the contrary.
                    --this is an Algol convention that
                    --does not apply to Ada.
  begin
    c:=4;
    x:=3;             --usage of x
                      --this is not consistent with an Ada
                      --procedure heading, which would
                      --require that x have the out
                      --attribute.
    ..
  end g;
begin
  ..
  c:=2;
  g(4, d);            --call by value - usage is illegal
                      --cannot assign to a constant
  g(c,d);             --call by name - usage is c:=3;
  g(e(3),d);          --call by name - usage is e(3):=3;
  g(e(c),d);          --call by name - usage is e(4):=3;
end f;
```

If the last call of g uses call by reference, the assignment to x assigns to e(2), since the value of c was 2 when g was called. On the other hand, if the language uses call by name, the assignment is made to e(4), since c has the value 4 when the assignment to x is performed. Other simpler situations are depicted in previous lines of the program.

Table 3-7 summarizes the Algol and PL/1 parameter interpretation rules. Ada is not included in the table because its interpretation rules have a different basis, which we discuss now.

The Ada interpretation of a parameter is controlled by the presence or absence of the reserved words **in** and **out** associated with the formal parameter declaration in the procedure specification. Rather than specifying parameter interpretations in terms of name resolution rules, the interpretations are made by specifying value copying operations. We examine the rules and then we discuss their significance. The reserved word **in** signifies that the actual value of the parameter will be copied to the formal parameter when the procedure is called. The reserved word **out** signifies that the actual value of the formal parameter upon completion of the procedure will be copied to the location named as the actual parameter. If the actual

TABLE 3-7 PARAMETER INTERPRETATION IN PL/1 AND ALGOL

Actual Parameter		Interpretations	
Class	Example	Algol	PL/1
Expression	$x + 5$	Value	Value
Simple name	x	Reference	Reference
Component name	x(i)	Name	Reference

parameter was an expression and the formal parameter's mode included **out**, the program is erroneous. Furthermore, it is an error for a function to have any parameter with the **out** attribute. A literal interpretation of these rules would impose a large overhead if the parameter were a vector or an array that needed to be copied. The Ada designers realized this fact and left the implementation of these cases at the discretion of the implementer. The wording from the Ada standard is: "For a parameter whose type is an array . . . an implementation may likewise achieve the above effects by copy. . . . Alternatively, an implementation may achieve these effects by reference . . . . The execution of a program is erroneous if its effect depends on which mechanism is selected . . . ." Thus the program of Example 3-21 is erroneous as an Ada program.

We try to relate these Ada rules for scalar objects to the name interpretation rules. We easily see that an **in** parameter behaves like a call by value. However, the use of **out** does not match either call by name or call by reference; one significant difference is that in an Ada program the value of the object seen from the calling context will not be changed unless the procedure successfully exits. By contrast, an Algol parameter passed by name will be modified in the calling context whenever the procedure writes to the name denoting the formal parameter. The net result is that an Ada program is more modular because each module either performs its complete function or else its visible effect on the rest of the program is limited to control flow changes.[15]

In Section 3.4 we will see how these naming issues influence the design of the underlying system.

3.2.3 Locators

A locator object contains an object's name, in the sense that the "value" of a locator describes the present location of another object. A locator at the high-level-language level corresponds to an indirect address at the processor level. It may be necessary to introduce locators into programs in order to properly describe addressing algorithms, in particular to access dynamic objects or procedure parameters. An Ada declaration of a locator object (which is called an "access variable") can be detected by the reserved word **access** as the first word of the type declaration.

[15]This difference is important for a procedure using exceptions for abnormal exit (Section 6.2.1.6) and for reasoning about program properties; it isolates the issue of the procedure's correctness from its modular separation from its caller.

Some naming questions related to the use of locator objects are: (1) "Does the name of the locator denote the value in the locator itself or the value in the object described in the locator's value?" (2) "How are the contents of the locator distinguished from the contents of the designated location?" and (3) "How freely can a locator value be passed around the program?"

The Ada answers to these questions are: (1) the locator's name refers to the locator itself; (2) the entire contents of the object can be denoted by the locator's name with "**.all**" appended to the end; and (3) a locator value may be passed freely around a program as long as the interpretation of its contents is not changed by the act of passing it to another context. The copying allowed by the latter rule must be consistent with strong typing if the language demands strong typing.[16] This restriction could be violated if the pointer within the locator object has a context-dependent interpretation, because that interpretation might change the type of the described object.

3.2.4 Summary

Numerous naming conventions are used in high-level programming languages. Some of these conventions, such as static nested name resolution rules, suggest certain implementation structures that can be supported at lower levels of the system. In Section 3.4 we will see how the high-level-language naming rules have influenced processor addressing designs.

3.3 PROGRAM ADDRESS SPACE

A program address space is created when a set of translation modules is combined to form a complete program. The linker resolves the names of ED objects used in the constituent translation modules; to complete the resolution, the linker may have to find a module in a library file and add it to the program; this act expands the program address space. The program address space defines the complete context for name resolution during program execution.[17] Actually, the act of linking translation modules to form the complete program can be performed before or during program execution.

A program address space is necessary to combine the separate program modules created when a programmer divides a large task into smaller pieces. To amass the complete program, the pieces must be combined into a coherent whole. The linking process glues the pieces together by coupling the usages of external names with named entities declared in other modules. This process constructs a "program address space" containing all objects declared in each constituent module. One could

[16]This amounts to saying that the value of a locator cannot be copied to another locator object unless the types of both are identical, where the locator's type implies the type of the object to which the locator points.

[17]Although this statement may make it sound as though name resolution must be performed during program execution, this is not the situation in most languages.

consider this process as building an encompassing block surrounding the naming trees of the constituent modules. An important naming question concerns the selection of the modules to be included within the complete program.

The process that finds the declaration corresponding to an ED name is called "resolving" the ED name. Each unresolved ED name must be matched with an EV definition appearing somewhere within the set being linked together. The matching process involves a scan of the lists of EV names associated with the files in a directory. The search path thus consists of a list of directories. This search path could be constructed automatically from the file tree's structure, but customarily, the user specifies a list of directories as a parameter of the link or run command.[18] The system's structure is not affected by this selection, but it is affected by the need for linking. In fact, we will see that special support must be provided at a low level if the system is to support efficient linking during program execution.

The definition corresponding to an ED name is taken as the first matching EV name found along the search path. The search process examines the list of EV names associated with every program file in each directory along the search path; the first match of an unresolved name found by this process is taken as the declaration of the object. To include the object within the program, the file associated with the EV declaration is added to the program.

Two quite different scenarios are possible. In the first, all linking is performed *before* the program is started; a system following this scenario uses *static linking*. In the second scenario, the program is started before all linking has been completed, and the linker is invoked as required if an unlinked reference is encountered during execution. A system following this scenario uses *dynamic linking*. A low-level failure detection mechanism is required for the system to be able to detect the unlinked condition during program execution.

To define the object denoted by a reference to an external object E, the linker must find the externally visible definition of the corresponding object. Usually, the corresponding object was declared to have the same name (E) and to have the same type.[19] Two data structures per module are required to perform the linking process: a list of all ED names used in the module, and a list of all EV names defined in the module. If we wish to enforce strong typing, each entry on each list must specify both the declared name and the declared type. We will learn more about these lists in Section 5.3.2.

Example 3-22

To illustrate ED name resolution, we ignore typing constraints. Consider this set of translation units and the EV names defined within each one:

```
f: a, b, c, j, k
g: b, e, t
h: c, j, p
```

[18]The choice of link versus run depends on the timing of the linking process.

[19]Type matching is required in a strongly typed language but may not be part of the check in other situations.

If a program using ED names a, b, and p is linked using the search order f, g, and h, the objects used will be f.a, f.b, and h.p. If, on the other hand, the search order were changed to g, h, and f, the objects used would be f.a, g.b, and h.p. This search process is illustrated in Figure 3-14, which shows the EV lists within the modules; the search order is reflected in the order of the modules across the figure.

It should be obvious how the name matching process can be generalized to require type matching and thereby to enforce strong typing.

A designer can choose the processor's addressing modes so that they support easy access through linked references to ED objects. In addition, the designer has the option to support context-dependent address interpretation at the processor level; this selection may be used to shorten processor programs. We explore these issues and options in the next section and in Chapter 5.

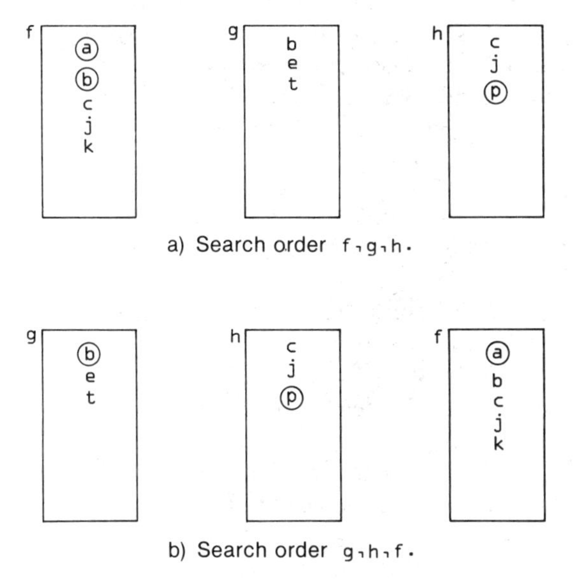

Figure 3-14 Declarations found during linking searches (marked with circles)

3.4 PROCESSOR-LEVEL NAMES

Processor-level names are found in assembly language programs, in data and programs produced by language translators, and in algorithms produced by either compilers or high-level language programmers. The detailed nature of these names and algorithms depends heavily on the processor's innate addressing mechanisms. We reviewed some conventional addressing mechanisms (used in the MC68020) in Chapter 2; here we elaborate those techniques and show the connections between these mechanisms and the designs used at the higher levels. We also introduce other naming options that move processor-level names closer to higher-level names.

In this section you will learn about the addressing modes and address interpretation mechanisms used in diverse processor architectures. You should understand the connection between the designs at this level and those at higher levels. You should also be prepared for the implementation option discussion in the following sections.

We start with an elaboration of processor-level address construction modes, based on the basic addressing modes of the MC68020. This processor, like many, interprets an address as a single integer. After we present many optional interpretations of such "one-dimensional" addresses, we turn to "two-dimensional addressing." We will cover designs that support efficient naming for block-structured languages and support the implementation of systems constructed from sets of cooperating but separated modules.

A processor program will have to compute an object address to access a component from an array, a record, or another data structure. These computations must occur during program execution, implementing a dynamic name binding. An address resulting from a processor-level name mapping is called an "effective virtual address." It is "effective" since it is an actual address used during object access. It is, at the same time, "virtual," since further translations under control of the operating system (discussed in Section 5.5) may be used to map the virtual address into a physical address that can be handled directly by the logic within the memory system.

3.4.1 One-Dimensional Processor Addressing

Any one-dimensional address can be considered to be an integer, without loss of generality. We denote an effective address by the symbol EA. An EA selects a memory location. An EA should not be confused with a register designation, which assumes a different role in the system. We denote an address register by the symbol AR, and we use C(AR) to denote the contents of address register AR. The actual value in an address designation, if it is present,[20] will be denoted by the symbol A. In addition, we use M(i) to denote the contents of memory location i. The values in the foregoing entities are considered to be integers.

The processor can compute an address by executing a sequence of instructions or by using one or more built-in addressing modes. To make an intelligent selection of address modification mechanisms to be supported in the processor, the designer must balance the answers to many questions, including the following:

1. Must a program be modified?
2. How quickly can a data structure component be accessed?
3. How easily can a programming error be detected?
4. How quickly can a procedure parameter be accessed?
5. How much address computation hardware must be provided?
6. How many different objects can be accessed?

[20]Since not all instructions access memory, some instructions do not contain any address designations.

In the following, we present two general approaches to performing an address computation during processing. We consider program modification, which we rapidly discard, and then we turn to address computation algorithms supported within the processor.

3.4.1.1 Program modification. Every instruction is a bit pattern and can be manipulated as a numeric quantity. By using arithmetic instructions, a program can compute an arbitrary bit pattern and then attempt to execute it as an instruction. In principle the program could obtain access to any arbitrary memory location in this manner. The use of instruction modification to sequence operand accesses within a program loop was first suggested by von Neumann. In contemporary designs iterative programming is supported by addressing modes using indexing and indirection. Why not modify instructions to compute object addresses? The reasons include:

1. The program will be difficult to read.
2. The program will not be reentrant.
3. There is no protection against an access beyond the bounds of a data structure.
4. The instruction manipulations themselves take many instructions and can be slow.

For these reasons, we seek other ways to modify addresses during program execution.

3.4.1.2 Processor addressing modes. Since it seems unwise to manipulate instructions as data, the processor must permit other types of address computations under program control. This requirement leads to indexing and indirection address computations. Indexed addressing was first introduced in the English Manchester MADM computer [WILK56].[21] In a functional sense, either indexing or indirection alone is adequate to provide general accessing to memory. However, providing only one of these addressing modes may not give an efficient design. Contemporary processors support many varied addressing modes which correspond closely to address computation algorithms used to access constituents of compound data objects.

An addressing mode specification contained within an instruction determines how the processor should use instruction bits and other information to compute the effective address for a memory access. Seven basic operations are used in effective address computations:

1. Select (the operand from a register or a program element)
2. Base (add a value)
3. Scale (multiply by an operand width)
4. Index (add a scaled integer)
5. Indirect (read a value from a given address)
6. Increment (add a constant to) a register or memory location
7. Decrement (subtract a constant from) a register or memory location

[21]Index registers were called "B-tubes" in this system; in later English designs index registers were called "B-lines."

These addressing operations correspond to basic steps used to access a component of a compound object: Selecting a value fetches an addressing parameter. Adding a base value to an address finds the origin of an object within a set of objects. Multiplication by a scaling quantity adjusts an index quantity to reflect the size of a vector's components. Indexing selects an element from a vector. Indirection selects the next component of a linked data structure. Finally, incrementation or decrementation applied to an index value supports a sequential scan through the components of a contiguously stored compound object.

By convention certain names describe particular addressing algorithms or modes:

1. Implicit addressing
2. Immediate addressing
3. Direct addressing
4. Register indirect addressing
5. Relative addressing
6. Memory indirect addressing[22]
7. Indexed addressing

We illustrate each addressing mode by an example from the MC68020; the reader may wish to specify the semantics of each mode in terms of a sequence of the seven basic address computation operations.

An instruction using *implicit addressing* does not contain explicit address information. The instruction's function code defines how to locate the instruction's operand(s). The possible operand locations include a processor register or the top of a stack held in memory. A pointer to the top of a memory stack is stored within a processor register designated by convention (and processor implementation). For example, the MC68020 uses register A7 as the stack pointer in operations (such as JSR—jump to subroutine) that access the implicit stack.

An instruction with *immediate addressing* obtains its operand value from the instruction stream. The operand may be located within an instruction field or in the program stream immediately following the instruction. A "quick" arithmetic operation in the MC68020 finds one operand value inside the instruction itself. If the operand comes from the instruction stream, the program counter accesses the operand value; after reading memory to find the operand, the program counter must be incremented to point to the next program element. The increment quantity must reflect the operand size, which is determined from the instruction's function code or address mode specification.

With *direct addressing* some instruction bits contain the complete effective address. The instruction format defines which bits hold EA. A designer may wish to select the instruction formats so that the same bits are used for addresses in all instructions. In the MC68020 two absolute addressing modes provide direct addressing to the memory.

[22]This is often called just "indirect addressing."

With *register indirect addressing*, the processor interprets the contents of a register specified in the instruction directly as a memory address. With this mode, an instruction requires only a register number to specify its operand; this number is much shorter than a memory address, so instructions are shortened by using this operand addressing mode. In some designs (e.g., DEC PDP11) the same set of processor registers is used for addressing and data manipulation. In other designs (e.g., CDC 6600 and MC68020) one register set is dedicated to holding addresses. The CDC 6600-series machines use register-indirect addressing exclusively in their central processor instructions, with the set of A registers holding addresses; there is no address mode selection available. Similarly, the MC68020 selects an address register (except when a PC-based addressing mode or a register direct operand is specified), but unlike the CDC 6600, many addressing modes are available.

With *relative addressing* the operand's address is specified relative to the contents of the program counter. In the simple case, there is a "displacement" in the instruction, which specifies the location of the operand relative to the location of the address itself.[23] For flexibility, a relative addresses is interpreted as a signed integer. Thus a relative address field with 12 bits could specify a displacement of up to 2047 locations following the instruction, and either 2047 or 2048 locations preceding the instruction, depending on whether one's-complement or two's-complement encoding is used. Figure 3-15 illustrates the range of possible branch destinations.

Relative addressing eases program relocation. Many branch instructions implement loops or conditional execution, and their targets are close to the branch instructions specifying them, so relative addresses can be short. As a consequence, relative addressing is commonly used to specify the destinations of control flow instructions, such as branch instructions in the MC68020.

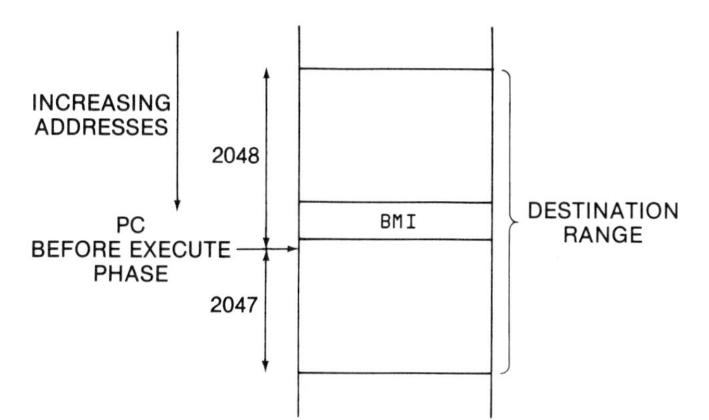

Figure 3-15 The range of possible branch destinations for PC-relative branching (12-bit displacement value)

[23]Actually, the origin for counting is the contents of PC at the time the relative address is evaluated; this value is the address of the next program element after the relative address. Note that the PC was incremented to point to the program element after the relative address when the relative address was fetched.

A *memory indirect address* specifies a direct memory address where the operand address is to be found. One design issue determines how the system will interpret an indirect address: in particular, should it be possible to specify further indirection. One option forces single-level indirection; the operand address is taken directly from the memory location addressed by the instruction. This mode is analogous to the use of a locator in Ada. Under another option the processor reads the memory value, uses its bits in place of some instruction address specification bits and restarts the effective address computation. This option allows multilevel indirection and may create a nonterminating loop of indirections. By adding a bound on the number of indirect references that can be used in any single address computation, such an infinite indirection loop can be forced to terminate. Another indirection option based on object tags is discussed in Section 3.4.4. The MC68020 provides two complex addressing modes, of which simple memory indirection is a special case.

A second design decision concerns the size of the indirect address. The obvious option is that the indirect address is to be interpreted exactly like a direct address that might appear in an instruction, and therefore should have the same size. But one way to permit a program to access a large address space is to specify that an indirect address will contain more bits than an instruction's format allocates for addresses.

Example 3-23

The DEC PDP8 [DIGI70] architecture provided 12-bit instructions fitting into 12-bit words. In one addressing mode, seven instruction bits select one of the first 128 memory locations. In another addressing mode, the same seven bits are concatenated with the leftmost five bits of the program counter to construct an address near the instruction itself. In any case, using the selected location indirectly causes the machine to interpret all 12 bits found there as an address, allowing access to any word within a block containing 4096 locations. Other techniques (discussed later) were used to enlarge this address space to 32,768 locations.

An *indexed address* is computed by adding[24] the contents of a selected register to the address specified within the instruction. In simple indexing, the instruction contains a register specification and a "displacement address." The effective indexed address is:

$$EA := A + C(AR);$$

Here AR designates the index register number from the instruction. As in BRISC, by forcing the register AR(0) = 0, the mode suppresses indexing; this design and coding trick may save bits in an addressing mode specification. Indexing requires an addition to generate the effective address; often, an adder dedicated to index addition is included in the processor hardware.

Example 3-24

An address specification in an IBM 370 instruction contains a "displacement" value D along with the numbers of one or two registers (depending on the instruction format) to

[24]Or, less frequently, subtracting (the IBM 704 series used subtraction); fortunately, subtractive indexing appears to be obsolete.

be used as the "base" (B) and "index" (X) registers. When both B and X are specified, the effective address EA is computed according to the following steps:

1. **if** B = 0 **then** base := 0 **else** base := R(B);
2. **if** X = 0 **then** index := 0 **else** index := R(X);
3. EA := D + base + index;

Note that the index amount is not scaled by the operand length; the program must include specific adjustments to account for the element size while computing the index values.

This addressing mode is useful when accessing an element of an array which itself is part of a record, with the record allocated on a stack. In this situation, the origin of the record on the stack is in a known position relative to the "base" of the activation block; this offset can be placed in the displacement portion of the instruction (see Figure 3-16). The origin of the activation record cannot be known until run time; it is placed in the "base" register. Now the index of the desired array component can be placed in the X register.

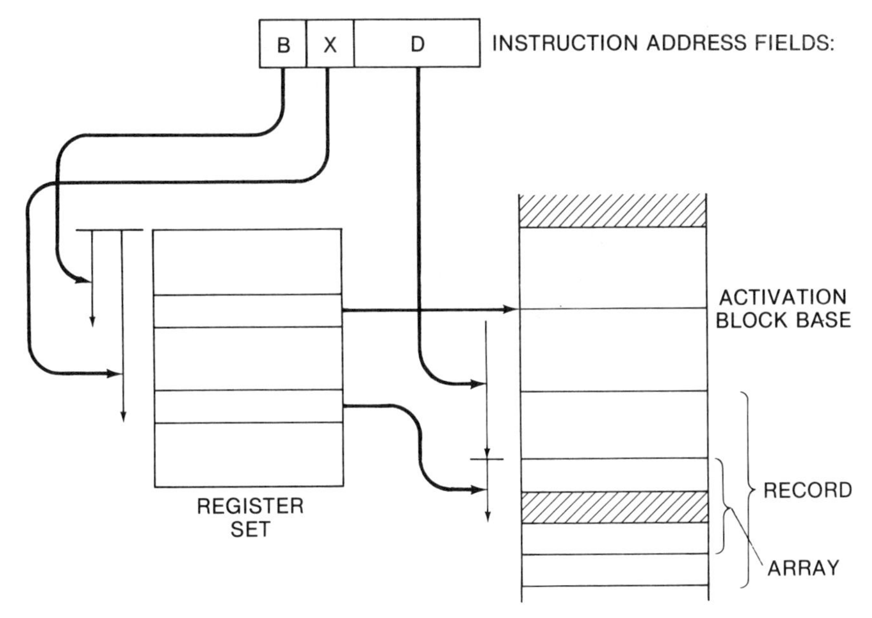

Figure 3-16 Double indexing to reach an element of an array within a record stored in an activation block

Example 3-25

In support of stack operations, the complementary modes corresponding to push and pop must have inverse orderings of the operations using the contents of the stack pointer register and modifying its value. The MC68020's complementary modes "address register indirect with predecrement" and "address register indirect with postincrement" support stacking. Their semantics are:

With predecrement

```
A(r) := A(r) - size;
EA := A(r);
```

With postincrement

```
EA := A(r);
A(r) := A(r) + size;
```

Here r is the register number, and size is the operand size,[25] determined from other information within the instruction.

3.4.2 Two-Dimensional Processor Addressing

A two-dimensional virtual addressing scheme can support the implementation of a block-structured language, it can ease the difficulty of combining separately compiled programs to form a single larger program, and it can assist in providing program protection and data security. The basic distinction between one-dimensional and two-dimensional addressing is found in the effective address computation. If additions performed during this computation can affect all address bits, the addressing scheme is one-dimensional. If the carry chain is broken between two bit positions, this break separates the segment number from the index portion of the two-dimensional address. This terminology does not agree with all writers or manufacturers; we choose these definitions so that there is a functional difference between segmented (two-dimensional) addressing and conventional (one-dimensional) addressing.

The segmented address of a simple object contains its segment number and its location relative to the origin of the segment. These two integers together comprise the segmented address (s, i), with s the segment number and i the item index. A segmented address is not the same as a one-dimensional address, since the act of indexing cannot change the segment number in a segmented address.[26] Figure 3-17 illustrates the structure of the segmented address space; the shaded element in Figure 3-17a is selected by the address (s, i). Figure 3-17b illustrates the indexing operation applied to a segmented address; notice that the segment number cannot be modified by indexing.

In this section we explore the use of two-dimensional addressing for block-structured languages and for combining translation units to form programs. The use of two-dimensional addresses to support security and protection is described in Chapter 4 of Volume 2.

[25]There is an exception for byte operands if the register is A7, which is the stack pointer. Since this pointer is restricted to a word (2-byte) boundary, the "size" used in these algorithms will be 2 when the operand width is either a word or a byte and A7 is selected.

[26]We defined a segmented address space as one in which this rule applies.

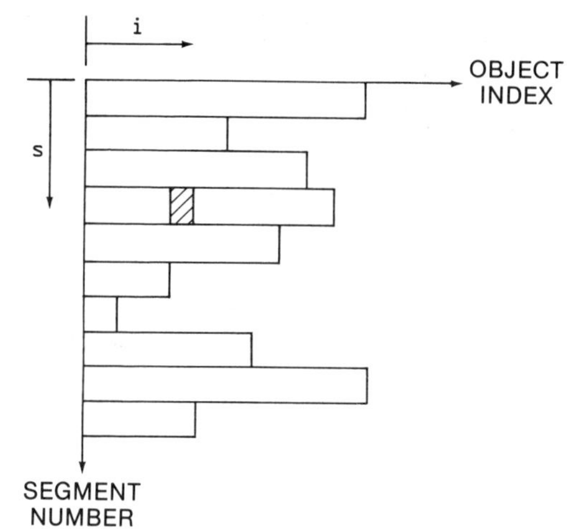

a) The two-dimensional space view

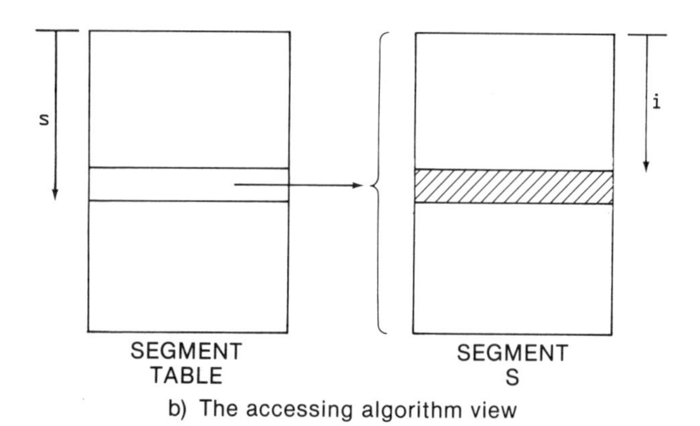

b) The accessing algorithm view

Figure 3-17 Two versions of two-dimensional addressing by segmentation. [The address is (s,i).]

3.4.2.1 Statically nested naming. The first processor-level implementation supporting stacks appeared in the Burroughs B5000 processor [BURR61]. A run-time allocation and addressing scheme based on statically nested naming had been suggested by Randell and Russell [RAND64] for a soft implementation of Algol60 programs; this scheme formed the basis for the addressing design used in subsequent large Burroughs systems (B5700, B6700, etc.) [BURR69]. We review the Randell and Russell design and then turn to the processor-level details.

Algol60's static nesting rule governing name visibility is the basis for the Randell and Russell design. They realized that within any single program block unique object names could be created by specifying two aspects of the object's name:

1. The block in which the referenced entity was declared
2. The position of that entity among those allocated in the same block

Furthermore, Randell and Russell noted that within one usage context one could identify each visible block uniquely by its level in the static nest. This works because under static nesting only one block is visible at each nesting level from any particular usage context. Therefore, the name N of a visible object can be mapped into a two-dimensional address of the form (level_number, index), where index identifies the entity N within the set of objects declared at its level.

The B5700 addressing scheme is based on two-dimensional addresses constructed according to the Randell and Russell scheme. For reasons that we discuss later, the levels are numbered (in user programs) in increasing order starting with 2 at the outermost program block. Objects within each block are numbered in order of appearance, starting with 2 for the first parameter or local object (if there are no parameters). We discuss later the reasons for these two 2's. In examples of this addressing scheme, we use the B5700 numbering convention.

Example 3-26

Here is the skeleton of an Ada program, showing all procedure and object declarations:

```
procedure main is
  a, b : integer;
  procedure g(x, y : integer) is
    c, d : integer;
    procedure h(u, v : integer) is
      e, f : integer;
    begin
      ..
    end h;
  begin
    ..
  end g;
  procedure k(r : integer) is
    u, v : integer;
  begin
    ..
  end k;
begin
  ..
end main;
```

The addresses of the items declared in this program, including the parameters (which are assigned to the first locations within each block of objects), are listed in Table 3-8. All visible names, including procedure names, are assigned addresses.

Note that the same address describes different objects; consider, for example, (3, 3), which names both g.y and k.u. However, these two objects are never simultaneously visible as a consequence of the static nesting rule. Thus the fact that their names have the same representation does not introduce ambiguity. This is seen clearly by examining the sets of objects visible from the using contexts k and h (see Table 3-9).

This use of two-dimensional addressing for the implementation of a statically nested language is a case of high-level semantics reflected in a processor-level design. The address bit savings given by this technique are discussed in Section 3.5. This encoding technique does give context-dependent addresses; this fact imposes

TABLE 3-8 TWO-DIMENSIONAL NAMES FOR THE OBJECTS DECLARED IN EXAMPLE 3-26

Object	Address
main.a	(2,2)
main.b	(2,3)
main.g	(2,4)
main.k	(2,5)
g.x	(3,2)
g.y	(3,3)
g.c	(3,4)
g.d	(3,5)
g.h	(3,6)
h.u	(4,2)
h.v	(4,3)
h.e	(4,4)
h.f	(4,5)
k.r	(3,2)
k.u	(3,3)
k.v	(3,4)

TABLE 3-9 OBJECTS CORRESPONDING TO CERTAIN NAMES IN BLOCKS h AND k, FOR THE PROGRAM IN EXAMPLE 3-26

	Object Denoted by Address from:	
Address	Block h	Block k
(2, 2)	main.a	main.a
(2, 3)	main.b	main.b
(2, 4)	main.g	main.g
(2, 5)	main.k	main.k
(3, 2)	g.x	k.r
(3, 3)	g.y	k.u
(3, 4)	g.c	k.v
(3, 5)	g.d	illegal
(3, 6)	g.h	illegal
(4, 2)	h.u	illegal
(4, 3)	h.v	illegal
(4, 4)	h.e	illegal
(4, 5)	h.f	illegal

further requirements on the processor-level design, as we shall see in the following section and in Section 5.4.2.

3.4.2.2 Combining translation units. It is a simple matter to combine a number of separate translation units to form a program if the addressing within each translation unit is one-dimensional and the processor's addressing is two-dimensional. All that is required is to assign a segment for each translation unit. Then we form two-dimensional addresses by placing the proper segment number into each address. Consider the address used to access the object called x, which was declared in the translation unit whose segment number is t. And suppose that x was assigned the one-dimensional address a_x. Then the complete address for x is (t, a_x). This merging process combines separately translated translation units, as depicted in Figure 3-18.

All methods for computing effective addresses that are valid with one-dimensional addresses are equally valid with two-dimensional addressing, provided that the segment number is not modified during indexing operations. Thus two-dimensional addressing is a processor design option directly reflecting high-level semantic and functional requirements. It is used in the Burroughs B5700 machines.

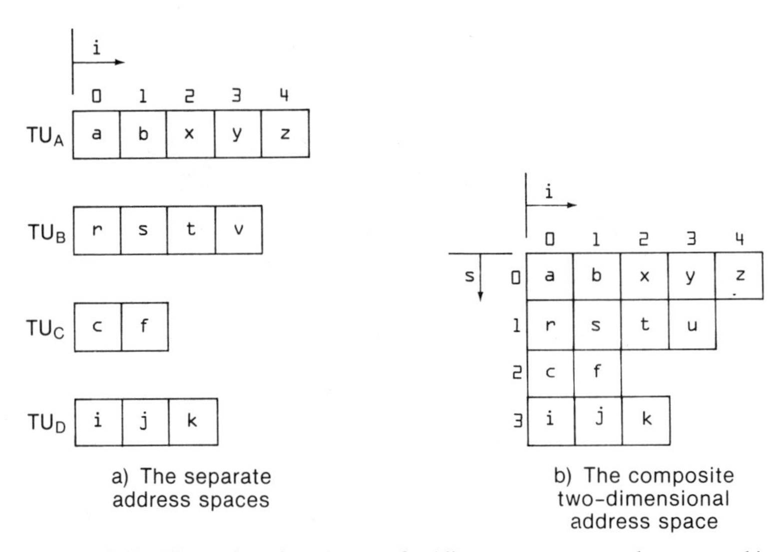

Figure 3-18 Illustrating the process of adding a segment number to combine separate modules

3.4.2.3 Moving addresses and objects between contexts. There is no difficulty in moving an address A from context C_1 to context C_2 if A has the same interpretation in both contexts. However, difficulties can arise from moving an address if its interpretation is context dependent. If the meaning will change as a result of the move, the address itself will have to be changed as it is moved. We need to identify the places where the problem might arise and then propose techniques for fixing the addresses to be moved. This issue is not an idle academic issue; among several important situations in which a name may be moved between two contexts, we find:

1. Locator sharing
2. Parameter passing
3. Result returning

Locator sharing naming problems may arise if a locator object is declared at nest level L_1 and then is assigned an address from a nest level $L_2 > L_1$. This pattern is illustrated in the following example.

Example 3-27

The following program[27] illustrates the naming problems arising from passing a context-dependent address between two contexts.

```
procedure b is --this overall program is not legal Ada!
  type accinteger is access integer;
  d : accinteger;
  procedure c is
    e : accinteger;
    ..
  begin
    e:=new integer; --create new integer and
    ..              --get a pointer to it
    d:=e;
  end c;
  procedure s is
  begin
    d.all:=4;       --the reference in question
    ..
  end s;
begin
  ..                --body of b
end b;
```

Suppose that the new object (to which e points) is located in the block associated with the call to c, which is at level 3 in the program. Suppose therefore that the address of the allocated object is (3, 5). When the assignment "d:=e;" is executed, the address (3, 5) is placed in location d. Then suppose that s is called and it proceeds to make the assignment of "4" to the location whose address is in d. The address within d is still (3, 5), but now the program is executing in procedure s, where level 3 corresponds to space within s. So the assignment will be made to location 5 within s's space. We have detected a problem, since this action is clearly not what was intended.

Parameter passing naming problems may arise if an access variable is passed as a procedure parameter. As with sharing, the problem occurs if the parameter moves upward in the naming nest and contains an address with a higher level number. In particular, the program in the previous example can be modified so that s is called from c, with e as an actual parameter. The contents of e, which have a context-dependent interpretation, are moved into s's context where they are subject to a different context-dependent interpretation.

[27]Although this program appears to make sense, it in fact is not a legal Ada program; the illegality is a consequence of certain Ada allocation rules, which have an indirect connection with the naming issues we are discussing here.

Result returning naming problems may arise if a locator value is passed from a subroutine to a calling module. This action may occur when a parameter is called by name or reference, when a procedure parameter has the **out** attribute, or when the function returns a result.

Our cursory examination of these situations leads us to the conclusion that the implementer must be wary of using context-dependent addresses and may have to insert special handling to modify an address before sending it out into an unknown context. In Section 5.4 we see how the B5700 designers provided a processor instruction precisely to handle this set of problems.

3.4.3 Systems with Tagged Objects

A *tag* associated with an object states some attributes of the associated object. For example, a memory word might be tagged with one of the codes shown in Table 3-10 to distinguish instructions from data and integers from reals. For addressing and naming, a basic distinction separates objects whose contents are relevant for address computations from objects that play no part in address computations. Further distinctions may clarify each relevant object's role in an address computation. In fact, introducing tagging into a design can move some addressing mode selection decisions from the translator or the object program to the run-time mechanism that interprets tag values.

In this section we explore ways that tagging can be used to simplify address specifications. We see how tags can be used to control indirection, how they can be used to support call-by-name parameter passing, and how they can be used to control indexing.

TABLE 3-10 TAG VALUES TO DISTINGUISH PROGRAMS FROM DATA

Code	Meaning
0	Instruction
1	Integer data
2	Real data

Before presenting the details, we state one important tagging property. Neither the system nor a programmer should be permitted to tamper with the association between a tag value and the object it describes. If a program could substitute an arbitrary tag value for a correct tag, it could change the interpretation of the associated object, and thereby sidestep all controls. Such a violation would be similar to writing a program that violates the type constraints specified within a strongly-typed programming language.

3.4.3.1 Tag-based indirection. To assist with indirection, we mark each pointer object with a specific tag value. In addition, we design the system so that it knows, for each operand of each instruction, whether that operand should be a value or could be an address. For example, normally, addition will not have a pointer as an operand. In fact, an addition operation should have data, and not control information, within both its operands. So if an operand for ADD is being sought and a pointer object is encountered, the processor can detect that the operand's type is incompatible with the operation. If the operand is a pointer, rather than data, the processor could be designed to use the object as an indirect address. Note that it is possible to construct an infinite loop of tagged indirect words; a counter or a timer could be used to terminate such a loop. For example, the B5700 uses a timer that causes an interrupt if a new instruction has not been started within an allotted time interval.

One advantage of tag-directed indirection is that a called procedure does not have to know whether a parameter was passed by value, name, or reference. When the procedure wishes to read the parameter's value, it simply performs a read instruction to obtain a value. If the actual parameter was passed by reference, the read will find a tagged indirect address; the tag will initiate the indirection, and the proper parameter value will be read to the processor.

The tag-based indirection scheme can be extended to assist accessing parameters passed by name. In Algol parameters are passed by name unless specified otherwise, and the semantics of call by name require that the value of the subscripts in the parameter's specification be reevaluated upon every access to the parameter from the called procedure. The addressing design specifies how to represent the parameters of the call-by-name and how to distinguish the call-by-name from other types of object access. One could assign special tag values to identify call-by-name parameters. One parameter would be a pointer to the data structure's origin; the other parameter would point to the object holding the current value of the index quantity. To complete the design, one must provide processor logic to interpret these tagged objects and construct the proper effective address. This scheme works well for a one-dimensional vector component that is passed by name, but does not generalize easily to multidimensional arrays.

Another method using tagging to support the Algol call-by-name specifies a tag value designating a pointer to the entry point of a parameterless procedure that returns the address of the desired object (defined by the actual call-by-name parameter) as its result. The processor will encounter the tagged entry point pointer while seeking a data object; at this point the processor simply calls the procedure and uses the (tagged) returned result as an indirect address. The mechanization could then interpret this result as a data item, the effect being that the address interpretation process starts anew. In principle the procedure's result could be another pointer to an object or to a procedure entry point (see Problem 3-22).

Example 3-28

```
type ai is access integer;
procedure g(d : ai) is --d is passed by name
  e : integer;            --the call by name
begin                     --is not legal within Ada
  e:=d+6;          --need to evaluate d here
  ..
end g;
```

We impose various parameter passing disciplines on this program. First, consider a call-by-reference discipline. In this case the actual parameter passed can be a tagged pointer to the location holding the value to be used. Suppose that procedure g were called from this program:

```
procedure h is
   k : array (1 .. 10) of integer;
   m : integer;
   ..
begin
   ..
   m:=4;
   g(k(m));
   ..
end h;
```

The actual parameter passed will be a tagged pointer to the object k(4). When the addition is performed in g, the processor will know that it is looking for a value; when it reads the parameter it will find the tagged pointer and perform the indirection to find the value.

Now consider passing the parameter by name. In this case the passed entity is not a pointer to the array k but rather a pointer to the entry point of a procedure to compute the pointer to k(m). When the processor reads the parameter and finds an entry point descriptor, it will call the procedure and use its result as an operand. Since the returned result will be tagged as a pointer, the processor will initiate indirection to find the value.

It may appear at first glance that indirection using tagged objects is the same as indirection without tags, but there is a subtle, yet important difference. A conventional design places indirection bits in instructions (or in their addressing mode specifications), with the result that the instruction unequivocally specifies the interpretation of the item being accessed. With tagging, on the other hand, the accessed item is self-describing and the instruction does not have to anticipate the type of object that will be found at its operand location. This difference is significant when the operand is a procedure parameter. If the language were Algol, a parameter could be passed either by name or by value, and the compiler of the called procedure cannot tell which case applies. In fact, each call of the procedure could present a different situation! There are several approaches to solving this dilemma, which we discuss more fully in Chapter 5. We have seen one approach that uses tagging to distinguish pointers, data, entry points, and other addressing specifications from each other. The processor can determine which case applies during execution of the procedure, and all cases can be handled easily with a single version of the called procedure.

3.4.3.2 Tag-based indexing. Several different designs can support indexing with tags. We discuss two options:

1. Generalizing indirection to permit indexing
2. Tagging indexed and unindexed descriptors differently

The first option is similar to the tag-based indirection scheme discussed above. There the indirect word was interpreted as an origin; here the tagged indirect word contains both an index specification and a base value quantity to be added together. When the tagged word is accessed during an attempt to access a value, the indexing is performed and the resulting effective address is used to find the object.

Under the second option, the tagged object may contain either the descriptor of a compound object or a pointer to a component of a compound object. The tag (or a flag in the value) indicates which format applies. The descriptor of a compound object contains the object's origin and the limiting index value (which exceeds the object's limit). Alternatively, the tagged object may contain the address of a component within the compound object. By performing a processor instruction to index the descriptor, the descriptor of the compound object will be changed to a descriptor of one of its components. A component's location could be represented by the origin of the compound object together with a separate index value or by a single value pointing directly to the component's location.

Example 3-29

The Burroughs B5700 processors support descriptors of both compound objects and their components; they distinguish a descriptor of a compound object from a descriptor of a component by a flag contained within the descriptor. An indexed address contains both the origin of the compound object and the index of the component. There is a processor instruction (index descriptor) that indexes a descriptor of a compound object. During this instruction, the processor checks the index value against the limit in the descriptor, replaces the limit with the index quantity, and sets the indexed bit within the descriptor; all of this is conditional on the index value being within the range limit specified in the initial descriptor. The indexing operation is depicted in Figure 3-19.

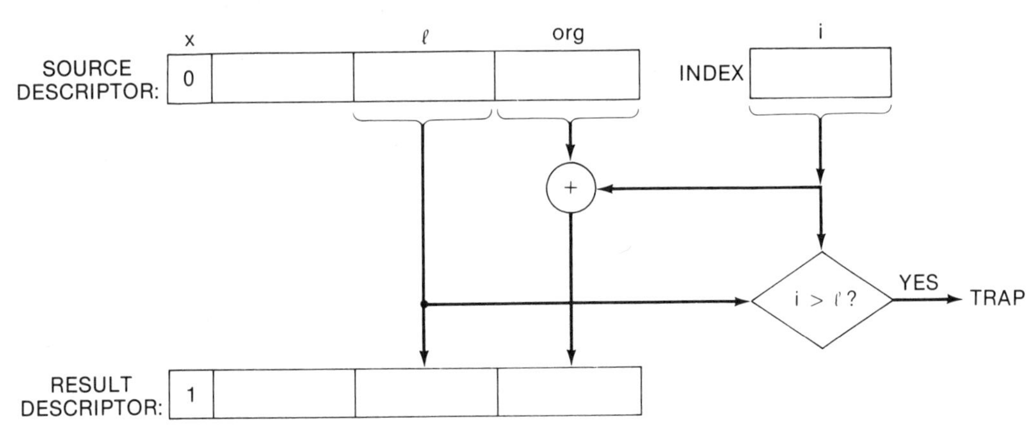

Figure 3-19 Descriptor indexing in the B5700

3.4.3.3 Capability addressing. A capability contains a description of a compound object along with a field specifying access rights. The access rights information specifies the types of memory accesses[28] which the possessor of the capability

[28]The types of access might include READ, WRITE, and EXECUTE (read for interpretation as an instruction).

is permitted to make to the object described by the capability. If the capability is to effectively limit access to the object it describes, it must be protected against unauthorized modification. One method for protecting a capability from modification is to mark each one with a special tag value and then restrict the operations that can be performed on (tagged) capabilities. This design uses tag values not to specify automatic indexing or indirection during accessing, but to restrict processing that could modify the capability's contents in an undesirable manner. We save the discussion of capabilities for Chapters 3 and 4 of Volume 2, where we discuss their roles in support of multiprocessing and system security.

3.4.4 Instructions That Compute Addresses

A fourth processor design option related to object addressing includes processor instructions that compute an object's address without actually accessing the object. Many machines have "load effective address" (LEA) instructions to support call by reference. By executing an LEA instruction the program can determine the address of an object and pass it as a parameter. Other instructions related to addressing perform useful index arithmetic.

We look at some examples of these instructions. First consider determining an effective address.

Example 3-30

The MC68020 instruction LEA (Load Effective Address) places an effective address[29] in a designated address register.

The processor can support address computations with an instruction that performs useful index computations. One such computation finds the address of an element within a multidimensional array.

Example 3-31

The VAX11/750 [DIGI77] has three address-related instructions. Two—push address and move address—use a regular addressing mode to compute an address that is either copied into a specified destination or pushed onto the stack. INDEX, the third address instruction, performs the computation

outindex := (inindex + insubscript) * object_size

which is useful in translating a subscript vector into a component address. All the parameters on the right side of the assignment are instruction operands, as are both the lower and upper limits on the subscript value. A violation of these range constraints produces a processor trap.

Example 3-32

The IBM System/38 [IBM80] instruction CAI (Compute Array Index) performs the multiply-add that reduces a two-dimensional subscript to a one-dimensional

[29] This address can be determined by any mode that both produces an address and does not increment or decrement the address register used in the effective address calculation. Addressing modes that violate these conditions are illegal with an LEA instruction.

subscript. There is no limit checking in this instruction. The instruction

CAI w, x, y, z

performs the following assignment:

$$x := y + (z - 1) * w$$

Here w, x, y, and z are the names of memory locations. A sequence of these instructions can be used to reduce any multidimensional subscript to an index into the space where the array is stored.

3.4.5 Summary of Processor-Level Addressing

We have covered a lot of ground concerning processor support for object addressing, so a quick survey is in order. We started with the basic notion that an instruction could be treated like an integer and therefore could be manipulated to set its address specification so that a desired operand would be accessed. Thus the basic ability to access any object can easily be attained (in a logical sense), but at a great loss in program understandability and execution speed. So processor designers insert features to assist object addressing. The most common designs support provides various modes of address computation that can be selected in any instruction.

Two-dimensional addressing can be used in various ways to support language semantics. Context-dependent addresses can be formed to name all entities visible within a statically nested program structure. If a set of translation units have each been translated into a one-dimensional address space, the second dimension can be used to identify the translation unit, simplifying the linking process. We have identified a problem that can arise while passing a context-dependent address among contexts; we left its solution open for the moment.

We have shown a tagging option that permits a procedure to be independent of the actual form of each parameter passed to it; these tags can be used in other ways, including assisting with system security (but that topic is left for Chapter 4 of Volume 2).

Finally, we have seen that the processor designer can provide instructions that compute addresses or address-related quantities, thereby speeding execution of programs that either pass parameters by reference or access components of multidimensional arrays at random.

Now we turn to the implementation of some of these features, showing how the designer can use clever encoding and interpretations to save program space. Other aspects of processor-level interactions with the system's memory will be covered in Chapters 4 and 5.

3.5 ADDRESS REPRESENTATIONS AND SEMANTICS

Address encoding can save bits in program representations and consequently reduce the memory bandwidth required to fetch instructions. On the other hand, the size of an effective memory address, an important processor design decision, should be large enough that programs are not unduly constrained by address size limits. It has been observed [BELL76] that the choice of the effective address size is one of the most important system design decisions, since the address size imposes an ultimate limit to system expansion. If a designer chooses to decrease the size of addresses within instructions, she has to provide a means for generating addresses larger than those that can be represented directly in an instruction. With such an escape route, the address space limitation no longer logically confines the programmer, although constructing longer addresses may be cumbersome. Any alternative means for address generation, which may include wide address registers or special registers for address generation, must be visible to the processor-level programmer, who may have the responsibility for controlling the contents and use of these special registers. However an address may be compressed, eventually it must be expanded to form a complete effective virtual address. How large should these addresses be? And how much memory space should each addressable object span? The answers to these questions define the system's address size and granularity.

In this section we discuss these issues. You will learn several techniques for reducing the number of program bits consumed for operand addresses. You will see the relationship between address compression techniques and high-level language structures. You will learn some consequences of each option in the programming domain. You will learn some issues related to address size and the granularity of memory addresses. Further implications of these choices at the hardware level are discussed in Chapter 5.

3.5.1 Address Compression

Since compressed addresses are shorter than uncompressed addresses, a program with compressed addresses will be shorter than one using uncompressed addresses, and will require fewer memory accesses to read its instructions. Therefore, if memory bandwidth is a performance bottleneck, address compression may ease that bottleneck simply because each program becomes smaller after its addresses have been compressed.

The second method using compressed addresses reduces bandwidth needs on he he processor–memory address path. The processor passes a compressed address to memory, where it is expanded into a full memory address. One "cost" of this change is that the address translation function must be moved from the processor complex to the memory, thereby making it "smarter." This technique is important only if the processor chip pin-bandwidth limitation is a performance bottleneck. This technique is amplified in Problem 3-18 and in Chapter 5.

We know that compressed addresses can be used to alleviate some performance bottlenecks. What are "reasonable" techniques for encoding addresses in programs? We will examine:

1. Using context-dependent addressing
2. Using processor registers
3. Encoding to minimize useless bits

Context-dependent addressing was used in the Randell and Russell naming scheme for nested block structures discussed in Section 3.4.2. In this scheme each address consists of a level number and an index. The size of the level number must be large enough to represent an integer corresponding to the depth of the program's nesting. And the index field must be large enough to represent the maximum number of objects that can be referenced at one level of the nest. We discuss these sizes further in Example 3-33.

The designer can use *registers more and memory less* by providing addressing modes in which register contents are used to generate wide addresses. One version of this approach uses wide index registers. In this design an index addition results in a complete memory address; without indexing, only one or both ends of the address space can be accessed. Figure 3-20 illustrates the mechanism and the two address options.

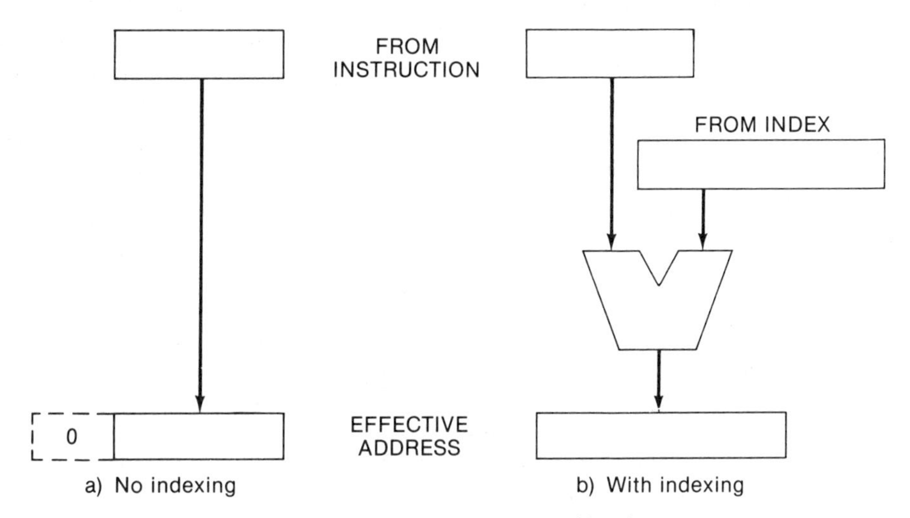

Figure 3-20 Wide index register addressing

Another technique for generating a wide address from a small program address specification uses a "field" register whose contents are concatenated as the most significant address bits; Figure 3-21 illustrates this address computation.

Several *clever encoding* approaches reduce the number of address bits in the program. Three encoding options will be covered:

1. Field width depends on nest depth.
2. Field width depends on a static program property.
3. Field contents are optimally encoded.

The *field width* can vary with a program's nesting depth. At low levels, only a few bits are needed to represent the level number, and more bits can be allocated for object indices. At higher levels, more address bits are required to represent the level

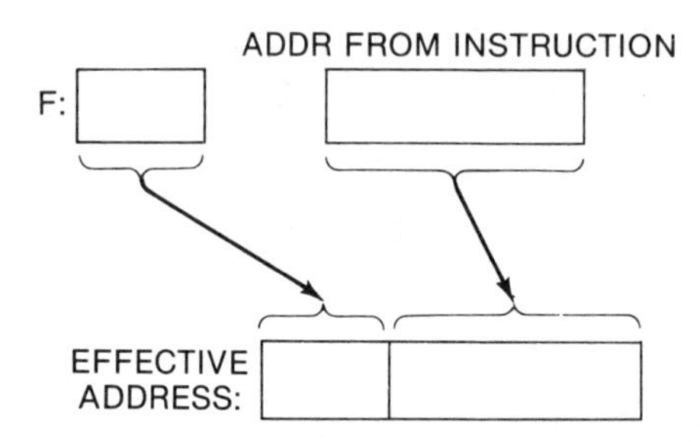

Figure 3-21 Field register addressing

number, but fewer bits are needed for the object index. The basic argument for reducing the size of the object index at higher levels states that blocks deeper in the nest will perform simpler algorithms and access fewer objects than blocks farther out in the nest. With respect to the level numbers, we know that any address used in a block at level k cannot contain a level number greater than k. So addresses in blocks at the top of the nest require few bits for level numbers, while addresses used deeper in the nest require more bits to specify the level number. However, since fewer objects are referenced from blocks with higher numbers, the object selection index in such addresses can be shorter than the index field in addresses used in blocks with lower numbers. These observations suggest using a context-dependent field assignment in block-structured names.

Example 3-33

In the B5700-series machines the executing procedure's level determines the bit assignments to level number and object index, as shown in Table 3-11. A variant on the obvious encoding reduces the number of different paths for address bits: level numbers are reverse encoded, with their least significant bits on the left end. Then every address bit may be used in only one or two different ways. For example, the leftmost address bit is always the least significant bit of the block number, and the next bit is either the most significant bit of the object index or the second least significant bit of the level number (see Problem 3-26). Only four address bits have two different uses, dependent on the execution level (see Figure 3-22).

TABLE 3-11 ADDRESS FIELD SIZES IN B5700 MACHINES

Level of Executing Procedure	Address Bit Allocation	
	For Level Number:	For Object Index:
0–1	1	13
2–3	2	12
4–7	3	11
8–15	4	10
16–31	5	9

A simplified context-dependent addressing scheme dedicates a single bit to distinguish a local address from a global one. Under this scheme any object must be

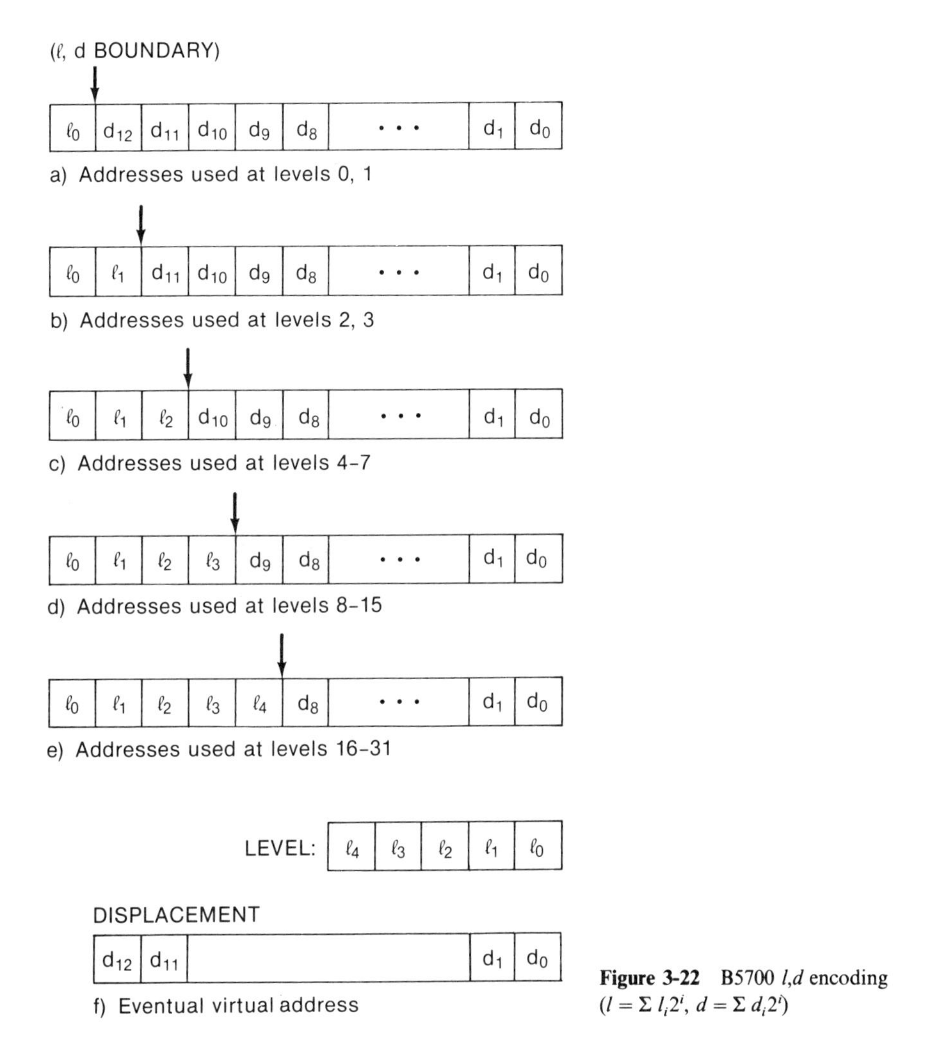

Figure 3-22 B5700 *l,d* encoding ($l = \Sigma\, l_i 2^i$, $d = \Sigma\, d_i 2^i$)

in either the local block or a single global block; this processor-level restriction is not present in the language, so the software must be designed to circumvent this limitation.

Example 3-34

The B5000 processor address encoding[30] included a single bit L to distinguish levels, along with an index field i. The value of L designated whether the index was to be used with respect to the outermost block or with respect to the innermost (local) block. We use the encoding L = 1 for a local block address in the example.

To access an object that is not local and is not in the outermost block, the program must manipulate locators, as described in Section 5.4. This program skeleton illustrates the difficulty.

[30]This was changed in the B5500 and succeeding machines.

```
procedure main is
  b : integer;
  procedure f is
    c : integer;
    procedure g is
      d : integer;
    begin
      d := b;
      d := c;
    end g;
  begin
    ..
  end f;
begin
  ..
end main;
```

The source location in the first assignment statement is declared in the outermost block; it can be directly named as (0, 2). The destination is local, and can be directly named as (1, 2). The source location for the second assignment statement (c) is neither local nor in the outermost block; it can be accessed only after manipulating some access variables.

Under this scheme, an object's address depends on both the context of its definition and the context of its use; Table 3-12 lists the declared names and corresponding addresses, considering all possible names and usage contexts for this program skeleton.

TABLE 3-12 ADDRESSES CORRESPONDING TO THE NAMES DEFINED IN EXAMPLE 3-34

	Usage Context		
Name	Main	f	g[a]
b	(0, 2) or (1, 2)	(0, 2)	(0, 2)
f	(0, 3) or (1, 3)	(0, 3)	(0, 3)
c	—	(1, 2)	v/na
g	—	(1, 3)	v/na
d	—	—	(1, 2)

[a]"v/na" indicates a visible object with no address.

The two-level L encoding saves address bits, but the example showed that it is difficult to reference a global object that is not in the outermost block from within a nested block. How could we modify the processor so that the limitation is circumvented but two-level addressing is preserved? One way is to allow the program to (dynamically) change the identity of the single nonlocal block that is accessible. The pointer to the visible nonlocal block would be in a processor register, so we just permit the program to load the register, which is used like a base register when an effective address is computed. Problem 3-19 is concerned with these details.

The second way to reduce address bits is to *redefine field sizes based on a static program property*. Within a single naming context or program, we could count the number of visible objects and assign just enough address bits to be able to specify any visible object. The address width for each program or program module would be determined by the translator. The designer would add a new processor instruction that sets the address field width; the translator would insert that instruction each time the naming context changes. This scheme adds processor complexity to handle the dynamic instruction format (see Problem 3-16).

A third way to use encoding to save address bits is to choose an *optimal encoding* for addresses. Optimal encoding is based on usage statistics. Once the usage statistics are known, address encodings can be selected to reduce the average address length. Huffman coding [HUFF52] should be used if the minimum length is desired.[31] The disadvantage of Huffman encoding is that every encoded value may have a different width. Thus the processor must determine dynamically the locations of both field boundaries within instructions and instruction boundaries. Problem 3-27 presents some of these issues.

A fourth way to save address bits is to *use a fixed set of address lengths*. Each address specifies its actual width, or some auxiliary length information may accompany the address. This technique makes a large address space available, but permits the use of short addresses for frequently referenced objects. By right-justifying the addresses and stuffing zeros on the left end, a short address designates an object located near the beginning of the address space.

Example 3-35

Table 3-13 lists the address length[32] options in the iAPX432 system [TYNE81]. All addresses are two-dimensional, of the form (s, i). The fully expanded segment and displacement fields contain 16 bits each. An instruction may include three fields specifying the address of one object; the effective virtual address is (s, b + x). There are two

TABLE 3-13 INTEL iAPX432 ADDRESS LENGTH OPTIONS

Address Field	Lengths	Comments
Segment number	4, 8	To obtain a 16-bit segment number, use indirection from the stack
Object base	0, 16	
Index	7, 16	
Branch destination	10,16	The short version is relative; the long version is absolute

[31]Huffman coding is discussed in more detail in Section 6.3.4.

[32]The zero length means that the value is taken from the top of the stack rather than from the instruction stream.

length options for the base and index specifications, so for each a single "length control" bit in the address specification specifies the width of that field. The segment number determination process is controlled by an "access mode" field, which can specify four modes, as listed in Table 3-14. For interpreting an indirect address, new rules come into play. For example, indirection taking the indirect address off the stack is the only way to obtain a full 16-bit segment number.

TABLE 3-14 HOW ACCESS MODE ENCODINGS DETERMINE SEGMENT NUMBER LENGTH IN THE iAPX432

Mode	Segment Number Length	Indirect Address Source
0	4	
1	0	Stack
2	8	
3	—	Memory

3.5.2 Address Sizes

The selection of an address compression scheme may determine some address field lengths. Another important address size question concerns the size of a complete virtual address—the one obtained from the effective address computation. This size determines the maximum number of objects that can be visible to a program without resorting to the file system, since the size fixes the number of address bits. Bell and Strecker [BELL76] emphasize the importance of a correct choice: "There is only one mistake . . . in a computer design that is difficult to recover from—not providing enough address bits . . . ."

A designer must choose what shall be included in the virtual address space. An important, relevant question is: "How will the virtual address space be managed?" In the IBM System/38 [IBM81a], for example, all information within the system, including files on removable media, is included within a single virtual address space. Furthermore, virtual addresses are not reused by the memory allocator. Thus the virtual space size determines not only how many objects can be accessed, but also how long the system can operate before running out of space. The timeout is inversely proportional to the rate at which space is acquired for objects. In the System/38, 16 megabytes are allocated on each allocation request,[33] and each virtual address contains 48 bits. As a consequence, 2^{23} allocations can be made before the system runs out of virtual space. If a system does not include files in the same virtual address space as main memory, main memory virtual addresses can be much smaller, yet still provide a sufficient number of different addresses.

[33]But note that an individual process can manage the space it obtained from a single system allocation so that the same space holds different sets of objects at different times. Thus smart local management will reduce the number of global space allocation requests.

With a wide virtual address, it would be folly to provide enough bits in the address field within each instruction so that the address in an instruction is as large as a complete virtual memory address. Thus the instruction's address field may be designed to be shorter than a complete virtual address, and a scheme to obtain additional address bits must be devised. We discuss four options:

1. Use indirection.
2. Use the contents of a selected processor register.
3. Use an implied register.
4. Use a special register array that maps addresses.

The indirection option works if the size of an indirect address is larger than an instruction address field. Then indirection can reach any virtual address, independent of the sizes of addresses in either instructions or address registers. One penalty of this scheme is the additional memory cycles required to fetch an indirect address whenever a wide address is needed. Clearly, this scheme is functionally general, in that an indirection can be inserted to reach any far-off location.

The second option chooses the size of the index quantities to match the size of a complete virtual address. Under this option indexing is used whenever a wide virtual address is needed (see Figure 3-20). An argument analogous to the indirection argument concludes that this option is functionally general also. Wide indexing is used in the IBM 370 machines.

The third option uses an extra register or set of "field" registers to hold the leftmost address bits of the wide addresses formed by the program. The particular register used in an address computation is selected during the effective address computation process.

Example 3-36

The DEC PDP8 [DIGI70] had 8 address bits in each instruction referencing memory and could find a 12-bit address through indirection, but the machine could be expanded to have 32,768 words of memory, requiring 15 address bits. The three additional bits were taken from one of two "field" registers, IF and DF (for "Instruction Field" and "Data Field," respectively). All addresses were formed with IF, except addresses determined by indirection, in which case the DF field was used. An address field in an instruction contained only 8 address bits plus an indirect bit. The most significant address bit selected whether bits 11 .. 7 were set to zero or were taken from the PC. This scheme further reduced the need for address bits in instructions, but made programming awkward, as any direct address had to be located in either low memory ($IR_7 = 0$) or the 128-word "page" where the instruction being executed was located. Figure 3-23 illustrates the spaces accessible directly and indirectly under this scheme.

The fourth option for generating additional address bits includes a set of address registers in the processor. Let there be 2^r such registers, so that r bits selects one of them. Now use the r most significant bits from the address to select a field register, and then concatenate the contents of the selected register with the rest of the address. Figure 3-24 illustrates this scheme, which was used in the SDS 940 to compute operand addresses [SDS66].

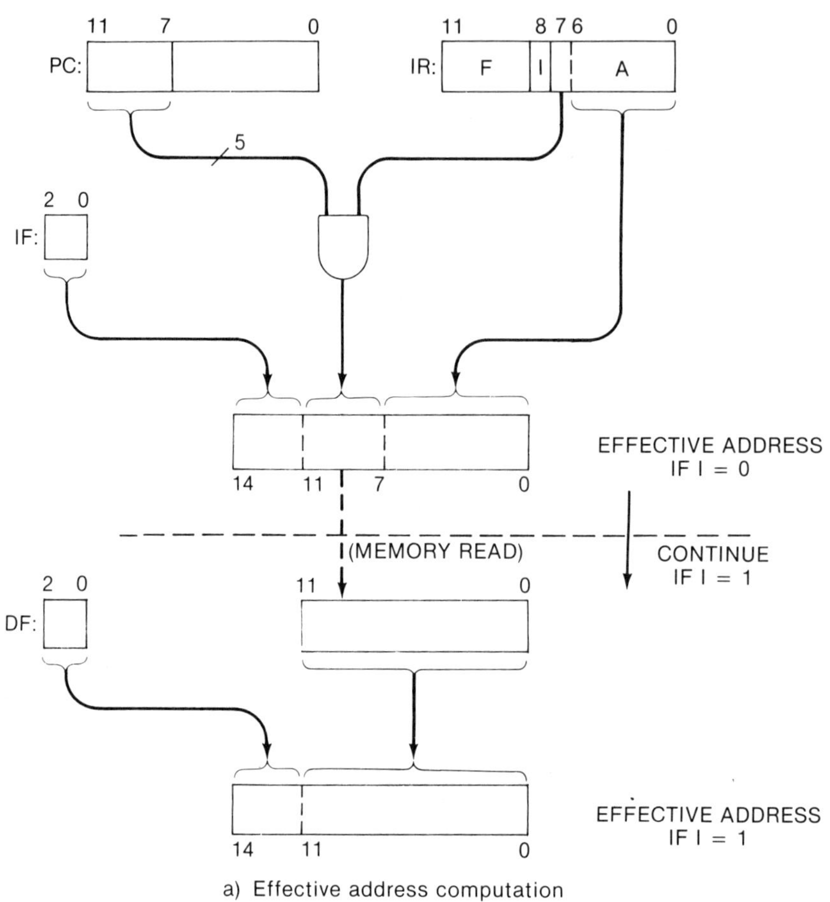

a) Effective address computation

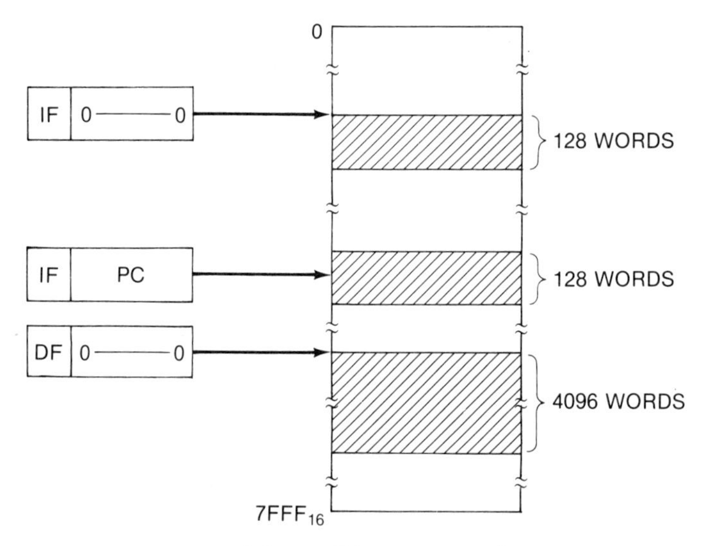

b) Accessible memory regions

Figure 3-23 PDP-8 addressing

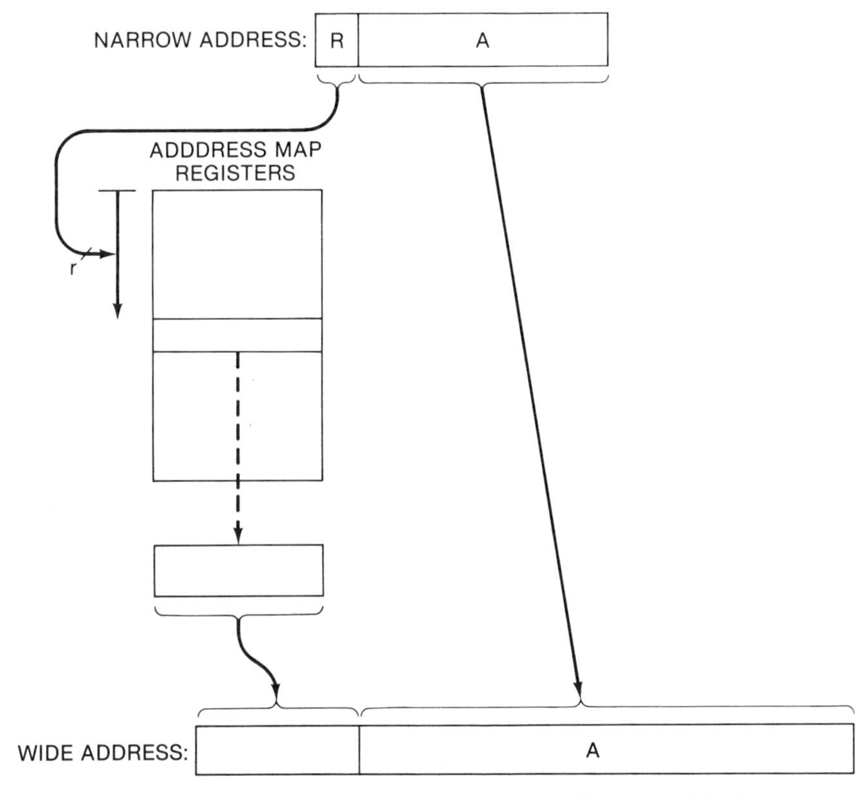

Figure 3-24 Using a register file to map a narrow address to a wide address

Notice that both the third and fourth options somewhat insulate the program's structure from the selection of the size of a complete address.

3.5.3 Address Granularity

The final size issue concerns the size of each object referenced by a distinct address. The distance between two items with consecutive addresses is machine's addressing granularity. For a more precise description, write out the individual memory bits. Now mark the first bit located in each separately addressed location, as shown in Figure 3-25. The number of bits between two address marks is the addressing granularity. The figure illustrates a 4-bit granularity.

The designer selecting the address granularity trades the flexibility of small granularity against the additional address bits needed to specify an individual operand from a fixed amount of memory (measured in absolute units, such as bits, not in flexible units, such as words). Most contemporary system designs address memory to the byte level. Others use words. The word width is defined differently for different system families.

It is important to note that the address granularity choice does not directly affect the size of an object accessed during one memory cycle. In Section 5.6.5 we

```
ADDRESS             BITS
0000        - - - - - 0
                      1
                      1
                      0
0001        - - - - - 0
                      1
                      0
                      1
0010        - - - - - 1
                      0
                      0
                      1
0011        - - - - - 0
                      1
                      1
                      1
0100        - - - - - 1
```

Figure 3-25 Memory bit map showing an address granularity of 4 bits

show how the processor–memory interface can be supplemented to support varying addressing granularities.

3.6 SUMMARY

In this chapter we have explored the formation and use of names in high-level languages and at the processor level. We discussed representation options for these names. We have seen how naming can be used to access constituent parts of compound objects. We learned that a name can be interpreted either globally or within a limited context. Nested naming rules are important in this regard. We know that context-dependent naming and other techniques can be used to save instruction bits.

To complete our study of the design of a computer's memory system, we turn to space allocation in the next chapter, and to accessing algorithms in Chapter 5.

3.7 PROBLEMS

3-1. An Ada procedure contains a set of declarations such that the names listed below are legal names for objects locally declared in the procedure. Write a set of Ada declarations that makes all of these names legal. Try to obtain the smallest set of declarations possible while meeting the legality constraint. Would your answer be changed if you were told that some of these names refer to the procedure's parameters? Explain.

```
a(3).b.c(4)      x(8)       a(7).g(2)
d.b.e            a(6).h     x(-3)
d.all
```

3-2. A programmer would like to define a package named P which will be used only in a subroutine S which is declared within a main program M. Furthermore, she does not want to use P anywhere else in the program. She has thought of two ways to structure the program; these two techniques are outlined in the following program structures.

Program A

```
package P is
  ..
end P;
package body P is
  f, g : integer;
  ..
end P;
procedure M is
  a, b : integer;
  procedure S is
    m, n : integer;
    ..
  begin
    ..
  end S;
begin
  ..
end M;
```

Program B

```
procedure M is
  procedure S is
    package P is
      ..
    end P;
    package body P is
      f, g : integer;
      ..
    end P;
    m, n : integer;
  begin
    ..
  end S;
  a, b : integer;
begin
  ..
end M;
```

The designer wishes you to compare these alternatives.

(a) Is there any logical difference between the two options?

(b) Is there any efficiency difference between the two options?

3-3. Consider the dynamic nesting example of Example 3-10. For the given history, construct the history of the stack in which nonvisible values are stored, and show the correspondence between the entries on that stack and the symbols in the parenthesized representation of the naming context. Make a separate picture showing the conditions after each context change during the program's flow. In your diagrams label each stack entry with the name of the entity whose value is stored in the location. Assume that all entities have the same size.

3-4. Devise a reasonable scheme that allows a programmer to specify within the defining module which modules may import each declared object. If object x is allocated in module m, your scheme should permit the programmer to specify as part of module m's text that x may be imported into another module b, but not into another module c. Both of these types of specification should be explicit in the text of the exporting module (module m in the example).

(a) Specify a syntax for this feature.

(b) Define the semantics of your proposal; be sure that you specify exactly the conditions under which an object will be visible within an importing module.

3-5. Explain the logical reasoning behind the following true statement: It is not possible to explicitly declare *both* importation and exportation of name visibility unless the space of program names is limited to a two-level structure.

3-6. The list structure depicted in Figure 3-26 is constructed from records of the type list_bead declared in the following Ada program fragment:

```
type list_bead;
type list_point is access list_bead;
type list_bead is
  record
    first : integer;
    second : real;
    third : list_point;
end record;
```

For each shaded element shown in the figure, write an Ada program fragment to read the element. The starting point for all accessing to the list is the access value stored in an object named "list." Your answer should contain three separate program fragments.

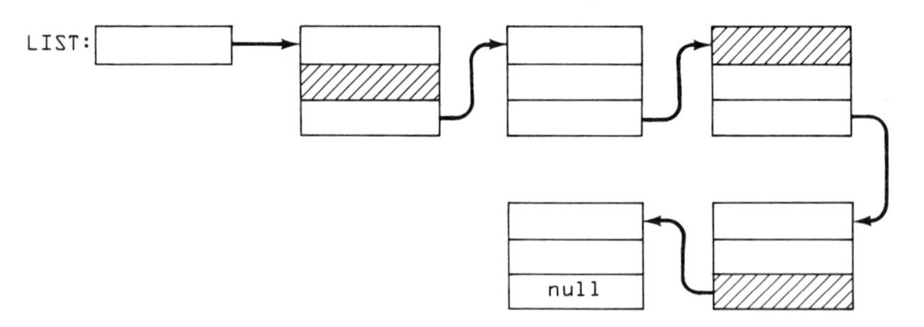

Figure 3-26 A list containing some objects to be named in Problem 3-6

3-7. Figure 3-27 shows a simple tree structure that was created by a program that built the tree incrementally as new data arrived. Notice the ordering among the values at the nodes. Each bead, as shown, contains one value-holding location and two pointers to successor nodes. Items in this tree are named by starting at the location "root," which contains a pointer to the tree's root bead. The components of each bead are named according to the following declaration:

```
type tree_bead;
type atree is access tree_bead;
type tree_bead is
  record
    topson : atree;
    bottomson : atree;
    it : integer;
  end record;
```

(a) What is the name of the place where the value 84 is stored?

(b) Given a pointer to a value in the tree, can you algorithmically construct a name for the object which holds the next smaller value in the tree? Explain.

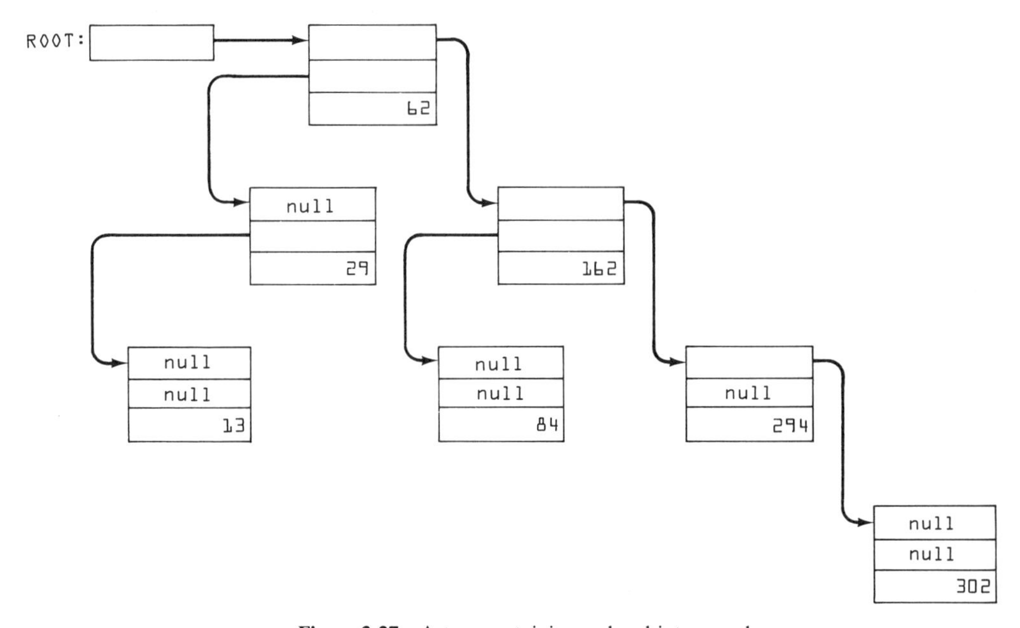

Figure 3-27 A tree containing ordered integer values

3-8. A system designer claims that a useful general program linking scheme could be defined as follows. Start with the usual static nesting rules and add the following linking command: "Place program P within block y[34] of program h from file F." This command still does not clarify how the act of placing program P in the specified block may change object naming in program h. Some interesting ways to interpret the act of nesting are:

1. The act of nesting can affect only names that were ED when h was compiled.
2. The act of nesting can change the meaning of any name used in h.
3. The act of nesting can change references to any procedures and subroutines but not to data-holding objects that were P when h was compiled.

Answer the following questions for all the interpretations of the act of nesting. (It is possible that the answer to a particular question not depend on the option chosen above.)

[34]Assume that the name y is unambiguous.

(a) Construct a set of program modules in which procedure m (defined in file FM) is statically nested within procedure b, which itself is defined within file FB, whose program has an outer block named main. Describe a (sequence of) linking command(s) that puts all of this structure together.

(b) Under the proposed scheme, which system element (e.g., the compiler or linker) determines the final form of the linked addresses?

(c) Discuss the degree to which module insertion affects program modularity.

(d) Specify the information that must be contained in the symbol tables kept with filed programs. Be sure that you provide enough information in the tables so that all necessary links can be established after the insertion request has been made.

3-9. Specify the semantics of each of the seven basic processor-level addressing operations. For each operation, write a programmed procedure that describes the operation.

3-10. For each addressing mode of the MC68020, describe a data structure such that the atomic constituents ("leaves of the structure") of the data structure are directly accessed through the mode. You may have to relate the declared data structure to data structures not visible in the high-level program that are used to support run-time structures. For example, memory indirect postindexed is useful when an access object (itself stored in memory) points to the top of a stack (also stored in memory) which is growing toward low memory addresses and the user program wishes to pop an item off that stack. In your answer, place emphasis on the structure eventually accessed, but also describe any structure-definition objects that are necessary to establish the connections at run time.

3-11. Write out the semantics of each of the following MC68020 addressing modes. Use the seven basic addressing operations as atomic steps whenever possible.

(a) Address register indirect.

(b) Address register indirect with postincrement.

(c) Absolute long.

3-12. Choose a familiar processor and compare its addressing modes with those of the MC68020. Which one has more modes? What data structures are supported by the additional modes?

3-13. Modify the effective addressing algorithm of Example 3-24 to include a scaling operation applied to the index quantity. You may assume that a quantity named SCALE was previously loaded with the scale factor when the control section interpreted the function code. The possible values of SCALE are 1, 2, and 4.

3-14. Consider a processor that supports multilevel indirection. It is designed so that the programmer may specify the point in the indirection chain where indexing is performed. Only a single index value can be specified in an instruction, but the timing of the indexing operation (with respect to the indirect chain) can be specified. Consider all logically different options regarding the timing of the indexing within indirection chains that include two reads of indirect addresses.

(a) For each option describe a data structure that is efficiently accessed by the option.

(b) Of the structures you identified in part (a), which do you think have an important effect on system speed? Discuss.

(c) Do any of these options speed parameter accessing compared to the simple scheme in which indexing always applies only to the address used in the first read of an indirect address?

3-15. Suppose that you are writing a program for a machine using register indirect addressing. Further, suppose that this mode is the only one available to access memory for data (the CDC 6600 is such a machine). Suppose that there is no way to use an address directly from the instruction stream, but that you first have to load an address into a register from an immediate operand. For this problem assume that the processor operations are like those of the MC68020. Show a program fragment that loads register X3 with the contents of memory location 100.

3-16. This problem is concerned with techniques that access nonlocal objects in a nested environment. Assume that the processor, like the B5000, maintains pointers to objects declared in the most recently entered block and the outermost block. To reach an intermediate level in the nest, the program must maintain a chain of pointers among the blocks mirroring the nesting structure, in reverse (i.e., the pointer chain reflects the search order for resolution of statically nested names). Assume that this chain has been established (i.e., in this problem you are not to worry about how the chain was set up). The pointer to the next ancestor block in the chain is in a fixed location within each block; this location is named CHAIN. Write an algorithm to obtain a pointer to the block at level L, given that the value of the current level is in location C. Leave the result in the location named B. The levels are numbered so that the lowest level number is associated with the outermost block of the nest.

3-17. The text suggested that the program of Example 3-27 could be modified simply to illustrate a naming problem that arises if a context-sensitive name is passed as an actual procedure parameter. Write a modified version of the program to illustrate the difficulty.

3-18. Write a fragment of a System/38 program that computes the index of the array element xarray(i, j, k, l) when the array was declared as

```
xarray : array(1 .. 10, 2 .. 4, 3 .. 9, 1 .. 3) of integer;
```

Do not check the subscripts to determine whether they lie within range; rather, just assume that they are valid. Table 3-15 lists some computational instructions in the machine that might be useful; in addition, the CAI instruction described in Example 3-32 will be useful. All instruction operands signify memory locations. An integer occupies one addressable location.

TABLE 3-15 SOME SYSTEM/38 COMPUTATIONAL INSTRUCTIONS

Instruction	Effect
ADDNS A, B, C	A:=B+C;
SUBNS A, B, C	A:=B−C;
MULTS A, B, C	A:=B * C;

3-19. Repeat Problem 3-18 for a familiar machine.

3-20. Show how you could use tag-based addressing to emulate the MC68020 addressing modes which do not increment or decrement address parameters during the address computation. Discuss briefly the reason for this exclusion.

3-21. We want to design a tag-based addressing mode which supports stack data structures. On a "pop" (read) access the processor would postincrement the last tagged indirect address object encountered along the path to the data object. In a symmetric manner, on a "push" (write) access the processor would predecrement the last tagged indirect address object along the path to the data object. Write out the accessing algorithms for read and write accesses, including the updates of the indirect address object. Start with the B5700 addressing mechanism in formulating your answer. You will have to impose a restriction that the last indirection was not performed through a computed indirection (as designated by the presence of an entry point descriptor in the indirection chain). Design your algorithm to handle the simpler case with no indirection in the addressing path (in this case there is no address word to be updated, and push and pop reduce to write and read, respectively).

3-22. Write out an algorithm that describes accessing a data object in a system using tag-based indirection with both indirect addresses and call-by-name entry points. The result of your algorithm should be the address of the data object, not the value contained therein. Use three tag values to signify data, entry, and pointer objects. In fact, define the data type "tag" as an enumerated type:

type tag **is** (data, entry, pointer);

Then the words "data," "entry," and "pointer" denote the possible tag values. Design your algorithm so that any arbitrary sequence (along the indirection path) of access variables and call-by-name procedure entry points will be properly interpreted.

3-23. Consider a system that supports tag-based indirection. Each indirect word can specify indexing to be applied to the indirect address included within the same indirect word. Let x denote the index specification in an indirect word. The index quantities are selected by the value of x as follows:

1. If $x = 0$, there is no indexing.
2. If $x = 1$, the index value is popped from the top of an implicit stack.
3. If $x > 1$, processor register x contains the index value.

Construct an indirect path to read the value 84 in the data structure shown in Figure 3-27, under the following restrictions:

(a) All index values are taken from the stack. This determines one indirection path.

(b) All index values are taken from processor registers. This determines a second indirection path.

In your answers show all values that determine the eventual address, whether located in the instruction, in processor registers, or in memory.

3-24. The Fairchild F8 microprocessor [FAIR75] designers reduced the bandwidth of address information flowing along the system bus by removing the contents of PC from the processor and placing it in the memory system. The processor's interface with the memory was therefore changed for instruction fetches. Two important primitive operations were provided. The first requested that the memory read the next program word. The second stated that the address being sent out along the address lines was to be loaded into the PC.

(a) This question is concerned with the need to increment the value in PC. We desire a solution such that the two operations described above are sufficient to implement arbitrary program structures. Describe which operations include PC incrementation. For each operation requiring PC incrementation, define the timing of the PC incrementation relative to the execution of other portions of the operation's execution by the memory system.

(b) Some instructions span more than the information fetched in one memory request. Define how such a long instruction would be fetched under this scheme.

3-25. The text claimed that using a wide indirect address to construct a wide virtual address is a general scheme, in the sense that there are no logical constraints that limit addresses under this scheme. In other words, the claim implies that any program P_w written for a processor with an arbitrarily wide address field in each instruction can be changed algorithmically into an equivalent program P_n for a processor that has only a narrow address field within each instruction. Discuss why this claim is true. Be sure that you consider all cases with indirection in program P_w.

3-26. The address in a B5700 instruction contains both a level number and an index, encoded according to the level of the executing procedure (as specified in Figure 3-22). This problem is concerned with the logic that separates the fields. Let PL denote the register that contains the level of the currently executing procedure. Assume that the address information from an instruction is placed in the 14-bit register ADDR before interpretation. The separated address should reside in registers L and I, with the level number in L and the index in I (both values should conform to the customary representation conventions).

(a) How wide is register L? Register I?

(b) Draw a diagram illustrating the data paths to load the L and I registers.

(c) Specify the control logic used to determine the logical values to be placed on the selector lines.

3-27. This problem is concerned with a scheme to dynamically change the address width in each instruction and thereby to save instruction bits. The processor contains a 6-bit address field width register AFW. The value in AFW is interpreted as the number of bits in the displacement field taken from an instruction. Now suppose that the IBM 370 instruction set were augmented by an instruction (SETAFW) whose single immediate operand is loaded into AFW. When the processor enters a new context, the SETAFW instruction may be executed to define the address encoding that will be used in the context.

(a) Let a(i) denote the maximum number of bits required for an address in context i. Let $n(i)$ denote the average number of addresses that appear in the program fragment executed in context i. Write a mathematical expression for the average number of address bits used in context i if the dynamic width scheme discussed above is implemented in the system.

(b) Write an inequality that will be true if the AFW coding scheme reduces the overall program length compared to the base IBM 370 system, which has 12-bit displacement fields in the address field for each memory reference in an instruction.

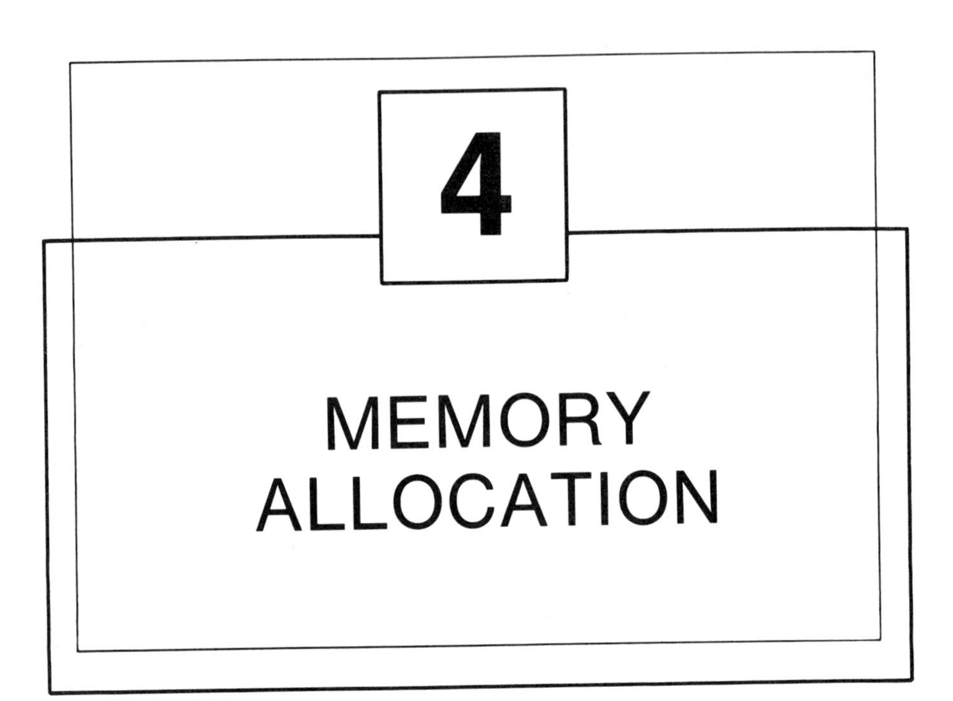

Have a place for everything and keep the thing somewhere else;
this is not advice, it's merely custom.
— Mark Twain

Yea, from the table of my memory
I'll wipe away all trivial fond records.
— Shakespeare, Hamlet

Allocation is our second major memory system issue, naming and accessing being the other two parts of the memory puzzle. In Chapter 3 we saw that memory naming and visibility issues can be utilized in designing processor addressing structures that are "close" to those required to implement high-level language naming semantics. Another semantic aspect of a language concerns the lifetimes of the entities holding named values. In this chapter we see how the allocation semantics from high-level languages can be mapped into space allocation strategies at different system levels, ranging from the compiler's allocation of main memory to the hardware's allocation of cache memory. We will see how designers can include support for allocation activities.

After reading this chapter, you should understand the important space allocation options and see how they relate to naming semantics and to using the system's memory resources efficiently. In addition, you will know how the low levels of the system can be designed for automatic implementation of simple, yet adequate allocation policies for cache memories.

In the next chapter we complete the memory presentation and see how actual accesses are completed. The methods used and the data required depend on the allocation decisions that we discuss here.

4.1 THE PROBLEM

A memory object cannot be accessed until space to hold its contents has been assigned within the memory address space. The allocation act performs this essential step.

Definition. *Memory allocation* is the act of assigning memory locations for specific uses.

When a translator program assigns addresses to declared objects, it is performing an allocation action. Similarly, when the linker assigns a memory region to hold a library module required for execution, it is performing allocation. Allocations are also performed by run-time support software and by the processor during program execution. Some of this allocation is requested directly by the program being executed, while other allocation requests are implicit in the language semantics without any overt allocation request appearing in the high-level language program.

The allocation strategy affects not only where objects will be stored but also how long the space will be allocated for the objects. The major functional requirement imposed upon an allocator is

Lifetime Requirement. An allocation A for the object X is functionally correct if the period of existence of allocation A encompasses the required lifetime of X.

The lifetime requirements for high-level languages will be described in Section 4.3.

In this chapter we discuss allocation problems and solution techniques for single process systems. The solution selection criteria include, as usual, functionality, cost, and speed. We will see not only how main (primary) memory space can be allocated but also how secondary memory allocations can be related to primary memory allocations and how these allocations can be implemented in a memory-management module within the operating system. When we consider the relationships among space allocations in primary (main) and secondary memory, we must face the trade-off between the speed and costs of the memory media themselves. In particular, we cannot minimize cost and maximize speed simultaneously because faster devices cost more, and larger quantities cost more. Thus we devise techniques to combine efficiently large, slow, cheap memories with smaller, faster, more expensive memories to form a memory hierarchy. We wish to coordinate all of this without undue overhead or complexity. Several structured approaches to these problems have been developed and are in wide use. Other, more sophisticated techniques may cost more overhead and may be used in large systems or when hardware support can be provided.

Before we turn to allocation issues, let us briefly outline the memory allocation module and its relationships with the remainder of the computer system, from which allocation and deallocation requests arrive at the allocation module. It may be possible to design the system so that explicit deallocation calls are not required. In the following discussion we assume that the system requires an explicit procedure call to free allocated space. We indicate where this assumption is not made.

If an allocation is to be meaningful, it must be respected within the system. Ensuring this respect may require adding an enforcement mechanism that assures consistency with the allocations that have been made. If all programs are "good," there is no problem. But there is a problem if only one "bad" program exists, since it could access an object not in its allocated space easily by specifying an address outside its space. Should the system automatically check for such errors?[1]

An allocation enforcer requires sufficient information that its checks can be completed correctly. What information is required? First, consider a single allocation, giving a block of contiguous memory locations to the requesting program. The enforcer's checks depend on the form of the address in an access request. If each address is interpreted relative to the block origin, the enforcer needs to know the block length to check whether the address exceeds that length limit. On the other hand, if an address is interpreted relative to a larger address space, the enforcer must know both the origin and length of the allocated block. This information could be collected into a single object of type space_descriptor, an instance of which contains both the origin and length of a contiguous block of allocated space. Figure 4-1 illustrates a single descriptor and the space it describes. The addressing and checking processes are more complex when a single process can be allocated several diverse blocks of memory; by analogy with segmentation (Section 3.4.2), a check of the segment number followed by a check of the object index against the length of that particular segment provides an adequate validity check.

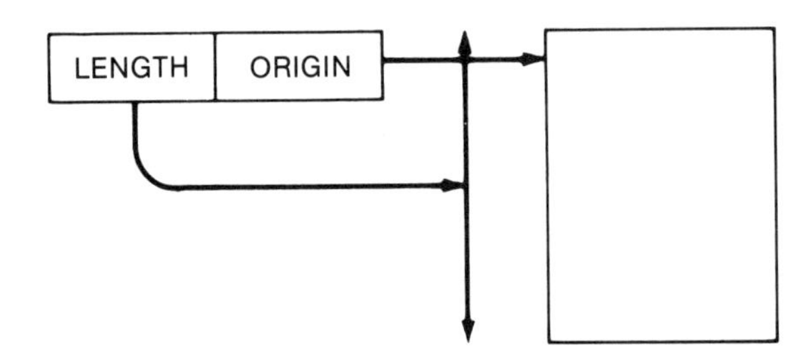

Figure 4-1 A space descriptor

Four aspects affecting any allocation design arise in this brief discussion:

1. The need to satisfy the functional requirements
2. The need for modules to handle allocate and free requests
3. The need for address validity checks
4. The selection of the result returned by the allocator

These aspects will reappear as we discuss allocations in the remainder of the chapter.

[1]In other words, should the system be designed under the "everything checked" philosophy, or under the "nothing illegal" philosophy?

4.2 ALLOCATION POLICIES AND THEIR IMPLEMENTATIONS

Almost every allocation decision can be divided into two phases. In the first phase, a space pool from which the allocation is to be taken is selected. In the second phase, some space from within that pool is selected to satisfy the allocation request. This decomposition of the problem is reflected in a picture showing a set of pools from which a portion of one pool is allocated to satisfy an allocation request. The pools are shown in Figure 4-2.

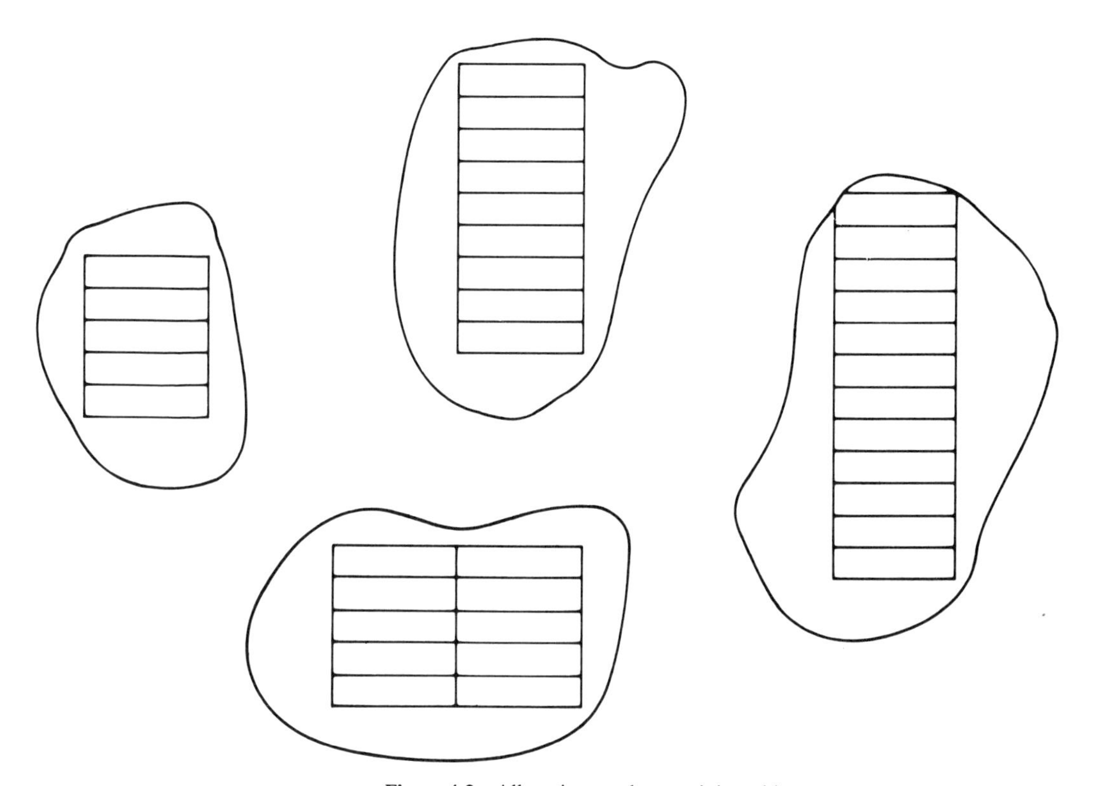

Figure 4-2 Allocation pools containing objects

4.2.1 Pool Selection Policies

The space resources are divided into *pools*, themselves managed as items in larger pools. Each individual allocation request is satisfied from a single pool. Within one pool the space selection decision is a simpler allocation decision than the selection of space on a system-wide basis. An advantage of the pool structure is that the pools themselves can be allocated and deallocated in a manner reflecting the program's structure. Creating this structure simplifies deallocation, especially if all space allocated within a pool can be automatically deallocated at the same time.

The following discussion is based on these assumptions:

1. Allocated space will be divided into pools.
2. When a pool is deallocated, all space within it is automatically deallocated.
3. Pool lifetimes and allocations will mirror the program's execution structure.

These assumptions are consistent with the hierarchical allocation strategy discussed above. All of our allocation discussion rests on these assumptions. The third assumption implies that pool allocations can change only when the program's execution point moves across a boundary separating program modules. Procedure call and return are two instances of execution point motion across a module boundary. Figure 4-3 depicts the pools and space allocations with each pool.

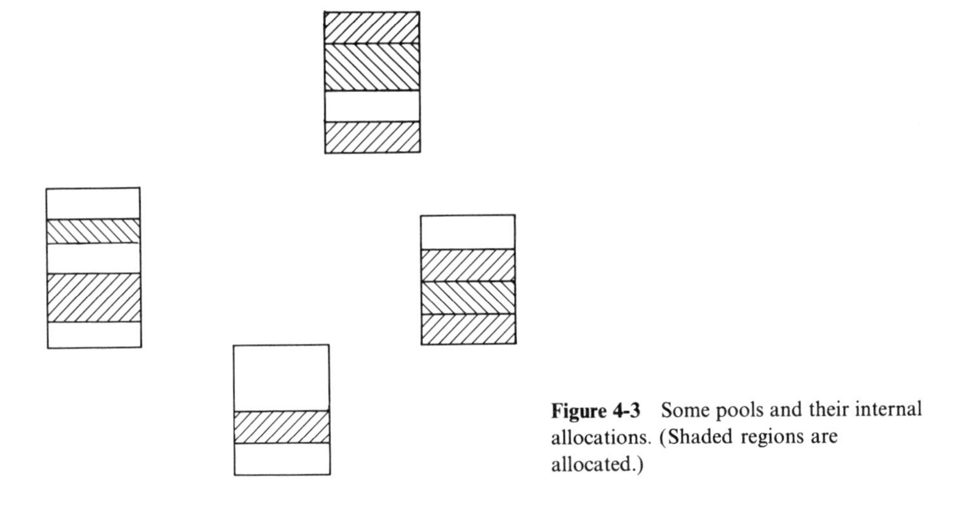

Figure 4-3 Some pools and their internal allocations. (Shaded regions are allocated.)

The space pool selection decision is partly determined by the lifetime requirement, since the pools themselves have lifetimes, and no object can easily outlive the pool of which it is a part. Our policies are based on the assumption that an allocation within a pool becomes invalid when the pool is deallocated. Consistent with this assumption, the basic pool selection policy is:

Basic Pool Selection Policy. Make an allocation for an object from the available pool whose lifetime is the smallest lifetime (of the available pools) that encompasses[2] the lifetime of the object.

Program semantics determine the required object lifetimes. This viewpoint suggests that the allocation problem must be solved at the object granularity level. In reality, however, the allocation problem can be divided into two parts: at the top level

[2]We use the following definition: A lifetime L_1 encompasses another lifetime L_2 if either $L_1 = L_2$ or if the start of L_1 does not follow the start of L_2 and the end of L_1 does not precede the end of L_2.

we have contexts with lifetimes; at the next lower level we have objects in those contexts with their own lifetimes.

We describe options for the allocation of space for an object in relation to a set of contexts $C_1, \ldots, C_n$. We assume that the higher order allocation decision has produced an allocation pool for each context. Let P_i denote the allocation pool associated with context C_i.

The choice of an allocation pool is influenced by the relationship between the object's lifetime and the pool's (or context's) lifetime. Several interesting relationships are depicted in Figure 4-4. We see four interesting cases:

1. Object lifetime matches context lifetime.
2. Object lifetime nested within context lifetime.
3. Context lifetime nested within object lifetime.
4. Neither lifetime nested within the other.

Simple allocation policies suffice for the first two cases. The other two cases are handled by reduction to one of the first two. This transformation is accomplished by finding or creating an artificial context within which the object's life is nested.

In the first case the match between object and context lifetimes means that X (an object in block C_j) has the same lifetime as P_j. Object X can be allocated within P_j upon entry to C_j, and when P_j is released (upon exit from C_j) the space for X will also be released. Under this policy, X will exist for the life of C_j.

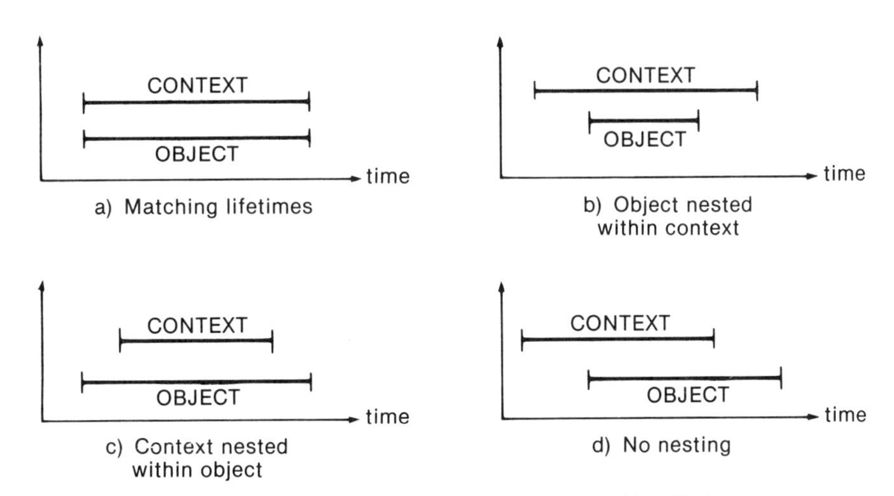

Figure 4-4 Some relationships among context and object lifetimes

Example 4-1

Object declarations in an Ada block, such as a procedure or function block, define local objects with lifetimes synonomous with the lifetime of the block. Therefore, space for these objects can be allocated when the block is entered and freed when the block is exited.

In the second object–context nesting relationship, the lifetime of the object is nested within the lifetime of some context C_j. It would certainly be adequate to allocate space for X within P_j, the corresponding allocation pool, keeping X's space allocated for the life of P_j. In this way the lifetime for the allocation of X encompasses the required lifetime for X (see Figure 4-5a). In another design the system performs a specific allocation for X when its life begins (for example, as a consequence of a use of **new** in an executable Ada statement) and a specific deallocation when X's life ends (for example, as a consequence of a call to free[3] in Ada) (see Figure 4-5b). Under the latter design, the space for X could be allocated within P_j, since the pool will not disappear while it is still needed to hold X.

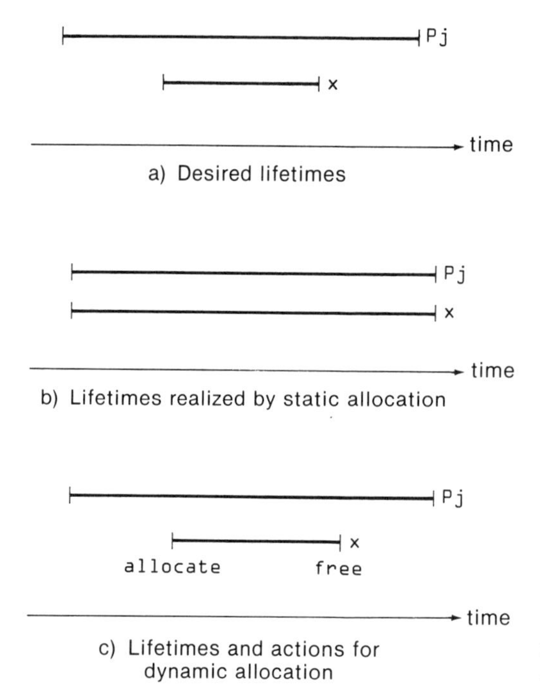

Figure 4-5 Static versus dynamic allocation with nested lifetimes

4.2.2 Allocation within a Pool

The problem of allocating space within a pool has two aspects. First, we may wish to group several objects to reduce the number of allocation decisions. Second, we must allocate a specific location for each object within the pool.

Any set of objects that have identical lifetimes and that are visible in the same places can be collected together for allocation purposes. Then the allocation of space for the objects within the collection can be handled just like the allocation of space within a pool.

[3]The function free is not built in to Ada; rather, an instantiation of a freeing procedure must be requested. These details are presented in Section 4.3.

The within-pool allocation problem can be divided into two situations according to whether:

1. All objects can be statically allocated for the life of the pool;

   or

2. Some objects require dynamic allocation during the life of the pool.

The latest time that a static allocation can be made is when the pool is created. In many situations the static allocation can be made during program translation. In this case the act of allocating space for an object "within" a context is simply the act of assigning a within-context (local) address for the object.

4.2.2.1 Static allocation. Two static allocation policies are:

1. First-declared-first-allocated (FDFA)
2. Grouped by common attribute

A first-declared-first-allocated static allocation is adequate for most situations, but it does require that all object sizes be known at the time of allocation. Under this policy the first object (in order of declaration) is assigned to the first address, the second object to the first remaining address, and so on. For example, the objects w, x, and thing declared in the statement

```
w, x, thing : integer;
```

would be assigned adjacent locations by an allocator using a first-declared-first-allocated policy.

We can describe this allocation policy in different terms: Consider an allocation as being made in response to a request which is a call to a function named allocate, whose parameters are a size requirement and a name. When a request arrives, the first free space is allocated to satisfy the request. Internally, the allocator keeps track of the free space available within each context; the index of the first unallocated, or "free," location is adequate for FDFA allocation. The free index can be bound to the name in the next allocation request, and the free pointer would then be updated to reflect the allocation. This policy is implemented by the following program fragment:

```
free : index;          --a global object
..
function allocate(n : integer; x : name) return index is
  temp : index;
begin
  add_to_name_map(x, free, c);  --c the context
  temp:=free;
  free:=free + n;
  return temp;
end;
```

The second static allocation policy groups all objects that share a common property, such as object type. Using this policy can be viewed as establishing a separate allocation pool for each object type. Most compilers, for example, allocate instructions and data to different regions of address space.

Example 4-2

```
type xtype is
  record
    a : integer;
    b : real;
    c : integer;
    d : integer;
    e : real;
    f : integer;
  end record;
x: xtype;
```

Suppose that the allocator collects objects according to their types and allocates integers first. If each real and each integer requires one location to hold its value, the allocation will be that listed in Table 4-1 for items within record x.

TABLE 4-1 TYPE-BASED ALLOCATION

Name	Location	Type
a	1	integer
c	2	integer
d	3	integer
f	4	integer
b	5	real
e	6	real

4.2.2.2 Dynamic allocation. A dynamic allocation is an allocation made during program execution. Dynamic allocation can improve space utilization. Dynamic allocation may be necessary for an object whose lifetime does not match the pool's lifetime. If the set of object lifetimes is structured so that space previously allocated for one object can be reallocated to hold a different object at a later time, a program using dynamic allocation may require less space than the same program using static allocation. Dynamic allocation may be necessary if the sizes of the allocated objects cannot be specified until the program runs.

The choice of dynamic allocation policy depends on the relationships among the lifetimes of the objects sharing the allocation pool. If the object lifetimes are nested, simple stack allocation policies can be used. If the lifetimes are slewed, a queue allocation policy can be used. More complex heap allocation policies are required when neither of these two relationships holds among the lifetimes of the allocated objects. We examine four policies in the following sections:

1. Allocation from a stack
2. Allocation from a queue
3. Fixed-size block allocation from a heap
4. Variable-size block allocation from a heap

The discussion of each of these policies will contain the following parts:

1. Conditions for the use of the policy
2. How the allocator module is invoked (its calls)
3. Data structures used to implement the policy
4. How an invocation is handled
5. Uses for the policy

In addition, if there are important variants of the policy, we will survey them in a final paragraph.

All descriptions of module invocations will assume that the following type declarations are visible:

```
type space is ..;
type access_space is access space;
```

4.2.2.2.1 *Allocation from a Stack*

Conditions: Stack allocation can be used if the lifetimes of the allocated objects form a nest. In particular, the allocate and free requests must form a nested set of events with the requirement that any matching pair must correspond to allocating and freeing space for the same object.

Example 4-3

Here are two histories,[4] one compatible with stack allocation and the other not. The capitalized names in the histories represent object types that were declared in the program.

HISTORY_1	HISTORY_2
a:=new Ta;	a:=new Ta;
b:=new Tb;	b:=new Tb;
c:=new Tc;	c:=new Tc;
f:=new Tf;	f:=new Tf;
free(f);	free(b);
g:=new Tg;	g:=new Tg;
free(g);	free(g);
free(c);	free(c);
free(b);	free(f);
d:=new Td;	d:=new Td;
e:=new Te;	e:=new Te;
free(e);	free(e);
free(d);	free(d);
free(a);	free(a);

[4]We use a history to depict an actual sequence of (important) events that occur during the example situation. The sequence depicted in a history must be compatible with all constraints governing the situation at hand, but need not be the only such possible sequence.

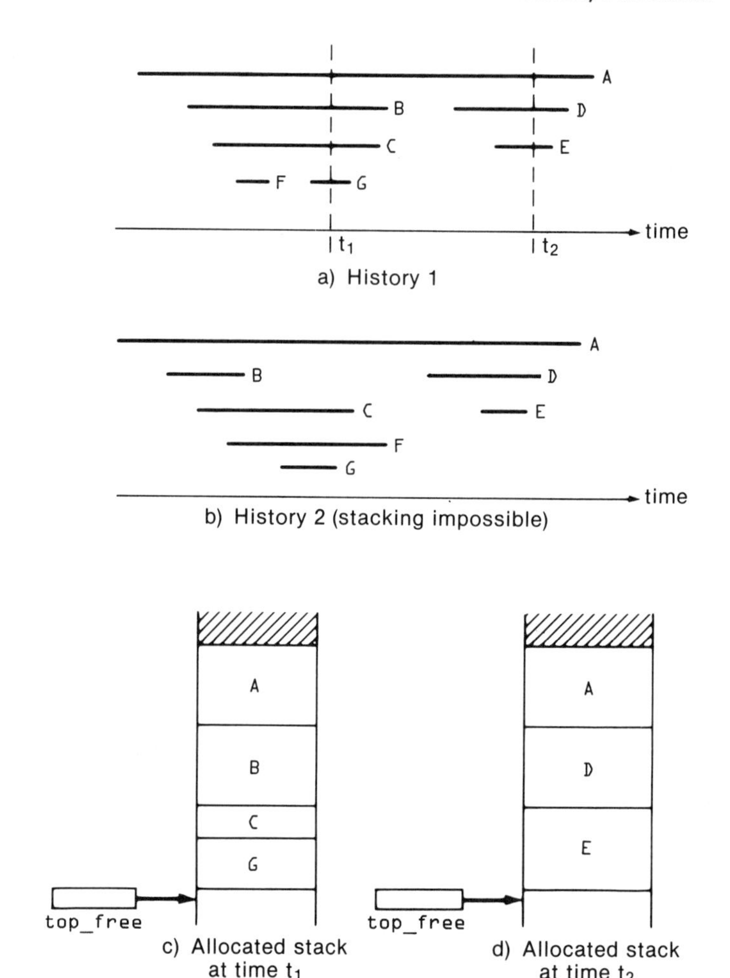

Figure 4-6 Stack allocation for Example 4-3

These histories are identical except for the timing of the deallocation of objects b and f. Figure 4-6 illustrates the object lifetimes for these two histories; it is easy to see the HISTORY_1 obeys nesting, whereas HISTORY_2 does not. Figure 4-6c and d show two snapshots of the allocation stack and the object lifetime nest, taken at the snapshot times indicated on Figure 4-6a.

Calls:

```
function allocate(size : integer) return access_space;
procedure free(new_top : access_space);
```

Implementation Structures: The implementation of a stack allocation policy requires a stack, which is the space pool, and a pointer top_free holding an index into the stack space. The top_free index is the management information, being the index of the first free location in the stack; it separates free space from allocated space. This distinction between allocated and free space is sufficient to manage the pool; the separations among spaces for individual objects within the allocated part of the stack is handled by the program(s) using the space.

Processing Requests: To make an allocation, the allocator first checks whether the remaining free space is large enough to satisfy the request. If the space is insufficient, the allocator traps. If there is enough free space, the allocator saves the current value of top_free to return as the locator result. It completes the allocation by increasing[5] the value of top_free by the amount of space that was requested. For deallocation, the allocator resets the value of top_free to the origin of the block being freed.[6]

Uses: Stack allocations can be used for the allocation of activation records in a block-structured language. An activation record holds the set of objects local to a block; it is allocated when the program enters a new naming context. We discuss processor support for this important allocation situation in Section 4.4.2.

4.2.2.2.2 *Allocation from a Queue*

Conditions: At first glance it probably seems that queue allocation would never make sense. A little thought should convince you that in order for the queue structure to apply, it would be necessary that an unrealistic relationship hold among the lifetimes of the objects allocated within the pool. In particular, a slewed "revolving door" relationship would be required, as illustrated in Figure 4-7. We shall see, however, that a queue allocation policy can be used to good effect in specific situations.

The slewed lifetimes directly map into a first-in-first-out allocation, which corresponds to a queue structure. This is easily seen by viewing the queue as a circular structure. Figure 4-7 illustrates the allocated blocks within a queue.

Calls:

```
function allocate(size : integer) return access_space;
procedure free(point : access_space; size : integer);
```

Implementation Structures: Within a queue allocation module, free space can be described by two pointers: one to the head of the queue of free space and the other to its tail. These pointers are equivalent to pointers to the tail and head, respectively, of the allocated space.

Processing Requests: The details of the queue manager's responses to allocate and free requests are straightforward; see Problem 4-4.

Uses: We will see some uses of queue allocations made under control of the operating system in Section 4.5.

[5]This assumes that the stack "grows" toward higher addresses.

[6]This does not verify that the stack discipline is actually followed; it assumes that the stack discipline is known to be appropriate for the situation. A similar assumption is made with respect to other allocators in the following discussions.

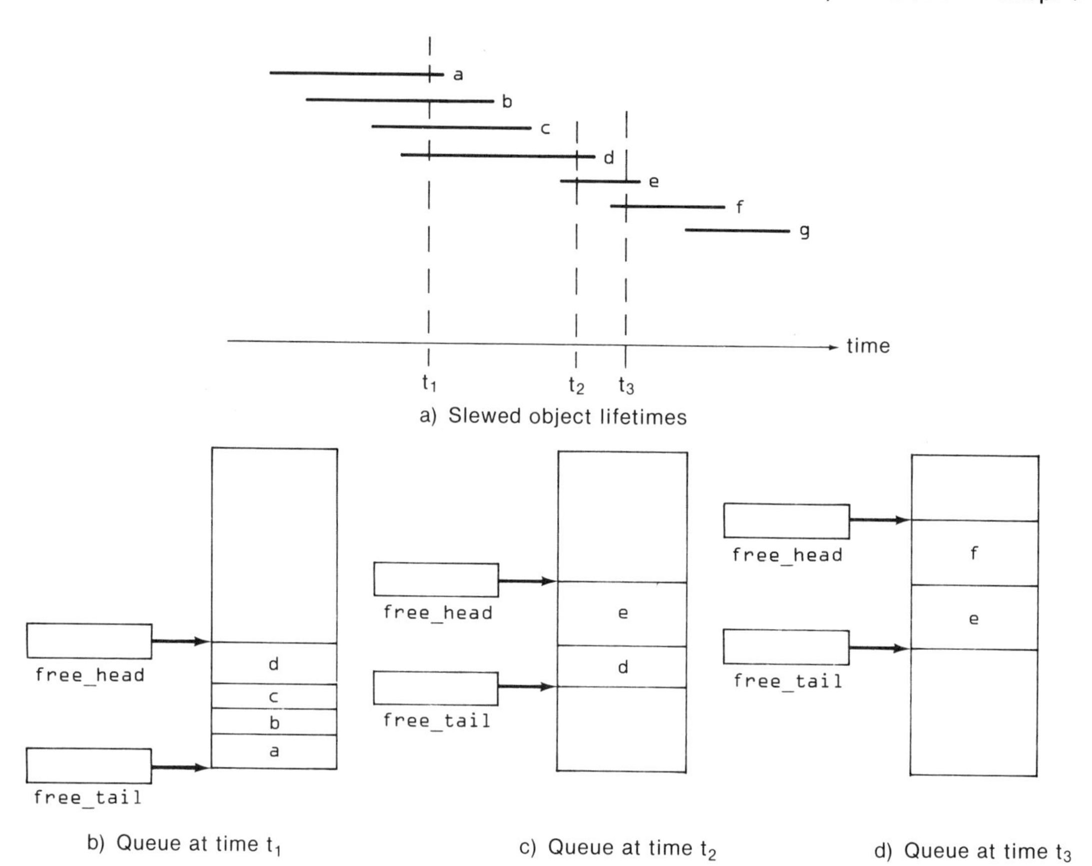

Figure 4-7 Allocation from a queue with slewed object lifetimes

Variations: If all programs using the allocator are assumed to operate correctly, one or both of the parameters of the free call could be eliminated, but additional status would have to be maintained by the allocator.

4.2.2.2.3 *Fixed-Size Allocation from a Heap*

Conditions: All allocation requests must ask for the same amount of space. Heap allocation is required when the allocate/free pattern does not match either the stack or the queue lifetime discipline.

Calls:

```
function allocate return access_space;
procedure free(point : access_space);
```

Implementation Structures: Although it is possible to manage a heap so that all the free space is always collected into a contiguous block, such a contiguous-free-space policy complicates the allocate and free operations, and consequently, may slow system operation. When free space is compacted into a contiguous block, the information in some allocated blocks will have to be relocated, and all locators describing the relocated information will have to be modified to reflect the changed allocation. To avoid these disadvantages of a contiguous-free-space strategy, the allocator must be designed to deal with a free space divided into a set of blocks.

In this section we discuss the simplest heap management situation in which every allocation is given the same amount of space; call that amount object_size. In this case the heap can be divided a priori into a set of *frames*, each containing an amount of space equal to object_size (see Figure 4-8). This division of the pool can be made before any allocation requests are satisfied.[7] The division of the pool into frames never has to be changed.

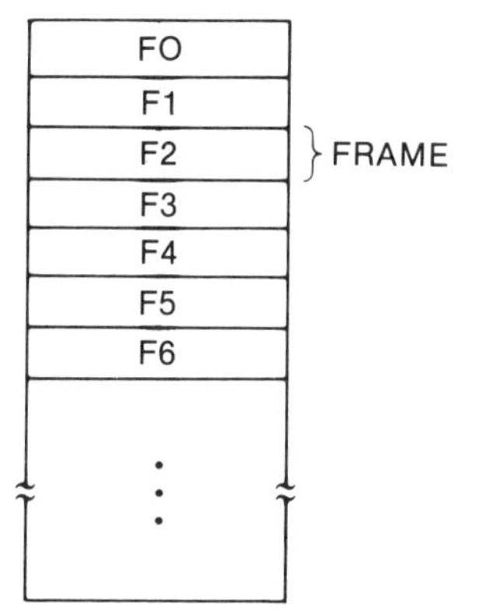

Figure 4-8 A heap divided into frames

With frame-based allocation, free-space bookkeeping can be based on either a table containing a "free" bit for each frame or a linked list with each bead describing a free frame. Figure 4-9 depicts these options. We discuss the list approach in the text, leaving the bit vector approach for the problems.

Processing Requests: To satisfy an allocation request, the allocator chooses a free frame off the free list, marks the frame "busy," and then returns a pointer to the chosen frame. To satisfy a free request, the allocator adds the freed space to its free list. No result is returned.

The free list must be updated during allocation and deallocation. Since the frames are the same size, they are logically interchangeable, and it may seem that free list management is not a significant issue. Although the selection of the free list management algorithm is not important in a uniprocessor system, it may be important in a multiprocessor system. We discuss two simple free list management policies: stack and queue management. Under the stack (or LIFO) policy the frame at the head of the free list is used to satisfy an allocation request, and a freed frame is added at the head of the free list. This policy maximizes the amount of space that never need be allocated (Problem 4-3 asks for a proof of this fact). Under the queue (or FIFO) policy the frame at the head of the free list is used to satisfy an allocation

[7]The size of the divisions can be selected during system design or programming, and the divisions themselves can be made during programming or system initialization.

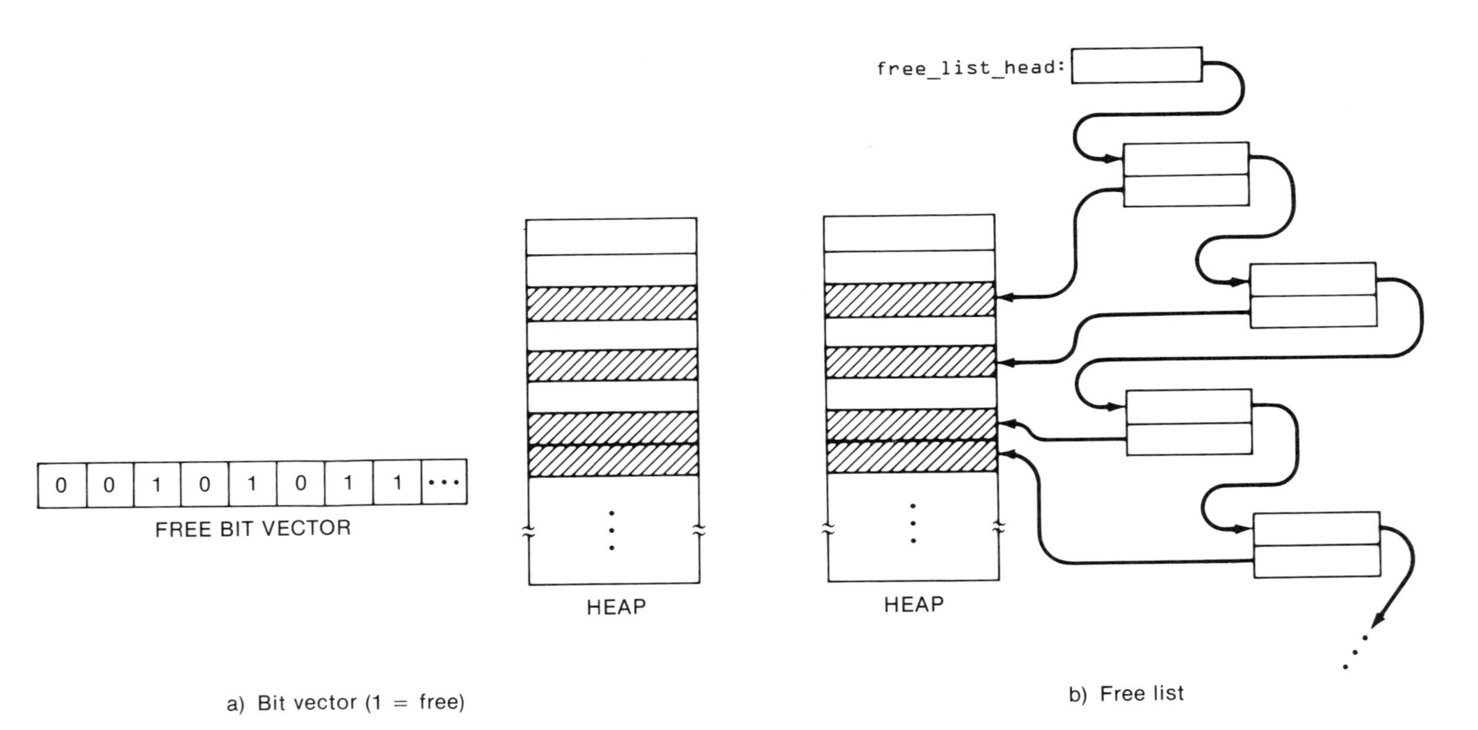

Figure 4-9 Free space bookkeeping options for fixed size allocations. (Free space shaded.)

request, and a freed frame is added at the tail of the free list. This policy has the advantage that the allocation and deallocation activities are somewhat independent (until the list becomes almost empty); the queue policy may be preferred in a multiprocessor system for this reason.

Whatever free space management policy is used, if the free-space list becomes empty, there is no remaining free space. If an allocate request arrives and only one process is using the allocation pool, there is no way that the pool can be used to satisfy the request. Thus the new allocation request must fail and raise an exception, the space manager must expand the allocation pool, or the manager must find another pool where space can be found to meet the allocate request. On the other hand, if the allocation pool is shared with other processes, the allocator also has the option to suspend the incoming allocate request until a frame in the pool is freed by another process.

Uses: Heap allocations of fixed size are used in page-based memory management schemes; these are basic elements of memory management by the operating system in many contemporary computer designs. In these designs, low-level hardware support for the framing and free space mappings can be built in during system design.

4.2.2.2.4 *Variable-Size Allocation from a Heap*

Conditions: None! The fourth policy option for run-time memory allocation from a pool supports dynamic allocations of variable-sized objects. This situation arises when a heap is required (because the allocate/free history does not match a stack or a queue discipline) and the allocate requests may ask for different amounts of space.

Calls:

```
function allocate(size : integer) return access_space;
procedure free(space : access_space; size : integer);
```

We will see that the space manager can be designed so that the size of each allocation unit is retained within the management module, in which case the process freeing some space need pass only a locator pointing to its origin (see Problem 4-11).

Implementation Structures: Since the object sizes vary, the allocation pool's space cannot be divided a priori into frames with the assurance that every allocation request could be satisfied by doling out a frame. The variable size requirement implies that the allocator will have to keep accounts about free space distributed in blocks of various sizes. Under the three simpler allocation policies, there was an obvious simple implementation that intuitively seemed to be a very efficient, and maybe the best possible, implementation. In the situation at hand, however, no simple implementation strategy stands out as the obvious best solution for all applications. Two issues require a deeper look. The first issue concerns the strategy for selecting space to satisfy an allocation request. The second issue concerns the management of the free space database. The two issues are coupled because the difficulty in satisfying a request would be lower if the free-space information were organized to shorten the allocator's search for a block to satisfy the request. In a similar manner, the data structure choice could simplify deallocation. Unfortunately, the structures that simplify allocation make deallocation more complex, and vice versa. A complete overhead accounting includes the overhead of both allocate and free operations [SLEA85].

The general situation contains the following important elements:

1. A set of free blocks (each containing contiguous space)

$$\{B_1, \ldots, B_n\}$$

2. The size of each block

$$\{s_1, \ldots, s_n\}$$

3. The origin of each block

$$\{a_1, \ldots, a_n\}$$

We wish to design the allocation policy to minimize the amount of time expended in management activities, measured across an arbitrary sequence of allocate and free requests. Formally, we wish to choose a policy that reduces the management overhead for the allocation history. Since the allocation history is not known a priori, a model of the situation would include a probabilistic characterization of the random process that generates the requests. We could evaluate each candidate policy against this model. A comparison of the resulting expected overhead times would complete the policy selection process.

Since such an evaluation doesn't always give the same choice, we describe here three important alternatives. One could keep a table of bits giving the allocation status of each allocation unit, but the table requires a bit for each word in the space,[8] and clearly the bit table would occupy many bits, in addition to being difficult to process to find space to allocate. The information regarding what space is free and what is not free (is "in use") can be expressed in terms of the origins and lengths of all free blocks.[9] Either a table or a list can be used to hold this free-space information. Figure 4-10 illustrates these alternatives for a small set of free blocks (the free spaces are denoted by shading in the figure). Linked lists describing free space are commonly used in support of variable allocation heap management.

Processing Requests: Since the allocated objects have different sizes, the free-space blocks have different sizes. Therefore, a simple searching strategy will not be adequate, since the first block in the free-space list may not be large enough to satisfy the current allocation request. Of course, the allocator must find a free block that is large enough to satisfy the request. It, however, may not be the best policy to use just any block that is at least as large as the request. If the allocator chooses a free block much larger than the requested size, the allocator may be designed to subdivide the

[8]Actual allocations could be based on other granularities; the important point is that the free-space table must describe the status of each atomic allocation unit. In the text we assume granularity at memory word or byte level.

[9]Origin information is a complete description when the allocated spaces are all of the same size, but when we have variable-sized allocations (see Section 4.2.2.2.4), length information will also be required.

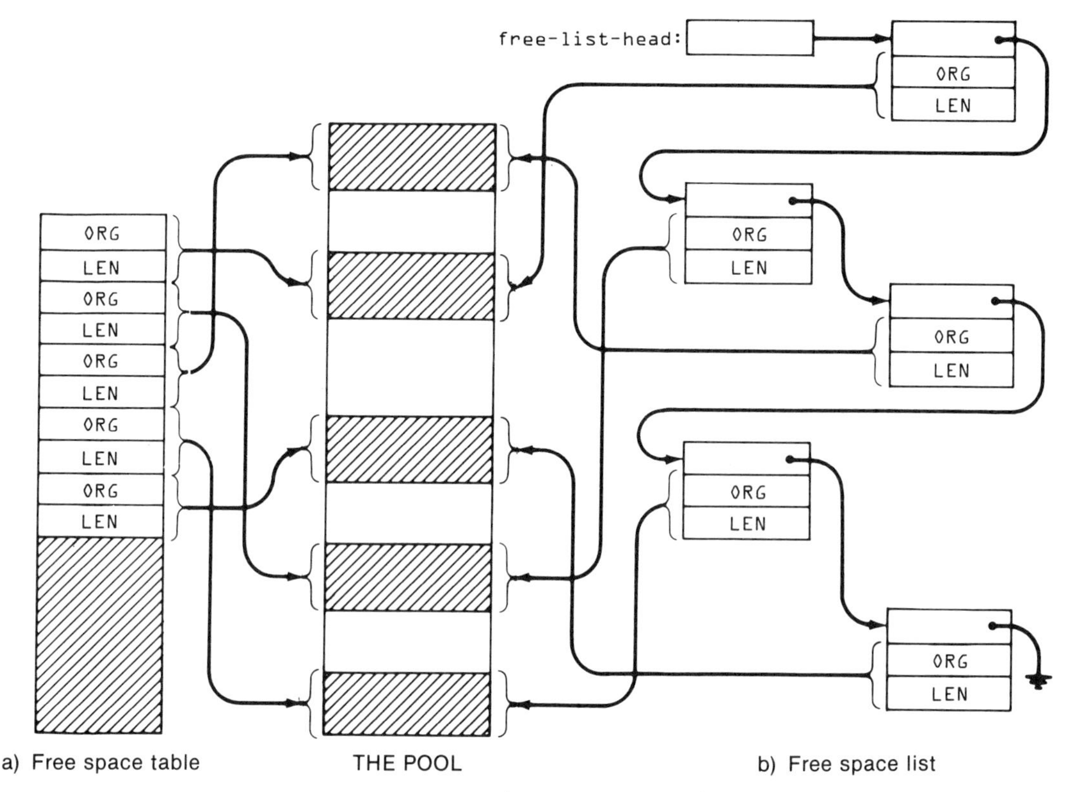

Figure 4-10 Free space bookkeeping options for general allocations

free block into a set of smaller free blocks.[10] Conversely, when a block is freed, the allocator might combine it with neighboring free blocks to create a single larger free block. If blocks are not combined, the allocator will eventually run out of blocks that can satisfy requests for large spaces.

Despite the option to combine free blocks to form a larger free block, it is still possible that the heap contains sufficient free space to satisfy an allocate request, but because the free space has been fragmented into a set of noncontiguous blocks, there is no contiguous block large enough to satisfy the request. If this condition arises, the allocator must either deny the allocate request or reallocate the heap to reorganize the free space into a single continuous block. Collecting free space in this manner is called "garbage collection" and is necessary in the implementation of list-processing languages. Recall that any change in an allocated block's location must be accompanied with a change in the contents of all pointers to the allocated block. It will be difficult to find all of these pointers unless they are embedded in a management data structure.

[10]If blocks were never subdivided, the first request for any space would allocate the whole pool!

We must explore designs for the following functions:

1. Selecting the block to use to satisfy a request
2. Subdividing a large free block to create smaller free blocks
3. Combining small free blocks to create a larger free block

The answers to the first two issues affect the design of the allocate procedure, while the answer to the last issue affects the design of the free procedure.

We consider three space allocation strategies and the corresponding allocator designs. The strategies are described by the search method used to find space to satisfy an allocate request:

1. First fit
2. Best fit
3. Buddy system

The *first-fit* allocation policy satisfies an allocate request with the first[11] free block that is larger than the requested size. A freed block can be placed on the list in a LIFO or a FIFO manner; in either case, this policy is not as good as the best fit policy.

The *best-fit* allocation policy satisfies an allocation request with the smallest free block that is larger than the space requested. The selection criterion suggests that the blocks on the free list should be ordered on the basis of their sizes. This choice places a burden on the free procedure and simplifies the allocate procedure. Note that remarks concerning the distribution of the overhead between the allocate and free procedures are not important, since each block has to be allocated and freed exactly once. By using a best-fit allocation strategy, the distribution of free block sizes may be skewed toward small sizes. It may be wiser to try to anticipate future allocation needs when dividing a free block to satisfy an allocate request [KAUF84]. The simple policy leaves the residue of the best-fit block as another free block. A slightly better policy places a lower bound on the size of a free block; if the best-fit block leaves less than the minimum free block size, the entire best-fit block is allocated and no new free block is created. Since the free list is ordered by block size, the act of allocating a block may imply two list searches: one finds the best-fit block, and the other inserts the new free block onto the free list.

When a block is freed, how is the free space managed? It might be wise to recombine (if possible) the newly freed block with neighboring free blocks to create a larger free block that could satisfy a request for a large block, if such a request were to arrive. To recombine free blocks in this manner, the allocator must determine whether a newly freed block is adjacent to any free block(s). If so, the contiguous free blocks can be combined to form a large free block. A free block list ordered by origin is useful for this activity.

[11]Here "first" refers to the order in which the free-space list is searched.

The *buddy system* is like the best-fit policy in that the block with the smallest remainder after allocation is used to satisfy an allocate request. This policy is different from the best fit policy in that the block sizes are constrained to a predetermined set of values. A block splitting rule governs the division of a free block that contains extra space beyond that required to meet the allocate request. The rule specifies the fractional parts of a block that will comprise separate blocks after block splitting. The set of these fractions determines the set of possible block sizes. Figure 4-11 illustrates some blocks created by a buddy system with the fraction sets $\{\frac{1}{2}, \frac{1}{2}\}$ and $\{\frac{1}{2}, \frac{1}{4}, \frac{1}{4}\}$. Suppose that the system is initialized with a single block of free space whose size is a power of two. Then, with these fraction sets, every free block in the system will have a size that is a power of 2. The allocator will satisfy an allocate request with a block whose size is the smallest power of 2 not smaller than the requested size.

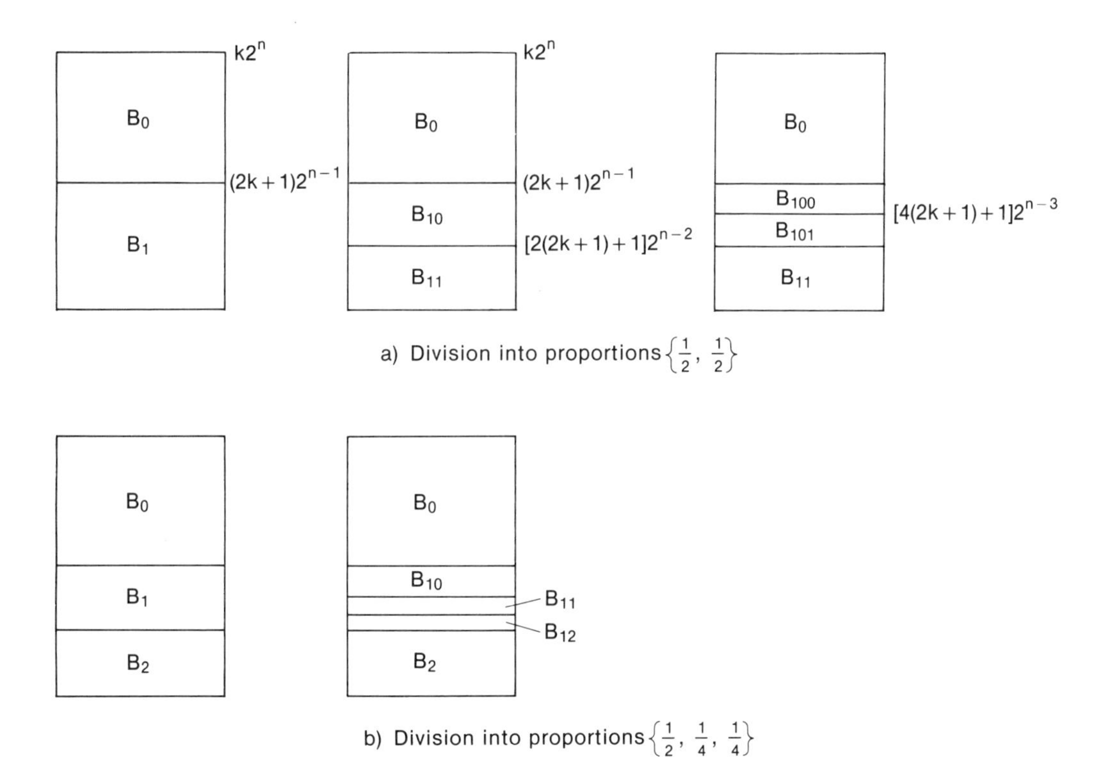

Figure 4-11 Buddy system space partitions

The management problem of combining small free blocks to form larger free blocks is handled easily under the buddy system, since the act of combining blocks is the inverse of the act of separating free blocks. Thus each freed block can be combined in exactly one way with its buddies to form a larger free block. Therefore, it is possible to compute the origins of the blocks that would have to be free to construct a larger free block C. After forming the combined block, the same free procedure might be called again to see whether C could be combined with its buddies. Although it may seem attractive to combine free blocks whenever possible, it is easy to see that creating an excessively large block in this manner may, in fact, make the block too large to meet a later allocate request. If this situation occurred, then when a later allocate request arrived, the large block would simply be divided into smaller pieces again. We see that the complementary acts of merging and division were wasted in this case. Due to this possibility, it can be attractive, especially with buddy systems [KAUF84], to delay free block recombination until such recombination is required to form a block large enough to meet a specific incoming allocation request.

Uses: Variable allocation from a heap is required to manage any space from which programmer-controlled allocations are made.

4.2.3 Policy Summary

We divided the memory allocation process into two parts: the allocation of pools and the allocation of space for objects within pools. The problem of acquiring space for the pools is the same as the problem of acquiring space within a pool for an object.

Free-space management is central to memory allocation. Different techniques can be used, including stack and queue management (which are feasible only if the lifetimes of the allocated objects have specific interrelationships), and heap management of fixed- and varying-sized objects. These policies can be adapted to specific environments, as we shall see in the remainder of the chapter.

Our discussion rested on two assumptions. The first assumption was that every time an object becomes free, the executing program will inform the memory management module. In some systems or languages the overhead[12] required to meet this constraint is too great, and the memory management system must be designed differently. We discuss this situation later.

The second assumption was that the allocator always responds to an allocation request with a contiguous block of space. This requirement makes allocation more difficult. If the assumption were relaxed, and the allocator were allowed to satisfy an allocate request with a set of blocks of space, the program using the space must be aware of this structure and access it properly. This option will be revisited in Chapter 5.

4.3 PROGRAMMER-CONTROLLED ALLOCATION IN HIGH-LEVEL LANGUAGES

The semantics of high-level languages specify the lifetime requirements of the objects declared in a program. There are three different classes of object lifetimes:

1. Static
2. Automatic
3. User-controlled

[12]This overhead is incurred in the bookkeeping required to know that a space has indeed become free.

A *static* lifetime matches the lifetime of the executing program. Static objects in an Ada program include the program itself, all links established to bind program modules together, and all objects declared in the body of any package (not including those declared within the body of a procedure or a function). Why are the module links static? Because the search path used to resolve ED names does not change during program execution. Why are objects inside a package static? Because they are used to hold the state internal to the package between invocations of program modules within the package. The seed of a random number generator, for example, is a static value within the random number generator package.

An *automatic* lifetime matches the lifetime of some invocation of a procedure, function, or block. In most languages, the lifetime of an automatic object X matches the lifetime of the procedure, function, or block that contained X's declaration. Automatic objects typically hold intermediate results during the execution of the procedure. When the procedure, function, or block is invoked again, a new set of automatic objects may be allocated.

A *user-controlled* lifetime does not match the lifetime of any program-related module. Explicit program actions signal the beginning and (usually) the end of the object's life. The program will invoke an allocate function when the object is to be allocated, and may invoke a free function when the object is no longer needed.[13] Note that since the program's execution flow may not be discernible by the translator, the translator cannot know the lifetimes of the programmer-controlled objects appearing within the program. Therefore, all allocations related to user-controlled objects must be made during program execution.

The position of a dynamic object D allocated by the run-time allocator cannot be known when the program is translated. Therefore, the translator cannot replace a reference to D by a static address. Rather, access to D must be made through an access object A that contains a pointer to the actual space allocated for D. The programmer must write statements that request the allocation for D and then place the returned pointer in A. Afterward, the programmer accesses D indirectly through the access object A.

Example 4-4

In Ada the size of a programmer-allocated object is defined by its type and the pool selection is implementation dependent. One way to request space allocation is to execute the Ada run-time allocation statement

```
⟨pointer⟩:= new ⟨data_type⟩;
```

Note that no parentheses surround the data_type name, despite the fact that that name is used like a parameter of the allocation request. In the following program fragment the assignment statement allocates a new instance of the object type bead:

```
type bead is
  record
    a : integer;
    b : real;
    c : character;
  end record;
```

[13]In Section 4.2 we saw that the explicit free may not be required in some situations.

```
type ba is access bead;
ptr : ba;
..
ptr:=new bead;
```

The single parameter of the allocate request is a type name; this name defines the space required to hold a representation of an instance of an object of that type, and therefore the amount of space to be allocated. Parameterized type names can be used to specify varying similar objects. Therefore, the actual discriminant values for a variant object type must be specified in the **new** allocation request, as in

```
type arr(n : integer) is array(1 .. n) of integer;
type accessarr is access arr;
this : accessarr;
..
this:=new arr(9);
```

A similar example using record variant discriminants is illustrated in Problem 4-15.

Example 4-5

In PL/1 a new instance of an object is created by executing a statement like

```
ALLOCATE RECORD TYPE IN AREA A SET POINTER;
```

The type name TYPE specifies the type of the object to be placed in the space that will be allocated (the type information implies the amount of space required for the object). The area name A specifies the pool (which had been declared as a vector) from which space for the object is to be allocated. The name POINTER in the SET clause states which pointer should be set to point to the new object.

At the end of an object's lifetime, the programmer may request object deallocation by calling the "free" procedure with (a) parameter(s) describing the space to be deallocated.

Example 4-6

Ada semantics imply that a user-controlled object created by **new** should continue to exist as long as the object or one of its components can be denoted by a name. This rule defines the timing of automatic deallocation actions that may be performed by the system. A programmer can instantiate an instance of the generic procedure UNCHECKED_DEALLOCATION and then call that instance to deallocate an object. Consider this program fragment:

```
type T is ..;
type aT is access T;
procedure freeT is new unchecked_deallocation(T, aT);
                                      --See footnote14
b : aT;
..
b:=new T;  --allocate an instance of T
..
freeT(b);            --deallocate the instance
```

[14]The two parameters specified here are the actual values of the generic parameters of the procedure template unchecked_deallocation. The instantiated procedure (here called free) has only one parameter of the type of the second generic parameter.

Note that the deallocation procedure is instantiated for the specific object type that will be explicitly deallocated. Upon a call to the freeT procedure that is produced by this instantiation, the system may[15] free the object even though there might exist another locator describing the object being deallocated;[16] that is why the word "unchecked" appears in the name of the generic procedure.

The possibility that there might exist a pointer to an object which has been deallocated can cause programming errors that can be difficult to detect. These remaining pointers are called *dangling pointers*; they can be used to access space that might have been reallocated for another object. If the dangling pointer is used to assign a new value to the object, something else will seem to change "magically!" Although it would be useful to detect whether dangling pointers are going to be left as a result of deallocation, the overhead cost for the management structures needed to find dangling pointers is quite high. Writers of language descriptions may say that a program using a dangling pointer is an illegal program, but there is no cheap way that this error can be caught by an implementation.

The LISP programming language, in which list data structures play an important role, provides for list creation and reassignment of pointer values in the course of list manipulation. It is possible that a list becomes inaccessible as a result of making an assignment that breaks the only accessing path by which the list could be reached. Due to speed considerations, the implementation of the assignment operation cannot be burdened with checking whether an old pointer that is overwritten is actually the last accessible pointer to another object. Therefore, the memory in a LISP system quickly becomes filled with old lists ("garbage") which have to be purged from the system to refresh the free space pool.

A high-level language programmer specifies object lifetimes through the positions of the declarations and through explicit calls to system functions that allocate or free space. In succeeding sections we see how these semantics can be supported in the system's implementation.

4.4 SYSTEM-CONTROLLED ALLOCATION IN PROCESSES AND HIGH-LEVEL LANGUAGES

The implementation of a high-level language must perform hidden (in the sense that the programmer need not be concerned about them) run-time allocations. Also, it must support calls to the memory allocator for user-controlled object allocation. The hidden allocations provide space for:

1. The process
2. The program
3. Static objects
4. Automatic objects

[15]The Ada specification states that the implementation has the option to reclaim any space automatically deallocated, but that it is not required to do so.

[16]If such a "dangling" locator is used to attempt an access to an object, the program is in error. (Many implementations will not detect such an error.)

In this section we explore design options for these allocations. We find stack allocations useful for parameters and automatic objects and process-private spaces useful for static objects. Finally, we show sample processor instruction sequences which invoke these important allocation functions.

4.4.1 Process-Level Allocations

Informally, a process is the execution of a program.[17] The system must provide memory space for use during the execution of each process. This includes space for the program itself, space for its static objects, and space for its dynamic objects. In addition, the process may require a space pool within which programmer-controlled objects could be allocated during program execution. In the following, we refer to this space pool as the heap, since heap management will be required, the lifetime relationships of the allocated objects being unknown.

If the processor supports two-dimensional addressing, the pool allocation problem can be solved simply—allocate one segment for the static object pool, one segment for the automatic object pool, one segment for the program, and a fourth segment for the heap.

If the processor supports only one-dimensional addressing, the process can be allocated a single pool which is subdivided by allocating these individual pools contiguously from the start of the process's space pool. Figure 4-12 illustrates this division of allocation pools. Another allocation approach allocates two separate static spaces for the program and the static data, leaving a common space to be shared by the automatic object pool and the allocation heap, as shown in Figure 4-13.

The system must allocate space for individual objects within each pool. In the static pool, FDFA allocation is adequate and can be performed by the compiler/linker combination. The program space is divided up if separately compiled modules

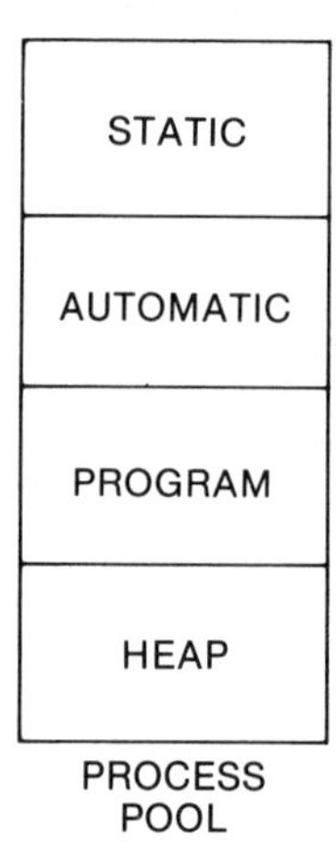

Figure 4-12 Static pool allocations

[17]This "intuitive" explanation is actually about as precise as one can get while trying to define a process. One's intuition is certainly adequate to deal with this notion.

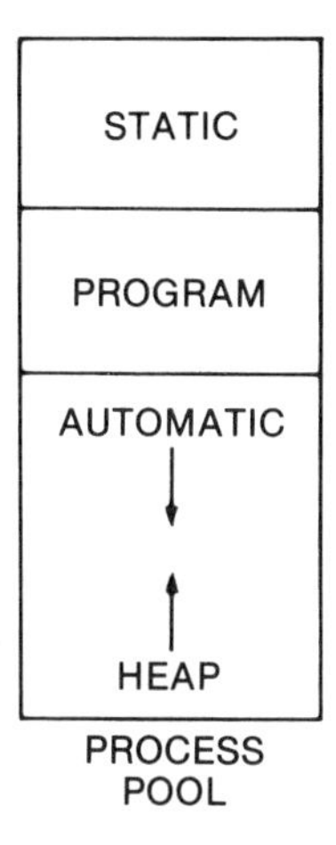

Figure 4-13 The automatic and heap pools sharing space

are combined to form the program. This breakdown cannot be ascertained until the modules are linked together. The automatic object pool is allocated during program execution using a stack discipline, as detailed in the following.

4.4.2 Allocation of Space for Automatic Objects

In a block-structured language with static nesting, an object is an automatic local object if its declaration appears in the declaration section of a procedure or a function block. An automatic local object is visible and known only during the lifetime of the activation of the program block immediately enclosing its declaration. Therefore, all objects local to a procedure or a function block have lifetimes synonymous with the lifetime of the program block, and their space can be allocated when that block is entered and freed when that block is exited. The allocation pool created in this manner is called the "activation block" for the invocation of the program block. Since lifetime of a block activation is synonymous with the lifetime of a procedure or function invocation, invocation lifetimes are nested, and stack allocation can be used

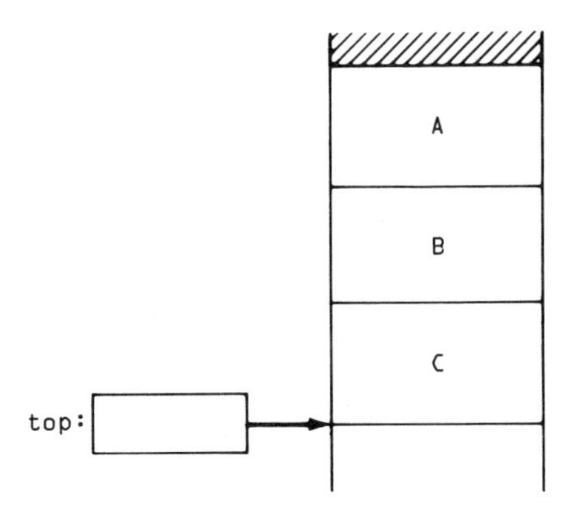

Figure 4-14 An allocation block stack

for the activation blocks. A stacked activation block structure is shown in Figure 4-14. This nested lifetime rules applies to Ada program and function blocks, but not to Ada package blocks.

To allocate an activation block, its size requirements must be determined. The size may be a constant or may depend on run-time values. If the sizes of all local objects are known at translation time, the size of the activation block can be computed by the translator and placed in the program as a constant.

Example 4-7

Consider this block heading:

```
type access_integer is access integer;
a, b, c : integer;
d, f, e : access_integer;
```

If both integers and pointers require one addressable memory unit, this block will require six locations. The compiler can place the constant "6" in the object program to denote the block length.

The size of a dynamic block cannot be determined during program translation. Thus, rather than placing the value of the block size into the program, the compiler generates instructions to compute the required space and places them at the procedure's entry point. The basic procedure calling scenario includes the following steps:

1. Save the TOS and the activation block pointer;
2. Copy the actual parameters to the stack;
3. CALL the procedure, updating the activation block pointer from the saved previous TOS;
4. Adjust TOS to allocate space for automatic objects;
5. Perform the procedure;
6. On completion, (a) deallocate automatic objects, and restore the TOS and activation block pointers to their saved values; then (b) push the procedure's result (if any) onto the stack.

Step 4 constitutes the procedure's "prologue," which includes computing the size of the activation block. Step 6a constitutes the procedure's "epilogue."

Example 4-8

```
procedure m(n : integer) is
  c : array(1 .. n) of integer;   --This is not Ada
begin
  ..
```

Here the array c is dynamically dimensioned based on the actual value of the parameter n. If the activation block contains both parameters and local objects, it requires n + 1 locations.

We have identified two allocation problems requiring further study: allocation for parameters and allocation for the activation block itself.

4.4.2.1 Allocations for parameters. Since the lifetime of all parameters matches the lifetime of the procedure invocation, the parameters can be grouped into a block whose lifetime matches the lifetime of the activation block. This observation shows the similarity with the activation block, and elicits the question, "How do we relate the placement of the parameters to the placement of the local objects?" There are two options:

1. Merge the parameters into the activation block.
2. Separate the parameters from the activation block.

Figure 4-15 illustrates the difference between these two options. The activation block and the parameter block shown are both associated with the same procedure call. The reader can see that the basic procedure calling scenario given above is consistent with the first allocation option and is not consistent with the second allocation option. We will detail both options by describing one machine design supporting each option. The Burroughs B5700 design [HAUC68] merges the parameters with the automatic objects, whereas the HP3000 [HEWL73] keeps the two groups separated.

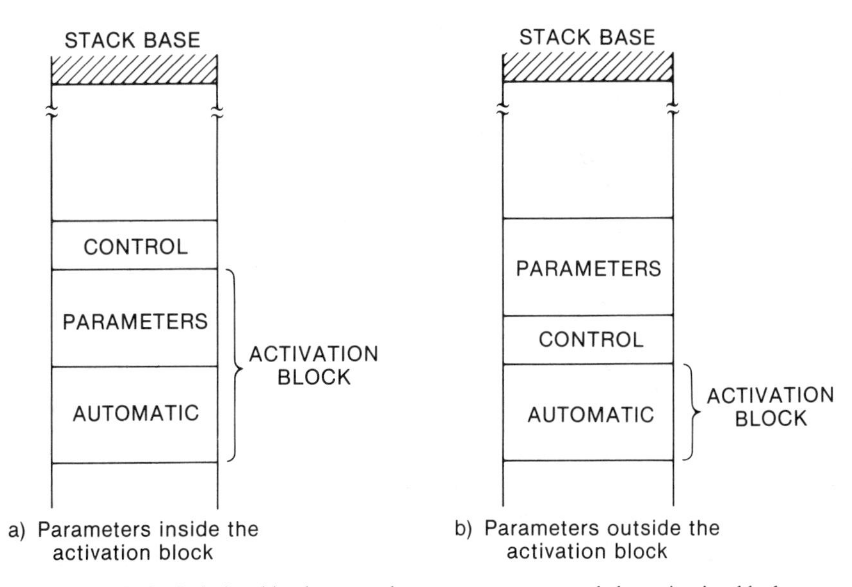

Figure 4-15 Relationships between the parameter space and the activation block

Example 4-9

In the Burroughs B5700 machines ([HAUC68], [ORGA73]) a single stack is used for saving the procedure call state, for procedure parameters, for activation blocks, and for storing temporary operand values and the results of operand manipulations. Every memory word (of 48 bits) has an additional 3-bit tag whose value distinguishes data objects and control words of various types.[18] The bottom of each activation block is marked by a control word of type "mark stack control word" (MSCW). During execution of the called procedure, the MSCW, along with the next word, holds saved processor state and stack state information. Immediately above this state information are the called procedure's parameters. The local objects used during the execution of the called procedure are located above the parameters. This structure is illustrated in Figure 4-16a.

The procedure calling steps that establish this stack structure are:

1. Save the TOS;
2. Push the actual parameters;
3. Perform the CALL;
4. Allocate space for the local objects.

To detail the B5700 implementation, we first describe the control words that play key roles in the implementation. The following declarations describe the fields within each of the three control words:

```
type stuff_flag is (unstuffed, stuffed);
type INDIRECT_REFERENCE_WORD(stuflag : stuff_flag) is
                                        --also called
                                        --IRW (stuflag = unstuffed)
                                        --SIRW (stuflag = stuffed)
  record
    case stuflag is
      when unstuffed =>
        level : integer;
      when stuffed =>
        stack_no : integer;
        block_base : index;
    end case;
    offset : index;
  end record;
type MARK_STACK_CONTROL_WORD is      --also called MSCW
  record
    active : boolean;                --true if program is active
    different_stack : boolean;
    stack_no : integer;
    block_base : index;              --points to statically
                                     --containing block
    level : integer;                 --of called procedure
    offset : integer;                --location (relative to here)
                                     --of preceding MSCW on stack
  end record;
```

[18]In figures we depict the tag value to the left of the accompanying word.

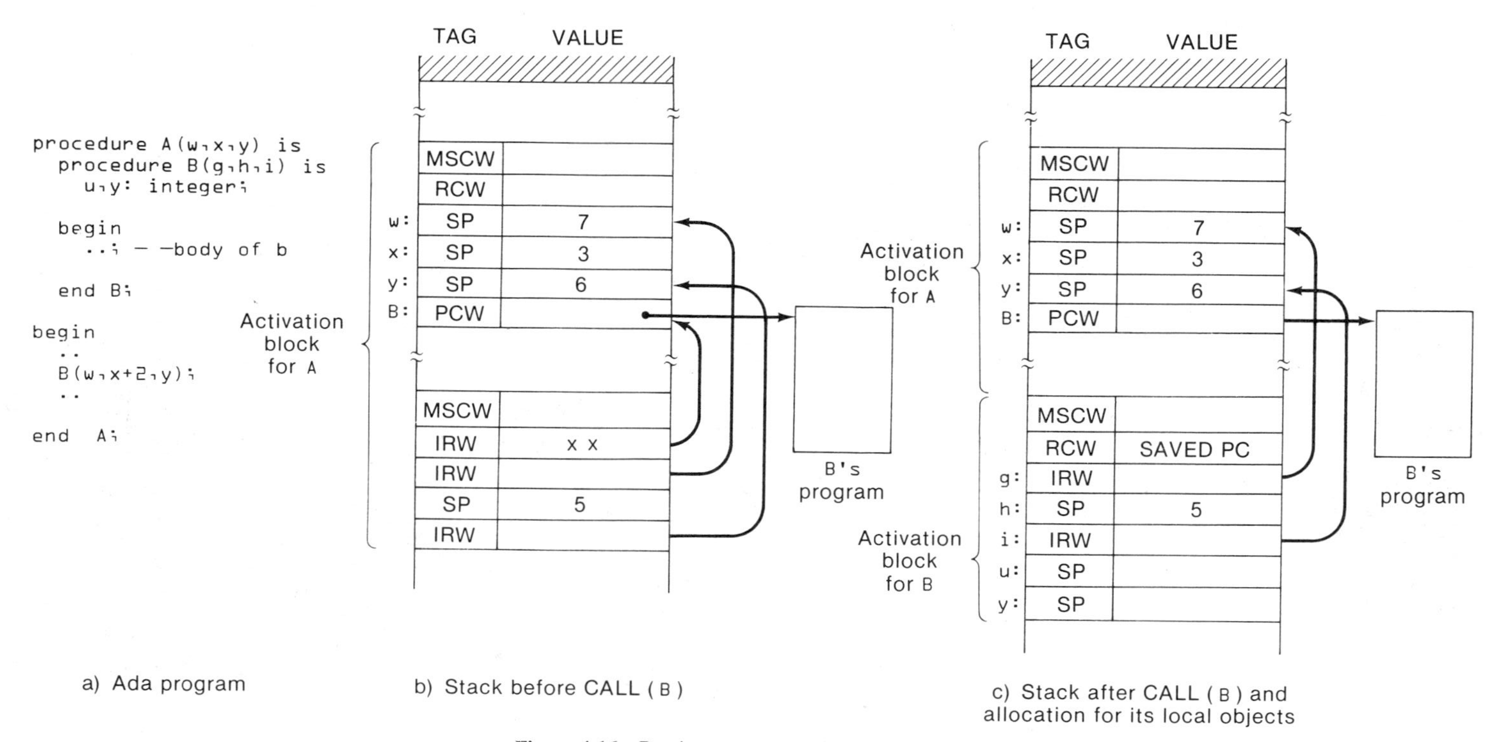

Figure 4-16 Passing parameters in a stack (B5700)

```
type RETURN_CONTROL_WORD is          --also called RCW
  record
    p_status : bits;                 --processor status bits
    p_counter : seg_address          --return point
    level : integer;                 --of caller
  end record;
```

The four types MSCW, RCW, IRW/SIRW, and PCW (see below) have different tag values. The stuflag that distinguishes between an IRW and a SIRW is located in the word. With one parameter passed by value, the calling sequence looks like

```
MARKSTACK
LOADNAME (entry point)
LOADVALUE (parameter) --repeat to load more parameters
ENTER
```

Step 1: TOS saving occurs during execution of the instruction MARKSTACK, which places a tagged Mark Stack Control Word (MSCW) on the top of the stack. The new MSCW is loaded with the difference between the present top of the stack and the previous value stored in the processor's F register. This difference will be used to restore F upon return from the procedure. The F register is set to point to the new MSCW. Thus the F register is the head of a list of all MSCWs on the stack.[19] The new MSCW is marked "inactive," meaning that it is ready for use in a procedure call that has not yet been executed.

Step 2: The next step is a LOADNAME instruction which pushes on the stack an indirect reference word (IRW) describing the pointer to the entry point being called. The pointer placed on the stack points to a "Program Control Word" (PCW) which itself contains a pointer to the entry point. This data structure (see Figure 4-16b) will be used to establish the naming environment for the called procedure, as detailed in Section 5.4; the use of a pointer to the entry point has no connection with space allocation issues.

Step 3: Push the actual parameters on the stack. This step may entail many processor instructions to evaluate the actual parameter values;[20] these details do not affect allocation. Figure 4-16b illustrates the stack structure after the parameter values have been pushed (just before ENTER is executed). In the figure XX denotes the PCW describing the entry point.

Step 4: The ENTER instruction is executed. During this instruction, the processor performs many actions to support the allocation, accessing, and naming of local objects, in addition to several control actions. The important allocation activity is the creation of a new activation block, which is effected by activating the topmost MSCW. Certain accessing control structures and the naming environment are updated; this activity is discussed in Section 5.4. One control activity saves the program counter in the word above the MSCW, changing this PCW into an RCW ("Return Control Word"); it also places the level of the calling program in the RCW. Finally, the program counter is set to the entry instruction of the called procedure (found by evaluating the indirect address that was in the IRW above the MSCW).

[19] Since the list is chained using relative locations, it can survive stack relocation.

[20] In fact, parameter evaluation may itself require procedure calls.

Since the MSCW occupies location 0 of the activation block, the MSCW, the RCW, and the procedure's parameters are all accessible as local objects in the new block. The local objects are also located in this block, above the parameters. Because the control information (the MSCW and the RCW) occupies two entries, the first parameter[21] is located at block address 2.

There is no run-time check to guarantee that a procedure does not modify the control information at the beginning of the block; the system requires correct programs. Therefore, the B5700 follows the "nothing illegal" design philosophy.

Procedure return is easily accomplished; to return the procedure executes the EXIT operator, which deallocates the top of the stack back to the topmost MSCW and restores the saved processor state so that the calling program can be resumed. The RETURN operator is used to return a result; RETURN behaves like EXIT but retains the value at the top of the stack during its execution. Thus the value last pushed on the stack by the called procedure is the result that it leaves at the top of the stack when control returns to its caller.

Example 4-10

Suppose that a function call is required to evaluate a subroutine parameter. This function call is straightforward under the B5700 mechanism, but it will leave an inactive MSCW within the stack during the execution of the function that evaluates the parameter. In particular, consider the call

```
f(x, g(y));
```

where both f and g are functions. Following the B5700 subroutine calling scenario, the MSCW, IRW, and first parameter for f's call are stacked and then g is called. Thus the configuration shown in Figure 4-17 exists during the execution of procedure g. Notice that the topmost MSCW is active, since g has been called, but the MSCW beneath it is inactive, since f is yet to be called.

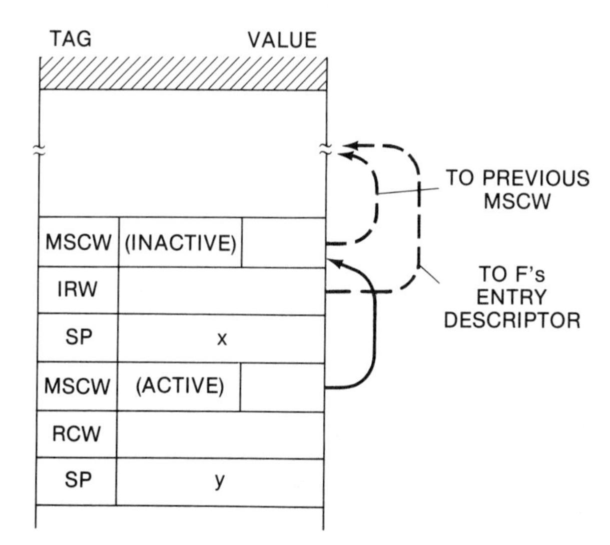

Figure 4-17 The B5700 stack during a function called to evaluate a procedure parameter (Example 4-10)

[21]Or local object, if there are no parameters.

Example 4-11

The HP3000 activation block format separates a procedure's parameters from its automatic objects, with the parameters stacked beneath the new activation block (see Figure 4-18). The procedure calling steps have to be ordered differently from the B5700; for the HP3000 they are:

1. Copy the actual parameters to the stack;
2. CALL the procedure, saving the processor's state and the stack block pointer and then updating the stack block pointer from the TOS;
3. Allocate space for the automatic objects;
4. Execute the called procedure;
5. On return, restore the TOS to the beginning of the parameter block;

Step 2 is performed by executing the processor instruction PCAL fentry (the operand is the address of the instruction at the entry point). During the PCAL instruction the processor state is saved (see Figure 4-18) and a pointer to the location holding the saved state is captured in a processor register.

A similar allocation is used in the HP9000 Series 500 system [OSEC84].

Comparing the B5700 design with the HP3000 design, we see that the HP3000 design allows the caller to push parameter values before saving any state; this removes the need for inactive state-holding words. On the other hand, the HP3000 must support more addressing modes, making its implementation more complex.

4.4.2.2 Allocation for the activation block.

There are three ways that the space for the activation block could be obtained upon procedure entry. First, initial values for all local objects could be pushed onto the stack. Second, the TOS pointer could be changed to allocate space without initializing it. And third, the CALL instruction could acquire the space for the called procedure. Pushing initial values onto a stack is straightforward, so we do not discuss it here.

Changing the TOS pointer to grab stack space is simple and easily implemented; it is not very pleasing from the language point of view, since all local objects will have initial values that are residues from previous activity. Nevertheless, this technique is used in many systems. In the B5700, the program could simply add an integer to the TOS, replacing the TOS value with the sum. The Data General Eclipse provides a catchall operation:

Example 4-12

The Eclipse operation SAVE [DATA74] has a single integer parameter, which is the amount of space to be allocated for local objects. This value is found in the program in the word following the SAVE instruction (placing the value in the program makes it inconvenient to deal with dynamically allocated spaces). The operation first saves the processor registers on the stack and then increments the stack pointer by the parameter's value. The SAVE instruction thereby incorporates the procedure's prologue functions; it is the first instruction executed at the entry to the procedure.

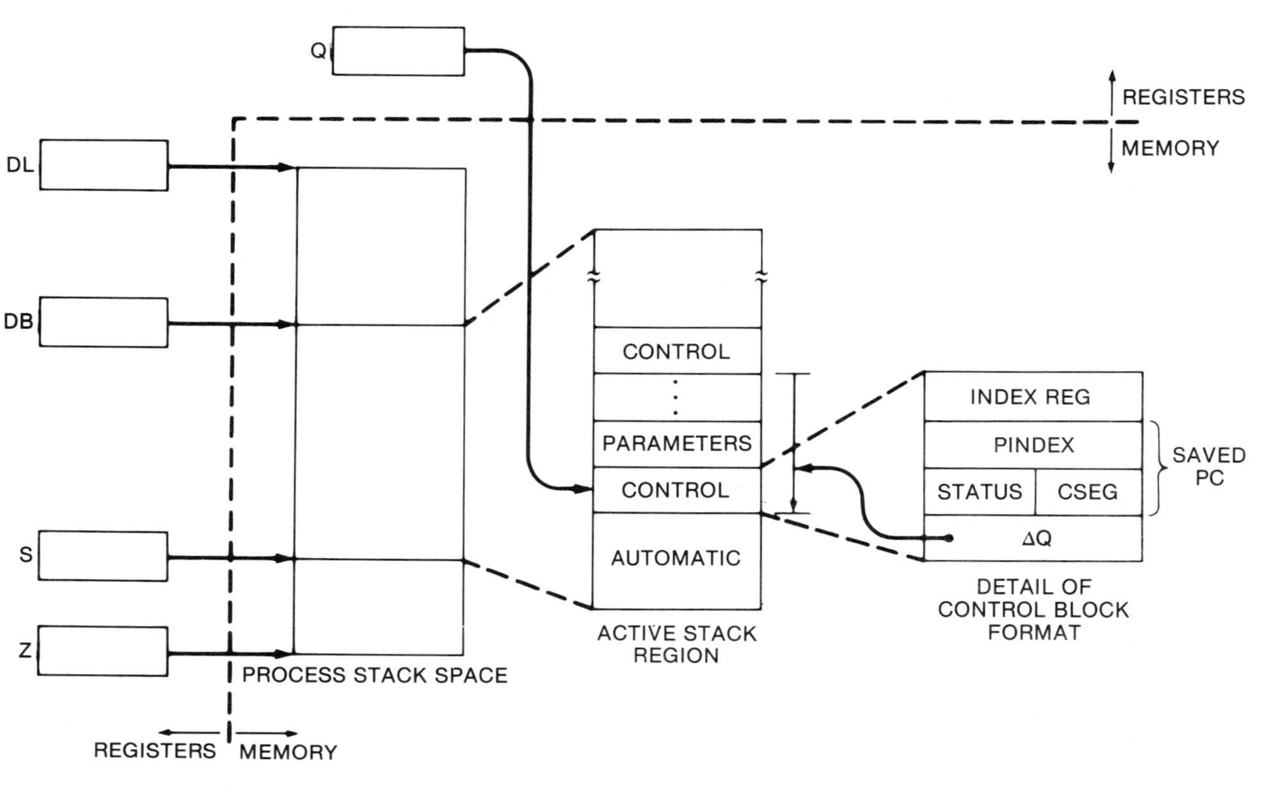

Figure 4-18 HP3000 stack format. After [HEWL73] © Copyright 1973, Hewlett-Packard Company. Reproduced with permission.

The third way that the automatic space for a procedure's invocation could be allocated is to perform the allocation during the CALL operation. This is the approach used in the IBM System/38.

Example 4-13

In the IBM System/38, each procedure or function entry point has several attributes. One of these specifies the amount of automatic storage that the invocation will require. During the CALL instruction that invokes the procedure, the processor acquires the stated amount of stack space.

We see that a stack mechanism provides a uniform way to pass parameters and to define local storage space for each procedure. The two actions are interdependent; the design choice affects the stack management mechanism and the call and return actions.

4.4.3 Space Allocation within the Activation Block

Space within the activation block must be allocated for each automatic object declared within the program text. If the sizes of all of the local objects are known at compile time, this allocation can be performed by the compiler. An Ada compiler can perform this object allocation, since the type of each object must be declared in the program text, and every Ada type declaration implies a size specification. What allocation strategy should be used within the activation block?

The first-declared-first-allocated policy can be used to allocate individual local objects. Another option collects together all objects having the same base type, allocating these groups on a FDFA basis and the space within each group in a similar manner.

Example 4-14

The following fragment contains all local object declarations for a parameterless procedure.

```
a : integer;
b : real;
c : integer;
type rec is
  record
    d, e : integer;
    f : real;
  end record;
g, h : rec;
k : real;
```

Suppose that each integer takes one addressable unit and each real object takes two addressable units. The object allocations, relative to the beginning of the activation block, for overall FDFA and type-based object grouping, with FDFA allocations of the spaces for each type and FDFA within the single-type type spaces are shown in Table 4-2 and Figure 4-19.

TABLE 4-2 LOCAL ADDRESSES (HEX) FOR ALLOCATIONS UNDER TWO ALLOCATION POLICIES

Object Name	Allocation Scheme: FDFA	Allocation Scheme: Type Grouped
a	0	0
b	1	2
c	3	1
g.d	4	6
g.e	5	7
g.f	6	8
h.d	8	A
h.e	9	B
h.f	A	C
k	C	4

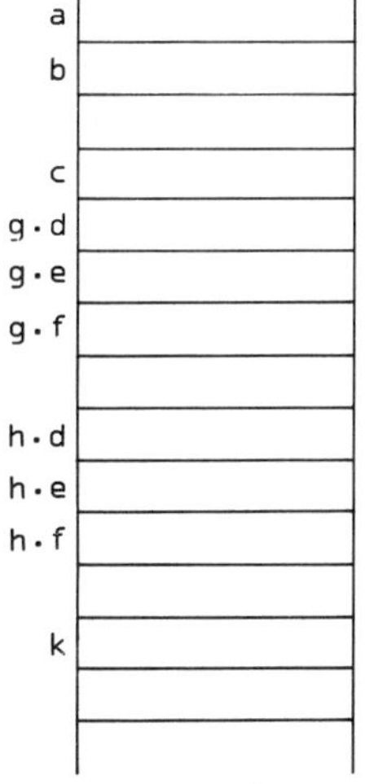

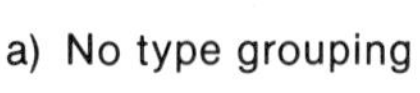

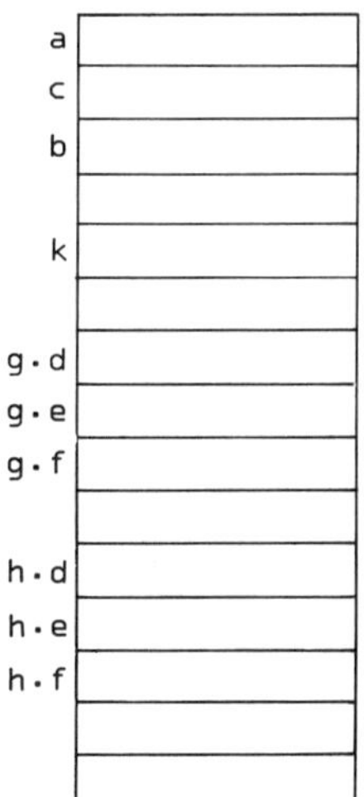

b) Type-based grouping

Figure 4-19 Two allocations in an activation block (Example 4-14 and Table 4-2)

If the activation block contains an object whose size is dynamically determined, such as an array with data-dependent dimensions,[22] the block allocation problem is more complex. Assume that FDFA allocation is used and at run time the system computes the actual object sizes. The size of an object X affects the sizes of all objects allocated space beyond X. Suppose, for example, that three objects n, x(10), and y are declared. If each component or simple object occupies one address, the addresses of the objects within the block are 0, 1, and 11, respectively. Notice that y's address

[22]Data-dependent allocations cannot be specified in Ada through a static object declaration; the language was designed so that all static objects within the block can be allocated during compilation.

is fixed by the compiler and that the compiler can place y's location in the instruction(s) that access y.

Now suppose that we have three objects declared as n, x(n), and y. The object y is located at address (n + 1) within the block. Since the value of (n + 1) cannot be known during program translation, the translator cannot put the address of y as a direct reference in any instruction. This example has only a single dynamically sized object, so the translator could circumvent the difficulty by allocating x in the last part of the automatic block. This strategy decouples all object addresses from the size of x.

We cannot decouple object addresses from the allocations and insert direct object addresses into instructions if the block contains more than one object whose size is dynamic. If the block contains several dynamically sized objects the statically declared objects cannot be allocated contiguous locations in a fixed manner. It is possible to avoid this difficulty by allocating all dynamically sized objects in a separate region, reserving the statically allocated region for statically sized objects. An access variable (locator) would be used to access each dynamically-sized object; since the size of the access variable is fixed, one corresponding to each dynamically sized object could be statically allocated with the static objects and used to access the dynamically sized objects indirectly.

Example 4-15

```
procedure sample(a : integer;
    b : array (1 .. a) of integer) is --Not Ada
  d : integer;
  e, f : array (1 .. a) of integer;    --Not Ada
  ..
```

This procedure heading specifies one dynamically dimensioned array (b) passed in as a parameter and two dynamically dimensioned automatic arrays (e and f). Assume that this procedure is going to be executed in a B5700 addressing environment, with the procedure parameters included within the local address block. If the translator used FDFA allocation, disregarding whether an object is dynamically sized or not, the objects would be allocated space in accordance with the name map shown in Table 4-3.

TABLE 4-3 THE FIRST ALLOCATION FOR EXAMPLE 4-15

Name	Origin
a	2
b	3
d	3 + a
e	4 + a
f	4 + 2*a

Notice that some addresses depend on the value of a, which cannot be known until the program is executed.

If the compiler allocates all dynamically dimensioned arrays at the end of the block and uses access variables to locate them, the locators can be placed in fixed locations, as indicated in Table 4-4. This arrangement is depicted in Figure 4-20.

TABLE 4-4 ALLOCATION FOR EXAMPLE 4-15 USING LOCATORS POINTING TO DYNAMIC ARRAYS

Name	Location	Contents
a	2	value
b	3	locator to 7
d	4	value
e	5	locator to 7 + a
f	6	locator to 7 + 2*a
—	7	first component of b
—	7 + a	first component of e
—	7 + 2*a	first component of f

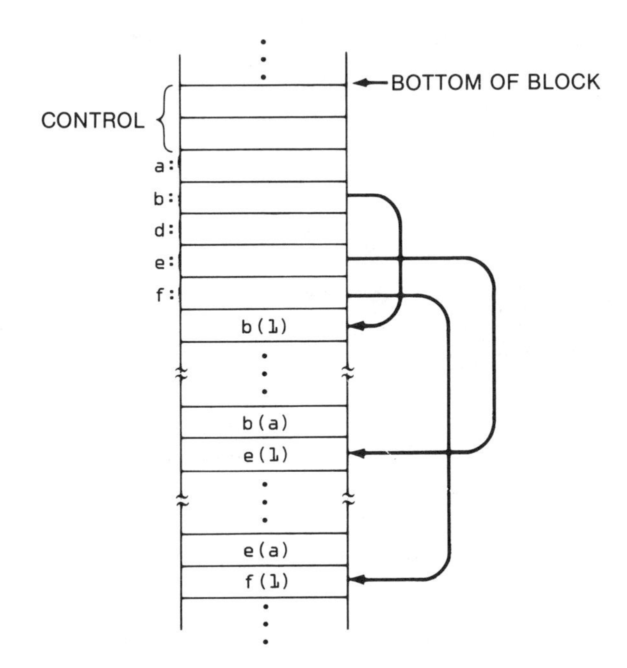

Figure 4-20 An activation block allocation with dynamic arrays (Example 4-15)

4.4.4 Summary

We have seen how an executing program acquires space for the objects that it must have present for proper execution. Static objects, automatic objects, dynamically sized objects, and user-controlled objects all require space. Some of these spaces can be acquired automatically by expanding the instruction semantics to make the desired allocations.

4.5 OPERATING SYSTEM MEMORY ALLOCATION

A computer system serving many processes simultaneously must efficiently allocate its resources, including its memory, to those processes. In this section we discuss memory management performed by the operating system. The operating system's memory management algorithms must be able to respond to uncertain situations unless the particular programs to be executed are known a priori. We will see that the system may have to relocate programs and data. We will see how the system can automatically allocate, free, and relocate user programs and data while leaving the user unaware of this underlying activity (this invisibility requires system support for run-time reinterpretation of addresses; see Chapter 5). As a side effect of this automatic activity, the operating system manipulates the lifetimes of its space allocations, thereby providing better service to the collection of users.

We present several space allocation policies for user program and data objects. First we present a static allocation policy and discover some of its inherent problems. Then we present the dynamic policies preferred in many environments.

4.5.1 Static Allocation Policies

The argument against a static allocation policy can easily be made from two cases. We hasten to point out that the arguments against static allocation may not apply to a particular situation. As we shall see in the sequel, static allocation can be useful in a deterministic environment, among others.

Under the first static allocation policy, the system allocates space for every program beginning at the same address A. To switch from process X to process Y, the information for process X has to be moved out of the way and that of process Y put in its place. The information for only a single process can occupy main memory at one time, and that information must be removed from main memory each time the operating system wishes to swap from one process to another. This static allocation policy suffers because the space allocations of all processes overlap.

The second static allocation policy overcomes this problem by assigning a different origin to each process in such a manner that the memory spaces of any pair of processes do not overlap. To do this well, one should know which programs will be sharing memory. With a static mapping policy, all allocation decisions are made before program execution begins. If the a priori policy decisions fix process scheduling, compatible memory allocations may be fixed a priori. Alternatively, this strategy could be used on groups of processes selected such that all members of one process group share the same block of space. Under this group allocation policy, at most one process from each group can occupy memory at any time instant. So to make the allocations we must know which program will be present during which time interval. Problem 4-18 discusses this situation in detail.

A static space allocation policy may be attractive for a dedicated application. In this case all program modules are known a priori and can be assigned memory space before execution. The interplay between scheduling and allocation can be avoided if the execution intervals of all program modules are known beforehand. Both a static execution schedule and a static memory allocation can be determined in this special situation.

4.5.2 Dynamic Allocation Policies

The need for a priori knowledge to attain a reasonable static allocation is an important constraint. What can the designer do if the usage environment is unpredictable? A static allocation is not likely to be attractive. As designers, we must devise effective dynamic allocation policies. We will also need efficient support mechanisms, for without support mechanisms we will see that the implementation of a dynamic allocation policy can be truly expensive! We should be on the alert for a system design that permits the software designer to implement a range of different policies efficiently. By concentrating on gross properties of candidate policies, we may be able to select a small set of dynamic allocation policies for which we can provide low-level support in the system design.

We discussed static allocation assuming that the memory space for each individual program was allocated as a single contiguous memory space. Alternatively, the system could allocate main memory space for only a portion of all memory space required for the complete execution of the program module, *provided* that the system contains a mechanism which hides this partial allocation from the programmer. Such a design hides the system's memory allocation decisions from the programmer.

Detailed policy options depend on whether the dynamic relocation and address mapping mechanisms support partial allocations. In our discussion we refer to these broad classes of mapping techniques in terms of the information present or absent. Our phrases are:

1. All information must be present.
2. Some information may be absent.

If all information must be present for a process to execute its program, the allocation strategies are trivial—all information must be loaded in main memory before the process can be executed. All the information can be dumped after process completion.

A scheme allowing absent information can be economical for two reasons:

1. Processes reference memory in patterns.
2. Cheaper, slow memory devices can be used for secondary memory, where the system can allocate space to hold information not present in the expensive, fast main memory.

If a process references only the fraction of its memory allocated to main memory, its execution speed will not be affected by the absence of the unreferenced information. There will be slight slowdowns due to occasional requests to access the inaccessible information. Thus the absence of the information may not affect speed significantly. But this design does reduce cost since secondary memory space is cheaper than primary memory space. So we have a cheaper system that can execute programs almost as fast as an expensive system, with enough fast memory to hold all the information for each process. We amplify these points before turning to specific memory allocation schemes allowing absent information.

Memory management policies allowing absent information perform well because most programs possess referencing locality, in the sense that in most program executions the memory references tend to be limited to a small set of objects while the program executes within a small region, such as a loop body. On a larger scale, locality occurs because each program module is specialized, accessing only those objects required to perform its function. The set of objects accessed while the program remains within a local region will be a small subset of the set of all objects accessible from the program. This observation can be phrased in terms of the continuity of the program's behavior, as in this statement:

Principle of Locality. The referencing behavior of a process in the near future is likely to be similar to the referencing pattern it exhibited in the recent past; furthermore, this property is true at almost all times during the execution of the process.

Locality has two aspects: temporal locality and spatial locality. Temporal locality suggests that the near future will be similar to the recent past. Spatial locality suggests that in a typical short time interval the number of objects that a large program will access will constitute a small fraction of the total space accessible to the program. Spatial locality is closely related to temporal locality because time continuity suggests that the set of objects accessed recently is similar to the set of objects about to be accessed. In other words, those objects that are accessed are accessed during a significant time interval, which means that they are accessed to the exclusion of other objects in the program's address space.

It is extremely important to realize that locality is a statistical property, not a certainty. In particular, our goal is statistically good behavior, which does not imply good behavior for each individual program that might be executed on the system. Certainly there will be exceptions—processes whose referencing patterns are problematical for the memory allocation scheme being used; such processes will exhibit poor performance. Their existence does not invalidate any statistical claims about locality or performance made for the allocation scheme. Any system design that is based on a statistical property of the environment may perform poorly on a specific program under a specific memory management policy, but this limited observation cannot be used to argue that the policy is bad. A valid statistical evaluation must be based on a sufficiently large, diverse set of observations.

The *reference string* concept is useful while discussing program referencing behavior. The reference string is a sequence of symbols denoting the sequence of memory addresses (or address blocks) actually accessed by the executing program. The reference string is a dynamic property of the program's execution. It cannot be determined effectively before the program begins execution, because the outcomes of data-dependent control decisions cannot be known beforehand.

To aid the visualization of locality patterns, consider Figure 4-21, which presents another depiction of a reference string. To construct the figure, a spot is placed at position (a, t) if an access to address a was made at time t. The fine resolution of the figure might make it difficult to see large-scale trends. To show these patterns better, construct a similar figure, but change the resolution to blocks of addresses and

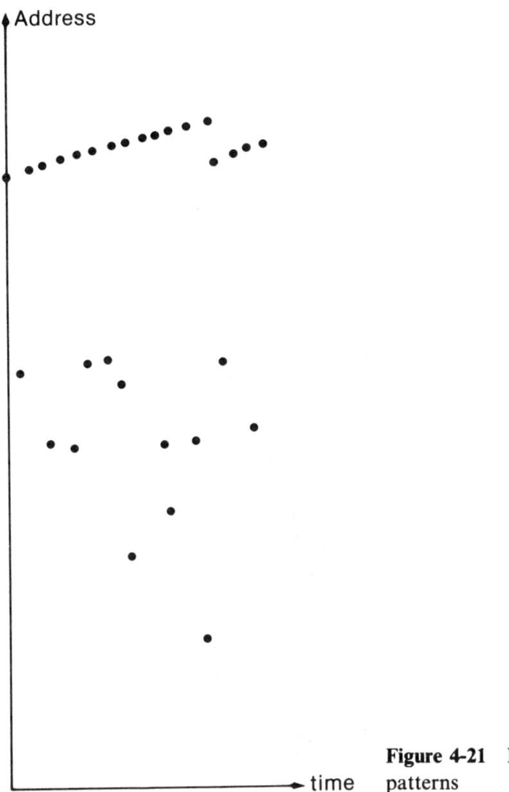

Figure 4-21 Memory referencing patterns

blocks of memory accesses. In Figure 4-22 a spot indicates that at least one reference to the corresponding block of addresses was made within the corresponding block of accesses. The figure depicts the referencing pattern of an actual program. Notice the strong patterns of blank spaces. A blank region indicates that the information in a memory block M was not referenced during a time block T. During T, M need not be present in main memory, because its absence will not affect execution of the program's instructions during T.

Referencing locality is one reason that allocation schemes allowing absent information are successful. The second reason is that memory devices can be arranged in a hierarchy based on cost and speed. The highest cost and performance memory occupies the top of the hierarchy. ECL memory, which is very fast and expensive, is at the top of the hierarchy of contemporary technologies. MOS memory is not as fast and not as expensive as ECL memory. The progression continues with magnetic disks and then magnetic tapes; each successive memory device is slower and less expensive than its predecessors. Information not needed in the fastest (primary) memory can be moved to slower (secondary) memory, where it can be stored less expensively.

We have set the stage for our discussion of operating system memory management—programs exhibit locality and memories form hierarchies. We are ready to

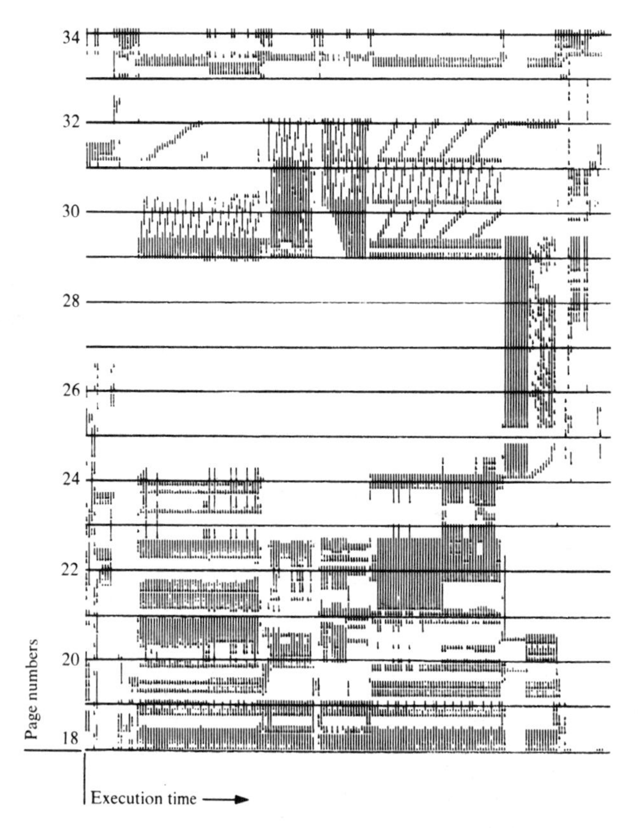

Figure 4-22 Locality referencing patterns (from [HATF72]). Copyright 1972 by International Business Machines Corporation; reprinted with permission.

turn to policy issues concerning memory hierarchy management. The designer of a dynamic relocation policy must define how the mechanism makes three important decisions:

1. *Loading*: when to load information in main memory
2. *Placement*: where to locate information being loaded
3. *Replacement*: when to replace information in main memory

Replacement is tightly coupled with placement; after all, if the system always had a place available, it would never have to replace any object! In some dynamic allocation schemes, loading and/or placement are trivial decisions; on the other hand, replacement decisions are difficult under most schemes. To make better allocation decisions, a system can be designed to collect usage information, including:

1. What objects were accessed
2. What objects were modified

By knowing which objects have been accessed, the operating system can better decide which information should be present in main memory. Further, if the system keeps track of which objects have been modified, and if it keeps a shadow copy of main memory within secondary memory, an unmodified main memory block can be discarded without copying it out to secondary memory when its space is to be reused. To determine which objects have been modified, the supporting (hardware) mechanism sets a modified (or "dirty") bit when the associated space is modified. Eventually, the system will copy each modified object to secondary memory and clear the associated dirty bit. This memory cleaning could be performed speculatively, that is, in anticipation of space needs. Such speculative behavior might improve system performance simply because it reduces the probability that a load request will require swapping out a dirty object before the desired object can be loaded. There is, however, a cost for speculative swapping because the swapping consumes bandwidth in the primary memory–secondary memory data path and because the memory references for swapping contend with memory references for program execution.

Now we are ready to face the important allocation decisions that the operating system's memory allocator must make. The first decision concerns the time when a block of information is loaded into main memory. We know that the memory management system must allow absent information and that the memory manager requires a nontrivial loading policy. Two important loading options are: (1) anticipatory loading (a block is loaded before actually being needed); and (2) demand loading (a block is loaded only when an access to one of its members is actually attempted). In a static (dedicated) environment, the process schedule might be predetermined so that anticipatory loading could be useful. In a dynamic (general-purpose) environment, however, the process schedule and the memory needs are not known a priori, so demand loading is always used. Memory management policies with demand loading differ only in their placement and dumping policies.

In the following sections we face the two remaining allocation decisions: placement and replacement. We emphasize the design of a general-purpose system operating in a nondedicated environment. Two important aspects of the memory allocation system concern the method for subdividing memory into allocatable units and the policy for managing these units of memory.

4.5.2.1 Memory subdivision. Memory can be subdivided into variable-length segments or fixed-length pages. A division based on segments can be related to the program's use of the memory objects contained therein. A division based on pages cannot be related to any properties of a user's program; the page-based division is made strictly for management convenience.

4.5.2.1.1 *Segmentation.* Segments have different sizes. Their lifetimes with respect to residence at a level of the memory hierarchy are not nicely related. A segment-based allocator must use a variable-sized heap allocation policy or force a queue discipline on its allocations. To use queue allocation the system forces skewed lifetimes by dumping segments from main memory as they arrive at the end of the allocator's queue. When an absent segment is accessed and must be loaded, segments at the end of the queue are dumped from main memory until there is enough free space to hold the incoming segment.

4.5.2.1.2 ***Paging.*** Pages have identical sizes; under a paging scheme the managed memory is divided into page frames of identical size, so any free page frame can satisfy any space request. Clearly, this space division is made for the benefit of the operating system; there is no reason to confine programs or data to fixed-size memory blocks. The assumptions permitting fixed-size heap allocation are satisfied by a paged system. Paging can be added beneath any existing memory system design because the accessing system can be designed so that all paging operations and manipulations are functionally transparent to all higher-level programs.

Under paging two of the three memory allocation decisions have trivial answers—a page will be loaded on demand, and it may be placed in any free page frame. To complete the design, we must select the page size(s), select the page dumping policy, and design hardware support for both statistics collection and address translation. Here we discuss page-size selection, dumping policy options, and statistics collection mechanisms. Address translation is covered in Chapter 5.

Several costs enter into the page-size question:

1. Address translation complexity
2. Page fault frequency
3. Waste data space
4. Descriptor table space

Address translation complexity is discussed in Chapter 5.

The *page fault frequency* measures the rate of occurrence of page faults, which occur when the accessing system detects that an object that is to be accessed is, in fact, absent from main memory. Upon detecting a page fault, the system causes an interrupt to invoke system software for memory allocation. The total interrupt processing overhead is proportional to the page fault frequency. How is the page fault frequency affected by the page size? There are two interesting aspects. First, if more pages were present in main memory, the fault probability would decrease. For a fixed main memory size, more pages can be present if each is smaller; this change might reduce the number of page faults, so one might conclude that the number of page faults would decrease as the page size decreases. However, with larger pages, more consecutive information will be moved to main memory on each page fault; having larger consecutive blocks should reduce the number of page faults, so one might conclude that the number of page faults would increase as the page size increases. Some statistical information concerning program behavior is required to determine the best page size.

Paging causes *waste data space* because the last page allocated to a block of contiguous virtual addresses will be partly empty if the entire page is not required to hold the end of the object. If the statistical distribution of object lengths is sufficiently random, the average amount of this "internal waste" will be one-half page per block of contiguous virtual addresses. The amount of this waste depends on the page size and the average size of contiguous blocks (measured in units of pages).

Finally, paging consumes *descriptor table space*. These tables describe the memory allocation and are used by the address translation and allocation modules.

The table space should be charged to management overhead. The amount of table space is proportional to the number of pages in the virtual address space, so the table size depends inversely on the page size. This space overhead increases with decreasing page size.

The two types of paging space costs are opposite functions of the page size—the amount of waste data space rises with increasing page size, whereas the amount of table space decreases inversely with increasing page size (assuming that the space to be described has a fixed size). The page size that minimizes the total space cost can be determined analytically if both functions are given analytically. The page size choice is not quite that simple, however, since the size choice must reflect software costs that depend on the page fault frequency.

The factors above must be balanced to determine the system's page size. How do system designers actually select the page size for a new design? Usually, they collect a set of sample programs and emulate their behavior under various page sizes. The best page size can be found at the minimum cost point. Designers have found that page sizes in the range 1024 to 4096 bytes seem best for most application environments. In the IBM 370 [IBM81b], for example, the page size can be configured to be 2048 or 4096 bytes; a software-controllable flag determines the size. For applications using vector streaming for high computational rates, much larger pages are appropriate. The CDC STAR-100 [CONT70], for example, has two page sizes: the large page size (for vector objects) is 65,536 words, or 524,288 bytes.

4.5.2.2 Memory allocation policies for paged systems. The sole memory allocation policy issue for a paged system concerns page dumping, since the loading and placement policies are trivial. The page dumping policy choice affects system performance and system complexity. Consider two disparate policies: random dumping and "expert" dumping. Random dumping is easy to implement but produces poor performance; the actual program behavior, which exhibits locality, is completely ignored by a random selector. A complex "expert" dumping policy would consume processor resources (time and hardware); it would require data collected during program execution and would give better performance than random dumping. Surely, there must exist a dumping policy that gives reasonably good performance using few statistics and few processor resources. During algorithm execution memory accessing statistics must be collected during every memory access. The policy selection question is more than just a software design issue because different statistics are needed to support different allocation policies. Only the execution machine can collect such statistics efficiently. Thus the allocation policy selection affects the hardware design.

We first discuss an idealized unrealizable "optimum" page allocation policy whose performance provides a performance limit for all allocation policies. Then we will turn to three realistic page allocation policies:

1. First-in-first-out (FIFO)
2. Least recently used (LRU)
3. Working set (WS)

All but the first require some data collection during every memory access. Data collection can be simplified if there are only a few objects to manage or a few statistics to collect. At the end of the section we describe use bit data collection, which simplifies the data collection hardware and yields approximate statistical information for the memory allocator.

4.5.2.2.1 ***Optimum Page Allocation.*** The optimum page dumping policy [BELA66] removes that page for which the time interval to its next access is the longest. It should be clear that this policy minimizes the number of page faults that will occur while the removed page is absent (because every other page that is present will be needed sooner than the removed page). The fundamental flaw in this fine policy is that it is necessary to know the program's future behavior in order to determine which page to dump. Of course, we cannot determine future page references (without running the program itself!), so this optimum policy is unrealizable. It is useful to consider the optimal policy not because it is realistic, but because it does define the best performance possible by a paged memory allocation system.

4.5.2.2.2 ***FIFO Allocation.*** The FIFO allocation policy dumps the page that has been present in memory for the longest time. The system keeps a list of page frame descriptors, ordered by the time they entered the memory. The entire memory can be managed as a circular buffer of pages, with the FIFO order being identical to the memory address ordering.

The FIFO policy is simply implemented since it does not require that any statistics be collected during program execution. Under a FIFO policy it is a simple matter to speculatively clean pages about to be dumped. Since under the FIFO policy the dumping sequence does not depend on future program behavior, the page cleaning module only has to know which pages are near the end of the queue of pages present in main memory. To effect this policy, the cleaning module maintains pointers that describe both the oldest present page and the oldest dirty page (see Problem 4-21 for details).

An intuitive justification for the FIFO policy is that it seems likely that a page that was brought in long ago is unlikely to be used again soon. Based on locality, one could argue that the oldest page is likely to be part of an old locality. Although this argument might apply to data, it applies less frequently to instructions. To be convinced, one has only to consider a program in which all the activity takes place within a loop that fits into a single page, yet accesses a lot of data in diverse pages. In this case an allocator following the FIFO policy will dump program pages periodically even though the process was continuously executing the program held in a page being dumped cyclically. One may argue also that this policy might cause the system to dump pages containing dynamically allocated activation blocks for the executing process. We know that the preceding arguments cannot be used to discard the FIFO policy, since the argument simply states that certain program behavior results in poor system performance. The argument makes no statements regarding average behavior.

Despite the simplicity of the FIFO allocation policy, systems do not use it because it performs poorly with real programs.

4.5.2.2.3 *LRU Allocation.* The principle of locality states that a process's referencing behavior in the near future will be similar to its referencing behavior in the recent past. This gives us one basis for estimating the future: measure the past. One simple statistic records, for each page, the time that it was last referenced. Recall that under the optimal allocation policy the manager dumps that page for which the time to next access is the longest. Based on the preceding interpretation of locality, the page whose next reference is furthest in the future is likely to be the page whose last reference is furthest in the past; this page is the least recently used (LRU) page in memory.

One LRU allocation problem concerns statistics collection and processing so that the allocator can find the LRU page. We discuss two options that show a trade-off between overhead expended on access and overhead expended on dumping; these are the time stamp and stack mechanisms.

Under the time stamp mechanism, during every access the current time is copied into the accessed page descriptor. When a page must be dumped, all these time stamp values are compared to find the smallest value; the corresponding page is the LRU page which should be dumped.

Alternatively, LRU data can be collected by stacking the page descriptors in order of recency of access. Whenever a page is referenced, the corresponding descriptor is moved to the top of the stack and all descriptors between the top and the previous position of the promoted one are pushed one position lower in the stack. The descriptor of the most recently used page is at the top of the stack; the bottom entry describes the least recently used page. Figure 4-23 illustrates how an LRU stack changes as references are made.

There is an obvious trade between overhead during access and overhead during allocation when one compares the time stamp and stack schemes. The time stamp

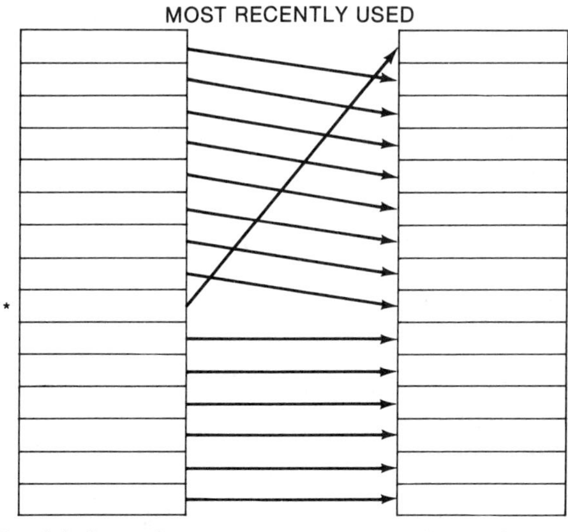

Figure 4-23 LRU motion of page descriptors. (Arrows denote motions.)

scheme has simple data collection, but the minimum value search required to make the dumping decision is difficult. The stack scheme requires complex data collection because the stack must be manipulated on every access, although finding the page to be dumped is quite simple. Hardware support for LRU page stacking was provided in the CDC STAR-100 and Cyber 205 machines; we discuss this scheme in Section 4.6.

One case is worthy of special note. If only a small number (n) of entries must be managed in an LRU fashion, a set of $n(n - 1)/2$ control bits can be used to collect LRU information; some are modified on each access and are examined to select the bottom entry on the stack. We encounter this mechanism again when we discuss cache memories in Section 5.6.2.

4.5.2.2.4 ***Working-Set Allocation.*** The working-set (WS) allocation policy [DENN70], like the LRU policy, is based on the locality assumption. Past behavior is used to make page dumping decisions. The WS policy uses a fixed window into recent memory accesses. Let W be the size of this window, measured in terms of access attempts. The WS dumping policy is to dump every page that was not accessed within the previous W access attempts. Those pages that have been accessed within the W access attempts immediately preceding time t are said to be in the program's *working set* at time t.

An exact implementation of the working-set policy requires both recording the time of access and checking the status of every page on every access attempt, since any page may leave the working set after any access. The check is made by comparing the time stamps in the page descriptors against the current time. Since there is no need for a free page until there has been a fault, a design option that defers all dumping testing until a page fault occurs could be attractive. In other related options, the entire set is not examined to process one page fault, and advance checking can be used to clean pages speculatively.

One major difference between the working-set and LRU policies concerns whether the total amount of main memory allocated for a process is static or may be dynamic. The LRU policy automatically produces a static allocation for each process if it always dumps a page allocated for the process that requires a new page. The working-set policy, however, cannot result in a static allocation unless the window size parameter is changed dynamically.[23]

Under the working-set policy, the decision as to whether a page should be dumped is based entirely on the contents of the corresponding page descriptor. In particular, comparisons between descriptors are not required (as with the LRU policy) to make the dumping decision. Thus the allocator does not have to scan all page descriptors to implement the dumping policy or to initiate speculative page cleaning.

4.5.2.2.5 ***Use Bit Approximations.*** Many studies of paging algorithm performance have been made. Various environments have been emulated. The results show that memory size is much more important than policy selection in determining

[23]In fact, with the working-set policy, there may exist no free pages and no pages to be dumped when a page must be loaded. Problem 4-23 presents some policies for handling that eventuality.

system performance, provided that a "reasonable" paging policy is used. We have seen that some reasonable policies require complex data collection, such as recording the time of each access, and others require complex dumping decisions, such as scanning all values within a table.

The use bit data collection technique is simple but provides only approximate data concerning recent referencing patterns. Under the use bit scheme the basic data collection step sets a "used" bit in the page descriptor when the corresponding page is accessed. Thus the value of the used bit states whether the corresponding page has or has not been referenced since the bit was last cleared.

To approximate the statistics collected for other memory allocation policies, the system can examine the use bits and update some auxiliary data structures after a page fault. The net result is that the processed data approximates the referencing behavior data that would have been collected by more complex data collection hardware.

To approximate the LRU algorithm, the page allocator maintains a stack of page numbers whose ordering approximates the recency-of-use page ordering. To update the stack, the number of every page whose used bit is set is moved to the top of the stack, and all used bits are cleared. Thus the set of pages referenced since the last stack update is moved as a block to the top of the stack (but the ordering within the block is arbitrary). Even though the bottom-most stack entry may not be the number of exactly the least recently used page, it certainly is the number of a member of the least recently used block of pages. The blocking is irregular with respect to time, being based on the occurrence of page fault interrupts.

Working-set statistics can be approximated in a similar way. In this case the allocator records the current time in the page descriptors when the used bits are scanned. Alternatively, a hardware mechanism can be designed to collect working-set statistics, as follows. Associate with each page descriptor a set of used bits arranged as a shift register that shifts from left to right. Upon access, the leftmost bit is set. When the used bit data are processed, all used bits are shifted one position and the leftmost bits are cleared. Pages that have not been referenced for the longest time will have the largest number of clear bits at the left end of their shift registers. The fidelity of the working-set approximation can be improved if the shifting times are evenly spaced.

Generalizing this fidelity argument, we see that the frequency of the data reduction activity affects the accuracy of the approximation. Two obvious choices of times to process the used bits are (1) periodically (based on a timer) and (2) on each page fault. Since most operating systems do not require regular interrupts and the added overhead of regular interrupts to improve the fidelity of the page usage information will not be overcome by a lower page fault frequency, data reduction is usually performed on page fault interrupts.

Any memory allocation policy that needs usage time information can approximate that information by sampling used bits. More fidelity can be obtained by more frequent sampling. The used bit design presents a trade between implementation accuracy and implementation efficiency. As excessively accurate information is not essential[24] for adequate page management performance, and because page dumping policies are based on the assumption that the near future will approximate the recent past—an approximation at best—a simple mechanization is often chosen. This means that used bit data will be collected on each memory access and processed on each page fault.

4.5.3 Summary

The operating system can allocate memory resources based on actual behavior of the processes and programs sharing use of the system, provided that some usage data are collected by the underlying mechanism. These data can be used to choose which information will be moved down in the memory hierarchy, with the hope that the dumping decisions will produce good system performance. Usage data collection can be implemented by the hardware or by the processor microcode, but not by software, since the data collection overhead will be too great. The used bit approximation scheme, however, employs hardware collection to obtain basic data that are processed by simple software to support memory management.

4.6 PROCESSOR SUPPORT FOR ALLOCATION POLICIES

In the preceding sections we have explored several memory allocation policies and shown how certain policies can be useful at different levels of the system design and implementation. We have seen how a list can be used as the free-space management database. We have seen that operating system memory management requires support from the underlying mechanisms to collect usage statistics upon which reasonable management policies must rely.

In this section we present briefly several ways that processor designs might be supplemented to support memory allocation decisions and their implementation. We show how a system can be designed to make memory allocations automatically. We discuss a list-searching instruction and statistical data collection mechanisms. We discuss the possible use of a coprocessor to speculatively clean memory pages that are likely swapping candidates. In addition to these specific design elements, the processor design should support efficient accessing to the allocated space; we discuss accessing in Chapter 5.

4.6.1 Processor Support for Automatic Allocation

The semantics of a processor's CALL instruction could be extended to include the prologue of the called procedure. In particular, the allocation of automatic space is always required, so it is a good candidate for inclusion within CALL. The System/38 has such a feature.

[24]If the converse applies, it is most likely true that the system's memory is too small; therefore, the situation would best be alleviated by reducing the number of active processes or by expanding the system's main memory.

Example 4-16

The amount of temporary spaces required for a procedure is known at compile time, if they are static. The System/38 [IBM81a] keeps the size of the automatic space as an attribute of an entry point to a procedure. When the entry point is called, the processor reads this space size attribute and acquires the required amount of stack space for the new invocation. Certain standard prologue instructions that would have been required otherwise are not needed.

4.6.2 List Searching

The implementation of a heap allocation policy with variable-sized allocations includes a linked list describing the free space. While servicing an allocation request, the allocator searches the list to find an appropriate block of free space. The best-fit policy, for example, requires finding the free block in the list whose size is the smallest value that is larger than the requested size. To implement an efficient search for such a list member the list should be ordered by block size. In a complementary manner, when servicing a free request, the allocator must insert the newly freed space into the free list while maintaining its size ordering.

The memory allocator may have to merge and split free blocks to provide an appropriate block size for each allocation request. Splitting free space is not difficult, as it can easily be built on the basic allocate and free operations. Merging free space, on the other hand, is more difficult, since one needs to find neighboring free blocks. If the free list is ordered by block size, it is hard to find block origins. One advantage of the buddy system is that the origins of a block's buddies can be computed (see Problem 4-24). With best-fit allocation, however, the allocator must search the free list to find the nearby origin addresses. The list ordering based on block origins will be different than the size-based ordering required for the best-fit size searches. A list structure in which each list bead contains two pointers would assist this flexibility.

The general goal is to search a list to find the first entry whose value meets a specified criterion. For memory allocation the search criterion uses an arithmetic comparison between the search parameter (the block size or the address) and a value in a bead element. A list operation that searches for the first entry whose value is not less than the value of an integer operand supports all memory allocation functions.

What result do we desire from a list search operation? The result should be an access variable which somehow describes the list element that met the search criterion. It is best if the result describes the predecessor of the bead that met the search criterion; this choice supports "easy" deletion or insertion in a singly threaded ordered list.

We may have to standardize some aspects of the list bead structure to provide low-level support for the search operation. In particular, the locations of the search field and the next-element pointer must be specified. Two different designs are discussed in the two following examples.

Example 4-17

The B5700 list search instruction ([BURR69], [BURR73]) relies on a fixed bead format. Each list entry is a single word containing the index of the successor list entry (in bits 19 .. 0) and the integer value v associated with this bead (in bits 47 .. 20). The complete list must be stored within one segment; the position index in a list bead specifies its successor's location relative to the segment's origin. Figure 4-24 illustrates the basic list structure. The list search operation has three arguments: a descriptor of the segment containing the list, the position index of the first word of the list, and a search value S (in bits 27 .. 0—this position does not match the position of v within a bead). To perform this instruction, the processor retains the indices of recently searched list entries. It examines the next list word, comparing its value v against S. If v < S, the search continues to the next bead in the list. If the value in the bead is not less than S, the search is complete, and the processor returns as its result the position index to the predecessor of the list entry where the completion condition was met. This situation is depicted in Figure 4-24.

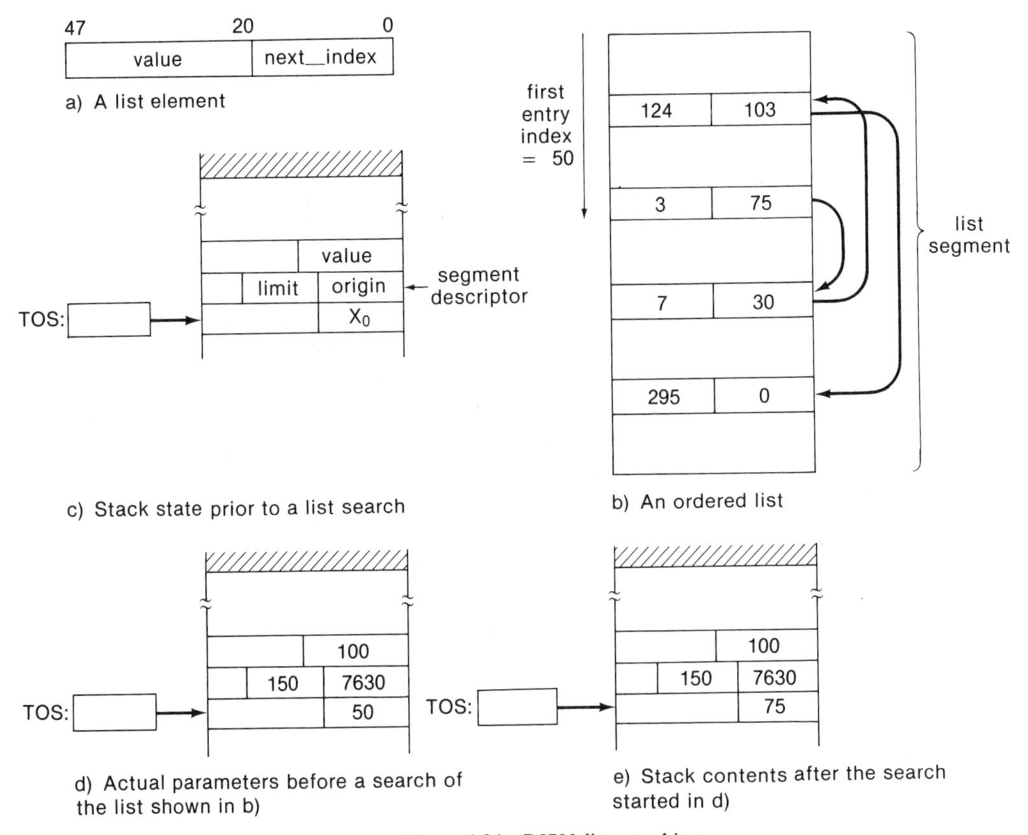

Figure 4-24 B5700 list searching

Example 4-18

The HP3000 processor [HEWL73] also supports a list search instruction, with a little more flexibility in the list format. In particular, the value and the successor pointer do not have to be allocated in a fixed relationship to each other. There are four operands of the instruction; the first two, like those in the B5700, are the pointer to the head of the list and the value to be found. The third operand specifies the number of words beyond the pointer where the value to be tested is stored. A final operand is a count that

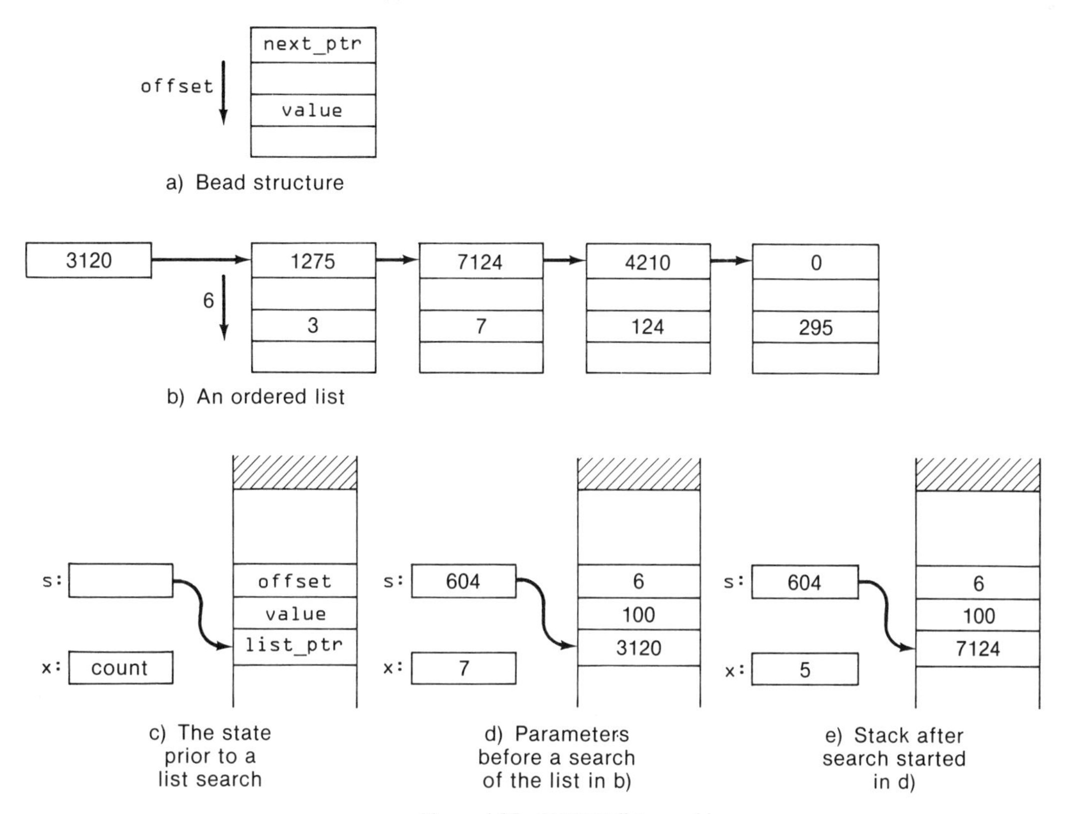

Figure 4-25 HP3000 list searching

limits the length of the search. The result of the search is a pointer to the node where the completion test succeeded, and not to its predecessor, as in the B5700. Figure 4-25 illustrates the data structures, including the result of a search through the list used in Example 4-17. The HP3000 list search instruction is privileged.

Comparing these two list search designs, we see more flexibility in the HP3000 scheme, but two memory accesses are required to read the (separated) bead value and successor pointer. Having the result be a pointer to the predecessor of the bead that met the search criterion (as in the B5700) makes bead insertion and deletion easier. These observations suggest that the B5700 scheme is the clear winner. However, the advantage goes back to the HP3000 design if the set of items must be ordered on more than one criterion. Let us examine this aspect in detail.

A free list ordered both by size and origin requires two different link chains. The structure shown in Figure 4-26 is attractive for this purpose. This structure cannot be described in an Ada program since one cannot perform arithmetic operations on access objects in Ada. The structure can be described in Ada by defining the pointers to point to the first item in each bead, with appropriate naming to specify the location (within the bead) of the successor pointer to be used during a particular search. For example, if next_address and next_size are the names of two access objects in the bead's record format, a program following the address sequence

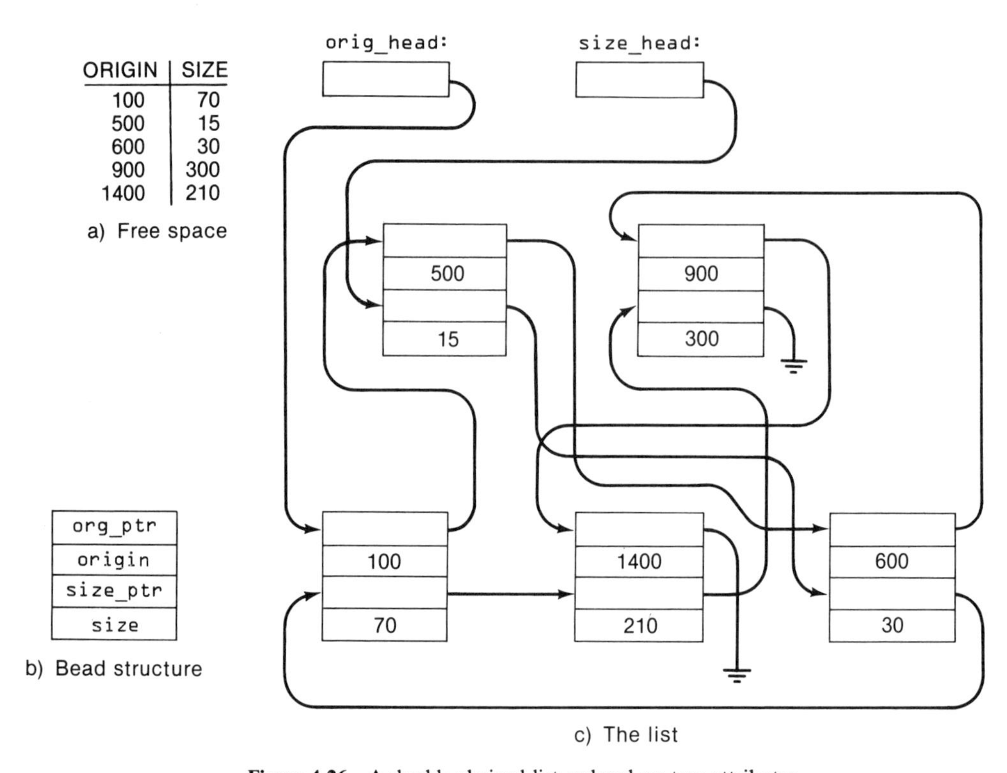

Figure 4-26 A double chained list ordered on two attributes

must update its current position (kept in an access object named "current") by one of these two assignment statements:

```
current := current.next_address;
current := current.next_size;
```

Another design that might be used to impose two different orderings on a single set of space descriptors uses another level of indirection. We make a separate singly linked list to order the elements on each attribute. The "values" in the two lists are access objects, each pointing to a space descriptor, as shown in Figure 4-27. Under this scheme, the double list design requires two beads for each free block. A simple processor list searching operation can be used within each list.

Both the B5700 and the HP3000 processors can be used to search a set of beads ordered on two criteria. Therefore, these designs support memory management algorithms.

4.6.3 Usage Statistic Collection Hardware

The hardware level is the only level at which reasonable statistics collection support for operating system memory allocation policies can be provided. The overhead inherent in implementing data collection in software is too great because data must

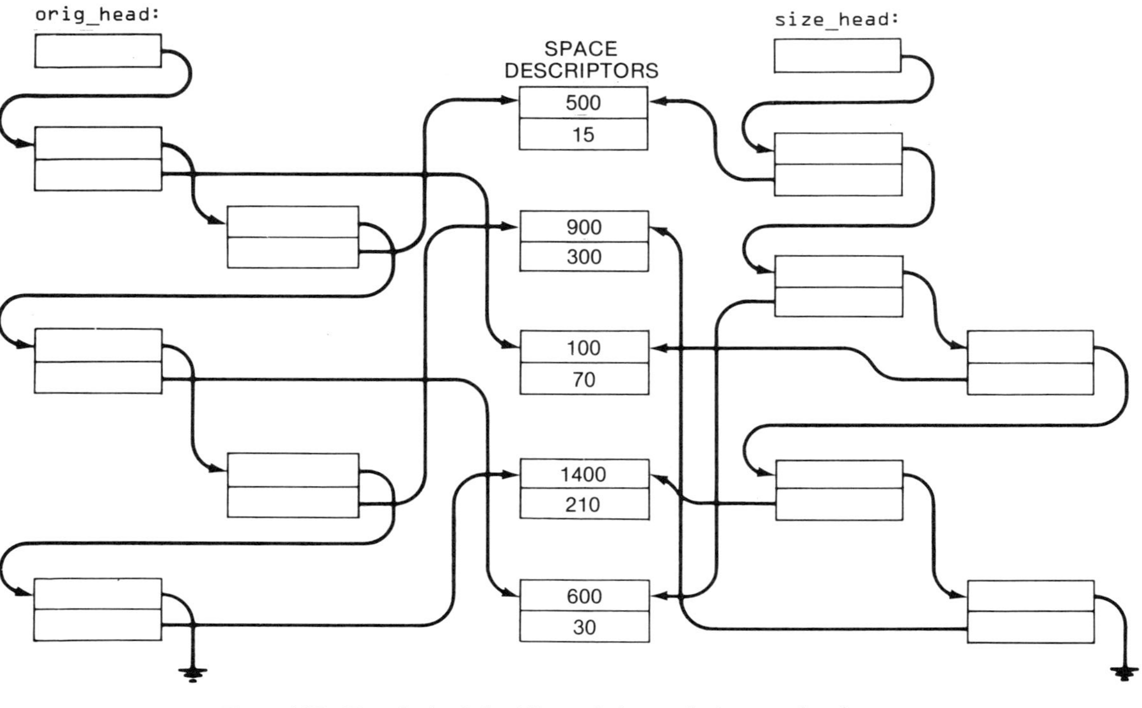

Figure 4-27 Two singly chained lists pointing to single space descriptors

be collected on every memory access. So we need data collection hardware. What data should be collected? The hardware can be specialized for one specific management policy, such as LRU statistics collection. Another option uses hardware designed to collect basic[25] usage information such as used bits; the simple usage information could be manipulated by the memory manager to support the chosen management policy. Such generic data collection can be used in support of many different management policies.

A basic policy-independent statistics collection technique keeps track of which regions have been accessed. Used bits are set by the hardware on any access. They are reset by the memory allocation software. In addition, the hardware can be designed to record writes (that indicate when a page becomes dirty). A "dirty" bit can be set by the hardware on every write access. We have already discussed how used bit and dirty bit information can be used by the software memory allocator.

A hardware LRU stack is a typical policy-specific hardware mechanism supporting memory allocation. Including enough hardware to hold the entire LRU stack can be expensive; a compromise design places some topmost stack entries in a

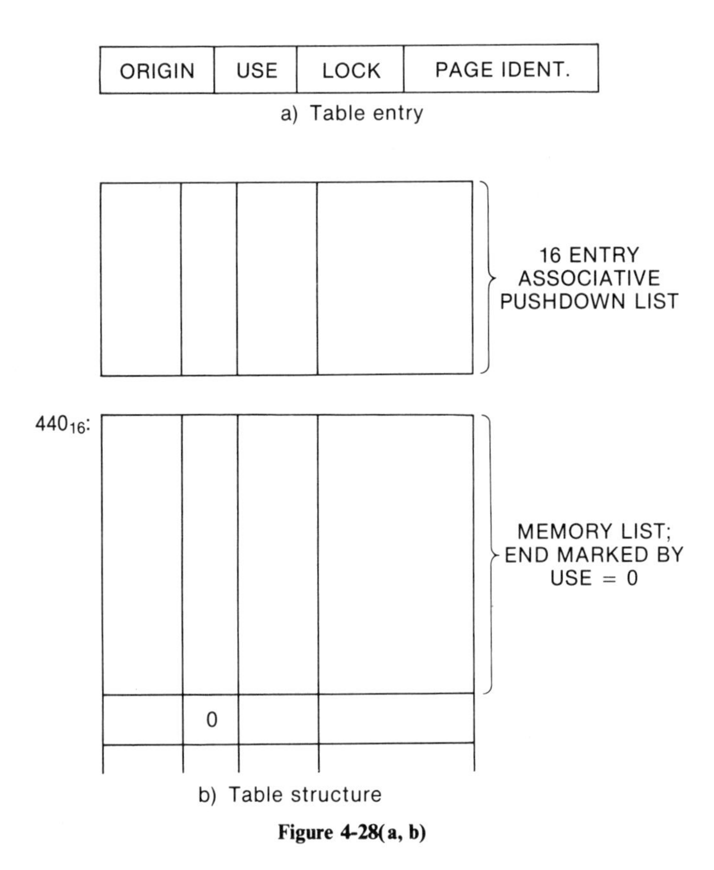

Figure 4-28(a, b)

[25]In the sense that the act of collecting information does not process (or select) information in such a way as to preclude the implementation of a specific memory management policy.

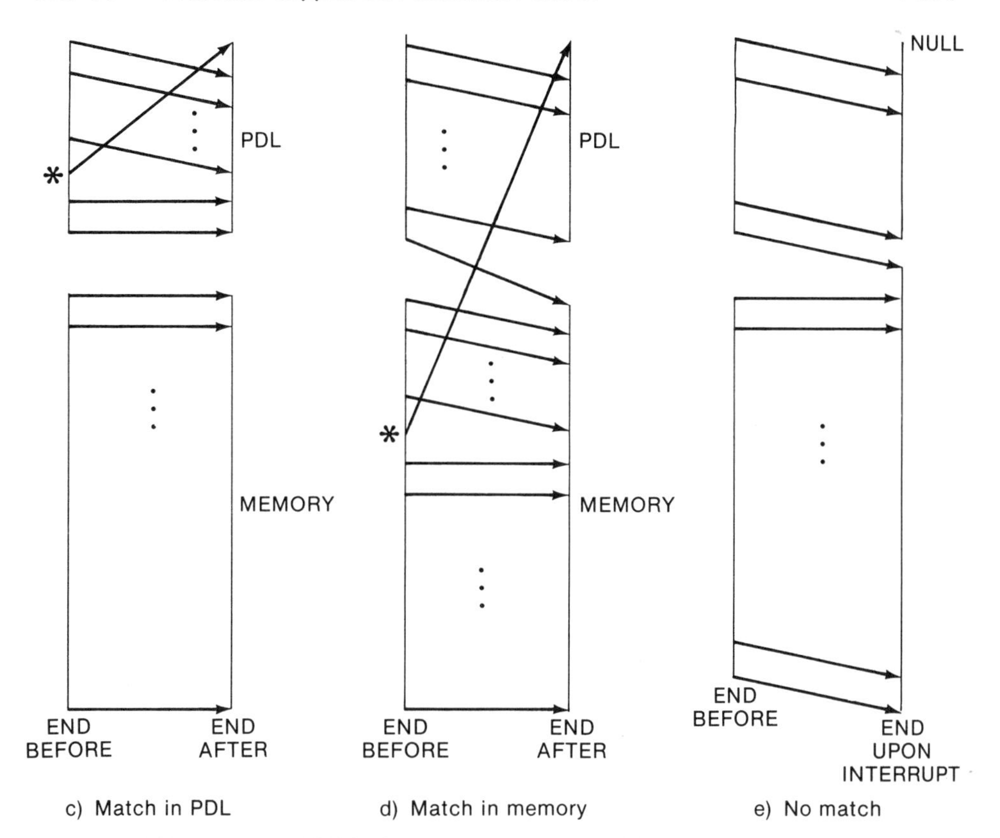

Figure 4-28(c, d, e) An LRU implementation (CDC CYBER205), cont. (* denotes matching entry.) After [CONT84]; courtesy of Control Data Corp.

hardware module, with the less frequently referenced descriptors (lower in the stack) stored in slower memory (in a location known to the hardware mechanism). In this manner the functionality of a complete hardware stack can be realized at a lower expense but with most of its benefits.

Example 4-19

The CDC STAR-100 [CONT70] used a hardware LRU stack containing 16 page descriptors (Figure 4-28). Upon each memory access associative comparison logic finds the descriptor of the page being used; intermediate descriptors are shifted down to the place that held the matching descriptor, as illustrated in Figure 4-28c. If the matching descriptor is not found in the hardware stack, the memory portion of the stack must be scanned to find the matching entry (see Figure 4-28d). If the matching descriptor is not on the logical stack, the scan will reach the bottom of the stack before finding a match. This condition indicates a page fault. Figure 4-28e illustrates this case. The CDC Cyber 205 system uses the same LRU statistics collection scheme, as does the ETA10.

We have seen that the hardware-level design may be influenced by the memory allocation policy used by the system to manage main memory. (Complementary hardware support for the accessing algorithms is discussed in Section 5.3.) By satisfying these requirements at the hardware level, the system efficiency can be improved markedly.

4.6.4 Coprocessors for Memory Swapping

It is straightforward to design a coprocessor that speculatively cleans memory pages; the coprocessor examines the memory allocator's database to find candidate pages for swapping out. After a page has been swapped out, its dirty bit is cleared, and another descriptor is examined. Since the swapping activity can get in the way of useful memory traffic, it is not wise to have the processor always looking for and finding pages to swap. Some statistics about the frequency of dirty pages could be used to limit the activities here. As far as this author is aware, several designers have proposed this sort of module, but it is not clear that one has actually been implemented.

4.7 SUMMARY

In this chapter we presented topics related to memory space allocation for objects used by executing programs. We looked at some static and dynamic allocation policies and their management requirements, including free-space bookkeeping. We saw how high-level language declarations can imply object lifetimes. We discussed ways to allocate space for static, automatic, and dynamic objects. Stacks of activation blocks are attractive for storing automatic objects and meeting the naming semantics of static nesting environments. We have seen how a process creator can allocate the spaces required to hold the programs and data for program execution. Beneath all these mechanisms, the operating system can manage space automatically based on the actual behavior of the programs executing on the system; hardware-level data collection is required for realistic implementations of this policy option. We briefly reviewed these hardware functions, to which we shall return when we discuss memory-accessing techniques in Chapter 5.

4.8 PROBLEMS

4-1. Pointers, descriptors, and capabilities all describe memory space. Briefly discuss their differences. For each one describe at least one situation in which it is useful.

4-2. This problem concerns the allocation strategy in which two stacks are allocated at opposite ends of a single vector. The stacks are set up so that they grow toward the middle as objects are pushed onto them.

- **(a)** Draw a picture illustrating the two stacks in the vector's space.
- **(b)** Write out the implementations of the push and pop operations for each stack.
- **(c)** A designer proposes using this structure to collect the stacks for two separate processes into a single space. The claim is that there will be a space saving without a time penalty. Discuss this claim. In particular, is the conclusion correct?

4-3. A system uses a stack allocation policy to manage free memory space from a space pool. Prove that if the block size is fixed for the problem, and if this policy allocates and deallocates fixed-size blocks only, it does maximize the amount of space that is never allocated to any object, for any given history of allocations and deallocations. Therefore, prove that the stack policy does minimize the amount of space that must be allocated for a given process to be able to execute. You may wish to consider an equivalent claim, namely that there does not exist another heap-based fixed-block allocation policy which uses less space. (*Hint*: Consider proving an analogous property with respect to the limiting behavior of policies in the designated class.)

4-4. Write a pair of allocate and free procedures using the queue allocation policy.

4-5. The picture in Figure 4-29 shows snapshots of four different allocation pools. The shaded regions are allocated and the clear regions are free. Fill in Table 4-5 with a mark in an entry if the corresponding combination of snapshot and allocation policy are incompatible. When you are finished, the clear table entries will represent the policy–pool combinations that are compatible.

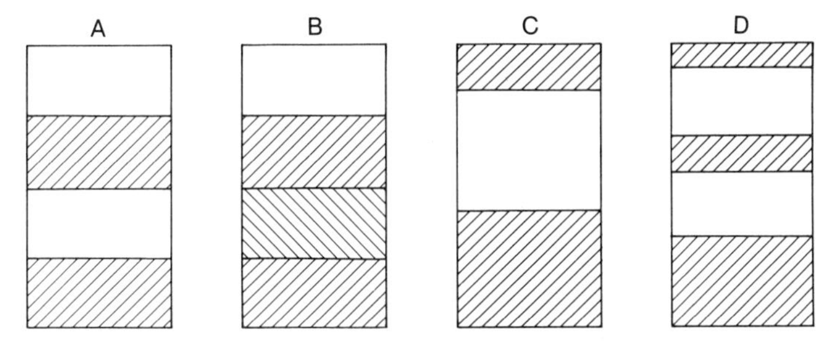

Figure 4-29 Four memory allocations (Problem 4-5)

TABLE 4-5 COMBINATIONS OF POOL CONFIGURATION AND ALLOCATION POLICY

	Pool Name			
Policy	A	B	C	D
Stack				
Queue				
Frames				
Segments (from heap)				

4-6. Write a pair of allocate and free procedures using the bit vector free-space management scheme for fixed-size allocation from a heap.

4-7. This problem compares the first-fit and best-fit allocation schemes.

(a) Write out the allocate algorithm under each policy. For first fit, assume that the free list is maintained in order of origins.

(b) Discuss the differences of the first fit policy between order by origin and LIFO ordering.

(c) What more would you like to know to compare these schemes?

(d) How could you obtain the information you desire? [See part (c).]

4-8. In the text's discussion of queue allocation, it was claimed that if the using programs were known to be correct, one or both of the parameters of the **free** calls could be removed from the call—it was implied that the removal would not have any effect on the program's semantics. (The two parameters were the origin and length of the space to be freed.) What property must the using programs satisfy so that both parameters can be eliminated? Explain.

4-9. In the text we did not present any algorithms that verify the consistency of free requests to an allocator. One way to include parameter checking is to perform these checks within the allocator's algorithms. Another method interposes a parameter checking package (Figure 4-30) between the outside world and the allocation module. The checker may change the parameters of free requests to force them to correspond to the combination of origin and length that was doled out by the allocator in response to an earlier allocate request. You are asked to write an Ada package that serves this function. Your package will keep an internal table which pairs each block origin with the corresponding block length. The entries to your package will be allocate_check(length)[26] and free_check(origin, length). If there is an error in the space specification of the free request received by your package, the actual allocation should be freed and an externally visible flag free_error should be set true. The system's allocation procedures that allocate and free space, without checking the parameters, are specified as:

```
function alloc(size : integer) return access_space;
procedure free(loc : access_space; size : integer);
```

(a) Explain briefly why the checking module is a package.

(b) Write the package.

(c) Comment on the advantages and disadvantages of the proposed method of responding to length mismatches.

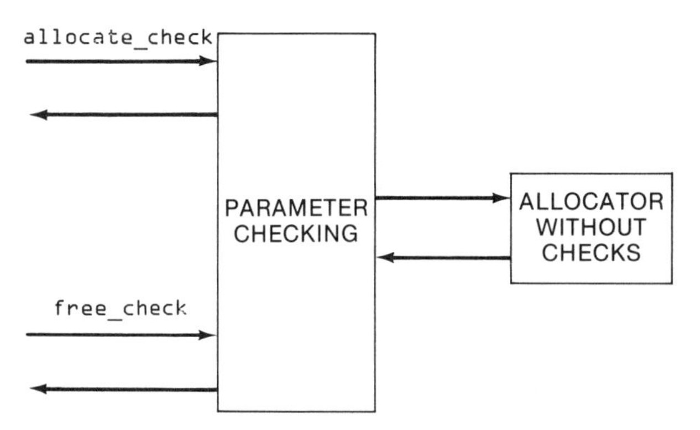

Figure 4-30 A parameter-checking module interposed between the users and the allocator

4-10. Construct an activity history to illustrate the fragmentation of free space as a consequence of a variable-sized heap allocation.

(a) Use explicit allocates and frees.

[26]We introduce new names for the entries to avoid overloading the name of the entry point of the built-in procedure.

(b) Use explicit allocates and access variable overwriting to remove references to an object (thereby freeing it implicitly). An access variable av pointing to Q would be deleted if a new access value pointing to R were written into av. This write implicitly deletes the pointer to Q.

(c) Show a pair of histories for access variable overwriting to illustrate that a specific overwrite operation cannot be examined in isolation to determine whether it implies that a free operation is needed.

4-11. This problem concerns the design of a space allocato using variable-sized allocation from a heap such that the allocator keeps a table showing the origin–size correspondences. The free call has only a single parameter which is the origin of the space to be freed.

(a) Show the data structures that you will use.

(b) Write the allocate and free algorithms.

(c) At least two assumptions must be made regarding the behavior of the programs using the allocated space so that the allocator will perform correctly. State two of them.

4-12. A variation on the best-fit allocation policy places a lower limit F on the size of a free block. It attempts to meet this constraint by choosing the free block to use in meeting an allocate request for S words as follows:

1. If there is a free block of size S, take it;

2. Look for the best fit for size (S + F);

3. If 2 fails, look for the best fit for S;

(a) Why is this variation attractive?

(b) Compare this allocation strategy against the ordinary best-fit policy.

4-13. A designer suggests the following allocation algorithm: If possible, the system chooses a free block close to the desired size. Failing this, it tries to split a block that is close to double the requested size. If this does not succeed, it tries for a block of four times the requested size, and so forth. If this progressive search fails, it takes the best-fit block (in relation to the original request).

(a) Comment on any relationships between the proposed strategy and the buddy system.

(b) Would you recommend this strategy over the best-fit strategy? If so, under what conditions? Explain your answers.

4-14. Write a space manager using the buddy system defined in the text. It can be called through the following interfaces:

```
function alloc(size : integer) return access_space;
procedure free(loc : access_space; size : integer);
```

Use the buddy version in which a block of size 2^n is divided into one block of size 2^{n-1} and two blocks of size 2^{n-2}. The size of the space pool is known.

4-15. In this problem we refer to the record variants of Example 3-6.

(a) Describe a way that the implementation might distinguish the two variants. (You need to have a distinguishing mechanism at both translate time and run time.) Can these be identical?

(b) Show how the **new** statement could be translated into a form consistent with your answer to part (a).

4-16. In Algol it is possible to define a new naming context within a procedure body by using the keywords **declare** .. **end**. Such a declare context is entered when the program flow reaches the **declare** statement. Upon block entry (before the statements within the block are performed) the local objects declared within the declare block are allocated and initialized. In a complementary manner, the block is exited to the next statement after the **end** that terminates the block. Upon block exit all local objects are deallocated. The previous rules define the semantics of the objects declared in an embedded **declare** .. **end** block. One implementation of these semantics allocates space for local objects when the block is entered and deallocates it upon block exit. The diagram in Figure 4-31a illustrates the allocation semantics of the **declare** .. **end** structure.

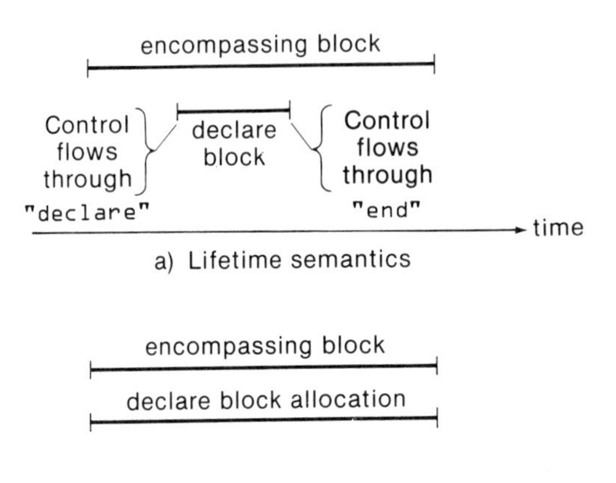

Figure 4-31 The **declare. . .end** block lifetime and allocation option (Problem 4-16)

In this problem we introduce and study an alternative implementation of the local object semantics. In the alternative implementation, all automatic objects declared within a **declare** block are allocated at the same time as the automatic objects declared within the enclosing procedure or function block. Figure 4-31b illustrates this proposed allocation.

As you answer this question, you may supplement the alternative design if necessary to match the semantics of the original design, but do preserve its basic allocation policy—that the automatic space local to the declare block is allocated with the objects declared local to the enclosing procedure or function block.

Discuss the following issues, comparing the two approaches.

(a) Object initialization.
(b) Object naming in the programming language.
(c) Object visibility in the programming language.

4-17. A designer suggests that access object embarrassments such as dangling pointers could be removed if only there were sufficient background bookkeeping to keep track of pointers. One way to eliminate dangling references is to associate with each dynamically allocated object a list of all the locators pointing to that object. Then when the object is deleted, the system is able to go through the list and replace all the locators by null. This problem is about designs with background locator bookkeeping.

(a) Specify such a data structure.

(b) Show how the block epilogue could use the locator list to delete dangling references.

(c) Write an Ada package managing the type "locator." The package should function so that a locator object is not the same as an access object (which behaves as defined in Ada); the package should guarantee that a locator object will never become a dangling reference. The trick is to chain together all locator objects that happen to point to the same allocated object. This structure is illustrated in Figure 4-32. The chain can be used as required to find all locators that point to an object. Design the package so that all locators that point to object X will be replaced by null when X is freed. Assume that all locators point to objects created by allocate operations (in other words, a program cannot construct a locator to an individual component of an area that was allocated by the allocator).

(d) Discuss the reason for the locator construction restriction stating that a program cannot construct a locator that points to a component of an object. In particular, show how removing this restriction will complicate the implementation.

(e) A designer proposes that the use of this scheme be made optional [the programmer specifies whether the locators pointing to a particular object shall be chained together by passing the value "yes" (or "no") to a third parameter of the allocate request that creates the first pointer to the object]. The proponent of this proposal claims that execution time can be saved for accesses to those objects for which dangling references will never be a problem. Comment on the designer's reasoning, and state whether anything would be lost by adopting the proposed modification. Which design philosophies apply to each design?

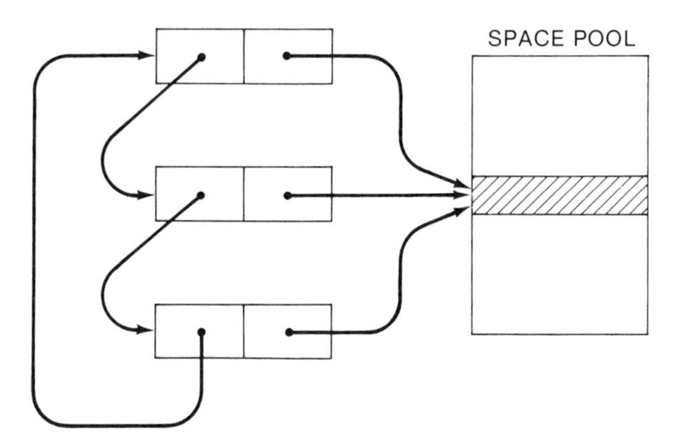

Figure 4-32 Chained locator objects (Problem 4-17)

4-18. This problem addresses the question, "How can an Ada implementation prevent dangling references?" One implementation strategy allocates spaces for all objects of type T at the nesting level where type T was declared; in this manner the dangling reference problem will be solved automatically, but an allocated space might be retained for a long time after it is actually needed. Another implementation strategy (to be investigated in more detail in the questions below) allocates space as deep in the module nest as possible, so that more objects can be deallocated automatically (upon block exit).

It is claimed that if we are going to try to move the objects deeper in the nest, we may be faced with the need to relocate some of the objects. To illustrate this claim, suppose that an object pointed to by an access variable called "here" is allocated in an area called "here_area".[27] Suppose further that the access variable "here" is allocated in a longer-lived context (such as an enclosing block). There is then the potential for dangling references. Figure 4-33a illustrates the pointers and the space just before the allocation containing here_area is freed. The pointer here will dangle if here_area is deallocated and the information that here accesses is not relocated.

One way to prevent dangling references is for the "system" to find automatically all access variables that describe space to be deallocated (like the one in our example) and move those objects which are described by these access variables into a longer-lived space. In our example, after the space called "here_area" disappears, the object pointed to from "here" should have been relocated to another area, say "there_area." The new allocation could be in a pool that will last as long as the access object which accesses the allocation.

You are to design an implementation of Ada containing this feature so that the programmer need not worry about whether there are dangling references. We allow two simplifying assumptions for this problem. You may suppose that there is a reserved area within each activation record reserved for holding the objects that may have to be moved

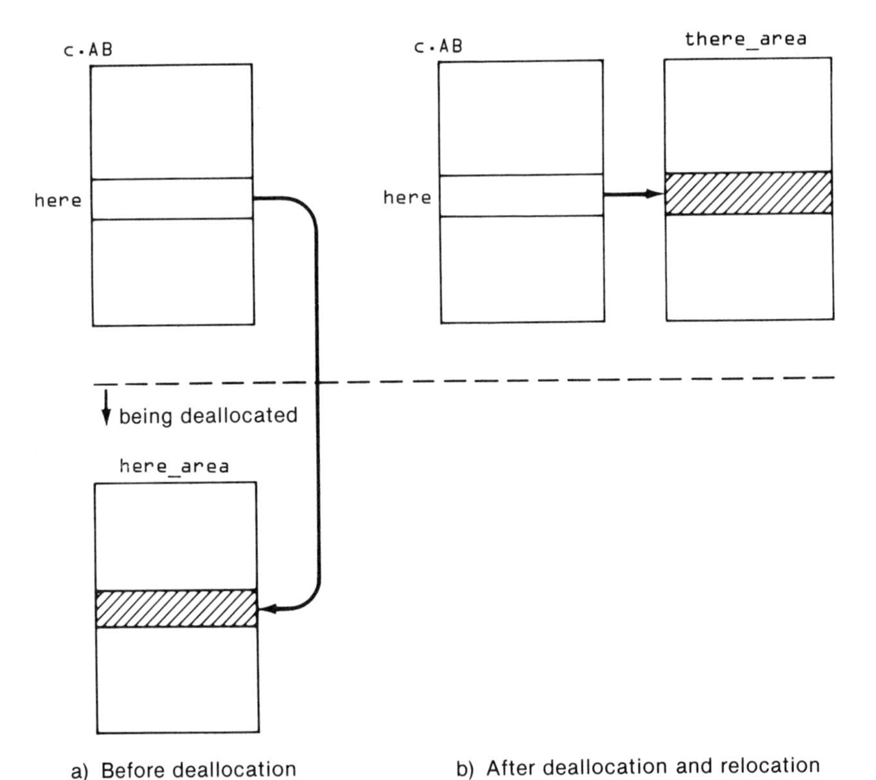

Figure 4-33 Pointer adjustments upon object relocation (Problem 4-18)

[27]This structure defining an area and specifying an allocation within that area is not possible within Ada. Nevertheless, this structure can be used in the implementation of Ada, since the implementation does not have to conform to the limitations of the language itself. So therefore the language itself does not have the problem presented in this exercise, but the implementer of the language must address the problem.

there. Further, you may ignore testing whether there is enough space in the local relocation area to hold the reallocated objects.

To satisfy the design constraints, you have to develop a scheme for representing and manipulating access variables (which may affect the implementation of all operations that can be performed on them) to satisfy the goals. Therefore, your answer should include a package supporting the data type "access_variable."

4-19. Suppose that a language allows a programmer to allocate objects from a global area and place their locators in local objects. Then when the local objects are deallocated at block exit, the system will find these locators and deallocate the objects.

(a) Write a block epilogue that finds all user-allocated objects and deletes them before block exit.

(b) Specify any data structures that you create to make this function work properly.

(c) Describe how the implementation of operations performed on access variables would be affected by your design (it is possible that the operator implementations would not be affected).

(d) Discuss whether the proposed scheme for automatic deallocation has any visible semantic consequences. (In other words, does the programmer ever write different programs if he knows that the proposed scheme is used in the implementation?)

4-20. This problem is about strategies for developing a static process schedule and memory allocation for a set of programs about which a lot of information is known. There are p programs. For each program P_i we have its execution time e_i, a deadline d_i before which the program should have completed execution, and the amount of memory m_i that the program requires for execution. Time zero is the present moment; no program can be executed before $t = 0$.

There exist dependencies among the programs such that the initiation of one program cannot precede the termination of another program. If there is a constraint that P_i must be completed before P_j can begin execution, we put the pair (P_i, P_j) in the scheduling constraint set. This information could be depicted as a process ordering graph. The process ordering graph has a node for each program and an edge for each pair in the scheduling constraint set. We draw the edge in the direction of increasing time; thus if (P_i, P_j) is in the scheduling constraint set, we draw an edge from the node corresponding to P_i to the node corresponding to P_j.

Finally, there are a set of memory constraints. Two programs, P_a and P_b, may share memory. Suppose that the scheduling constraint set includes (P_a, P_b). Then the memory that P_a used should be retained for use by P_b. We assume that P_a does not require more memory than P_b. Note that if the scheduling constraint set interposed a third program's execution between those of P_a and P_b, the shared memory space will have to be retained while the third program is executed. These constraint combinations may increase the instantaneous memory demand until it exceeds the demands of any single program.

There is a single processor on which the programs will be executed. The processor has a memory capacity M. Assume that no time is consumed for switching programs (this overhead time could be included with the processing time of the loaded program).

(a) Find an algorithm that finds a feasible schedule (one meeting the deadline requirements, the memory requirements, the precedence scheduling constraints, and providing the required execution times). If no feasible schedule exists, the algorithm should so indicate.

(b) Repeat part (a) if there are r processors on which the programs can be scheduled. Each processor's memory capacity is M. Two programs that share memory must be scheduled on the same processor.

(c) In what manner do the results of the algorithm from part b) determine the memory allocations within the system? [Note that this question can be answered even without a solution to either part (a) or (b).]

4-21. One way to reduce paging overhead is to speculatively clean pages in main memory when it seems that they are likely to be overwritten to swap in a new page. The allocator uses a FIFO allocation policy. The cleaner uses a FIFO searching policy to find pages that have been modified and not cleaned out (the FIFO ordering is based on the time of page allocation). Of course, only "dirty" pages have to be swapped out. For this problem, consider the relationship between this speculative cleaning policy and the FIFO page management policy. In the first two parts of the problem, you will examine two schemes for implementing this page cleaning strategy. The major difference between the two schemes lies in the manner in which dirty pages are found.

(a) In this scheme, the system maintains a pointer to the dirty page that is closest to the swap-out position in the FIFO structure (see Figure 4-34). Describe how this pointer is manipulated upon page swap (information flows from primary memory to secondary memory), upon reading an object located within the page (information flows from main memory to the processor), and upon writing to an object located within the page (information flows from the processor to the main memory).

(b) In this scheme, the system always searches for a dirty page by scanning the dirty bits starting with the page frame about to be overwritten, and working backward toward the most recently arrived page. Describe this page swapper design.

(c) List the page manipulation operations that you believe to have the largest effect on the "performance" of these algorithms.

(d) Based on the overhead of the schemes of parts (a) and (b) involved in performing the "significant" operations you identified in part (c), what would you recommend to a system designer considering these two options?

(e) Discuss briefly how these two schemes could be adapted for use in a system using an LRU memory management policy.

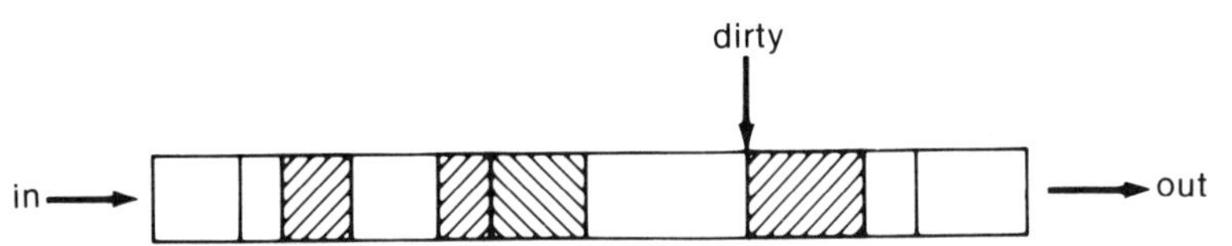

Figure 4-34 Dirty pages (shaded) and the dirty page pointer for speculative cleaning with FIFO allocation (Problem 4-21)

4-22. Consider reclaiming space in a Burroughs B5700 system for segments entering main memory. A round-robin basis is proposed. One pointer "first" describes the first allocated location, and another pointer "free" describes the first free location. A segment to be loaded is described by its descriptor, which contains

```
length: integer;
disk_address: index;    --how to find it.
```

Figure 4-35 illustrates two possible configurations of the memory and the pointers; the shaded areas indicate segments that have been allocated space in the memory.

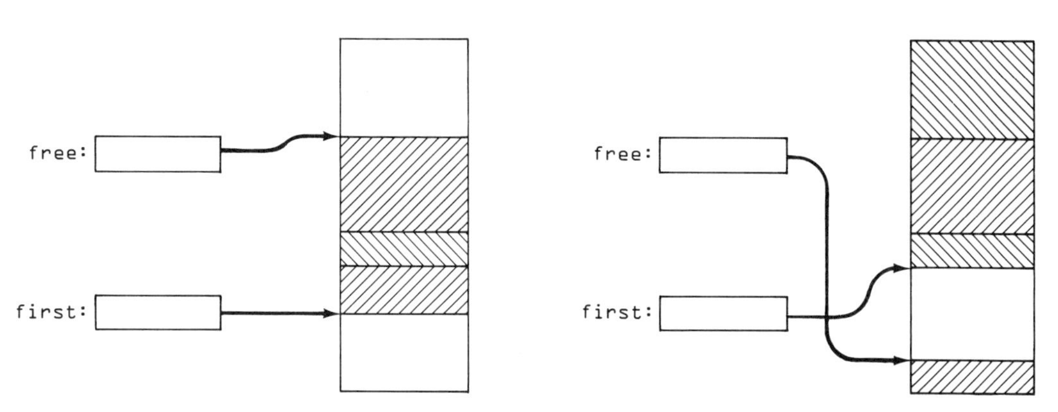

Figure 4-35 Two configurations of free space (Problem 4-22). Allocated space is shaded.

(a) Devise and describe a data structure that chains together the descriptors of the segments loaded in main memory so that a segment descriptor can be found easily when the information it describes must be moved to secondary memory to make room for an incoming segment.

(b) Using the data structure you defined in part (a), write an algorithm that takes as a parameter the descriptor of a segment to be loaded and produces a list of descriptors of segments that have to be removed to make room for the incoming segment.

4-23. This problem is concerned with difficulties that arise because the working-set management policy requires a dynamic space allocation for each individual task. With a fixed value of the window size, memory may be oversubscribed, and something has to be done to relieve the situation. Clearly, the working-set policy requires modification.

(a) Show how relief could be gained by dropping a task from the scheduled set.

(b) Discuss how relief could be gained by reducing the value of the working-set window size. Can you determine any useful bounds on the benefits obtained by dropping the window size by ΔT? (The bound might be a function of the window width.)

(c) Compare the two policies suggested in parts (a) and (b).

4-24. Given a buddy system based on the fractions $\{\frac{1}{2}, \frac{1}{4}, \frac{1}{4}\}$. You are given the origin and length of a block. Specify an algorithm that computes the lengths and origins of its buddies. All addressing starts at 0, which designates the first location in the pool being allocated. The length of the pool (a power of 2) is known.

4-25. The HP3000 linked list search instruction leaves as its result a pointer to the list bead that satisfies the matching criterion, rather than to its predecessor, as does the B5700 linked list lookup instruction. This difference can be significant because the processor does have to find the predecessor bead to insert a bead before the one found or to delete the found bead. A software designer proposes that this limitation could be alleviated by redesigning the list structure to place the search value associated with a bead B in B's predecessor in the list. Each bead's format is specified in the following record declaration:

```
type list_bead;
type list_bead_ptr is access list_bead;
type list_bead is
```

```
record
   next_pointer : list_bead_ptr;
   next_size : integer;
   present_value : origin_address;
end record;
```

(a) Show an algorithm to insert a bead into the list having this modified format. At the start of your algorithm the desired place has just been found by executing the HP3000 list lookup instruction, so you have a pointer to the first bead whose value meets the search criterion.

(b) Show an algorithm to delete a bead from the list having this modified format. As in part (a), you start with a pointer to the first bead whose value meets the search criterion.

(c) Compare the number of accesses to list entries required for the two list formats and make a recommendation for or against the proposed change in the list format.

4-26. One disadvantage of the HP3000 linked list search instruction was that the result pointed to the bead where the condition was met, not to its predecessor (which is useful for insertion and/or deletion). Show how a program can obtain a pointer to the predecessor by manipulating the count in the index register (X). Illustrate the operation of your program fragment for the list search depicted in Figure 4-25.

4-27. The processor-supported list searching instruction requires a fixed format for the list entries. At least *s*, the size of the search field, is fixed by the instruction's implementation. A software designer proposes that this length limitation could be overcome by constructing a "tree" of lists. This tree is constructed as follows: Let W denote the value in the desired wide search field. Let w denote the number of bits in the wide field. Divide W into narrow search fields $S_1, S_2, \ldots, S_p$, with S_1 containing the leftmost s bits of W, S_2 the next s bits of W, and so forth. The elements of the search space are thus represented in a p-level tree of lists. In this tree the lists at level i (level 1 is the root) are ordered by the contents of S_i.

(a) Draw a representation of the lists in a two-level structure. Show some instances of contents with their wide field values indicated on the corresponding leaf nodes.

(b) Specify which bead(s) you would like to obtain as a result of a list search in this tree. You want to be able to insert and/or delete an entry at the location indicated by the search. Be sure that you consider the situation that arises if one of the beads at one end of a lowest-level list is the one meeting the search criterion.

(c) Write out a search program to find the node meeting the search criterion (you can use greater than or equals, as in the B5700 and HP3000 machines, if you like). Your algorithm should return the result that you desired in part (b). Your algorithm can use the B5700 search operation to find a desired entry in a list.

(d) Write out a bead insertion program based upon the algorithm you developed in part (c).

5

MEMORY ACCESSING

The existence of forgetting has never been proved;
We only know that some things don't come to mind
when we want them. — Nietzsche

An effective memory accessing design provides access to information in the computer when the processor needs access. It does not let the computer forget, and it does not allow the information to get too far away unless the information is accessed infrequently. To do its job effectively, the accessing mechanism will have to move information closer to or farther from the processor, depending on its frequency of use. To implement these moves and keep track of the closest location of each object, the accessing mechanism will have to be able to map names among name spaces and move objects among memory modules. Clearly, these activities require assistance from the memory allocator.

In this chapter we discuss memory accessing for single process systems. To access an object, the system may first have to translate the object's name from one name space (such as the space of symbolic names in Ada) to another name space (such as the space of absolute memory addresses that can be interpreted by the memory system's hardware). The mapping may be performed in several stages. In this chapter we explore some structured techniques for implementing these mappings.

Since the structure of the memory space of a virtual machine may not correspond directly to the structure of the memory space of the underlying virtual machine, correspondences between names in the higher machine and locations in the lower machine must be defined by address transformations, which can be simple, complex, static, dynamic, system controlled, or programmer controlled. Since name transformations must be performed during program translation and execution, mapping speed can be an important criterion for selecting the mapping technique to be used. In addition, one could consider building special hardware to support useful name mappings.

In this chapter you will learn basic mapping techniques and then explore their usage in the implementations of languages and systems. You will learn the reasons for the selections designers have made. After completing the chapter you should be a good critic and an understanding and sympathetic observer of name mapping functions.

The structure of this chapter is as follows. We first present the basic techniques used to implement name mappings. Then we explore their usage at different levels of the hierarchy of system descriptions. We start with the translation of programs started by the compiler or assembler and completed by the linker before program execution. Then we turn to some mappings made during program execution. These include the computations of effective addresses and the interpretation of addresses that select one object from a dynamic structure, such as a stack that contains activation blocks corresponding to procedure calls that have been executed. Then we examine the mappings that are performed in the processor's hardware, such as the translation from a virtual to a physical address. We look at the interface between the processor and the memory system, where we examine the cache memory, memory interleaving, and other issues that have important effects on system speed. Finally, we present some implementations of associative memory functions.

We learn various techniques for memory accessing; different policies are appropriate depending on the characteristics of the environment. For name mapping and accessing, two important characteristics of the environment are the size of the name space and the density of name usage in the space. When the space is very large, usage will be sparse. But when the name space is small, it will be well used, and different mapping techniques will be chosen. We see the gradual transition from hashed table mappings to set-associative table mappings as the usage patterns shift along this continuum. First we catalog the basic name mapping techniques.

5.1 BASIC TECHNIQUES

We first cover basic name mapping formalisms and terminology. We then discuss several commonly used name mapping structures.

5.1.1 Object Designation Options

Memory objects can be selected on the basis of their locations or their contents.

Definition. An object may be selected by *location-addressing*, in which case it is selected because of its location within a memory address space.

Definition. An object may be selected by *content-addressing* (or associatively), in which case it is selected because a specified portion of its representation —the *key*—meets a match condition when compared with a selector value.

Location addressing is the usual method for selecting memory objects at the processor level. Location addressing can be implemented by using a decoder that activates one of a set of *word select* lines. This process chooses a row of bits in a memory array (see Figure 5-1). The information in this row comprises a single addressable item.[1]

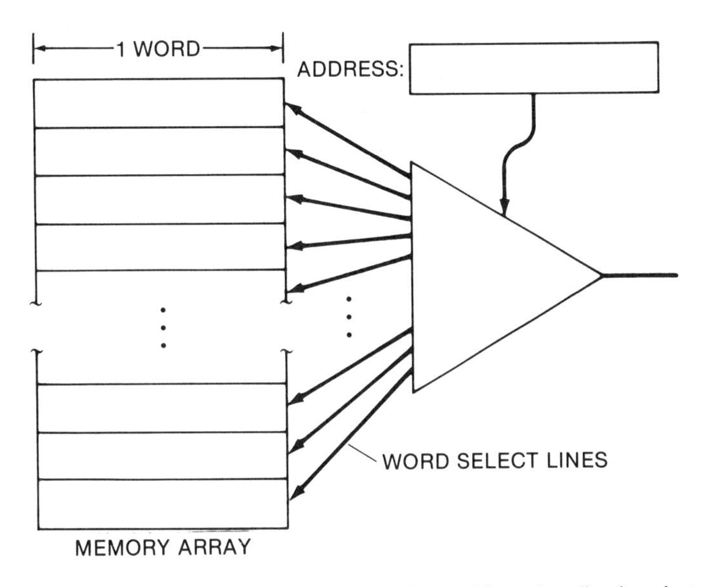

Figure 5-1 Memory array with word select lines; address decoding by selector

In specialized processors associative addressing may be used to select operands; our major interest in associative memories arises from their use to implement name mappings efficiently. In an associative memory used for name mapping the search information is all or a portion of an address. The important point is that the type and form of the search information is known before the hardware is designed. Therefore, the key can be assigned to a fixed field within the object. Furthermore, it is known that a match condition demanding equality between the selector value and the contents of the key field will be adequate for the associative memory functions needed to support name mappings. The match check is made against every word in the associative memory; the result of the match condition check against a word in the memory is stored in a *match bit* associated with that word. Later the system may want to access the memory words that met the selection test; to make such an access, each match bit can be used to drive the select line to the associated word (see Figure 5-2). An associative memory with fixed key field can be built from a conventional location addressed memory and a smaller associative module that contains match test logic in every bit. Other implementation options are presented in Section 5.7.

[1]This comment takes the viewpoint of the memory module; this view does not have to correspond to the processor's idea concerning what constitutes a single word.

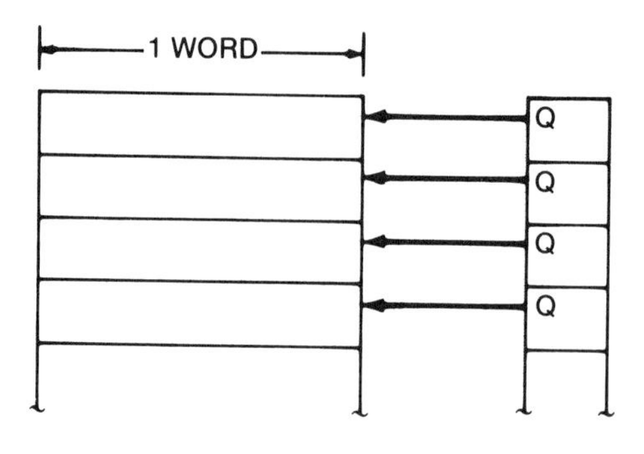

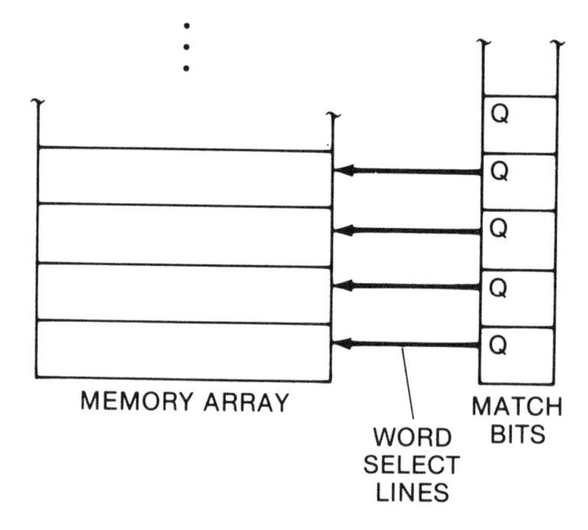

Figure 5-2 Associative memory array with word select lines driven by match bits

Example 5-1

Consider a single location in an associative memory that contains A3B672 (hexadecimal). Suppose that the associative memory has a loadable search mask. A "1" mask bit value denotes a bit position in which the selector value and the memory location's contents participate in the match decision. For an equality match condition, in all bits where the search mask is "1," the bit in the memory word must equal the corresponding bit in the selector word. Table 5-1 shows some search mask and selector values (in hexadecimal) and the corresponding match bit result.

TABLE 5-1 EFFECTS OF AN ASSOCIATIVE SEARCH AGAINST A WORD CONTAINING A3B672

Search Mask	Selector Value	Match Bit Result
F00000	A00000	1
F0F000	A0B012	1
F0F000	A3B149	1
FFF000	A3B149	1
FFF000	B3B149	0

One important difference between an associative memory and a location-addressed memory is that any valid address is the unique identifier of one word. Thus any access request to a location-addressed memory selects a single memory word. An associative memory, on the other hand, may contain several entries with the same key value, so an access request may set the match bits of several memory entries. It is also possible that the associative memory does not contain any matching entries. These points are important for the implementation and use of an associative memory within an address mapping module.

5.1.2 Name Mapping Strategies

Names serve a role similar to that of addresses in a location-addressed memory system. A name mapping transforms addresses between name spaces. A system may remap a name many times to obtain the hardware-recognizable address of the location to which access was desired. Since many maps may be used, and their time delays may be important in determining system performance, the efficiency of the mapping process can be a matter of concern. In this section we explore several name mapping options; in later sections we discuss their utility for various steps in the overall name mapping process. In this section we formally cover general mappings. We turn to practical mappings and present basic implementations of these mappings in Section 5.2. Some implementations may use an associative memory to effect the mapping function.

The translation from a name n_1 in name space N_1 to the corresponding name n_2 in name space N_2 is expressed by the formal mapping function f_{12}:

$$n_2 = f_{12}(n_1) \tag{5-1}$$

Such a formal description is conceptually complete, but not very useful in implementing the function.

We start the implementation discussion with two extreme designs, showing how the corresponding mapping functions might be implemented. The two extreme cases are:

1. Algorithmic maps
2. Tabular maps

An *algorithmic representation* of a name mapping can be encapsulated in a procedure. Any mapping can be implemented by a sufficiently complex procedure, which may execute slowly. "Simple" algorithms reduce the execution time, so they are interesting. We could specify a simple algorithmic mapping by giving the encodings of the input and output names and an arithmetic function that expresses the conversion between the encoded names.

A *tabular representation* of a name mapping is a table specifying the output name corresponding to each possible input name. Since the set of names actually used is finite, a finite table completely describes the mapping. Of course, the finite table can be large and therefore useless due to inefficiency.

Another representation of a tabular mapping treats the table as a binary relation. If two items I_1 and I_2 satisfy the binary relation R, we say that the pair (I_1, I_2) belongs to the relation R. The complete relation can be described by listing all pairs that belong to the relation. Clearly, the relation's pair list is equivalent to a tabular listing.

Example 5-2

If a compiler assigns the variables with symbolic names X, Y, and Z to memory addresses 100, 105, and 130, respectively, its name mapping relation is

$$R = \{(X,100),(Y,105),(Z,130)\} \tag{5-2}$$

Tabular name mappings are used frequently in computer systems—the table is called a *symbol table* when the input names are symbolic; it is called a *segment table* when the input names are segment names; and so on.

5.1.3 Name Mapping Lifetimes

An important attribute of a name mapping concerns the time interval during which the mapping remains valid. We will be concerned with the relationship between the lifetime of a program and the lifetime of the mapping of its names. This concern derives from the need to maintain a correct mapping as long as it is needed; if we are fortunate and the mapping's lifetime matches the program's lifetime, the mapping will never have to be changed during program execution; the translation of such a mapping can be performed before the program begins execution.

The following questions and definitions delineate some important situations.

1. Is the mapping identical during all executions of the program?
2. Does the mapping change during program execution?

Here are some terms that describe the categories.

Definition. A *fixed* name mapping is the same for all executions of a program.

Definition. A *variable* name mapping is not the same for all executions of the program.

Definition. In a *static* name mapping the same mapping function is used during an entire execution of the program.

Definition. In a *dynamic* name mapping the mapping function may change during program execution.

Example 5-3

A Fortran compiler's assignment of virtual addresses for objects is a fixed mapping, since the same mapping is used for all executions of the program. This type of mapping was illustrated in Example 5-2. The mapping is static.

An Ada compiler will allocate the objects local to a procedure P in an activation block that will be allocated on a stack for the duration of the procedure's execution. The resulting mapping of a local object's name to a stack location is variable and dynamic, since the procedure call history prior to the call to P affects the stack allocations during P's execution. However, the mapping of the name of a local object to an offset within the activation block is fixed and static.

A fixed name mapping can be performed during program compilation; first the compiler makes its allocations and stores the allocation information in a symbol table. Later when the compiler generates the program it determines target names to be inserted within the program by consulting the symbol table.

Name mappings that are not fixed cannot be performed during compilation; either the map is variable (and requires an adjustment for each program execution) or it is dynamic (and may change during program execution), so the translation cannot be completed until run time.

Since performing an allocation is tantamount to defining a name mapping for the allocated objects, some name mapping is implicitly changed whenever an allocation is performed. In Chapter 4 we noted three times when an allocation may be performed:

1. During translation (compilation or assembly)
2. During linking
3. During program execution

The name mapping function may be changed at any of the three times mentioned above. If the changes during program execution occur frequently, hardware support may be desired for effecting the mappings.

5.2 NAME MAPPING IMPLEMENTATIONS

Name mapping functions are implemented by one of these simple mechanisms:

1. Additive relocation
2. Locator structures
3. Table structures

In the following discussion, we assume that each name is an integer or a vector of integers.[2]

5.2.1 Additive Relocation

An additive relocation mapping uses the function

$$n_2 = f_{12}(n_1) = n_1 + R_{12} \tag{5-3}$$

[2]This does not represent a loss of generality, since symbolic names can be converted to integers by performing arithmetic algorithms on the internal codes used to denote printable characters.

Note that R_{12} is the origin of the N_1 (target) space within the N_2 (host) space. Figure 5-3 depicts this mapping. With n-dimensional addresses, all quantities in the mapping function are n-component vectors of integers.

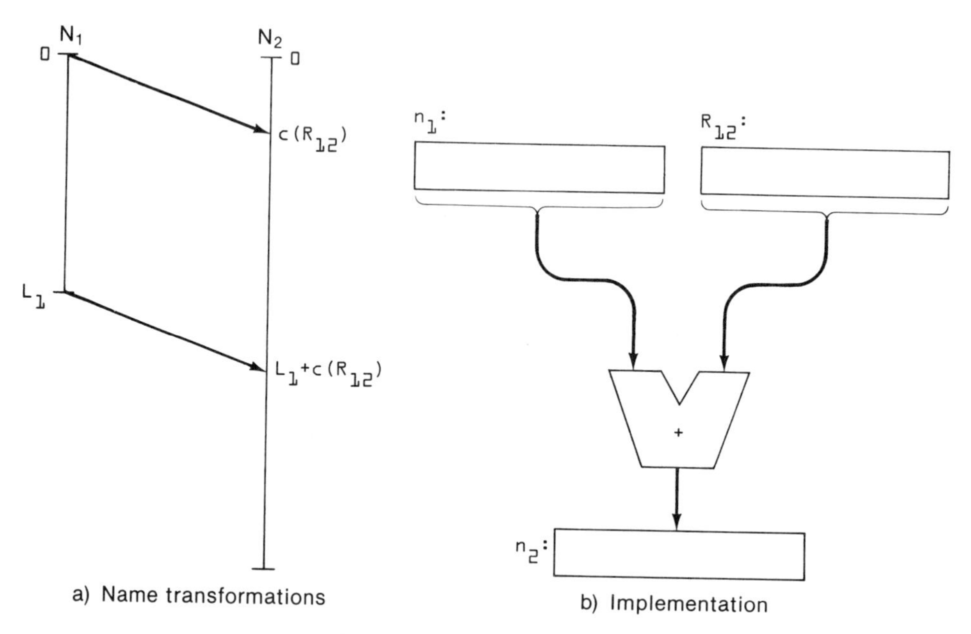

Figure 5-3 Additive relocation

Example 5-4

An additive relocation mapping in three-dimensional address space is

$$n_2 = n_1 + (5, 7, 3) \tag{5-4}$$

Under this mapping the N_2 name of the N_1 address (10, 3, 278) is (15, 10, 281).

Additive relocation is not always effective. In particular, consider multidimensional name spaces. The target space N_1 can be characterized by a dimensionality d_1 and a set of extents[3] in each dimension $e_1, \ldots, e_{d1}$. The extent in each dimension is independent of the actual values of the indices in every other dimension. Similarly, the host space N_2 is characterized by dimensionality d_2 and extents $f_1, \ldots, f_{d2}$. Additive relocation will work only when the target name space is a subset of the host name space. Additive relocation simply translates a replica of the target name space within the host name space.

Example 5-5

Take two three-dimensional name spaces, with Algol declarations

```
host : array(1 .. 10, 1 .. 25, 1 .. 4) of integer;
target : array(1 .. 4, 1 .. 10, 1 .. 2) of integer;
```

[3]The "extent" of a dimension is the number of permissible index values in that dimension.

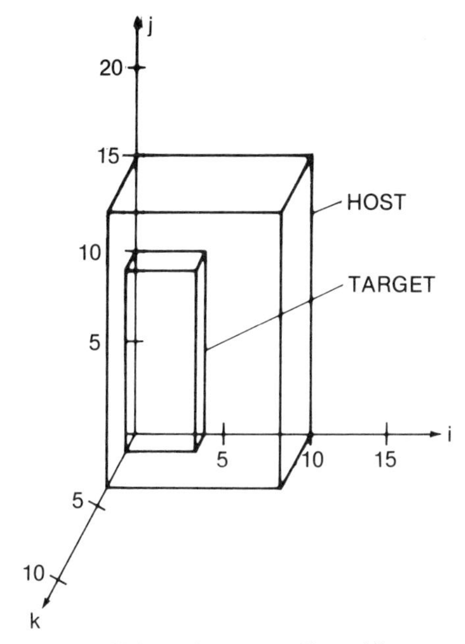

a) Objects in "normal" position

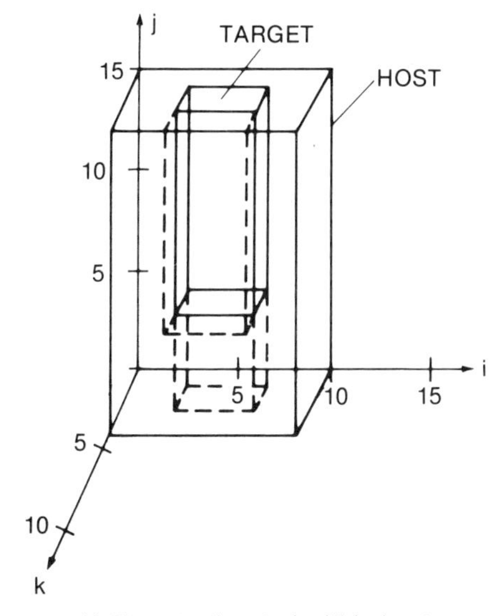

b) Target relocated within host

Figure 5-4 Three-dimensional additive relocation

Figure 5-4a illustrates these objects in the space of subscript values. Since the target structure is a subset[4] of the host structure, additive relocation can be used to map its components into the host object. Figure 5-4b shows the two spaces after an additive relocation mapping with the origin of the mapping set to (3, 5, 1).

[4]We make the subset notion precise below.

The additive relocation condition can be generalized by allowing subscript permutations; the advantage of a permutation is that it may allow us to fit "thick" dimensions of the target object into the host object. For precision, here is a formal definition of the general subset condition:

Definition. The target space N_1 defined above is a *subset* of the host space N_2 defined above if

1. $d_1 \leq d_2$, and
2. There exists a permutation of the coordinates of N_1 into the coordinates of N_2 such that the extents of the coordinates satisfy the conditions $e_k \leq f_k$, where e_k is the extent of the kth coordinate of N_1 after the permutation, for $1 \leq k \leq d_2$.

If N_2 has more dimensions than N_1, any set of the dimensions of N_2 can be used to satisfy the subset conditions. The coordinates of n_1 in the other dimensions will be fixed. Fixing the value of the subscript in some dimensions effectively positions N_1 in N_2.

Example 5-6

The space M = (3, 6, 2) is a subspace of the spaces P = (7, 4, 2) and Q = (4, 2, 2, 3, 8). There are several ways to map M into Q; here is one:

$$M(i, j, k) => Q(i, 1, 1, k + 1, j + 2).$$

Space M is not a subspace of the spaces R = (100, 2) or S = (2, 2, 3, 2, 2, 2, 2). Even though both of these spaces contain enough elements to hold all the elements of M, a simple address mapping will not suffice.

An additive relocation mapping is simple and easily implemented. However it has disadvantages:

1. N_2 must be larger than N_1.
2. N_1 must be a subset of N_2.
3. N_1 must be allocated contiguous space within N_2.
4. The map mechanism must include an adder that must propagate carries, slowing the mapping process.

Despite these disadvantages, additive relocation is frequently used, due to its simplicity. Furthermore, it is compatible with linear addressing mechanisms.

5.2.2 Blocked Pointer Relocation

A blocked pointer mapping divides the input address space into independently relocated blocks. Suppose that every name n_1 contains p bits, divided into a q-bit "block number" Q and a (p − q)-bit object address A (within the block). Then a 2^q-entry table MAP containing pointers defines the mapping, which is given by

$$n_2 = MAP(n_1.Q) + n_1.A \tag{5-5}$$

Figure 5-5 depicts this transformation.

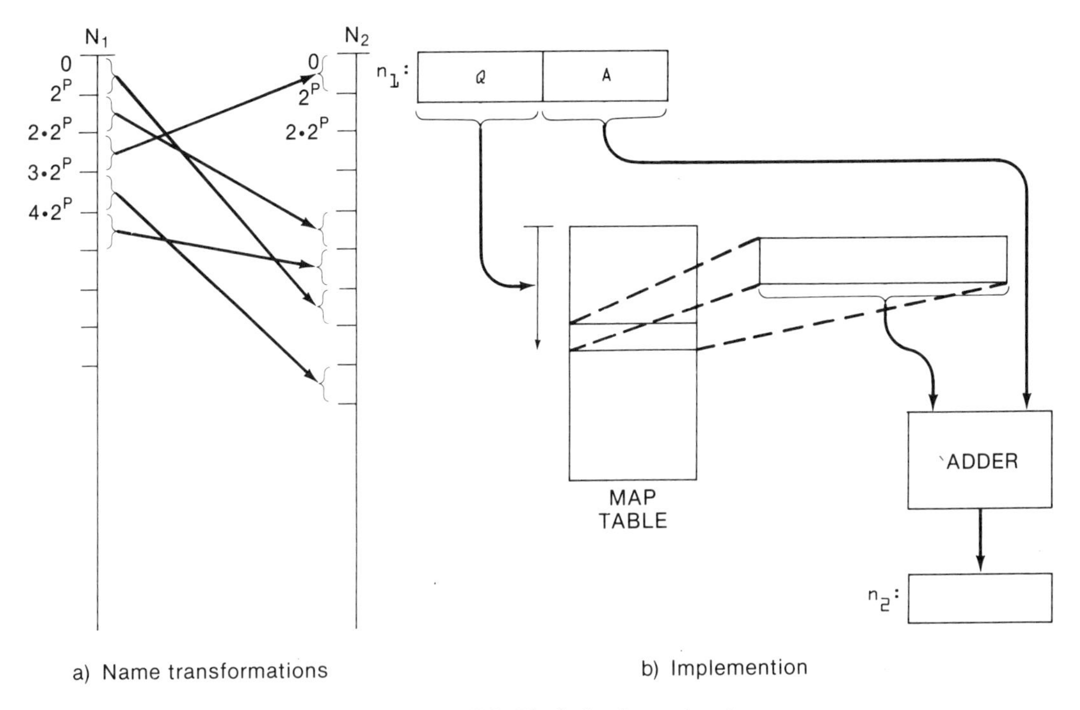

Figure 5-5 Blocked pointer relocation

Blocked pointer mappings are quite general; in fact, they can implement completely arbitrary mappings—consider the limiting case when $p = q$. In this case the entire name is the index into the MAP table. This situation may not be desirable, however, because the MAP table will be large. Nevertheless, with an appropriate selection of the block size, blocked pointer mappings can overcome some of the disadvantages of additive relocation schemes:

1. Additive relocation requires that the output name space be not smaller than the input name space. Blocked pointer mappings can circumvent this restriction since not all possible input names need to have images in the output name space; a null entry in the mapping table can be used to denote such an unmapped portion of the input name space.[5]
2. Additive relocation requires a contiguous allocation for all of N_1 within N_2. A blocked pointer mapping requires contiguous allocation within each block, but the blocks may be arbitrarily located. Thus, although an allocation for N_1 must utilize a fixed number of blocks, they may be located anywhere within N_2, and, in particular, need not be contiguous.
3. Finally, additive relocation requires an addition with carry propagation. This need can be removed in block mappings by allocating the blocks to spaces (in N_2) beginning at addresses whose last $(p - q)$ bits are zero. Then the address addition becomes concatenation, requiring no logic, as shown in Figure 5-6.

[5]The system must contain a mechanism to detect such null entries.

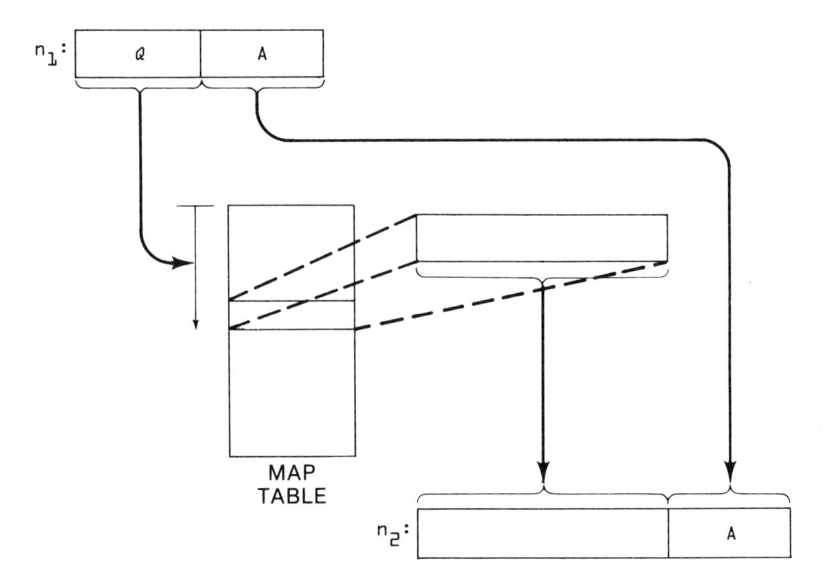

Figure 5-6 Blocked pointer relocation using concatenation

Block relocation does, however, have its own disadvantages:

1. If the block size is large, allocations for small objects require large space allocations that are not entirely used.
2. If the block size is small, the map table is large.
3. The map table must contain an entry for every block, whether used or not.

These conflicting observations give the designer an opportunity to trade space usage by varying the block size.

5.2.3 Tabular Mappings

A tabular mapping implementation of an address mapping independently describes the image of each discrete point of the input space. The appropriate table entry contains the mapped name; it may be selected by indexing if the input name is an integer, or by an associative fetch from the table with the input name serving as the search key. Options within this framework center on whether the table uses an integer selector and on how the lookup is implemented. The following paragraphs describe four alternative implementations of tabular mapping functions:

1. Indexed table
2. Linked list
3. General associative memory
4. Two-level associative table

Example 5-7

We illustrate the name mapping strategies with the mapping of Table 5-2. In addition to the target and host names, the table specifies the order in which the entries were made in the map.[6]

TABLE 5-2 NAME MAPPING FOR OUR RUNNING EXAMPLE

Target Name (hex)	Host Name (hex)	Entry Order (decimal)
0	1AB	9
1	—	—
2	—	—
3	0B2	1
4	—	—
5	—	—
6	1A6	8
7	—	—
8	110	4
9	—	—
A	—	—
B	—	—
C	—	—
D	—	—
E	1A1	2
F	1B7	12
10	006	3
11	—	—
12	—	—
13	138	7
14	—	—
15	—	—
16	10A	10
17	—	—
18	—	—
19	—	—
1A	032	5
1B	—	—
1C	05B	6
1D	—	—
1E	069	11
1F	—	—

5.2.3.1 Indexed table. An indexed table takes an integer input name. This integer is used as an index value to select the table entry that contains the result of the mapping. Figure 5-7a illustrates this mechanization of a tabular map.

[6]The history will be significant for some mapping strategies.

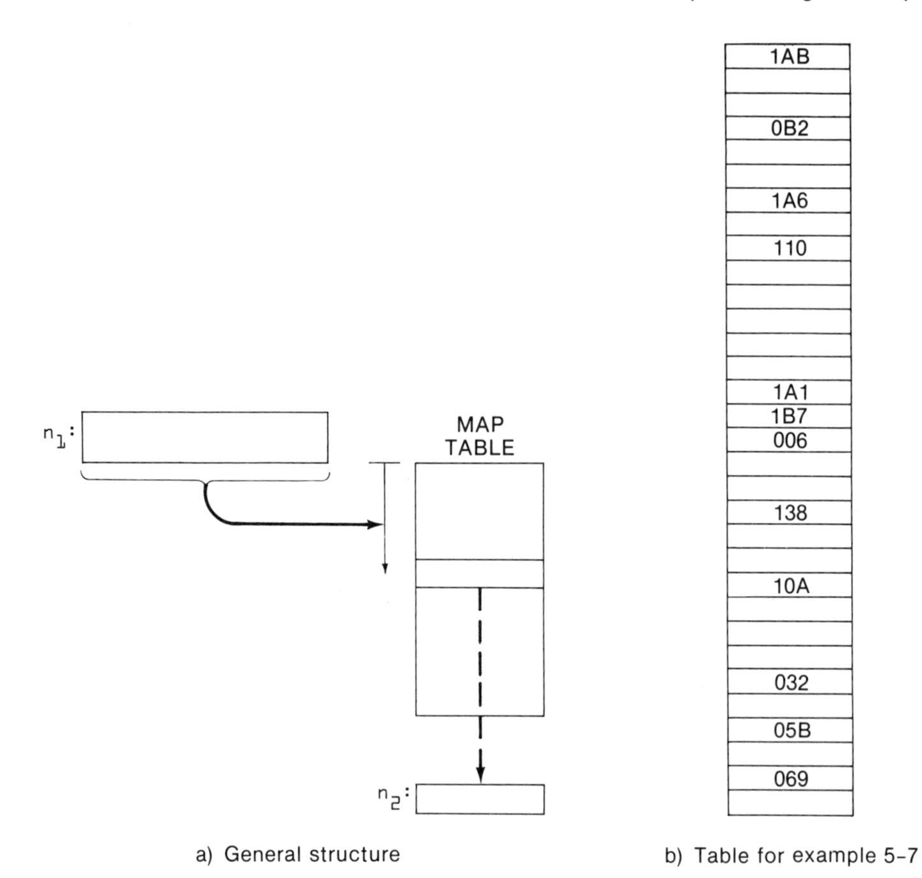

Figure 5-7 Indexed table mapping

Example 5-8

The entries in the first two columns of Table 5-2 specify the addresses and entries of the index table implementing the mapping of Table 5-2; the memory table is shown in Figure 5-7b.

An index table mapping can be useful when the name set is small and fills most of the target name space, since then the index table will be small and most of its entries will contain valid mapping information.

5.2.3.2 Linked list. In a linked list implementation each bead contains one pair from the relation describing the map. The input integer value is the key for an associative list search. The list could be ordered by the key value.

Example 5-9

The sorted linked list for our running example (Table 5-2) is shown in Figure 5-8.

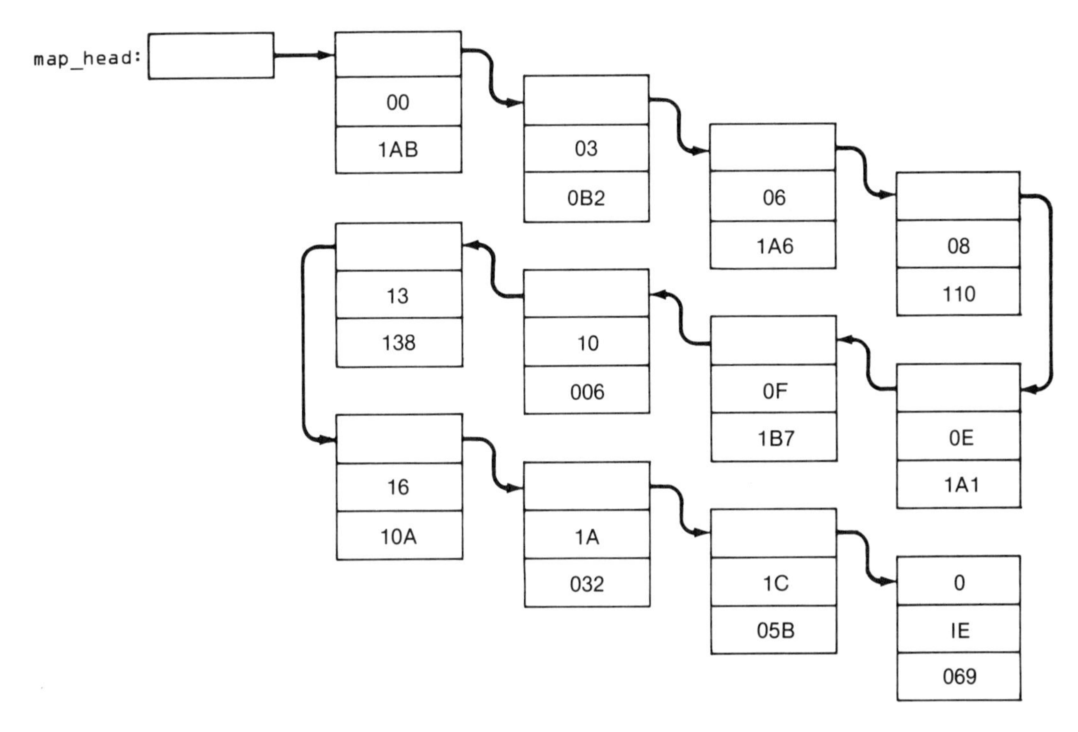

Figure 5-8 An implementation of the map of Table 5-2 using a sorted linked list

The linked list mapping is space efficient; it contains a bead for each member of the relation. Accessing the list is slow, as the pointers must be followed to traverse the list. Unfortunately, there is no practical way to compute the location of a list entry by evaluating an expression.

5.2.3.3 General associative table.

A general associative memory implementation of a tabular mapping contains all pairs that belong to the mapping relation. A search using the input name as the selector will find the entry containing the corresponding mapping pair which contains the mapped name. This type of search was used for the linked list implementation of the map. With an associative memory holding the table, many comparisons can be made simultaneously. The input name is compared with the key of each table entry using an equality test;[7] where the equality test succeeds, the match bit is set.

Example 5-10

Figure 5-9 depicts the contents of an associative memory implementing the mapping of Table 5-2. The memory entries have been allocated to table slots in the order of their definition. The search register and the match bit values reflect a search for the $06 key.

[7]In Section 5.7 we discuss a more general situation, with other boolean predicates being used to set the match bit.

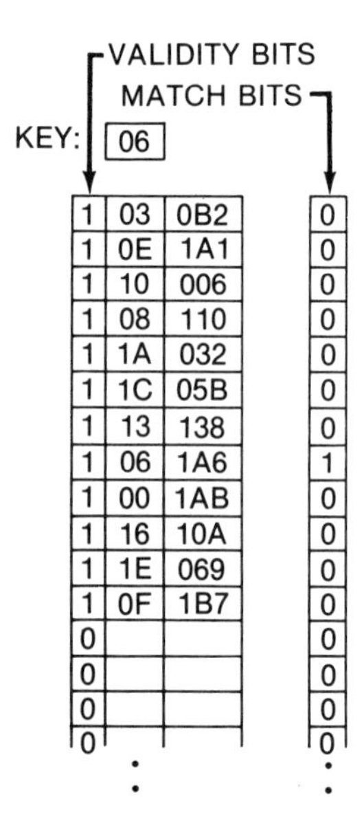

Figure 5-9 An associative memory containing the map of Table 5-2; search for 06 depicted

Since general associative tables are expensive or slow, they are not often used for name mappings—hash tables or simpler associative schemes are used whenever the performance requirements permit. Now we examine some of these options for implementing a table mapping.

5.2.3.4 Hash table. A hash table can implement a general associative mapping, provided that all search requests desire a match with a predefined key field. An entry in the table is a pair (key, answer). A search request is "Find the answer that corresponds to the key value K." Whether implemented in software or hardware, the hash table has some common functional elements, including an indexed table, a hashing function, comparison testing, and a secondary search algorithm. A hardware implmentation is shown in Figure 5-10. To search for an entry with key K in a hash table, one uses this general algorithm:

1. Compute a table index i from the selector value K (i:= hash(K);)
2. Access table(i);
3. If table(i).key = K, return the pair (i, table(i).value);
4. Invoke secondary search;
5. Return answer and success/failure status;

Step 4 is intentionally vague; there are many feasible options, as we shall see.

The "hashing function" used in the first step performs a many-to-one mapping to compress the space of key values to the space of table indices. Many different selector values will hash to the same table index,[8] so the table index is not a complete

[8]If the set of input names is known, one could ask "What hashing function avoids all collisions?" See [SEBE85] and [CICH80] for approaches to this limited question.

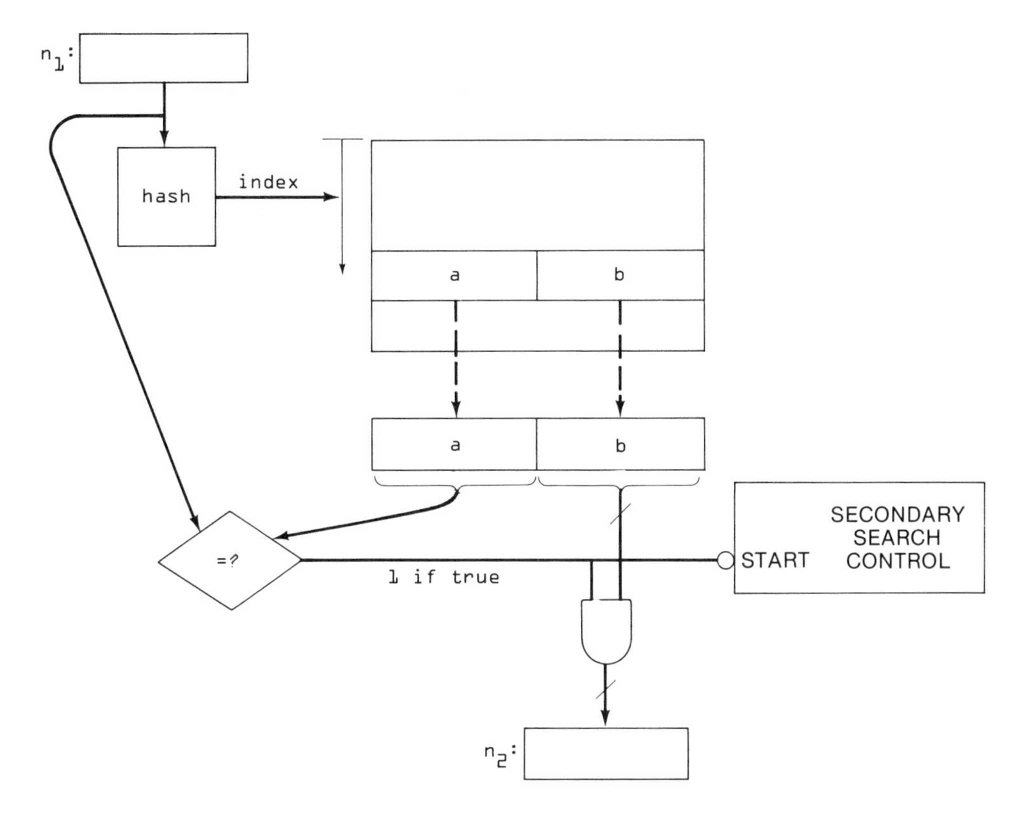

Figure 5-10 Elements of a hash table mapping

specification of the selector value. To resolve the uncertainty, each table entry must contain the key value corresponding to the answer it contains. We will use the term "table slot" to denote a position within the indexed table which may hold one or more entries from the tabular mapping. The table slot is being distinguished from a table entry, which contains a pair from the mapping function's binary relation. In step 3 the table slot indexed by the hashed selector value is examined to determine whether the key field in any of its table entries indeed matches the desired key value K. If the match test fails and the table slot is full,[9] we say that a *collision* has occurred. If the table entry is not full and the match test fails, we can deduce that the answer is not in the table; why?[10]

If the equality check in step 3 fails and the table slot is full, the desired entry may be located in another place. To determine whether the entry is in the table and to find it, the mechanism invokes the secondary search algorithm. One simple secondary search algorithm makes a linear scan of the table, starting with the entry after the one where the match attempt failed. If the linear search reaches the end of the table, it goes back to the beginning of the table. Let us see how the linear scan operates before we turn to other secondary searching options.

[9]The slot is full if every one of its table entries is valid.

[10]Because map entries are never deleted.

Example 5-11

The behavior of a hash table depends on the order in which entries are added to the mapping. We will describe the process of building a hashed implementation of our running example (Table 5-2). The entry history was specified in that table. Assume that each table slot can hold only one map entry. For simplicity in illustrating the building process, we choose a simple, arbitrary hash function:

$$\text{hash} := 2 * (K \textbf{ mod } 8) + \text{parity}(K) \tag{5-6}$$

The parity function yields zero (one) for even (odd) parity. Figure 5-11 shows an easy way to compute this hash function. Now we watch the accretion of the table, placing the hash values in the comments:

```
insert ($03, $0B2); --hash = $6
insert ($0E, $1A1); --hash = $D
insert ($10, $006); --hash = $1
insert ($08, $110); --hash = $1; collision
insert ($1A, $032); --hash = $5
insert ($1C, $05B); --hash = $9
insert ($13, $138); --hash = $7
insert ($06, $1A6); --hash = $C
insert ($00, $1AB); --hash = $0
insert ($16, $10A); --hash = $D; collision
insert ($1E, $069); --hash = $C; collision
insert ($0F, $1B7);--hash = $E; see text
```

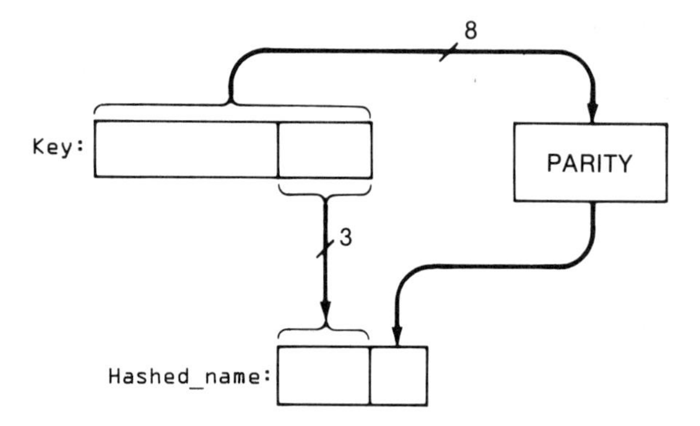

Figure 5-11 A simple hashing function

The process of adding these entries to the hash table proceeds without incident until the first collision, which occurs when the entry ($08, $110) is added to the table. The table configuration just before this insertion is attempted is shown in Figure 5-12a. The attempt to add the new entry to the table causes a collision, and the secondary search looks at location 2, which is empty. Therefore, the entry is inserted at index 2 (Figure 5-12b).

The next collision occurs when adding ($16, $10A), whose hash value is D. This overflows to location E. The next addition hashes to index C, which is a collision with the earlier entry placed at C. Since both D and E are filled, this entry is added at indcx F. Figure 5-12c illustrates the table at this point. The final entry hashes to index E, an

V	K	VALUE
0		
1	10	006
0		
0		
0		
0		
1	03	0B2
0		
0		
0		
0		
0		
0		
1	0E	1A1
0		
0		

a) Before first collision

V	K	VALUE
0		
1	10	006
1	08	110
0		
0		
0		
1	03	0B2
0		
0		
0		
0		
0		
0		
1	0E	1A1
0		
0		

b) After first collision

V	K	VALUE
1	00	1AB
1	10	006
1	08	110
0		
0		
1	1A	032
1	03	0B2
1	13	138
0		
1	1C	05B
0		
0		
1	06	1A6
1	0E	1A1
1	16	10A
1	1E	069

c) Before last entry is inserted

V	K	VALUE
1	00	1AB
1	10	006
1	08	110
1	0F	1B7
0		
1	1A	032
1	03	0B2
1	13	138
0		
1	1C	05B
0		
0		
1	06	1A6
1	0E	1A1
1	16	10A
1	1E	069

d) Complete table

Figure 5-12 Building a hash table (Example 5-11)

index value that has not appeared in the history. Nevertheless, the desired slot is occupied with an entry that was placed there after an overflow search. There has been a collision with an overflow entry! Whereas a human observer can see that this collision involves one of the overflow entries, the mechanism sees only that there is a nonmatching valid entry in the accessed place. This implies overflow, so the overflow search is instigated. The overflow search to insert the E entry cycles back to the top of the table and does not succeed until index 3 is reached. The final table configuration is shown in Figure 5-12d.

Here are the details of the sequential search collision resolution algorithm. In the program, i denotes the hash value and j denotes the index of a candidate table slot. As in the example, the algorithm is written for the case when there is one map entry per table slot. Sequential searching starts with $j := i + 1$ and proceeds circularly around the table looking for the desired entry. It is possible that an empty slot will be found, in which case the search is unsuccessful. It is also possible that the scan returns to the starting point (j = i), in which case the table is full and there is no entry matching the key. Here is this algorithm expressed as an Ada program:

```
missing_entry : exception;
type key_type is ..;
type value_type is ..;
type table_entry is
  record
    key : key_type;
    value : value_type;
    valid : boolean := false; --table is initially empty
  end record;
table : array(1 .. n) of table_entry;
..
function searchhash(K : key_type) return value_type is
  i, j : integer;
begin
  i := hash(K);
  j := i;
  while K /= table(j).key
  loop
    if not table(j).valid then
      raise missing_entry;
    end if;
    j := (j mod table'last) + 1;
    if j = i then
      raise missing_entry;
    end if;
  end loop;
  return table(j).value;
end searchhash;
```

The sequential search algorithm embodied in this program works only if no table entry is ever deleted. Name mapping tables can be managed so that their entries never have to be deleted.[11]

There exist many other secondary searching algorithms; we briefly look at an interesting one that uses a hierarchy of tables. Figure 5-13 illustrates a sequence of tables (the sequence shown reading from left to right). The mth table is named table(m). The figure suggests that all the tables are the same length, but this condition is not required. Our search strategy will use a different hash function at each table; these functions are denoted hash(m, key). The search strategy is as follows: first search table(1); if it suffers a collision, search table(2) using hash(2, K), and so forth. If the search in the last table suffers a collision, sequential searching in that table is used to complete the search.

[11]We achieve this by structuring the table usage so that the entire table is deleted. Notice the parallel with the allocations of objects to pools based on the lifetimes of the pool and the object being allocated.

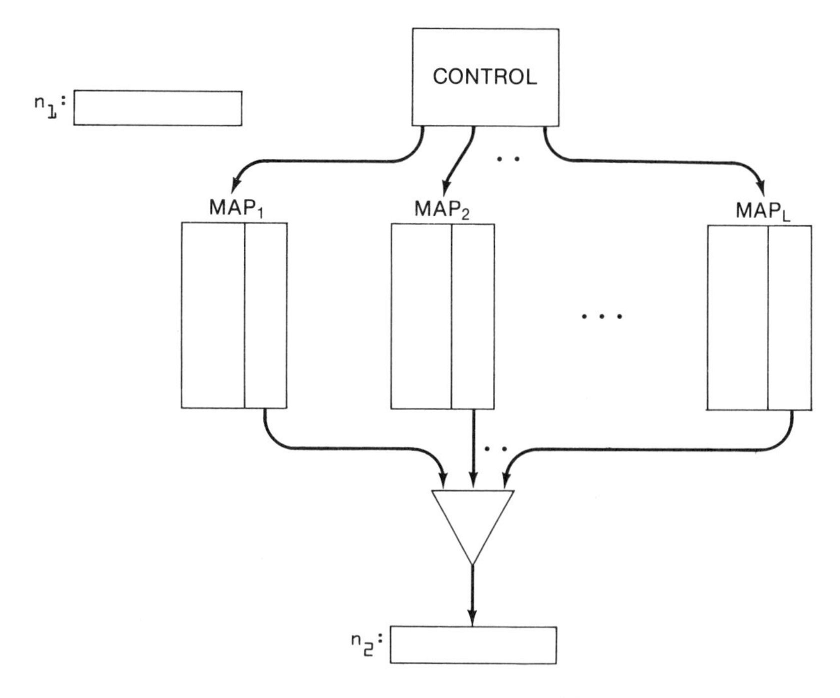

Figure 5-13 A multilevel map table

To measure the effectiveness of a hash table implementation, we estimate the time required to map a name. For a hash table stored in memory, the cumulative memory access time plus the cumulative entry comparison time will be used. Both of these times are proportional to the number of accesses to table entries made while looking for the matching entry. The shortest mapping time is attained with the indexed table, since only one table entry is read out and no comparison is required to verify the match condition. To make an estimate for a hash table, we need to know the collision probability, since that determines the number of table accesses used. If there were no collisions, a single access would suffice. In the worst case, all input names map into the same hashed index, and almost every access suffers at least one collision. With n entries in the map and an even distribution of requests over the set of map entries, we expect to scan n/2 entries to find the match. This exceptional case is improbable, fortunately. If the hash function is "good," there will be few collisions, and the search will require few table accesses. The computation of the expected number of accesses is beyond the scope of this discussion; see [KNUT73] for the details.

While hashed mappings have the advantage of a short access time, they do have disadvantages. These include:

1. The hash table size must match the size of the range of the hashing function.
2. A hash table cannot be expanded easily.
3. The entire hash table space must be allocated even if the table contains only a few entries.

In addition, several speed concerns may mitigate against the use of hash tables to implement an associative mapping; these include:

1. Hashing time
2. Search time after finding a collision
3. Time to make the equality test

The multilevel map table structures we discuss in the next section should be considered when the first two speed issues seem important.

5.2.3.5 Unordered multimemory mapping tables. A multimemory mapping table contains a hierarchy of mapping tables, but is not a multilevel hash table. In the multilevel hash table, each successive table contains different entries from its predecessors. In the table hierarchy, on the other hand, each successive table contains *all* the entries from its predecessor (and, by extension, of all its predecessors). All component tables in a multilevel hash table could reside in the same memory, but this would be unwise with the multimemory table, since there is little point in repeating all the entries from the predecessor within a new table occupying the same memory. The advantage of a multimemory mapping table is that the successive tables can reside in different levels of the memory hierarchy. A search failure in the first-level table initiates an attempt in a second-level table, accessing a slower memory system. Program locality suggests this strategy; as with virtual memory management, a table manager can move map entries among the tables to speed the mapping process. The goal is to have the first-level table hold frequently used entries, with less frequently used entries relegated to tables lower in the hierarchy. If this goal were achieved, the average amount of time spent to make a table access would be low, but the cost of the memory space for the map would be reduced compared to the single-level table implementation.

The important policy for a multilevel map table is the policy controlling the composition of the table at each level of the hierarchy. It is almost correct to reason that the strategy for deciding when to move a table entry among the levels could be similar to the strategy for managing virtual memory (see Section 4.5), since the goals are similar. The only flaw in this analogy arises because the map table entries might be rarely changed, and the complete table is always found at the bottom of the hierarchy. In the extreme situation the map is static, the table entries never change, and there is never a "dirty" entry. Thus once the complete table is stored at the bottom of the hierarchy, table entries never have to be written to any table lower in the memory hierarchy. In other words, there is no need to save any entry before overwriting it.

The simplest multi-memory map table, the two-memory table, is used with the set-associative tabular mapping. In many systems set-associative maps implement the name mapping for a cache memory and translate virtual memory addresses to physical addresses. Another interesting multimemory mapping is the tree structure, used to implement a map with a large domain,[12] often found in a file system or a large database system.

The set-associative mapping is a two-level map; the first level is a hashed table with a trivial hashing function (for speed). Often, the slot index is the verbatim

[12]In other words, many values are mapped.

contents of a selector subfield, such as the n least significant[13] bits. There are four significant differences between a set-associative mapping and a hashed mapping:

1. Simplicity of the hash function
2. Slot size
3. Mismatch handling
4. Table state after a collision

We just mentioned the hash function simplicity; in the set-associative mapping hashing is performed by field selection, sometimes supplemented by a trivial computation (such as parity).

The slot size for a simple hashed mapping is one. For the set-associative mapping, the slot size may be, and usually is, greater than 1, and the selector must be compared against all entries in the selected slot. If any slot entry matches the selector, the search process is complete. Multiple copies of the match checking logic will be required; Figure 5-14 illustrates the structure of a set-associative table with slot_size = 2.

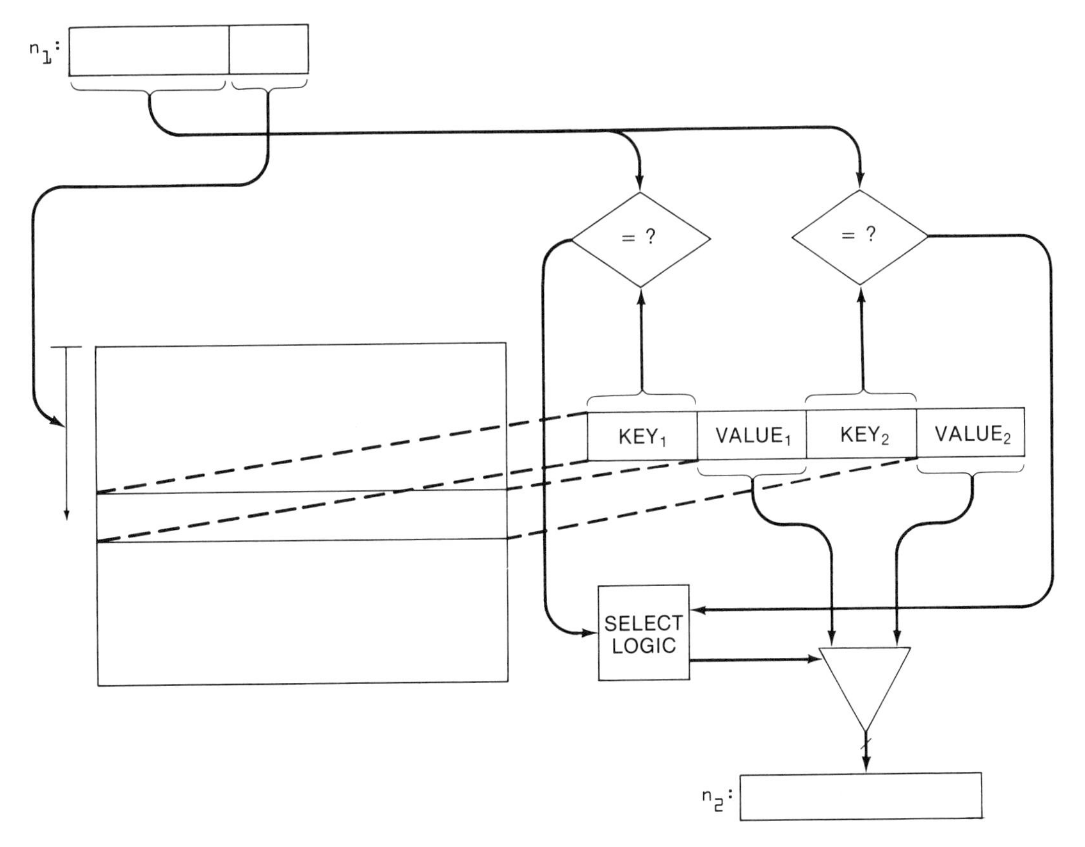

Figure 5-14 A set-associative memory

[13]The least significant end is chosen to obtain a better hashing distribution across the table indices.

After a mismatch[14] in a set-associative table, the secondary search is made in the secondary table, not by looking at other entries of the primary table (as with a hashed mapping).

After a mismatch is detected and the desired entry is found in the secondary table, the table manager may promote it to the primary table to speed future accesses.

The set-associative structure can be used with a second-level table implemented in any chosen manner.

Here are some important decisions to be made during the design of a set-associative memory:

1. Select the bits to be used for the index subfield.
2. Choose the hashing function, if any.
3. Determine the number of slots in the table.
4. Determine the number of table entries per slot.
5. Select the policy for placing entries in the first-level map.
6. Select the implementation of the second-level map.

The index subfield bit selection, along with the hash computation, determines which key information constitutes the slot index in the set-associative memory. The choice may affect the statistical slot usage pattern, which affects performance. Sizing the first-level table determines the statistical spread achieved through the use of the index to find the table's slot to be accessed. The hardware cost is also affected by this selection. By varying the number of slots the designer can move between a *fully associative* table (with all entries in one slot) and a *direct-mapped* table (with one entry per slot). The selection of the number of entries per slot affects both the hardware complexity and the table size (if the previous selections have been fixed). The policy for placing entries in the first-level map determines when an entry is put into the set-associative table and where in the table the new entry shall be placed. Selecting the implementation of the second-level map is not very important, since the system's performance is achieved by attaining a high hit ratio in the first-level table. The slower accesses to the second-level table are infrequent.

Comparing the set-associative mechanism against the other table searching mechanisms, we see that this mechanism requires wider table entries and more comparison logic per entry, but never requires more than one fetch from the table itself if the desired entry is present in the first-level table. Furthermore, the table index is easily determined from the selector, so the mechanism can operate very quickly when the desired entry is indeed found in the first-level table.

To assist in making intelligent decisions after a mismatch is detected in a set-associative memory, the mechanism should collect some usage and status information. Data collection hardware is necessary to obtain this status information. For example, when a new entry must be copied to the first-level table, information about recent usage can help select the entry to be displaced. One simple policy used when

[14]No entry in the slot matched the selector.

the slot has two entries is to enter the new entry (corresponding to the search that failed) so as to retain in the slot the entry that was accessed most recently; the manager replaces the other one (accessed less recently). This is a trivial special case of an LRU policy.

Example 5-12

Suppose that we implement the mapping of Table 5-2 with a four-slot direct-mapped table which uses the least significant two bits of the key value as the table index. The table has four slots, each holding one map entry. The primary table entries change with time. Figure 5-15a specifies a history of selector values presented to the table. Assume that the direct-mapped table is initialized with invalid entries, and that an LRU replacement policy is used. The resulting history of set-associative search failures is marked with plus signs in the figure. Figure 5-15b and c illustrate the table contents after the fifteenth access and at the end of the history.

Example 5-13

Consider the history from the previous example with an expanded four-slot set-associative table that has two entries per slot. The LRU replacement policy will be followed. Then the set-associative search fails on the access attempts marked with minus signs in Figure 5-15a. The table contents after 15 and 25 accesses are shown in Figure 5-15d and e.

These examples illustrate the mechanics of set-associative maps, but no simple example can illustrate their statistical behavior, since a properly configured map will have a low miss probability. The boundary of acceptable miss probabilities will lie lower than 5%; the exact value at the boundary depends on the ratio of access times for the memories holding the tables at different levels.

Set-associative maps are often used when rapid name translation is needed; often, they are implemented in hardware modules. Match failures may be handled by hardware, firmware, or software modules, depending on the speed requirements.

5.2.3.6 Ordered mapping tables. An address mapping function may be sparse in the sense that the mapping is defined for a very small fraction of its input name space. A general associative mapping, requiring special hardware, may be too expensive. Hashing and set-associative maps provide effective implementations simulating general associative maps, but require the entire table stored at the lowest level of the hierarchy. In some situations the map table has a very large domain; it is stored in several levels of the memory hierarchy. Ordering the table entries can assist accessing. A small ordered table can be searched using binary search, but this necessitates storing the table contiguously in some address space and having random access to the table. If the table is too large to be stored in a contiguous address range, a multimemory mapping might be considered by the designer.

There are several ways to organize a multimemory mapping; here we present the tree structure and one mixed variation—the indexed-sequential structure. In a tree-structured multi-memory mapping the access path depends on the selector value. The tree entries are ordered by key field values, so a simple search algorithm suffices. The search algorithm defines both the search process and the underlying data

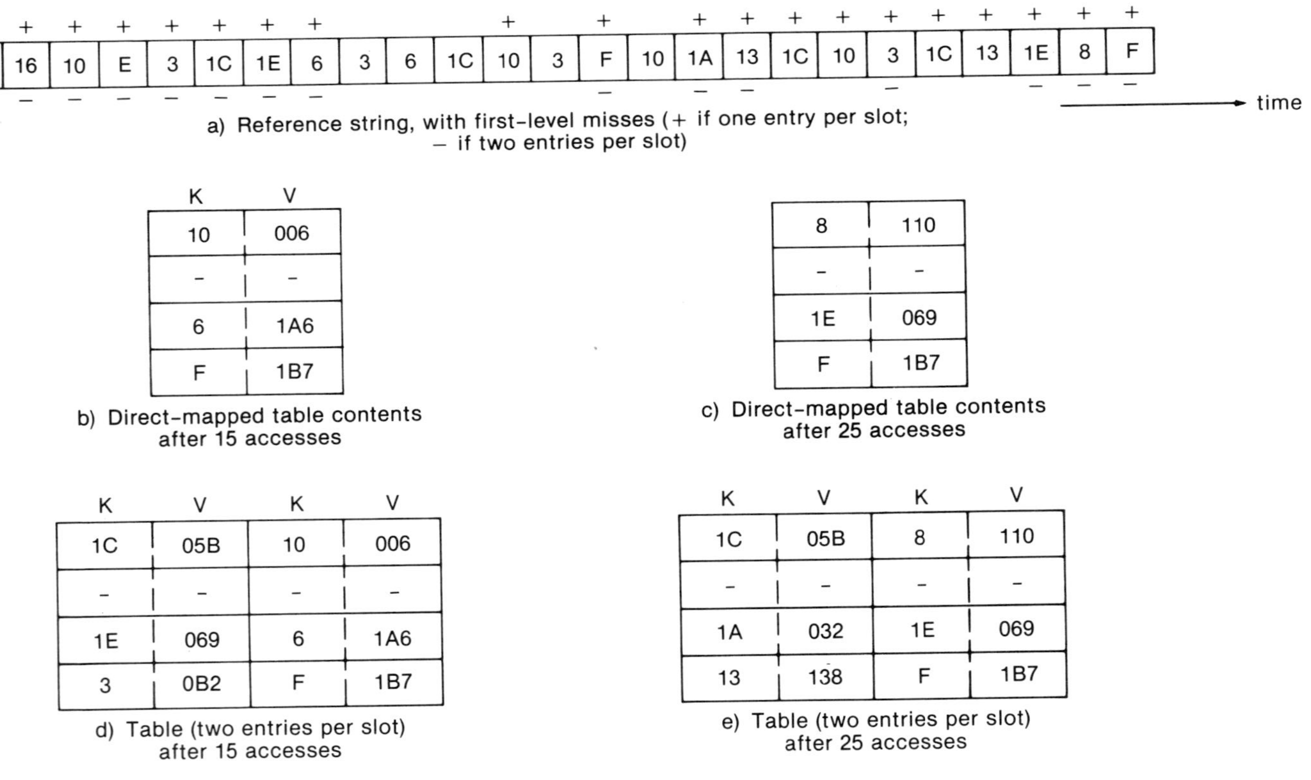

+ + + + + + + + + + + + + + + + + + + +
0 16 10 E 3 1C 1E 6 3 6 1C 10 3 F 10 1A 13 1C 10 3 1C 13 1E 8 F
– – – – – – – – – – – – – – –
time
a) Reference string, with first-level misses (+ if one entry per slot;
– if two entries per slot)
K V
10 006
- -
6 1A6
F 1B7
b) Direct-mapped table contents
after 15 accesses
8 110
- -
1E 069
F 1B7
c) Direct-mapped table contents
after 25 accesses
K V K V
1C 05B 10 006
- - - -
1E 069 6 1A6
3 0B2 F 1B7
d) Table (two entries per slot)
after 15 accesses
K V K V
1C 05B 8 110
- - - -
1A 032 1E 069
13 138 F 1B7
e) Table (two entries per slot)
after 25 accesses

Figure 5-15 A short history of a set-associative memory

structure. We will not discuss algorithms for operations other than table search since they are easily determined once the search algorithm is known.

For an ordered table implementation it is essential that the table be accessed through a single key field so that its entries can be ordered uniquely by their key values. At each stage of the search process an arithmetic comparison determines search success, search failure, and directs the continuation of the search, if required. For example, binary search works in a table fragment contained in a linearly addressable address space in a random-access memory; that algorithm makes a less-than/equal/greater-than test to direct the search. For binary search, the search time is proportional to the logarithm of the table size.

In a tree-structured table the result obtained at one level of the table might indicate the conclusion of a successful search, but it might command a move to a lower level of the tree to search for the desired entry in another portion of the table. In a *balanced* tree the distance from the root to every leaf is approximately the same. The search time in a balanced tree-structured table is a logarithmic function of the table size. When a new entry is inserted in the table, it may be necessary to adjust the tree to maintain the balanced property. The details of this activity are beyond the scope of this discussion (for details, see [KNUT73]).

A disadvantage of a tree structure is that pointers have to be traversed to effect the search algorithm, and chasing pointers is often slower than performing address arithmetic. The tree's use of pointers can be considered to be an advantage, since any pointer could direct the search to information in slower memory. One might place all second-level nodes on the disk and use disk addresses as pointers. A wise designer would consider a balanced n-ary tree, whose data structure is depicted in Figure 5-16. Notice the tags associated with the index values; each tag signifies whether the described space contains data or further pointers. Also notice the use of the highest key value in the entry that points to the next lower level of the table. This structure is tailored to a search that stops when the value from the table is not less than the selector. When the search stops, the flag can be examined to determine whether the desired entry has been found; if the tag signifies a pointer, the described space is then scanned following the same algorithm.

A second important ordered table structure is the *indexed sequential* table. The entries in this table are grouped into consecutive sets, much as the two-level tree. There are four levels of the mapping (see Figure 5-17). The key value in an entry at the first, second, or third level is the highest key contained in the set beneath. In the second level there is a table of the third level structures; alternate entries in the third level distinguish whether the actual entry is found in a sequentially stored sequence or in a linked data structure. The sequential list of entries is located in a fixed-length pool; the linked list chains together all "overflow" items—those that would not fit into the fixed-length pool. This whole structure may be used for a single large disk file containing records that will be retrieved individually. In this case the top-level table selects a set of "cylinders" on which the data reside. The second level selects one cylinder in the set. The third-level table is stored at the beginning of the cylinder selected; it serves as the index of all information on that cylinder. Its alternate entries starting with the first entry specify the sequentially stored information; the other entries specify the entries stored in the linked list holding overflow

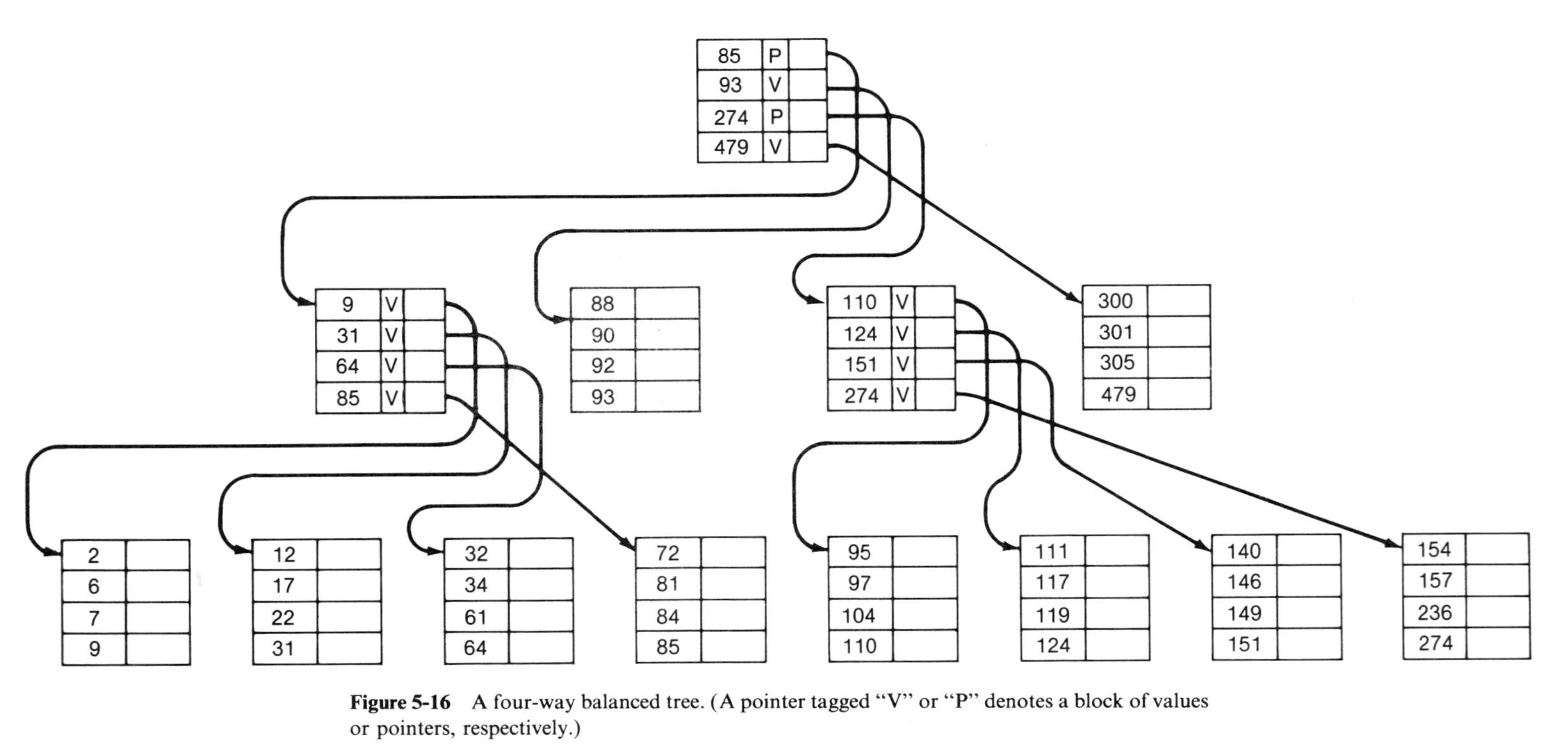

Figure 5-16 A four-way balanced tree. (A pointer tagged "V" or "P" denotes a block of values or pointers, respectively.)

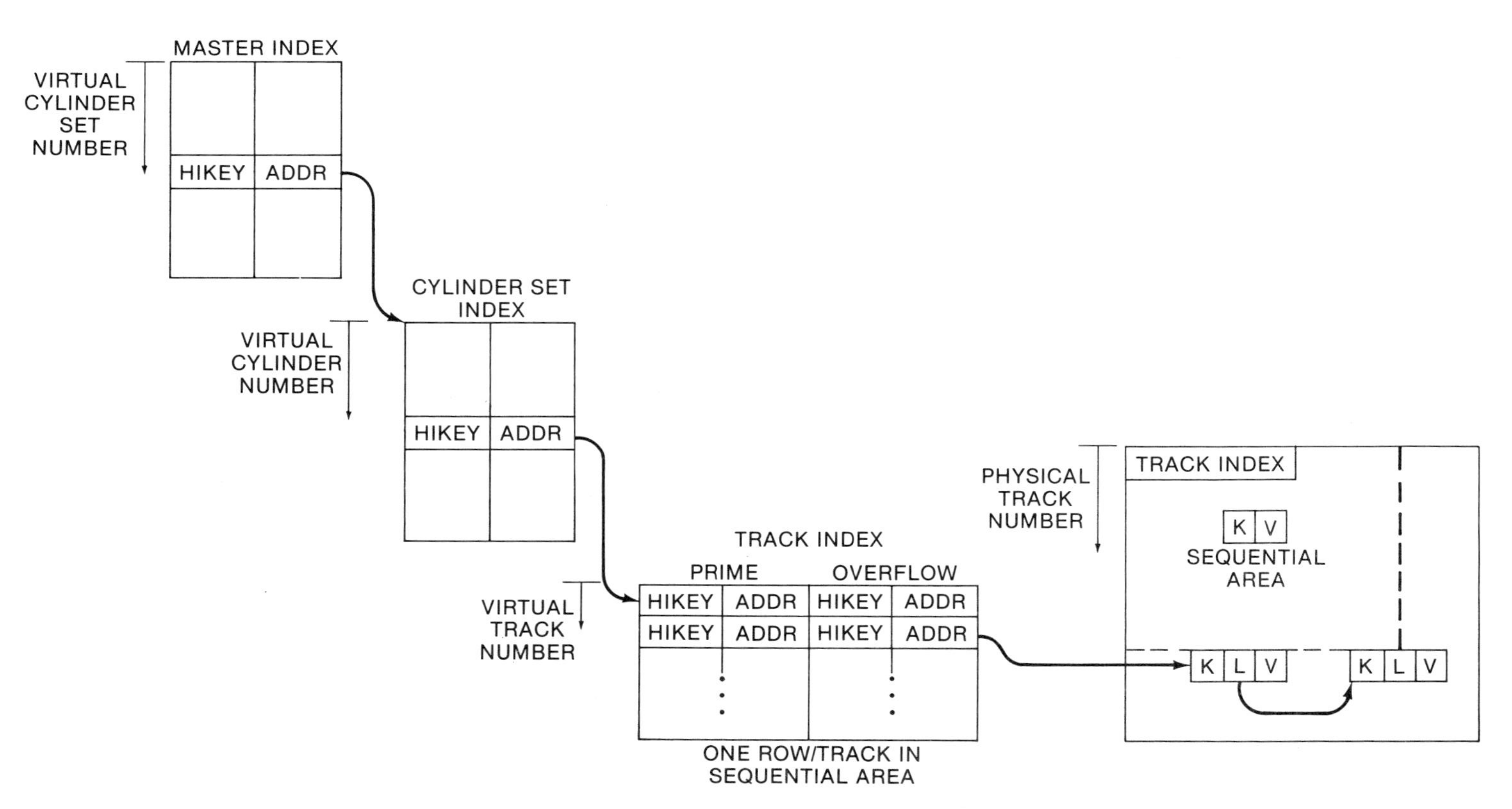

Figure 5-17 Indexed sequential file organization

information. A linked list is not used for all entries since following a linked list on a disk is expensive (a complete revolution may separate one list entry from its successor). Restructuring the database to remove the overflow records can be useful when the access time increase becomes noticeable. The restructuring operation is expensive, requiring a rework of all information in the database. Indexed sequential organization is used for large data files held on disk. The disk controller can be designed to support some of these searching operations without intervention from the central processor.

5.2.4 Summary

Name mappings are essential to the process of accessing an object in a computer's memory system. The complete name mapping may be implemented in several stages. At each stage the name map may be implemented by a simple mechanism that allows little usage flexibility, or by a complex mechanism that uses more space or takes more time to provide more flexibility. Three general name mappings suffice for all practical situations: additive relocation, blocked pointer mapping, and tabular mapping. Different mapping functions and implementations may be appropriate at the compiler, linker, and run-time levels of the system, in addition to the processor and interface hardware. After all, there is a different emphasis on speed, size, or flexibility in different situations. We explore these issues in the remainder of the chapter.

5.3 NAME TRANSLATION BEFORE PROGRAM EXECUTION

Static name mappings do not change during program execution, so they can be performed before program execution. We use the common compile-link paradigm to describe the preexecution activities. The compiler can define static allocations for block-local objects and for objects local to the compilation unit. These static allocations provide the basis for a static name translation performed before program execution. In a similar manner, the linker allocates space and thus defines names that link a set of program modules to each other; these names can be translated before program execution. The compiler maps names within one module; the linker maps names that couple modules to each other. Between them all names can be mapped before program execution. There is some benefit (in some environments) to deferring the linking process until the program executes on the processor.

5.3.1 Mapping Names in an Isolated Program Module

Whether the translation program is an assembler or a compiler, it must perform name mappings. Similar design issues arise; they have similar solutions for both the assembler and the compiler. We discuss compilation, without loss of generality.

Four major issues relate to the name translation process:

1. Structure of the input name space
2. Structure of the output name space
3. Choice of the name mapping techniques
4. Implementation of changes in the map

5.3.1.1 Structure of the input name space. For compilation the input name space is the space of symbolic names constructed according to the rules of the language. The space is structured by the rules defining how a programmer can name components of data structures. This space is sparsely used.

5.3.1.2 Structure of the output name space. For compilation the output name space is the space of address specification techniques that can be used in object programs. The space can be simple if the program makes only simple references to memory and only simple data structures appear in the program. Dynamically allocated objects, however, must be accessed through locator objects, indirection, or algorithms that compute addresses. Here are four important name representations:

2a. Integer value
2b. Parameters for a processor-supported addressing mode computation
2c. Search algorithm
2d. Index within a table filled by the linker

5.3.1.3 Name mapping techniques. The name mapping process involves both name definition and name replacement, which can be separated into two phases. During the name definition phase the translator scans the program, accumulates a list of all input names, and allocates space, as appropriate. During the name replacement phase, the translator scans the program and replaces each input name with its output name. If each name's definition precedes all uses of that name, these two compilation phases can be accomplished during a single scan of the input text. On the other hand, if name usage may precede name declaration, the text will have to be scanned twice; this process is known as "two-pass" translation.

Since the input name space is sparsely used, the compiler might use an associative name mapping for the symbol table. Although associative mappings may be supported by hardware, translation speed is not critical, so the use of specialized name translation hardware is not indicated. Therefore, software-implemented hash tables are used to effect the name mapping within a compiler.

5.3.1.4 Changing the map. There are two situations in which the translator's name map must be changed dynamically during the translation process. One situation occurs when a new name is declared in the program; this name must be added to the program's name map.

A map update is required as the compiler's scanner moves across a naming context boundary. As the naming context changes, so must the translator's name mapping table change. If the scanner leaves a completed context, the translator can discard the old symbol table and start a new one for the new context. Ada programs have nested naming contexts requiring that the compiler maintain every naming context until it is closed off by the final **end** signaling block termination. With such static nesting, the compiler can stack the mapping tables, there being one for each naming context in the nest. Each map table can be a hash table.

Whenever the scanner enters a new name context, a new name table is created by pushing it on a stack, and initialized empty. As the scanner leaves a completed name context, the name table at the top of the stack is deleted. The stack ordering reflects the static block nesting, placing the current block's map table at the top of the stack. When a declaration is scanned, the new name and its attributes are entered in the table at the top of the stack. Whenever a name has to be translated, the tables are searched backward from the top of the stack. If all hash tables are the same size, stacking these hash tables is quite easily accomplished.

In summary, the translator converts the symbolic names from the input program to names in the translator address space associated with the *translation unit*, the set of programs translated together. The translator uses a hash table to hold the names mappings that it requires. The output names produced by the translator are input to the linking step in the composite name-translation process. During linking the translator name spaces of several independent translations may be combined.

5.3.2 Combining Translated Program Modules

The linker builds a program from separate translation units. It combines appropriate translation units to form one logically consistent program. These links can be established prior to or during program execution. During this process, the linker combines the translator address spaces and modifies program addresses to be compatible with the space allocations in the composite program. Figure 5-18 depicts the roles of the translator and linker, if linking occurs prior to execution. The figure shows three separately compiled programs which the linker has found in the process of determining the meaning of the ED names in the programs. The linker was given a file search order to be followed when looking for the definitions of ED names.

The figure also shows the act of loading the program for execution and then executing the program. In many designs, the program's parts must be gathered into a single address space before the program can be executed. In many of these designs, the linker is designed both to make the logical connections and to place all the required programs into the same address space. This pattern was assumed for the situation shown in the figure. Since these actions do not always go together, we define linking and collection to be separate acts. Thus the act of establishing the logical connections between separately translated programs is called *linking*, while the act of gathering together all the separately translated programs into a single program occupying a single address space is called *collection*.

The linker's main job is to find an external object corresponding to each name that was ED in a using program. To do this, the linker searches files that contain object definitions, following the search order prescribed in the search list. Once the linker finds the corresponding definition, the linker links the defining module into the composite program by adjusting the access path to the referenced ED object so that it reaches the defining module. To achieve this, it may replace all references to the object with the correct address, or it may complete an indirect address to the desired object.

One design decision concerns the timing of the linking process. There are two major options, static linking and dynamic linking. *Static linking* occurs before program execution. *Dynamic linking* occurs during program execution. It is easy to guess that static linking is more efficient but less flexible than dynamic linking.

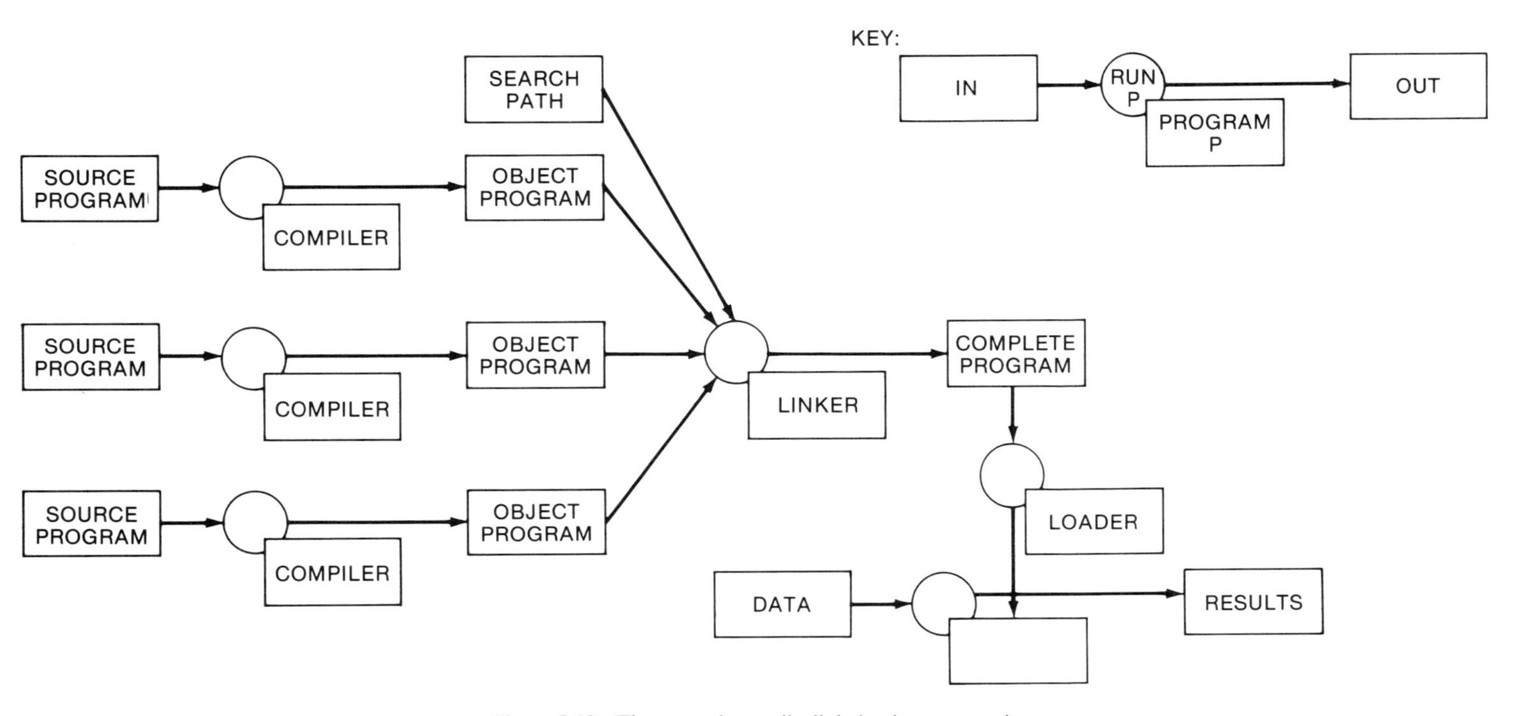

Figure 5-18 The general compile–link–load–run scenario

Dynamic linking requires a supporting mechanism to test each access attempt to ascertain whether it is, in fact, a reference to an unresolved link. This requirement has a significant impact on the processor design; it is discussed in detail in Section 5.4.4.

The final step in the linking process modifies addresses in programs so that the correct references will be completed during program execution. Several data structures and addressing modes play important roles in making address modifications. In addition, the choice of static versus dynamic linking has a profound effect on these aspects of the design. After all, the underlying support for dynamic linking must be visible during program execution to detect links that have not been resolved.

The data structures used during linking include:

1. A list of all (ED) symbols imported by a module
2. A list of all (EV) symbols exported from a module
3. A list of file names specifying a search path

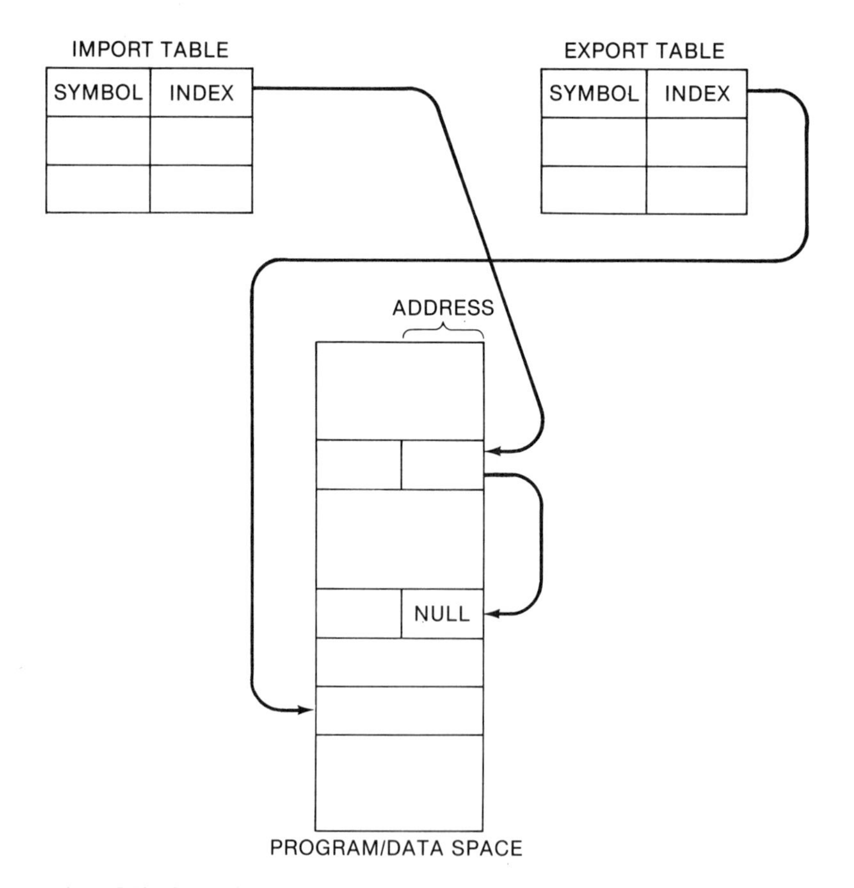

Figure 5-19 Import/export name lists. (The pointer structure links together the uses of the imported name.)

4. The address of the (defining) location within the module to which an EV symbol corresponds
5. A list of all locations where each ED symbol is used

All these data must be provided by the compiler. The first two comprise a table expressing the imported symbols and their usage in the program module; this is called the *import table*. Similarly, the externally available symbols and their definitions are collected into an *export table*. The symbol definitions in the export table are relative to the origin of the spaces allocated by the compiler. The ones that are program locations (entry points) are relative to the origin of the program space. Figure 5-19 contains a diagrammatic representation[15] of these import and export tables and the data structures connecting them to the program. We discuss two methods to link modules together and mention a variation on one of them.

In the first method, the linker changes addresses in the importing module. To support this linking method, the translation program creates a list of all uses of each imported symbol. This list could be an appendage of the symbol table. It is usually more effective to structure this list as a linked list using the address field of an instruction that references the external object to hold the relative (or absolute) offset of the next usage of the external address. With this chaining of all uses of each imported symbol, as shown in Figure 5-20a, the linker can simply follow the chain of address pointers and thus find all locations where the imported symbol is used; at each of these locations, the address should be changed to reference the external object. The result of this operation is shown in Figure 5-20b. This technique is very efficient and straightforward; the only disadvantage is that the importing program is modified. Thus this technique cannot be used if a program is to be shared among different environments.

Here is a sketch of the reference replacement algorithm that is used to replace the chained uses with the definition.

1. Let S be the next unlinked imported symbol; (If none remain,exit.)
2. Let A be the address in the entry where S was found;
3. Find the declaration linked to S, and let D be its value;[16]
4. Let B be the contents of the address part of M(A);[17] (This is the pointer to the next entry.)
5. Store D in the address part of M(A);
6. Copy B into A; if this is not 0, go to step 4;
7. Go to step 1;

In the second method the translator replaces every reference to an imported object with an indirect address pointing to a table that will hold the addresses

[15]This applies only to one linking scheme.

[16]This value is actually an address.

[17]This denotes the contents of the location with address A.

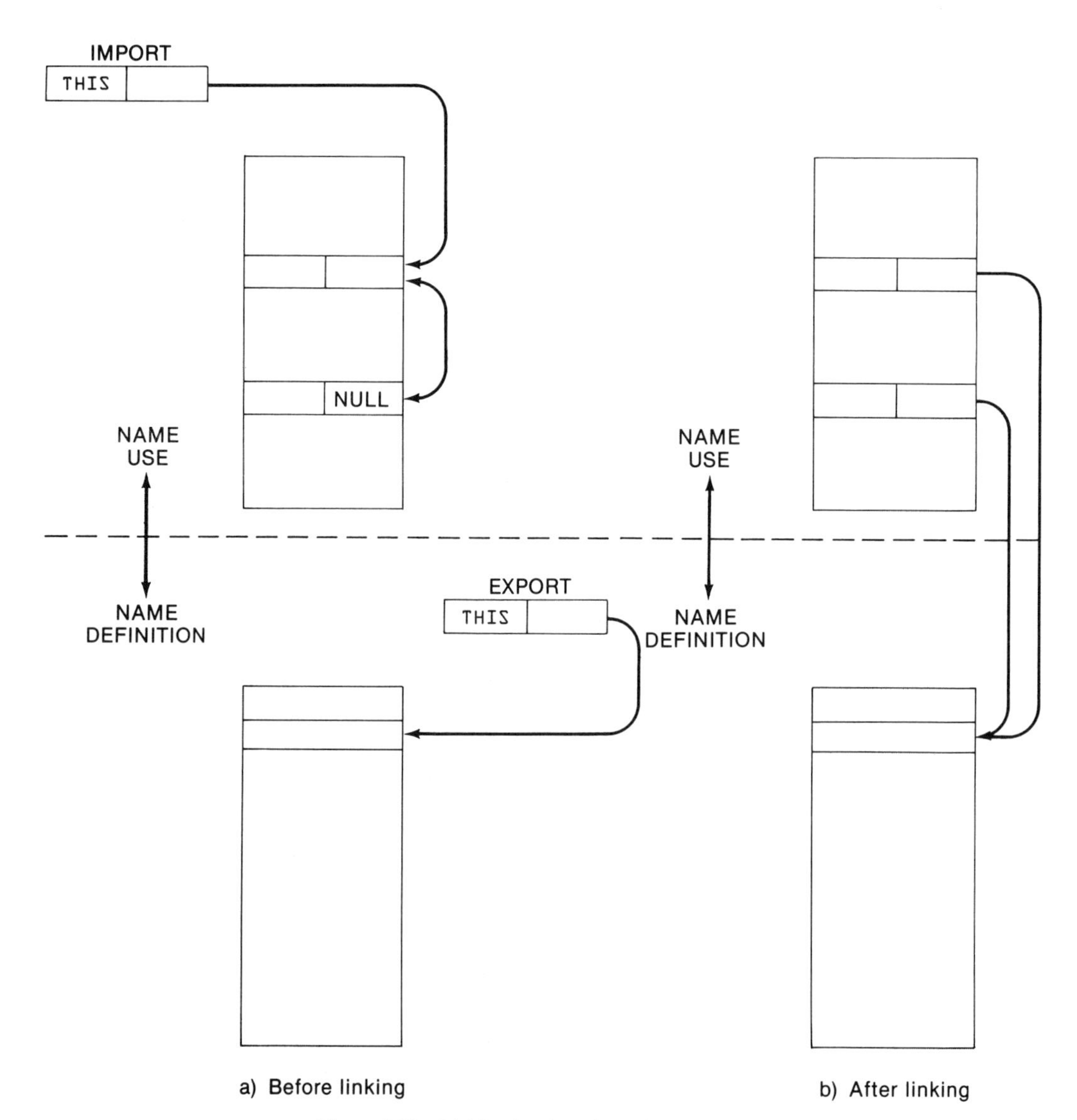

Figure 5-20 Linking by changing addresses in the program

corresponding to the imported symbols. The compiler has translated every reference to an ED object into an indirection to an entry in this table. When the imported symbol is defined by the linker, the table entry is filled in. During execution the imported object is accessed indirectly. Note that under this method the using program is not changed during linking. Thus this method permits a program to be shared even though it may be linked to different environments. Also, few memory accesses are needed to complete the link. However, more memory accesses and more memory space are required during execution, compared to the first linking method. Figure 5-21a shows the data structures created by the translator to support this linking method. The effect of linking is shown in Figure 5-21b.

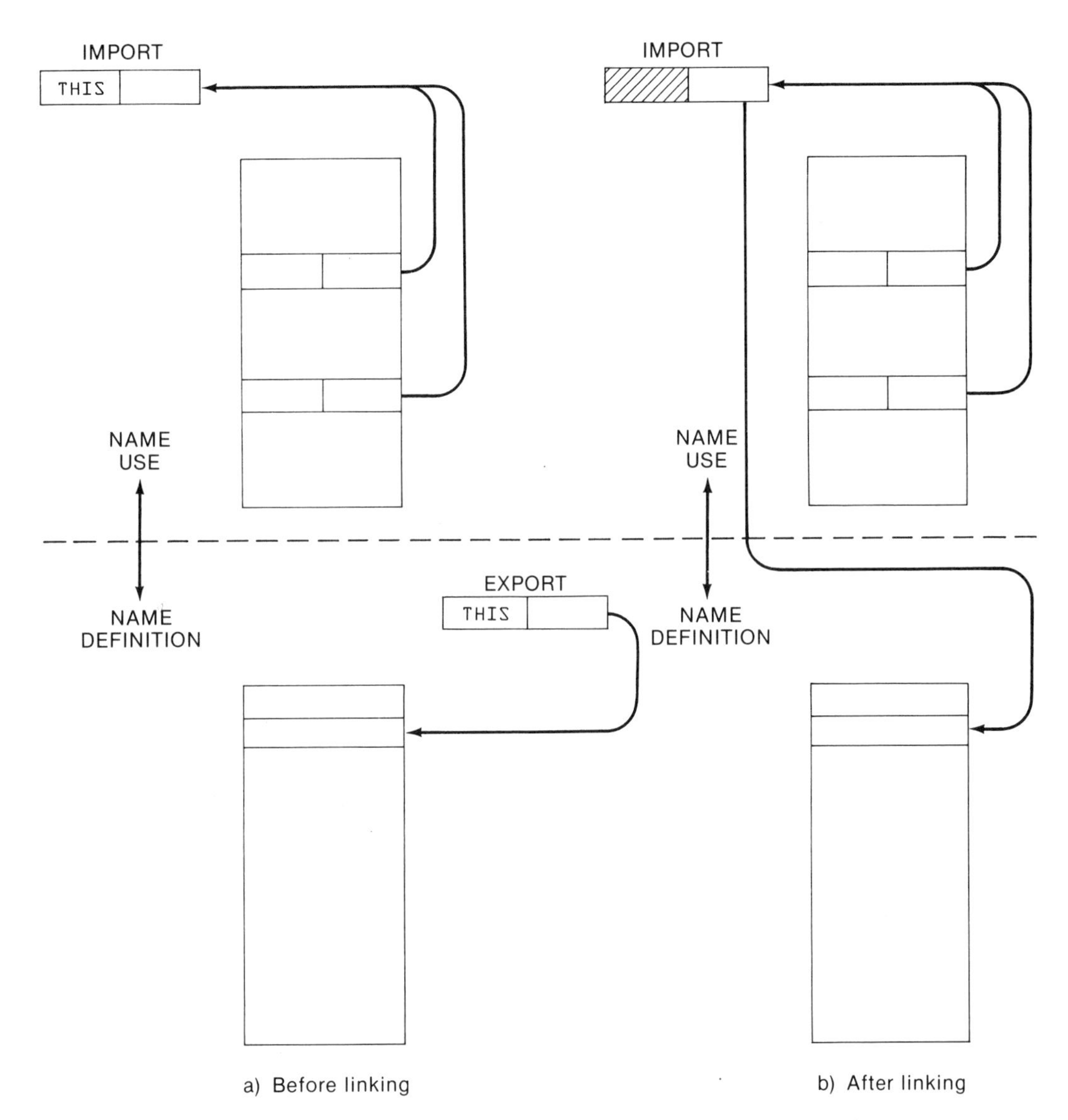

Figure 5-21 Linking by indirect accessing using simple indirection

The variant linking technique uses indirection through the export table of the defining module instead of a direct reference to access an imported object. This option is not useful in most environments, as it requires yet another memory access to reference an imported object, and it adds only the flexibility to redefine the exporting module without having to relink the environment. Figure 5-22 shows the data structures under this variation.

The following examples illustrate some situations in which various linking techniques are attractive.

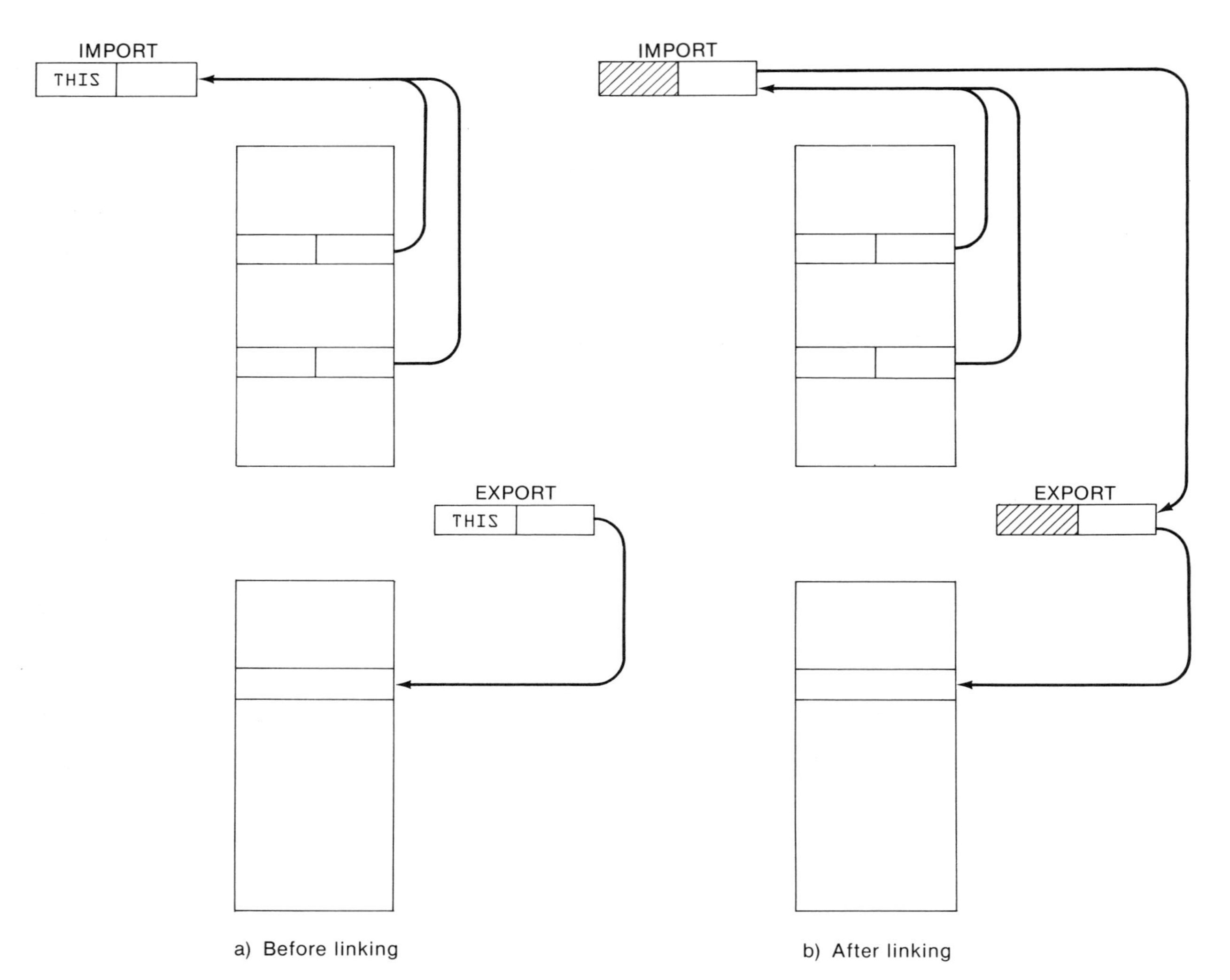

Figure 5-22 Linking by indirect accessing using double indirection

Example 5-14

We wish to defer the definition of imported symbols until program execution so that programs could be executed without being completely linked together. It is necessary that each indirect address to an unlinked reference be marked so that the processor can take an interrupt and the linker be invoked on any attempt to use such an unlinked reference. After the link has been established, succeeding access attempts may proceed without linker intervention.

Unlinked entries can be flagged by placing the flag value in a special mark bit or by using a reserved address value (such as all 1's). The mark bit or address[18] must be checked before each reference to any item anywhere in the system. This imposes two forms of overhead:

1. Space for the mark bit
2. Time for checking the mark bit and invoking the linker when the bit indicates an unlinked reference. Such tests can be incorporated in either hardware or firmware.

Example 5-15

We want to design a system so that a programmer can use the same copy of a program, without modification, in different linking environments. Several needs must be met to solve this problem. First we must keep variable data out of the shared program. This creates a program that is never modified; such a program is called a *pure procedure* or a *reentrant program*.[19] Second, we need to allocate a separate memory space for each user's local variables.[20] Third, we need to keep the linkage information separate for each process.[21] All these needs can be met by giving each process its own copy of the linkage information, referenced indirectly through a locator private to the process.

Collection is the final process that might be performed while linking separately compiled program units. The collector program allocates memory space for each program that is needed to resolve the links in the other programs. If addressing is one-dimensional, the collector can allocate these spaces in a sequential manner. The process of collecting may require that addresses internal to a program be modified to reflect the new location of the program. We might ask, "What was the original location of the program?" The answer is simple: A compiler assumes that the object program will be located starting at memory address zero; all addressing is relative to this assumed origin.

The details of the collection process depend on the addressing modes supported by the processor. Internal addresses that are expressed relative to the program counter do not need to be changed on relocation, since the relative positions of the instruction and an object declared in the same address space cannot be changed by the relocation process. Addresses that serve as links between separate compilation

[18]The address has to be checked to determine whether it is equal to the reserved value which flags an unlinked table entry. All bits of the address may have to be examined to make this decision.

[19]Informally, a reentrant program can be reused without housecleaning, whether a previous invocation of the same program may have been suspended, exited, or terminated.

[20]This requirement means that each program will have to access its private objects through an access object.

[21]This requirement demands a separate copy of the link vector for each copy of the program.

units or that are not PC-relative do have to be changed by the collector. The locations of such addresses must be marked by the compiler or translator so that the collector can find those addresses that require modification. If the instruction formats allow addresses in only one or two locations within the word, a bit vector with a bit for each possible address location suffices to mark the addresses requiring modification upon relocation. This vector is often called a "relocation vector." With more options regarding the use of external names in address expressions, the relocation information must provide more information for use when the addresses are defined; see Sections 2.6 and 2.7 of [ORGA72] for a description of the way that multiple options are handled in the Multics system.

Example 5-16

Some MC68020 instruction formats contain addresses, but only in extension words used by certain addressing modes. All addresses are therefore word aligned, but some contain 16 bits and others contain 32 bits. The collector must know the difference in order to perform 32-bit relocation arithmetic on the longer addresses. Therefore, a relocation vector for an MC68020 program would have to include not only a bit to indicate the presence of address information, but also another bit to indicate the length of the particular address. Figure 5-23 shows these data structures and illustrates the effect of relocation on a small program segment. This example is a bit strained since a reasonable assembler would not allow the programmer to specify address widths and then permit an arbitrary relocation of the program. The figure nevertheless illustrates the relocation actions.

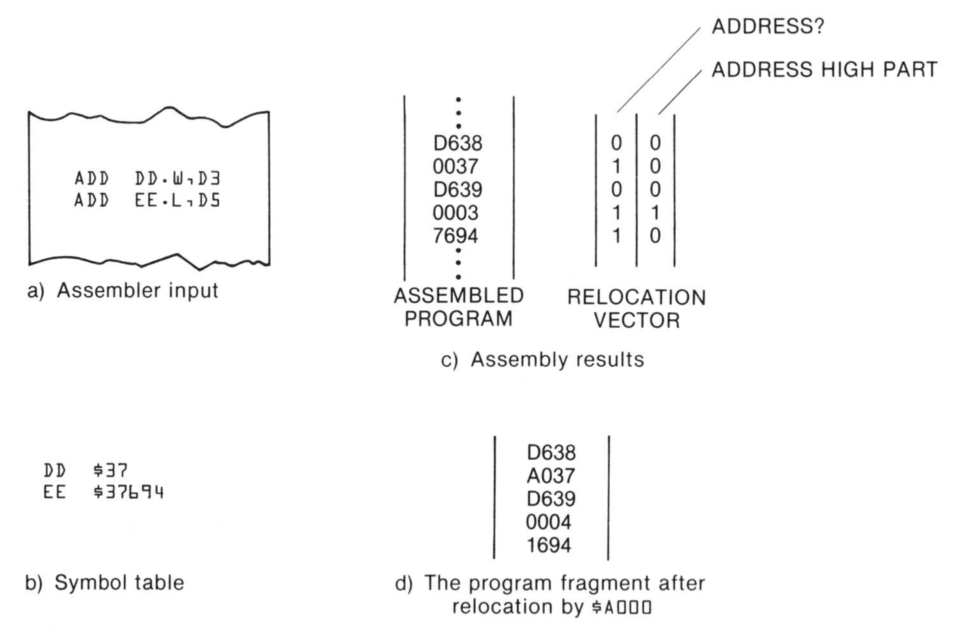

Figure 5-23 Relocation with two address sizes

There is one special case in which linking is somewhat trivial. Suppose that addresses within modules are one-dimensional, and that the processor can handle a second address dimension. The second dimension can be used to hold module identification numbers provided by the linker, and intramodule addresses will not require modification during the collection process. This scheme does not support hierarchical collection since every collection step using this technique adds an extra dimension to each address.

Example 5-17

In the Burroughs B5700 family, each module collected to form a complete user program is allocated a separate slot in a user-level vector of descriptors stored at level 1 of the address space. In a corresponding manner, system module descriptors occupy a system-level vector at level 0. These structures are depicted in Figure 5-24. The system-level collection of these procedure segments is a static collection made when the system is generated. The user-level vector is created during linking and collection. As the collector constructs the user-level vector of descriptors, it constructs a "program control word" (PCW) for each ED entry point and a space descriptor for each ED data object. These PCWs and descriptors are stored as constant values in the program. Each program control word describes a single entry point, giving the level (0 or 1), the segment number, the word offset, and the byte offset of the first instruction of the procedure. In Example 4-9 we saw how a PCW is loaded onto the stack in the procedure's prologue for each procedure nested within the block being entered. This operation is effected through the special processor instruction MAKE PCW, which pushes a word-length immediate constant from the program stream onto the stack, tagging it as a PCW. The linker/collector places this constant value into the calling procedure's instruction stream. Since a procedure body can be accessed only through level 0 or level 1, there is no need for more than one bit for the level number in the PCW, which then has a fixed format.

In the figure we show the execution of this process as task number 47; thus its stack descriptor is found in word 47 of the stack vector, which is found from the descriptor at offset 2 in the segment pointed to from D(0). From D(1) we reach the segment labeled "USER LIST," which contains descriptors of the segments collected to form the program being executed. In this segment the first entry describes the program whose structure is outlined in part (b) of the figure, and the second entry describes a segment of library programs where the sin function was found by the linker. The entry for the sin function is at byte 3 of word 214_{16}. This location information, plus the level at which the function should be executed (level 2, since it is externally visible from the library), was stuffed into the constant (whose value is $00062140A001_{16}$) in the prologue of main, as illustrated in the insert in part (d) of the figure. When the MAKEPCW instruction is executed (upon entry to main), the constant is completed with the stack number to form the constant 04762140A001, which is pushed on the stack in the level 2 block. Just before the ENTER calling the sin function is executed, the top of stack contains the parameter value (a) above a pointer (2, 6) to the PCW, which describes the entry to sin.

5.3.3 Comments

There are many steps in the name translations made before program execution, including compilation and linking. We have seen several strategies for implementing these mappings. The results of the mappings are address specifications which can be

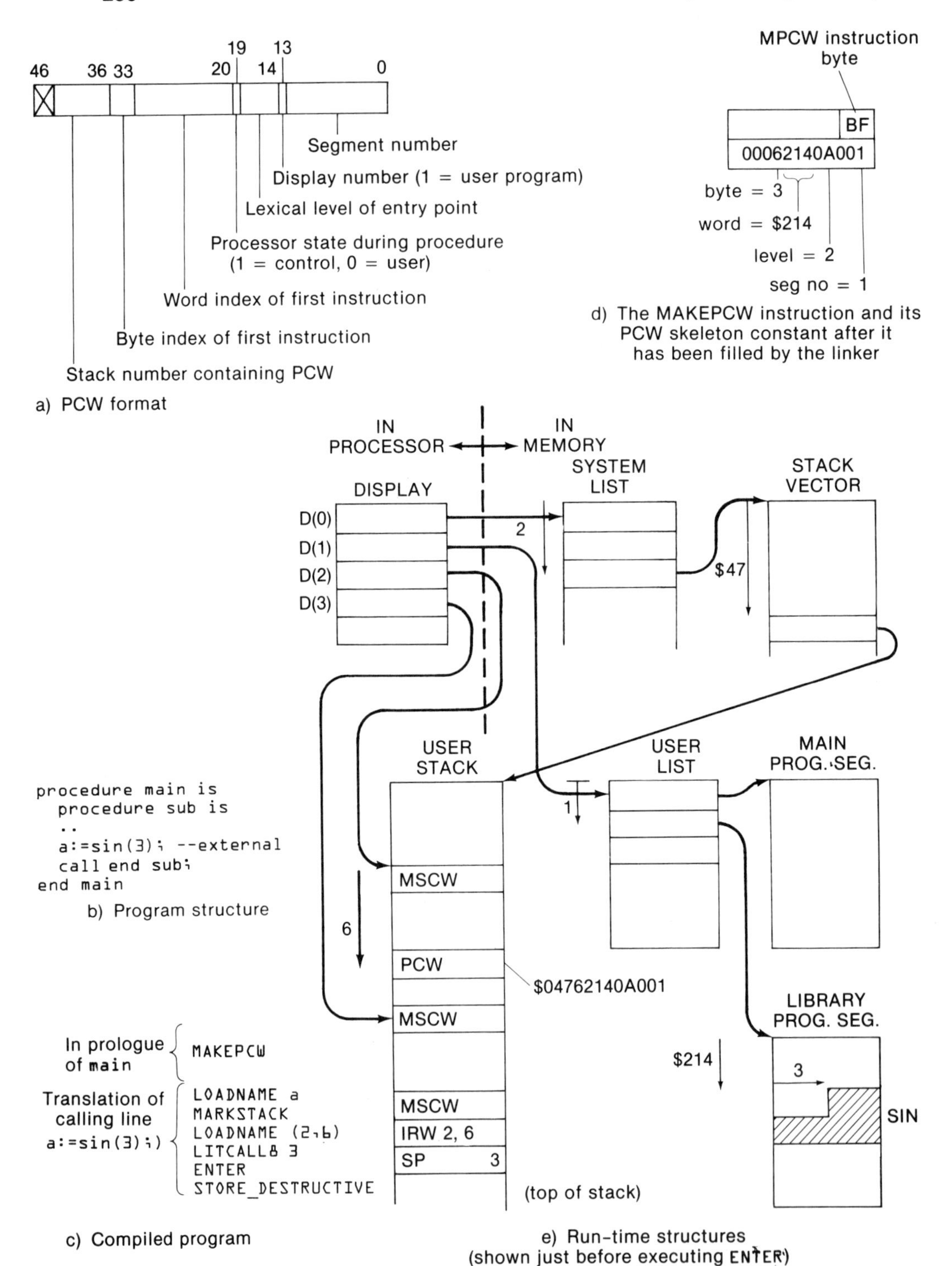

Figure 5-24 B5700 link/call data structures

used by the processor's effective address computation mechanisms, which will be discussed next.

5.4 NAME TRANSLATION BY AN EXECUTING PROGRAM

Processor programs may translate object names and compute object addresses at run time. These actions may have been deferred until run time because some information required to determine the address did not become available until the program was executed. Here are some reasons why an object address cannot be determined before the program executes:

1. A virtual address is data-dependent.
2. Locator values are used in the address determination.
3. A physical address is context-dependent.

A *data-dependent virtual address* accesses an element from an array, a record, or another data structure. A conventional addressing mode's computation suffices for most of these situations.

A *locator* might be passed as a procedure parameter whose value depends on the data values passed from the calling program. Again, the address computation of a conventional addressing mode suffices.

A *context-dependent* address might be used to access a dynamically allocated space, such as a stacked activation block. In this case conventional addressing modes cannot be used directly, unless the mapping between the level number and the physical origin of the corresponding activation block has been established in a structure compatible with a processor-supported addressing mode.

An address resulting from a run-time address computation is called an effective virtual address (EVA). It is effective since it is an actual address used during object access. It is virtual since further translation[22] may be required to determine the corresponding physical address.

In this section we summarize briefly the development of virtual addresses that can be computed from conventional access modes. Then we turn to the mapping issues that arise from the use of level numbers to specify an activation block on the stack. Finally, we discuss the design of addressing schemes to support dynamic linking.

5.4.1 Addresses within Dynamic Structures

The virtual address of a dynamically allocated object cannot be determined until the allocation has been made or until the dynamically determined parameters of the object have been fixed. Each of these situations involves adding a static index value to a dynamically determined value to compute the EVA. Table 5-3 summarizes these situations.

[22]This (set of) translation(s) is controlled by the operating system. They are discussed in Section 5.5.

Example 5-18

```
procedure ex(..) is
  type four_type is
    record
      that : integer;
      this : integer;
    end record;
  black : four_type;
  ..
begin
  ..
  black.this := 3;
  ..
end ex;
```

TABLE 5-3 SUMMARY OF RUN-TIME EVA COMPUTATIONS

Data Structure	Address Components	
	Variable Part	Fixed Part
Dynamically dimensioned array[a]	Component index	Structure origin
User-controlled object	Object origin	None
Component of user-controlled object	Object origin	Component index
Automatic object	Block origin	Object offset

[a]Note that this case applies to an array having at least two dimensions even if the subscript values are fixed in the program text.

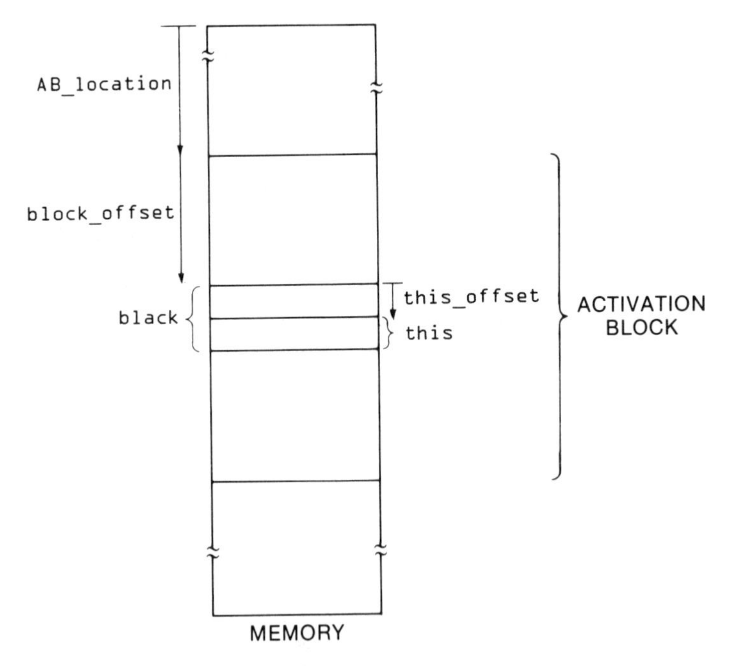

Figure 5-25 Accumulating offsets to access an item in a record in a block on a stack (Example 5-18)

In this program fragment, the object black is a record with a static internal structure. This means that the compiler will allocate space for the component named this relative to the origin of the record; let this_offset be the amount of the (static) offset by which this is displaced from the record's origin. Since black is declared local to the procedure, space will be allocated for it within the activation block allocated (on the stack) on entry to procedure ex. Let block_offset denote the (static) offset of the origin of the record named black with respect to the origin of the activation block, and let AB_location denote the origin of the activation block.[23] Then the element black.this will be located at the address A given by

$$A = AB\_location + block\_offset + this\_offset \quad (5\text{-}7)$$

Figure 5-25 depicts these entities and shows the computation of the EVA reaching black.this.

5.4.2 Two-Dimensional Addresses

A *two-dimensional address* containing two integers selects one element in an activation block. The first integer is the level number, which has to be translated into the activation block origin before the EVA addition can be performed. We want to find a technique that efficiently translates the level number to the origin of its activation block. The design issue is to select the best mapping technique and to implement that mapping technique. Since there is no algorithmic relationship between the level number and the origin of the corresponding activation block, the address mapping must be enumerated in a table, a list, or a combination of those two. We look briefly at the list map implementation and of a combination using a table for fast translations and a list for efficient mapping function management. Then we turn to the important problem of designing the system to properly maintain the (block_number → block_origin) map.

The list representation of the tabular name map is constructed as a tree structure with the pointers pointing back toward the root of the tree. There is a list bead for each active context. Each bead contains information about the location of the corresponding activation block and a pointer to the statically enclosing activation block.

Example 5-19

Figure 5-26 depicts this tree structure for the following program skeleton[24] and history.

```
procedure a is ..
  procedure b is ..
  procedure c is ..
  procedure d is ..
    procedure e is ..
  procedure f is ..
    procedure g is ..
    procedure h is ..
..
```

[23]The value named AB_location is not visible to or accessible within the high-level program. The name is used only for expository purposes.

[24]The skeleton omits the **end**s and procedure specifications which would be required to make the program correct.

```
call a;
call b;
call c;
call d;
call c;
call d;
call e;
call f;
call g;
call h;
call f;
call h;
```

In the figure notice that a branch always connects a node at level m with a node at level $m - 1$. The tree has several branches that appear to be duplicates; these correspond to procedures c, d, f, and h, which have more than one activation in use. There is no ambiguity about the execution context since that context is determined by following the pointers back toward the tree's root from the activation most recently created, which corresponds to the currently executing context.

Recall the linked list implementation of a tabular name map. In this situation a list entry in the current map contains the origin of an activation block which corresponds to a program context visible from the execution environment. The list is linked according to the static program structure, with the current context at the head of the list. This structure is related to the tree structure containing all activation blocks of a program. Each list for a current context starts at the leaf of the tree that corresponds to the current context and extends backward to the root of the tree. The processor traverses the list to translate a name. The number of list beads that must be traversed depends on the level numbers of the execution point and the address desired.

The third implementation technique is a combination of the table and linked list approaches. A linked data structure defines the map, and the processor transforms the list data into a table format to speed accesses during program execution. As the execution context changes, it will be necessary to modify the list and/or reload the tabular version of the map.

The map representation issue is just the first part of the mapping problem; we also have to provide a mechanism that updates the map whenever the addressing environment changes. One basic decision concerns whether the map will be updated by hardware or software. We discuss implementations with processor support for map updating on context changes. This design may be coupled with the design of the mapping mechanism itself, as it is in the Burroughs B5700 designs.

Example 5-20

The B5700 processor contains 32 "display" registers, named D(0), . . . , D(31). During program execution register D(i) contains the addrss of the MSCW at the bottom of the activation block for the visible nested block at level i. If the processor is executing a

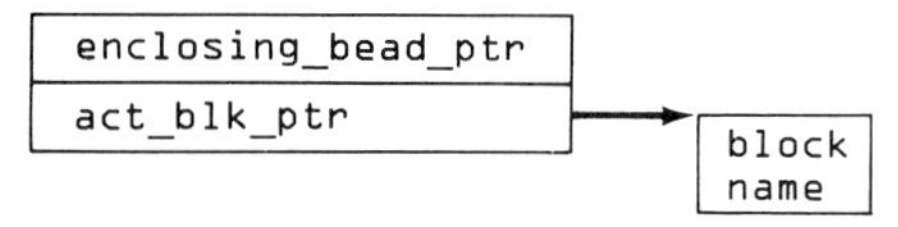

a) Format

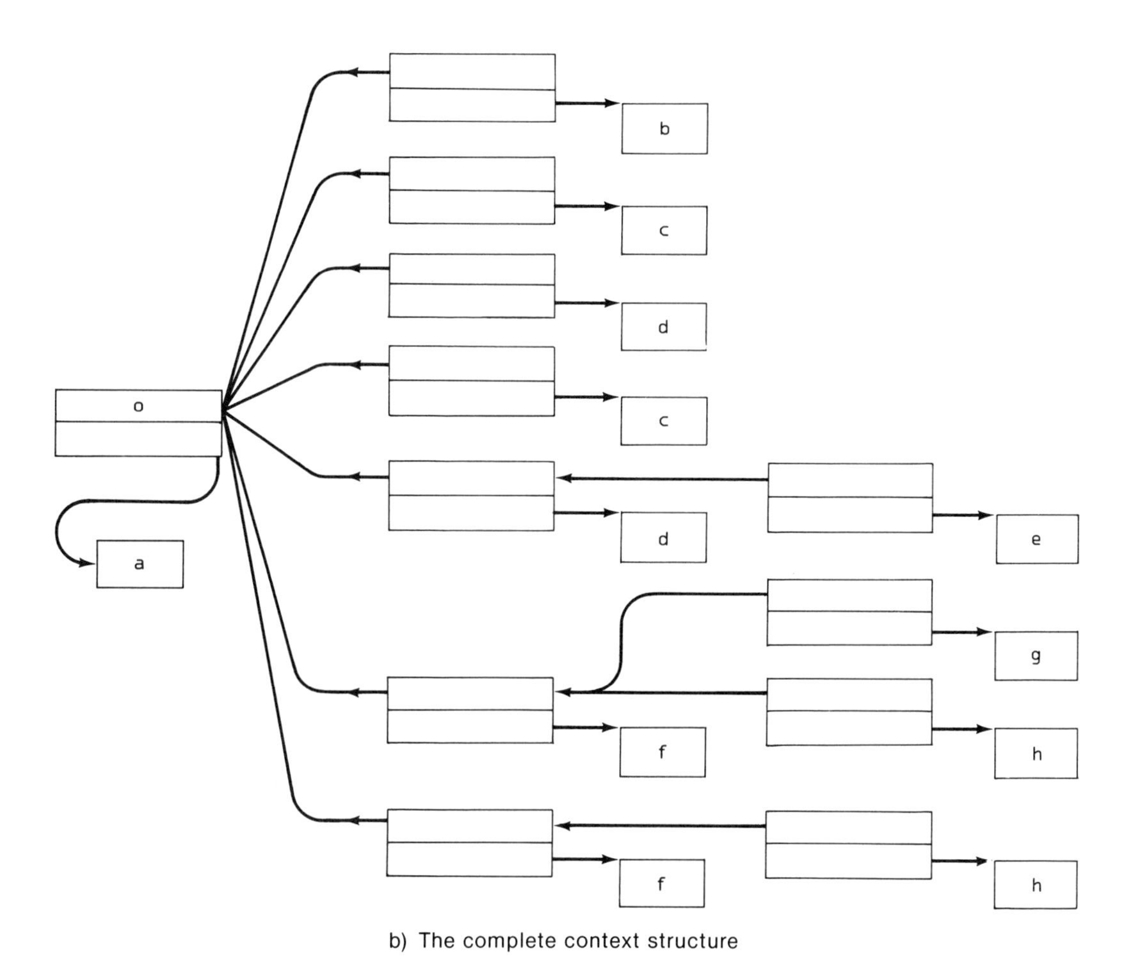

b) The complete context structure

Figure 5-26 A list representation of a context structure

program at level j, the contents of D(k) are irrelevant for k > j. The translation of the virtual address (n, i) is

$$EAR := D(n) + i;$$

This address mapping process is depicted in Figure 5-27.

Now that we understand the address mapping process, we turn to the question: How does the processor maintain the map with correct entries? First, when does the

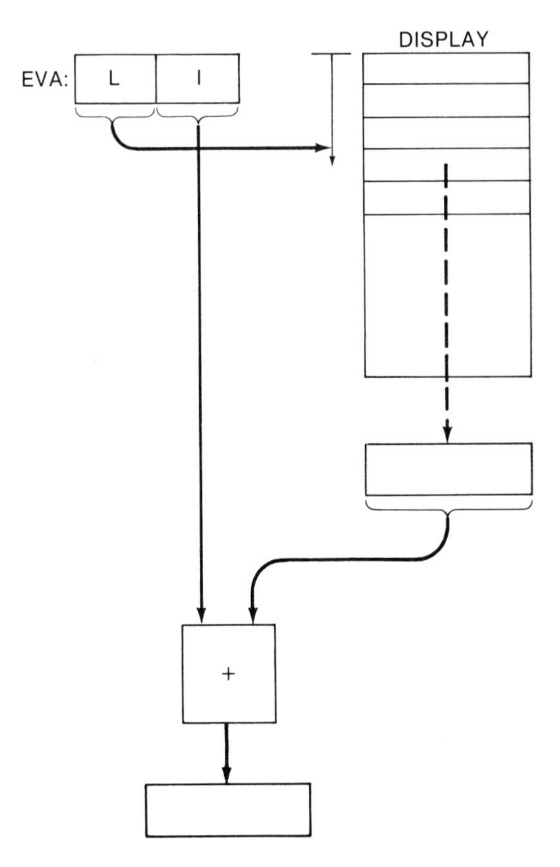

Figure 5-27 B5700 address computation

map get changed? A change is necessary only during procedure entry or exit, at which time the processor reloads its display registers. Second, how does the processor reload the registers? The reloading process starts with a pointer to the head of the list structure defining the new mapping and the level of the program block corresponding to that list element, which we will call L. The display updating algorithm proceeds according to these steps:

```
  type list_bead;
  type list_ptr is access list_bead;
  type list_bead is
    record
      next : list_ptr;
      org : address;
    end record;
  display : array (0 .. 31) of register;
procedure update_display(L : integer; context : list_ptr) is
  level : integer;
  here : list_ptr;
```

```
begin
  here := context;
  for level in reverse 0 .. L loop
    display(level) := here.org;
    here := here.next;
  end loop;
end;
```

Since the list structure mirrors the nested program structure, it is unlikely that an execution of this update procedure will actually modify the contents of the display registers with low numbers. Thus the display register reloading process can be shortened if the algorithm is modified to detect when a register update does not actually change the register's contents. The reloading process can terminate when the no-change condition is detected. Problem 5-26 asks for details of the corresponding algorithm.

We left open the question: Where does the processor get the list pointer and the level number to start the update process? The answers to these questions relate closely to the answer to the third design issue—how is the list updated as new contexts are entered? First we explain the machine's representation of the list. Each activation record starts with a MSCW; this word contains both a pointer to the MSCW of the statically enclosing block and the level of execution for the procedure block corresponding to the activation block starting at that MSCW. Therefore, the MSCW serves as a list bead in the name environment list. Since the MSCW contains the level of execution, only a pointer to the MSCW at the head of the list is required to initiate the display update procedure.

Now how does the processor find the head of the MSCW list? The easy case is procedure return, in which case the head of the list describing the new environment is the (active) MSCW for the activation block immediately beneath the topmost block on the stack. This MSCW can be found by scanning the dynamic MSCW history chain linked by the deltaF fields in the MSCWs.[25] The desired MSCW is the first active[26] MSCW beneath the topmost one. Procedure return cannot be achieved simply by popping the topmost display register since the calling procedure may not correspond to the block enclosing the called block (see Problem 5-25).

The complex case is procedure call. After procedure call, the topmost MSCW, placed on the stack by the MARKSTACK operator executed at the beginning of the calling sequence, will be the origin of the list for the new environment. How do we find the execution level of the new block and the identity of the enclosing block? These two pieces of information must be determined during procedure call. The statically enclosing block is an activation block corresponding to an execution of the procedure statically enclosing the called procedure. The entry point description is a program control word (PCW) within that block; it points to the first instruction of the called procedure. The description of the entry point is an indirect word whose block information points to the MSCW at the base of the relevant activation record, and whose index finds the PCW within that record (see Figure 5-28). So when the processor performs the ENTER instruction, it uses the entry point pointer (which was pushed just on top of the topmost MSCW) to find the MSCW that will be the successor of the new (topmost) MSCW in

[25]The deltaF field is loaded by the MARKSTACK operation, and the topmost MSCW can always be found through the contents of the F register (see Example 4-9).

[26]Imtermediate inactive MSCWs are ignored—they do not correspond to active procedure calls.

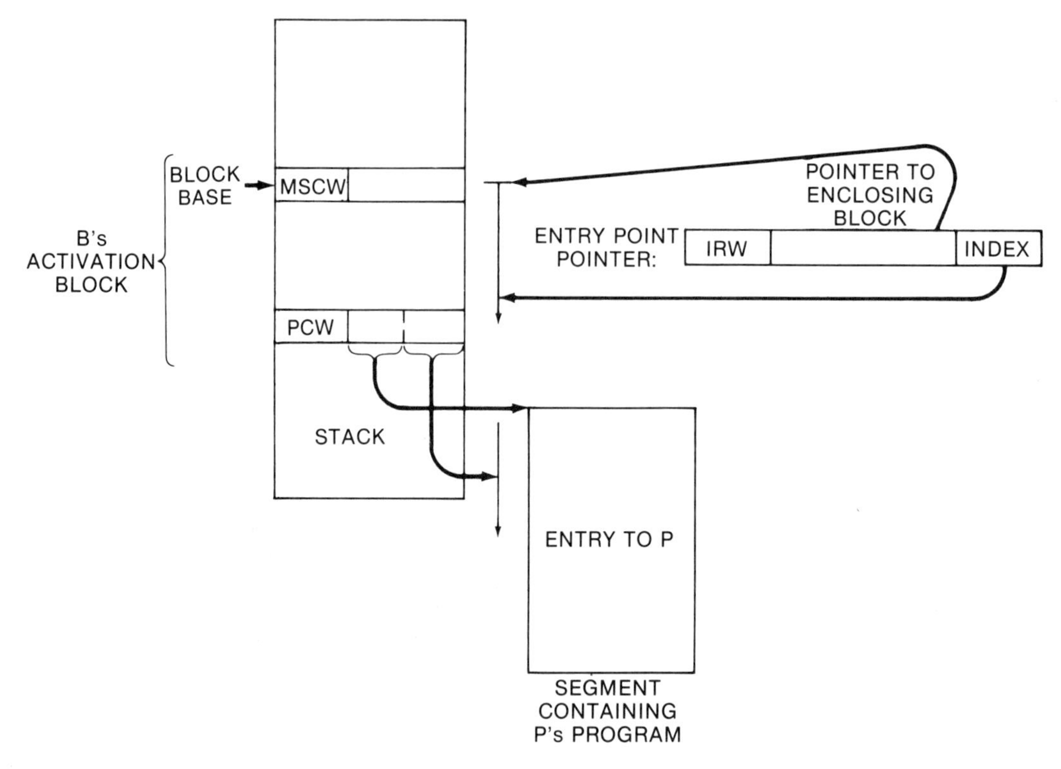

Figure 5-28 The enclosing block environment is found from the entry point pointer (B5700 tag types shown)

the environment list. During ENTER the static link pointer to the successor MSCW is written into the topmost MSCW.

The next question concerns the level number—where did it come from? This level number describes the context for the new procedure; it was determined by the compiler when it scanned the program's nested blocks. The compiler then placed that number in the constant destined to become the PCW of the entry point. This constant became the PCW contents during the execution of a MAKEPCW instruction in the prologue of the enclosing procedure. Thus the PCW contains both the level number and the address of the entry point of the procedure being described.

With this understanding of the display register updating and usage, we can complete the presentation of the B5700 addressing options. Figure 5-29 shows the relationships among pointers and translation tables related to addressing in this system. The four different types of addressing entities that can appear in a user program are listed in Table 5-4. Using the notation M(x) to denote the contents of memory location x, the translations of the addresses are listed in the table. In some address specifications the single DS bit is used to indicate that a different stack contains the object being described. The SU bit may appear to have a similar effect; actually, it distinguishes a program defined at level zero from one defined at level one.

The base of the activation block containing a PCW word must be found to

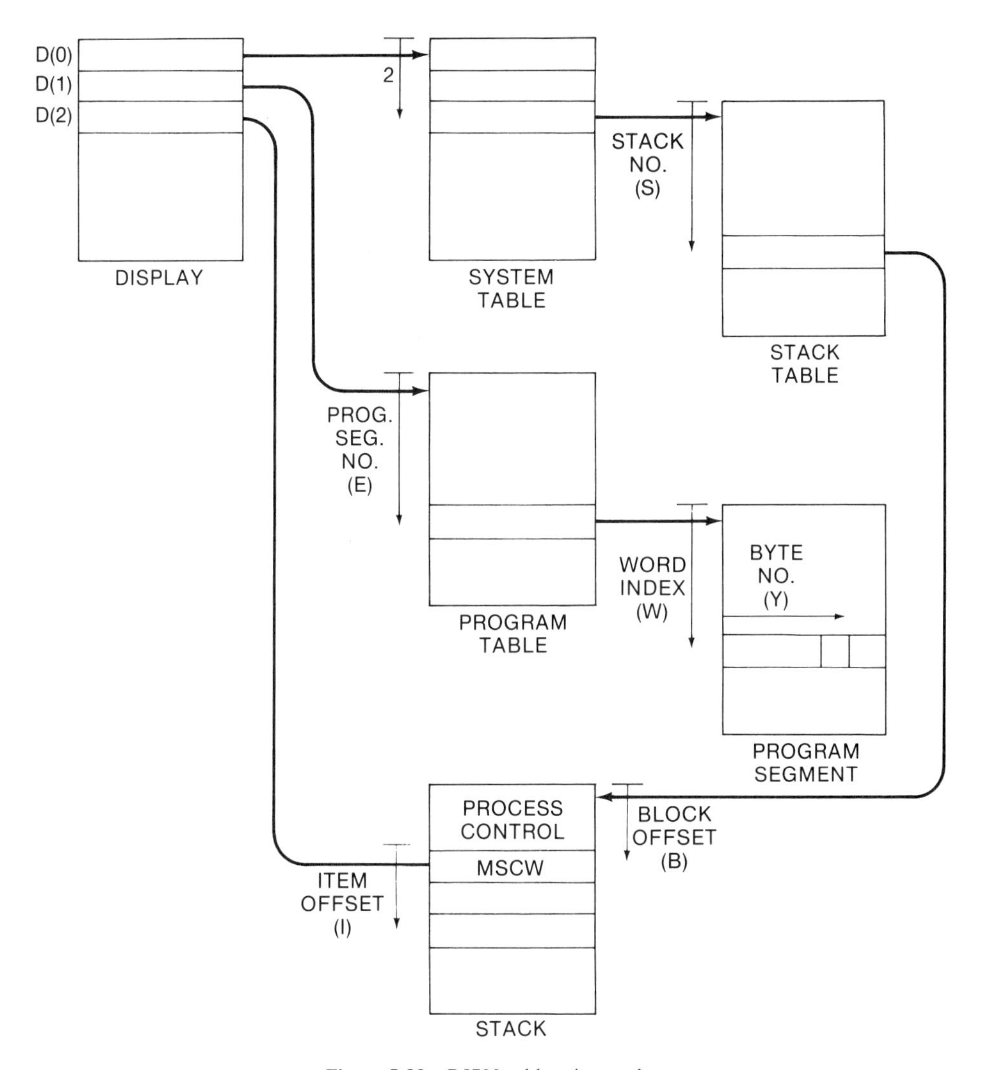

Figure 5-29 B5700 addressing paths

complete an ENTER that calls the program; this can be found from the SIRW address form or from the (L, I) form by performing the indicated computation with $I = 0$. Notice that the conversion between an indirect word and a stuffed indirect word (which is performed by the operation STUFF ENVIRONMENT) simply translates the level number to a pointer to the base of the activation block; it is important that the complete address is not changed into a single pointer to the value. Why? Because the single pointer to the value does not provide an easy way to find the bottom of the block, which must be found if the indirect word is used to find an entry point.

The PCW address form is used in PCW words and in the RCW (return control word) which holds the PC value saved upon interruption or procedure call. In this form both a word and a byte number must be specified.

TABLE 5-4 ADDRESS FORMS USED IN THE B5700 SERIES

Address[a]	Address Translation	Use
L, I	D(L) + I	Instruction
L, I	D(L) + I	IRW
S, B, I (DS)	**if** DS = 0 **then** BOS + B + I **else** M(M(D(0) + 2) + S) + B + I	SIRW
S, B (DS)	**if** DS = 0 **then** BOS + B **else** M(M(D(0) + 2) + S) + B	SLINK[b]
E, W, Y (SU)	WORD ADDRESS: M(D(SU) + E) + W BYTE NUMBER: Y	PCW

[a]A component shown in parentheses is a single bit used to guide the translation process.

[b]This form is used to locate the bottom of an activation block; it is used in the linked pointer structure defining the addressing environment.

Example 5-21

The MC68020 instructions LINK and UNLK (unlink) form a complementary pair that allocates and chains together stack activation blocks. The instruction LINK An, # <displacement> pushes the contents of An on the stack, loads An with the stack pointer, and then adds the displacement to the stack pointer. If the selected address register was used as the pointer to the topmost activation block, this instruction reloads that pointer with the address of a new block created at the top of the stack. Figure 5-30 illustrates these changes. UNLK simply reverses the allocation by reloading SP from the address register and reloading the address register with the value that had been previously pushed on the stack.

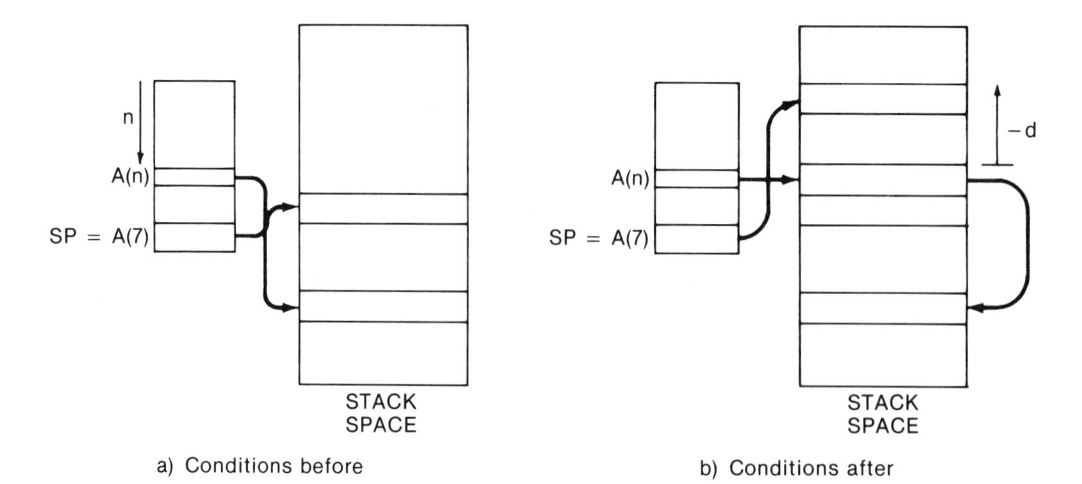

Figure 5-30 The MC68020 link An, #d instruction ($d < 0$)

In register-transfer style these operations perform the following algorithms:

LINK An, # d	UNLK
SP := SP − 4;	SP := A(n);
M(SP) := A(n);	M(SP) := A(n);
A(n) := SP;	SP := SP + 4;
SP := SP + d;	

These operations do not affect any address mappings, but they do create and maintain the data structure that chains the activation blocks together to form a dynamic chain.

To select the best of these options for a system, the designer must consider both the frequencies and costs of the following operations:

1. Mapping an address
2. Loading the table
3. Updating the map

5.4.3 Procedure Parameter Lists

Special memory accessing modes may be required to access efficiently the actual value of a parameter from within a procedure. The details depend on the method that the processor supports for placing parameters on the stack. In Section 4.4.2.1 we discussed options for positioning the parameter block relative to the activation block allocated for the called procedure. One option places the parameters in the first part of the activation block; the other option places the parameters below the activation block. In the former option, illustrated in Figure 5-31, parameters are included with local objects, and the addressing modes used to access local objects can access

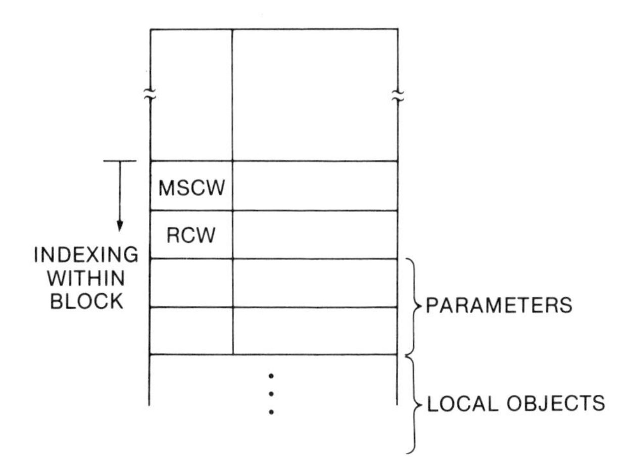

Figure 5-31 Parameters located within activation block (B5700 stack details used)

parameters as well. When the parameters are placed outside the activation block, as in the HP3000 design (Example 4-11), a special accessing mode may be required to access the parameters. We explore this case in the following example.

Example 5-22

Three registers in the HP3000 processor point to the stack space; they are S, which points to the top of the stack,[27] Q, which points to the top of the control region of the activation block, and DB, which points to a space at the bottom of the stack segment which is the base of the stack (but not necessarily the beginning of the segment containing the stack). Recall from Example 4-11 that HP3000 procedure parameters are placed in the stack before the control words that start the activation block. This means that the parameters are found at addresses beneath that designated by Q, whereas the local objects are stored in locations above that in Q. Since there are likely to be more local objects than parameters, the addressing mode encoding is designed to permit longer displacements going positively from Q (toward local objects) than going negatively (toward parameters).

The particulars of the HP3000 addressing modes are summarized in Table 5-5 and Figure 5-32. The P-relative modes are used to access objects within the program segment; this is used for control instructions and for access to constant values. The DB-relative mode is used to access static objects allocated for the process at the base of the stack space. The next two modes are the subject of our present discussion, while the last is used to access intermediate results stored near the top of the stack. From the table you can see that the design permits direct access to up to 63 parameter words and up to 127 automatic object words for the current procedure. Note that the compiler can translate a name into an address using the appropriate addressing mode.

The HP3000 addressing modes do not support direct access to objects declared in immediately enclosing blocks, there being no addressing options corresponding to the use of the display registers of the B5700 processor. Global data can be referenced by using indirect addresses relative to the bottom of the stack. In this processor an indirect

TABLE 5-5 ADDRESSING MODES FOR THE HP3000

Address Mode	Address Field Bits 6	7	8	9	10	11 ··· 15	Address Computation
P+	0	0	←			d →	P + d
P−	0	1	←			d →	P − d
DB+	1	0	←			d →	DB + d
Q+	1	1	0	←		d →	Q + d
Q−	1	1	1	0	←	d →	Q − d
S−	1	1	1	1	←	d →	S − d

Source: [HEWL73]; © Copyright 1973 Hewlett-Packard Company. Reproduced with permission.

[27] Actually, there is a register SM which points to the top of the stack in memory and a register SR which counts the number of stack words held in processor registers. Ignoring the effects of buffering the stack contents in processor registers, the combination of SM and SR define the logical top of the stack, which is the basis for addressing.

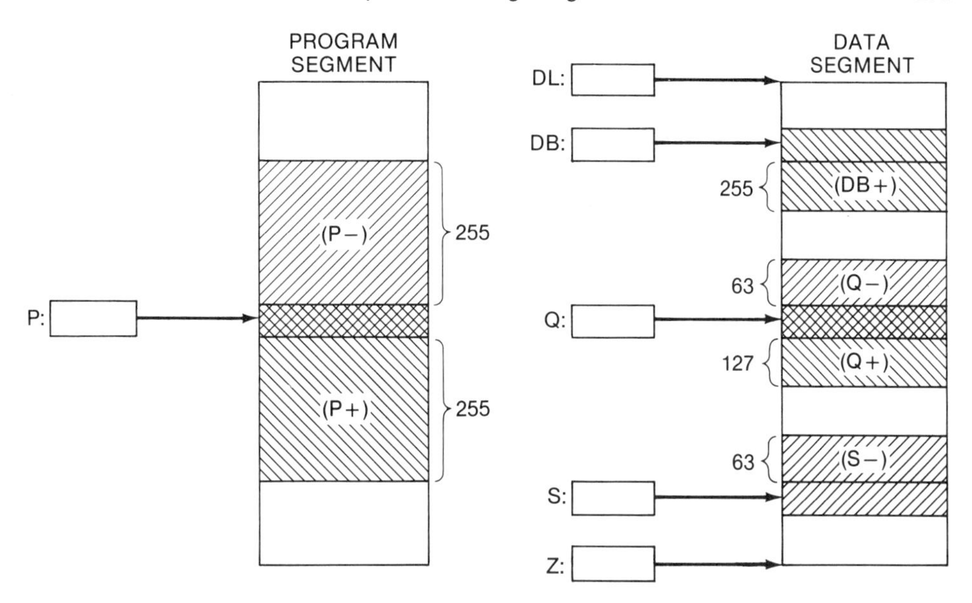

Figure 5-32 HP3000 addressing—directly addressible spaces shaded. (See Table 5-5 for list of modes; some modes are available in some instructions.) From [HEWL73]. © Copyright 1973 Hewlett-Packard Company. Reproduced with permission.

data address is always interpreted as a distance beyond the location described in the DB register. Indexing can be used with these modes to obtain access to various portions of the memory. Indexing is always applied after indirection, if any, and the index quantity is always added to the address, whether the addressing mode specified subtraction or addition to the processor register used in the indexing process. Problem 5-20 describes one way that these address modes could be used to achieve the effect of two-level addressing.

Problem 5-27 describes an alternative design[28] that combines programmer accessible registers to both hold the display information and problem data, if that is more valuable. This approach gives a difficult register assignment problem in which the register optimizer in the compiler must determine the "value" of having another register dedicated for data.

5.4.4 Dynamic Linking

Processor instructions and processor mechanisms are required to support dynamic linking among compilation units. Recall that the linking process connects imported symbols to symbols exported from other program modules. Under static linking all such connections are established prior to program execution. Under dynamic linking the links are evaluated (the jargon word for this is "snapped") during program

[28]The reader is encouraged to evaluate this design proposal in the questions asked in Problem 5-27. We neither disparage nor endorse the proposal here.

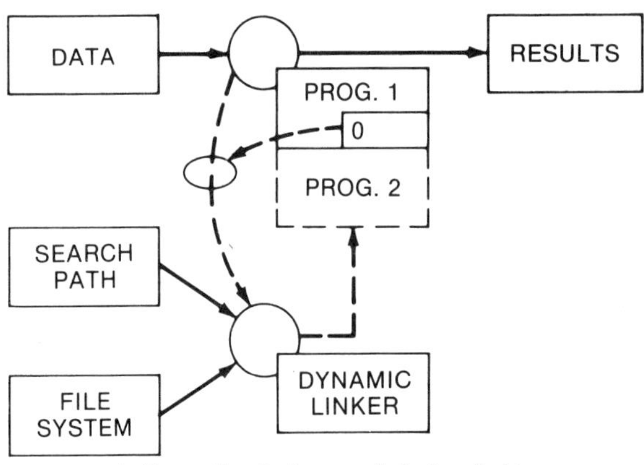

a) Execution before and during linking

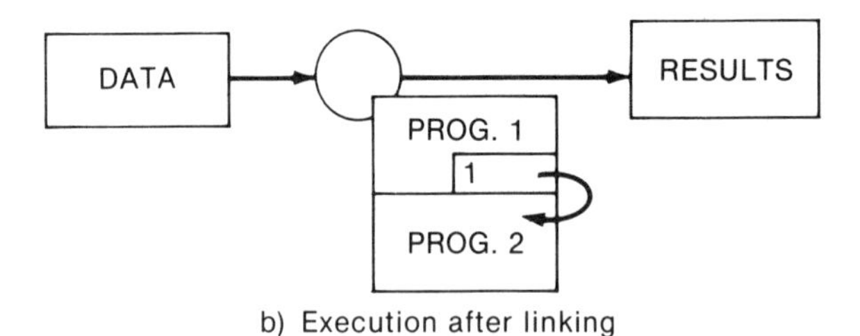

b) Execution after linking

Figure 5-33 Dynamic linking

execution. Figure 5-33 illustrates this dynamic linking scenario. As a consequence of dynamic linking the link vector may contain a mixture of snapped and unsnapped links. To support dynamic linking, both the processor and the support software must be designed to detect when an access attempt reaches an unlinked entry in the import table. An interrupt (to activate the dynamic linker) should be signaled when an unlinked entry is detected. The following description of the situation is generic, as it does not depend on whether the instruction space is shared with other programs. First we describe the situation for *every* access using an entry in the link vector as the pointer to reach the actual object.

1. A processor register B_{link} has been set to point to the link vector for the compilation unit.
2. The processor makes an indirect reference through $B_{link} + k$.

To complete this indirect reference, the hardware must know whether the link vector entry has, in fact, already been linked. We put a flag in each link vector entry; that flag will be true if the corresponding entry has been linked; the format is shown in Figure 5-34a and b.

The accessing process becomes

1. Fetch the indirect word into ADDRESS;
2. If the linked flag is false, interrupt the processor;
3. Access the address in ADDRESS;

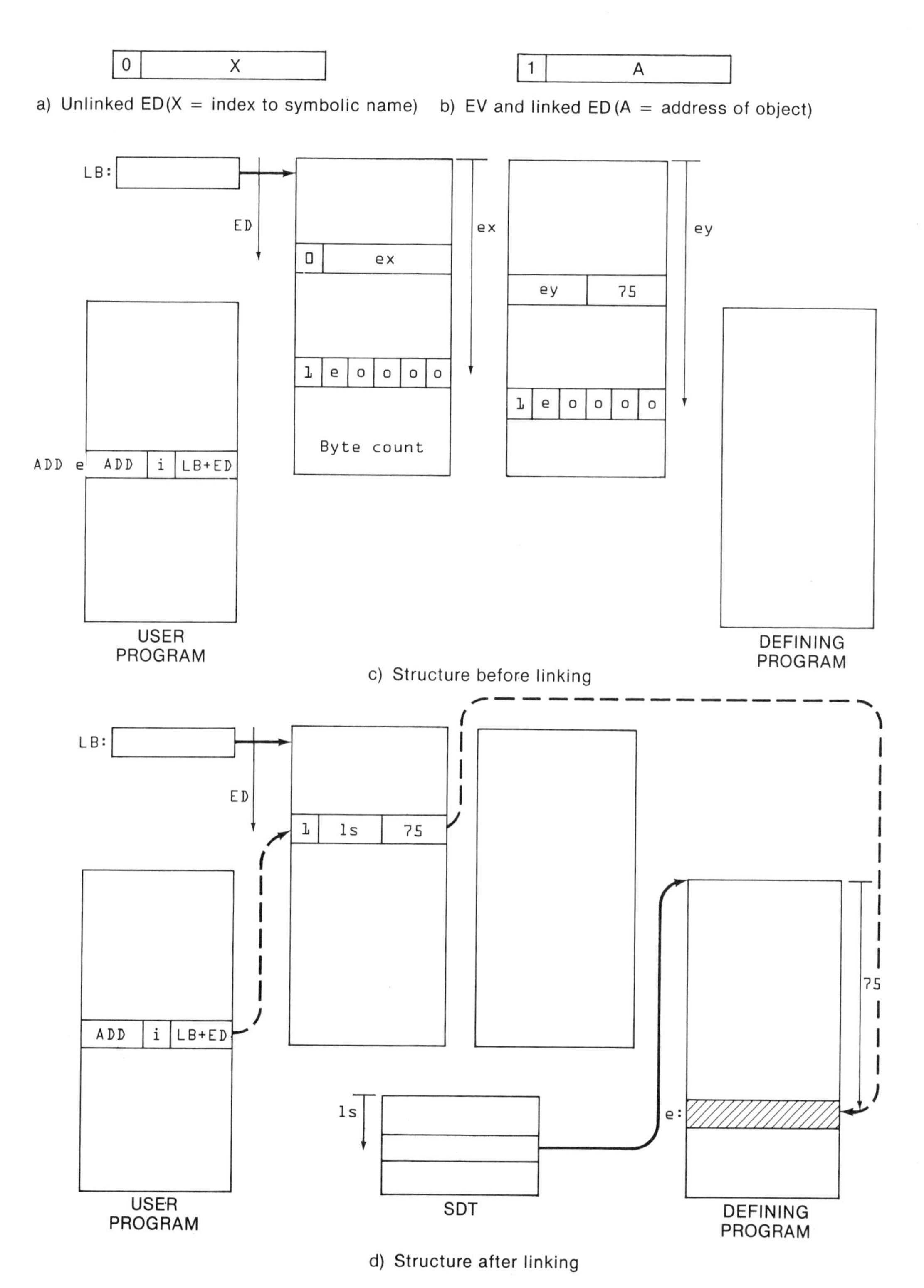

Figure 5-34 Multics dynamic linking (simple conceptual case—access direct to a simple object)

Figure 5-34c and d illustrate the access paths and pointers used with dynamic linking. In Figure 5-34c we see the situation before the link has been snapped. Notice that the pointer in the link word is used to point to the symbolic ED name requiring linking; the first byte of the name space is the count of the number of bytes comprising the name. When the linker has been invoked, it searches for the corresponding object definition and then replaces the unsnapped link with an indirect word, completing the double indirection used in future accesses to the ED object. By changing the link vector entry (see Figure 5-34d) upon snapping the link (rather than changing the instruction referring to the link vector), the snapped link can be used to complete other references to the same link vector entry without further linker calls. The cost of this saving is the extra memory access made to complete the second indirection. After the linker has made these changes, it returns control to the interrupt handler, which directs the processor to retry the instruction that caused the trap.[29]

An important option is provided in the Multics dynamic linker design [ORGA72]. The problem is that when a module is loaded the first time, its objects must be initialized in accordance with their declarations. One cannot support this functionality by just initializing the values when the module is entered because the initialization should occur only when the module is loaded for the first time. So the Multics design provides a flag interpreted by the linker; the linker causes a trap before the object has been loaded and the trap response is to initialize the objects.

5.4.5 Summary

In this section we have explored several design issues concerning the computation of addresses during program execution. We introduced several addressing modes and techniques that could be added to the "conventional" addressing modes. We saw how these modes could support certain important high-level language constructs, such as parameter addressing, accessing objects in nested blocks, and accessing imported objects through link vectors.

5.5 OPERATING SYSTEM CONTROLLED ADDRESS TRANSLATIONS

The system must translate each EVA into a physical memory address (PMA). The operating system allocates memory resources, so the EVA $\rightarrow$ PMA mapping must be controlled by the operating system. The map parameters are stored in tables maintained by the operating system's memory allocator. The address translation mechanism retrieves table values to compute the physical addresses for the program in execution. In this section we discuss the connection between memory allocation policies and the EVA $\rightarrow$ PMA mapping. In particular we show how additive relocation and blocked-pointer mappings have been used.

[29]This way the linker does not have to know about the internal register we called ADDRESS in the algorithm.

5.5.1 Additive Relocation

When an additive relocation scheme is used for the EVA → PMA mapping, the address space can be divided into several subspaces. A design with one subspace is mainly of historical interest, since it forces the memory manager to allocate a single contiguous memory block for each complete program. Two selections complete a multiple-subspace design:

1. The number of relocation registers
2. The policy for choosing the relocation register to be used

The effect of varying the number of registers can be studied by simulation. Register selection can be based on the value of the high-order address bits; this scheme reduces to a blocked pointer mapping that is logically similar to a segmented or paged mapping. A more flexible register selection mechanism compares the EVA against values held in the address mapper. The Univac 1108 system typifies this approach:

Example 5-23

The Univac 1108 [UNIV65] had two relocation registers (B_I and B_D) and a third (threshold) register B_B. All registers handle only bits 17 .. 10 of 18-bit virtual and physical addresses. Let the subscript H denote these high 9 bits selected from the entity whose name is subscripted. Thus A_H denotes the upper 9 bits of the virtual address A. Since the three registers contain only these 9 bits, their names will not be subscripted. In the 1108's EVA → PMA mapping the upper bits of the physical address PMA_H are given by this program fragment:

```
PMA_H : physical_address; --upper 9 bits called PMA_H
..
if A_H > B_B then PMA_H := B_D + A_H;
  else PMA_H := B_I + A_H;
```

The lower part of PMA is copied directly from the lower part of A. Figure 5-35 illustrates this mapping. Due to the 9-9 division of the virtual address, physical memory space is managed with a granularity of 512-word blocks.

The register name subscripts (I and D) reflect the designer's intention: a program's instruction and data regions should be located in different parts of the virtual memory address space. Then the instruction and data regions can be separately mapped into physical memory. The operating system would try to allocate the two regions in distinct memory modules so that the overlapped processor can simultaneously access instructions and data. This overlap, which requires that instructions and data be located in distinct memory modules, speeds processing (see Chapter 1 of Volume 2). The compilers and linkers are designed to separate instructions from data and to load them from opposite ends of the virtual address space. Thus the two regions can be separated easily.

5.5.2 Blocked-Pointer Mappings

Both segmented and paged allocations produce address space structures that are easily translated to a physical address using a blocked-pointer mapping. We explore these two cases in this section.

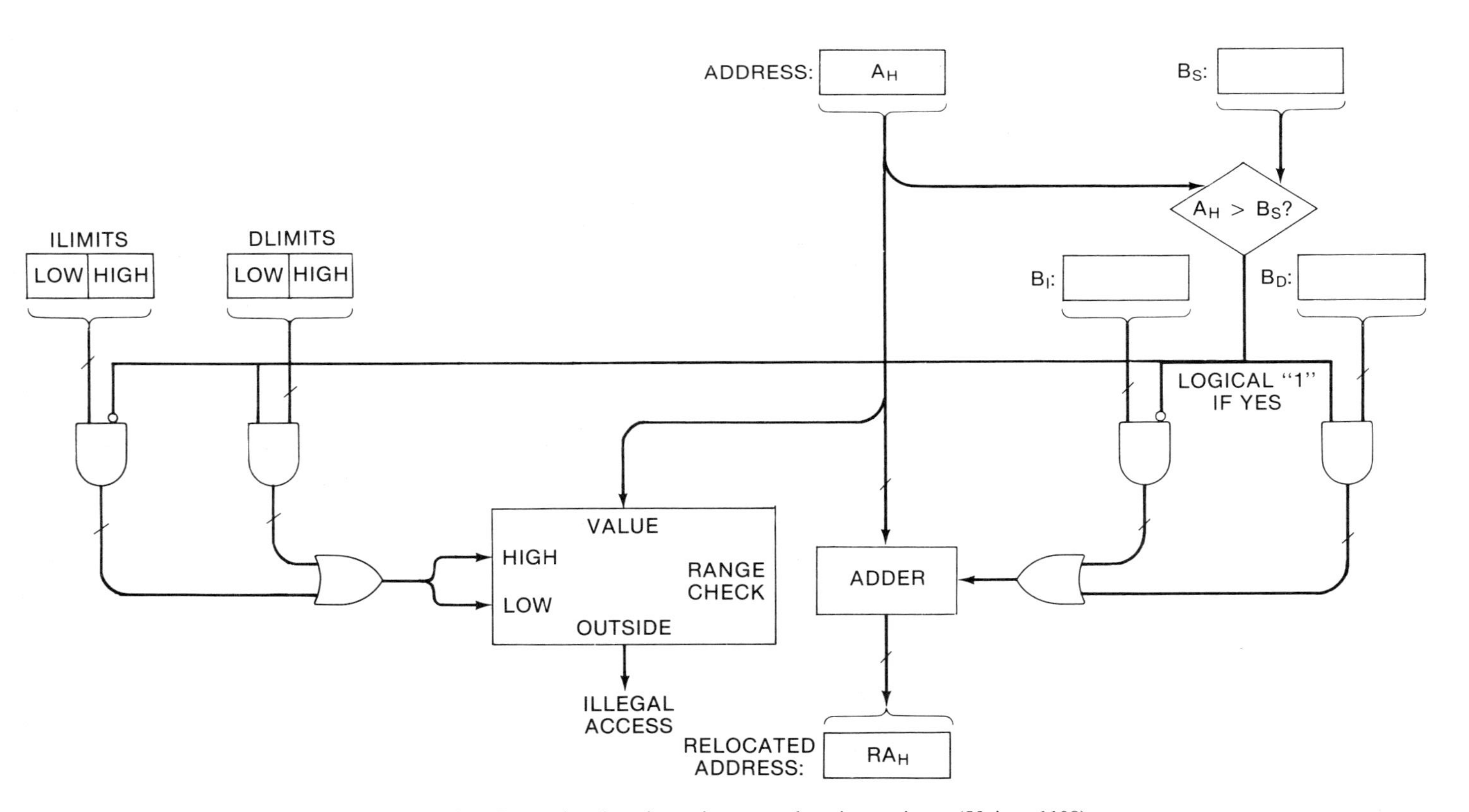

Figure 5-35 Dynamic relocation using two relocation registers (Univac 1108)

5.5.2.1 Segmentation. Since segment lengths vary, the address translation mechanism must check that the segment's length and the index in the virtual address are compatible. In addition, the EVA → PMA mapping must be performed. We study this mapping now.

Under segmentation each EVA is separated into two parts: a segment number s and an item index i. The *segment descriptor table* (SDT) is indexed by the segment number; a segment table entry contains at least the physical address[30] PMA of the origin of the segment and its length:

```
type segment_descriptor is
  record
    PMA : address;
    length : integer;
  end record;
```

The complete address mapping is

$$PMA = SDT(s).m + i \tag{5-8}$$

While one adder performs the mapping addition, another adder can subtract the actual index value from the segment's length to determine whether the address actually reaches beyond the end of the segment. The comparison logic signals an interrupt if the index value exceeds the length. Figure 5-36 illustrates this addition and checking process.

The SDT represents the tabular mapping of the process' segment number space into another address space. The user program and/or the compiler/linker determine which segments are loaded into the SDT. The operating system's memory allocator determines the addresses in the SDT entries.

Logically, the SDT is a single table, and it could be implemented as one table. Alternatively, the SDT could be implemented as a tree of tables, with some bits of s selecting the subtable and the remaining bits selecting an entry. This design may be chosen for the convenience of the operating system; like paging, its existence would not be visible to the executing program. By managing the segment table like a set of pages, the system's table and memory management functions might be simplified.

Another design option divides the segment table into pieces in a manner visible to the executing process. The B5700 system separates system objects (described at level 0) from user program objects (described at level 1). A global address is specified by a segment number and an index; the most significant bit of the segment number indicates which display register to use to translate the address. Figure 5-24 showed this mapping.

The Intel iAPX432 system [TYNE81] also uses segmentation; its segment space is divided into four portions described by separate tables. The segment table used for a particular address translation is selected by the value of the two *low-order* segment

[30] If the system implements paging beneath segmentation, the SDT entry contains the PMA of the first entry in the segment's page table.

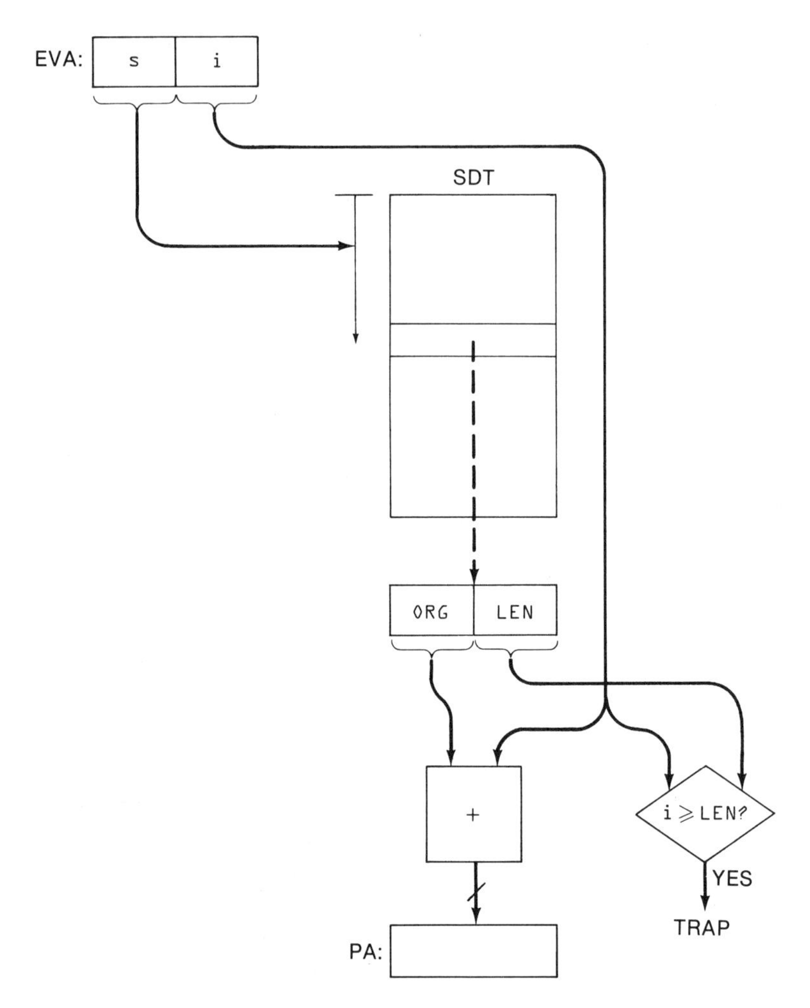

Figure 5-36 Segment descriptor table address mapping

number bits. User programs may reload three of the four[31] table entries, thereby changing the set of accessible objects. Figure 5-37 illustrates this mapping strategy.

5.5.2.2 Paging. A memory page is a fixed-size contiguous block of memory allocated as a unit. The page size is fixed to one (or sometimes two) value(s) when the processor is designed. A typical page contains between 2048 and 8192 addressable units; this size was determined by simulations. There are many pages within the virtual address space. Pages are independently allocated memory space, so a blocked pointer mapping is used; the complete mapping is described by the *page*

[31]The segment table numbered "0" contains pointers to the description of the process itself; therefore, it cannot be changed during program execution.

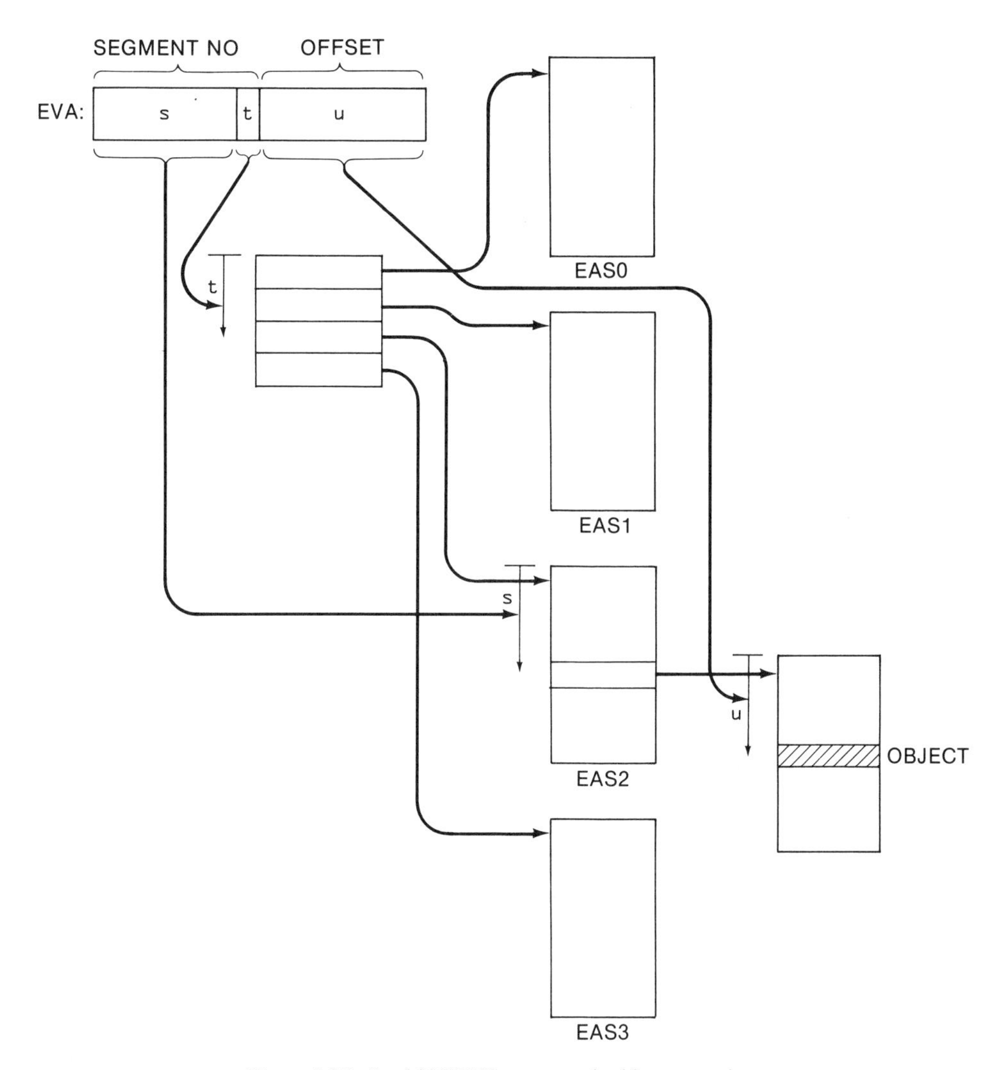

Figure 5-37 Intel iAPX432 segmented address mapping

table. Since there are many pages and since programs exhibit locality, page address mappings may be performed by a two-level mapping table (see Section 5.2.3.5), with a set-associative table in front of the complete page table. In the IBM 370 the first-level table is called the Translation Lookaside Buffer (TLB). Figure 5-38 illustrates the page address mapping through a TLB backed up by a complete page table contained in memory.[32]

To obtain maximum mapping speed, the TLB hardware must both compute the set-associative mapping and also manage the TLB's entries. Software intervention is not appropriate since it would be too slow for this frequently exercised

[32]Of course, the page table must not be accessible to user programs.

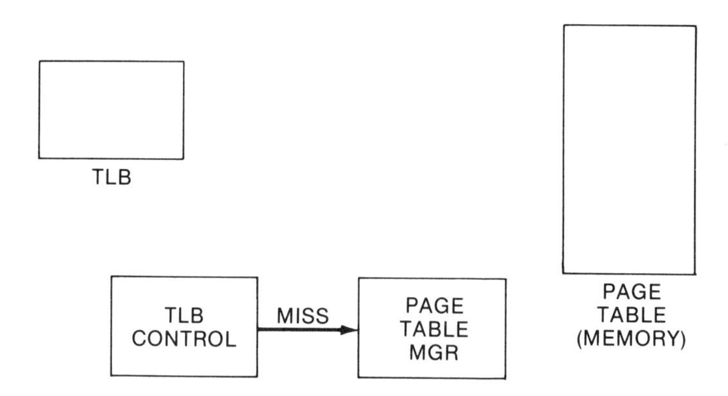

Figure 5-38 TLB and page table structures

function. When the EVA has a "hit" in the table, the PMA is constructed by concatenating the table entry with the "index" portion of the EVA. When the EVA's page is not present in the TLB, the hardware TLB control logic accesses the complete page table in main memory and loads the proper page description into the TLB, displacing some TLB entry. The entry to be deleted might be chosen by an LRU policy, described in Section 4.5.3.3. The TLB can use a small set size and the LRU data can be recorded in a small set of recency-comparison bits.

5.6 THE PROCESSOR–MEMORY INTERFACE

The interface between the processor and the memory determines many system properties, including its performance. A hardware designer can increase system speed by incorporating mechanisms that speed memory accesses or that generate and translate memory addresses. The memory hardware design affects system expansion possibilities, system speed, and system reliability. Finally, special modules in the processor–memory interface can modify the addressing granularity, thereby decoupling the memory granularity seen at the processor from the granularity of the memory modules themselves. We discuss these issues in this section.

The time required for the processor to access an item stored in memory often is a fundamental limit to system speed. Under many designs, the memory access time is not identical for all memory access attempts, so the performance of the memory system is characterized by the *average* amount of time required for a memory access. This time is called the *effective memory access time.* The effective memory speed can be improved by changing logical structures in the processor–memory interface or by changing the memory technology. A technology change does not directly change the system's architecture and therefore is beyond the scope of this book.

The architectural techniques we discuss in this section include:

1. Memory management units
2. Cache memories

3. Multiple independent memory modules
4. Memory bandwidth improvement
5. Memory granularity adjustments

A memory management unit reduces access time by speeding the memory address mapping process, which must be performed before most memory accesses. A cache memory statistically reduces the access time. Having multiple memory units statistically reduces the waiting time until an access attempt can be initiated at the memory, and therefore reduces the effective access time as seen from the processor. Memory bandwidth improvements can increase system speed by decreasing the address sizes or increasing the amount of data accessed during one memory cycle. Data width increases are helpful if the additional information accessed can actually be used by the processor. Granularity adjustment decouples the actual memory design from its logical interface viewed from the processor; this technique can be used to create one or more system(s) with different or flexible word sizes from the same set of memory modules.

5.6.1 Memory Management Units

The memory management unit (MMU) is placed between the processor and the memory (Figure 5-39); it transforms virtual addresses to physical addresses and may check access rights to validate the acceptability of an access attempt. The MMU may also contain the memory bus control logic; this functionality is simply moved from the processor, so its inclusion in the MMU does not change the logical structure of the system.

We discuss the major memory-related MMU functions: address mapping and access right checking. We will see that the latter function is added easily once the former function has been supported, so we emphasize the mapping function here.

Assume, without loss of generality, that the MMU performs memory mapping on a page basis. Thus the MMU logically maps each page number to the memory

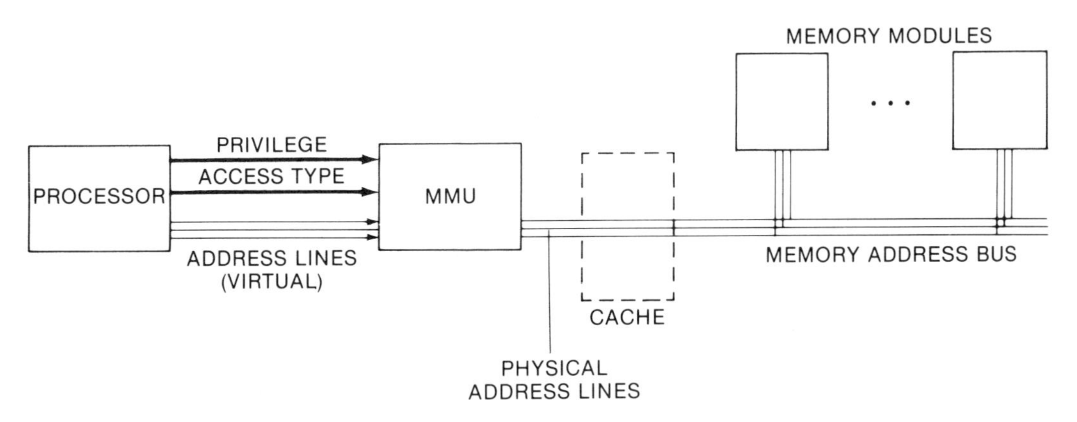

Figure 5-39 MMU module placement

address of the corresponding page frame. The logical map table has one entry per virtual page frame. If the MMU receives a virtual address, which is usually the case, its mapping function has to be different for each executing process and must be changed when the processor switches processes. The map table must span the virtual address space—a large address range. For good performance, speedy accesses are required, at least for those pages likely to be accessed. Thus while the translation time for pages likely to be accessed must be short, the translation for pages unlikely to be accessed can be slower. These observations suggest the use of a set-associative table held within the MMU backed up by the complete address map held within main memory. MMU control logic must manage the composition of the set-associative table. Typically, an LRU policy is used; the LRU statistics are represented by a set of recency-comparison bits within the table slots.

In a multiprogrammed system the MMU's map table includes both physical location and access rights information for each page frame. The access rights bits define the types of access permitted to the executing process; these access rights must be checked on each access attempt. The access rights may specify permissions based on the type of access (write, for example).[33] To enforce this level of access control, the processor must notify the MMU of the type of each access being attempted. In some designs the privilege attributes of the executing process may be sent to the MMU with each request. These considerations suggest the processor-MMU interface signals shown in Figure 5-39.

For system integrity, the map table must be controlled by the operating system's memory management modules. This control ensures that the address mapping and access rights are consistent with the memory allocation and permission policy being enforced. Thus the manager must control the contents of the memory copy of the memory map table, and it must define which map table is to be used by the MMU. There is no requirement concerning copying between the set-associative map and the mapping table because this copying is controlled at the MMU hardware level. There must be a way for the operating system to invalidate all set-associative table entries when the scheduler dispatches a new process.

Example 5-24

During a transition between executing the operating system and executing a user program, it is necessary to instantly change the MMU's mapping function to that of the operating system. This requirement could be satisfied in two ways. One way is to include the operating system within the memory image of every user program and to have the operating system granted access to any section of the memory space. Another way is to include the operating system in the user's memory image, as before, but provide a second set of access permission bits in the map. The set of access rights bits to be used on an access is selected based on the processor's mode. A third way to approach this dilemma is to provide two mapping tables and a means for instantly switching from one to the other. Figure 5-40 illustrates these options.

The MMU must correctly restrict access to the map tables while the processor

[33]This fine granularity of access control is required in systems with memory sharing; see Chapters 3 and 4 of Volume 2.

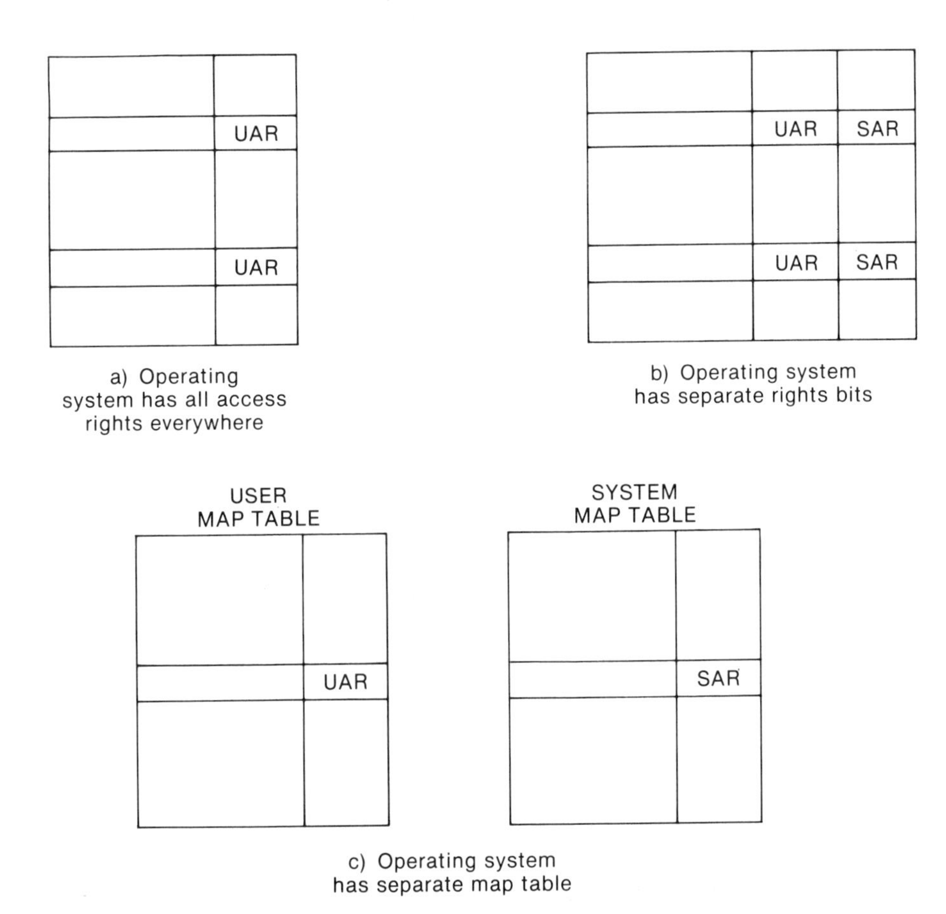

Figure 5-40 User/operating system separation in the MMU tables (UAR = User Access Rights; SAR = System Access Rights)

executes a user program, lest the user's program modify the table, thereby obtaining unauthorized access to information in the system. This issue may appear to be circular—the system must control accesses so that the access control mechanism works correctly! Actually, one way to approach this cycle is to deny access to the tables when user programs execute and permit table access only when the processor is executing in supervisor mode. Another approach to this problem isolates the memory map information in a special device to which access is permitted only by executing special "privileged" instructions executable from supervisor mode.

Now consider the location of the map table. It could be forced to be located at a fixed ("wired-down") location by the design of the MMU. If the MMU expects to find the memory map table at a fixed physical address, the system must copy the map table for the next process that will be dispatched to the fixed location where the MMU will find the table; this copying must occur before dispatching the process, and consumes many memory cycles. To remove this delay, the MMU could be designed so that the table origin address (within main memory) is passed from the processor to the MMU. In this case, the system must assure that the correct origin information is passed to the MMU upon process switch. Since the table does not have to be copied, this option permits changing the map more quickly. Note that the MMU's activity to reload its map is the same under all designs.

The mapping techniques just presented are appropriate for user processes, but the operating system itself may require memory accesses subject to fewer access restrictions. In fact, to manage memory the system may have to access memory on the basis of physical addresses. Thus, when executing memory management algorithms, the processor may have to be able to bypass the MMU's memory mapping logic. How would this bypass be specified? One method for specifying the bypass decision uses the processor's mode. From supervisor mode, for example, it could be ruled that all accesses bypass the MMU map and are made directly to the memory. This choice is not wise, since many parts of the operating system will have to be written using absolute addressing, thereby placing a greater burden on the programmers. It would be much better to provide a means by which the memory management function could be "buried" deep within the system, with the outer layers of the operating system written using virtual addressing. One design alternative makes the MMU bypass choice switchable while the processor is executing in supervisor mode. With this option the lowest levels of the operating system can use absolute addressing, but the levels above the memory manager can all be written using virtual memory addresses.

5.6.2 Cache Memory

A cache memory may be inserted between the MMU (if there is one) and the physical main memory (Figure 5-40) to give the processor the appearance of a faster main memory. The cache serves as the fastest, most expensive level of the memory hierarchy; it is inserted to decrease the average main memory access time as seen from the processor.

From a logical point of view a cache memory is similar to a paged memory—information may be absent, the memory is the fastest in the system, and management algorithms are required. As with paging, the selection of the dumping policy is important. The problem of selecting the cache's dumping policy is not the same as selecting the page dumping policy because the speed ratio between the two memories involved is drastically different. With a high speed ratio, the cost of a poor decision is high, and the use of a complex decision algorithm can be justified. Thus with a high ratio a complex management policy can be implemented in software. On the other hand, if the speed ratio is low, the cost of a poor decision is low and it is more important to make a quick decision than to make a really good decision, so a simple dumping policy can be adequate. The latter case applies to cache memory design, because the speed ratio between the cache memory and the main memory is less than 10 : 1, whereas the ratio of main memory speed to secondary memory speed may be 10^3! Also, the cache memory is fast enough that very few logical operations can be performed during one cache memory cycle. Hence all cache address translation and space management algorithms must be quite simple and must be implemented in hardware.

The cache provides fast access between the processor and any object stored in the cache. Frequent fast accesses reduce the average memory access time. The access time is expressed in terms of the cache hit ratio h, the fraction of access attempts that find the desired object within the cache. If m is the average main memory access time and c the cache access time, the average memory access time s is given by

$$s = hc + (1 - h)m \tag{5-9}$$

The hc term should be replaced by just c if the main memory access cycle is not initiated until after the cache miss is detected. However, since h is close to 1 for realistic designs, this detail makes little difference in the overall results. The average memory access time is a linear function of h.

Since the cache memory is small and expensive, the size of the swapped unit must be much smaller than a page. Cache swapping units are called blocks or lines; their size lies in the range from 8 to 32 bytes. This size selection is based on hardware cost, physical space, the speed improvement, and the cost.

The high speed of the cache memory would be wasted unless there were a high-speed mechanism that translates a memory address to a cache location. Due to program locality a cache using a set-associative mapping will give good performance.

Example 5-25

Figure 5-41 shows the complete TLB/cache mechanism used in the IBM 370/168 processor. The cache slot selection is independent of paging address translation, which speeds up address translation because the cache index and the TLB can be accessed simultaneously. The longest signal path through the TLB/cache passes through the encoder, the TLB accessing process, the equality check on the table row read out, the selection of the proper page number for the cache equality check, the cache equality check, and finally, the multiplexer selecting the double word to pass to the processor.

Within the framework given by the set-associative cache located between the processor and memory, several policy issues must be resolved to complete the cache design:

1. When to clean a cache block
2. When to load a cache block
3. When to dump a cache block
4. Cache position

5.6.2.1 Cache block cleaning. A cache memory, like a primary memory in a memory hierarchy, must occasionally receive new information to reflect a changed locality pattern. Old information must be replaced. Will the cache block to be replaced be clean? Suppose that it is not clean. Then its contents have to be copied to main memory before a new block can be read in to take its place. The time required for this copying may reduce system performance. If the performance is unacceptable, we need to look for an alternative design. Could we design the cache

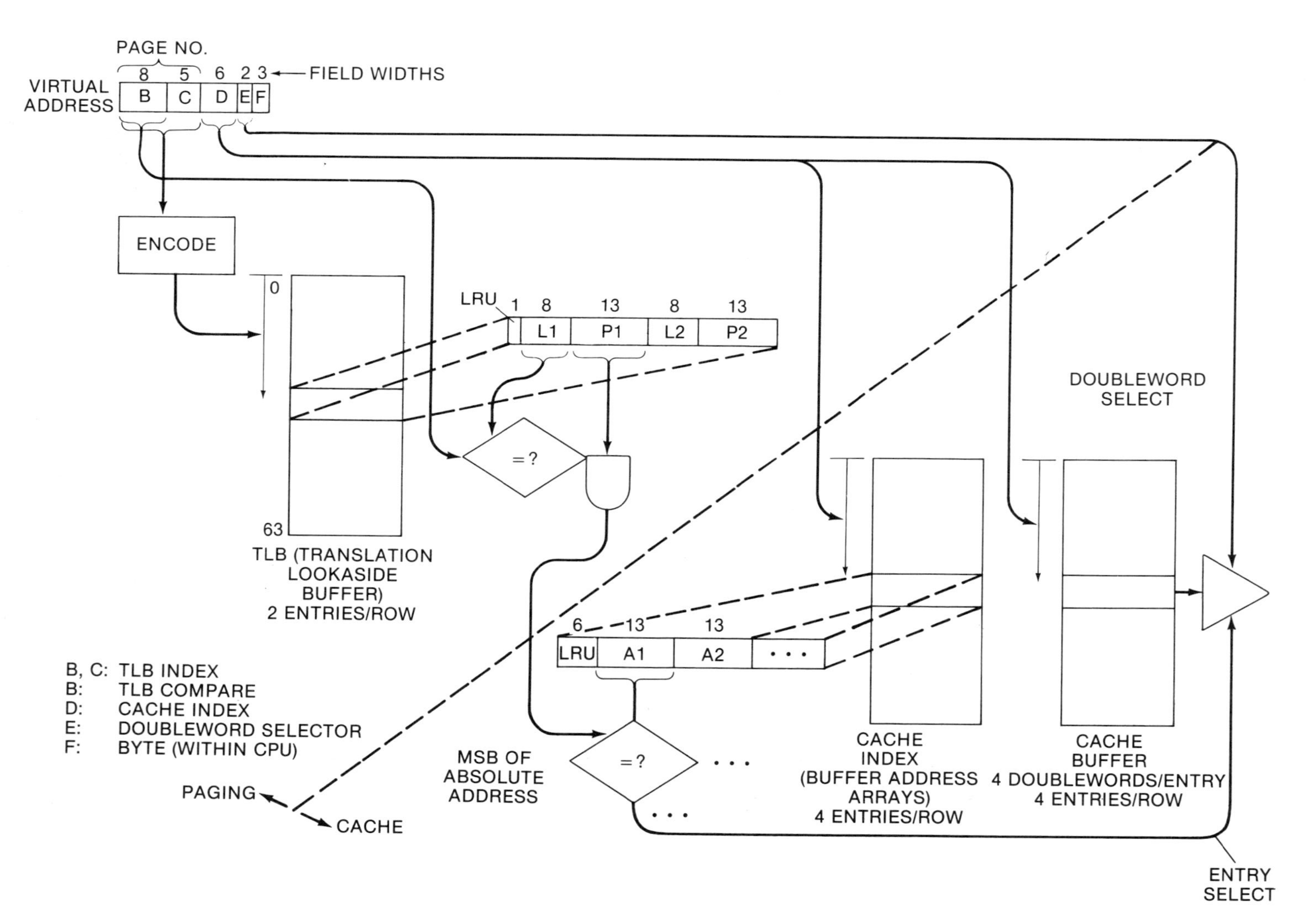

Figure 5-41 IBM370/168 paging/cache mechanism

so that its blocks are usually clean? Since a write cycle is the only activity that can dirty a block,[34] we consider the cache actions on a memory write.

What policies could be used for cleaning[35] cache blocks? A cache block is clean when its contents match the contents of the corresponding block of main memory. The only way that a dirty cache block can be cleaned is by writing it to main memory. We consider two policies:

1. Write-through
2. Copy-back

The policy selection affects both the system's logical properties and the speed of memory write operations through the cache. If the cache is associated with the processor (see Section 5.6.2.4), the selection affects the logical properties, since delayed writing may affect the consistency of the memory views seen by different processors. On the other hand, a system with memory-associated caches always presents the external world with a single view of the memory, regardless of the policy for writing information to memory. The effective memory speed is affected by the choice of the cache block cleaning policy because a memory write operation takes longer when the block must actually be written to main memory. The slowdown only affects write accesses, which are typically about 15% of all memory accesses. Now we consider the two policies.

Under the *write-through* policy, during any write cycle, the cache generates a request to write the same information to main memory. A cache block never need be considered "dirty" if this policy is followed. This policy may slow the system since there will be many memory write requests.

Under the *copy-back* policy a block is not written to main memory until the cache decides to dump it, and then it is written to main memory only if it is dirty. This policy results in fewer main memory writes than the write-through policy. Under write-through the slowdown affects only memory write operations, whereas under copy-back, the slowdown may affect any memory access that causes the cache to be loaded.

A mixture of the two policies can be implemented by adding a flag to each memory page or segment, the flag value signifying which policy is to be used for the associated information. We discuss this option further in Section 3.9.2 of Volume 2.

5.6.2.2 Cache block loading. Another cache design decision concerns the cache loading policy. It should be clear that if there is but a single program in the system it always pays to load a block into the cache when the block is first read, for locality predicts that the program is likely to read other information from that same block in the near future. On write, however, the issue is not quite so clear. It could be argued that once a block is written into, the same block is likely to be written into

[34]Other situations requiring special attention, such as the action in the cache when a direct-memory-access (DMA) device writes to a memory location that happens to be present in the cache, will be considered later.

[35]Cleaning a cache block is like cleaning memory space, as discussed in Section 4.5.2.

again soon. This argument suggests that the block should be loaded into the cache when the write operation is performed. This argument does not apply if the cache uses write-through, since under write-through each write operation initiates a write cycle in the main memory, whether the block is located within the cache or not. It is easy to see that there is no advantage to loading the written block into the cache if the cache uses the write-through policy. Furthermore, the written block will occupy cache space that otherwise could hold another block whose read accesses would be speeded up. Thus loading written blocks into the cache will decrease the read hit ratio, which may increase the average memory access time.

Example 5-26

> Each page descriptor in the Fairchild CLIPPER [FAIR85] contains a flag indicating which cache cleaning policy is to apply to the information within that page when (and if) it is cached. The option chosen for a page is encoded in the "System Tag" field in the page descriptor. Whereas a page of shared information must follow a write-through policy (see Section 3.9 of Volume 2), a page of information private to one process is not subject to any logical constraints, so its system tag may specify either write-through or copy-back.

5.6.2.3 Cache block dumping.

A cache dumping policy is needed if each cache slot includes more than one block. The dumping policy, like a page dumping policy, determines which block will be removed from the cache when a new block must be loaded within the slot. Since there are few blocks per slot, an LRU policy with usage data stored in a set of comparison bits (Section 4.5.3.3) can be used. If there are n blocks in each slot, the LRU information requires $n(n-1)/2$ comparison bits—bit b_{ij} $(i < j)$ is set if block i has been referenced more recently than block j. While making an access the system forces new values into $(n-1)$ of the control bits to make it appear that the block being referenced is more recent than any other block in the slot. To make the block dumping decision, n AND gates, each with fan-in of $(n-1)$, are provided. The output from gate i is high if the ith item is the least recently used block in the slot.

How does the selection of the dumping policy affect the cache performance? Recall that cache performance is characterized in terms of the "hit ratio," the fraction of access requests that are actually satisfied by the cache without reference to main memory. It is difficult to obtain any analytic characterizations of cache hit ratios except under unrealistic assumptions, so simulation must be used. Simulation studies are only as accurate as the characterization of the system's environment. With these caveats up front, let us look at one typical simulation study. We choose the study by Smith and Goodman [SMIT83], which is typical of these studies except that it studied only instruction referencing patterns. First the authors obtain a "workload characterization;" memory reference strings are collected by an interpreting program. These reference strings are presented as input to the simulator. Different simulations emulate different cache policies for each reference string. The cache size and configuration were also varied. Each reference is made to a 4-byte instruction word. The data in Figure 5-42 show the variation of the effective access time with the cache structure, its replacement policy, and its size. It is clear that the size of the cache is the most important factor determining the hit ratio.

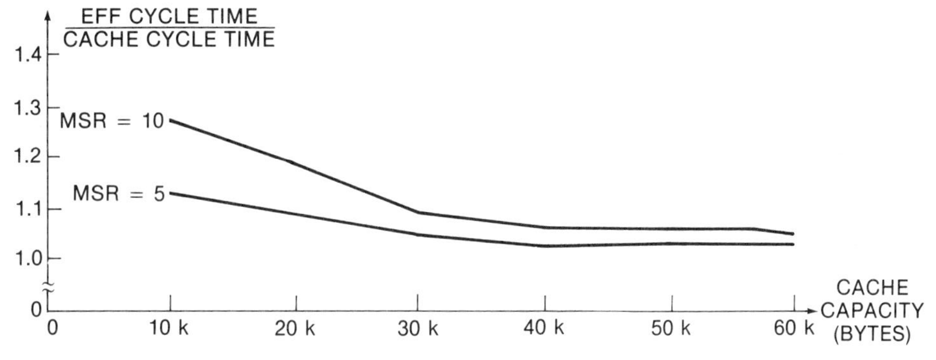

a) General effects of cache size and memory speed ratio (MSR) (curves based on data from [SMIT82])

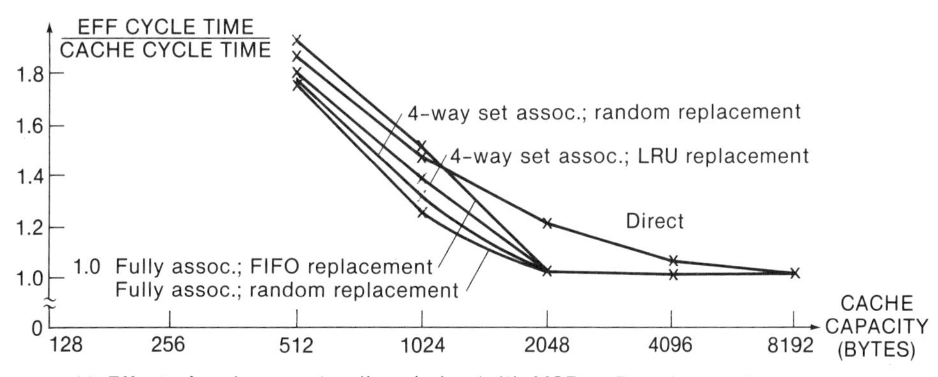

b) Effect of replacement policy choice (with MSR = 5) on instruction cache (curves based on data from [SMIT83])

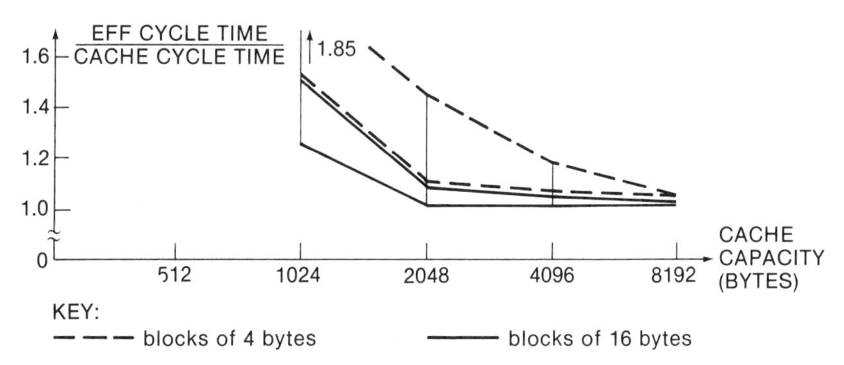

c) Effect of block size (with MSR = 5) (curves based on data from [SMIT83])

Figure 5-42 The effect of cache design parameters on cache performance

These results are hardly surprising since caching is like paging and since the page dumping policy does not have much effect on the performance of the paging system. While the simulation results in the table suggest that the cache structure does not make much difference, we should look at the dependency of the access time on the block size. This relationship was shown in Figure 5-42c. The bars in the figure indicate the range of hit ratios across the range of policies.[36]

5.6.2.4 Cache position. Should the cache memory be considered to be associated with the processor or with the memory? Figure 5-43 depicts the two alternatives. Our question raises an important design issue. If the cache is associated with the processor, only the (single) processor can submit access requests that will be handled by the cache. On the other hand, if the cache is associated with the memory, any memory requestor can submit access requests to the cache.

Several issues complicate the selection among these alternatives:

1. Speed
2. Request competition
3. Multiple copies of data

The *effective cache speed* is affected by both the speed of the cache itself and the signal delay between the processor and the cache. If the cache is associated with the processor, the signal delay from the processor to the cache will be short, and the effective cache access time will be the smallest possible for the given cache implementation. For this reason the cache memory is usually associated with the processor.

Request competition can be a problem if the cache is associated with the memory, since all processors and input/output devices may send access requests to the cache.[37] Competing requests may make the cache unavailable to a processor; this lengthens the average access time. Recall that this effect is not present if the cache is associated with the processor.

Multiple data copies may be present in a multiprocessor system; the fact that there can be several copies of the same memory item in different caches introduces a problem if any processor changes its copy. Immediately, the other copies contain obsolete information. This problem is known as the "cache coherence problem." Other aspects of this situation are covered in Chapter 3 of Volume 2. To meet the logical requirements, in one solution to this coherence problem each cache monitors all memory write requests on the system bus and takes an appropriate action when it sees a write request. The cache may have to invalidate a block or write the new value into the copy held in the cache. The overhead of these activities may decrease the cache speed. The effect is present only if the caches are associated with the processors. If all caches are associated with the memory, a cache entry effectively replaces the memory copy for all access attempts so that there is only a single (visible) copy of each memory item. Therefore, all processors see the result of any memory

[36]Information about which policy is best or worst is not significant, since the point is that the results are almost independent of the policy, especially in the region of interest (where the effective access time is small).

[37]At first reading this statement might make the reader conclude immediately that there is no reason to want the cache at the memory. Actually, placing separate caches in front of separate memory modules has the effect of spreading the demand, and the effect of the competition may not be more serious than the contrary effect of the cache coordination problem discussed in the next paragraph.

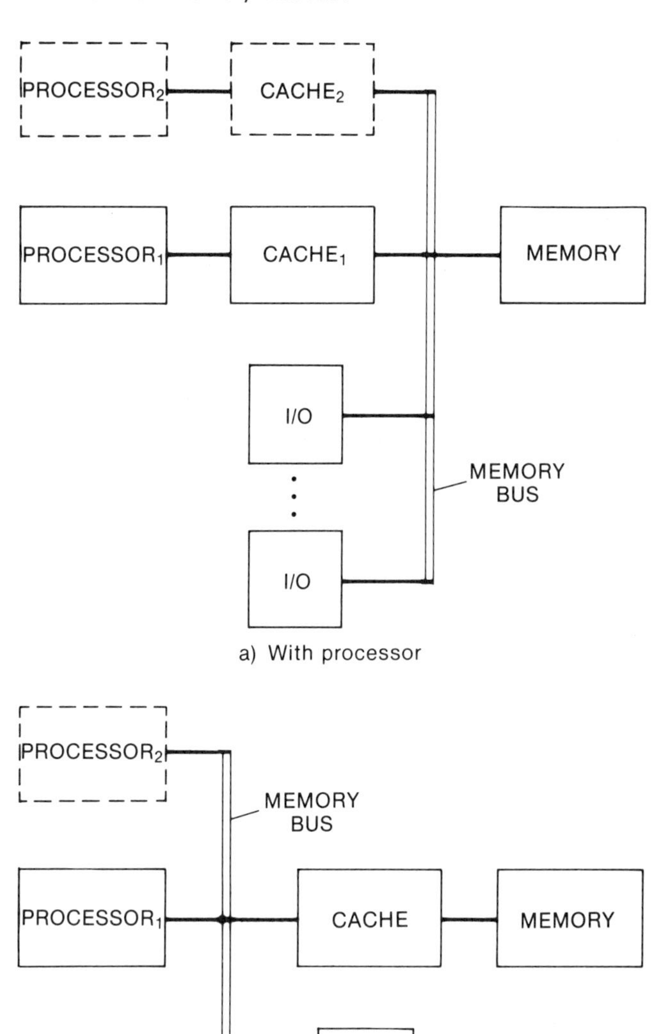

Figure 5-43 Cache positions

write, and the coherence problem vanishes. Many designers have preferred to associate the cache with the processor to obtain higher speeds, even though this structure introduces the coherence issue if the system has multiple processors.

Example 5-27

IBM 370 cache memories are associated with the processor, using the write-through policy for coordination. On the other hand, Amdahl 470 cache memories are associated with the memory; writing is done when a block must be dumped from the cache.

5.6.3 Memory Interleaving

It is possible to construct a complete memory system using a single memory module, but there are many reasons why this strategy is undesirable. First, the design poses reliability problems. Second, the design limits system expansion. Third, the design cannot allow overlapping access requests from several different requesters, because the module cannot handle a second access request while another one is being completed. Request overlapping can improve system performance; we discuss this effect in Chapter 1 of Volume 2.

Here we present some alternative methods for constructing a memory system from several separate memory modules. The design issues center on the method used to select which memory module contains the object being addressed. It is safe to say that memory module selection is based on the values of some memory address bits; although this is certainly true, the observation does not illuminate the selection issues or the designer's options. In this section we discuss several options, including interleaving.

If the number of modules is a multiple of 2, the module selection should use bit values taken from the ends of the physical address, but not from its middle. The design decision concerns how many bits are to be used from each end of the address; the selection affects the randomness of the request distribution among modules, the memory expansion possibilities, and the effects of failures on the system's capacity.[38]

If the number of modules is not a multiple of 2, nontrivial address mapping logic will be required. In the following subsections we discuss some interleaving options, as follows:

1. No interleaving
2. Power of two interleaving
3. Prime-way interleaving

5.6.3.1 No interleaving. For no interleaving, the memory module number is taken from the most significant address bits. Each memory module will hold a set of contiguous addresses, as illustrated in Figure 5-44. The accessing pattern is not likely to be randomly distributed across the set of memory modules, because a long block of consecutive addresses[39] is located in the same module. This design does, however, have a memory system expansion advantage; the expansion increment is a single module, providing system configuration flexibility.

[38]This concern may not be important unless the system should be able to operate in a degraded mode after a module failure; we do not discuss it in detail.

[39]Recall that consecutive addressing is common inside loops and when processing many data structures.

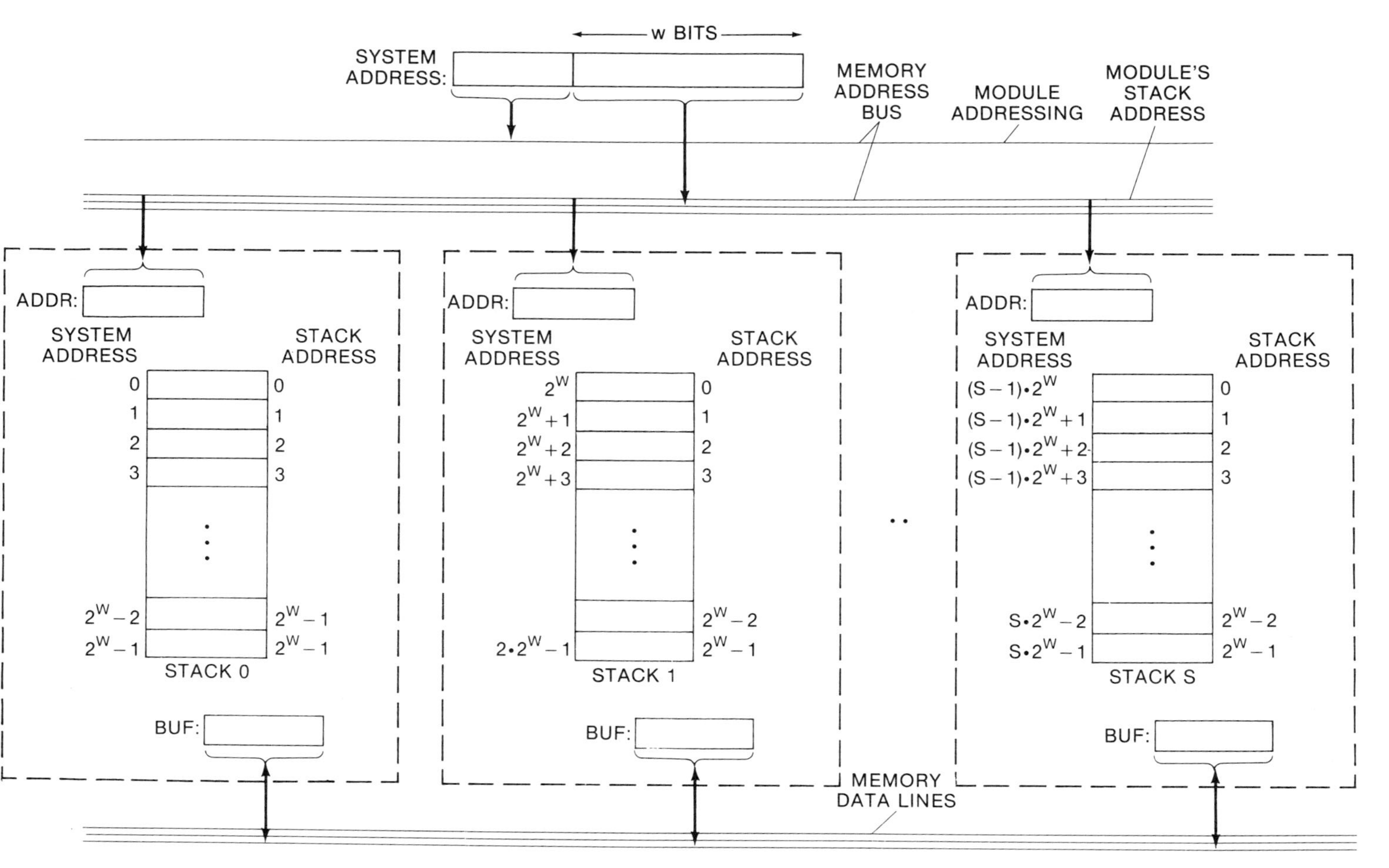

Figure 5-44 A set of noninterleaved memory modules

5.6.3.2 Interleaving by a power of 2. Memory interleaving maps any pair of consecutive addresses to different physical modules. The degree of interleaving is the length of the cycle by which addresses are mapped into module numbers. Suppose that address zero maps into module zero (a common condition!) and that the next address that maps into module zero is L. Then L is the degree of interleaving. With L-way interleaving a memory address M is converted into a module number N and a local address A using the relations

```
N := M mod L;
A := integer_part_of(M/L);
```

With this module selection scheme memory must be expanded by adding a complete interleaved set of modules, thereby adding a contiguous set of addresses to the memory.

When L is a power of 2, the residue and quotient operations amount to selecting physical address bits. In particular, N is the set of $\log_2 L$ bits from the right end of M, and A constitutes the remaining bits of M; see Figure 5-45.

At the module level, the referencing pattern to an interleaved memory will be randomly distributed among the modules unless the program exhibits a repetitive pattern with an addressing increment which satisfies a particular relationship to the degree of interleave. Otherwise the probability that an arbitrary memory access request will select a particular memory module will be 1/L.

The randomness advantage of interleaving can be traded against the small expansion increment advantage of a noninterleaved system by taking some module selection bits from each end of the address. Such a configuration can be viewed as a set of memory "banks," each containing a set of L-way interleaved modules, as illustrated in Figure 5-46. The randomness is preserved within a bank (each module gets 1/L of the references), but not among banks.

5.6.3.3 Prime-way interleaving. It might seem that prime-way interleaving would be terribly inefficient and its implementation awkward due to the need for division by the prime number. It is possible to exploit some properties of prime numbers to simplify the design, provided that some waste space can be tolerated. First we present a simple way to find the module number N from the address M. Then we tackle the determination of the local address, which does require either a division or an allocation that leaves unused space.[40]

To find the module number, we must divide the address M by the prime number P (we use P rather than L, as before, to emphasize the fact that the value is a prime number). Now express M in terms of its binary representation:

$$M = \sum m_i 2^i \tag{5-10}$$

The module number N is given by

$$N = M \textbf{ mod } P = \left[\sum m_i 2^i\right] \textbf{ mod } P = \left[\sum m_i (2^i \textbf{ mod } P)\right] \textbf{ mod } P \tag{5-11}$$

[40]This scheme was first described in [LAWR82]; also see [TENG83].

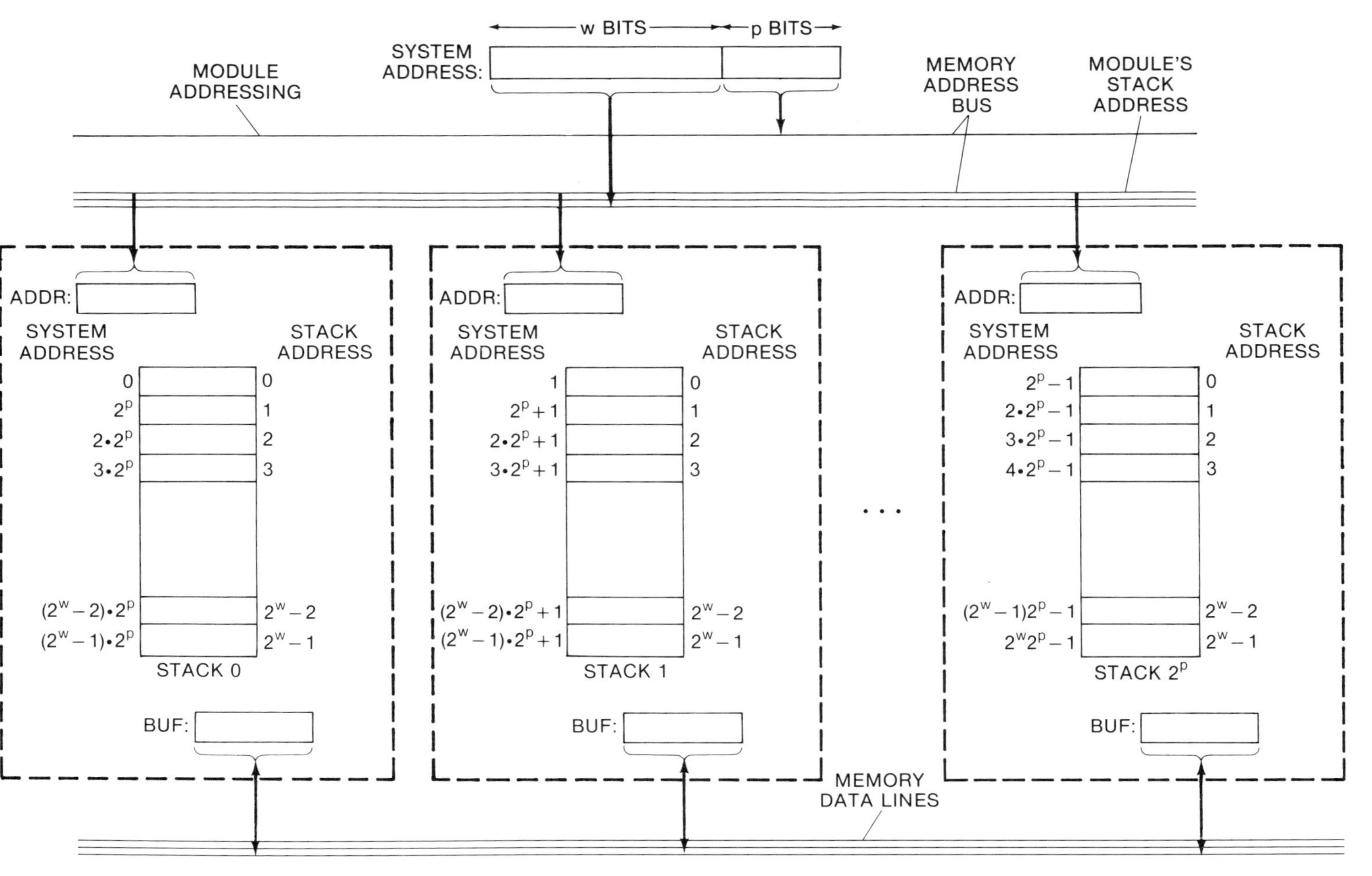

Figure 5-45 A set of totally interleaved memory modules

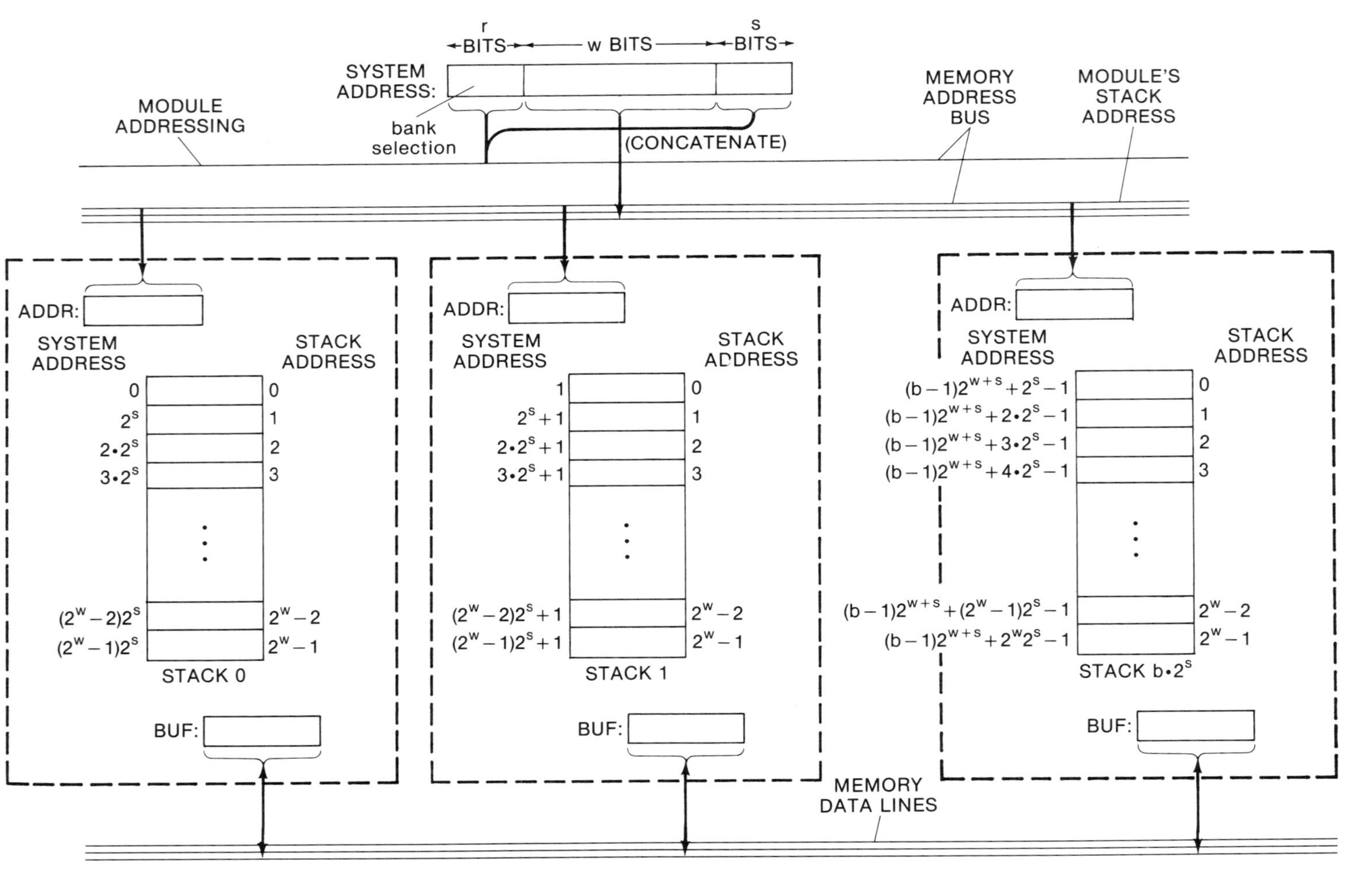

Figure 5-46 A set of b banks composed of totally interleaved memory modules

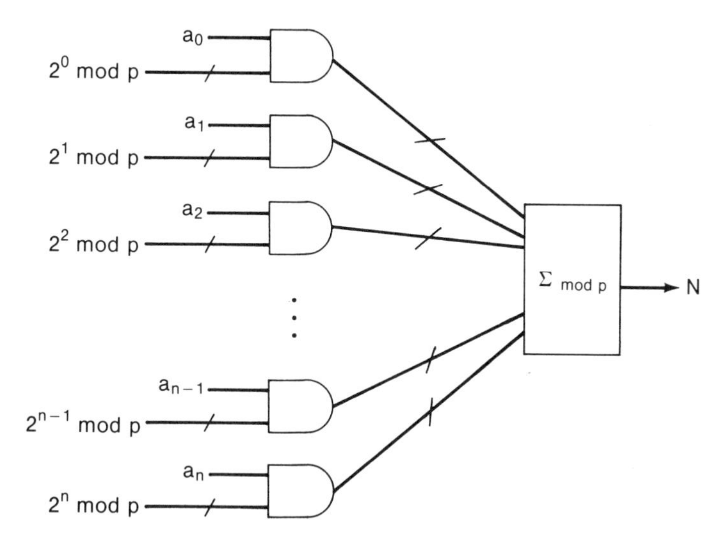

Figure 5-47 Module number determination for prime-way interleaving

The quantity in parentheses is a constant for each i, independent of the value of m_i. In other words, Equation (5-11) states that the m_i's select some constant values to be summed (see Figure 5-47), with the summation being performed modulo P. The constants exhibit cyclical values as a function of i, as shown in Table 5-6 for a few interesting values of P. We can easily argue that the period of this cycle is a divisor of $(P - 1)$. Among the entries in the table, $P = 17$ has the shortest period, namely 8. The structure of the module number determination circuit for $P = 17$ is shown in Figure 5-48.

TABLE 5-6 RESIDUES OF 2^i mod P

	P				
i	11	13	17	19	37
0	1	1	1	1	1
1	2	2	2	2	2
2	4	4	4	4	4
3	8	8	8	8	8
4	5	3	16	16	16
5	10	6	15	13	32
6	9	12	13	7	27
7	7	11	9	14	17
8	3	9	1	9	34
9	6	5	2	18	31
10	1	10	4	17	25
11	2	7	8	15	13
12	4	1	16	11	26
13	8	2	15	3	15
Period	10	12	8	18	36

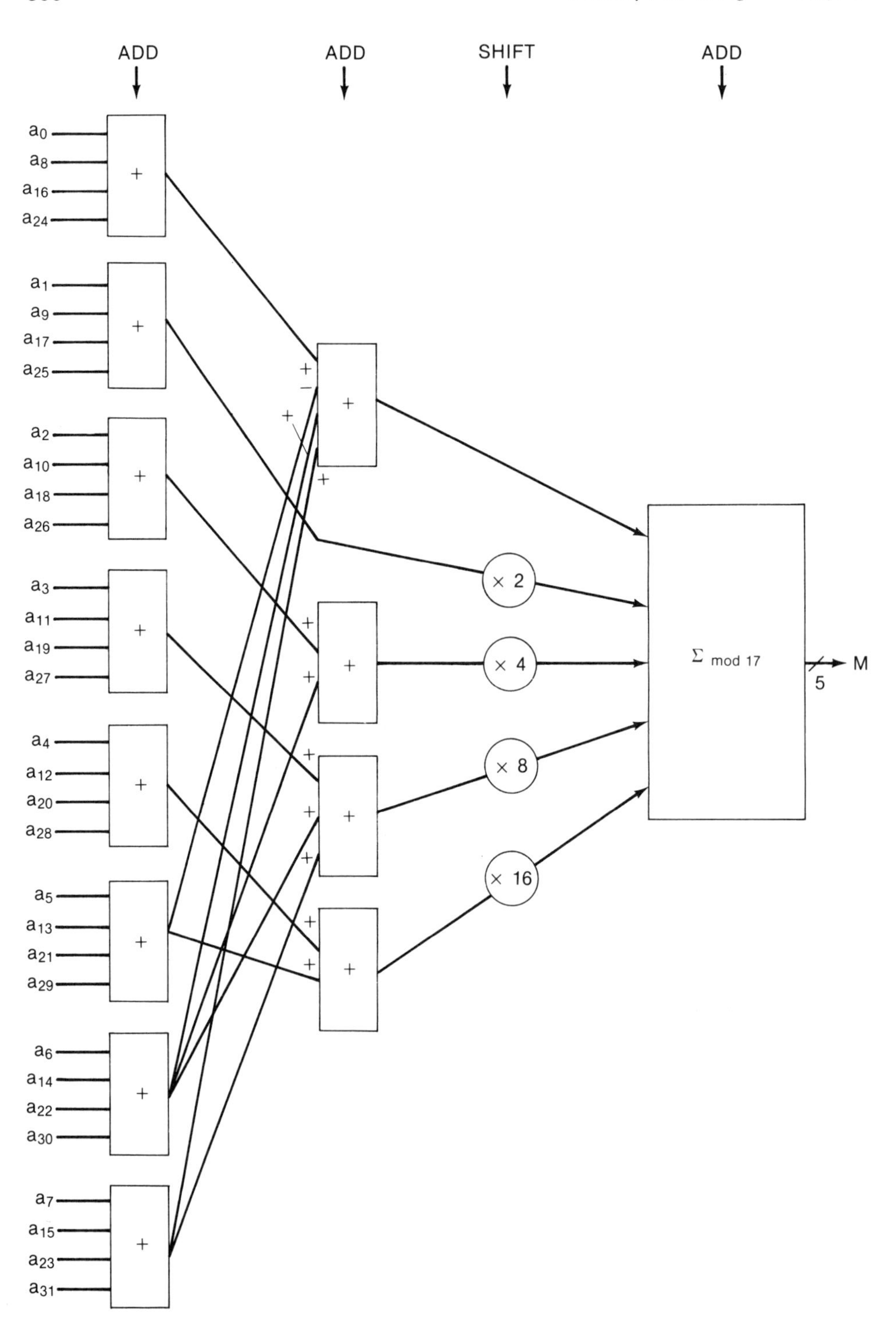

Figure 5-48 Computing the module number from the 32-bit address $a_{31} \ldots a_0$ for 17-way interleave

The remaining part of the prime-interleave design concerns the selection of the local address A. Theoretically, we should use the quotient of the division of M by P; we have already noted that this requires a difficult computation (which could itself take longer than a memory cycle!). If we are willing to sacrifice some memory space to obtain simplicity in the addressing mechanism, we use instead the quotient upon division by a power of 2 less than P. This choice guarantees that (1) the address can be found by bit selection, (2) every address is at least as high as the correct one, and (3) the mapping from M to A is one-to-one. Let R denote the selected power of 2. With $P = 17$, we choose $R = 16$. Figure 5-49 illustrates the mapping of physical addresses into the memory modules for $P = 17$ and $R = 16$. It is easy to see that the fraction of space used is R/P, which indicates that the greatest power of 2 less than P should be used for R and that choosing P close to a power of 2 is desirable.

The Burroughs Scientific Processor [KUCK82] used 17-way interleaving.

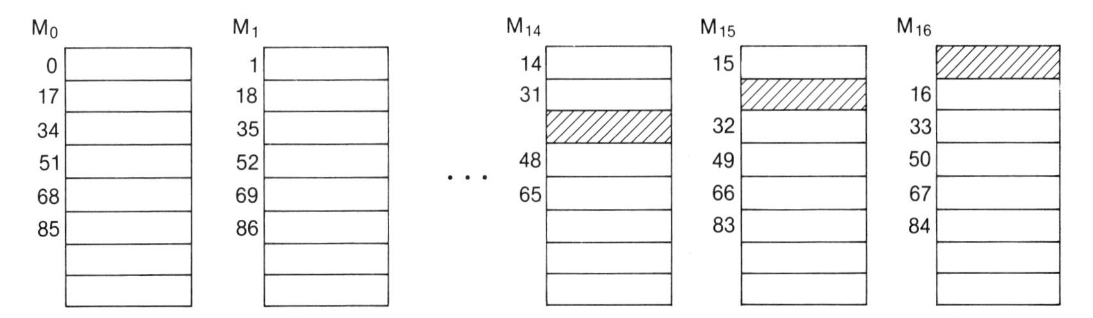

Figure 5-49 Address mapping with 17-way interleave. (Unused space shaded; addresses decimal.)

5.6.4 Memory Bandwidth

The bandwidth of the memory system can be a system bottleneck. Drastic system restructuring that allows several operations to be performed on an object between the time it is read from memory and the time a result is written back to memory can reduce the impact of any memory system bandwidth limitation. Some such designs are discussed in Chapter 1 of Volume 2. Here we present some simple system structuring techniques that modify the processor–memory interface. These techniques reduce the address bandwidth requirement or increase the data bandwidth by increasing parallelism. First we discuss address bandwidth reduction techniques.

Address bandwidth affects the bus traffic patterns. The address bandwidth is less likely to be a bottleneck than the data bandwidth. The address bandwidth requirement can be reduced by moving address translation from the processor. The processor would send a short address across the bus and the memory system would translate it to its long form. The processor must modify the mapping mechanism on every mapping change; this transaction consumes bus bandwidth. For example, using this strategy to translate the B5700's context-dependent addresses in memory would require that the display information be available within the memory system. The address bandwidth can be reduced by using a simpler form of context-dependent addressing for instruction fetching. Suppose that every instruction is the same size. Now move the program counter logic to the memory system. For sequential instruction fetching, a single-bit request "fetch next instruction" is adequate; no address need be sent from the processor to the memory. A new address must be sent from the processor only when a branch is to be taken. The Fairchild F8 microprocessor system used this bandwidth reduction technique. Another way to reduce the instruction bandwidth requirements is to insert an instruction cache to buffer program words near the processor; the CLIPPER system uses this technique.

Data bandwidth constraints are more likely to affect system performance than address bandwidth constraints. A simple approach to relieve this bottleneck is to access many objects in parallel during one memory access. If the additional information is likely be used, the parallelism may be worthwhile. With a specialized application such as vector processing, it is very likely that the additional information will be used. Thus vector-oriented large-scale machines are designed with a wide data path to memory.

Example 5-28

The CDC STAR-100, a vector machine, was designed to access 512 information bits and 16 parity bits on every memory cycle. This was achieved by interconnecting a set of smaller memory modules, each one holding 64-bit words. All modules in a parallel set receive the same address. The wide data path to the processor is constructed by concatenating the data paths to the modules in the parallel set, as illustrated in Figure 5-50.

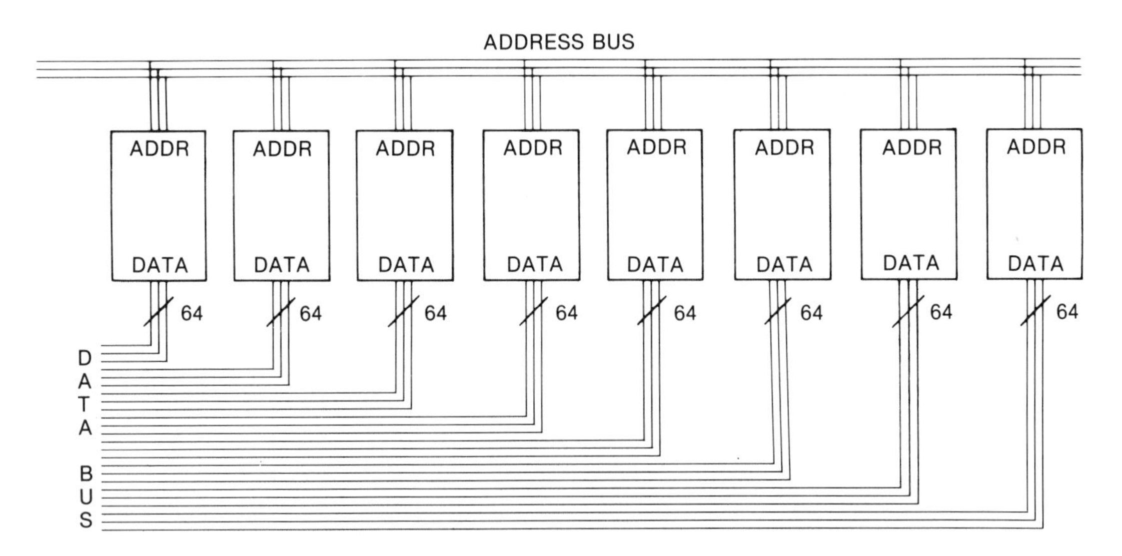

Figure 5-50 CDC STAR-100 memory organization

A memory with a wide data path can be used to speed transfers between a processor cache and main memory. Many bits from the same cache block can be accessed simultaneously during one memory cycle. The bits can be communicated on the data path as a sequence of smaller words, with each word transfer taking much less time than a complete memory access. The cache response time is reduced even further if the memory's control logic sends the addressed word in the first bus transaction that passes data. Sequencing through the remaining words starting from the addressed one is adequate to load the complete cache block.

Example 5-29

Suppose that the memory width is eight words, and that a block of eight words is to be loaded into the cache. The cache missed when it attempted to access location 35_{16}. The memory then accessed locations 30 .. 37. The words are then sent to the processor in the order 35, 36, 37, 30, 31, 32, 33, 34, which allows the cache to respond to the processor immediately after the first word is received from the memory.

5.6.5 Granularity

The width of the data path at the processor does not have to match the width of the data accessed in a single fetch from a memory module. The memory with a wide data path is a simple case of this general situation. A granularity adjustment module (GAM) interposed between the memory system and the rest of the computer (Figure 5-51) can provide more width flexibility. In the figure each memory module accesses

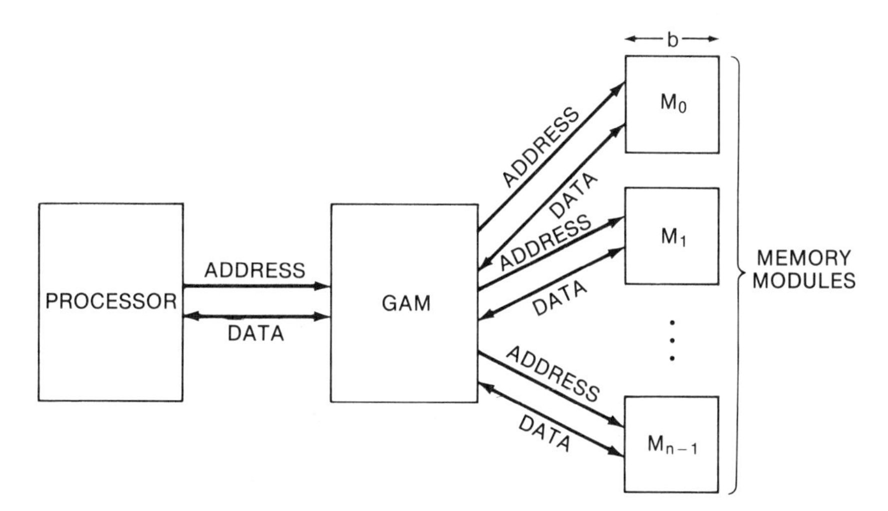

Figure 5-51 GAM module placement

b bits in a single cycle. Bit addresses are interleaved among the n modules in b-bit chunks. Thus the sequence of the addresses of the bits within module 0 begins

$$0, 1, 2, \ldots, b-1, nb, nb+1, nb+2, \ldots, (n+1)b-1, 2nb, \ldots$$

In any reasonable design both n and b should be powers of 2, so we assume this condition as we continue the discussion.

The GAM divides the incoming address into fields as shown in Figure 5-52. To illustrate the GAM's computation, consider accessing a single bit located at address A. By examining the N field of A, the GAM can determine which memory module

D	N	B

Figure 5-52 Address fields for a memory with a GAM (see text)

contains the addressed bit. The B field tells which of the bits within the "word" accessed in that module is being designated. The D field selects the word within the selected module where the addressed bit is stored. If the request asked for more than one bit, the bits immediately following the first one may be located within the same word as the first bit, or if the addressed one was the last bit of the word, in the next module (next being interpreted modulo the number of modules). It is easy to see that, in general, the GAM sends addresses to the modules according to the following:

GAM Addressing Rule. The module-local word address w of the information is $D + 1$ in module i for $0 \le i \le N - 1$ and D in module i for $N \le i \le n$.

Using this addressing rule the GAM can guarantee access to at least $(n - 1)b + 1$ consecutive bits starting at any bit address.

After the GAM has accessed the desired bits, it must reformat them for presentation to the processor, which expects the accessed data to be aligned within the processor–memory data path. For reading, the alignment process will require both shifting and masking. To write into the memory, the GAM must supervise a sequence of actions: read, shift, mask, and write.

Example 5-30

In the Burroughs B1700 series [BURR72] memory addressing was to the bit, and the processor could make variable-length memory requests for up to 24 consecutive bits. The configuration parameters were $n = 4$, $b = 8$.

5.7 IMPLEMENTATION OF ASSOCIATIVE MEMORY FUNCTIONS

Associative fetches from tables play a large part in the implementation of memory accessing functions. The logical requirements on an associative memory are complex, and it might appear that the cost of associative fetching would be high in terms of either speed or logic gate count. We have seen that hardware and software designers have devised ways to implement the lookup feature without building a general associative memory; the hash table and set-associative table typify these alternatives. Despite these options, some designers still desire general associative memories. They may try to use an associative system to permit a large degree of parallelism in a specialized application. For example, an associative system could locate, in parallel, many situations requiring immediate attention, and the processing could then proceed at these critical points of the problem space.

In this section we explore some ways to implement a general associative memory. We start with the required operations. Then we develop a partial system design to implement the required operations. Subsequently, we outline several approaches that provide most or all of the desired associative functions.

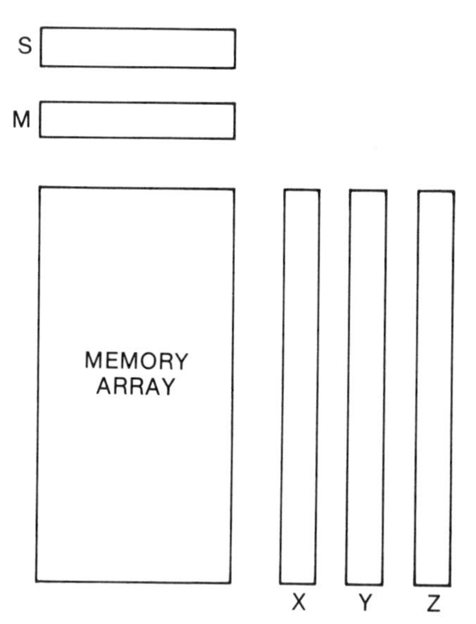

Figure 5-53 Associative memory registers

5.7.1 Associative Memory Operations

The major operation in an associative memory is the search operation, which finds all entries in the memory that satisfy a given search (or match) condition. Additional operations are required to insert and manage entries within the associative memory. We first discuss the search operation and its results; then we turn to other associative memory operations.

We will need a validity bit V(i) with each memory entry. The bit will be set ("true") if the corresponding memory entry contains meaningful information, and will be cleared ("false") otherwise. We will see that many, but not all, associative operations are performed only on valid entries.

The parameters of a search request are a search value, a match predicate, and a mask that specifies which bit positions are to be considered when making the match test. Two registers called S and M will hold the selector value and the mask value, respectively. These registers are the same width as all memory entries; let w denote this width. Further, let h denote the "height" of the memory, which is the number of entries in the memory. The result of the search operation may be the value of an entry meeting the match condition or the result may be a set of bits, one for each entry in the memory, specifying whether the corresponding entry meets the match condition. The "match bits" are stored in a "register" named X, containing h bits, one for each memory entry. An additional result is a status value specifying how many entries satisfied the match condition. Figure 5-53 depicts the memory array and the associated registers.

The match predicate MP might be stated as a boolean expression. The "match"[41] should succeed for all memory entries for which the match predicate MP

[41]We use quotes because the English word "match" may imply that the predicate is an equality condition; equality is just a special case of a match predicate.

evaluates to true. The MP governing the value of x(i) (i is an integer index denoting the location address of the entry) may involve the contents of the M and S registers, and the corresponding memory entry E(i). We can express any match condition as a boolean expression. We use vector indices as subscripts to designate the bit positions in a field within a register or location. The complete value in a register or memory entry is designated by the name of the register or entry without any subscript. An MP requiring an exact match in all bit positions is

$$\text{MP(i)} := \text{V(i)} \textbf{ and } [\forall \text{j}, (\text{E(i,j)} = \text{S(j)})] \tag{5-12}$$

Note that we use the assignment operator to denote result determination; this must be distinguished from the simple equals sign, which denotes the equality predicate. The previous equality predicate tests all entries in the memory; occasionally, it is convenient to have an equality test confined to those entries where X(i) was previously set. An MP for this test is

$$\text{MP(i)} := \text{V(i)} \textbf{ and } \text{X(i)} \textbf{ and } [\forall \text{j}, (\text{E(i,j)} = \text{S(j)})] \tag{5-13}$$

Another interesting match predicate requires a match only in those bit positions where the mask's bit is set. This condition to test all memory entries is

$$\text{MP(i)} := \text{V(i)} \textbf{ and } \{\forall \text{j}, [(\text{E(i,j)} = \text{S(j)}) \textbf{ or not } \text{M(j)}]\} \tag{5-14}$$

The masked equality match predicate is sufficient to implement all memory accessing algorithms presented in this chapter. In fact, since in memory name mapping the mask value can be fixed at design time, an explicit mask register is not required,[42] and the matching logic and algorithm can be tailored for the specific mask pattern.[43] In the following we discuss general associative memories; this means that we will include the mask register and obtain search results in the X register.

The major associative memory operation is the masked search, expressed as

$$\text{SEARCH: X} := \text{MP(S, M, X)}$$

The simplified specification omits the validity bits and the status condition left in the condition code register, as will be discussed presently.

Next consider READ and WRITE operations; write is required to load the memory. In a location-addressed memory these operations access a memory entry whose address was specified as an operand, and data flows through a memory data register D. In an associative memory, these operations also use a data register, but the selection of a memory entry is made through the X register. For simplicity, first assume that only a single bit of X is set. Then READ and WRITE pass data between D and the entry E(i) where X(i) is set. The WRITE operation also sets V(i) in the

[42]Because a multiple match signifies an error, logic to find the first match (see below) will not be required.

[43]This means that many gates and tests can be eliminated from the general design.

selected entry. Thus, if there is a single bit of X set at location i, these operations amount to

```
READ: D := E(i);

WRITE: E(i) := D; V(i) := true;
```

The SEARCH operation leaves status information in the associative memory condition code register (AMCC). The three bits of this register indicate the number of X bits that are set, as indicated in Table 5-7. The distinctions made by the status values are important. They allow the program to test whether an upcoming associative memory operation can be meaningfully performed. For example, if AMCC(2) is set, a READ operation probably should not be performed. Since AMCC reflects the status of X, whenever X changes, AMCC may change accordingly.

TABLE 5-7 ASSOCIATIVE MEMORY CONDITION CODE BITS

Bit Position	Meaning
0	No bits set in X
1	One bit set in X
2	More than one bit set in X

Two operations are required to control the existence of associative memory entries. ENTER places the contents of D into one previously invalid entry; this operation can be emulated by a short sequence of other instructions,[44] but is so useful that we designate it as a separate operation. DELETE clears the validity bit of every entry where X is set. In other words,

```
DELETE: V(i) := V(i) and not X(i);
```

To permit general logical operations on the match information, which may be useful for application algorithms using complex entry selection criteria, we provide Y and Z registers, each containing *h* bits. The associative memory supports the following logical and copying operations between the V, X, Y, and Z registers:

1. SET P;
2. NEGATE P;
3. COPY P TO Q;
4. P AND Q TO R;
5. P OR Q TO R;
6. EXCHANGE P AND Q;

Here P, Q, and R designate any of V, X, Y, or Z.[45]

[44]This is possible only if the contents of V can be explicitly manipulated. Our design that follows does permit this kind of manipulation.

[45]The set of operations embodied in this instruction set obviously greatly exceeds the logical minimum, but it makes function selection orthogonal to operand selection for these logical operations.

An important special operation finds the first bit of X that is set, setting the corresponding bit in Y, while clearing all other bits of Y. In addition, the bit of X that was selected is cleared. This operation would be performed after the memory finds a multiple match, yet only one of the matching entries is to be manipulated. The multiple match condition can be detected by testing AMCC(2). The operation to find the first set bit of X will be called

```
FIRST
```

It is very expensive of logic, program steps, or signal delay to implement FIRST, since the value of each bit of the result depends on the values in all preceding bits of the operand. Therefore, we forgo orthogonality and only permit this operation to use X to determine Y.[46] We choose this combination because then a loop that individually processes all selected entries can be written easily. The program begins by performing the search and saving the results:

```
SEARCH          --clearly not an Ada program!
if AMCC(0) then
  ..            --handler for the no match situation
  end if;
while AMCC(2) or else AMCC(1) loop
  FIRST;
  EXCHANGE X AND Y;
  ..            --perform operation on one entry
  EXCHANGE X AND Y;
end loop;
```

In the following we examine the implementation of these operations, along with some variants that may be useful if the associative memory system is not implemented directly in hardware.

5.7.2 Implementation Options

First consider the implementation of the search operation, undoubtedly the most difficult operation. The search process must examine the mask-selected bits in all memory entries to find all matching entries. Three searching methods can be used:

1. Fully parallel
2. Word-slice
3. Bit-slice

These names reflect the amount of memory information examined during a single stage of the search.

[46]We do it this way so that an implementer could use a logic circuit to perform this operation, and the logic can use the time between operations to propagate the signals down the chain. If the operation used an intermediate register and implemented FIRST between arbitrary registers by copying, the signals within the FIRST logic could not start propagating until the intermediate register was loaded.

A **fully parallel search** simultaneously compares all the mask-selected bits of all entries against the corresponding selector bits. For simplicity, start by setting all bits in X. Then the outcomes of the comparisons at each bit position of word i can be combined electrically to signal mismatch, which clears the X(i) bit; this logic is depicted in Figure 5-54. Of the SEARCH implementation options, parallel search is fastest, requires the most hardware, and is the most expensive.

A **word-slice search** implementation can be used to build an associative memory from a conventional location-addressed memory. The word-slice search process consists of a loop that reads a table entry and compares its mask-selected bits against the selector value. The loop terminates when a matching entry is found. With the conventional memory hardware there is no register analogous to the X register of the parallel design; the SEARCH result is the address of the first entry meeting the match predicate. If there is no matching entry in the memory, the search will terminate by reaching the end of the memory address space. If more than one entry meets the match predicate, the search finds the first one; others can be found by continuing the search loop starting from its previous (matching) position. One advantage of this option is that conventional memory components can be used to implement the associative memory. Another advantage of this option is that general match predicates are easily accommodated. A disadvantage of this option is the large number of memory accesses to make the search; compare this against a hashed implementation

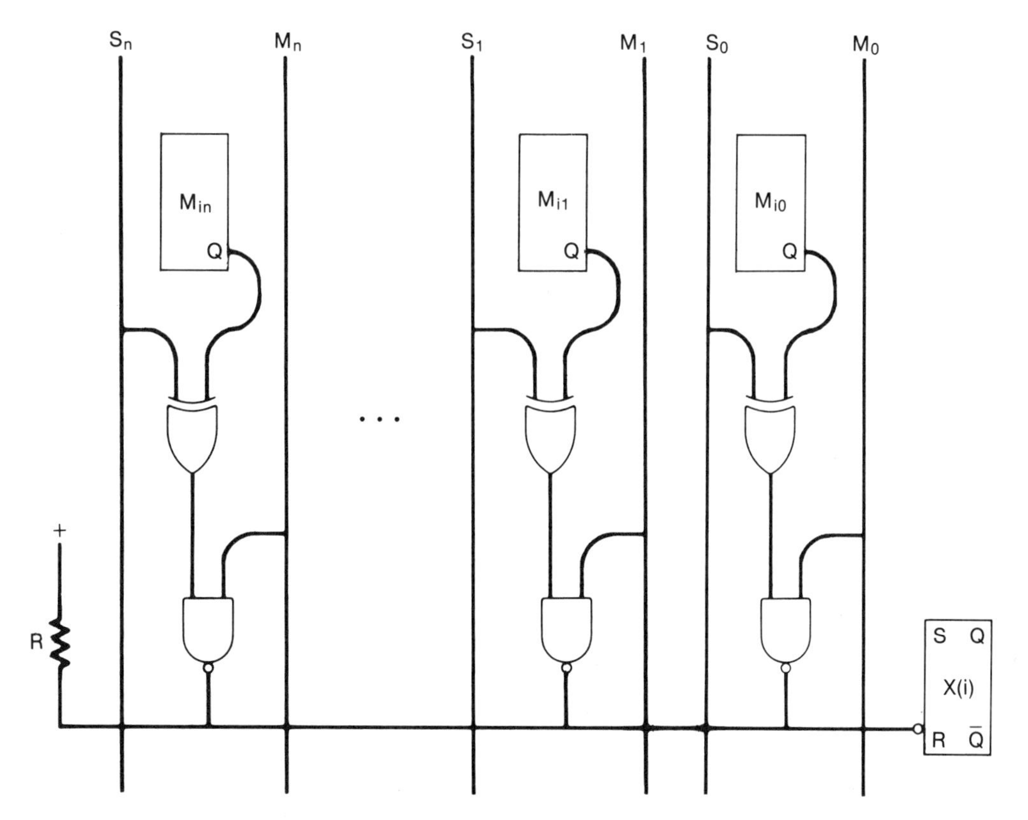

Figure 5-54 Equality match logic—parallel search (open-collector NAND gates)

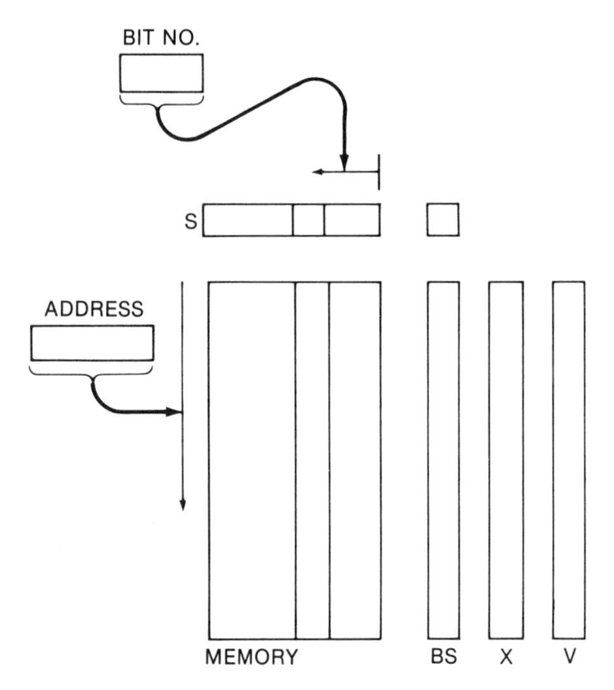

Figure 5-55 Structure for a bit-slice search

of a name table; in both schemes individual table entries are examined to find one satisfying the desired criterion. The major differences between the hashing scheme and the word-slice search are:

1. Word-slice searching must scan all table entries if the desired entry is not in the table.
2. Word-slice searching starts at the same table entry regardless of the search request.

From these observations we see that on the average a hashed search uses fewer accesses to find the matching entry than a word-slice scan. In fact, if the hashing function is sufficiently random (i.e., if the names actually mapped hash into quite different indices), there is a good chance that the first access will succeed by finding a matching table entry. One disadvantage of hashing is that only one search field can be accommodated.

A **bit-slice search** requires special hardware, but its complexity is lower than that of a parallel search implementation. For bit-slice searching, the memory hardware is designed so the memory can be read or written either along a single word or along a single bit (of every word).[47] The buffer register BS (bit-slice) receives the information read out from a bit slice. The structure of this bit-slice implementation is shown in Figure 5-55. This memory has X and V registers (and possibly Y and Z).

[47]Bit-slice WRITE is not necessary unless X and V are contained as columns in the memory.

To search the memory the X register is set and a loop that scans the selected bits is executed. In the loop body one mask-selected bit is read into BS, and BS is compared against the corresponding bit of S; in any bit position where there is a mismatch, X is cleared. The cost of a bit-slice memory lies between the cost of a word-slice memory and the cost of a fully associative memory. The bit-slice memory has one advantage, which is that it is easily adapted for match predicates with arithmetic comparisons, such as greater_than. An arithmetic comparison could be performed by software controlling a fully associative memory, but the program is tedious, as it must inspect bit slices and check the condition code to decide how to proceed.

After an associative search has set the match bits, it is still necessary to ascertain whether there is one match, more than one match, or no matches at all. Trying to implement these functions in logic circuits illustrates the logical fan-in requirements. Figure 5-56 shows one method for determining the match information. The dashed logic can be added to clear out all match bits except the first one; this logic therefore implements the FIRST operation. It is not the most efficient, however, because it includes a logic path that passes through $2h$ gates.

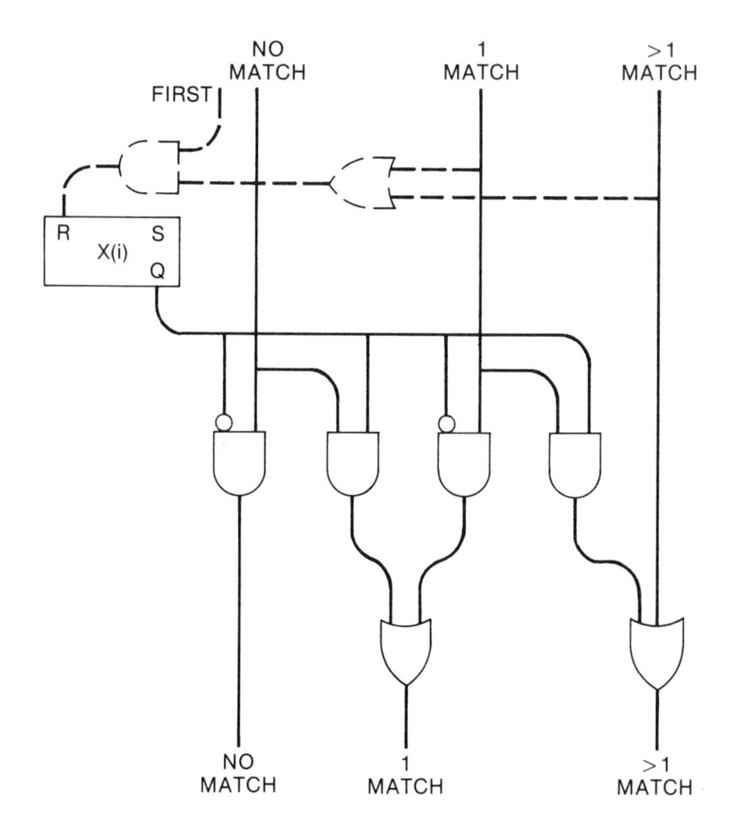

Figure 5-56 Match information logic

5.7.3 Comments

Associative memories are useful in memory mapping algorithms because the domain of the mapping function is large, yet only a small fraction of the domain is mapped. We have shown several alternative implementations and the basic operations of a general associative memory.

A few parallel computer systems based on associative searches used to enable other operations, such as arithmetic, have been proposed. A few have been built. The Goodyear STARAN system [BATC74] used variant of bit-slice searching and can be programmed as though it performs general associative operations. The details of these designs are beyond the scope of this book.

5.8 SUMMARY

This chapter closes our triple-chapter tome on computer memories. In this chapter we covered the address mappings required to translate a high-level name into a sequence of signals that would access the correct location in a physical memory. We showed different implementations of general address mappings, including the use of associative memories, hash tables, computed addresses, and set-associative memories. We showed the use of these techniques in different stages of the accessing sequence. For example, hash tables are used in compilers, tabular mappings are used in segmentation and paging, and set-associative mappings are used to speed up page table and cache mappings. All of these perform the same basic address mapping, translating names from one name space to another name space. Table 5-8 summarizes the name mapping problems encountered at the different stages of accessing.

TABLE 5-8 SUMMARY OF MEMORY NAME MAPPINGS

	Input Name Space		
Address Mapper	Form	Size	Usage Density
Translator	Symbolic	Vast	Very low
Linker	One or two integers	Large	Low
Processor	One or two integers[a]	Large	Low
Operating system	(Virtual) integers	Large	High (in blocks)
Memory interface hardware	(Absolute) integers	Large	High (in blocks)
Cache controller	(Absolute) integers	Large	High (in blocks)
Memory module	Integers	Moderate	High

[a]Or parameters of an algorithm that produces an integer.

In addition, this chapter has shown other architectural techniques, such as cache memories and interleaved memory modules, that reduce the average access time for memory accesses. These techniques achieve a speed improvement while using the same basic memory elements. This benefit is possible because programs exhibit locality and because processors can be designed to issue two or more simultaneous memory access requests (see Section 1.6 of Volume 2).

In these three memory chapters we have covered many important aspects of the computer's memory system. In Chapters 1, 3, and 4 of Volume 2, we consider other memory-related issues, showing how parallelism and sharing can yield speed or logical improvements, but at the same time can create problems of consistency and privacy.

5.9 PROBLEMS

5-1. Write a generic Ada procedure that will take as input two records describing array dimensions, having the following formats, and produce as output a permutation of integers in which the ith entry specifies the number of the dimension into which the ith dimension of the first array should be mapped to achieve a subset mapping of the first space into the second one. If the first space is not a subset of the second, have the procedure raise a "not_a_subset" exception. The generic parameter of the procedure is the number of dimensions of the spaces; we use n to denote that parameter in the following. The two input records have the format:

```
type input_dim_vector(n : integer) is
  record
    low, high : array(1 .. n) of integer;
    --vectors of lower and upper bounds on index
    --values
  end record;
```

5-2. This problem asks you to specify a mapping of multidimensional subscripts into one-dimensional subscripts which requires a minimum number of multiplications for execution. The mapping is to be performed during program execution.

(a) Specify such a mapping.

(b) Give formulas for the numbers of additions and multiplications required to map an n-dimensional subscript vector into a single index value.

(c) Specify the minimum set of parameters needed to define the function.

5-3. An address mapping is implemented using a hierarchy of hash tables. Let htab(i, j) denote the jth $(1 \le j \le N)$[48] entry in the ith $(1 \le i \le L)$ table of the hierarchy. The same hashing function is used to access the tables at all levels of the hierarchy. In case of a collision in the ith table, the next search is made in table $(i + 1)$—using the same hash function. If there is a collision at level L, one of the following strategies is used:

1. Use sequential searching in the table at level L; if this fails, quit.

2. Search sequentially, as in strategy 1, but if that fails, try sequential searching in table $(L - 1)$, and so on; failure occurs if the sequential search at level 1 fails.

[48] Yes, all tables are the same length! Why?

(a) Write out the steps of the search algorithm for each design.

(b) Contrast these designs with the following more conventional designs:

(i) A single hash table with one entry per slot and LN slots.

(ii) A single hash table with L entries per slot and N slots.

5-4. You are given a hashing function

```
function hash(key, size : integer) return index;
```

Its parameters are a key and a table size. Its result is an index value within the range 1 .. size. You will use this hashing function to construct a hash table using sequential searching after a collision.

(a) Specify a hash table search procedure that will work correctly even if the hash table is completely filled (i.e., there are no null entries in the entire table). If a search fails, have the procedure raise the exception "missing_entry."

(b) Write a generic hash table package supporting the following operations: insert, search, and initialize. The generic parameter is the table length.

5-5. Hash table search procedures can have problems if table entries may be deleted. To alleviate this problem, a designer proposes that one include in all hash table entries a special mark bit called "reserved." The idea is to set this bit when an entry is deleted from a location.

(a) Why not just make the deleted entry null?

(b) Write out as a sequence of steps the algorithms supporting this type of hash table, with the operations: insert, search, initialize, and delete. Be sure to specify all important values.

(c) Write an Ada package incorporating the algorithms of part (b).

5-6. Write a description of the hash table search algorithm if the table uses a set of J different hash functions to perform the secondary search. Write out one version in which the Ada function naming conventions are obeyed. There is only one table.

5-7. Specify a procedure that will expand a hash table, placing its former entries properly into a larger table space. Assume that there is a hash function:

```
function hash(key, size : integer) return index;
```

When should this reconstruction/expansion procedure be invoked?

5-8. Write an Ada package that specifies and encapsulates all operations on objects of type hash_table. The package should be generic, with the size of the hash table being the parameter.[49] Use sequential searching to handle collisions. The hash table operations to be supported are SEARCH, CLEAR, ENTER, and REPLACE.

5-9. Write an algorithm that searches a hash table with p (>1) entries per slot. Use sequential search for collision resolution.

5-10. Construct a table that shows how many hash table entries are searched to find each table entry in Example 5-11.

5-11. Consider a set of entries to be entered into a hash table. For each entry E_i its probability of use p_i is given. Let arrangement A be the arrangement of hash table entries achieved

[49]There will be a problem in finding a hashing function that works well for all possible size values; ignore this problem and just use an external function hash(n, size), where n is the name to be hashed and size is the table length. You should not worry about writing a program for the hash function or whether it is reasonable to assume that such a function does exist.

by inserting the entries in a time sequence ordered by the decreasing order of their usage probabilities. Show that arrangement A is optimal in the sense that the expected number of table fetches to retrieve an entry will be minimized.

5-12. A hash table controller resolves collisions by using a sequential search starting just after the location at which it discovered the collision. Table entries are never deleted. The search keys are alphabetic strings. The simple hashing function uses the alphabetic position of the first letter in the string as the table index (this simple hashing function is not recommended for general use!). Thus a string starting with "a" hashes into the first table entry, while one starting with "d" hashes into the fourth table entry.

A snapshot is taken and the contents of the table are observed; Table 5-9 shows the hash table contents at the snapshot. Based on the snapshot, write inequalities that state the strongest timing relationships that you can find concerning the ordering of the times that these entries were added to the table. For example, if you conclude that "ellen" was entered after "alan," write

$$\text{ellen} > \text{alan}$$

Do include a relation concerning any pair of keys about which you can determine a timing relationship from the information in the snapshot. Do not include redundant relations. For example, if you decide that the following three relationships are true, omit the third one from your answer, since it can be discerned from the other two. The three relations are

$$\text{ellen} > \text{alan}$$

$$\text{alan} > \text{brad}$$

$$\text{ellen} > \text{brad}$$

TABLE 5-9 SNAPSHOT OF A HASH TABLE

Location	Key
1	alan
2	brad
3	alex
4	dick
5	ellen
6	cindy

5-13. You need to access an entry in an ordered table containing n entries. Two designs are being compared; they are a binary balanced tree with one value at each intermediate node (see Figure 5-57) and an ordered list which is searched by using a binary search algorithm. It is argued that since both searches will examine the same table entries, the choice between the two designs is arbitrary (in other words, the two are equally desirable).

(a) Is the premise of the search statement correct?

(b) Is the conclusion correct? Explain your answers.

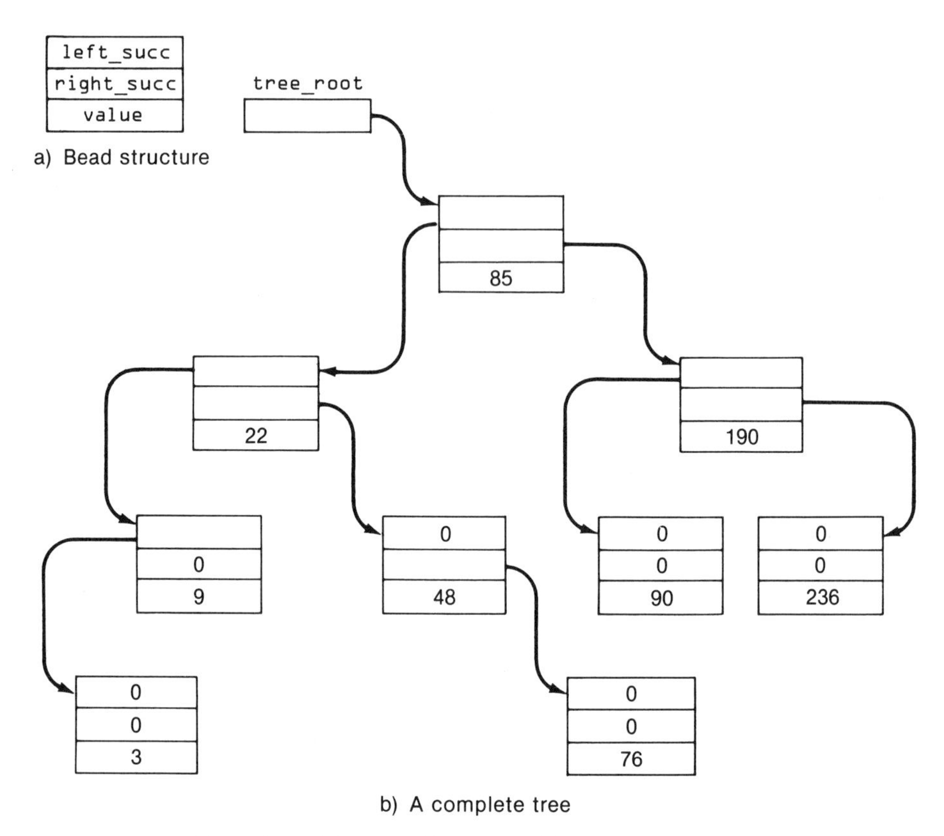

Figure 5-57 A balanced binary tree with a value at each node

5-14. This problem concerns the implementation of a mapping function through an n-ary tree structure. Let T denote the number of entries in the complete table (which comprises the entire tree).

(a) Find a mathematical expression that gives the processing time expended at one node as a function of n. The binary search algorithm is used to search the node.

(b) Find an expression for the total time expended in a complete search to find an arbitrary table entry (for a fixed total table size) as a function of n. (Do not account for the access time to reach a new mode—which might have to come from a slower memory.) Assume that all table entries are at leaves of the tree.

(c) How is the answer to part (b) changed if each internal node contains n table entries in addition to the tree links? To answer this, you must take into account the probability of finding a match at an internal node of the tree.

5-15. Draw a figure describing the allocation and effective address computation for each situation described in Table 5-3.

5-16. Here is an Ada program and an execution history for the program:

```
procedure a is
  procedure b is
    procedure c is
```

```
        ..
      begin
        ..
        d();
        ..
      end c;
      ..
    begin
      ..
      c();
      ..
    end b;
    procedure d is
      ..
    begin
      ..
    end d;
    ..
  begin
    ..
    b();
    ..
  end a;
HISTORY:
  call a;
  call b;
  call c;
  call d;
  return;
  return;
  return;
  return;
```

Draw pictures of the MSCW linked data structures in a B5700 implementation and execution of this program. Show the linked structures after each call.

5-17. This problem is concerned with a designer's choices regarding the implementation of the display vector to support the execution of programs written in a language that uses static nesting for name resolution.

(a) Identify factors that influence a designer's decision whether to automatically store the old display vector in an activation block when calling a new context. Assume that all display entries contain absolute addresses.

(b) Repeat part (a) if the display entries contain addresses relative to the origin of the stack object.

(c) Evaluate the factors for the execution of Ada programs, and make a recommendation regarding Ada's implementation on a system using display vectors.

5-18. Here is a proposal related to the retention of the display information across a procedure call. Recall that the B5700 scheme recomputes the display each time that a new context is entered. A speedup is achieved by adding a check about whether the display register is actually changed or not. The scheme to be considered in this problem saves all display information on the stack when a new context is created (as in procedure call), and restores the saved information to the display registers when the new context is exited (as on procedure return). A designer proposes saving the following information for each display register:

1. The offset of the base of the block (relative to the bottom of the stack)
2. A different stack flag (DS), true if it is a different stack
3. If DS = true, the stack number

The first two items are stored in the same memory word and the third item (if needed) is stored in a second word.

(a) Would this scheme work properly if the stack were relocated while the display information was pushed on the stack?

(b) Draw a picture illustrating the saved display information while a subroutine at level 3 is in execution, having been called from a procedure at level 4. You might want to use the following program and history as a specific example. The conditions for your diagram pertain to the display information on the stack during the execution of k.

(c) Does this scheme offer any savings over the Burroughs scheme? Explain.

```
procedure f is
  procedure g is
    procedure h is
    begin
      ..
      k()
      ..
    end h;
  begin
    ..
    h();
    ..
  end g;
  procedure k is
  begin
    ..
  end k;
begin
  ..
  g();
  ..
end f;

History
call f
call g
call h
call k
```

5-19. A designer proposes that the context dependency of addresses be automatically removed by stuffing the environment into an address whenever it is loaded into a register. Discuss the advantages and disadvantages of this proposal. Consider two cases.

(a) The environment is specified by the absolute address of the activation block base.

(b) The environment is specified by the pair (stack_no, index), where the index specifies the position of the activation block's base relative to the base of the stack object.

5-20. Design a method to implement call-by-name in Algol for the MC68020.

5-21. Write a machine language program for a familiar machine for the calling sequences for a procedure using each of the parameter passing conventions described in Section 5.4.3.

5-22. One option for passing subroutine parameters is to place them in the calling sequence (i.e., in the calling program itself). A designer proposes to use this convention to call recursive procedures. Is this feasible? Describe what additional manipulations the recursive procedure would have to perform (in addition to those necessary if the procedure were nonrecursive).

5-23. A compiler designer for a HP3000 Pascal compiler proposes to allocate the first word of each local space to a pointer that describes the value of Q (relative to DB) for the statically enclosing activation block. In this manner the activation blocks would be linked together to form the tree structure required for global references. Further, she proposes that locations DB through DB + 31 be allocated to hold the display information for an executing procedure, with DB + i holding the location of Q for the block of lexical level i.

(a) Show how a nonlocal object at location j within the activation block at level s would be accessed from the processor.

(b) Write an algorithm that updates the display information in the DB block.

5-24. Five "needs" that may enter into the selection of one linking scheme over another are:

1. The ability to establish linkages during program execution
2. The ability to change existing links during program execution
3. Speed of program execution
4. Speed of establishing links
5. The ability to share instruction segments.

Order these five "needs" in relative importance for each situation:

(a) Execution of FORTRAN programs.

(b) Execution of Ada programs.

5-25. This problem concerns the number of beads of the context tree that the processor must examine to fill its display. Let n denote the current level; the numbers start from the user's outermost program block, which is at level 2. Using the Burroughs B5700 design, how many block pointers will be examined to construct the new display in each of the following situations? Write a skeleton of a program in some block-structured language (specify the language you are using) to illustrate the situations in parts (a) through (d).

(a) The main program calls a procedure declared within the declarations of the main program.

(b) A program at level n calls a procedure declared within its own declarations.

(c) The program returns to its caller, the call having been made in a situation like that described in part (a).

(d) The program recursively calls itself.

(e) The operating system schedules another process for execution; the new process will resume execution in a block at level n (n should be a parameter of your answer). Do not attempt to write a program skeleton for this situation.

5-26. Rewrite the display loading procedure of Example 5-20 so that it will terminate when it finds that the value it wishes to write to a register is already located there.

5-27. A designer proposes using one set of registers to serve both the display register and data register functions. Her basic idea is that the registers could be used for computational

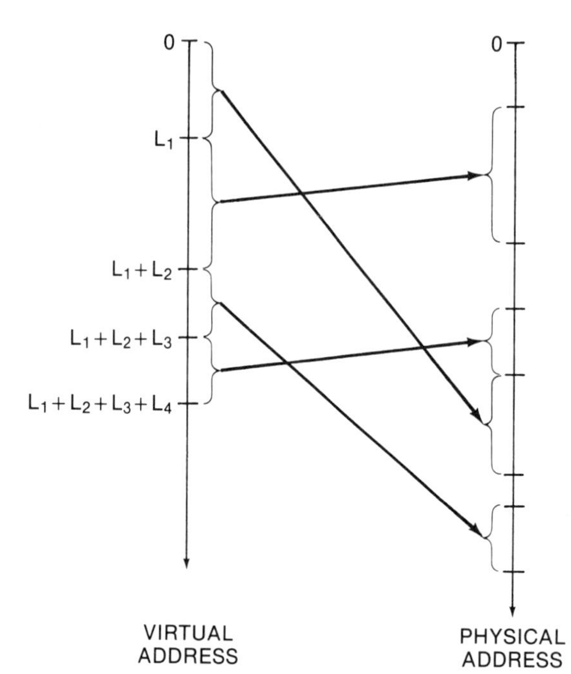

Figure 5-58 An address mapping (Problem 5-28)

purposes if they were not needed for making global references. Her design and supporting arguments are summarized in the following paragraphs:

Design. The CALL instruction automatically fills the processor registers with complete display information, with register R_i holding the pointer to the activation block for level i.[50] During program execution within the called program, registers that were loaded with display information may be overwritten with data. (The compiler will keep track of which registers are holding display information and which are available for data.) The register allocation module of the compiler decides (for each context) which registers should be used for nondisplay information.

Rationale. The processor will use fewer cycles to fill the display registers if it does that automatically during the CALL instruction (fewer cycles than would be required if the same operation were performed by a sequence of instructions in a user program). If the called procedure does access a global object, the new design might run faster than a "conventional" machine design. If the program does not access any global objects at a certain level P, the register allocator would be given this information and it could then use register R_P for data; therefore, there does not have to be any loss of efficiency due to register allocation for data unless the usage patterns suggest that the display information would be useful.

Here are some questions concerning this design proposal.

(a) Is the claim justified that the processor can fill the registers faster when it does this automatically? Explain.

(b) Presuming that the scheme does provide correct behavior, how does the register allocator decide whether to take another register from the display set and use it for data? Specify what characteristics of the program would affect this decision.

(c) What would the system have to do during a return instruction?

(d) Comment on the overall feasibility of the proposed design.

[50]Use the B5700 system for numbering levels.

5-28. Consider a system having four relocation registers R_1 .. R_4. Each relocation register contains both the physical origin of a block of memory and the length of the contiguous block of memory that it describes. The virtual addresses of the information in the four blocks are contiguous in the order of their relocation register numbers. In other words, register R_1 contains the origin and length of the first block, whose first virtual address is zero. The first virtual address of the block described in R_2 is equal to the length of the block described in R_1. This pattern continues through the end of the fourth block, whose last virtual address is equal to the sum of the four lengths. Figure 5-58 describes the relationships among the virtual and physical addresses.

(a) Choose formats for the information in the registers, and use those formats to describe the address translation process.

(b) Suppose that the program wished to coalesce blocks 1 and 2, moving block 3 down to block 2, and adding L more locations in the new block 3. Figure 5-59 depicts this change. Describe the steps that the system must perform to effect this change.

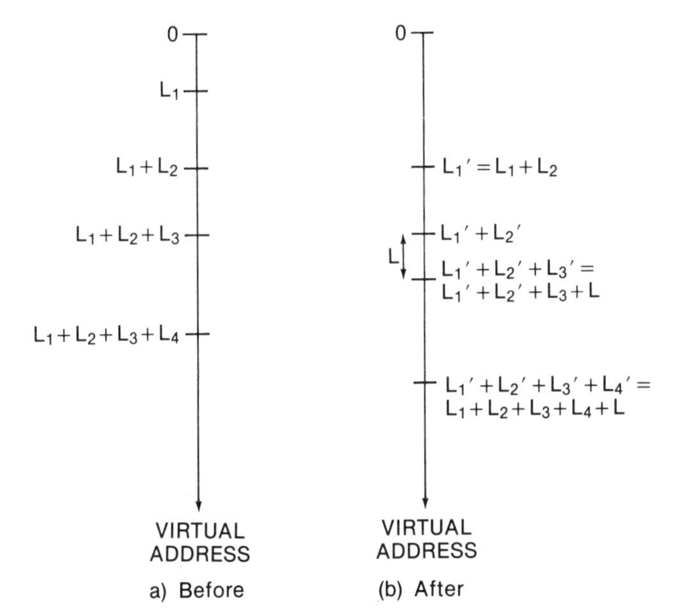

Figure 5-59 Changing the address subdivisions (Problem 5-28)

5-29. Here is a proposed method for keeping usage data for pages. Place a counter in each page descriptor in the main memory map. The counter manipulation rules are: (1) A counter is incremented on each attempt to access the page; and (2) all counters are decreased by the same value, which is proportional to the number of memory accesses made to the entire memory since the last time a page fault occurred, whenever a page fault occurs. The pages having the lowest count values are the first candidates for replacement.

(a) Discuss the relationship of the proposed scheme to LRU management.

(b) What do you suggest for the initial value of the counter for a new incoming page? Explain.

(c) Discuss the advantages and disadvantages of the proposed scheme.

(d) Consider a modification of the count decrease rule in which the amount of decrement in a count value is proportional to the present value held in the counter. Does this variation approximate LRU better than the original scheme?

5-30. We wish to consider changing the assignment of stack numbers to processes while the B5700 system is in operation. Since the system is in operation, you must assume that there do exist within the system processes whose execution has not been completed.

(a) What information in memory would have to be modified to change the stack number assignment? Try to make your answer as general as possible. (A general answer would be "All PCWs have to be changed.")

(b) Discuss the desirability and usefulness of changing the stack number assignments during system operation.

5-31. In Section 5.5 the text suggested two methods for selecting one of several relocation registers. Another possibility not mentioned there is to use some low-order bits from the EVA to select the relocation register. Discuss this option, and compare it with the other two options.

5-32. A paged system might utilize three tables (described below) to assist in memory accessing and memory management. Two of these tables, which we will call the "short table" and the "long table," are searched using the virtual page number. The third table, which we will call the "reverse table," is searched using the physical page origin.

When a virtual address is to be translated, the short table is consulted. If the desired entry is not found in the short table, the long table is used for a second search attempt. The reverse table might be used during page fault handling.

In this problem you are asked to determine what information should be stored in the entries in each table. You should try to shorten the table entries as much as possible (in other words, an answer stating that all information is in each table is not satisfactory). Your selection criterion should be that you wish to maximize the speed of common operations, while providing sufficient information to implement the management policies and to provide logically correct behavior. Fill out a table formatted like Table 5-10, placing marks that indicate information that should be present in a table entry.

You are asked to complete the table twice—once for LRU and once for FIFO management. If you think that other information should be present that is not listed in Table 5-10, add more rows to your table.

TABLE 5-10 INFORMATION PRESENT IN TABLE ENTRIES

	Short Table	Long Table	Reverse Table
Virtual page origin			
Physical page origin			
Dirty bit			
Time of last use			
Length			
Access rights			

5-33. A set-associative memory is designed specifically for use to map page numbers into origin addresses (this might be used inside an MMU). Here is the design: The associative memory is a buffer in front of a memory-resident table whose origin is 800_{16}. Each associative memory entry contains a validity bit V (which is set if the entry is valid). The V bit value can be controlled from the processor by executing one of two special instructions CLRV and SETV, which clear and set the V bit of the page selected by the address in the instruction, respectively. These operations have no effect if the page fails the associative search (i.e., is not found in the associative memory). When a new entry is written into the memory, its V bit is automatically set. The associative memory inserts a replacement entry from the memory-resident page table whenever an associative match (used to try to find the mapping of a page number) fails. An LRU discipline is used to determine which entry should be replaced.

(a) Is there any need for a WRITEAM instruction that writes a new entry from a processor register into the associative memory? It would select an associative memory entry by using the memory address as the selector. Explain.

(b) Discuss the need for the SETV instruction.

5-34. A designer proposes that a cache memory be constructed from a fully associative memory. Another designer favors the set-associative approach. The fully associative proponent argues that that design can do everything that the set-associative memory can, and also is more able to adapt to changing loads and referencing patterns. Discuss this argument and describe why the set-associative implementation is always preferred.

5-35. State one (simple) reason why hashing is not recommended for finding cache entries.

5-36. A designer proposes using (level, index) addresses (as in the B5700) and passing them to the cache memory. This means that the address matched during the cache search process would be the (level, index) address of the object desired.

(a) Assuming that this suggestion is adopted, when would the cache have to be invalidated? Explain.

(b) Would you recommend this strategy? Explain.

5-37. It could be argued that the processor registers are another level of the memory hierarchy. After all, they are faster than a cache memory.

(a) If this argument were accepted, what form of operand specification would you expect to find in a processor ADD instruction? Explain.

(b) Do you think that this argument provides a basis for system design? In other words, would you recommend designing a system around this argument? Explain.

5-38. An interleaved memory system has m modules arranged in an n-way interleave. What is the probability that two successive memory access requests will conflict (desire the same module)?

5-39. Prove that in an L-way interleaved memory, an addressing pattern with the nth access to the address $B + nK$ will result in some modules never being selected if $\gcd(K, L) \neq 1$.

5-40. In this problem we examine techniques that could be used by a memory module to return data that it has read from its array to the module requesting the read. A split bus cycle is used. In the first bus cycle the request is passed to the memory, which then initiates a read cycle. The second bus cycle is used to transfer the data back to the requestor. Here are three techniques that could be considered:

1. Each request contains the requestor's name; the memory module routes the data to that module by placing (req_name, data) on the bus in the second bus cycle.
2. The requestor keeps the memory address that it asked to have read. The request contains only the address to be read. When the memory has completed the access, it places on the bus the pair (address, data), and the requestor recognizes the result by looking for the address match with its outstanding request.
3. The requestor keeps the number of the memory module to which the request was routed, and the memory module sends back the pair (module number, data).

(a) Compare the amounts of logic required under each technique.

(b) Discuss any relationship between the addressing techniques and the methods used to resolve conflicting requests for memory access from different request sources.

5-41. A designer proposes the following: We should associate a cache memory with each memory module. We could assign certain memory modules for instructions and others for data. Since program references are more local than data references, smaller caches could be used with the instruction memory modules, maintaining the same hit ratios, yet the overall system cost would be decreased in comparison to a design in which a separate (but equal) cache is associated with every memory module. Discuss:

(a) The hypotheses of the claim.

(b) The factors that influence the system cost of the proposed design.

(c) Any software support required to achieve the claimed advantages.

5-42. A designer proposes increasing the memory bandwidth by providing two memory buses: one handling READ requests and the other devoted to WRITE requests.

(a) Draw a diagram of this memory system configuration.

(b) Describe the bus event sequences to implement a READ/MODIFY/WRITE memory cycle.

(c) Compare the performance of this design against the performance of a conventional one-bus design with twice the bandwidth.

5-43. A system uses a GAM to cause the processor to feel that the memory contains 23-bit objects, even though the memory has 8-bit entities in its basic modules. The system is to be designed to permit arbitrary bit addressing for the origins of the 23-bit objects being accessed.

(a) What is the minimum number of memory modules that could be used if the system is to permit access to any contiguous 23-bit word in a single memory cycle?

(b) A designer proposes inserting a cache holding 23-bit items between the processor and the GAM. The cache would accept a bit address A and hold the values of the bits in locations A, A + 1, . . . , A + 22. Comment of this design, particularly whether it will provide the correct functionality (recall that any cache should be logically transparent). Be sure to consider both write-through and copy-back caching.

5-44. Compare the speeds of hardware implementations of parallel, bit-slice, and word-slice associative searches.

(a) First determine the significant parameters describing both system speed and the table's configuration.

(b) For what combinations of these parameters is word-slice searching the fastest technique? Assume that a gate's delay d is given in terms of its fan-in f by the relation

$$d = 3 + f \qquad (5\text{-}15)$$

(c) Repeat part b if the gate delay is given by the relation

$$d = 3 + 5 \log_{10}(f) \qquad (5\text{-}16)$$

5-45. To speed up word-slice searching, a designer proposes a new word-slice memory with a built-in rearrangement mechanism that attempts to keep the entries most likely to be referenced at the top of the list, so that they will be found faster when a search is made. The proposed rearrangement strategy is to move an entry to the top of the memory when it is accessed, moving down one position all those entries between the top and the former position of the accessed entry.

(a) Show that this policy can be implemented with only a single read-modify-write access to each table entry beyond the first entry.

(b) Under what referencing patterns would you expect the redesign to pay off?

(c) Another redesign option is to consider the table as a circular list. When a search succeeds, the list pointer is left pointing to the entry which was successfully found, so that the same entry is the first to be checked during the next access attempt. What are the advantages and disadvantages of this policy compared to the list rearrangement policy?

5-46. Describe the logic used to mark the first matching entry after a bit-slice associative search. Design the logic to minimize the delay while respecting a gate fan-in limit G. The logic should output a one at the position corresponding to the first entry in a vector (of length n) which is set to one, and a zero at the positions corresponding to all other entries.

5-47. In a general associative memory we may wish to allow entry selection based on an arithmetic comparison between the selector and the value stored in the key fields of the entry. Consider that all values are integers and describe search strategies that use the fewest bit-slice accesses and yet implement matches wherever the key value satisfies each of the specified predicates.

(a) key $<$ selector.

(b) key $\leq$ selector.

What representation do you desire for negative values?

5-48. Write a sequence of associative memory operations (from the set listed in Section 5.7.1) to set the bits in X according to the following predicate:

(entry.u = value_1) **or** (entry.v = value_2)

The fields u and v are selected by the masks u_mask and v_mask, respectively.

5-49. To answer the following questions, you will have to write short program fragments for an associative system. Assume that the system has the structure and the functions of the systems described in Section 5.7.1.

(a) Write a sequence of associative memory operations to set the bits in X according to the following predicate:

(entry.u = value_1) **and** (entry.v = value_2)

The fields u and v can be selected by using the masks u_mask and v_mask, respectively.

(b) Write a search algorithm to search for all entries that meet the search criterion

entry.u $<$ value_1

5-50. An associative search has been completed and it yielded a multiple match. Suppose that each table entry contains a field "dupl_position" which is to be filled with an integer whose value is the ordinal position of the entry among the matching set determined by the previous search. In other words, it is desired that the ith memory entry that met the search criterion have the value i placed in its dupl_position field. Starting from the search results in the M register, specify an algorithm that places the position numbers in the dupl_position fields. Use operations from the set introduced in Section 5.7.1.

6

SINGLE STREAM CONTROL

It is harder to command than to obey.

— F. Nietzsche

It is not enough to have a good mind.
The main thing is to use it wisely.

— Descartes

The computer's control section supervises the system's operation. To perform this function the control unit must "know" where to find individual program elements (statements or instructions), it must "know" the interpretation (meaning) of the program elements, and it must "know" how to command the other parts of the system to effect the desired functions. The control unit is responsible for all bookkeeping concerning the location of the execution point, and it may be responsible for performing certain auxiliary operations, such as those required to maintain memory address mapping information as the execution point moves among naming contexts. The conventional view of these operations includes a "control point" progressing through a "program." Some languages, like Prolog, take a radically different view. The Prolog view is that the program is activated when the user asks a question, and the system is then responsible for finding some way to meet the "goal" specified by the question. Along the way other actions might be performed, depending on the contents of the database.

In Chapter 2 we described simple microprocessor control structures. In this chapter we study control functions in a single virtual machine. We present sequence control constructs and describe how they might be implemented at lower levels. We also consider the location and representations of the instructions themselves and the use of lower-level sequencing in the implementation of higher-level functions. At the end we will review the nonsequential goal-directed control view typified by the Prolog language.

We present a small set of simple control structures, a set of constructs for high-level languages, and discuss the criteria for selecting modifications to the control function set. Then we present enhancements at various levels of system description, starting from high levels and working back to low levels. We show some techniques used to implement low-level control constructs.

After you have studied this chapter, you should be familiar with control functions and structures for single virtual machines. These structures provide the basis for generalizations to multiple process systems, which are covered in Chapters 1 through 3 of Volume 2.

6.1 BASIC CONTROL CONCEPTS

We divide the control design issues into four groups; design options for each are discussed at various levels of the system within this chapter. We phrase these issues in terms of a simple paradigm of the control function; this paradigm is depicted in Figure 6-1. The program is stored in an addressable "memory;" a "program counter" (PC) contains the location of either the current instruction or of the next instruction;[1] an instruction register (IR) holds the current instruction; and a sequencer issues

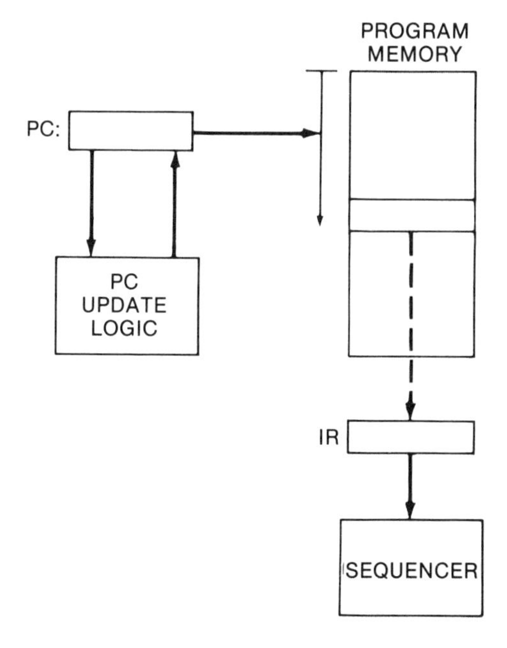

Figure 6-1 Basic control elements

[1]At some point during the execution cycle, the PC is updated to point to the next instruction.

control signals to system components to properly implement the desired functions. The PC contents satisfy the PC State Property (Section 2.3.2), which states that the PC points to the next program element to be interpreted. Every instruction affects the contents of PC, and therefore influences the sequence in which the program's instructions are executed. Once an instruction has been fetched for execution, the sequencer interprets its contents and issues commands that cause the appropriate function to be performed. The four design issue groups concern the choices of:

1. Program sequencing constructs
2. Program location
3. Control implementation techniques
4. Instruction representations

Program sequencing constructs determine the order of program execution. The choice of sequencing constructs may affect the readability of the program and the ease of correctly specifying the program. *Program location issues* determine the relationship between the memory holding programs and the memory holding data. Program location choices may affect the integrity of the program and the flexibility of memory management. *Control implementation decisions* determine the rigidity of the implementation. The selection of a control implementation technique may affect the ease of correcting implementation errors and the speed of program execution. *Instruction representation issues* determine how an instruction is encoded. Instruction representation decisions may affect program size, the complexity of the control unit, and the execution speed.

Design decisions taken within each of these issue groups have different effects. Now we examine these general options in more detail.

6.1.1 Sequencing Constructs

Sequential execution is a basic sequencing construct, with instructions executed in the order in which they are stored. In Chapter 2 we indicated that all control sequencing constructs can be developed from sequential execution plus a single conditional branch instruction (JNG). Although it is true that all conceivable control structures can be constructed using sequential execution and this single simple branch instruction as primitives, a program satisfying these constraints would be terribly inefficient because many steps may be required to implement other desired control constructs. In addition, the programmer would have to deal with many bookkeeping details; this chore would increase the chance that errors might creep into the program. For these reasons we desire a more comprehensive set of control structures.

Before going further, we dismiss one conceptually important issue that is not a real concern—namely, the logical completeness of the control sequencing constructs. From the discussion in Chapter 2 we know that a single conditional goto is logically complete for performing all control functions; therefore, obtaining a functionally complete set of control constructs is trivial.

The PC update logic (Figure 6-1) controls the execution sequence. For sequential execution the PC is incremented during instruction execution so that it points to the next instruction in sequence. If the instruction specifies a branch or jump, the PC is loaded with the destination of the branch. A complete specification of the system's control sequencing could be developed if one knew the update logic. Alternatively, the specification of the sequencing constructs can be used to design the update logic.

As we expand the set of control instructions, we must keep in mind reasonable selection criteria. We should consider all of these criteria:

1. Understandability (simplicity)
2. Provability and testability
3. Closeness to structures at neighboring abstraction levels
4. Performance

Understandability reflects the ability of human beings to comprehend (and therefore to use) the sequencing structures. Understandability is closely related to provability and the closeness of the structures to those used by the abstract machines adjacent in the hierarchy. For example, sequencing abstractions that closely reflect the requirements of an application would provide a convenient framework for programming that application. Simplicity is closely related to understandability; structures that are complex are harder to understand and fewer people can use them effectively and correctly.

Provability and *testability* are also closely related to understandability; to construct a correctness proof for an implementation of an algorithm, one must either understand both the algorithm and the implementation or construct an automated procedure that does. Any proof must be directly related to the sequencing structure since any proof must consider both the sequence of operations and their semantics. Sequencing must be considered so that the prover can equate the machine state after the execution of one instruction to the machine state before the execution of the next instruction. The semantics of each program step determine the relationship between the machine state before the instruction and the machine state after the instruction. For a more complex sequencing structure, such as a loop structure, the prover tries to find some property of the state which is invariant during the loop's execution; then the prover shows that this property is preserved by the loop body. Again, the sequencing among the loop's instructions is critical to this demonstration. To define the semantics of an instruction for proof purposes, one desires maximum generality, which means that one desires the minimum "preconditions" on the prior machine state that determine the maximum information about the posterior machine state.

The issue of test design is closely related to proof structures. Clearly, there is a similar intent; both proofs and tests are supposed to convince one that the system does in fact perform the desired functions. Just as proofs rely on the execution sequence, so tests must be designed based on the execution sequence. Therefore, system designs and implementations that improve understandability by improving structure will enhance both the test design process and the proof process.

Closeness affects the understandability of the relationship between neighboring levels of the implementation; if the structures being implemented and the structures available to implement them are similar, the implementation will require few steps.

Closeness may speed implementation, improve understanding, simplify proofs, and simplify testing. It may, on the other hand, degrade performance, since more implementation levels will be required between the application and the hardware implementation of the system. Having more levels does not necessarily slow execution, however, as it depends on how the level structure really affects the implementation.[2]

Performance is an important criterion in all computer designs. Some sets of system requirements may emphasize performance, whereas others may emphasize other system properties, such as cost or reliability. Performance is especially important at lower levels, as these levels form the basis for implementing the higher level functions. Performance can be improved by implementing high-level functionality in few atomic actions at lower system levels. But doing so requires closeness, understandability, provability, and ease of testing.

Thus we observe a trade of understandability against performance—schemes that are more understandable seem to require more support for adequate performance, and the maximum performance seems to be achieved by implementing the system with one of the least understandable schemes. One could, of course, construct counterexamples to this statement, which is not meant as a challenge for the reader to waste time.

6.1.2 Program Location Options

Two design issues concern the location of the program. The first determines whether there are separate memories for data and program. The second determines whether program and data memories can reverse their roles.[3]

One effect of providing separate memories for program and data (see Figure 6-2) is that the designer enlarges the memory space, since the two separate memories have separate address spaces. Therefore, an instruction may have the same address as a data object. The apparent ambiguity is easily resolved, since the sequencer

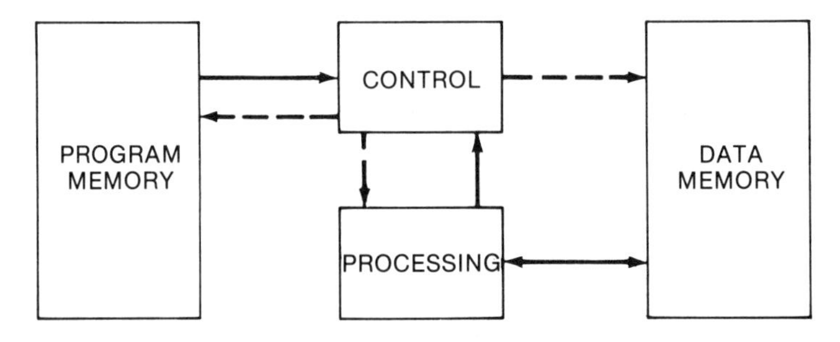

Figure 6-2 A Harvard architecture

[2]It is a straightforward matter to develop an algorithmic method for reducing a multilevel system implementation to a single program level, while preserving functionality.

[3]The issue concerns whether it is possible to read and write programs as though their instructions were data objects, and whether it is possible to execute data objects as though they were programs.

knows which memory addresses refer to instructions, and which to data objects. Information needed to make these distinctions is made available by the MC68020 control unit, which emits status codes to the bus that indicates the type of access being made during each memory access request. This illustration shows that it is not unreasonable to divide the address spaces according to their contents. We will see, however, that the scheme does have other problems.

Although it may seem that a scheme separating instructions from data is complete, it is not, since there must be some means for writing the program memory, at least to load a new program. Another exception to the simple rule separating the program memory from the data memory arises if the instruction set permits immediate data operands to be read from the program memory.[4] The program sequencer can be designed to detect immediate addressing and to make the appropriate memory request. This rule handles immediate operands but does not assist with loading program memory, since it is not possible by a simple examination of the program sequencer status to distinguish writes used for program copying from other data writes.

A machine with a separate program memory is often called a "Harvard machine," since the first computers built at Harvard in the 1940s used a separate paper tape for their programs; this tape was logically similar to a separate read-only program memory. Machines that intermix programs and data in the same memory are called "von Neumann machines" or "Princeton machines," since the first machine built by von Neumann at Princeton placed the program and the data in the same memory unit. Sharing the same memory has an allocation advantage, since there is a better chance that an arbitrary combination of program and data can be allocated space within a single larger address space than that they could both reside in a system with separated spaces. However, the different locality patterns for instruction and data references suggest that a designer consider using separate caches and memory management policies for programs and data. The Harvard architecture, although less common than the von Neumann architecture, has some advantages: it permits more overlap of instruction fetching with instruction execution.[5] In addition, the program memory can be a read-only structure during program execution; this feature implies that the program can be reentrant—that is, it can be shared by two processes without changing its logical properties.

The second location issue concerns reversing the program and data roles. This design decision does determine whether programs can be loaded and whether immediate operand values can be read from the instruction memory. One way to overcome the limitations is to design several processor instructions that access the program memory for data references. Simple store and load instructions would suffice (in a logical sense). To attain the advantages of the Harvard separation, the programmer would have to be limited in his use of these instructions. Another way

[4]There is no logical requirement for immediate addressing.

[5]If instructions may contain immediate operand values, an exception must be made to this statement; the fetch of an immediate value cannot be overlapped with the next instruction fetch, since both are located in the same memory.

to attain the separation is to permit the program to branch to the data memory.[6] Transferring control does not solve the immediate addressing issue.

What criteria might affect the selection between the two options? First, the size of memory addresses may differ. Second, program comprehensibility is affected.[7]

6.1.3 Control Implementation Options

Issues in the implementation option group affect the rigidity of the implementation of control functions, including instruction interpretation, sequencing to implement instruction semantics, and control sequence modification instructions. The control implementation can be *static*, in which case one would "wire" the implementation into the mechanism, or *dynamic*, in which case the implementation would be effected by a piece of software that interprets the instructions being executed.

The designer of a dynamic implementation must choose both the nature and timing of implementation changes. An implementation change might redefine the instruction set. The latter could be beneficial by specializing the processor to the needs of an executing program. For example, if the program handled only real data objects, integer arithmetic operations could be removed without penalty.

What system evaluation measures are affected by these choices? Flexibility is obviously increased if the implementation is dynamic. However, consulting dynamic tables to interpret each instruction clearly slows instruction execution. So system speed is another major concern.

6.1.4 Instruction Representation Options

An instruction, like all information in the computer, is represented by a set of bits. This issue group concerns the interpretation of the bits in each instruction. Some typical questions in this group are: How is the function code extracted from the instruction? Where are operand addresses, if any, to be found? Are there, in fact, any operand addresses?

The representation design determines the *instruction format*. One simple design dichotomy separates *fixed* from *variable* instruction formats. If the format is variable, can individual fields have lengths that may vary in different instructions? Can the length of a single instruction depend on the information in the instruction? The MC68020 has variable instruction formats and variable instruction lengths (all are multiples of 16 bits); this flexibility is used to accommodate certain operand addressing modes. In the MC68020, instruction execution and the function to be performed are determined by the contents of the first word of each instruction.

What advantages might be obtained by changing the instruction format? First, making instruction lengths variable and their formats variable can reduce overall

[6]This change might also imply a reversal of the role of the other memory. The advantage of such a simultaneous role reversal is that execution speedup by overlapping data and instruction fetches is still attainable.

[7]The ability to use data as a program or a program as data may mask the program's actual control sequencing.

program size, which reduces the number of memory references required to access the program; this effect might speed program execution. On the other hand, decoding and extracting instruction fields whose sizes may vary is more difficult than extracting fields from fixed-format instructions, so control units that can handle variable formats may be slower than control units that handle only a fixed instruction format. In addition, the data path structure in a hardware interpretation mechanism will be complex if formats are flexible; this will increase system design and implementation times and costs, and may slow program execution or force engineers to reduce the clock speed due to the longer physical interconnections required for the flexible format design.

6.1.5 Summary

We have many opposing forces acting to favor or disfavor design options. At different design levels different considerations may dominate, so different selections will be appropriate. Now we start with the high-level language level, where understandability is very important, and progress eventually to the microprogramming level, where speed is important and the understandability can be allowed to be very low.

6.2 HIGH-LEVEL LANGUAGES

In this section we consider control design issues and show how the basic language structure can affect the option choices outlined above. We use Ada and other languages for examples. Our discussion parallels the structure of Section 6.1—first we look at basic sequencing constructs. In this section we focus on languages following the "traditional" view of a program as a sequentially executed set of statements. A different view lies at the base of nonsequential languages like Prolog, which is discussed in Section 6.5.

6.2.1 Sequencing Constructs

At the high-level language level the "desirable set" of control constructs is selected based on the ease of understanding program structures. We start with Ada's basic control structures, adding control structures from other languages. We cover these basic control structures present in Ada:

1. Sequential execution
2. Conditional execution
3. Loops
4. Subroutine call and return
5. Goto
6. Exceptions

At the end of the section we introduce a few control structures that are not present in Ada but that can be useful for implementation, modularization, or understanding.

6.2.1.1 Sequential execution. Sequential execution is the "default" mode of operation; this sequencing pattern applies unless otherwise specified. In a high-level language, statements are executed in the order they are written in the program text until a specific sequence control statement or the end of the program block (such as a loop body) is reached. Figure 6-3a illustrates this sequencing structure. The rectangle represents a program fragement; the arrow depicts the execution sequence.

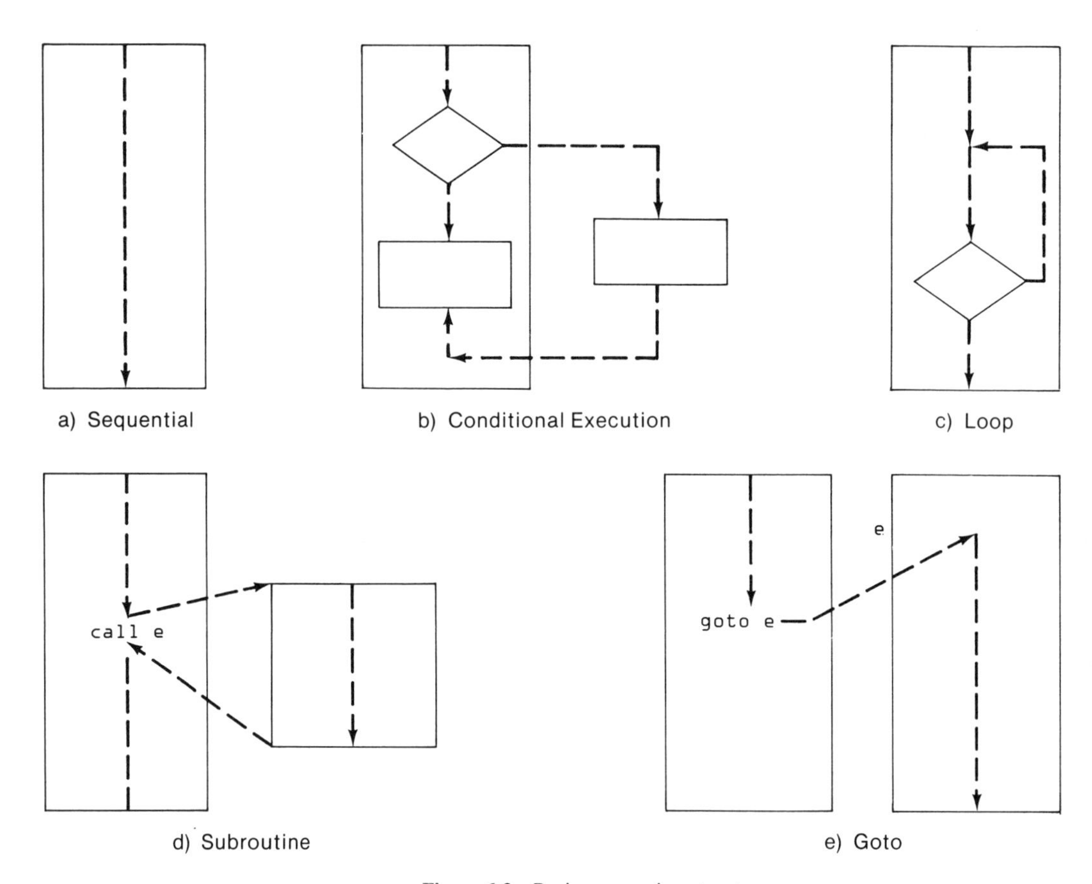

Figure 6-3 Basic sequencing structures

6.2.1.2 Conditional execution. A conditional execution structure specifies the execution of a set of statements only if a stated boolean condition is met, or more generally, if a stated expression has a specified value. In Ada these two situations are specified by the **if** and **case** control constructs. Figure 6-3b illustrates this sequencing structure with a two-way choice.

6.2.1.3 Loops. Loop structures specify the repetitive execution of a list of statements, which together comprise the body of the loop. The basic pattern of a loop's control flow is affected by its termination structure. The basic structures include[8] the indefinite loop, the **while** loop, the **until** loop, and the counting loop. Figure 6-3c illustrates these sequencing structures. The semantics of these structures can be expressed in terms of conditional execution using gotos, as follows:

```
       Ada                  Structure          Equivalent Program

                         Indefinite Loop
loop                                 《loop》
  ⟨statement_list⟩;                          ⟨statement_list⟩;
end loop;                                    goto loop;

                           While Loop
while ⟨boolean⟩ loop                 《loop》 if ⟨boolean⟩ then
  ⟨statement_list⟩;                            ⟨statement_list⟩;
end loop;                                      goto loop;
                                             end if;

                           Until Loop
until ⟨boolean⟩ loop                 《loop》 ⟨statement_list⟩
  --this is not in Ada                       if not ⟨boolean⟩ then
  ⟨statement_list⟩                             goto loop;
end loop;                                    end if;

                          Counting Loop
for ⟨name⟩ in ⟨range⟩ loop    if not_null (range) then
  ⟨statement_list⟩;             ⟨name⟩:= (first value in range);
end loop;                     《loop》 ⟨statement_list⟩;
                                if ⟨name⟩ ≠ (last in range)
                                  then
                                  ⟨name⟩:= (next value);
                                  goto loop;
                                end if;
                              end if;
```

The "normal" way to exit from a loop structure is for the termination condition at the "head" of the loop to be satisfied. This is not the only way to exit from a loop, however; exits can also be made by executing the **exit** statement, by an inner loop executing an **exit** statement that forces the termination of two or more nested loops, and by an exception condition arising and thus forcing termination of the block containing the loop.

The **exit** statement forces loop termination before the loop's normal termination condition is met. The **exit** statement obviates the need for a **goto** statement to exit the loop.[9] In Ada an **exit** statement with a loop name (see Section A.5.4) forces termination of (all nested) loops including the loop named in the **exit** statement.

The semantics of loop exits forced by exceptions are discussed in Section 6.2.1.6.

[8]Not all of these structures are provided in all languages.

[9]An exit using a **goto** statement is not favored because the goto statement provides a means for constructing flow structures that are hard to comprehend.

6.2.1.4 Subroutines. Decomposing a program into functions or procedures is an important modularization technique. From the point of view of the calling procedure, the call statement along with the execution of the called procedure can be considered as a single operation of an "enhanced machine," with the enhanced machine's program counter remaining at the call statement during the execution of the called procedure. In other words, we could take the view that the PC for the caller remains at the call statement while the function is performed. This view, ignoring the details of the called procedure, is consistent with procedural modular decomposition and with implementations (which "save" the program counter during subroutine execution). Figure 6-3d illustrates this sequencing structure.

Subroutine structures must be supported by control constructs for procedure call and return. We present simple cases in this section.

A call statement transfers control to a procedure or function. The procedure executing the call statement is known as the *calling procedure*, and the procedure to which control is transferred is the *called procedure*. A **return** statement transfers control from a called procedure back to the calling procedure. Using the hierarchical view, the execution of **return** signifies completion of the single high-level operation by the underlying implementation level. After **return**, execution in the caller can progress to its next action.

An important aspect of the call-return mechanism concerns whether the implementation permits *recursion*; with recursion a procedure can be called from a program even though that program currently has an uncompleted invocation of that same procedure. In the implementation a LIFO stack discipline is required to support recursion by saving the state of each invocation beneath the status of all later invocations of the same procedure. Most contemporary languages, including Algol, PL/1, Pascal, Ada, and Modula, permit recursion. On the other hand, early versions of BASIC and Fortran do not support recursion.

6.2.1.5 Goto statements. A goto statement specifies an immediate change in the execution point, not saving the location from which the **goto** was taken. Figure 6-3e illustrates this sequencing structure.

It may seem obvious that **goto**s are required for programming generality, since program completeness is guaranteed by the existence of the conditional **goto**, as discussed in connection with the MIN design in Chapter 2. This "obvious" conclusion is not correct. In fact, the **goto** is not necessary if conditional and loop control constructs are available. In other words, the conditional and loop control constructs together are logically sufficient to express any arbitrary control sequence, and the **goto** construct is not required!

Example 6-1

One can emulate the actions of any general-purpose computer using a single **loop** statement containing a single **case** statement. If the range of instruction addresses is 1 .. n, the emulation program is

```
procedure emulate is
  program_counter : integer range 1 .. n;
  range_error : exception;
```

```
begin
  loop
    case program_counter of
      when 1 => <first_instruction's_effect>;
      when 2 => <second_instruction's_effect>;
      ..
      when n => <last_instruction's_effect>;
      when others => raise range_error;
    end case;
  end loop;
exception
  when range_error => ..;
end emulate;
```

Since any of the instruction effect clauses can assign a new value to the variable program_counter, arbitrary control structures can be emulated by this program structure.

This example shows that though a syntactic program analysis may conclude that a program has good structure, in reality a complex semantic structure may be hidden beneath the beautiful syntactic structure. In fact, good structuring cannot be imposed simply by linguistic rules; the programmer must be committed to good structure in the first place. In a similar manner, we conclude that one cannot design a language translator to enforce good programming practices. Of course, language structures can be devised to make it difficult to circumvent good structuring practices. We hasten to point out before leaving this example that the reader should not take it as an example of good programming practice!

The **goto** statement is a very controversial addition to the basic repertoire. Since any **goto** can shift control to any visible labeled location in the program, a programmer can create complex flow structures using **goto**s. In fact, one can construct sequencing structures so complex that people may have difficulty comprehending them—even the original programmer may have trouble upon returning to the program after an extended absence. Nevertheless, the possibility of arbitrary sequencing supported by the **goto** can be useful for handling errors and exceptional conditions. Ada does permit **goto** statements (see Section A.5.5).

The control flow complexities of the **goto** statement prompted Dijkstra [DIJK68] to title a famous note "Goto Statement Considered Harmful."[10] Many advocates of structured programming over reacted by defining structured programming as the absence of **goto**s. Although complex sequencing structures can be created without using **goto**s, albeit with difficulty, this strict definition of structured programming is not realistic.

Although the **goto** construct is not desirable in structured programs, it is necessary for the efficient implementation of system functions. After all, there is a basic requirement to be able to violate the restrictive sequential sequencing strait jacket. Consider, for example, how to design an efficient implementation of the Ada

[10]Not only did this note start the structured programming movement in earnest, it also prompted a spate of papers with titles of the form "__________ considered harmful!"

conditional execution construct. There is no way that the program can be arranged so that no **goto**s are required. The difficulty is that there must be a way to skip past the instructions that correspond to the statement_list that was not selected. A **goto** construct in the underlying machine is clearly needed for an efficient implementation of the **if** .. **then** .. **else** construct.

Dynamic gotos have destinations that cannot be determined from a static examination of the program. This complicates matters because the program is hard to understand and because run-time support software must determine the actual destination each time the dynamic **goto** is executed and must detect and make all context changes implied by the actual destination's location within the modular structure. Furthermore, proofs of program properties are difficult with static **goto**s and almost impossible with dynamic ones. Nevertheless, some languages support dynamic **goto**s. Ada does not.

Two basic techniques for specifying dynamic **goto** destinations are:

1. Selected **goto**s
2. Label variables

The *selected* **goto**[11] statement contains a list of all possible destinations. One of the listed destinations is selected based on the value of an expression in the statement. In Fortran a computed **goto** looks like

```
GOTO (23,30,25,79,45)I
```

The value of I, which is an integer, is used as a (one-origin) index into the list of statement numbers to find the statement number of the next statement to be executed. Since all possible destinations are known when the program is translated, the translator can determine the legality of each possible destination and also can insert calls to appropriate deallocation and synchronization algorithms as needed. These compile-time implementation details can be "hidden" from the programmer's view.

Example 6-2

In Cobol, a branch destination may be selected from a list; the statement specifies both the destination list and an index variable, as in[12]

```
GO TO DEST-1,DEST-2,DEST-3,DEST-4 DEPENDING ON SELECTOR
```

Here SELECTOR is the index value. One-origin indexing is used.

What should happen if the selector value lies outside the range of the list? In Cobol, execution proceeds to the statement following the GOTO. In some other languages, an index value out of range is considered to be an error, and program

[11]This is called a "computed goto" in Fortran and is also available in APL.

[12]Hyphenation is used to construct compound names in Cobol; a hyphen in Cobol serves the same role as that of the underline in Ada.

execution is terminated if one is encountered. Cobol also permits one to change the destination of a GO TO statement under restricted conditions.

Example 6-3

Cobol's ALTER operation allows a programmer to change a **goto**'s destination in a restricted manner. To understand the restrictions, we must introduce several basic Cobol program structuring constructs. Each Cobol program is formed from "paragraphs," which are program blocks. If a Cobol paragraph consists only of a GO TO, its destination can be modified by executing an ALTER statement anywhere in the program. Suppose that the paragraph is defined by

```
A.
    GO TO FIRST.
```

Here A is the "name" of the paragraph. Execution of the statement

```
ALTER A TO PROCEED TO SECOND.
```

changes the destination of A's GO TO to SECOND.

Notice the difficulty in program understanding that this ALTER possibility introduces—an apparently static **goto** is really not static because another statement somewhere in the program might change its destination. This uncertainty cannot apply, however, to any GOTO appearing in a more complex paragraph.

Label variables constitute the second way to specify the destination of a dynamic **goto**. A label variable is an object whose values identify locations within the program. Making a new assignment to the label variable redefines the destination denoted by the variable. Execution of the statement

```
goto label_variable;    --not Ada
```

causes a transfer of control to the statement whose label is held within the label variable. Although this description makes the implementation sound simple, several complexities are not far beneath the surface! Recall, for example, that object name interpretation may depend on the execution context; this implies that after the transfer to the destination statement, the proper name interpretation rules must apply. How, then, do we arrange things so that the label variable's "value" can be used to find (or specify) the execution context (which defines the naming context)? There are two significant implementation questions related to this context identification question:

1. How to specify the execution context within the label variable's "value"
2. How to pass a label value from one context to another one

Since these questions are similar to the questions that arise when passing object names among contexts (see Section 3.4.2.3), a similar approach can be used to "solve" the problem—we include within the "value" of a label variable a pointer to the activation block which defines the chosen naming context.

The following example and Problem 6-3 introduce some of the execution context issues associated with label variables.

Example 6-4

Consider this program fragment using label variables:

```
    label1 : label;
    label1 := "success";  --not Ada
    for i in 1 .. n
    loop
      if a(i) <= 6 then
        label1 := "fail";  --not Ada
      end if;
<<fail>> y := y + 3;
    end loop;
    goto label1;           --not Ada
```

The **goto** statement will cause a transfer of control to the middle of the loop if for some i in the range 1 .. n, a(i) is less than or equal to 6. Such a transfer should be illegal, as it compromises the integrity of the loop module structure. If, for some execution of the program, every a(i) were greater than 6, however, the **goto** would not compromise the loop structure, and that execution of the program would not violate the program's structure. Since the legality of the **goto** is dependent on the data being processed, the compiler cannot tell whether the **goto** is legal. To be "safe," the compiler could be designed so that it would consider this program fragment to be erroneous.

A label variable may cause both data-dependent legality problems and data-dependent module exits. To avoid these problems, the designers of Ada did not permit label variables, and a label name is not visible outside the program unit where it is defined. These rules prohibit transferring control among parallel constructs, such as among exception handlers or subprograms declared within the same encompassing program.

Example 6-5

```
procedure f( .. ) is
    ..
    procedure g( .. ) is
    begin
      ..                  --goto a would be illegal here
    end g;
    procedure h( .. ) is
    begin
      ..
      goto a;             --illegal
    end h;
    ..
begin
    ..
```

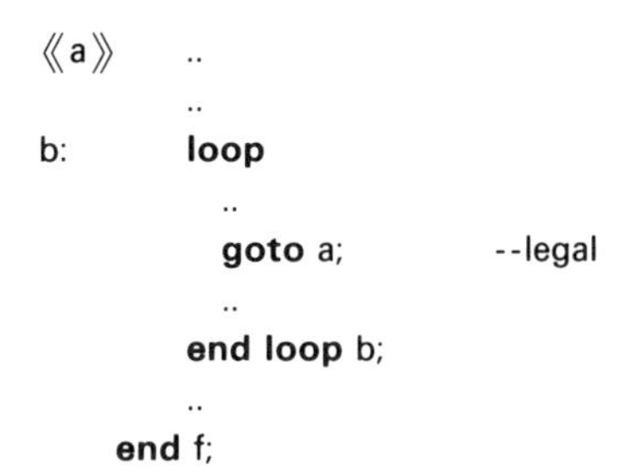

In this Ada program structure the label "a" declared within procedure f is visible inside f, but not in procedures g or h. Thus a **goto** statement with destination "a" is legal within f, the labeled statement being its successor in the execution sequence. Notice that the **goto** can be used to exit from loop b.[13] However, the same **goto** statement within g or h is illegal unless another statement labeled "a" appears within the same procedure. Thus a **goto** cannot be used to force a procedure exit (from procedure h to procedure f in this case).

Static **gotos** are a necessary complication of control flow, at least at the system's implementation levels. **Gotos** can be used to confuse the reader of a program, and therefore their use is strongly discouraged in structured programs. Dynamic **gotos** complicate both the interpretation and the ease of understanding, so their use is more strongly discouraged.

6.2.1.6 Exceptions. Many programming languages do not support exceptions. In those that do support them, exception constructs can be used to handle errors, asynchronous events, or unexpected operand values.

Three basic design issues concerning exceptions are (1) whether the execution point is permitted to return to the point where the exception was taken, (2) how the execution context to be used during the handler's execution is found, and (3) how the association of an exception handler with an exception event is established.

6.2.1.6.1 *What's Next after an Exception Occurs?* Suppose that an exception E has been declared and that a handler for E has been associated with E. Then if E occurs, control immediately passes to the associated handler, which is then executed. If the language permits handlers to return, the handler would be written like a subroutine; when the handler was completed, it would execute a **return**, which passes control back to the point where the exception condition was detected. Figure 6-4 illustrates this control flow; the circled numbers in the figure indicate the order of execution.

If the language does not permit handlers to return, then when the handler is completed, some default control action is taken. In Ada, exception handlers cannot return, and the procedure or function in which the handler was declared is terminated automatically when the handler has completed execution. This control structure is illustrated in Figure 6-5.

[13]The destination would be the statement labeled "a."

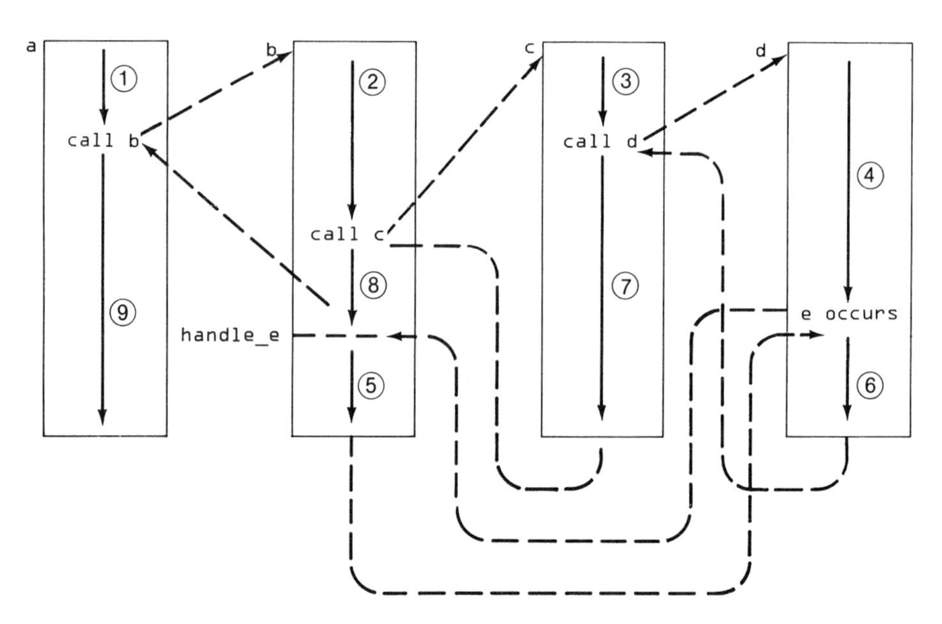

Figure 6-4 Control flow for exception handling with return allowed

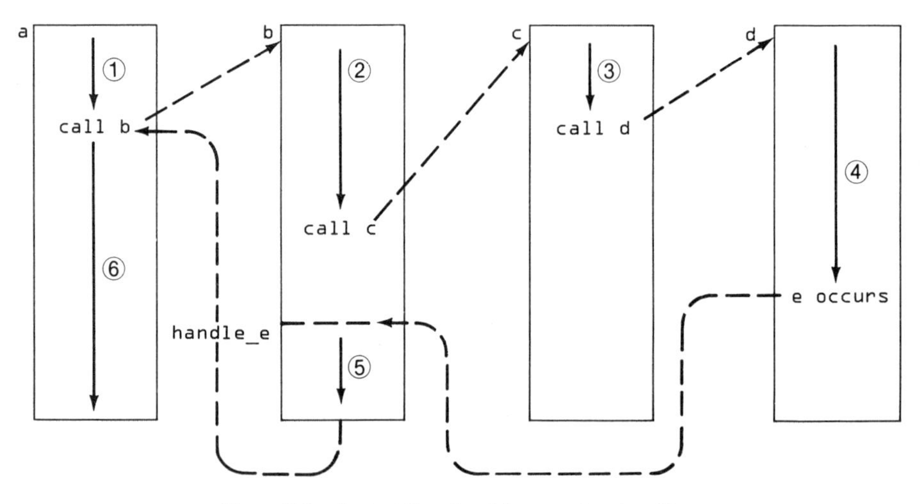

Figure 6-5 Control flow for Ada exception handling

6.2.1.6.2 ***What Is the Exception Handler's Execution Context?*** Every exception handler is declared within a context, be it a nested block or a program. Let C_E denote the declaration context for handler E. There are only two combinations regarding the handler's execution context.

In the simplest combination, the execution point happens to be in C_E when E occurs. Control passes to E without a context change; the prior context was correct for E's execution. In the second combination, the execution environment when the exception occurred (we denote this context by C_P—the context of the PC) is not the same as context C_E. The handler is found using dynamic nesting resolution rules (see Section 3.2.2.3.1, item 2); the search process may force the exception to be "propagated" to the next outer module in the (dynamic) nest. When C_E is reached by this process, both the handler and its execution environment have been found. The process of finding the handler and reaching its context pops one or more contexts off the activation block stack. The following example illustrates this situation.

Example 6-6

```
procedure a is
  E : exception;
  ..
  procedure b is
    ..
    procedure c is
      ..
    begin
      ..
    end c;
    ..
  begin
    ..
    c                    --call procedure c
    ..
  end b;
begin
  ..
  b
  ..
exception
  when E => ..;          --handler for exception E
end a;
```

Suppose that the history of this Ada program is

```
call a;
call b;
call c;
E occurs;
```

If the handler for E declared within procedure a is the appropriate one to take the exception, returns from blocks b and c must be forced before the exception can be handled. Figure 6-6 shows the activation block stack before E occurs and just as E's handler begins execution. After the handler terminates, block a is also deleted from the stack, as procedure a is automatically exited upon completion of E's handler.

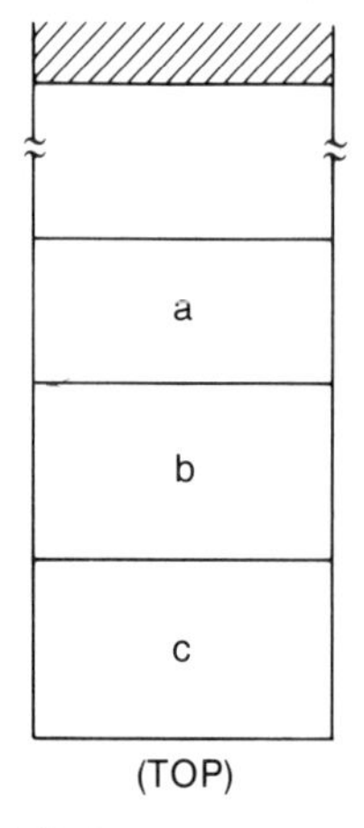

a) Before exception E

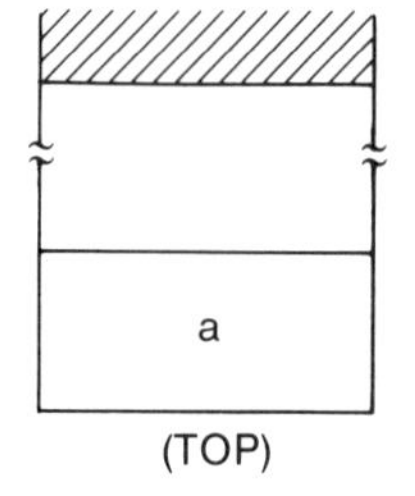

b) After exception E

Figure 6-6 Stack cleansing after exception occurrence (Example 6-6)

6.2.1.6.3 ***Associating a Handler with an Exception.*** The final exception design problem concerned how an association between an exception and a handler can be established. Languages differ greatly regarding the syntax used to specify this association, but these differences are not conceptually significant. We must be concerned, however, with whether the association is static or dynamic; a static association can be established only during compilation, whereas a dynamic association can be established during execution.

In Ada, the association between exceptions and their handlers is static; the handlers are defined at the end of a program block, and apply during the execution of that block. Thus block entry implies the automatic establishment of a handler–exception association for every exception handler declared at the end of the block. In PL/1 the handler–exception associations are dynamic. When a PL/1 block is entered, no automatic handler–exception associations are created. A new association can be established by executing the ON statement, which has the form

```
ON ⟨exception⟩ DO ⟨statement⟩;
```

The semantics of this statement are obvious from the keywords. Dynamic changes in the associations between handlers and exceptions may make a program difficult to understand.

6.2.1.7 Other control constructs. In this section we present several unusual variations on the control constructs. These constructs are not present in most languages, but they present interesting semantic possibilities. The three constructs we present are:

1. Routine replacement calling
2. **one_of** conditional execution
3. Guarded **do** conditional looping

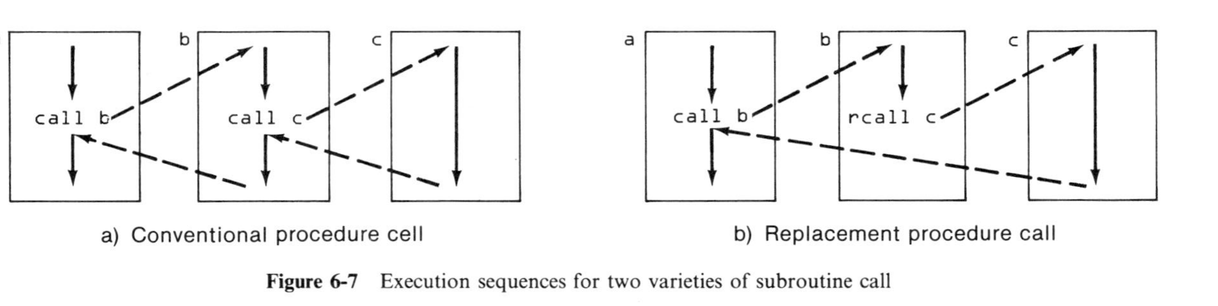

Figure 6-7 Execution sequences for two varieties of subroutine call

6.2.1.7.1 ***Routine Replacement.*** In routine replacement calling the execution of the called routine replaces the execution of its caller. In particular, the caller is not resumed when the callee completes its algorithm. Rather, the callee returns control to the caller's return point. We will use the keyword **rcall** to indicate a replacement call. Figure 6-7 depicts the **rcall** sequencing pattern, comparing it to the conventional call sequencing. The **rcall** semantics require destroying the caller's execution context (but saving its return conditions), creating an execution context for the called procedure, and transferring control to the called procedure. Figure 6-8 depicts the stack structures for this implementation.

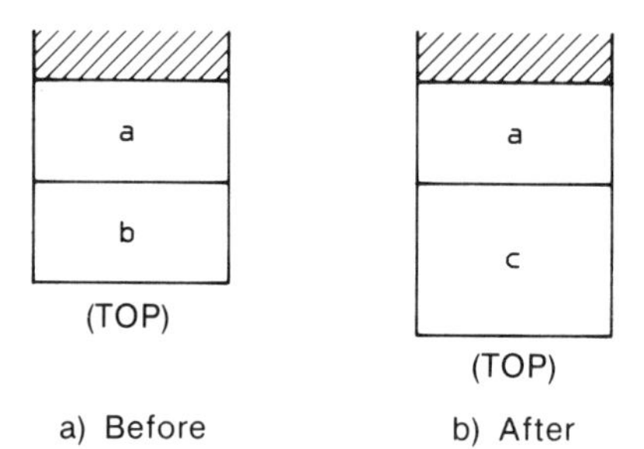

Figure 6-8 Stack configurations before and after the rcall shown in Figure 6-7

The **rcall** activity is similar to exception handling in Ada; but it is not identical to exception handling (Why?).

6.2.1.7.2 ***One_of.*** The **one_of** and guarded **do** are two generalized conditional execution constructs which flexibly select statements (to be executed conditionally) based on data conditions that pertain during program execution. These two structures can be useful for specifying program behavior because their semantics relate simply to conditions on data values. These conditions can be used when reasoning about program properties.

The **one_of** alternation construct is somewhat like a **case** structure. Think of the **case** structure as a specification of a set of (trivial) boolean conditions. When the **case** is executed, the boolean conditions are evaluated, and the set of statements associated with the true condition[14] is executed. Because the conditions all demand equality with the same expression, they are both trivial and nonoverlapping—only one of them can be true (because the right sides of the equalities are all different). In the **one_of** structure, the boolean conditions can be independently written by the programmer, and more than one of them may be true. The execution of the **one_of** statement specifies the execution of some statement list selected randomly from among those associated with true boolean conditions. We express the **one_of** statement in a manner similar to an Ada case statement:

```
one_of                              --Not Ada
  when <boolean_1> =><statement_list_1>;
  when <boolean_2> =><statement_list_2>;
  ..
  when <boolean_n> =><statement_list_n>;
end one_of;
```

[14]It may be that all conditions are false, in which case no parts of the **case** statement are executed.

A **one_of** statement does not include an **others** condition; if none of the booleans are true, execution proceeds to the next statement immediately; in that situation the **one_of** is like a no-operation. To execute a **one_of** statement, the system first evaluates all the boolean conditions. It then selects one of those which was true, and executes the associated statement list. Control then proceeds to the next statement. This construct is useful for specifying and modeling policies that seem arbitrary at the level of abstraction of the model. Ada does not have a **one_of** statement, but it does contain a **select** construct which has many similarities with the **one_of** construct. The **select** construct is used in conjunction with interprocess message communications, as discussed in Section 2.5.3 of Volume 2.

6.2.1.7.3 ***Guarded do.*** The guarded **do** statement is a looping version of the **one_of** statement; like the **one_of** statement, a guarded do statement contains a set of boolean conditions, each associated with a list of statements. Each time the statement is executed, all the boolean conditions are evaluated. If all are false, the loop is terminated. If, however, one or more are true, one of the true ones is arbitrarily selected and the corresponding statement list executed. The set of conditions is then evaluated again, and the loop continues until all conditions are false. Here is our syntax for the **guarded do**:

```
do loop                          --Not Ada
   when ⟨boolean_1⟩ =>⟨statement_list_1⟩;
   when ⟨boolean_2⟩ =>⟨statement_list_2⟩;
   ..
   when ⟨boolean_n⟩ =>⟨statement_list_n⟩;
end do;
```

After the guarded **do** loop has completed execution, the union (OR) of all the boolean conditions specified within the **do** must be false. This fact makes the guarded **do** an attractive structure for reasoning about program properties.

6.2.1.8 Summary. In this section we have reviewed many sequencing constructs; most of them are present in some programming language, but most are not functionally required in any language. The richness of the constructs eases program construction and understandability.

6.2.2 Program Location

The design decision concerning a separate program memory is simple at the high-level language level, since most languages clearly separate the roles of program and data objects; the only exceptions being label and locator variables, which can contain values that act as pointers to memory program locations. Therefore, the conceptual view that there are separate program and data memory spaces is upheld. In many languages there is only a single name space, since names used for data objects cannot be the same (symbolically) as names referring to label objects. This constraint is not present in Ada, since any ambiguity arising because name H refers both to a data item and a label object can be resolved by using the types of the objects in question.

In Ada there is a clear separation between program entities and data entities;

there is no way that data can be a program and no way that the program can be data. In LISP, on the other hand, data structures can be interpreted; in simple cases, the LISP EVAL function executes the function which is the first element in the data structure argument of that EVAL command; the remainder of EVAL's list argument is the list of arguments for the function. Thus EVAL(f ⟨list⟩) has the effect of f(⟨list⟩).[15] A similar feature is available in Snobol. In Prolog there is no clear separation of program and data; in the programming model the computer contains a set of data and those data are always processed by the same built-in algorithm.

6.2.3 Implementation

The implementation of the high-level control semantics must provide the proper control sequences. Whether these are implemented by compilation or interpretation makes no difference with respect to the semantics. The performance is affected, however. In this connection, we take note of some statistics that have been gathered regarding the frequency of use of the various types of high-level programming constructs. Table 6-1 illustrates statistics collected from typical Pascal programs. From the table we see that the statements with nonsequential control possibilities comprise about 50% of all statements. The high frequency of **call** and **return** emphasizes the importance of an efficient implementation of these constructs.

TABLE 6-1 STATEMENT FREQUENCIES IN PASCAL PROGRAMS

Statement Type	Frequency (%)
Assignment	45
If .. then	29
Call/return	15
Loop	5
With	5
Case	1
All others	<1

Source: [PATT82] © 1982 IEEE.

6.2.4 Representation

The design decision is trivial here—each program must be human-readable and therefore must be represented by a character string. It is also trivial to observe that the statement format is fixed in syntax but not in length.

6.2.5 Summary

A large variety of control flow constructs have been proposed for and included in high-level languages. Many of these constructs directly map to control constructs

[15]The binding of the name f is made during program execution when EVAL is used.

provided at the processor level, as we shall see in the next section. Some control constructs are useful for reasoning about program properties and may not have "clean" implementations. Nevertheless, their logical properties make them attractive.

6.3 PROCESSOR-LEVEL CONTROL ISSUES

The control designs of the high-level language may be supported by the control structures, representations, and implementations interpreted by the processor itself.

6.3.1 Sequencing Constructs

Sequential execution combined with a single type of conditional branch is an adequate basis for implementing (or simulating) all possible sequencing structures. But imposing this restriction drives one to very lengthy programs with little benefit. The set of sequencing constructs requires some enhancement beyond simple sequencing and simple conditional branches, if only to improve system performance. In this section we discuss such enhancements, after detailing the basic sequential and conditional sequencing constructs.

6.3.1.1 Sequential execution. Sequential execution at the processor level is supported by control logic which increments the program counter (PC) by the length of each (nonbranch) instruction as it is executed. If the processor has a set of instruction lengths, it is a trivial observation that those instruction fields that determine the instruction length must affect the PC update function. Since the PC cannot be completely updated until the instruction has been decoded, having a set of instruction lengths means that PC update can be completed only after instruction interpretation.[16]

6.3.1.2 Conditional execution. Conditional execution is supported by branch instructions which test conditions within the processor. The processor will change the control point to a different location if the tested value meets a specified condition. Conditional test instructions differ in the types of values that can be tested and in the kind of changes to the PC that can result. With respect to the values tested, either attributes of values can be directly tested or the condition code values established by a previous instruction can be tested.

The two primary variants are the branch instruction, which can transfer control to an arbitrary point, and the skip instruction, which can transfer to one of the immediate successors of the instruction.

Older processor designs base branch condition tests on the contents of processor registers. Contemporary designs, like the IBM 370, the MC68020, and the RISC

[16]Many processors, however, may increment PC at several points in the instruction execution process (when reading another extension word to complete an effective address computation, for example). Therefore, the contents of PC typically contain the address of the first program element that has not yet been considered.

machines discussed in Chapter 2, use condition code values as the basis for branching decisions.

There is not a simple one-to-one mapping between branching constructs in high-level languages and instructions in the processor program. For example, one simple branch instruction is not sufficient to directly support the high-level conditional execution expressed by the **if** .. **then** language construct, since the **if** .. **then** structure contains two alternatives. Nevertheless, the translation of the **if** .. **then** construct to a processor instruction sequence is straightforward; in fact, only forward jumps are required to implement the **if** .. **then** semantics.

Example 6-7

The MC68020 processor has a 16-bit condition code register within its processor status register; 5 bits in the condition code register indicate the conditions, which can be tested according to the status codes listed in Table 2-7.

Example 6-8

All computational operations in the IBM System/38 [IBM81a] machines have an optional form in which an extension of the operation code defines the set of conditions (on the result) under which the next instruction will be taken from one of (up to) three branch "targets." Another optional form sets an "indicator" in a memory location if the specified condition is true with respect to the result of the computation. For each computational operation, there is also an instruction form that forgoes condition testing.

The second question for the design of conditional branch instructions concerned how the destination of the branch could be specified. The most flexible situation uses processor addressing modes to determine the destination address. In the least flexible design (a skip instruction) the processor computes both of the possible next instruction addresses from the current value of the program counter; the programmer cannot change these associations between the location of the "skip" instruction and the locations of its possible successors. We discuss such skip instructions after we briefly cover the use of addressing modes to determine the branch destination.

Indexed branches supporting computed goto structures can be implemented at the processor level by using indexed addressing to determine the branch destination. An addressing mode in which indirection after indexing determines the branch instruction's destination gives a control structure analogous to Fortran's computed goto.

Example 6-9

The following program fragment illustrates how a vector of destinations for an indexed branch instruction implements the semantics of the FORTRAN indexed **goto** statement.

```
GOTO (3, 6, 14, 10)I

load Rx with I;
branch dest_vec - 1, Rx;
```

```
dest_vec: label_3;
  label_6;
  label_14;
  label_10;
```

Most processors provide a sequencing construct analogous to the **case** construct. An indexed branch could be used in conjunction with a jump table to achieve the desired effect if the expression on which the **case** decision is to be based assumes integer values.

Example 6-10

The VAX processors support a CASE instruction that combines the indexed jump table activities into a single processor instruction, in addition to placing the list of possible targets within the program. The VAX CASE instruction has the following arguments:

1. S, a selector value
2. B, a base value
3. L, a limit value
4. D(i), a list of destinations

If $S - B$ is positive and not greater than L, the value $S - B$ is used as an index into the list of destinations, and a branch taken to the address selected from the destination list. If, however, $S - B$ is negative or exceeds L, no branch is taken. The values S, B, and L are integers.

Skip instructions are like branch instructions except that when the condition is met, the next instruction location cannot be arbitrarily specified; rather, the next instruction must be the one immediately following the instruction after the skip instruction. Thus a skip instruction is a special case of a branch instruction. Why, then, introduce the skip construct? It is attractive because it removes the need for any branch destination specification in the branch instruction. If the basic instruction format includes a memory address, that address can be used to specify a memory operand to be tested. Even if the processor does not have a skip instruction with a memory address, the skip instruction can be attractive because it can be represented in fewer bits, since it does not require a memory address specification.

Example 6-11

The IBM 704 [IBM55] had an interesting skip-class instruction, CAS (Compare Accumulator with Storage). This instruction had one memory operand, whose contents Y were compared against the contents of the (single) accumulator A. The next instruction was one of the three immediately following the CAS instruction. If $A < Y$, the instruction after CAS was executed next. If $A = Y$, the second instruction after CAS was executed next. Finally, if $A > Y$, the third instruction after CAS was executed next. Notice the relationship between this sequencing structure and the Fortran three-way IF. This coincidence is interesting, since Fortran was originally designed for the IBM 704.

Notice the ease of implementing a skip instruction if every processor instruction has a fixed length, and its difficulty otherwise.

6.3.1.3 Loop support. Loop support at the processor level can take two forms. First, processor implementations can be "tuned" for fast loop execution, as discussed in Section 6.3.3. Second, instructions to test for loop continuation or completion can be provided. The MC68020 DBcc instructions (see Section 2.3.3.2) are in this class. We illustrate the spectrum of options in several examples.

Example 6-12

A classic integrated loop support instruction comes from the IBM 704; its TIX instruction included both a decrement value and a branch address, in addition to an index register designation. Let D, A, and X denote the decrement value, branch address, and register number, respectively. Also let R_X denote the index register selected by X. Then the operation of TIX was given by these steps:

```
1. If R_X < D then exit;   --test, branch not taken
2. R_X := R_X - D;         --decrease count
3. PC := A;                --branch to A
```

If R_X were loaded with the count for a FOR loop, a TIX with D = 1 could be used at the end of the loop to count, test, and branch to the head of the loop in case the loop had not been completed.

Example 6-13

The DEC PDP8 instruction ISZ [DIGI70] supported counting loops with the counter in a memory location M. The operation of this instruction was:

```
1. PC := PC + 1; --update to next instruction
2. M := M + 1;
3. If M = 0 then PC := PC + 1; --skip next on zero
```

To form a loop, the instruction location following the ISZ instruction should contain a branch instruction to return to the beginning of the loop. Location M would be initialized with the negative of the loop count.

Example 6-14

The PDP11 instruction SOB (Subtract One and Branch) can be used for counting loops; it has a register selector operand r and an offset word value w [DIGI75]. Its semantics are:

```
1. PC := PC + 2; --PC counts bytes but this instruction occupies 2 bytes
2. R_r := R_r - 1;
3. If R_r ≠ 0 then PC := PC - 2 * w; --to loop start
```

Note that the branch is always taken backward, to reach the beginning of the loop. By contrast, the VAX11-780 loop counting instructions do not impose this restriction on the direction of the branch [DIGI77].

6.3.1.4 Procedure call and return. During procedure calling the processor at least must save the PC and reload the PC with the location of the first instruction of the called procedure. One call design decision selects the type of location where PC will be saved—should it be in a register, in memory, on a stack, or elsewhere? Another call design decision chooses actions to include within CALL beyond the basic PC-saving function of the simple CALL operation. These added functions may save processor registers, acquire local space for the called procedure, or change the name map. The return instruction reverts control to the caller, so its functions are defined by the actions taken upon call, and there is very little to choose once the call has been specified. For this reason we concentrate here on the call design.

The performance of the processor for procedure calling can be measured by the number of processor cycles required to execute CALL and arrive at the first instruction of the called procedure, with all machine conditions established for the execution of the called procedure. For a fair comparison, this count should include both cycles in the CALL instruction and cycles expended during any additional state saving and space allocation steps required to establish the new procedure for execution. If the called procedure's prologue assists with these functions, the time to execute those prologue functions should be included in the procedure call time estimate. Moving those standard prologue functions into the CALL instruction reduces the overall CALL cycle count. This argument justifies placing enhanced features in CALL instructions. The high frequency of call/return instructions (see Table 6-1) emphasizes the importance of an efficient implementation of procedure call on the system's performance.

The preceding argument is based on the idea that all the functions performed during the complete call sequence are useful. The validity of this assumption depends on the complexity of the called procedure. Certainly, if the called procedure is complex, it will be useful to establish an independent environment for its operation. When the called procedure is short, however, the called procedure may not require many processor resources, and the state-saving effort will be wasted. Therefore, the designer might provide alternative ways to call procedures, depending on the number of the added features provided. In addition to a "complete" call instruction, a processor design might include a short version of CALL without the enhancements.

Example 6-15

The HP3000 processor [HEWL73] supports two call instructions, named SCAL (subroutine call) and PCAL (procedure call). The SCAL instruction provides minimum support, simply saving PC on the top of the stack and loading PC with the entry instruction address. When PCAL is used, a new activation block is created and the complete processor state is saved on the stack. The PCAL instruction is used whenever the called procedure is located in a separate instruction space.[17]

A complementary pair of return instructions, SXIT and EXIT, respectively, are provided. EXIT is also used to return control from an interrupt handler (see Section 6.3.1.5).

The first call design decision concerns the location where the program counter is saved upon call. Registers, memory, or stacks can be used to hold the PC contents saved during CALL.

[17] A separate instruction space will exist if the calling and called procedures were compiled separately.

With *register saving* the CALL instruction has two operands—one specifies the register in which PC is to be saved, and the other specifies the entry point of the called procedure. Letting R and P denote these two values, the CALL involves the following steps:

1. Update PC to point to the next instruction;
2. Save PC in register R;
3. Load PC with P;

Register saving is quick, but the called procedure may have to copy the saved PC value to a memory location.[18] One might assume that because the PC state was saved in a register, the other processor registers must be saved before they can be used by the called procedure. This assumption is valid for most register-based processor architectures, but the BRISC design overcomes this limitation by implementing the register set as a separate memory which is treated as a stack simply by adjusting a pointer on procedure call and return.

Example 6-16

On call, a BRISC machine saves some processor registers in a private register memory in the processor. When the CALL is performed, the mapping between register numbers and addresses in the register memory is changed. Thus some registers can be used for parameter passing, some for local storage, and others for global objects. The 10 lowest locations of register memory space are used for global registers. The remaining locations in the register memory form a stack structure working backward from the top of the register memory. Recall that BRISC appears to have 32 registers, so 22 of these are located in the stack growing downward. Upon CALL the topmost register address is reduced by 16; upon RETURN this process is reversed. The effect is that registers R10 .. R15 of the caller become registers R26 .. R31 of the callee. These registers can be used to pass parameters to the callee and to return results to the caller. Additionally, one of these registers can be allocated to store the PC upon CALL. Figure 6-9 illustrates these allocations. During the execution of the called procedure the registers can be used as follows:

1. R0 .. R9: global objects
2. R10 .. R15: outgoing parameters and saved PC
3. R16 .. R25: local objects
4. R26 .. R31: incoming parameters and return PC

Notice that the register numbers used in a calling CALL and in the matching RETURN are different. For example, if the CALL used R10 to save the PC, the RETURN should specify R26 to restore that saved value.

Notice also that the implementation of the register number remapping only requires adding the more significant register number bits to the relocation constant that is used to map register numbers above 9 to memory addresses.

[18]This extra copying does destroy the speed advantage obtained by avoiding the memory reference during the CALL instruction. For this reason, register saving is desirable if the called procedure requires few registers, and undesirable if the called procedure requires many registers, and will recopy the saved PC to make the registers available.

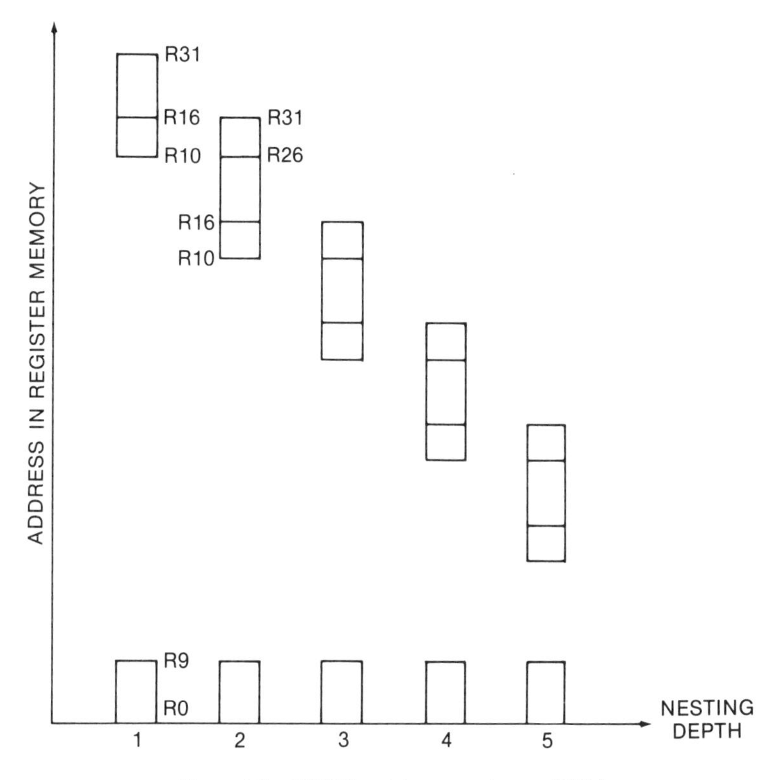

Figure 6-9 BRISC register renaming on CALL

Memory saving of the PC requires an extra memory cycle during CALL. Furthermore, the CALL instruction must specify two memory locations—one for PC saving, and the other for the first instruction of the procedure being called. Let these two operands be S and P. Then the execution of CALL requires:

1. Update PC; --Makes it point to the instruction after the call
2. Save PC in memory location S;
3. Load PC with P;

To reduce the number of instruction bits, a relation between P and S can be imposed. For example, the relation $P = S + 1$ could be used. This rule is used in the central processor of the CDC 6600 and in the DEC PDP8 processor. Figure 6-10 illustrates the CDC 6600 design, which does not have indirect addressing to simplify the return instruction. The constraint between P and S does save address specification bits, but this design does force an intermixture of saved state with instructions, so the procedures cannot be reentrant. Furthermore, since the saved PC value is located in a jump instruction within the instruction space, it is important that location S not be reached by sequential instruction execution. Thus the procedure entry point cannot occur in the midst of a sequential block of instructions.[19]

[19]It can be argued that it is useless to CALL in the middle of an instruction sequence anyhow, since the execution environment for the called procedure would not be properly established.

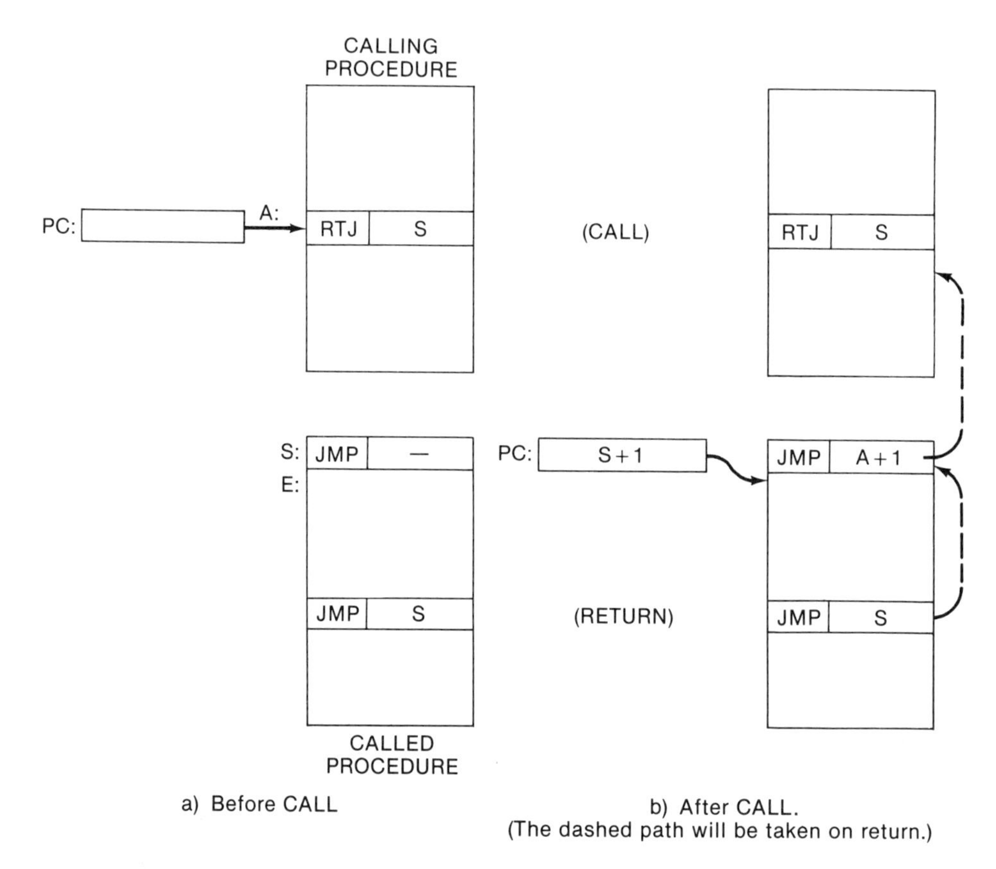

Figure 6-10 Procedure CALL/RETURN in the CDC 6600

The next option is to save the PC on a memory stack. Under this option, the CALL instruction's parameter that specifies where to save the PC is not required, since there is (conventionally) only one stack (described by the pointer SP) onto which the saved state will be placed. Suppose that SP points to the first free location, with the stack growing toward higher memory addresses. Then the semantics of the CALL instruction under this option are:

1. Update PC;
2. Store PC in the memory location whose address is in SP;
3. Increment SP;
4. Load PC with P;

Recursion is directly supported in such a design, since another call to P can be made immediately, the second saved state being stacked atop the first saved state.

A fourth possibility is a combination of register saving and stack saving. The PC is saved in a register after the former contents of that register are pushed on the stack. If the selected register is R, the semantics are:

1. Update PC;
2. Save R on the stack;
3. R := PC;
4. Load PC with P;

One advantage of this option is that parameters transmitted in the caller's program can be easily retrieved by using indexed addressing; register R can be used as an index register, and it points directly to the instruction object following the call. This location would contain the parameter values if parameters were passed in the instruction stream.

The second aspect of the procedure call structure concerns the complementary operation—procedure return. A return instruction restores the PC to the caller's block, with the processor state restored to the state before the call was executed. Semantics that reverse the calling process are in order. This includes restoring the PC to move the control point back to the calling program. This is relatively simple: If the PC was saved in a register, an indexed jump does the job. If the PC was saved in memory, the return instruction can be an indirect jump through that memory location. If the PC was saved on a stack, the saved value is popped from the stack and the stack pointer adjusted accordingly. The latter case certainly requires a special return operation that combines popping the saved PC off the stack with using it as a jump destination.

Example 6-17

The call instruction in the CDC 6600 series [CONT66] is RJ—Return Jump. With an operand address S, RJ stores the updated PC along with an unconditional jump function code at location S and places the address S + 1 in PC. Since there is no indirect addressing mode in this design, the return is effected through a jump to location S, where the JUMP instruction that was loaded by the RJ instruction will be found and executed. Thus the return is achieved by the execution of two consecutive jumps.

The final aspect of the CALL instruction design concerns the selection of additional functions within the call instruction. Such extensions could be designed to support high-level procedure structures, for example. One interesting extension of the CALL is to have the processor automatically save the old context. Another extension is to establish some of the new execution context as the CALL is performed. The following examples illustrate some of these options in actual machine designs.

Example 6-18

The B5700 ENTER instruction establishes a new stack frame and addressing context and also links the new stack frame into the static addressing hierarchy. To understand how this operation works, we must recall the configuration of the stack before the instruction is executed. The sequence of actions was:

1. Mark the stack (push an MSCW); --sets the F register
2. Push a pointer to the entry point descriptor;
3. Push the actual values of the parameters;
4. Execute ENTER;

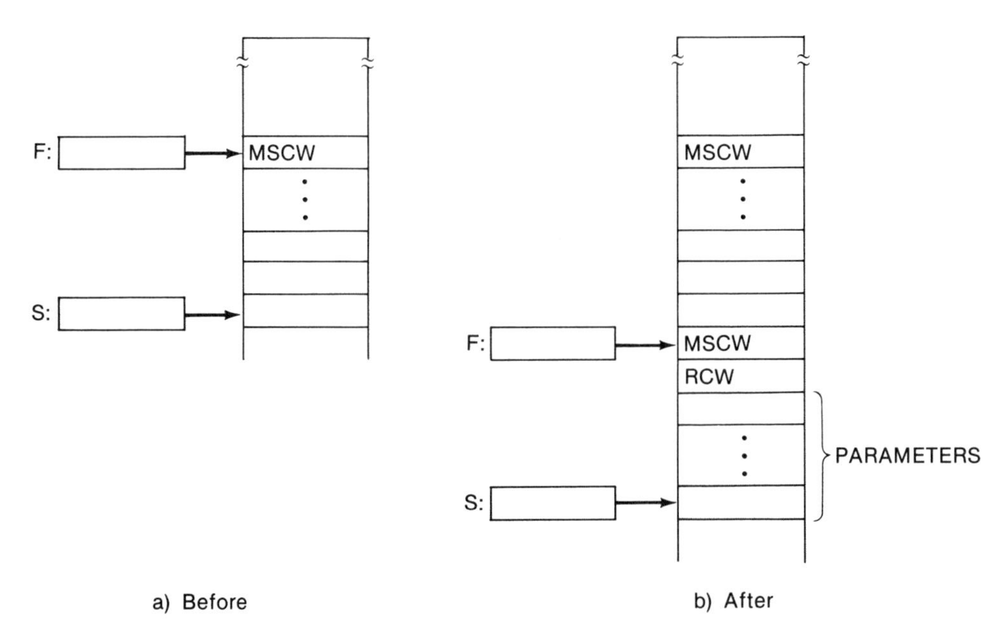

Figure 6-11 B5700 stack configurations across a subroutine calling sequence

This sequence of operation was described in Example 4-9; the stack configurations at the beginning and end of this sequence are depicted in Figure 6-11. Note that the beginning of the new activation block is defined by the location of the MARK STACK CONTROL WORD (MSCW) last pushed on the stack; the location of this MSCW is held in the processor's F register, which was set on execution of the MARKSTACK instruction. The rough sequence of steps to execute ENTER is:

1. Update PC;
2. Find the entry point and the location of the enclosing block's MSCW by indirection through the contents of MEMORY(F) + 1; --see commentary below
3. Save PC in MEMORY(F) + 1;
4. Save the static link in MEMORY(F);
5. Store the level of the callee in MEMORY(F);
6. Set the active bit of the MSCW in MEMORY(F); --marks the MSCW as one at the bottom of an AB
7. Load PC with the entry point;
8. Update the display registers (see Example 5-20);

The location of the enclosing block's MSCW, which is the "static link," is found from the pointer to the entry point descriptor. This pointer may be an "indirect reference word," which contains an address as a (level, offset) pair; the MSCW location is then in display(level). If the pointer is "stuffed," it contains the offset of the MSCW's location within the stack; this offset points to the MSCW of the enclosing block. The level of the callee is found in the descriptor of its entry point.

More elaborate execution environment specifications can change the local addressing environment of the executing process and/or the access rights accorded to the executing process. An entirely separate execution environment, including a new stack space, might be required. Changing both local addressing and access rights supports the visibility limitations of Ada packages, and changing to new static spaces also supports the use of Ada packages to hold global state internal to a package. By changing access rights during CALL, one can control information flows, as discussed in Chapter 4 of Volume 2.

Example 6-19

An external entry point in the original Multics machine (the GE645) was described by a pointer to a program fragment in the linkage segment to be used for external references during the execution of the called procedure [ORGA72]. Control was transferred to this fragment, which simply loaded the link vector pointer with the description of that segment and then transferred to the correct entry point. This structure was necessary because there were restrictions within the processor logic regarding the sources for loading the base registers in the processor. The structure of this program fragment is illustrated in Figure 6-12.

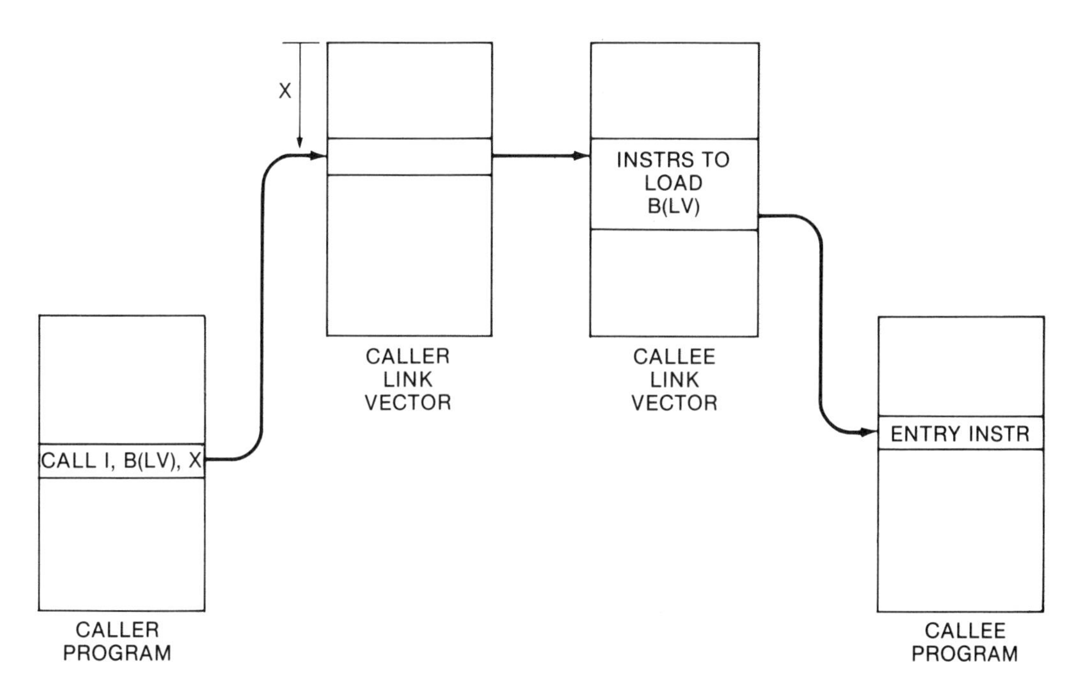

Figure 6-12 GE645 program CALL structures

Example 6-20

The VAX processors [DIGI77] support two elaborate CALL instructions, CALLG and CALLS, designed so that the act of calling a procedure does indeed act like a processor instruction with minimum effect on the processor state. First we discuss the most general variety, in which an argument list location is specified as an operand. The operand specified in the instruction is the "entry point," whose contents are an "entry mask" EM, which specifies initial settings of the overflow enable bits and contains a 12-bit mask whose bits denote which of the registers R_0 .. R_{11} should be stacked for restoration.[20] Registers R_{12} .. R_{15} have special fixed roles, as follows:

1. R_{12}: argument pointer
2. R_{13}: frame pointer
3. R_{14}: stack pointer
4. R_{15}: program counter

The argument pointer contains the address of the first word of the argument list; this word contains the length of the argument list, and the argument values are stored in subsequent words. The frame pointer contains the location of the base of the new activation record established by the CALL being made; it is used for activation block addressing and for restoring the stack pointer during RETURN. The stack pointer and program counter have obvious roles.

When the CALLG instruction is executed, the following actions are taken:

1. The stack pointer is saved in TEMP;
2. The stack pointer is adjusted to be doubleword aligned;
3. The registers selected by the entry mask are pushed on the stack;
4. PC, FP, and AP are pushed on the stack;
5. The register save mask, the condition codes, and other status bits are pushed on the stack;
6. A zero word is pushed on the stack;
7. Set values in condition bits (0 or set as per the entry mask);
8. FP := SP;
9. AP := operand value;
10. PC := entry + 2; --the address of the first program byte;

The effect of these actions is to place the processor in a known state, save the processor registers that will be used by the called procedure, and transfer control to the called program. Figure 6-13 depicts the machine state after this call operation has been completed. The return operator unwinds all these actions to restore the processor's state when it does return to the calling program (see Problem 6-19).

The CALLS instruction supports parameter passing on the stack. The operation is almost identical to the CALLG instruction, except that (1) a count word containing the number of arguments is pushed on the stack before step 2 of the CALL algorithm described above, and (2) in step 9, AP is set to point to the location of the stack word containing the argument count.

Example 6-21

The CALLM instruction of the MC68020 processor is used to call a module, which is a separately translated program running in its own execution environment. The instruction's operands include (1) a "descriptor" and (2) the number of bytes occupied by

[20]Since the entry mask information is a static attribute of the called procedure, placing it within the program space is consistent with having the program space be read-only.

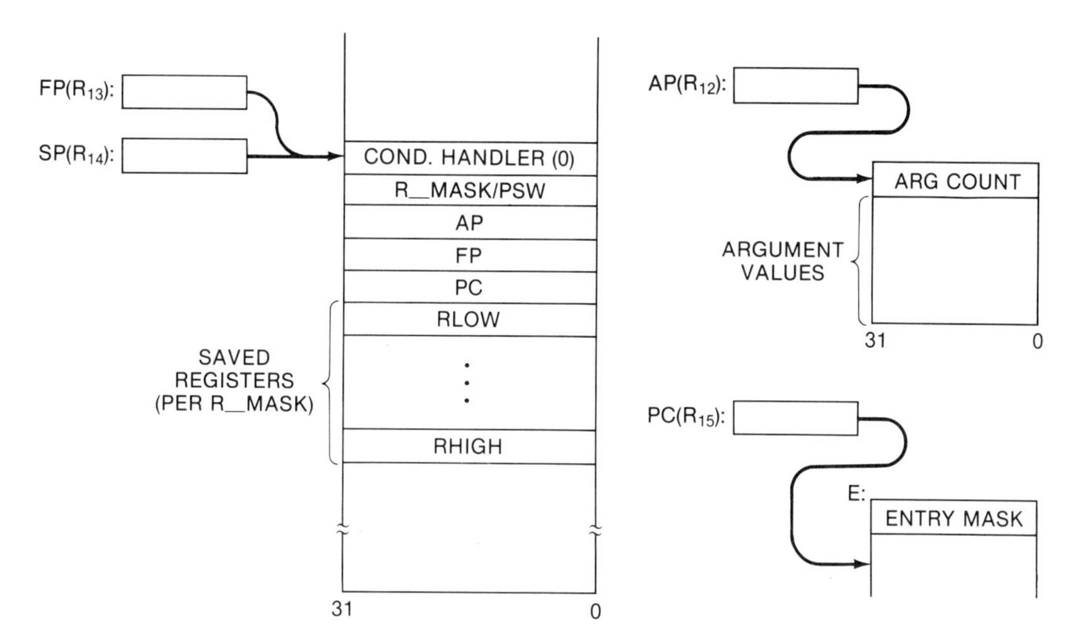

Figure 6-13 VAX stack configuration after CALLG E

arguments to be passed. The instruction's effective address is the location of the descriptor of the module, whose format is illustrated in Figure 6-14. The descriptor includes the entry point information, in addition to at least 12 bytes of information describing the module's entry point, whether the module requires a separate stack for execution (and the value of that stack pointer), and a pointer to the data area to be used by the called module. The use of this area is determined by how the module has been programmed; it could be used to hold the (private) link vector of that module (see Section 5.3.2). In addition, the entry point location is not the location of the first instruction to be executed

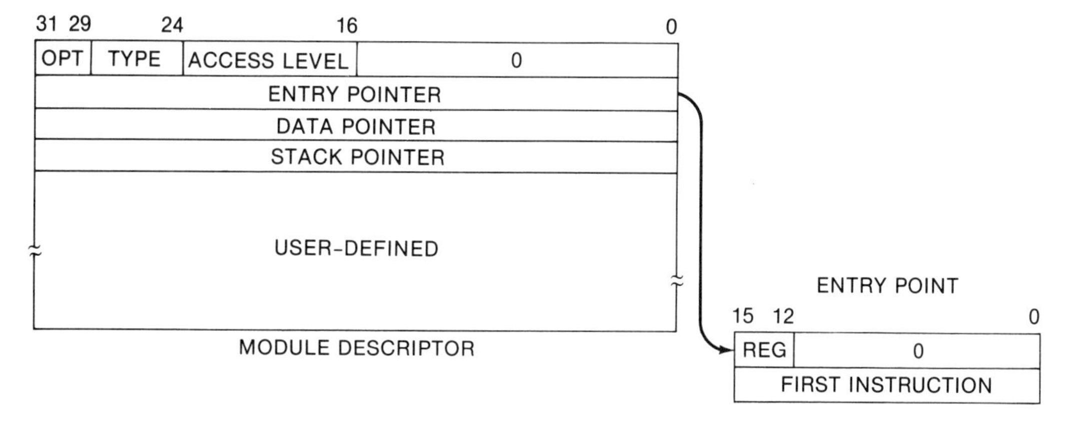

Figure 6-14 MC68020 module descriptor and entry point (after [MOTO84]; courtesy of Motorola, Inc.)

after the CALLM instruction is completed; rather, the first word at the entry point specifies which processor register is to be loaded with the pointer to the data area for the module; then this register may be used by the called program to access its link vector.

To complete the module call, the processor needs the (static) entry point location and other information that may depend on the program using the module. The latter information is found in the module descriptor, which is private to the executing process. The information concerning which register will contain the data space descriptor is contained in the program (at the entry point's location), as that selection must match the register specifications contained in the program's instructions—this selection is static.

When a module is called, processor state is saved according to the format shown in Figure 6-15. The information in this set of memory locations is used by the complementary return instruction RETM. Note that the module descriptor pointer is placed in

29	24	16	8	0
OPT	TYPE	ACCESS LEVEL	0	COND. CODES
0		ARG. COUNT	0	
MODULE DESCRIPTOR POINTER				
PC				
MODULE DATA AREA POINTER				
SP				
ARGUMENTS (OPTIONAL)				

Figure 6-15 The stack frame saved by the MC68020 CALLM instruction (after [MOTO84]; courtesy of Motorola, Inc.)

the saved state; this action permits the called module to access any user-defined[21] information that may have been placed in the module descriptor. The first word of the module descriptor and the first word of the saved stack frame contain access-level information related to data sharing and access control; its use is described in Section 4.6.2.2 of Volume 2. Here we need to know only that the contents of the access control information may force the processor to change stacks for the execution of the new module; if no change is required, the new activation block is pushed on the caller's stack.

It should be apparent that the CALLM instruction must require many processor cycles to complete; the actual number depends on the number of parameters passed and whether a new stack is required. The cycle count, in the worst case, reaches $71 + 6n$, where n is the number of parameter words passed. By contrast, the BSR instruction, which calls an "ordinary" subroutine, takes at most 13 cycles. Clearly, the CALLM instruction should not be used where not necessary. It is no surprise that the RETM instruction takes up to 35 cycles, compared to only 12 cycles (worst case) for the ("normal") RTS return instruction.

Example 6-22

The Intel iAPX432 [TYNE81], like the MC68020, has two complex call instructions: CALL and CALL_THRU_DOMAIN. Both instructions have two operands

[21]"User-defined" really means "not interpreted by the processor's built-in mechanisms."

containing three pieces of information:

1. Descriptor of the static link
2. Pointer to the domain definition for the new procedure
3. Pointer to the entry point's instruction segment (relative to the new context)

The operands of these instructions can be taken from the stack, from memory locations, or from an immediate operand (this processor has no programmer-visible registers). The last two values are taken from the same object, which contains only static information. The operand location flexibility is adequate to permit the compiler to place static operand information in the program itself and dynamic operand information in a process-local space.

The domain structure defined by these structures supports the Ada package concept; note that the domain can have different entry points (selected by the instruction segment index in the third operand) just as an Ada package can have several externally visible functions or procedures. However, the iAPX432 processor restricts the location of each entry point to the beginning of a segment.

The processor holds a descriptor of the current execution context in an internal register. Figure 6-16 illustrates the data structures affected by a CALL_THRU_DOMAIN, showing the configuration both before and after the CALL instruction. Each segment has an access part (shown above the wide separating line) and a data part (below the wide line). Entries in the access part contain 64 bits; each one describes a memory space, which might be a subspace of a segment. The drawing in the figure does not show the most general case, because it shows the local constants located in the domain segment. The TRACE and FAULT entries in the domain's access part describe the procedures that will be called if a trace or fault event occurs during the execution of a program running within that domain.

The first data in the instruction segment specifies static information about the execution environment for the called procedure. The first instruction follows this static information; it starts at bit offset 40_{16}. The figure indicates the sources of most of the information that is placed into the new context segment during the CALL instruction. The new context segment was obtained from a pre-linked list of contexts provided by the operating system; the data length and access length values in the new instruction segment state the size requirements of the new procedure; if these cannot be met by the next context on the pre-linked list, an interrupt occurs so that the system can reallocate memory, if desired. Notice that the GLOBAL_CONSTANTS are identical for both procedures; in fact, they are identical for all processes in the system.

The difference between the CALL and the CALL_THRU_DOMAIN concerns the degree of change during the execution of the instruction; the simple CALL does not change the context or domain information.

These examples show that complex context changes are quite useful in establishing the proper program execution context, but are time consuming. A study considering other design alternatives to reduce the number of memory references in the iAPX432 CALL [GEHR86] demonstrated that a reassignment of the locations used for state information plus an enhancement of the memory controller (to support an operation that clears a block of memory) could save over 50% of the CALL's memory references, reducing its cost to a level comparable to the cost of a CALL in

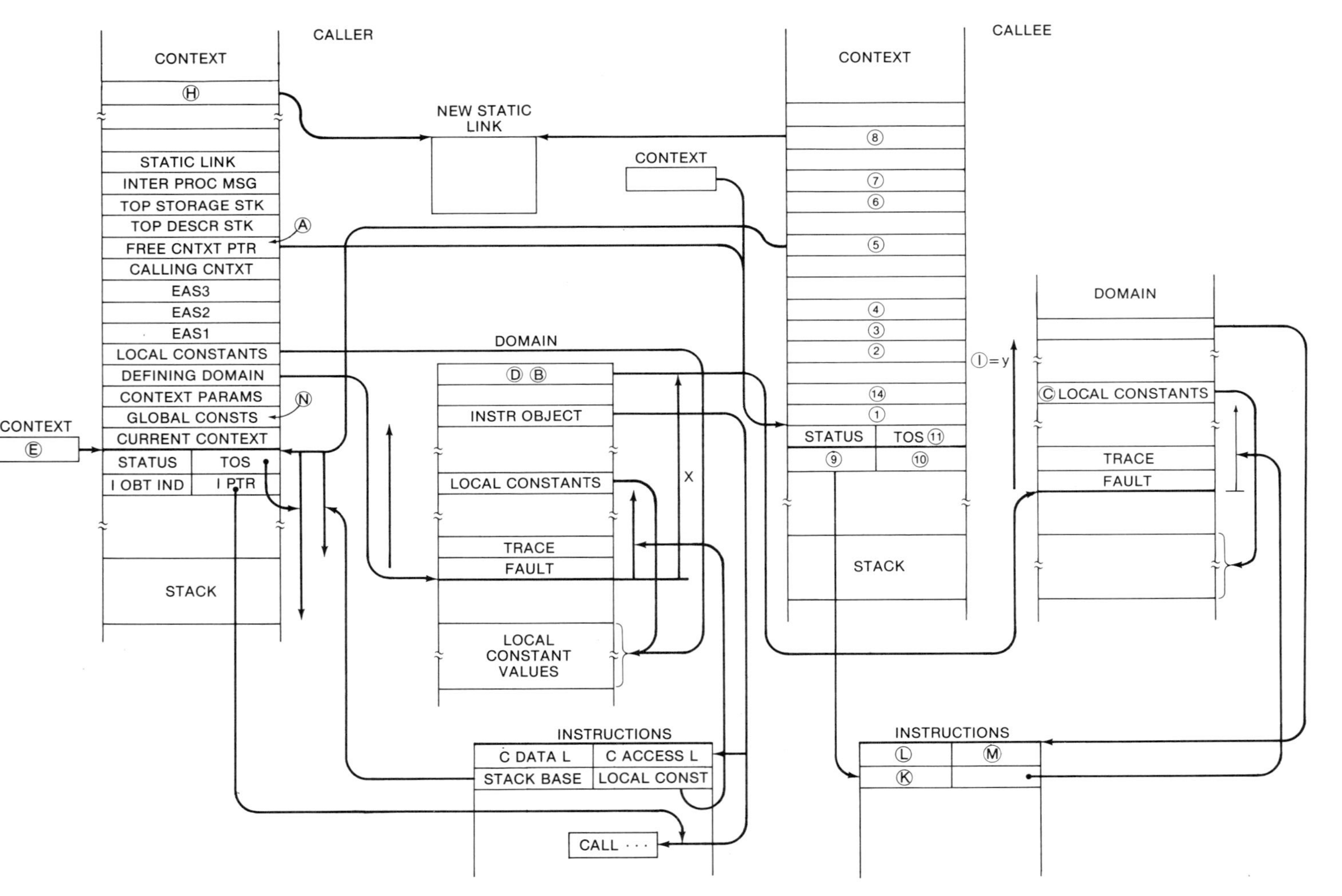

Figure 6-16 Important process-describing data in the Intel iAPX432 (ver. 3) and how it changes during CALL-THROUGH-DOMAIN. In each segment the thick line separates access objects (above) from data (below). The call parameters are x, y, and z: x, the domain index of the called domain; y, the domain index (within the called domain) of the instruction object; z, the address of a descriptor of the static link. The callee entities that receive new values are numbered, and the sources of their information are marked with circled letters. Item Ⓐ goes to location ①, etc., except: ⑥ and ⑦ come from the storage manager; ⑨ is set to 40_{16}; ⑫ and ⑬ are within the descriptor of the new context, being set from Ⓛ and Ⓜ.

the MC68020.[22] Complex context changes may include changes in the system's protection state; the consequences of this possibility are explored in Chapter 4 of Volume 2. Complex context changes are not required for every CALL, so designers should consider providing support for both simple and general calls (with complete context changes). Complementary return operators are also required.

6.3.1.5 Branch instructions. The options for unconditional branch instructions are quite limited. They are similar to the options for conditional branch instructions that have already been discussed. In reality, all processors have some form of unconditional branch instruction. The major differences among these instructions lies in the way that the target instruction address is specified. Both PC-relative and direct (absolute) specifications have been designed into machines.

6.3.1.6 Interrupts. Interrupts are caused by events external to the program in execution. Since there is no relationship between the program in execution and the occurrence of the interrupt, the system must be designed so that it can react to the interrupt and preserve the status of the program that happened to be in execution when the interrupt occurred. The conventional approach to this requirement is to design the processor to treat the occurrence of the interrupt like a procedure call, with the call operands taken from locations built into the processor. When the interrupt forces the call, the processor finds these implied call operands and then performs the call, which requires at least saving the executing program's state and then loading the interrupt handler's entry point into the PC.

Several design issues remain after it has been decided that the interrupt's occurrence will be treated like a call:

1. When may the interrupt be recognized?
2. Where is the process state saved?
3. How is the entry point found?
4. Where should execution be resumed after the interrupt handler is completed?

The first design issue is to decide when interrupts may be recognized. The basic requirement is that when an interrupt occurs, the processor must be able to save state in such a manner that the execution point can return to the point of interruption after the interrupt handler has completed execution. There are both microscopic and macroscopic aspects to this timing issue. The microscopic aspect concerns when an interrupt can occur within the execution of an instruction. The macroscopic aspect concerns when an interrupt can occur within the execution of a program. A partial answer to the microscopic version of the question is "before starting a new instruction." Additional interruption points may be added within long instructions so that the processor can meet response-time requirements. The macroscopic version of the question involves delving into interactions among interrupt modules. The following

[22]This demonstrates that there may be a significant opportunity to enhance the speed of complex instructions, and that the raw performance of one implementation cannot be used to judge the speed of a general implementation strategy.

requirement is necessary: for it to be permissible that a new interrupt B be recognized after one interrupt A has been recognized but before the A's handler has completed execution, the processor will have to be able to save the state of A's handler. A little thought is sufficient to convince one that there are three possible rules: (1) it is not possible to interrupt an interrupt handler, (2) interrupts cannot be "recursive,"[23] or (3) the saved states must be stored on a stack. Each possible rule leads to a decision concerning the times when an interrupt can be tolerated.

The second design issue is to decide where to save the process state when the interrupt occurs. If the processor architecture uses a stack to save PC during a CALL, the same stack is usually used for process state saving upon interrupt. If processor state is saved upon interrupt exactly like it would be for a procedure call, it would seem that the same RETURN instruction as for a procedure's return can be used to terminate the interrupt handler. The apparent parallel between interrupts and procedure call cannot be carried this far, unfortunately. The processor's mode may have to be changed to handle the interrupt. As a consequence, the execution mode before the interrupt occurred must be saved upon interrupt and restored upon completion of the interrupt handler.

Example 6-23

Upon occurrence of an interrupt, the B5700 processor saves state on the stack the same way that state is saved on procedure call. The same mechanism can be used for both situations because the system design is based on the "nothing illegal" philosophy. Therefore, one can be sure that mode information saved on the stack upon every call will not be compromised by any program.

If the system design is not based on the "nothing illegal" philosophy, the saved mode cannot both (1) be stored in a place writable by a user process and (2) be restored upon procedure return (see Problem 6-23), lest the system's integrity suffer. One way out of this dilemma is to define a privileged interrupt return instruction which restores the processor mode, in contrast to the procedure return instruction, which cannot change the processor mode. Another way out of the dilemma is to use a separate system stack on which interrupt handlers operate.

Example 6-24

The MC68020 has three stack pointers, a user stack pointer (USP), an interrupt stack pointer (ISP), and a master stack pointer (MSP). Bits 12 and 13 of the status register determine which of these three will be used for register A7. Upon the occurrence of an interrupt, the status register is saved on the interrupt stack and then set so that ISP will be used for interrupt processing. In this manner, the master stack can be reserved for the execution of system procedures that are directly requested from an application process. There are several return instructions differing in the amount of processor state information restored from the stack; those that may change the processor's mode cannot be executed while the processor is in user mode.

The third design issue is to decide how the system will find the handler's entry point. Most designs dedicate specific memory locations to hold interrupt entry

[23]Meaning that the same interrupt occurs a second time before the first occurrence has been handled.

points. Some information about how to save process state may also be stored in specific memory locations. The big decision concerns whether the processor selects the interrupt locations based on the type of the interrupt. If so, the effect is that the processor automatically decodes the interrupt.

Example 6-25

Upon an external interruption, an IBM System/370 processor saves the processor state (its PSW) in locations $24_{10} .. 31_{10}$ and takes the new PSW from memory locations $88_{10} .. 95_{10}$. This PSW contains a saved PC, which defines the entry point for the interrupt handler. A word containing the interruption code is stored at a memory location chosen based on bits in the PSW. (Similar activities occur for internal interrupts.)

A simple condition decoding design multiplies the interrupt number by a constant (usually a power of 2) and uses the result as an address or a table index. The addressed location will contain the first instruction of the interrupt handler or, in another type of design, the address of the first location in the interrupt handler.

Example 6-26

The MC68020 distinguishes among 256 different exception conditions (of which 192 can be defined by the programmer). A table containing 1024 bytes is used in interrupt processing, as described below. The origin of this table is held in the VBR (vector base register) processor register, which is accessible only when the processor is in supervisor state. A table entry contains 4 bytes holding the address of the entry point of the associated exception handler. This table structure is depicted in Figure 6-17.

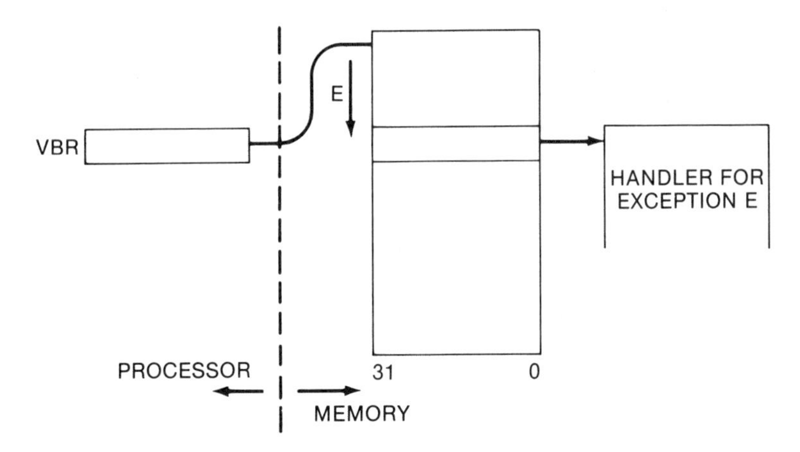

Figure 6-17 MC68020 exception entry table. The table offset is 4 * E(bytes), there being 4 bytes per entry.

Upon occurrence of the interrupt, at least 8 status bytes are pushed on the stack, following this format:

```
type exception_format is (short, throwaway,
  instruction_exception, m10bus_fault, coproc,
  m20short_bus_fault, m20long_bus_fault);
```

```
type byte(n) is array(1 .. 8 * n) of bit;
type exception_stack_frame is
  record
    status_register  : byte(2);
    program_counter : byte(4);
    format           : bit(4);
    vector_offset    : bit(12);
    case format is
      when short | throwaway =>
        null;
      when instruction_exception =>
        byte(4);
      when m10bus_fault =>    --see footnote24
        byte(50);
      when coproc =>
        byte(8);
      when m20short_bus_fault =>
        byte(24);
      when m20long_bus_fault =>
        byte(80);
    end case;
  end record;
```

The status register saved at the top of the stack contains the mode and the interrupt priority level (used for prioritizing interrupts). The vector offset is the index into the exception entry table; its value serves as an indication of the type of exception that occurred. The format field specifies the format of the status information saved on the stack; "additional processor state information" may contain from 0 to 40 (16-bit) words. For details concerning the contents of the additional saved information, see Chapter 6 in [MOTO84].

Upon completion of the interrupt handler, the processor executes the RTE instruction, which restores the entire state, examining the saved format information to determine which information was saved and how to resume the interrupted activity.

6.3.1.7 Routine replacement.

Of the "other" control constructs mentioned in Section 6.2.1.7, only routine replacement has appeared at the processor level.

Example 6-27

The IBM System/38 processor instruction "transfer control" (XCTL) performs a routine replacement call, passing an argument list to the replacement routine.

The control flow resulting from routine replacement was illustrated in Figure 6-7.

[24] This exception condition can be raised by the MC68010 processor, but not by the MC68020.

6.3.2 Program Location

Program location is the second basic issue concerning the control design space. Most processor designs are based on the von Neumann model and do not restrict program location. A few designs use the Harvard model, in which case the program must reside in the program memory.

Example 6-28

The Texas Instruments TMS320 signal processing processor uses a modified Harvard architecture. There are separate instruction and data buses, which usually operate independently. However, an interconnection between the two buses can be activated to permit accesses that violate the strict data-instruction boundary imposed in the Harvard paradigm.

Access control restrictions may be imposed on the memory to support protection and security of shared objects.[25] Such access controls may imply some restrictions on program location. In particular, a program can be executed only if it is located in a portion of memory to which the processor has execute access. Execute access usually does not imply write access. If write access is permitted to a program, the program cannot be protected against inadvertent modification. On the other hand, if execute access is independent of write access and the program is to be protected, the program cannot modify itself during execution. The CDC 6600 design (Figure 6-10) is therefore incompatible with program protection against inadvertent modification.

6.3.3 Implementation

Processor control implementation choices affect the complexity of the processor's logic, its testability, and its speed. Microcoding greatly enhances the regularity of the processor's implementation and makes its control section more easily testable. Microcoding, however, can slow execution. Microcoding is discussed in more detail in Section 6.4.

In addition, the control implementation affects the processor mode separation that protects the operating system from user access and modification. Most processors have a supervisor mode in which all instructions can be executed and in which system control can be exerted. In contrast, in user mode some processor instructions will be proscribed and memory access may be restricted. Memory access restrictions are discussed in detail in Chapter 3 of Volume 2.

Some implementation techniques speed the system; these include using instruction buffers and designing instruction representations to facilitate their interpretation. We discuss instruction buffering here and instruction representation choices in the next section.

An instruction lookbehind buffer is somewhat similar to memory cache. Their

[25]In Chapter 4 of Volume 2 we discuss protection and security in more detail.

rationale is also similar—since programs exhibit locality, recently executed instructions are likely to be executed in the near future. This is particularly true if the instructions are part of a loop. The instruction buffer can speed loop execution by permitting execution of successive iterations without having to access memory more than once for each instruction in the loop. The instruction buffer control logic is designed so that the processor can quickly find instructions that happen to be located in the buffer.

Conceptually, the instruction buffer is placed between the IR and the memory, as shown in Figure 6-18. Whenever the control unit wishes to fetch an instruction, it

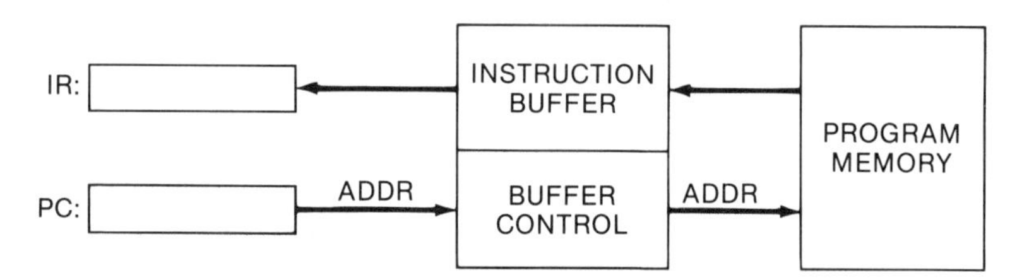

Figure 6-18 A lookbehind instruction buffer

passes the instruction address to the instruction buffer, and awaits a reply. If the buffer does contain the instruction, it responds with the instruction, and the control unit can proceed. On the other hand, if the buffer does not contain the instruction, the buffer requests the instruction from memory, and when the instruction arrives, it is passed to the processor and placed in the buffer, whereupon the processor can proceed.

The instruction buffer, being like a memory cache, presents similar design issues. In particular, loading, location, and dumping policies must be selected. The selection of the buffer's dumping policy is tied up with the implementation of the buffer's associative addressing; several options are described in the following.

One buffer design has the n-word buffer keep the n most recently executed instruction words, wherever they happen to be located in memory address space. This design requires within the buffer a general associative search mechanism, which must be either expensive or slow; for speed, one would include matching logic associated with every buffer entry. With this design any loop consisting of not more than n words will fit into the buffer. Since all instructions in any loop shorter than the buffer's capacity will be found in the buffer on the second and succeeding executions of the loop body, these loops will be executed with minimum time spent on instruction fetch. The flexibility to hold any loop is gained at the expense of lookup logic complexity. Observe that most loops contain sequentially executed instructions and that all of these instructions can be placed in consecutive memory locations by the compiler. Therefore, designing the lookbehind buffer so that it can handle the general case may not be a good strategy.

How can we simplify the instruction buffer if we assume that each loop body will be contained within instruction words that occupy sequentially addressed memory locations? First, we can simplify the search logic, since the set of words contained in the buffer comes from a contiguous set of memory locations and the set of locations can be described by the first and last memory addresses whose contents are present in the buffer.[26] The test to determine whether an instruction word is present in the buffer requires two arithmetic comparisons against address bits from PC (see Problem 6-26). Could the buffer location selection mechanism be simplified in this contiguous case? Yes! We could use a direct mapping cache, with the least significant memory address bits being the buffer index. The contiguity restriction does require that the buffer's contents must be marked invalid upon the execution of any branch instruction whose destination lies outside the range of the buffer's contents.

Another approach to speeding instruction fetching is to provide a separate instruction cache, designed in a manner similar to the general memory cache described in Chapter 5. One important difference between instructions and data is that the pattern of instruction referencing is more predictable than that of data referencing, since instructions tend to be executed sequentially. A *prefetching* policy can be used; under this policy, upon each cache reference, the cache is searched for the next block *after* the one referenced; if that block is absent, it is fetched in anticipation of a future need. The Fairchild CLIPPER uses this strategy, which was used in the ILLIAC IV instruction buffer (that buffer design was not as flexible as a cache, but it incorporated prefetching—see [BARN68] and [BOUK72]).

6.3.4 Instruction Representation

Several issues relate to the representations used for processor instructions. The designer must decide between the competing goals of implementation simplicity and representation shortness.

Control unit *simplicity* can be enhanced by encoding instructions so that each bit within each instruction is used in only a few different ways. The RISC design epitomizes this approach, using almost all instruction bits in almost the same manner in all instructions. The MC68020 instruction set, on the other hand, requires complex decoding. For example, in Table 2-13 we saw that the "dow" information is sometimes part of the function code and sometimes specifies a particular instruction variant.

Length savings can be achieved by allowing variable-length instructions. The actual length of an instruction may be determined by the function code or other parameters. Another option defines a mechanism whereby the lengths of individual instruction fields can be independently varied. One aspect of this issue concerns the *granularity* of the extensions; another aspect concerns *how* the length is specified, which affects the difficulty of determining the actual format of an instruction.

Instructions with variable lengths can be used to allow flexibility in operand specification or to use frequency-dependent coding of field contents. Both techniques save instruction bits, thereby reducing the memory bandwidth required to access the program.[27] The Intel iAPX432 has bit granularity within programs and its instruction lengths vary greatly.

[26]We require a special case for an empty or a full buffer, depending on the details of the range encoding.

[27]We assume, of course, that the memory access time is fixed.

Instruction extensions can be supported easily when the extensions are a consequence of address mode specifications, and when each extension is itself the same size as an instruction. In this case the extension granularity matches the granularity of all program elements. When an extension item is required, it is fetched in a manner similar to any instruction in the program.

Example 6-29

Some MC68020 operand addressing mode options specify a register's contents as the operand. Other mode options use the register as an index register whose contents are added to an address found in an extension word; the sum is the address of the memory location whose contents are the operand. In the MC68020 the instruction length cannot be determined from just the function code. Some instructions have two operands, each possibly requiring an extension word to hold a memory address. As a result, instructions can have several different lengths, but all are multiples of a word length. The PC simply counts the instruction words as they are fetched and interpreted.

Instruction addressing and extension is simple when the instruction length is a multiple of one basic length, which we call the *instruction granularity*. In the MC68020, the instruction granularity is a word. In the B5700, the instruction granularity is a byte.

Example 6-30

If bit 7 of the first byte in a B5700 instruction is zero, the instruction length is 2 bytes. If bit 7 is 1, the first byte is the function code, and the instruction length depends on the remainder of the function code. In many cases the length is just one byte; the exceptions are described in Table 6-2.

By varying instruction lengths by bits, rather than by words, the designer can reduce program length. But the complexity of instruction fetching and decoding increases as the granularity is lowered, so mechanism complexity is the cost of shortening programs in this manner. Here we briefly discuss these topics, starting with the optimum encoding scheme.

To optimize the instruction length, all usage frequencies must be known. Then one uses the Huffman coding algorithm [HUFF52], which works from the least frequent case to the most frequent case. The Huffman algorithm produces a coding whose average code length is the shortest average code length possible for the given usage frequencies. Due to the drawbacks of fine granularity and decoding complexity, Huffman coding is almost never used to represent computer instructions. We illustrate both the Huffman procedure and the Intel iAPX432 system's use of function encoding at bit granularity. Then we examine some realistic compromises that give good average code length without too much complexity.

Example 6-31

Suppose that five different instruction codes are to be encoded using Huffman coding. First, their frequencies of use must be determined. In this example we use the frequencies listed in Table 6-3.

The first step of Huffman's code assignment algorithm finds the two lowest probabilities. In the second step, a zero code bit is assigned to one of the instructions with

TABLE 6-2 B5700 INSTRUCTION LENGTHS LONGER THAN ONE BYTE, BY FUNCTION CODE[a]

First Byte (hexadecimal)	Instruction Length (bytes)
00-7F	2
95	2
96	2
98	4
9A	3
9C	3
9E	2
A0	2
A1	3
A2	3
A4	3
B2	2
B3	3
BE	7
C0	2
C2	2
C4	2
C6	2
C8	2
DC	2
DD	3

[a]Some function codes have different interpretations when the processor is executing an "edit" sequence (initiated by the instruction "enter edit"); the edit mode interpretations of the function codes were not considered while making this table.

TABLE 6-3 HUFFMAN CODING

Instruction	Frequency	Code
instr1	0.6	0
instr2	0.3	10
instr3	0.08	110
instr4	0.01	1110
instr5	0.01	1111

the selected probabilities, and a one code bit is assigned to the other instruction. The added code bit is placed in front of any code bits previously assigned to these instructions.[28] In the third step, the two instructions are combined into a single instruction whose probability is equal to the sum of the probabilities of the two instructions. Making this combination defines a set of instructions; the same code bit value is

[28]This statement is necessary because the procedure will be executed recursively.

assigned to all set members when step 2 is performed with a set of instructions. The procedure continues by looping back to the first step, assigning two code bits and combining two entries each time that the loop is performed. One entry in the instruction list is removed from the list and combined with another list entry for each execution of the loop. The loop terminates when only one instruction set remains, so the entire procedure will require $n - 1$ iterations, where n is the number of instructions in the original list.

The Huffman codes for our instruction frequencies are shown in the table. These codes are designed to be read serially from left to right. (What happens if they are read the other way around?)

From the example we see that the number of bits that have to be interpreted to discriminate among the codes and find their lengths depends on the values of the previous bits in the code. This possibility makes Huffman codes difficult to interpret and confirms the complexity of the implementation of a decoder. In addition, it is hard to design a Huffman decoder to be tolerant of errors.[29]

The decoding difficulty that arises from small length granularity variations can be alleviated by choosing an encoding using a small set of lengths and placing a length field code in each code word. This strategy achieves some length reduction, but it may not achieve the maximum reduction obtainable from Huffman coding. A code design using a small number of lengths also has a simpler decoder.

It is difficult to quantify the trade between length and decoding complexity. We must be satisfied with the small number of publicly available examples. In one, Wilner [WILN72] reported a study measuring the trade of decoding time against space consumed by the instructions themselves. He studied instructions in the systems programming machine of the Burroughs B1700 processor [BURR72]. The time measure is specific to the microcoded interpretation scheme used, so the trade-off curve cannot be directly applied to other situations. Nevertheless, the results are instructive. Figure 6-19 shows time versus space at three points in the design space. The shortest time and largest space corresponds to function codes that have a single fixed length. The time and space measures are normalized to this "best time" case. The smallest space and longest time correspond to Huffman coding. The third point corresponds to choosing three fixed code lengths and assigning codes for the most frequent instructions to the shortest length, and the least frequent instructions to the longest length. Although this midpoint does not achieve either the space or the time minimum, the differences between this point and the optimum points are quite small. The B1700 study graphically illustrates the importance of choosing length granularities wisely.

Another system using a small number of lengths is the Intel iAPX432, in which operand specifications and instruction codes are both encoded in varying lengths. Since a single instruction may contain a number of variable-length fields, a single instruction may attain any of a large number of lengths.

Example 6-32

Intel iAPX432 function code specifications can use a varying number of bits; class and format information at the beginning of the instruction specify the function code

[29]It is impossible to recover synchronization if a bit is dropped or inserted, for example.

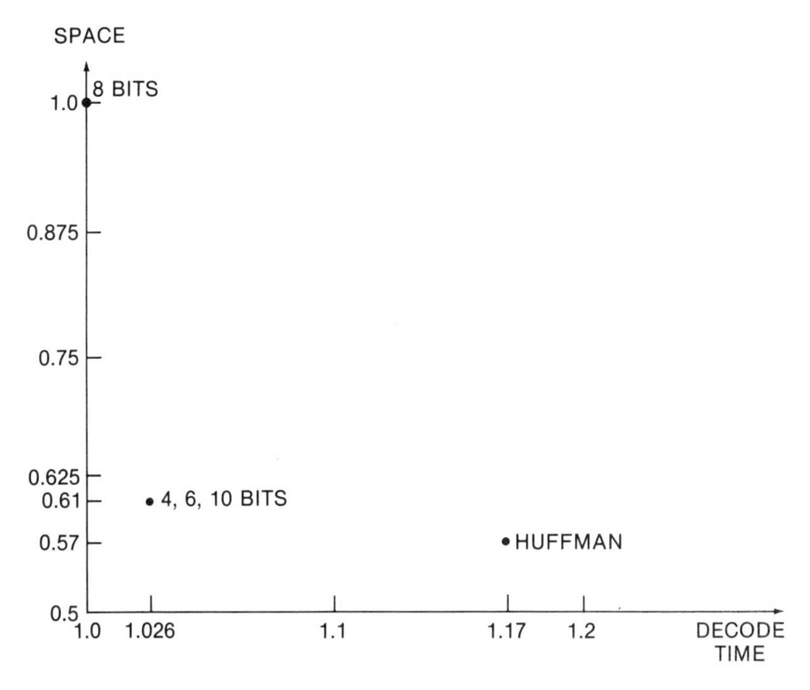

Figure 6-19 B1700 space-time trade-offs (from [WILN72])© AFIPS Press, used with permission.

TABLE 6-4 REPRESENTATIVE iAPX432 INSTRUCTION LENGTHS[a]

Operation	Possible Lengths (bits)
ADD/SUB/MPY/DIV	16, 20, 25, 29, 34, 38, 43, 47
INCR/DECR	14, 15, 18, 19, 23, 24, 27, 28 32, 33, 36, 37, 41, 42, 45, 46

[a]The other operand and the result are on the stack.

lengths. Table 6-4 illustrates all possible lengths for the single operand versions[30] of arithmetic operations on integer operands.

A third method for shortening instructions uses implied register contents for operand specifications. Relative addressing, for example, saves bits in branch instruction destinations by specifying displacements relative to the PC's contents. Since many loops and conditionally executed statement lists are short, short relative address specifications are adequate in most branch instructions. In a long loop a long addressing mode may be needed to specify the destination of the branch instruction that closes the loop. On the average, the time penalty due to the long addressing mode required to complete the long loop is only a small percentage of the loop's total execution time, which is large.

[30]One scalar operand from memory—not from an indexed data structure; the other from the stack.

6.3.5 Summary

Processor designers have made diverse design selections in their attempts to move high-level language semantics into processor functions. We have presented several attempts in this direction; many associated with loop control and function calling. These design decisions result in very complex instructions. Compared to a RISC design, these processors might be considered "very complex."

There is also a wide variation among the instruction representation techniques. Perhaps the two ends of the spectrum are the iAPX432, with bit granularity, and the IBM System/370, with only three instruction lengths (2, 4, and 6 bytes). Within a fixed width, the architect does have many coding and representation options. Choosing a consistent encoding of the instruction bits simplifies the instruction interpretation process, which reflects directly in the structure of the microprogrammed host system.

6.4 MICROCODE CONTROL STRUCTURES

Microcode implementations of processor functionality are commonplace. The basic idea is to implement the processor's control section as a programmed module, the program being called the microprogram. The implementation has several advantages, including regularity of the logic structures in the system. The implementation regularity is a great advantage, making microcoding attractive. Figure 6-20 depicts

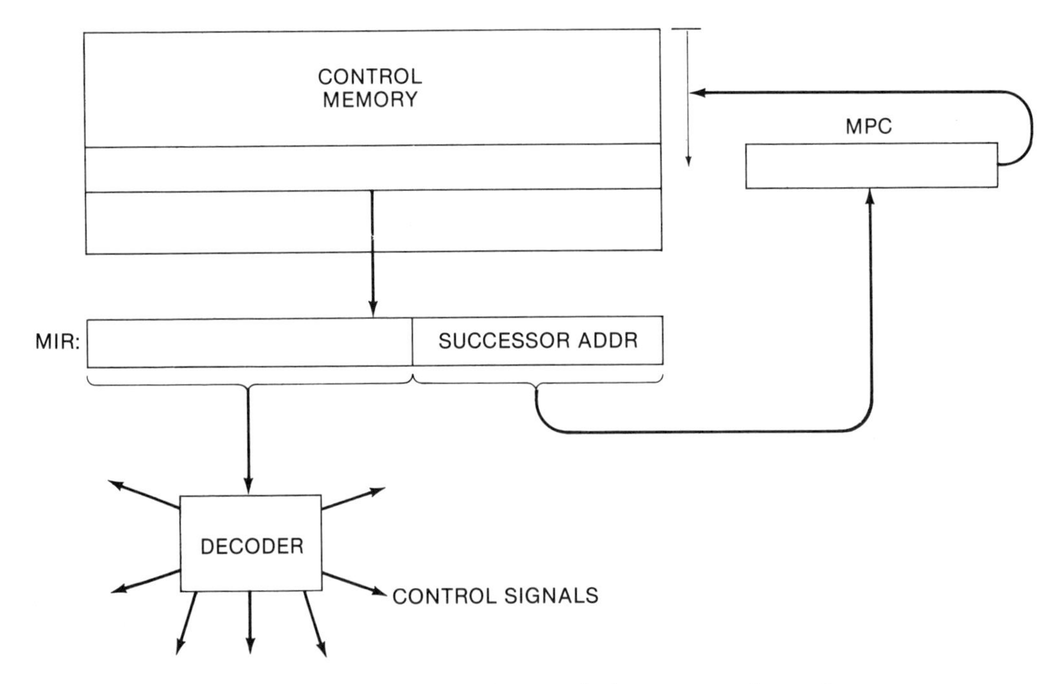

Figure 6-20 Basic elements of microprogrammed control

the general structure of a microcoded control unit. The microprogram counter MPC determines which microinstruction will be fetched from the control memory; the fetched microinstruction is placed into the microinstruction register MIR, whence it is decoded to produce control signals that enable register transfers or pass values around the system. A sequence of microinstructions executed in this manner performs the actions of a single processor instruction.

To compare different implementations of the same target system, one must first ascertain that they are functionally equivalent and then one can make a comparison based on nonfunctional criteria. So the first question is: Given a host system structure and two different implementations of the control section, how can we tell whether the control units are equivalent? A simple equivalence test demands that both have the same input/output behavior, when they are considered to be finite-state machines. We could arrange the set of equivalent microprogrammed control units that implement the desired target architecture according to their microinstruction widths.

We consider two designs near the ends of the spectrum based on microinstruction widths as we investigate system complexity and regularity. Let C denote the number of control signals output from the control unit; this value is a (fixed) attribute of the control unit. A conceptually simple design has C microinstruction bits that directly specify the control signals to be produced and N_1 bits that specify the address of the next microinstruction to be performed. The microinstruction does not have to be decoded. Let L be the number of microinstructions in this control memory; the complete control memory contains $L(C + N_1)$ bits. Another implementation could use a separate microinstruction to produce each control signal. In this design, each microinstruction requires $\log_2 C$ bits that select which control signal will be produced, and N_2 bits to determine the sequencing, with $N_1 \leq N_2$. (Why?) The second design has a single decoder which generates the single control signal from the $\log_2 C$ bits that select that signal. The size ratio N_2/N_1 is almost equal to the average number of control signals that are active in each of the "wide" microinstructions.

One basic design decision for a microcoded implementation of a target architecture concerns the microinstruction width; the terms *vertical* and *horizontal* microcode are used to describe the two extreme approaches in this design continuum. Although neither of the two extreme designs presented above represents an interesting implementation possibility, they do depict the extremes in the vertical–horizontal spectrum.

Now let us consider realistic design options. One realistic design near the vertical end of the spectrum has microinstructions that can be described like processor instructions performed by the host architecture. The control unit has its own sequencer that produces the correct control signal sequence that implements each kind of microinstruction. The sequencer's functions are similar to those of a processor's control unit, but all instructions are simple, so the sequencer's complexity is much lower than the complexity of a sequencer for the target machine implemented without microprogramming. The "missing complexity" has been replaced by the larger control memory, which has a regular structure. A control unit implementation following this paradigm is said to be "vertically microprogrammed." Its microinstruction width may be as small as 16 bits. The typical vertical microinstruction is divided into fields that have interpretations similar to those of a processor instruction, such as the function code, the address field, and a field choosing the instruction variant to be performed.

The second design option lies near the horizontal end of the spectrum. This design is based on a functional classification of the control signals in the implementation. To make this classification, we partition the host machine according to module or function, such as the register memory, the arithmetic unit, the shifter, and the condition selector. Examining one functional group, the designer can identify all useful control signal combinations that govern the activity in that host machine partition. After studying all host partitions, the designer divides the host's microinstruction, in a similar manner, into "fields," with the contents of each field being decoded (if required) to choose the particular combination of control signals that should be sent to the corresponding partition of the host's logic. This design approach leads to the decoder structure shown in Figure 6-21. A control unit implementation following this paradigm is said to be "horizontally microprogrammed."

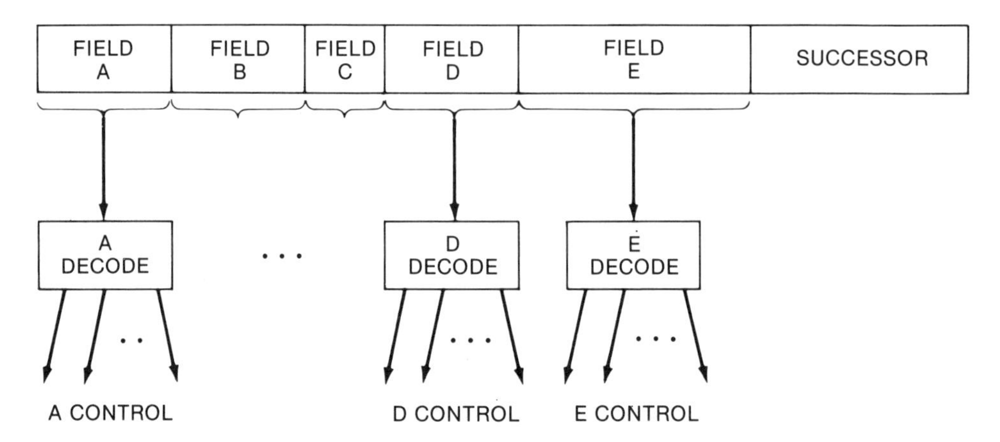

Figure 6-21 Decoding of a field-based microinstruction

Its microinstruction width may be greater than 100 bits. There may be more than 15 fields in a horizontal microinstruction; some may be decoded and others not.

Another way to reduce the microinstruction width is to interpret a microinstruction field differently depending on the contents of another field. Because of its increased speed and higher regularity, the horizontal microcode approach may be desired for realizing a large or fast system.

The problem of designing microcode control structures is quite different for vertical microcode than it is for horizontal microcode. Since vertical microcode is somewhat like a conventional processor program, the control design decisions for vertical microcode and for processor instructions are quite similar. Therefore, the control design selections for a vertical microcode implementation parallel those for processor control instructions, and the discussion of Section 6.3 applies to the design of vertical microcode control structures.

In this section we emphasize horizontal microcode. We use our common control paradigm, with a program memory (microcode designs usually follow a Harvard architecture), a microcode program counter (MPC), and a microcode instruction register (MIR). Figure 6-20 illustrated these basic elements of the control section. In addition to these elements, a sequencer attached to the MIR outputs will be used to govern the issuance of the control signals that implement the desired functions.

6.4.1 Sequencing Structures

In microcode many conditional sequencing decisions must be made; they decode the instruction being interpreted and they select execution sequences based on the data values being processed. Therefore, there is little benefit to be gained by providing a mechanism for sequential execution, whereas there may be a great payoff from supporting fast multiway branching. In this section we examine the general sequencing constructs to see whether they can be useful in or adapted to microcoded controllers.

6.4.1.1 Sequential execution. Sequential execution is not generally useful for horizontal microcode, since incrementing MPC takes time. Also, incrementation requires special hardware, and conditional branches are quite frequent. Under one view of an incrementation design, the incrementer determines each next microinstruction address (NMA) during instruction execution. But notice that one could precompute NMA and store it in the microinstruction, thus saving execution time at the cost of microcode memory space. In such a design each microinstruction contains a field to hold the NMA, as depicted in the format and data flow structure of Figure 6-20. This NMA scheme was used in Wilkes' first proposal for microcoded control [WILK53].

With the NMA field, there need be no relationship between the program's flow structure and its memory addresses. The microprogrammer may construct execution sequences that merge and flow arbitrarily through the address space without incurring any execution time penalty. However, sophisticated program development tools are required to cope with the complexity inherent in the flexible control flow structures afforded by the NMA design. All serious microprogrammers use such program development aids.

6.4.1.2 Conditional execution. Two-way conditional branching, in the form used in processor instructions, is not attractive for horizontal microcode. One detriment is the time delay to examine the condition value(s) and subsequently to gate the next instruction address into the MPC. Another detriment is the number of consecutive two-way branches required to implement a multiway branch. So we look for a better branching design.

One way to make a two-way conditional decision is to stuff the value of the condition being tested into NMA. This NMA structure will branch to either of two locations depending on the condition value. Figure 6-22 illustrates this technique to test the carry bit by stuffing it into the least significant bit of NMA. In this design, the two branch destinations have consecutive addresses. This contiguity is not a

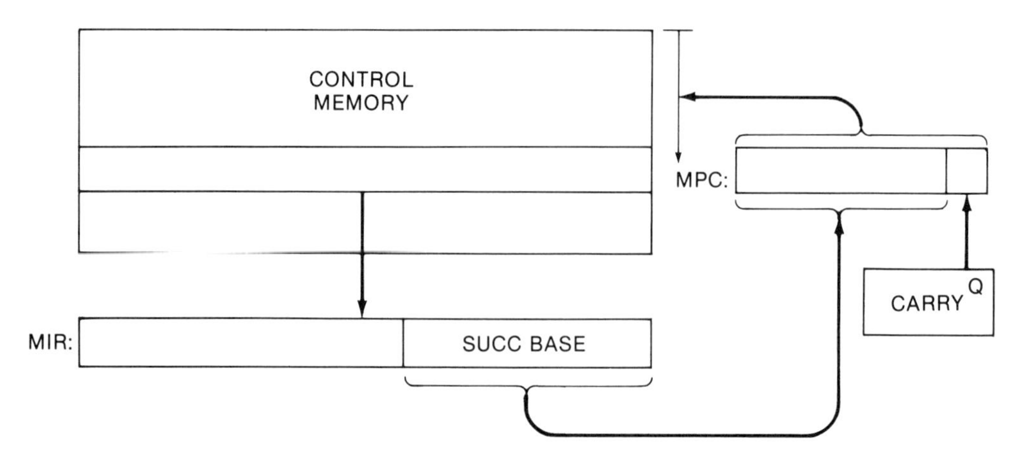

Figure 6-22 Condition bit stuffing for microcode sequencing

constraint, since these microinstructions can specify their successors' locations independently.

Example 6-33

Suppose that a microinstruction at location $A00_{16}$ specifies the selection of the carry bit (C) as the (bit 0) condition in the next address, and gives $AB0_{16}$ as the NMA. The next microinstruction will be taken from either location AB0 (C was zero) or location AB1 (C was one).

Another design that uses a machine condition to change the NMA ORs the condition being tested with the next instruction address (BASE) taken from the microinstruction. Figure 6-23 illustrates the structure of the next address determination logic for this design option. If condition C affects bit position k, and if $BASE_k$ is 1, the value of condition C will not affect the effective next instruction address. Thus the BASE encoding can be chosen to serve both as a base address and as a condition mask. Does this mean that no condition mask or selector is required? Probably not, especially if the number of conditions to be tested exceeds the number of NMA bits, as might be expected. Also, using BASE bits in this manner creates a bias toward addresses with bits set to 1; as a consequence, certain portions of control memory might be sparsely utilized.

We see that a fast multiway branching design requires a condition selector to choose the machine condition bits that will affect the branch outcome. The condition selection should be controlled by the contents of a microinstruction field. This structure implies a chain of logic gates: first, the selector value must be decoded to obtain a selector enable signal, and then the condition bit must be ANDed with the selector enable signal. Since several conditions could be directed to the same bit of NMA,[31] an OR gate will be required to combine the alternative status bits. Due to the length

[31]This fan-in will be logically necessary if the number of testable conditions exceeds the number of NMA bits.

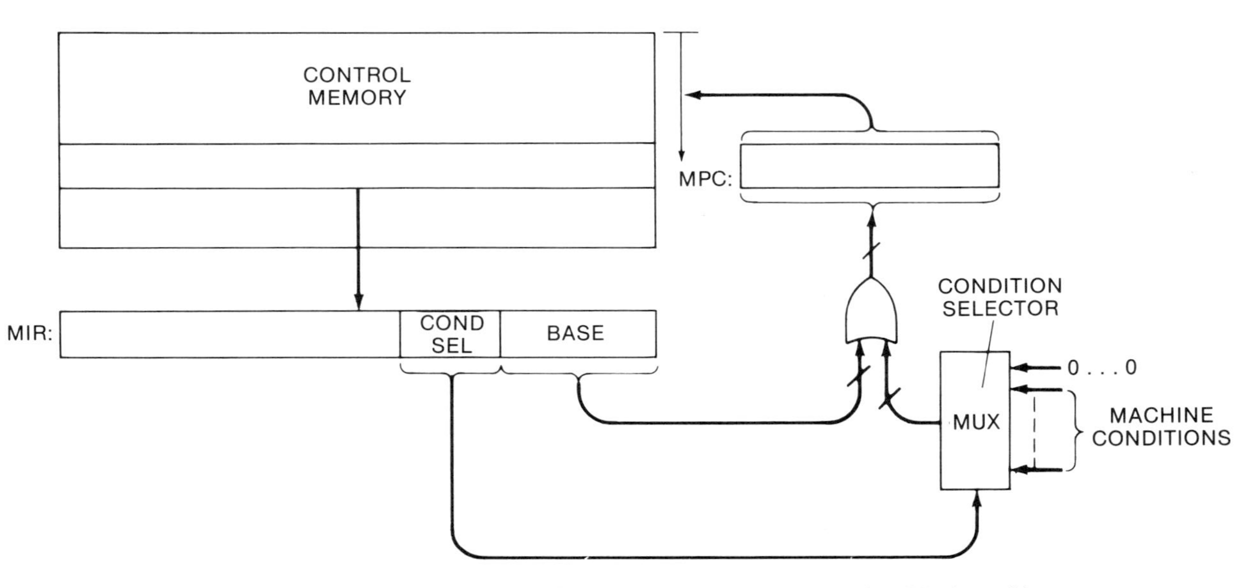

Figure 6-23 Conditional microinstruction sequencing implemented by ORed machine conditions

of this logic path, NMA determination could become a system performance bottleneck. One way to eliminate this bottleneck is to defer the use of the conditions until the next microinstruction has been executed. The execution scenario under this deferred branch design is:

1a. (See text below.)
1b. Read control memory into MIR;
2a. MAR ← NMA ‖ HOLDNEXT;
2b. The condition selector field of MIR is decoded;
2c. Perform the microinstruction in MIR;
3a. The selected condition bit pattern is selected and its value stored in HOLDNEXT;
3b. Read control memory into MIR;
4a. MAR ← NMA ‖ HOLDNEXT;

The actions with the same numeric label may be performed in parallel to speed execution. Step 1a is identical to step 3a. Steps 1b, 2a, 2b, 2c, 3a, and 3b together comprise the actions taken to execute the microinstruction read out in step 1b. Figure 6-24 illustrates the parallel execution of these steps. The control flow through

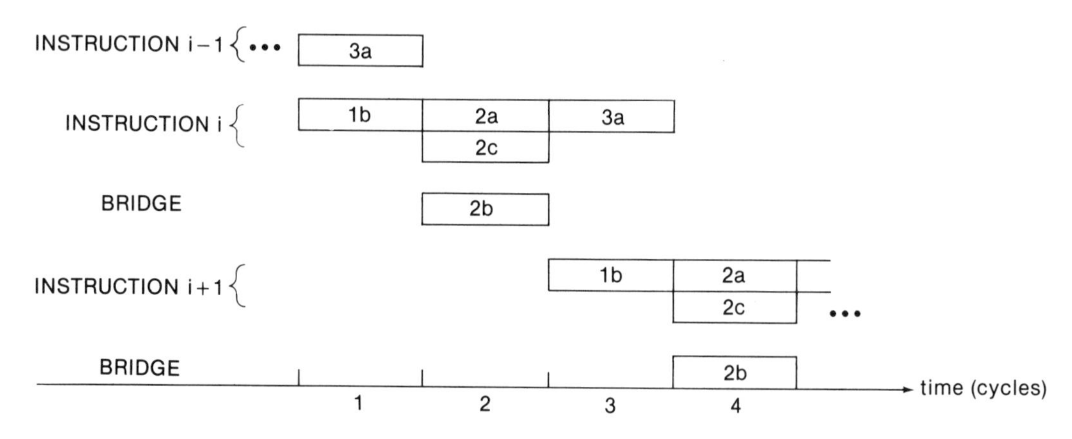

Figure 6-24 Overlapping microinstruction execution using deferred branching

the microprogram is determined by steps 2b, 3a, and 4a. Since MIR is reloaded in step 3b, the BASE address used to determine NMA comes from the microinstruction loaded at time 3, whereas the condition selection for its branch possibilities was taken (in step 2b) from the microinstruction loaded at time 1. We see that deferred branching permits the microinstruction execution cycle to be shortened from 4 clock times to 2 clock times. Deferred branching is commonly used in microprograms for this reason, even though the deferral makes programming more difficult, just as it did with the BRISC architecture discussed in Chapter 2.

Example 6-34

The PDP11/60 microinstruction sequence control uses a 12-bit microinstruction address, constructed from a 3-bit page number and a 9-bit index within the page. The page number is held in a "field" register (which actually could be the high-order bits of the MPC), so page changing requires special register transfers.[32] Control flow is determined by the 9-bit base address **BA** in a microinstruction and one of 32 selectable combinations of 6 bits determined from the machine status. Selectable patterns include useful subsets or functions of the function code, selected according to the target processor's instruction format.[33] A 5-bit microinstruction field controls the pattern selection. The branch control field is ORed with the least significant bits of **BA**, as illustrated in Figure 6-25. Deferred branching is used.

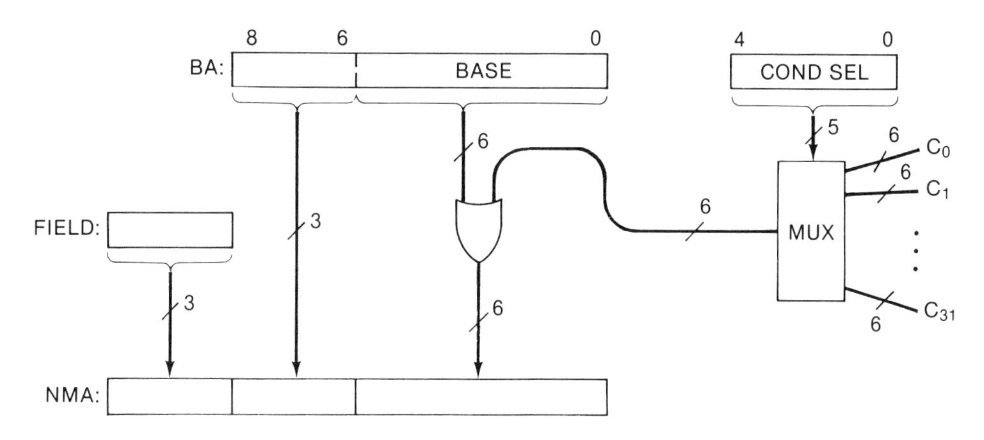

Figure 6-25 Information flows that determine the next microinstruction address in a PDP11/60

Two design decisions required to complete the multiway NMA branching design are:

1. Choose the portions of the machine state to be available for NMA determination.
2. Choose the NMA bits that can be affected by the selected condition.

The second decision is unimportant (see Problem 6-31). By contrast, a good selection of the parts of the machine state that can be tested can improve system speed by tailoring the host machine to the target architecture.

6.4.1.3 Loop support. Microcode loop support could be used to support the emulation of processor instructions such as bit shifting and bit serial arithmetic operations such as multiply and divide. The counting loop structure is adequate; a

[32]This is similar to one scheme for obtaining wide memory addresses, as discussed in Section 3.5.1.

[33]These patterns are selected to allow microcode to dispatch quickly to sequences performing important target processor functions.

loop termination test which determines whether a counter has reached a prespecified value, such as zero, will be sufficient. Arithmetic algorithms are not always amenable to a counting loop implementation. For example, Booth's multiplication[34] algorithm skips across contiguous blocks of identical multiplier bits and thus uses an unpredictable number of iterations to complete a multiplication. In contrast, the simple shift-add multiply algorithm requires a fixed number of iterations, so a counting loop in the controller would be useful.

To support microinstruction counting loops, the designer could dedicate a host register for counting and connect special loop termination test logic to the outputs of that register. The termination test output would be one selectable condition input for NMA determination.

Example 6-35

The 16-bit field length register FL and the 24-bit field address register FA in the B1700 microprogrammed processor [BURR72] contained the parameters for implementing an instruction whose operands could span many memory words. These two registers could be used in a microcode counting loop, with the COUNT microinstruction (this processor was vertically microcoded) controlling the loop iterations. One COUNT operand is the amount of the count. Variants of the COUNT microinstruction count these two registers singly or together, possibly in opposite directions. With an increment quantity of 24 (the ALU width), a loop could be easily constructed to perform serial operations on bit string operands. If the FL value should become negative or zero as a result of the COUNT operation, it would be set to zero and a flag would be set. This flag can be tested by a later instruction to complete the loop. The FL value is also used to define the width of the ALU operands; therefore, this loop structure will automatically handle operands whose lengths are not multiples of 24.

The B1700 loop counting scheme is related in a clever manner to the ALU width control; this simplifies the programming of operations on general operands. Other microcoded designs have used microcode counting for serial operation implementations.

6.4.1.4 Subroutines.

Microcode subroutine support is rarely provided, since speed is of concern, and the call/return overhead would be too great. A microprogrammer would not want to call a subroutine within the implementation of a commonly executed instruction. However, since the execution speed of an infrequent instruction does not affect system performance much, subroutine implementations for these instructions are quite feasible.

How much subroutine support should be provided? We consider only minimal subroutine support; in particular, the host could save only the MPC in a register, rather than in a memory stack. Although saving the MPC in a register prohibits recursion and subroutine nesting without further copying, these restrictions are not significant at the microcode level.

A host design that can be microprogrammed by the user should support a limited variety of subroutine calling.

[34] Booth's algorithm is discussed in Chapter 3 of [CAVA84].

6.4.1.5 Interrupts. Usually, microcode is not directly interrupted. The microprogram must emulate the host machine architecture, which includes responding to interrupts. A common way to support host interrupts is to include a specific flag or register summarizing their occurrence among the testable machine conditions. For example, a host register could capture the status of system bus interrupt signals. The interrupt status register test would be made only where it is convenient to respond to an interrupt. One simple rule governing interrupt testing times restricts the detection of interrupts to either the beginning or end of the execution of an instruction. (Both are not needed—why?)[35]

If microcode is not directly interrupted, there is no design issue concerning how interrupts are handled at the microcode level. We have just seen how interrupt conditions can be simply tested during instruction execution. To assist with this test, the host hardware might be designed to provide a single "interrupt present" bit that would be tested at the top level of the microcode.

6.4.2 Program Location

Harvard-style microcode is often used; the microcode memory is not visible from processor instructions. This design has several advantages, including: (1) The two levels of the system are separated, and (2) short addresses can be used for microcode sequencing. In this section we discuss three variations of the basic Harvard design:

1. Multiple microcode memories
2. Writable microcode memory
3. Microcode in main memory

The first Harvard microcontroller variation provides several control memories, each supporting a different processor architecture. The same effect could be achieved by increasing the size of the control memory. To avoid wide microinstruction address fields, the most significant address bits could be taken from a field register, whose contents would be controlled by executing a specific microinstruction, by executing a processor instruction ("change mode"), or by setting manual switches. With this design, support for different processor architectures can be provided; this flexibility can "bridge" customers from a previous architecture to a new design.

Example 6-36

The IBM 5100 computer supported BASIC and APL programming from two separate sets of control ROMs. The programming language was selected by a switch on the front of the machine. The switch position determined which set of control ROMs would be used to fetch microinstructions, and, therefore, which language was being emulated. Figure 6-26 illustrates how memory enables could be controlled to effect this scheme.

[35] A more complete discussion of interrupt design options is presented in Chapter 2 of Volume 2.

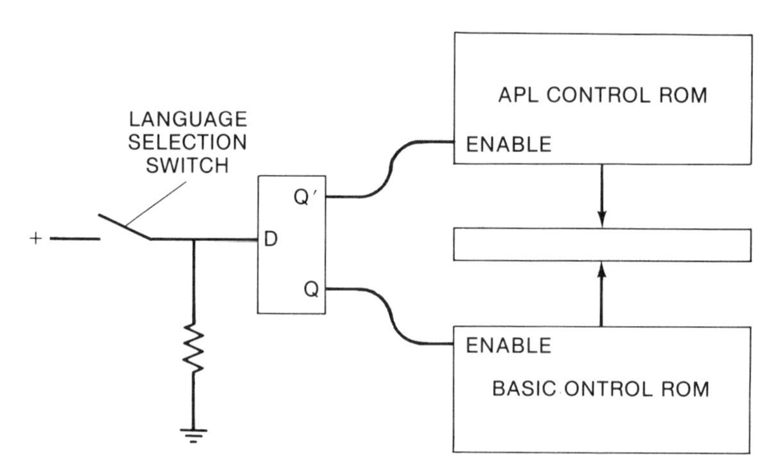

Figure 6-26 Control memory selection in the IBM5100 system

The second Harvard design variation permits writing into microcode from processor instructions. This flexibility allows a programmer to add interpretation sequences for function codes unassigned in the basic target architecture. Such an expansion of the processor's instruction set can be useful for the efficient implementation of operations on new data types or to speed the execution of programs written in a particular language. There are two difficulties with writable control memory. One problem is that the added microcode is part of process state. Thus if a process writes to control memory, the operating system must assure that these changes remain intact during all time intervals when the process is in execution.[36] A minor technical difficulty with writable microcode concerns the processor and microprogram word lengths. If the microcode word length is greater than the processor word length, to write one microinstruction word a sequence of write instructions has to be performed by the processor program. The control memory's controller could be designed to buffer the portions of the new microinstruction word until it is complete, whence the entire instruction word could be copied into the control memory at a designated address. For example, the PDP11/60 has a processor word width of 16 bits and a microcode word width of 48 bits, so three processor instructions are required to write one microinstruction. Experience shows that the ability to write into the control memory is seldom utilized in general-purpose systems, but it can be very useful for a machine operating in a dedicated environment. Notice that any program which relies on the ability to write into the control memory cannot run on another machine with a different host architecture. If the manufacturer, like many of them, markets compatible target architectures implemented on totally different host architectures, a program using writable microcode can be run on only one model of the host architecture. This constraint could constitute a severe program portability restriction.

[36]This requirement can be difficult to satisfy, since processor designs that support writable control memory may not provide an analogous ability to read the control memory—as would be required to save the process state.

A third Harvard design variation takes microinstructions from the processor's main memory. This feature could be used to emulate several different machine architectures that support different languages efficiently. The feature could also be used to cut system cost (if control memory is significantly more expensive than main memory). The microcode for the System/360 Model 25 was taken from main memory. System speed suffers and the usable memory space is diminished. With today's lowered memory prices, this reason for choosing to place the control program in main memory has vanished.

Example 6-37

The Burroughs B1700 system supported several languages through "soft" interpreters. The person implementing a language on the B1700 designed both a compiler and a "good" soft host machine for the language. The microcoded soft host machine was then implemented by microcode that ran on the hardware host machine. Each compilation output was labeled to identify the soft host under which it should be executed. The operating system ensured that the proper microcode was loaded before the program was executed. Such a design requires some overlap between the control store for each language S-machine and the control store supporting the operating system (see Problem 6-34).

By placing microinstructions in main memory, the designer can eliminate the cost of a control memory. If microinstructions are executed directly from main memory, the microcode word width should equal the main memory word width, but it could be a multiple of the main memory word width. In the former case, vertical microcode must be used. To improve performance, microcode caching, to be discussed next, can be added. This change also loosens the instruction width restrictions.

Example 6-38

The B1700 systems placed the (vertical) microcode in main memory, but the larger models included a fast microcode memory that could be loaded under microcode control. Figure 6-27 depicts (a simplified version of) the logic for accessing microcode in this structure. The FFIELD register holds the value of the most significant address bits for the block of microcode currently held in the fast memory. A comparator examines MPC and FFIELD to emit a memory enable to main memory or to the fast microcode memory. The fast microcode memory is loaded by a specific microinstruction.

In summary, we have seen that a microcode Harvard architecture is attractive, but there exist viable variations that can be useful in special situations.

6.4.3 Implementation

Several microcode-level implementation tricks may improve system performance. We consider microcode caching, field extraction logic, and indirect specifications of common control program elements.

6.4.3.1 Microcode caching. Caching microcode in a manner similar to placing a memory cache between processor-level memory and the processor itself is

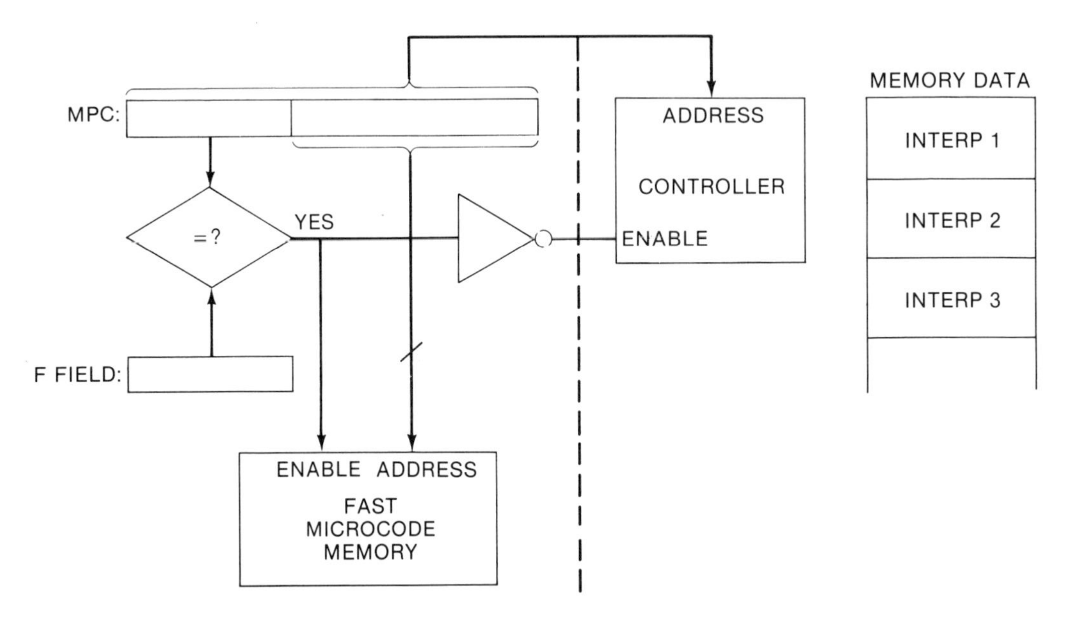

Figure 6-27 B1700 microprogram access structures

not useful. Why not? The processor-level cache succeeds because there is a great speed difference between the cache and the next slower memory, and because there is locality in the referencing patterns of processor programs. At the microcode level, neither of these properties are true. Regarding the first property, the control memory itself must be fast (for fast microcode execution). No cache memory technology is fast enough to realize a significant speed advantage over the fast control memory by inserting a cache. Regarding the second property, processor-level reference strings exhibit locality for at least two reasons, neither of which applies well to horizontal microcode. First, there is a lot of sequential execution in the processor's program. Horizontal microcode with a branch after each microinstruction does not fit this pattern. Second, a processor-level program may execute a long sequence to perform a "simple" function (at a higher level of abstraction); thus many instructions reference the same set of data, thereby enhancing the program's locality. In contrast, microcode, whether vertical or horizontal, executes the same function for the emulation of a single processor instruction—a relatively short interval. So one might conclude that caching is never worthwhile in microcode.

This conclusion (that microcode caching is never worthwhile) may be incorrect, however, if the microcode itself is not stored in a special fast memory. For example, a design placing microcode in processor memory can be enhanced by caching microcode in the processor, especially if the cache is big enough to hold a significant fraction of the entire microcode for the emulation. By carefully adjusting the microcode layout, one could collect related functions in small regions of microprogram address space, caching the set of related functions for the duration of the execution of instructions utilizing these functions.

6.4.3.2 Field extraction units. A field extraction unit selects and aligns a contiguous subset of a register so that the subset can be processed as a single entity. This facility could be used in many ways within a microcoded host processor; it could dissect an instruction's fields, it could separate the exponent part of a floating-point value from the mantissa, or it could separate addressing mode specifications from addresses. The major control-related usage is to separate target machine instructions into their constituent fields. Then the separate fields could be used independently to select registers and microcode sequences as required to perform the emulated instruction.

The control inputs to a field extraction unit specify the position p and width w of the field to be extracted. The internal logic can be simpler if the field position is measured with respect to the end at which the output is aligned. For example, if the output field is right-justified, p should be measured from the right end of the word. The data input contains the field to be extracted. Figure 6-28 depicts a field extraction module. Many gates will be required to construct the field extraction logic, and there will be many gates along a data path through the extraction unit.

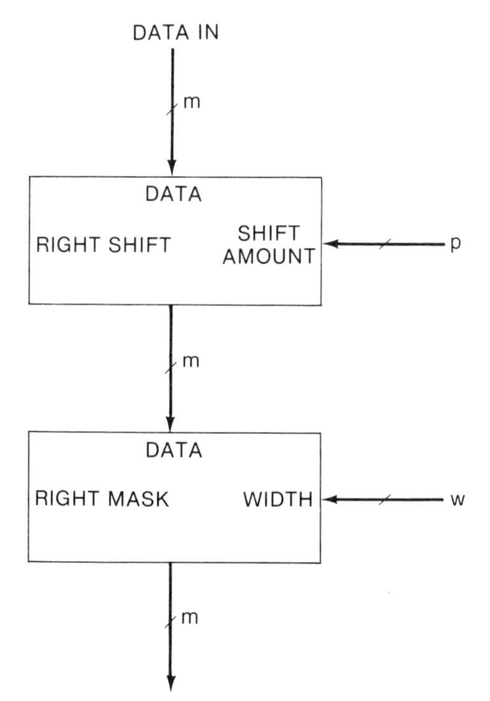

Figure 6-28 Field extraction logic (right-aligned output)

Why use a field extraction module? After all, any given field can be extracted by routing wires from the source to the proper destinations. If the host machine is designed to emulate a single target architecture, all instruction formats are known and all fields to be extracted are also known, so the host hardware register designations and selection logic can be designed accordingly. On the other hand, if the host machine must emulate several target processors, different instruction formats may have to be decoded, and specialized field extraction units may be useful. We could think of this design selection issue as a binding time selection. If hardware paths are used for field extraction, the field formats are bound at hardware design time. If general field extraction units are used, the field formats are bound when the microcode is written.

Example 6-39

The B1700 processors were designed to support a number of different target architectures, not all of them known when the hardware was designed. The designers chose to implement many divisions of the information in the registers and give them names, as though they were registers. For example, the F register in that architecture is divided into several named parts, as indicated in Table 6-5. Fields FA and FL, holding the values manipulated by the COUNT microinstruction (see Example 6-35), are both pieces of F. Both registers and (named) subregisters could be specified as operand locations.

TABLE 6-5 SUBREGISTERS OF THE 48-BIT F REGISTER IN THE B1700

Name	Bit Range
FA	47 .. 24
FB	23 .. 0
FU	23 .. 20
FT	19 .. 16
FL	15 .. 0

Source: After [BURR72].

Wiring-in field definitions improves system speed, just as wiring-in the machine conditions to be tested does. In both cases, wiring-in the definitions tailors the host machine to a specific set of target architectures. If another target machine architecture is to be emulated, the field definitions wired into the host might not be appropriate any longer, and the microcode would have to be changed to use a sequence of shifts followed by a masking to isolate individual field contents. This alternative is slower than using a field extraction unit.

Due to the delays they introduce, general field extraction units are not an attractive option for a high-performance host. Typical high-performance microcoded designs are tailored for a particular target architecture and use wired-in field extraction.

6.4.3.3 Short codes for common control elements. Microcode can be shortened if common elements of the microprogram can be assigned short codes. Some common elements that could be given short designations are: constant values, register numbers, and sequences of microinstructions. We discuss the program simplifications that short coding can produce, and warn of the decreased system speed that might result.

Many host machine designers have provided short selector codes that feed constant values to ALU inputs. Others have organized an array of constant values like a memory, permitting "normal" addressing to select the desired constant value. Designs that do not support short names for constant values must have some way of placing a complete constant value within a microinstruction. Since only a few constant values will be needed to emulate a host architecture, a small memory holding these constants can be advantageous.

The second possibility for shorthand names lies in register naming. If all host registers are arbitrarily placed into one register address space, each will require an address adequate to distinguish it from all other registers. In the spirit of Huffman coding, we should consider assigning short codes for registers referenced frequently. The host registers that emulate the target's address, data, and instruction registers are candidates for this special consideration.

Example 6-40

The PDP11/60 host architecture includes a 16-register memory addressed by a 4-bit code. The last four entries in the memory can also be selected by a 2-bit code in certain situations; these four entries contain three constant values (0, 1, and 2) and the memory buffer register.

The final technique for shortening microcode is to define short names for common sequences of microinstructions. Under this option, sometimes called *nanoprogramming*, a microinstruction may be implemented by a sequence of nanoinstructions, the latter specifying the host's behavior at a very low level of detail.

Example 6-41

The Nanodata QM-1 host [NANO72] was designed for general emulation; vertical microinstructions are implemented by nanoprogram emulation.

One conceptual generalization of the scheme assigning short codes for common patterns defines a small code to be used as the address of a wide entry in a translation memory that contains wide microinstructions. To provide variations, other microinstruction fields could be stuffed into the wide microinstruction before it is performed. This design is depicted in Figure 6-29. This two-level structure is similar to the two-level microinstruction-nanocode design, but it is not identical to nanoprogramming.

6.4.4 Representation

Since the representation of vertical microcode instructions is similar to the representation of processor instructions, there is little to discuss. With horizontal microcode, we have seen that the representation can be chosen so that decoding is reduced, especially if each field has a specialized unchanging function. Then only a small amount of decoding is needed. Although this desirable state of affairs requires wide microinstructions, it does speed execution. Some designers compress microinstructions by using the contents of one field to select how another field is to be interpreted. An implementation of this dependency may increase the decoding delay.

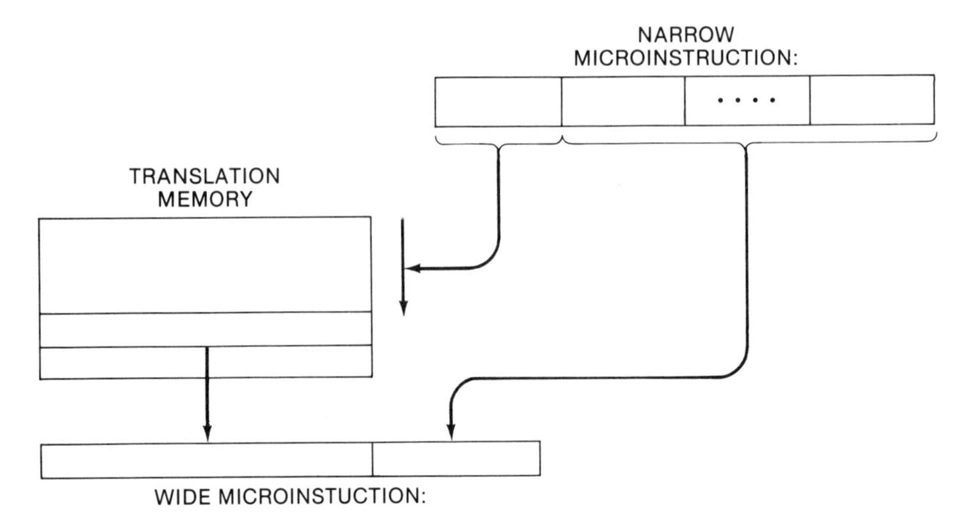

Figure 6-29 Translating a short code into many microinstruction bits

6.4.5 Microprogramming Control Summary

Microprogramming is an important implementation technique since it gives the manufacturer a simple regular implementation and it allows modifications of the control mechanism after the hardware has been completely designed. Control designs for microprogramming are slightly different from those used at higher levels, since the microprogram will be used for a long time and it is invisible from almost all people. Therefore, it can be worthwhile to precompute the addresses of successor instructions and to place those values directly into the microinstructions themselves. In addition, stuffing machine conditions into the successor address gives a powerful and speedy mechanism supporting multiway branching. Other microcode control designs, such as those that directly support looping and subroutines, can be implemented in a manner similar to their implementation at the processor level.

6.5 CONTROL STRUCTURES IN PROLOG

Prolog control structures are quite different from the conventional control structures to which most of us are accustomed. For this reason alone, we describe them apart from the conventional structures discussed earlier in this chapter.

Prolog comes in a number of incompatible versions, all sharing the same control philosophy and structure; they differ with respect to their built-in functions and a few representation conventions. Our presentation is based on [CLOC87], the third edition of an early Prolog book that has attained status for presenting a widely-accepted "standard" version of the language. This version is sometimes called "Edinburgh Prolog." Most other Prolog implementations include the features we describe. A Prolog overview is presented in [COHE85].

Several important assumptions affect Prolog's control structure; they include:

1. There is a single homogeneous database—a space containing both program steps and data.
2. Program execution is directed toward satisfying a specified goal.
3. A basic strategy for searching the database to satisfy a goal is built into the system.
4. Many operations work through "side effects."

Now we study these aspects in more detail.

6.5.1 The Prolog Database

Prolog supports reasoning about facts to draw logical conclusions, so Prolog terminology is oriented toward predicates, facts, and rules of inference. Thus we say that the Prolog database contains *facts* and *rules.*

A *fact* states that a predicate is true. It is written like a function or a word:

```
thing.
brother(john, bob).
```

Notice that each line is terminated with a period. The first fact states that "thing" is true. Therefore, if the system is looking to find whether "thing" is true, this fact shows that it is true, and we could say that the fact "satisfies" the goal. The second fact is a *structure* which states that john and bob (in that order) satisfy the predicate "brother." In other words, this structure might mean that john is a brother of bob. The ordering of the structure's parameters is important; we cannot conclude from this structure alone that bob is a brother of john. There may be another database entry stating that the brother predicate specifies a commutative relationship. A rule can be used to state such a general relationship.

A *rule* states a relationship between some facts or structures. Many rules contain variable names, which are distinguished from constant names by the fact that each variable name starts with a capital letter, whereas each constant starts with a lowercase letter.[37] Here is a simple rule:

```
brother(X, Y) :- brother(Y, X).
```

This rule states that the predicate brother(X, Y) is true if the predicate brother(Y, X) is true; in other words, it establishes the commutativity of the brother relationship. You see that the combination ":-" can be read "if." Notice that ":-" is not read "if and only if" because there could be other rules or facts in the database which specify other ways that the brother relationship could be satisfied.

[37]You may have been wondering why the proper names in the predicate were not capitalized; now you know why.

Let us look at another, more complex rule concerning the brother predicate.

```
brother(X, Y) :- father(V, X), father(V, Y), male(X), male(Y).
```

This rule is read "X is the brother of Y if there is a V such that V is the father of X and V is the father of Y and X is a male and Y is a male." You see that a comma is read "and." You also see that Prolog supports existential quantification ("there exists a ________ such that ________"). As Prolog attempts to satisfy its goal, it will, in effect, find one object whose existence was postulated, for if it cannot exhibit such an object it cannot claim that the goal can be satisfied.

The "or" relationship between two facts can be stated in two different ways:

```
alphanumeric(X) :- alphabetic(X).
alphanumeric(X) :- numeric(X).
```

or

```
alphanumeric(X) :- alphabetic(X); numeric(X).
```

So the semicolon is read as "or;" it may be used to shorten the database or to express a goal that could be satisfied in several possible ways.

6.5.2 Prolog Goals

Prolog is interactive; execution is initiated when the user enters a fact, a rule, or a query. When a new fact or rule is entered, Prolog simply adds it to the end of the database and the system awaits another user input. When a query is entered, Prolog initiates its goal-satisfaction algorithm. Here is a simple query:

```
?- brother(jim, john).
```

This asks whether there is some set of facts and/or rules in the database which leads to the conclusion that the relation brother(jim, john) is true. Given this query, the Prolog system will search the database trying to find a set of facts and a sequence of rules that together imply the truth of the query. If the search is successful, the Prolog system will answer with "yes;" otherwise, it will answer "no."

To complete the search, the system may have to assign values to one or more variables. All such assignments have to be consistent within the scope of a single rule. If some variables were assigned particular values to satisfy the goal, the system will print out these assignments before its "yes" answer is printed. If the answer is "no," there is no way to assign values to variables to satisfy the query, so no assignment of values to variables can be printed.

One may phrase a query containing a variable name. This type of query will find a specific object (if that is necessary) that satisfies the query. For example, the query

```
?- brother(john, Brother).
```

asks for a person who is a brother of john. The identity of that person will be presented among the variable assignments listed before the "yes" answer is presented.

Looking inside the system just a bit, the text of the user's query is taken as the system's goal, and the system uses its search strategy (see below) to determine whether the goal can be satisfied. The search terminates (1) when it finds a way[38] to satisfy the goal, or (2) when the search ends in failure because there are no ways to satisfy the goal. If the system indicates success, it has found one way to satisfy the goal and the user does not know whether there are other combinations that satisfy the goal. If the user responds to the answer by typing a semicolon, the system will search for a different solution. Repeated semicolon responses will produce a list of all solutions, followed by the answer "no," produced when there are no more ways to satisfy the goal.

6.5.3 Prolog's Searching Strategy

The execution of a Prolog program consists of a sequence of attempts to satisfy goals. To describe the execution sequence, we describe how a goal can be satisfied and how the search process proceeds.

There are two basic ways to satisfy a goal:

1. It matches a fact in the database.
2. It matches the left side of a rule in the database, and the right side of that rule is true.

To apply these rules, we need a definition of "matching" between a goal and a fact or the left side of a rule. The two objects being matched are structures. They match if their corresponding components match. This is a recursive match condition that eventually reduces matching to a comparison between two "simple" elements (i.e., elements that are not themselves structures). If neither simple element contains a variable, they match if they are identical character strings. If either or both is a variable, those variables may have to be assigned values to complete the match process. Table 6-6 summarizes the possible situations. In the table we characterize

TABLE 6-6 PROLOG ELEMENT MATCHING

Status		
Goal Free?	Rule Free?	Action
No	No	Match fails if they are not equal
No	Yes	Assign value of goal's entry to the rule's variable
Yes	No	Assign value of rule's entry to the goal's variable
Yes	Yes	Replace the rule's variable with the name of the goal's variable

[38]Some implementations find all ways to satisfy the goal, but Edinburgh Prolog and many others find just one way per query. In this text we remain consistent with Edinburgh Prolog and terminate searching when one way to satisfy the goal has been found.

the status of each element (in the goal and the rule or fact) by whether the element is a free variable. The word "free" indicates that the element in question is a variable which has not yet been assigned a specific value. An element is said to be *instantiated* if it has been assigned a specific value. The last row of the table merits special attention. When two variables are matched, a consistent assignment requires that both be assigned the same value. This is forced by renaming the rule's variable to match the goal's variable. This action does not assign a specific value to the variable; it just renames the variable. It is important to note that the name of a variable appearing in a rule is local to the rule; all the rules could use the same local names without conflict.

Given this matching rule, we turn to the process for satisfying a goal. We picture that process in terms of traversing a conceptual tree structure, looking for a way to *satisfy* the goal at the root of the tree. We describe the tree satisfaction process recursively, as follows. Each tree node is associated with a fact, a rule, or a goal. A fact node is always satisfied.

A rule node is satisfied if the subtree rooted at the node (call it N_R) is satisfied. The configuration of branches from N_R is based upon the structure of the right side of the rule; the subcases follow: First, if the right side of the rule is a single goal, that goal is associated with the only child node of N_R. If the right side was a conjunction of some goals (which were separated by commas in the rule), the rule node becomes an "AND" node whose children are the goals within the conjunction, listed in the order of their appearance in the rule. An AND node is satisfied if all of its children are satisfied. If the right side of the rule was a disjunction of some goals (which were separated by semicolons in the rule), the rule node becomes an "OR" node whose children are the goals within the disjunction, listed in the order of their appearance in the rule. An OR node is satisfied if any one of its children is satisfied.

A goal node has a child for each database entry that matches the goal. In the (conceptual) tree, the goal node is an OR node with these alternatives as its children.

The recursive goal satisfaction algorithm seeks to satisfy its "current" goal by seeking to satisfy the subtree rooted at the node in the tree corresponding to the current goal. Child nodes are processed in a left-to-right manner. The process amounts to a left-to-right depth-first search of the tree, whose progress can be controlled using a pushdown stack and recursive backtracking. To manage this search properly, each time the system makes a choice it records the search position and information about the current node on a pushdown stack. If it has to resume the choice search, it can pop the saved state and resume the previous scan.[39] When the user's goal succeeds, the stack's contents reflect the database entries used to satisfy the goal.

If the search to satisfy G reaches the end of the database, G cannot be shown to be true. If G is the user's goal, the system responds "no." If G is a subgoal, the system will backup and try again to satisfy the original goal, using new matching choices. Recursive backtracking organizes the search.

[39]We will see that additional information will have to be stacked for correct behavior.

Here are a few steps that describe parts of the tree searching process:

1. If G_i is satisfied and is part of a conjunction (a list joined by commas), the next goal to check is the successor of G_i in the list. If G_i is the last entry in the list, the goal appearing on the left side of the rule has been satisfied.
2. If G_i is not satisfied, the term in which G_i appears cannot be satisfied using the current assignment. The system must backtrack to the last point where a choice was made and retry that search.
3. A choice is made whenever one rule is selected to be satisfied. When several terms appear in a disjunction ("or") on the right side of a rule, a choice is made when one of these terms is chosen. If it fails, the remaining terms of the disjunction must be tried before the complete rule is considered to have failed.

These steps are not a complete description of the search rules. One aspect of this process not described here concerns managing the assignment of values to variables in a manner consistent with the semantic rules. Each time that a rule selection instantiates a variable or forces a rule's variable to match the goal's variable, corresponding entries in other goals may have to be changed. Making a new copy of the goal list each time that a new rule is selected is part of one solution to this consistency requirement. The reader can fill in the details to obtain a complete scanning algorithm.

6.5.4 Controlling the Search Process

We are ready to see how a Prolog programmer can exercise some control over the search process. The first control method relies on the order of the database entries. Improper ordering can result in incorrect answers or infinite loops.

Example 6-42

These two databases differ only in the order of their entries.

Database A:

```
brother(john, bob).
brother(X, Y) :- brother(Y, X).
```

Database B:

```
brother(X, Y) :- brother(Y, X).
brother(john, bob).
```

Given the query

```
?- brother(bob, john).
```

a Prolog system with Database A will answer "yes," having used the second entry to reverse the goal's parameters and the first entry to find its truth. In contrast, a Prolog system with Database B will loop indefinitely, repeatedly interchanging the parameters of the goal. Note that the complete satisfaction tree is infinite in either case.

Generalizing the problem encountered in the example, we see that a Prolog programmer should place more specific facts and rules ahead of rules expressing more general properties of the predicates in the database.

Not only must the Prolog programmer properly order the database entries, but he also needs some primitives to control the search process. Three special control terms are provided: success (expressed as "true"), failure ("fail"), and cut ("!"). Success is so simple that you might think it redundant; you are correct, but it is convenient, so it is built in. Fail looks even more obvious, but it is absolutely necessary to be able to force a failure.[40] You will see its importance in connection with the cut operator. Cut is a very important search controller. If cut is encountered as a goal, it immediately succeeds, *and* it fixes all selections made since the parent goal (the one on the left side of the rule containing the cut) started its search through the database. This means that any options selected since the parent goal was the current goal are forced be the only option once cut has been encountered as a goal. The cut effectively commits the satisfaction of the parent goal to the choices that have been made in that rule up to the point of the cut. The cut states that there shall be no other ways to satisfy the parent goal, *unless* the search backtracks far enough to remove the parent goal from the search path. When the cut is processed, the stacked backtracking possibilities are removed back to the choice of the parent goal.

This database contains a simple use of the cut:

```
not(X) :- call(X), !, fail.
not(X).
wednesday.
```

The primitive named "call" initiates a search with its argument (X) as the goal. We follow the system's actions in response to two queries. The first query, not(tuesday), clearly is true. Here is how the Prolog system determines this answer:

1. Rule 1 is attempted; it matches the goal if X were assigned the string "tuesday," so the system binds tuesday to X;
2. Subgoal call(tuesday) is chosen;
3. Goal tuesday is chosen (since call always succeeds if its argument does);
4. Rule 1 is attempted; it does not match the goal;
5. Rule 2 is attempted; it does not match the goal;
6. Rule 3 is attempted; it does not match the goal;
7. There being no more rules, goal tuesday has failed;
8. Backtrack to the last choice, which was made at step 1 when rule 1 was selected. Go back to trying for the goal that was current at that point ["not(tuesday)"] and start the search just after the failure point. So the next step will try rule 2;

[40]In a strict sense, fail does not have to be built-in because one could simply insert a goal that does not match the left side of any rule. In fact, one could name it fail!

9. Try rule 2; this succeeds because the left side can be matched by setting the variable X to "tuesday;" this satisfies the user's goal since no unsatisfied subgoals remain on the list;
10. There being no unsatisfied goals, the question is answered in the affirmative;

Now follow the system as it processes the false query

```
?- not(wednesday).
```

The process proceeds:

1. Rule 1 is attempted; it matches the goal if X were assigned the string "wednesday," so the system binds wednesday to X;
2. Subgoal call(wednesday) is chosen;
3. Goal wednesday is chosen (since call always succeeds if its argument does);
4. Rule 1 is attempted; it does not match the goal;
5. Rule 2 is attempted; it does not match the goal;
6. Rule 3 is attempted; it does match the goal;
7. The goal being satisfied, the system goes back to the goal list it was processing, where it finds the cut;
8. The system drops the alternatives for a retry of the parent goal "not(wednesday)" (this means that the retry of the first search starting from rule 2 is canceled);
9. Cut having succeeded, the system moves to the next goal on its list, which is "fail;"
10. Clearly, fail is not true, so the system tries to backtrack; there are no remaining options, so the system responds to the user's query with "no;"

What would have happened if the cut were removed? In this case the database contains

```
not(X) :- call(X), fail.
not(X).
wednesday.
```

Again we present the false query

```
?- not(wednesday).
```

Execution proceeds as in the last case through step 6. Step 7 is almost identical except that the system finds "fail" next on the list. The final search steps are:

7. The goal being satisfied, the system goes back to the goal list it was processing, where it finds the fail goal;

8. Backtrack to the last choice, which was made at step 1 when rule 1 was selected. Go back to trying for the goal that was current at that point ["not(wednesday)"] and start the search just after the failure point. So the next step will try rule 2;
9. Try rule 2; this succeeds because the left side can be matched by setting the variable X to "wednesday";
10. There being no unsatisfied goals, the question is answered in the affirmative;

This result is not what we intended. Thus we see the utility of the cut and the need for the fail goal.

It is instructive to note that the program we have just studied does not really correspond to the conventional meaning of "not," but rather, the program returns "true" only if it cannot show that the argument ("X") could not be proven to be correct with the given database. This is not the same as proving that X is false.

Prolog includes other built-in predicates that allow the programmer to test conditions within variables and their values; some of these are listed in Table 6-7.

TABLE 6-7 BASIC PROLOG PREDICATES

Predicate	True if . . .
true	always
fail	never
var (X)	X has not been assigned a specific value (it is still a "free variable")
nonvar (X)	X has been assigned a specific value
integer (X)	X has a whole number as a value
atom (X)	X is not an integer and contains no spaces
atomic (X)	X is an atom or an integer
X = Y	X matches Y (also holds for integers)
X \= Y	X does not match Y (also holds for integers)
X = = Y	X matches Y, but with restrictions on assignments to variables
X \= = Y	Negation of the previous
X > Y	Both arguments are instantiated integers; the first is larger
X < Y	Use analogy with X > Y
X = < Y	Use analogy with X > Y
X > = Y	Use analogy with X > Y
A is B	B evaluated as an arithmetic expression is equal to A (see text)

The is operator forces the evaluation of the expression on its right side; without the is operator, the expression would be treated as a pattern to be matched. In a sense the is operator serves as both an assignment statement and an equality test. It amounts to an assignment (to a temporary variable) when its left side is an uninstantiated variable. It amounts to an equality test if the left side is either a value or the name of an instantiated variable.

In the next subsection we complete our Prolog discussion as we look at the ways that the state of the Prolog machine can be changed and show that any general algorithm can be expressed as a Prolog program.

6.5.5 Operations by Side Effects

The basic Prolog searching process is sufficient to answer many queries, but it does not provide general computational power or any way to modify the database permanently. In this section we show how Prolog can change its database through the side effects defined into some primitive Prolog predicates. We also will show how the execution sequence can be controlled to emulate conventional program sequencing structures. This exercise demonstrates Prolog's generality; despite this property one should not consider Prolog for inappropriate applications, such as numerically intensive problems.

We start with the use of side effects to make permanent changes in the database. There is only one basic way that a Prolog program can permanently change the database—by scanning a built-in predicate with appropriate side effects. Notice that the value-variable assignments made during the basic Prolog matching process do not change the database; these value assignments are only temporary assignments to local variables.

To make permanent database changes, the scanning process must encounter one of the basic language predicates defined with side effects. Some of these basic operations[41] are listed in Table 6-8. All basic operations must be considered to be goals; nonconditional operations always succeed, so when considered as goals the operations listed in the table should be considered always to be true.

TABLE 6-8 SOME PROLOG OPERATORS

Action	Description
asserta(X)	Add X to the beginning of the database
assertz(X)	Add X to the end of the database
retract(X)	Find the first database entry that matches X and delete it from the database

The operators asserta, assertz, and retract modify the contents of the database; they are similar to write and read operations. Two forms of assert,which is similar to write (actually, append), are required because the order of entries within the database is crucial to the goal-matching process. The retract operator deletes a selected database entry.[42]

We close the section on Prolog control structures with a short discussion concerning the possibility of writing conventionally expressed sequential algorithms in

[41]We have excluded input/output and file system actions to simplify the presentation.

[42]Note that the sequence retract, assert is not the same as write because the newly asserted entry may occupy a different position in the search order.

Prolog. To construct a simple straight-line procedure using Prolog primitive operators, place the procedure's specification (its name plus its formal parameters) on the left side of a Prolog rule and place the procedure's body, expressed as a conjunction, on the right side of the rule. Since the scanning rule will scan the members of the conjunction in the order of their appearance, the elements of the conjunction will be executed sequentially. One must be careful about the interactions between backtracking and the sequential operations, because any side effects are not retracted if the search process backtracks.

Example 6-43

The Prolog rule

```
f(X, Y, Z, A, B) :- V is Y+Z, V is V * (A+B), X is V * A.
```

is analogous to the following Ada procedure declaration:

```
procedure f(x out integer; y, z, a, b : integer) is
  v : integer;
begin
  v:=y+z;
  v:=v * (a+b);
  x:=v * a;
end f;
```

Notice how the existential variable serves as an automatic local variable.

This method for writing a Prolog analog of a conventionally expressed algorithm is adequate for a strictly sequential program, but does not work for other conventional control structures. Consider writing a Prolog program analogous to a conventional loop.

Example 6-44

One way to express a loop structure uses a cut and a universal subsidiary goal. The universal subsidiary goal "repeat" defines the beginning of the loop. It really defines a pseudo choice point to which the backtracking process will return each time that the main goal (performing the loop) fails (which will occur if the termination condition has not been met). Here is the loop structure, along with the definition of repeat:

```
loop(⟨var_list⟩) :- repeat, ⟨body_text⟩, ⟨term_test⟩, !.
repeat :- true.
repeat :- repeat.
```

The meta symbols (in angle brackets) indicate where the loop body and the predicate (true when the loop terminates) should be written. The cut at the end is necessary to prevent further executions of the loop if some predicate scanned after loop completion causes backtracking. This case is important for loop nesting. The reader should fill in the body and test for a simple example and trace the execution of this program.

We see we can argue that the Prolog language is general-purpose and that conventionally expressed algorithms could, if necessary, be expressed within a Prolog program. It should also be obvious, however, that thinking in terms of conventional control structures is really not appropriate for Prolog programming.

6.5.6 Prolog Summary

Prolog execution is based on a complex internal process which attempts to certify the truth of a query on the basis of facts and rules of inference stored within its database. Conventional program execution can be specified in the language, albeit awkwardly. It may appear that the truth of falsehood of a query would be based solely on the combination of facts and rules in the database. Although this is the case for simple databases, with complex rules the order of the information within the database is extremely important, for this order determines the sequence in which the facts and rules will be searched. A Prolog programmer can modify the order of scanning the database by means of the true, fail, and cut predicates.

The Prolog database may be modified when the scanning process encounters a predicate having side effects. Input and output activities are activated in a similar manner. In fact, any program can be mapped into a Prolog program, but the remapping of control constructs makes the program's structure appear to be different.

The Prolog scanning rules actually define a recursive left-to-right depth–first tree searching process. The implementation of this scanning process would be greatly assisted by efficient stack operations that keep account of the tree searching process. The recursive scanning process requires many stack operations. Unfortunately, it is also true that the required sequential search rules imply sequential execution; this fact makes it difficult to design a Prolog execution mechanism that effectively uses parallelism while following a strict interpretation of the defined semantics. Parallelism can be used effectively to search for all patterns that satisfy a query, or when the coupling among clauses (through variables) is weak.

It is possible to speed up the Prolog scanning process. One technique creates an internal division of the facts and rules into groups such that any one scan can be confined to a single group. Each Prolog database scan looks for a rule or fact that matches the current goal. One invariant during this scan is the name of the predicate (or the first word of the fact, if the goal is a fact). We simply use a name mapping strategy (Section 5.2) to map predicate names into group identifiers; the search can be confined to the group whose identifier is the mapped version of th goal's predicate name.

In Section 7.5 we discuss LISP, a predecessor of Prolog with which Prolog shares many aspects. In particular, LISP is interactive, its data types include character strings, its programs can be manipulated like data (this is true of Prolog, but we excluded it from this short summary), and database entries can be changed as a result of side effects within functions. Among the important differences between Prolog and LISP is the difference in emphasis on certain datatypes. Prolog emphasizes character strings, whereas LISP emphasizes lists.

6.6 SUMMARY

We have discussed the control of a single process in a computer system. We addressed several important design decisions, such as the selection of sequencing structures and the representation of the instructions themselves. We saw that "functional" languages (like Prolog) have different control sequencing rules.

At high levels, where programs are frequently rewritten, the control structure choice should be dominated by the desire for clarity in the program's structure. At lowest levels, by contrast, the designer is not very concerned with these niceties and many control structure decisions are dominated by system speed requirements. Similarly, program location selections vary from a data/program memory at the highest levels to separate control memories at the microcode level. The representations of the instructions themselves become more complex as the lower levels are reached. Implementation techniques must be carefully selected at each level.

We also explored Prolog, a language with an unconventional execution model based on searching a database to find a way to satisfy a query presented by the user. We showed some essential parts of an argument to convince you that Prolog is indeed a general-purpose programming language. Although this generality may be reassuring, it should not be taken as an argument that every application should be programmed in Prolog.

6.7 PROBLEMS

6-1. Consider a **case** structure in which the selector expression may have values in the range 0 .. 63, with all values within that range equally probable. Let c_i denote the count of the number of instruction words corresponding to a direct translation of the statement list for expression value i. (This count does not include any branch instructions that might be inserted at the end of the statement list to skip over the others and reach the instructions corresponding to the statement after the **case** statement.) Table 6-9 specifies a frequency distribution of c_i.

TABLE 6-9 FREQUENCY DISTRIBUTION OF STATEMENT LENGTHS

Number of instruction words	0	1	2	3	4	5	6	7	8	9	10	13	15	18
Number of cases	2	4	10	18	9	7	4	3	2	1	1	1	1	1

In this problem you will evaluate some design options concerning the implementation of the **case** branching using computed destination addresses. The branch address computation will use the value of the selector shifted by an amount that you will select; the result will be the destination address of the branch instruction. Figure 6-30 illustrates this destination address computation. Note that the initial instructions of the **case**

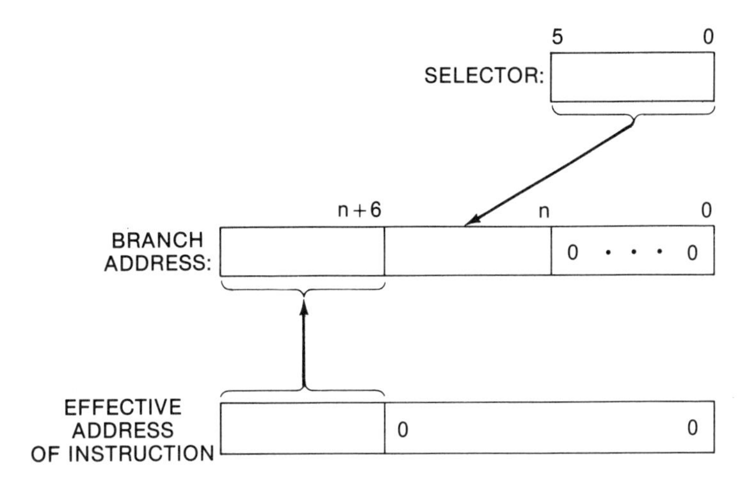

Figure 6-30 Determining the CASE destination address

statement blocks are separated by 2^n words, where n is the amount of the shift. Define the "branch target area" to include the locations between B and $B + 2^{n+6}$, where B is the "base" branch location used if the **case** selector is zero. In this problem consider $n =$ 2, 3, and 4 only. If an instruction sequence does not fit into the space between branch destinations, the maximum possible subsequence of the instruction sequence will be placed there and the last word will be filled with a branch instruction which occupies the whole word. This branch instruction takes the execution point away from the branch target area. Figure 6-31 illustrates this program flow.

(a) Outline a strategy for placing the instruction words within memory.

(b) Determine I_n, the total number of instruction words required for the complete implementation of the **case** statement, for $n = 2$, 3, and 4. Why is $I_n > \Sigma\, c_i$?

(c) What is the smallest n such that $I_n = I_{n+1}$?

(d) Let J_n denote the number of instruction words within the branch target area that contain instructions executed for statements in the **case** statement lists. Find J_n, for all n. Include those branch instructions that pass control to the next statement as part of the set of instructions executed for the statements in the **case** lists. Do not count any additional branch instructions that may have to be inserted to overcome the limitations imposed by the branch address computation.

6-2. Describe a strategy for converting a Cobol program that contains dynamic **goto**s changed by ALTER to another Cobol program which uses only the selected **goto** for dynamic branching.

6-3. We are trying to solve the following problem: A label variable, like an entry point variable, must be associated with an execution environment. In recursive situations each block may have been invoked several times. Labels associated with any of the invocations might have been passed through parameter passing to contexts where the label's execution environment is not part of the current execution context. We want the system to move to the proper context if asked to goto the label variable.

Discuss and compare the following two proposed solutions to this problem:

1. The "value" of each label variable contains a pointer to an activation block defining the appropriate execution environment.

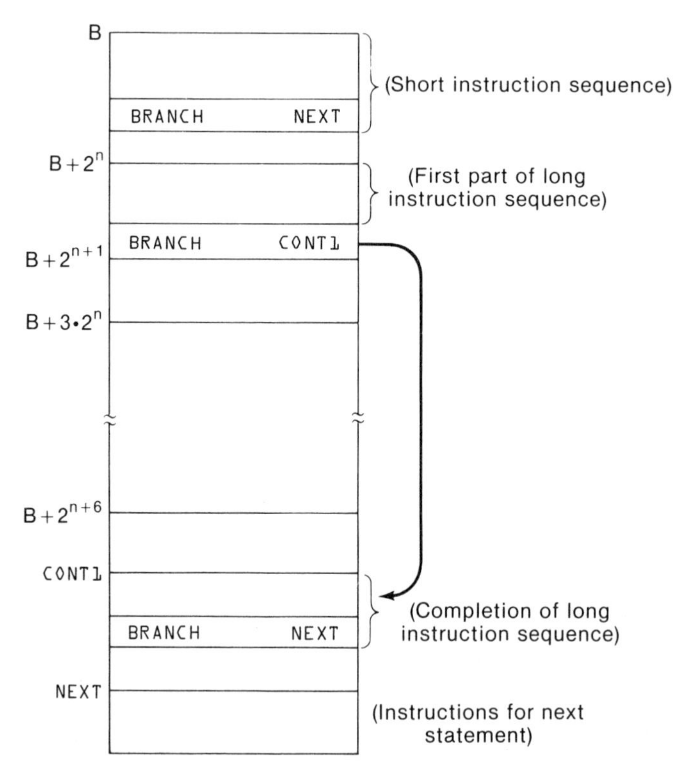

Figure 6-31 Program structure for Problem 6-1

2. The "value" of each label variable does not contain any execution environment information. Rather, the dynamically most recent activation of the program block containing the label value's declaration will become the execution environment after the goto is taken.

For an example that illustrates the different semantics of the two proposals, consider this program structure:

```
procedure k is
  procedure f(lab : in out label; .. ) is    --not Ada
    b1, b2, b3, b4 : boolean;
    procedure g is
      h1 : label;          --not Ada
    begin
      ..
    《h》 if b2 then
           h1 := h;        --not Ada
         else
           h1 := lab;      --not Ada
         end if;
         ..
         lab := h1;        --not Ada
         f(h1, ..);
    end g;
```

```
        begin
          ..
          if b1 then
            g;                    --function call
          end if;
          ..
          if b4 then
            goto lab;
          end if;
        end f;
      begin
        ..
        f(place, .. );
        ..
      《place》  ..
      end k;
```

Take this execution history:

k calls f
f calls g
g calls f
f calls g
g calls f

After the last call, the stack contains six activation blocks.

Now assume that in this (third) activation of f condition b4 is true and the **goto** lab statement is executed. What is on the activation block stack after the goto? Under proposal 1, it would contain either 1, 3, or 5 blocks. Under proposal 2, it would contain either 1 or 5 blocks. The exact numbers depend on the values of the boolean quantities during previous invocations of the procedures. All activation blocks corresponding to modules that must be aborted (because there is no way to complete them) as a consequence of the **goto** are to be discarded upon execution of the **goto**.

6-4. This problem explores the relationship between exception control flow rules and the use of the stack by the exception-handling program. There is but one stack per process.

(a) Show an example that illustrates how the exception handler could use addressing relative to the top of the stack to access objects stored during the execution of the "normal" program for the block where the exception handler is defined. Assume that the Ada exception control flow model is being followed.

(b) Now construct an example to show why the scheme of part (a) cannot be used if the exception control flow rules allow a return to the procedure where the exception occurred.

6-5. The following program includes a guarded **do** statement. There is no information available about the properties of the functions f and g. Despite this lack of information, what can you say about conditions in the visible objects (x and y) after the **do** completes execution? Assume that the **do** does, in fact, terminate. (Can you actually tell whether this is the case or not?)

```
x, y : integer;
..
do loop
  when x > 7 => f(x,y);
  when x < 5 => g(x,y,3);
end loop;
```

6-6. Construct an Ada program whose control flow structure is equivalent to a guarded **do**. Do not use **gotos**. Provide two different solutions, one for each of the following options regarding the selection of the enabled statement that will be executed. Each solution should be equivalent to a strategy for converting an arbitrary guarded **do** statement into an "equivalent" Ada program.

(a) Perform the first (in order of appearance in the program) enabled statement each time the **do** loop is performed.

(b) Perform a randomly selected one of the enabled statements each time the loop is performed.

6-7. Consider a processor in which some instructions are shorter than one word; these short instructions may be packed into single words.

(a) Assume that all instructions are the same length (16 bits) and that the word length is double the instruction length. The memory data interface passes words between the processor and memory. Write an instruction fetch procedure (named fetch_next) to be used in the following package specifying the processor's program execution.

```
generic
  n : integer;
package program_type is
  type program is array (1 .. n) of word;
  procedure execute(p : program);
  procedure load(p : out program; b : buffer);
    --makes the contents of buffer b become a program,
    --loading it into the program object p
end program_type;

package body program_type is
  counter : integer;
    --program counter for indexing to a word of the program
  left_next : boolean;
    --indicates which half of the word indexed by
    --the counter contains the next instruction;
    --when true, the left is next (it is first)
  function fetch_next (counter : in out integer; side : in out boolean)
    return instruction is
  .. --etc.
end program_type;
```

Write the program to minimize memory accesses. It will help to keep the most recently fetched program word in a location local to the program_type package.

(b) Now assume that all instructions that can perform sequence control functions by modifying the contents of the counter may, in fact, load or store the counter's value, but left_next is always set true when counter is loaded. Are there restrictions on the location of branch destinations in the program space? How might an assembly program enforce this restriction without requiring that a programmer know which half of an instruction word is occupied by any specific instruction?

(c) Define the interrupt response time to be the elapsed time between the (asynchronous) occurrence of the interrupt signal and the fetch of the first instruction of the interrupt handler. With the combined assumptions of parts (a) and (b), are there restrictions on interrupt response times? What are their consequences? Relate the worst-case interrupt response time under these assumptions to the worst-case interrupt response time achieved if the left_next value could be loaded and stored.

6-8. In this problem you will evaluate the effects of varying the amount of information accessed during one memory cycle on the time required to access instructions. Let W_i denote the width of a single instruction, and let W_m denote the data widths of the memory and of the processor–memory interface (which has the same data width as the memory). Consider a typical instruction execution sequence, including both instruction fetch and execution.

(a) Consider a fixed program without branch instructions. Sketch the curve of the total time used to access instructions as a function of W_m. Although W_m values that are not multiples of W_i may not have a simple interpretation, interpolate a smooth curve through the meaningful points (for those W_m values that are integer multiples of W_i). Assume that the processor can hold all the information obtained in a single memory access in an internal program buffer. An instruction held in the program buffer can be executed without requiring a memory reference to fetch the instruction. The program buffer does not retain old information after a later memory access is made for an instruction fetch. In other words, the program buffer can hold only the most recent program word(s) read in one memory access.

(b) Let f denote the frequency of jump instructions. Plot a curve showing the total instruction access time as a function of W_m for $f \neq 0$. Explain any differences from the answer to part (a).

6-9. A Harvard architecture contains a program memory separate from the data memory. A designer proposes that the same separation could be achieved by providing two memory maps in the MMU—the instruction address map would be used when fetching instructions and the data address map would be used when accessing data objects. Would this scheme provide all/some/none of the benefits claimed for the Harvard architecture? Explain.

6-10. One could design a "two-address" processor in which each instruction specifies the location of the next instruction to be executed, even if no branch is required. Two next instruction addresses must be specified in a conditional branch instruction or a CALL instruction. This capability might be useful for a number of reasons, including:

1. Instructions might be stored in a non-random-access memory device.

2. Instruction execution times might be variable.

Discuss the degree to which these reasons apply to the following cases. For each case recommend whether two-address instructions should be used. All data objects are stored in the same memory device as the instructions.

(a) All instructions and data are stored on a physically rotating memory device, and executed directly from this device (i.e., they are not buffered in a random-access memory). A word stored in the rotating memory can be accessed only when the word is passing a fixed "read station."

(b) Instructions are stored in a serial shift-register memory which requires frequent refreshing (by reading all objects in the memory). The memory's shift control logic permits an external controller to suspend shifting for a limited period of time. The shift control logic limits the suspension time by forcing shifting whenever the time since the last shift exceeds T.

6-11. A system designer argues that there is no logical requirement that a system support branch instructions with run-time modifiable destinations. It is trivial to see that a solution which simply emulates all statements will do the job. We seek other approaches to the problem.

(a) Show how the effect of label variables in a high-level language could be emulated in a system that allows only selected **gotos**. If your approach requires help from the compiler or the linker, specify the assistance needed from each.

(b) Explain why a designer might want to think of implementing dynamic destinations at the processor level.

(c) Discuss the relationship between this problem and the issues presented in Problem 6-3.

6-12. A designer is proposing a new processor instruction set. He suggests that the design would be simpler if the only conditional execution support were through conditional skip instructions. Each of these instructions tests processor status in a manner specified within the function code. The processor then skips the next instruction in the program if the condition is true.

Discuss the viability of this design philosophy at the processor level and also at the microcode level. In thinking about the microcode level, assume that the machine is to implement the instruction set of a general-purpose processor of conventional design, such as the IBM 370.

6-13. Select a familiar machine and determine whether its processor instruction set includes skip instructions. If so, show how that particular set of skip instructions could be used to implement counting loops, such as Ada **for** loops.

6-14. Select a familiar machine and list all machine conditions that can be tested by its conditional branch instructions. Are there any machine conditions that can be set during program execution but that cannot be tested by conditional branch instructions?

6-15. A designer proposes a new general CASE instruction to be included in a processor design. The operands of the proposed instruction are a value V and the addresses of two tables. Value V is treated as an unsigned integer. To execute the instruction, the processor sequentially scans through table1 until an entry is found that exceeds the operand value. Let i denote the position in table1 where this inequality test is satisfied. Thus we know that

$$V \geq \text{table1}(j) \quad \text{for all } j \text{ such that } 1 \leq j < i$$
$$V < \text{table1}(i)$$

The program counter will be loaded from table2(i).

(a) Discuss the relationship between this instruction and the Ada **case** statement.

(b) Compare this instruction to the VAX CASE statement presented in Example 6-10.

(c) Do you recommend the inclusion of the proposed CASE instruction? Explain. Consider the execution of Fortran and Ada programs.

6-16. Here are six techniques that could be used to provide subroutine capability

1. Provide data paths between the program counter and other addressable registers in the machine. Explicit copying instructions are provided to effect these transfers, but there is no other way to get at or modify the contents of the program counter except during sequential execution or through a conventional "jump" instruction.
2. Provide a special register R for saving the program counter. The only transfer path into or out of R or PC is a single bidirectional path between the two registers. Register R cannot be copied to memory or other registers. There are instructions that perform the replacement $R := R + C$, where C is an operand value. The program counter PC can be changed during sequential execution or during the execution of branch instructions.

3. Provide a hardware stack (fixed length) of registers with PC logically at the top of the stack. The stack is implemented by shifting values through a flip-flop array. Entries within the hardware stack are not accessible except by shifting them back to PC. There is no access to the bottom of the stack.
4. Same as technique 3 except that the bottom of the stack is an addressable register named Q. Values in Q can be manipulated by explicit instructions. In particular, they can be copied to and from memory.
5. The processor contains a stack pointer register that holds a memory address denoting the top of a stack; during CALL the PC is pushed onto the stack. During RETURN the top of the stack is popped to PC.
6. The PC is saved in memory location 4 on every CALL, and restored from location 4 during RETURN.

Answer each question for each technique. When you answer a question about a particular technique, assume that the technique is used without any additional features provided by other techniques on the list.

(a) Describe all actions necessary to manipulate PC values to effect subroutine call and return activity. Consider nonreentrant (simple), reentrant,[43] and recursive routines. If the implementation requires software support, mention in your description the activities relegated to the software.

(b) Are any restrictions imposed on potential subroutine structures by the option being discussed? What are they?

(c) Discuss the advantages and disadvantages of the option.

(d) Assign importance ranks to each of the advantages and disadvantages you described in part (c). For evaluation use terms like "irrelevant," "not very important," or "extremely important." Complete this evaluation for each of these two cases:

(i) Assembly language programs are implemented using the technique. In other words, the actions described in part (a) take place when the machine instruction CALL is executed.

(ii) The microprogram to emulate a general-purpose machine is implemented using the technique. A CALL within the microprogram uses the actions described in your answer to part (a).

6-17. This problem concerns two ways to realize **while** loops, one using software and the other using a new processor instruction.

(a) Show that the effect of the construct

```
while ⟨boolean⟩ loop
   ⟨statement_list⟩;
end loop;
```

can be implemented using the construct

```
until ⟨boolean⟩ loop
   ⟨statement_list⟩;
end loop;
```

without any **goto** statements.

[43] A reentrant routine can be used by several different processes that are executing independent programs without any communication between the processes which happen to share use of the routine.

(b) Propose a processor instruction to assist the implementation of the **while** structure. Specify the operand(s) and semantics of the proposed implementation. Show how and where your proposed instruction would be inserted into the program by a compiler translating the **while** construct.

6-18. The examples in Section 6.3.1.3 cited several different processors and their instructions that support counting loops. We will use the three Fortran DO loops whose headers are specified below. The structure of the general DO statement is

```
DO n I = N1, N2, N3
```

Here n is a statement number, I is an integer variable name, and the Ni's are integer-valued expressions.[44] The semantics are: (1) The expressions N1, N2, and N3 are evaluated once before the loop body is executed; (2) the statements following the DO, up to and including the statement labeled n, constitute the loop body; (3) the mth time through the loop the counter I has the value

```
I = N1 + (m - 1) * N3
```

and (4) this progression of I values continues until $I > N2$, at which time the loop body is not executed, and the loop is completed. The loop body is always executed at least once, regardless of the values of the expressions Ni. Here are the three loop headers to consider:

```
DO 3 I = 1, 10
DO 3 I = 1, 10, 2
DO 3 I = 6, 20, 3
```

The first header implies a default value $N3 = 1$.

(a) For each cited processor, state how you would initialize the counter and its decrement (or increment) quantity (state which you are defining).

(b) For each cited processor, draw the structure of the loop control flow.

(c) Discuss any changes you would make if N3 were an expression to be evaluated during program execution.

6-19. Here are three alternative proposals to provide the capability of saving processor state during the procedure calling process:

1. Save all registers as part of the CALL instruction.
2. Add a single instruction that saves all registers in a block of consecutive memory locations beginning at the effective address specified in the SAVE instruction.
3. Each register can be saved by a separate STORE instruction, which is executed within the called routine as needed.

In each case, a complementary capability to restore the processor's state will be provided.

(a) What are the advantages and disadvantages of the three proposals?

(b) To compare the speeds of these three designs, make the following speed assumptions:

   1. Unless specified otherwise in the following list, each instruction requires two time units (this time includes both the instruction fetch and its execution).
   2. In design 1 each instruction fetch and each register store takes one time unit.

[44] N3 must be positive, and may be omitted, in which case it takes the default value of 1.

3. In design 2 each register save requires two time units.
4. In design 3 the register-saving program loop takes seven time units per register saved, plus three time units for initialization.

You are asked to determine combinations of the frequency of procedure calls and the number of memory cycles used to execute an "average" procedure such that each design is better than the other designs. The comparison criterion is the execution time averaged over all procedures. Assume that the frequency distribution (probability density function) of the number of registers i required by a procedure is given by $f(i)$. The value of the function $f(i)$ gives the fraction of function calls (measured dynamically) for which the called procedure uses exactly i processor registers.

(c) Compare these schemes against the MC68020 scheme in which the entry mask specified with the entry point is consulted to determine the registers to be saved on the stack. Discuss the differences between the designs.

6-20. Some of the subroutine implementation techniques discussed in Problem 616 do not support reentrancy in a single-processor system. Reentrancy is defined as the ability for two processes to be executing instructions from the same procedure body without either having completed that body yet.

(a) Which techniques do not support reentrancy in a system with one processor?
(b) Now consider a system in which each process is assigned to a separate processor, with the program located in a shared memory. Which techniques now support reentrancy? Explain.

6-21. Example 6-20 described the VAX CALLG instruction. Recall that the argument list for the called procedure is not located on the stack. The VAX also has a CALLS instruction which would be executed after the procedure's argument values (4 bytes apiece) have been pushed on the stack; CALLS establishes conditions for the execution of the procedure. The CALLS operands are an argument count (the number of 4-byte-long words) and the address of the entry mask for the procedure. A calling sequence is structured:

```
PUSH argument_n;
PUSH argument_(n-1);
..
PUSH argument_1;
CALLS n, proc_entry;
```

An address in the VAX is a byte address.

(a) Write a sequence of register transfers that performs CALLS.
(b) Draw a diagram showing the machine conditions upon completion of the CALLS.
(c) Write out the steps for performing the return instruction. Note that there is only one return instruction; a flag (saved with R_MASK on the stack upon CALL) indicates whether the call that entered the routine was CALLG or CALLS. If the call was CALLS, the return instruction removes the arguments from the stack.

6-22. The text claimed that the system's integrity could be compromised if the processor's operating mode were available to the user's program. Detail this problem and show how the system could be compromised if the mode were saved and restored during "normal" call and return instructions.

6-23. This problem relates to details of the iAPX432 procedure calling instruction described in Figure 6-16.

(a) Of the information placed in the new context during CALL, which is static information and which is dynamic information? Explain your answers and relate them to the sources of the information. In other words, if r was static and came from the instruction segment, you would state that the instruction segment was a static object, so the static nature of r's information and its location are consistent with each other.

(b) Write a sequence of steps that properly finds the new procedure and establishes its context. In other words, make an implementation of the semantics of CALL_THRU_DOMAIN.

6-24. A processor uses a hardware pushdown stack to save PC during subroutines. Since the capacity of the stack is limited by the hardware configuration, the stack control must be designed to prevent stack overflow. Notice that stack overflow could occur on any call. Interrupts and traps are handled like calls, necessitating saving PC on the hardware stack. This problem concerns the design of a hardware stack controller that interrupts the processor if any action is attempted that would imply future stack overflow. Describe all control information needed to implement this feature and discuss (1) how it could be managed, and (2) the tests that check for stack overflow.

6-25. A processor designer proposes to include an instruction lookbehind buffer to decrease instruction fetch delays. The buffer holds the n most recently executed instructions, using a fully associative search to determine whether a desired instruction is present in the buffer.

(a) For what control flow patterns would the inclusion of the buffer actually decrease program execution times?

(b) Our designer further proposes that the processor-level program be allowed to explicitly control the loading of the lookbehind buffer. Two new processor instructions—"Start instruction saving" and "Stop instruction saving"—are proposed. The lookbehind buffer retains the n (different) most recently executed instructions that were fetched while the processor was saving instructions. The instructions controlling instruction saving are not themselves saved in the buffer. You are to recommend whether the designer's new instructions should be included in the repertoire. Answer the following questions related to this decision.

(i) Are there any situations in which program speed would be improved by including the new instructions? Explain.

(ii) Are there any situations in which program speed would be degraded by including the new instructions? Explain.

(iii) Do you recommend that the new instructions be included?

(c) Compare the proposed design against one with processor instructions BEGINLOOP and ENDLOOP. BEGINLOOP would initiate lookbehind saving and ENDLOOP would stop saving even if the buffer was not already filled. If the buffer filled up during the loop, it would automatically stop saving when it filled up, preserving the instructions that it had saved before it filled up.

6-26. Consider a processor with a lookbehind instruction buffer and relative addressing on branches. A designer proposes that the buffer be controlled according to the following rules:

1. The buffer will be declared invalid if the processor executes a jump to an instruction not located within the buffer.
2. After a jump to a location within the buffer's address range, the processor will obtain the instruction from the buffer if the buffer location is valid.
3. Every instruction fetched from memory is loaded into the buffer when it is about to be executed.

(a) Define the logic for determining whether the destination of a jump instruction lies within the buffer. Be sure to consider cases in which jumps are taken from the middle of the buffer.

(b) Draw a register level diagram showing the registers holding the information needed to determine where an instruction is found (include the PC). Show the logic modules needed to make the decision, indicating the data paths between the registers and the decision modules. Also describe the functions of all the modules.

6-27. This problem is concerned with the policies for changing register contents and validity bits that control an instruction lookbehind buffer. Suppose that the program counter is divided into two fields:

```
type pc is
  record
    p : integer;
    i : integer;
  end record;
program counter : pc;
```

The two registers pp and j specify the buffer's range in such a way that the validity of a buffer entry can be determined from the logical expression

$$\{[(i < j)\textbf{and}(p = pp + 1)]\textbf{or}[(i \geq j)\textbf{and}(p = pp)]\}\ \textbf{and}\ \text{buffer}(i).v = \text{true}$$

Here buffer(i).v denotes the validity bit associated with the ith word of the buffer. Note that this test not only tells how to test a buffer entry for validity but also implies how the buffer entries must be managed as the program is executed. The test is designed to allow the buffer to hold all instructions for a loop whose instructions are located in contiguous addresses and which is short enough to fit into the buffer.

Specify completely a consistent set of policies concerning changes in the values of the pp and j registers and the v bits in the buffer entries. Your solution should be compatible with implementations of the processor's functionality without the instruction buffer; in particular, you should not have to add processor instructions to control the buffer. A solution with the smallest number of special cases is considered to be best.

6-28. Contrast the use of an instruction cache with the use of an instruction lookbehind buffer (as described in Problem 6-25) with respect to:

(a) Performance versus complexity.

(b) The types of program structures that are speeded up by including the cache or buffer.

6-29. Write out a sequence of steps that will fetch a complete MC68020 instruction. Recall that the need for extension words is determined by the addressing mode specifications.

6-30. Here is a designer's reasoning and claim: The destination address for an unconditional microcode branch instruction could be computed by the same technique used for conditional branch instructions. For any conditional branch, the host forces a machine condition into the low-order bits of the MPC. The machine condition to be used in this manner is selected based on the contents of the "condition select" microinstruction field. One way to implement an unconditional branch is to take the selected condition bits directly from a microinstruction field (this has the effect of forcing a constant into the selection bit positions). A second way to implement unconditional branching places the complete destination address in the next instruction address field of the microinstruction; no selection is used.

The claim is that the former scheme allows shorter microinstructions than the latter scheme. Discuss this claim.

6-31. Consider a microcoded host design in which NMA bits may be modified by selected machine conditions while a next instruction address is being computed. The text claimed that the detailed selection of which bits were modified was not important. Consider two designs, A and B, which differ only in the selection of affected bits. In design A, a condition set C can affect bit i of NMA, whereas in design B set C affects bit j ($j \neq i$) of NMA. Assume that bits i and j are not affected by any conditions not in set C in either design. Justify the claim by showing that a rearrangement of A's microprogram suffices to construct an equivalent microprogram for B.

6-32. A designer proposes a microcode control instruction that behaves like the VAX CASE instruction (see Example 6-10). The claim is that this structure would be useful for multiway branching such as used for dispatching based on the function code of an instruction being emulated. Comment on this proposal.

6-33. Consider the following suggestion. A microcoded host machine designer wishes to remove the need for MPC saving during subroutine calls. He proposes to design the microcode so that conditional branches can be used to return from the microcode subroutines. By selecting the branch conditions in the branch that performs the return to be identical to the branch conditions that caused the control flow to reach the point from which the call was made, the designer proposes to achieve a return flow that corresponds to each call. As an example, pick a microcode routine that might be called during the execution of a MPY instruction or during the execution of a DIV instruction. Within the subroutine's return instruction function code bits (from the target's IR) can be selected to distinguish the two instruction codes and thereby to reach the proper return points. In particular, a different return point would be reached depending on whether MPY or DIV was being performed.

(a) Discuss the reasonableness of the assumptions behind this design.

(b) In a second design (call it E) the microprogram establishes some coded conditions in a register R and then calls the routine; R's contents are used to select the branch destination that achieves the return. For the original design and design E, discuss whether the design restricts the use of subroutines in microcode. Explain your conclusions.

(c) For both designs, discuss whether the design saves anything when compared to a design with microprogram subroutine calling supported by saving MPC on a hardware stack.

6-34. In Example 6-37 the text claimed that there must exist some overlap in the B1700 design between the S-interpreter for a language and the S-interpreter for the operating system programs. Justify this claim.

6-35. A designer proposes building a microprogrammed host with two control memories having different speeds. The proposed strategy places the microcode for all frequently executed target instructions in the faster memory and the microcode for less frequent target instructions in the slower memory. Further, the designer proposes allocating a buffer within the fast memory into which a block of the slow memory's contents could be copied. This copying would be achieved by dividing the microcode in the slow memory into blocks based on the pattern of data types of the target instruction's operands. When one instruction from a block of slow memory is executed, the entire block within which it is contained will be copied into the fast control memory, from which it will be executed.

Comment on this design proposal. Would it be functionally reasonable? What addressing logic would be required? Would it provide a reasonable cost/performance figure? Would you recommend implementing it? Explain.

6-36. Show that one could design an operating system for a processor with writable microcode which would allow process swapping, despite the fact that the microprogram could not be read. Furthermore, there need not be any restrictions on the writing of microcode by any process in the system. The proposed strategy for achieving this goal is to force all microcode writing to be performed by a service within the operating system.

(a) What data would the operating system have to buffer to perform this task correctly?

(b) What steps related to the writable microcode should be performed by the operating system to swap processes?

6-37. We wish to modify the logic suggested in Figure 6-28 so that (1) the fast microcode memory address space is divided into four blocks, (2) a microinstruction within a block but not present in the fast memory will be loaded into fast memory only when some microinstruction in the same "slot" (of four microinstructions) is fetched, and (3) the selection of the four blocks that might be swapped into the fast memory is controlled by the microprogram. A BLOCK_CHANGE microinstruction is added to control which blocks are present in the fast memory. There are two operands for this instruction: (1) the block number (which is the most significant bits of the memory addresses within the block), and (2) the number of the block frame within the fast memory where the new block is to be positioned.

(a) Specify the controller's rules used to determine which memory will be used to read a microinstruction.

(b) Draw a picture of the modified control logic.

(c) Specify the actions required to implement the BLOCK_CHANGE instruction.

6.38. The text claimed that the logic within a field extraction unit would be simplified if the field's position were specified relative to the end of the register at which the result will be aligned. Justify this claim.

6-39. A designer claims that the use of a translation memory TM (Figure 6-29) has the following advantages and disadvantages:

1. System speed could be enhanced by overlapping execution; thus the TM design has little speed penalty.
2. The cumulative number of memory bits required to specify an emulator will be reduced by using the TM design.
3. The TM memory's contents effectively replace decoding logic.
4. Determining a good TM implementation of an emulator to replace one that was horizontally microcoded is a straightforward task.

Comment on these claims, taking a position about whether each claim is justified (completely, partially, or not at all) and explaining your positions. If your answer claims that something is possible, your answer should demonstrate an approach to making that possible. If your answer claims that something is difficult, support your answer with a sketch of a difficult instance.

6-40. Draw a functional diagram showing the major components of a field extraction unit. There are n bits in the input word, and the output is to be a copy of the w bits starting in bit position b. The bit positions are numbered from right to left. So if $n = 32$, $w = 10$, and $b = 15$, the output is to be a copy of input bits 15 .. 6. The output is to be right justified within the n-bit output data path.

6-41. Comment on the relationship between the design of a field extraction unit and the design of a granularity adjustment module (see Section 5.6.5).

6-42. Write a Prolog program fragment that corresponds to an Ada **while** loop. Be sure that your solution can be used inside a nest of loops.

6-43. Write a Prolog program fragment that corresponds to an Ada **case** statement.

6-44. Write a Prolog program fragment that corresponds to an Ada **if** ⟨boolean⟩ **then** ⟨s_list1⟩ **else** ⟨s_list2⟩ statement.

6-45. Explain why the use of the Prolog cut forces the programmer to pay attention to the order of the database entries. An example showing that the order makes a difference is sufficient.

6-46. Write a Prolog program that accepts the query

```
?- replace(⟨before⟩, ⟨after⟩).
```

The intent is to change the database by replacing the fact (or rule) in the first parameter with the fact (or rule) in the second parameter. Replacement means that the search order should be the same as before, with the "after" fact (or rule) in the position in the order where the "before" fact was located. (*Hint*: It may be necessary to write a recursive routine to perform the task.)

6-47. When Prolog attempts to match two elements and finds that both are variables, it preserves the variable name that appears in the goal by changing the rule's variable name to the goal's variable name. Explain why the reverse assignment should not be used.

6-48. Draw the structure of the Prolog search tree for the program in Example 6-44.

6-49. Write a program in a familiar conventional programming language to perform the database search inherent in Prolog's semantics. Omit the possibility that a clause actually causes the execution of a program.

6-50. Explain the claim that Prolog is a general-purpose programming language. Can you write a general emulator of an Ada program in Prolog? Do not try to do it!

7

OBJECT TYPES AND OBJECT MANIPULATION

The formula 'Two and two make five'
is not without its attractions.

— F. Dostoevsky

Spurious moral grandeur
is generally attached
to any formulation computed
to a large number of decimal places.

— D. Berlinski

The computer's ability to manipulate information makes the computer more than just a filing system. An inefficient, but logically complete computer system can be constructed using only one manipulation operation—integer subtraction. We need to add both operations and data types to implement general algorithms efficiently. We need a programming language that is "close" to the application. In particular, we desire a programming language with a set of object types and corresponding operations that are themselves close to the application. Abstractions based on object types are very useful because they encapsulate details of value representation and operation implementation. In this chapter we explore the creation of new object types, operation specifications, object representations, and operation implementations. We will see how designers can provide efficient, yet extensible, language and system implementations. We also present the design of a LISP-oriented processor.

How do these design decisions affect the structure of the underlying system? At the top level, adding a new object type specification may have little effect on processor design. An Ada programmer may use **package**s to build abstractions that support new data types; these extensions create software procedures within the program. Such extensions have no effect beneath the compiler, which implements operations for the new data type with calls to appropriate procedures. However, adding hardware modules at the processor level that operate on real objects would significantly enhance system performance if the Ada compiler were modified to produce programs that took advantage of the hardware assist. This compiler-hardware interaction suggests that we should take a comprehensive view of the type implementation options.

Many texts and articles cover the representation of traditional numeric and character data types and the implementation of operations on these objects (see [CAVA84], for example). In light of this other coverage, we concentrate here on techniques for adding new types and on nonstandard techniques for implementing object manipulations.

When a program contains an expression such as x + y * z, what does the system have to know and do in order to perform the intended evaluation? Here are some issues:

1. What is the type of each operand?
2. What are the operands of each operator?
3. What is the representation of the value of each operand?
4. How is each operator performed?

There are three operands and two operators in the expression. If this were an Ada expression, the object types would all have been declared before the expression appeared in the program, so the compiler would know the type of each operand when it encounters the expression. An Ada compiler uses algebraic precedence rules to determine that the operands of "*" are y and z, and that the result of this operation and x are the operands of "+." The value representations depend upon the object types and affect the method by which each operation is performed. All of the questions above seem to have simple answers for Ada programs. Actually things aren't quite this simple in all cases, because in Ada it is possible to define new interpretations for operators and functions, with the selection of the particular operator to be applied depending upon the types of its operands. Thus there is a fifth question:

5. How is each operator defined?

In this chapter we explore the answers to these five questions, and present optional approaches to each of these issues. Ada is designed so that all the above questions can be answered unambiguously during program compilation, but there exist other languages to which this observation does not apply. It is possible that all these questions have to be answered during program execution!

This chapter begins with a general description of system extension by introducing new types and operations. We will show the effects of binding time choices and how they lead to different ways of thinking about the implementation process. Our customary top-down structure will be followed within the first six sections—we start with a general description of the problem, the approach, and some solution options, and then we move to progressively lower system levels. Sections 7.2 through 7.7 address the five issues mentioned above.

The chapter begins with a discussion of techniques for type definition and implementation. We present the essential elements of type definitions. In Section 7.2 we discuss some ways that object types can be bound to objects; type binding is important because it affects the way that object contents are interpreted, and therefore how the contents should be manipulated when an operation is being performed. In Section 7.3 we survey techniques for defining operator-operand associations; these choices affect the interpretation of programming language statements and of processor instructions themselves. We consider the options regarding the sources of operands for object manipulation operations. These decisions may affect program understandability and execution speed, often in contradictory ways.

In Section 7.4 we discusses object representations. Object format and field encoding options are emphasized. A carefully chosen encoding can simplify operation implementation. A good field layout can simplify the important process of separating an object into its component parts prior to manipulation. In Section 7.5 we detail techniques for specifying operations on objects. The major issues concern how the high-level type specification is converted into an implementation and how the implementation can be made more efficient. In Section 7.6 we present some options for selecting the correct version of an overloaded operator and some ways that the processor design can be selected to make the system execute operations more quickly.

In Section 7.7 we describe the LISP language and architecture of a processor designed for the execution of LISP programs. This design utilizes some techniques introduced earlier in this chapter.

After reading this chapter you will be familiar with the use of type-based abstractions and some modern approaches to supporting diverse data types and their operations. You will see how frequently used operations and types can be supported at the hardware level, with infrequently used operations and types supported by optional coprocessors or software.

7.1 TYPE SELECTION AND SPECIFICATION

In this section we cover type selection and type specification, emphasizing relationships among type specifications and their influence on specification techniques. More options exist at high levels, so low-level aspects of type selection are given only brief mention.

Type selection chooses a set of types appropriate for an application. This process is more an art than a science. Types might be selected to match how one thinks about the application's problems. There are two levels: first one chooses some "basic" types useful for the application class, and later one may add specialized types chosen for one or more particular applications.

7.1.1 Basics

A *type specification* can define both the representation of an object of the new type T and the semantics of the basic operations on objects of type T. Ideally, both aspects are associated with a type specification, but some languages do not support such a complete encapsulation of a type definition.

What are the goals? Our main goal is to encapsulate type specifications so that few people have to be concerned with object representation details. In line with this goal, the type specification should distinguish externally visible attributes and operations from the (larger) internally visible set used in the realization.

A complete type specification includes both (1) the public, or visible, aspects of the type being defined, and (2) the private, or invisible, aspects. Good encapsulation suggests a simple external interface that defines the type name and an adequate (but not excessive) set of operations. Figure 7-1 illustrates the simple interface for an integer_matrix type. Each complete type declaration specifies all these elements:

1. type_name;
2. interface_specification;
3. representation_definition;
4. operation_definitions.

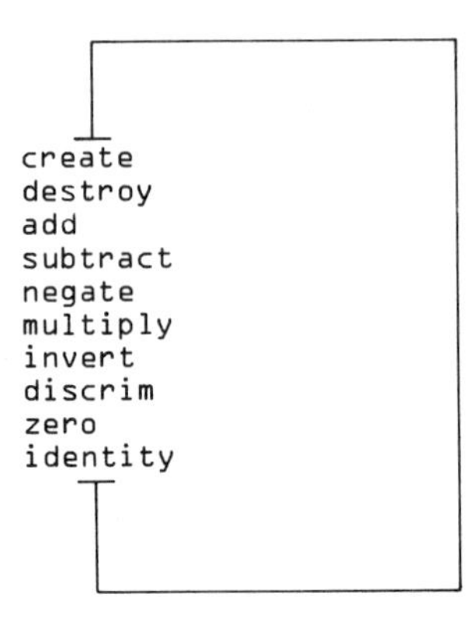

Figure 7-1 The interface of an integer matrix package

The type name and interface specification describe the externally visible attributes of type T. The operations are usually described as functions or procedures whose operands and/or results include objects of type T. The representations and operation definitions detail the actual implementation of type T; they are discussed in Sections 7.4, 7.5, and 7.6.

Example 7-1

The external attributes of the type integer_stack are its type name (integer_stack) and the externally visible operations (push, pop, and the predicate is_empty). The formal Ada **package** specification of this information could look like

```
package integer_stack_pkg is
  type integer_stack is private;
  procedure push(s : integer_stack; v : integer);
  function pop(s : integer_stack) return integer;
  function is_empty(s : integer_stack) return boolean;
```

```
private
  type stack_space is array(1 .. 100) of integer;
  type integer_stack is
    record
      space : stack_space;
      index : integer;
    end record;
end integer_stack_pkg;
```

The elaboration of the private type declarations given in the **private** part of the package specification is required in Ada so that a program in another module can know how to copy and compare (for equality) values of the newly declared type.

A complete type definition must detail the four essential elements listed above. This statement, however, does not mean that details must be recreated or reentered for each type definition—to avoid such drudgery one could incorporate some parts by referencing previous type definitions or by creating a specific instance of a parameterized type definition. If one is able to build on previous definitions, one can write a modular, understandable program that will be maintainable. We detail some hierarchical type definition techniques as we present some type-related features of high-level languages in the next section.

7.1.2 High-Level Languages

One type-related design decision selects the *base types* of a language. Base type selection considers the anticipated applications for programs written in the language. It is easy to suggest the base type selections shown in Table 7-1.

TABLE 7-1 PREFERRED DATA TYPES FOR PROCESSOR SUPPORT BASED ON APPLICATION AREA

Application Area	Most Preferred Data Type(s)
Scientific	Reals, integers
Business	Character strings, decimal integers
Artificial intelligence	Lists

When a language is being defined and its base types are being selected, it is almost impossible to anticipate the range of actual needs of program creators and of people's views of application algorithms. For expansion, the language might support new type definitions and type-based modularization.

Type declarations can be used for language expansion. What are our desires? We wish to provide a flexible base that can be expanded by new type definitions that support various applications areas. We wish that these expansions be made easily. We wish that the type specification and usage mechanisms permit hierarchical modular program structures. We also wish to be able to reuse definitions without too much waste.

The ability to reuse definitions is not related to the time of binding between a type name and its definition. Both Ada and Smalltalk [GOLD83] support the definition of new types, but differ with respect to the binding times. In Ada, all type definitions are bound to specific implementations during compilation and linking.[1] Ada's early binding time forces some awkward implementation details, but Ada's type definition facilities do meet many of our desires. Smalltalk permits changes in type definitions during program execution.

Since the program context of a type definition may include other type definitions, structures and interrelationships between type definitions can be constructed. While talking about this situation, we use T to denote the name of the type being defined, and we call any visible type other than T a *defined type*.

The simplest type definition context contains only the base types built into the language; these types can be used to construct the representation of and operations on any new type T. For example, the type integer_stack can be defined in terms of integers and arrays, both elements of the base language. In general, any new type can be defined in terms of the language's base types, using a progression of replacements. The ensuing complexity may make a type definition in this basic form hard to understand. Type definitions constructed using relationships between T's type definition and the set of defined types may be easier to understand. Here are four possible relationships between T's definition and other defined types, denoted by subscripted D's:

1. T's definition uses D_1 .. D_n.
2. T is similar to D_i.
3. T is a subset of D_i.
4. D is a parameterized type and T is an instance of D with specific parameter values.

Note that including these four relationships does not alter the capabilities of the language, but by recognizing and using these relationships among types, one might write a more understandable program.

7.1.2.1 Type nesting by usage. Usage-based nesting occurs when T's representation includes some objects of other user-defined types D_1 .. D_n. For example, consider

```
type T is
  record
    a : D1;
    b : D2;
  end record;
```

[1]The only dynamic aspect is the discriminant value(s) in variant records, which can be bound when an object is allocated during program execution.

A conventional nest structure cannot be imposed on this situation if all the types have to be visible on the outside—in a nest all the nested things are visible from the inside, but only those at the outermost level are visible outside. Whether the program is expressed using static module nesting, still there does exist a usage-based nested relationship between two types when one's definition uses the other.

7.1.2.2 Type similarity. In a simple case of type similarity we define type T in terms of one defined type D_1. To complete T's definition, one specifies how type T is different from type D_1. The differences may remove or add features relative to those of D_1. Since feature deletion is simpler, we discuss it first.

Type similarity with deletion could be specified easily:

```
type T is D without ⟨exclusion_list⟩; --not Ada
```

Type similarity with deletion can be visualized as blocking T's interface to exclude the deleted elements of D's interface. Note that due to similarity, T's specification does not include details about the representation or implementation of type D. One practical difficulty with the widespread use of this technique is that the first type defined (call it F) must incorporate all the features of the types that may be declared similar to F; building up by expansion from base types is more useful.

Example 7-2

A double-ended queue object type needs six operations: insertion and deletion at either end of the object, and object creation and deletion. A single-ended queue could be viewed as a double-ended queue with the backward operations removed. Figure 7-2 illustrates the encapsulation of a single-ended queue implemented under this deletion viewpoint. The declaration might be

```
type SEQ is DEQ without back_insert, back_delete;
```

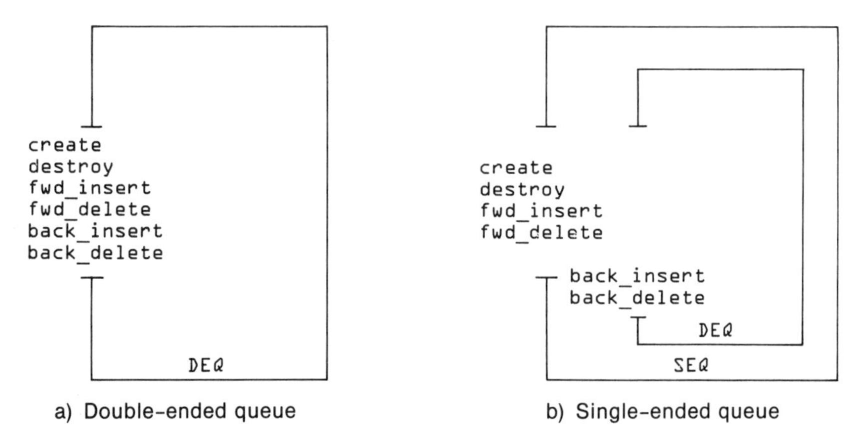

Figure 7-2 A single-ended queue as a restriction of a double-ended queue

Here is an argument that two different types should not share implementations [SNYD86]: If the types are truly encapsulated, the implementer of type D should be free to modify its implementation, provided that the properties seen through D's external interface are not changed in the process. Now if T shares D's implementation, a modification to D's implementation may also modify T's implementation; this would constitute an unacceptable violation of encapsulation. Therefore implementation sharing should be discouraged.

7.1.2.3 Value restrictions. As with type similarity, a type T defined by value restriction from type D shares D's value representation scheme and operation set. With type similarity, the differences between T and D lay in the set of available operations. With value restrictions, the differences between the two types lie in the range of possible values that can appear in the objects.

A typical value restriction rule limits the range of values of type T objects to a contiguous subset of the values of type D objects. The implementation of T can be identical to the implementation of D, with a simple range check added to determine value legitimacy.

In Ada value restriction may be used to define a *subtype* that inherits both its representation scheme and its operations from its parent.

Example 7-3

```
subtype ten_only is integer range 0 .. 9;
```

Since ten_only is an integer, one can add two ten_only objects. All other integer operations are also available for ten_only objects. Within the implementation, the check whether the result actually does lie within the specified range can be made by an inequality test for each limit of the range.

An important intertype relationship exists when types T_1 and T_2 share value representations and semantics. In this case, the value within a type T_1 object could be copied unmodified into a type T_2 object. The system then can *coerce* two objects to a single compatible type before performing an operation of which both are operands. This simplification can save a programmer the trouble of defining the interpretation of each operation for all combinations of types and subtypes that could occur among its operands.

7.1.2.4 Parameter setting. Great savings can be realized by collecting the common features of a number of types in a comprehensive parameterized definition. In the Ada model, a generic package can be declared and later its parameters can be set to create a new package. In Ada the generic parameters of a package or procedure can be either object values or object types; the option of having types as parameters makes it possible to collect together the common features of structurally similar types. For example, we could define a generic stack package that performs functions on stack objects. The type of the stack entries could be a parameter of the generic stack package. This is especially simple since only copying is performed on objects within the stack.

To specify a parameterized type in Ada, its parameters are attached to a **generic package** which includes an externally visible definition of the type. The **new** operator used in a package declaration creates a specific copy of the parameterized **package**, and the use of **new** implicitly creates a new externally visible type based on the type declaration within the **package**. Since all copies of the package declare the same type name, a qualified name may be required to distinguish among the types created when the generic package is instantiated.

Example 7-4

If we have defined a **generic package** for stack operations, we can create a **package** and thus a type for a short stack of integers simply with

```
package short_int_stack is new stack_type(20, integer);
```

Suppose that the generic **package** specification for stack_type contains the type declaration

```
type stack is
  record
    space : array(1 .. size) of T;
    top : integer;
  end record;
```

Then the new type created in the short_int_stack declaration above is named short_int_stack.stack. An instance of this kind of object is declared thus:

```
stack_instance : short_int_stack.stack;
```

An obvious advantage of parameterizing type definitions is the ensuing saving of coding and debugging effort.

7.1.2.5 Comments. A programmer can create type relationships and thus can simplify type declarations and encapsulate certain semantic details. These possibilities are quite useful in high-level programming. Unfortunately, elaborate type declaration features are not available in many programming languages. Pascal, for example, permits type declarations that define object representations, but there is no facility for encapsulating these type representations, since they are visible wherever the type is visible.

7.1.3 Processor-Level Designs

The processor-level design should support some basic operand types and may provide a way to define operations on new types. The designer chooses the basic type set from the expected usage and the "cost" of supporting each type and each operation. The processor design may allow the programmer to extend its instruction set to support new data types; this option is presented in Section 7.5.3.

What types should be in the processor's *base type set*? The MIN processor example shows that minimal support of one operand type is functionally complete and also terribly inefficient. We have noted that type selection is an art; here we will look briefly at the selections that have been made. Table 7-2 lists some object types

TABLE 7-2 OPERAND TYPE SUPPORT FOR SELECTED PROCESSORS[a]

Type	Processor Family										
	S/38	IBM370	MC68020	DEC VAX	CDC 6600	CDC STAR	Cyber205	CRAY-1	B5700	i80286	iAPX432
Integer	×	×	×	×	×	×	×	×	○	×	×
Real	×	×		×	×	×	×	×	×		×
Boolean	×	×	×	×	×	×	×	×	×	×	×
Stack	×		×	×					×	×	×
List			×	×					×		
Queue	×			×							×
Character string	×	×		×		×			×	*	×
Decimal integer	×	×	×	×		×				+	×

[a] ×, Support for most operations; ○, supported as a special case of real; *, no edit instruction; +, adjustment from integer operation only.

supported by processor instructions in various processors. All processors support integers and booleans. Most support reals, either in the processor or in an optional piece of additional hardware. High-performance scientific processors support only a few data types. In this vein, notice that decimal and character string operations were removed from the CDC STAR when it was redesgned to become the Cyber 205. We see little support for queues and lists, despite their important role as data structures within the operating system.

7.1.4 Host Type Selection

A microprogrammed host may not directly support the implementation of all types visible in the (virtual) processor it emulates. An important design decision chooses the set of types that will be supported at the host level. The cost of increased support is processor complexity; the benefit is performance improvement. Operations not supported directly in the host hardware could be supported either by host firmware routines or by processor software routines invoked in response to an interrupt caused when the operation is not recognized.

Example 7-5

The DEC MicroVAX 32 [SUPN84] designers studied usage statistics to divide the data types into three categories for implementation in the processor chip, in the optional floating-point chip, and in conventional routines invoked from interrupt handler software (called "macrocode" in the paper). The type division is tabulated in Table 7-3.

TABLE 7-3 MICROVAX 32 TYPE SUPPORT

	Means of Support			
Data Type	Host	Microcode	Optional Chip[a]	Macrocode
Byte integer	×			
Word integer	×			
Longword integer	×			
Quadword integer		×		
Variable bit field		×		
Variable character		×		
String		×		
Real (d-format)			×	
Real (f-format)			×	
Real (g-format)			×	
Real (h-format)				×
Octaword integer				×
Leading separate numeric				×
Trailing numeric string				×
Packed decimal				×

[a]If the chip is not present, these types are supported by processor macrocode.
Source: Based on data from [SUPN84]; © 1984, IEEE.

The usage statistics and the microprogram sizes for this design are summarized in Table 7-4. Notice that the space required for the microcode itself is reduced to 20%, yet less than 2% of the instructions executed (counted on a dynamic basis) by the processor cannot be executed from the processor's microcode. To approximate the performance loss, one must know the execution times of the instructions in question and the performance penalty for execution of an instruction outside the microprogram. The MicroVAX designers provided some performance assists within the chip's instruction set, thereby reducing the time penalty for execution outside the microcode to a factor of 4. The overall performance degradation in this situation amounted to 4%.

TABLE 7-4 MICROVAX INSTRUCTION STATISTICS

Percentage of Instances Based On	Locus of Implementation		
	Processor	Optional Chip	Macrocode
Static processor instruction count	57.6	23.0	19.4
Static microinstruction count	20.0	20.0	60.0
Dynamic microinstruction count	98.1	1.7	0.2

Source: [SUPN84], Table 2; © 1984, IEEE.

7.1.5 Comments

Relationships between type definitions are very important in high-level programming. These relationships not only simplify programming and type specification, but they may also simplify the implementation. Type definitions and object operations can be built up from a basic set of types and operations. At high levels we seek comprehensive coverage, but at low levels we can obtain good performance by providing support for a small set of statistically selected types and operations.

7.2 OBJECT-TYPE BINDINGS

It is essential to know the type of an object to determine the semantics of each operator of which the object is an operand. Here we discuss the type–object relationships; the operand type–operator relationships are studied in Section 7.6. Type–object bindings may be static or dynamic. Static typing can be established by a simple declaration, such as

```
x : integer;
```

This declaration states that the object contained in location x shall be treated as an integer. Dynamic typing does not require an object type declaration; rather, the actual type of an object is held in the system during program execution and may be examined as needed to determine the type of the object's current contents.

7.2.1 Basic Options

A global object type declaration like the one shown above is but one of five conceptually different options for specifying or finding an operand's type. The complete list of options is:

1. Type declaration
2. Type information along the access path
3. Type information along the operator path
4. Type information within the object itself
5. A combination using one of the above for the object's type class, and another to declare the object's variety within the type class.

Figure 7-3 illustrates these five options. In the figure we show an operator (think of it as a general instruction) with two operand specifications; the first one points to a descriptor of a location holding a descriptor of the object, which contains a pointer to the object itself. You will not be led astray if you assume that the operand descriptor points to a register that contains the memory address of a descriptor of the object itself.

Not all of these five conceptual alternatives will necessarily be available in a single system. The first option was illustrated above; the global object type declaration removes any need for run-time data specifying the object's type. Figure 7-3a depicts this option; dashed arrows indicate that the type declaration influences both the function code and the object's representation.

The second option places type information along the access path reaching the object. Such type information may be contained in a descriptor of the object or of the space within which the object is located. Figure 7-3b shows an object descriptor holding both the object type and a pointer to the object itself. The other alternative places a group of objects of the same type into a single space whose descriptor contains the type information for all the objects in the space.

The third option finds operand type information along the path specifying the operation to be performed. For example, at the processor level type information may be implied by the instruction's function code (see Figure 7-3c).

The fourth option places type information within the object itself. A typical design under this option places type information in a tag associated with the object (see Fig. 7-3d). In Section 3.4.3 we discussed tagging in connection with object naming and learned how type information within an address object can guide its use in object accessing. In a similar way, type tags on operands can guide their use in performing operations.

The final option separately declares two aspects of the object's type; a pair of the preceding options are used to specify each aspect of the type. For example, with Ada variant records the record type may be declared and the discriminant value(s) within each object complete the type information by indicating the particular variant that is present in that object (see Figure 7-3e).

As we work our way down the hierarchy, notice how the set of interesting

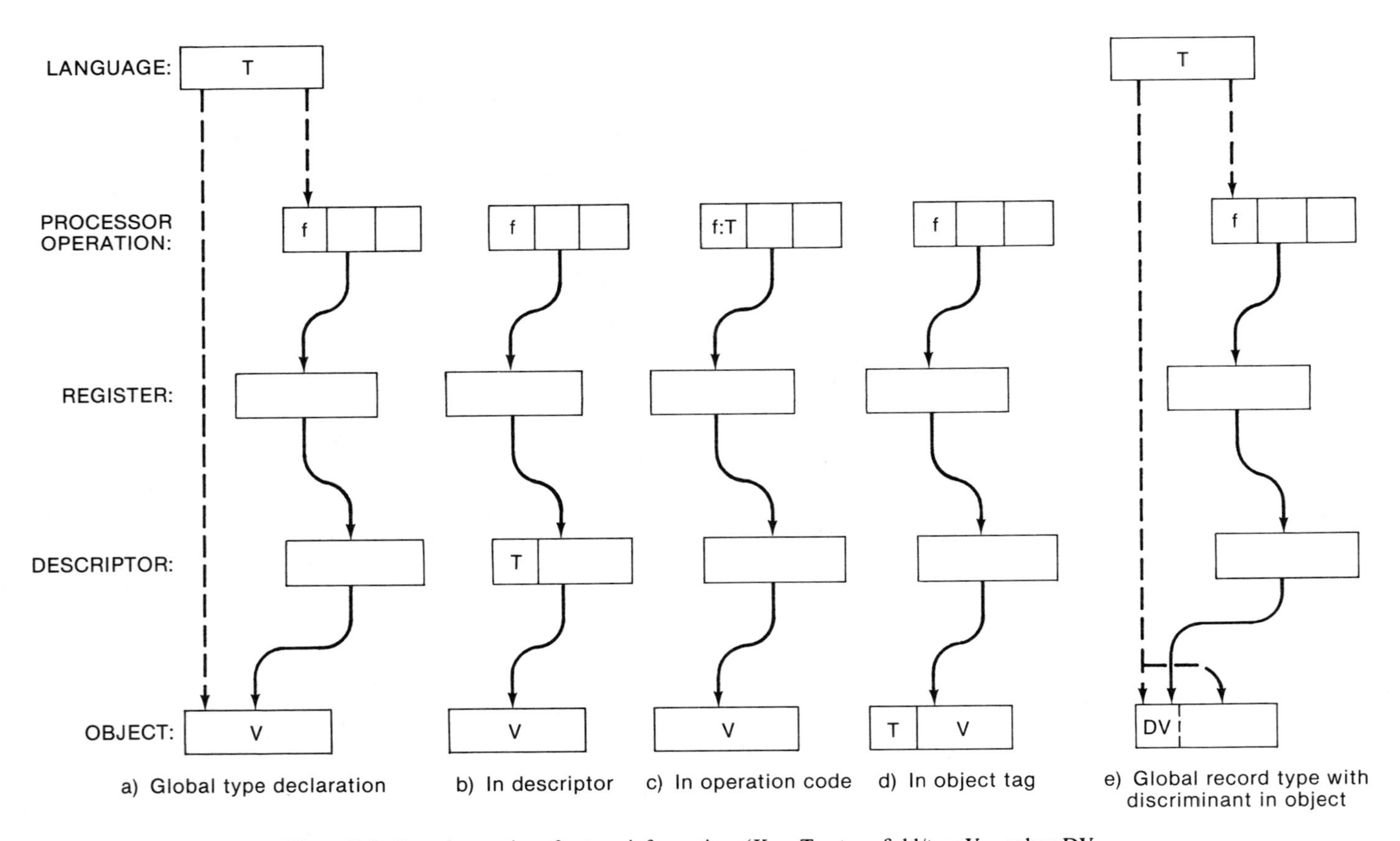

Figure 7-3 Location options for type information. (Key: T = type field/tag; V = value; DV = discriminant value)

options moves away from the type declarations that are so useful for creating understandable programs. Implementation correctness is assured by making correct transformations among these schemes as the high-level description is transformed into a representation used during instruction execution.

7.2.2 Object Types in High-Level Languages

The most common object declaration syntax declares the type of an object within the declaration of the object itself, thereby assigning a static type to the object. Like Ada, most typed languages force some static typing on all objects, but may allow dynamic types to handle variants.

Every object-type binding scheme (except operator based) can be found in some language. The importance of knowing object types and of choosing correct operator variants according to the operator types cannot be overemphasized; an error may cause results that depend on the internal value representation schema—a possibility that we hope to remove by encapsulation so that it would not be possible to write high-level language programs that have representation-dependent behavior.

Representation-dependent behavior may occur if the language is not strongly typed.

Definition. If language L imposes object–type rules such that every path to object X forces its interpretation as the same type, for all objects X, we say that L is *strongly typed.*

Ada is strongly typed. If a language is not strongly typed, we say that it is *weakly typed.* In a weakly typed language there exists some way to create two or more access paths to the same object (by two different names that are aliases, for example), giving two or more interpretations of the object's type. By writing a value using one access path and then reading that value using a different access path, we may obtain a representation-dependent result. Then our desire to encapsulate the representation scheme would not have been realized. Since pointers can be used to create access paths and aliases of objects, correct pointer typing is critical to the success of a strong-typing scheme.

Example 7-6

Often a magical property is attributed to strong typing; it has been claimed that it is hard to write bad programs in a language that uses strong typing. This example will illustrate that it is possible to misuse strong typing. In particular, we show how a weakly typed language could be emulated by a program written in a strongly typed language.

We sketch the construction of an emulator E_L for an arbitrary weakly typed language L that includes a set L_B of base types. The compiler for E_L converts the representations of all objects to a single type, which we call "thing". Each object of type thing contains two integer fields: a tag and a value. For every operator f defined for a type within L_B, f is redefined for type thing operands. To perform f, the emulator first reads all operand types from the first fields of their representations. Having all operand type information, E_L selects a procedure that correctly performs the desired operation on the value fields of the type thing objects.

> Nothing in this implementation prevents dynamic object typing, since operand type information is examined during the execution of each operator. Thus the emulator appears to be strongly typed, but actually dynamic type assignments could be made.[2]

We hasten to point out that this example presents an academic emulation designed to dispel the apparent magic surrounding strong static typing. In practical situations, however, there is a lot to be said in favor of strong static typing, in terms of both implementation ease and program understandability.

Despite the advantages of static typing, limited dynamic typing may be quite useful. We consider two different, yet related techniques for dynamic typing:

1. Dynamic arrays
2. Variant records

As we look at these dynamic situations, try to notice how the restrictions imposed on the programmer limit the extent of dynamic changes and thereby simplify the implementation.

A *dynamic array* is convenient for declaring a temporary local array for use during procedure execution. Typically, the dimensions are fixed when the array object is allocated. The implementation stores the actual dimensions and consults them as required.

Example 7-7

In Algol60, a dynamic array can be declared as a local object within a procedure body; its dimensions are evaluated during the procedure's prolog and appropriate space allocated at that time. Using Ada-like syntax, a procedure header might look like:

```
procedure f(a, n : integer) is
  b : array(n, n) of integer;   --not Ada
```

A *variant record* declaration groups a number of related record types beneath a single type declaration. This construct is useful for building a data structure whose elements all have the same record type, but with a small number of variations.

Example 7-8

```
type name is string(1 .. 30);
type sex is (male, female);
type married_person(p_sex : sex) is
  record
    first_name : name;
    middle_name : name;
    last_name : name;
    case p_sex is
      when female =>
        maiden_name : name;
      when male =>
        null;
```

[2]It could be argued that the processor's representation encapsulation has not been violated; see Problem 7-7.

```
        end case;
      end record;
    type mar_list is array(integer range < >) of married_person;
    marrieds : mar_list(1 .. 100);
```

The first part of this declaration fragment is identical to the declaration appearing in Example 3-6. The last two lines define a type which is a vector of married people, which can be of either sex in any order. The object named marrieds is such a list with 100 entries. If the two sexes had had to be separated because they had different record formats, it would not have been possible to construct the single list.

Despite the advantages of strong typing, some languages allow the program to assign a value of any type to any named location. To ensure type consistency and thereby to avoid the possibility of representation-dependent results, we must either tag all objects with their types or rely on correct programming. If all objects are tagged, the system design follows the "anything goes" approach. Reliance on correct programming follows the "nothing illegal" approach. The nothing illegal approach does not introduce any architectural problems, in the sense that there are no options that could be used in the lower levels to assist the system's correctness.

Language variants that add object typing to a LISP or Prolog-like environment are under active use and development. Such variants include Flavors (based on LISP; see [MOON86]), CommonLoops (based on LISP; see [BOBR86]), and SPOOL (based on Prolog; see [FUKU86]).

7.2.3 Processor-Level Typing

In many processor designs, the way that each object is manipulated is determined solely by the function code in each instruction manipulating the object.

Example 7-9

The IBM 370 instruction set contains several different ADD instructions, including:

A (add binary integers—signed)
AP (add decimal strings—packed decimal representation)
AH (add a halfword integer to an integer—all signed)
AL (add logical integers—unsigned)
AE (add normalized; short format—reals)
AD (add normalized; long format—reals)
AXR (add normalized; extended format—reals)

Thus in this design the operand types are conveyed within the function code. The three real formats use 32, 64, and 128 bits.

Other type definition methods have been used in processor designs:

1. Types in descriptors
2. Types in object tags
3. Types limited by object location

We examine these options through examples; first we look at two systems placing object type information in object descriptors.

Example 7-10

The Intel iAPX432 accesses objects through storage descriptors. In case the object's type is not built in, the storage descriptor contains a field with a code for the object type, a pointer to a type definition object, and a pointer to the space containing the object's representation.

A type manager package can create a new typed object by executing the processor instruction CREATE_TYPED_OBJECT, which returns a descriptor of the new object.[3] One operand of this operation is a descriptor of the type object. The conditions after the typed object has been created are depicted in Figure 7-4a. To prepare to pass

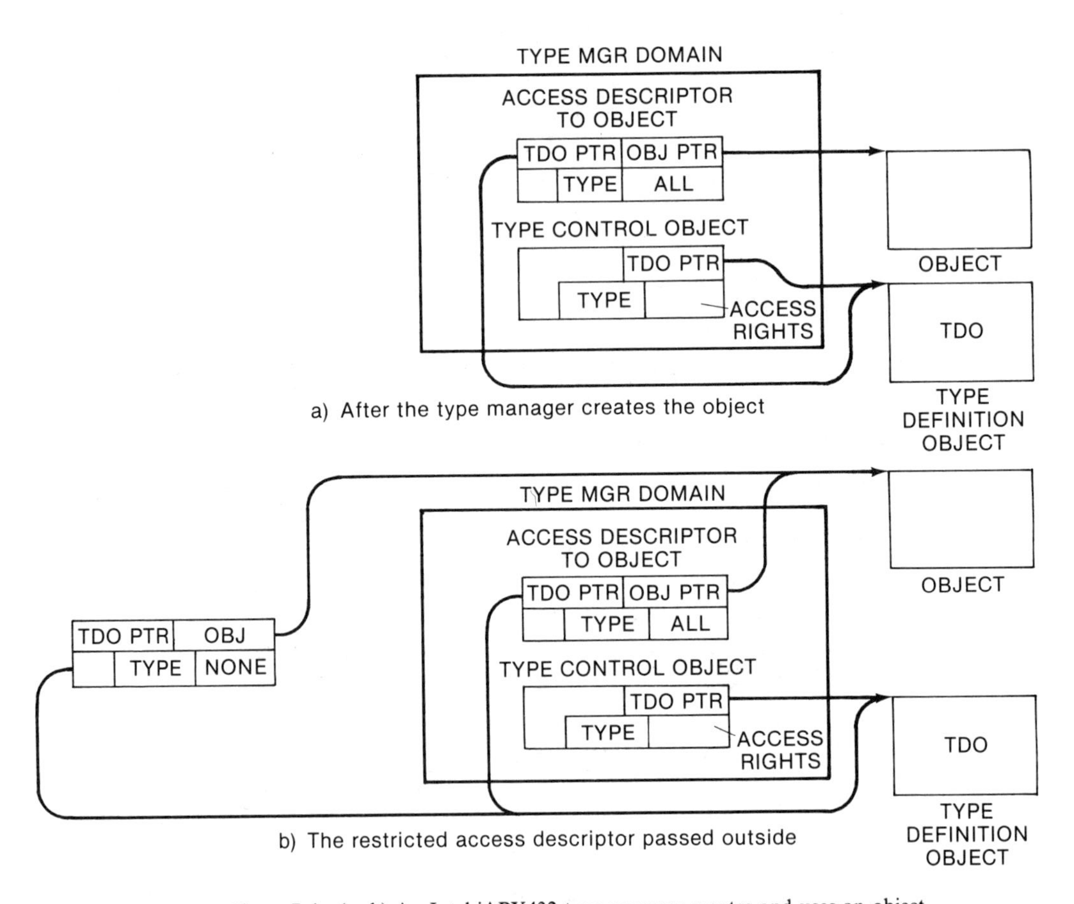

Figure 7-4 (a, b) An Intel iAPX432 type manager creates and uses an object

[3]A similar operation creates a "refinement," which is a subpart of a complete object, and assigns it a type. This is an important feature because it permits the type manager to collect a set of representation objects into a single storage segment, thereby saving memory allocation overhead.

out a descriptor to the object, the type manager makes a copy of the descriptor and then restricts the holder of the copy from direct access to the object by executing the RESTRICT_ACCESS_RIGHTS instruction; Figure 7-4b shows the restricted descriptor passed outside the type manager's domain. The using program can copy the restricted descriptor and eventually can ask for an operation to be performed on the object by passing the restricted descriptor back as an argument to the type manager. Figure 7-4c illustrates the arrival of the restricted descriptor within the type manager. The manager can take the restricted descriptor and amplify its rights, provided that it is the proper type manager. This condition is tested by requiring that the manager wishing to expand the access rights also holds the type description object for the type of the object described by the restricted descriptor. The amplification is obtained by executing the AMPLIFY_RIGHTS instruction, which has two operands: the descriptor to be amplified and the type control object pointing to the type definition object (see Figure 7-4d).

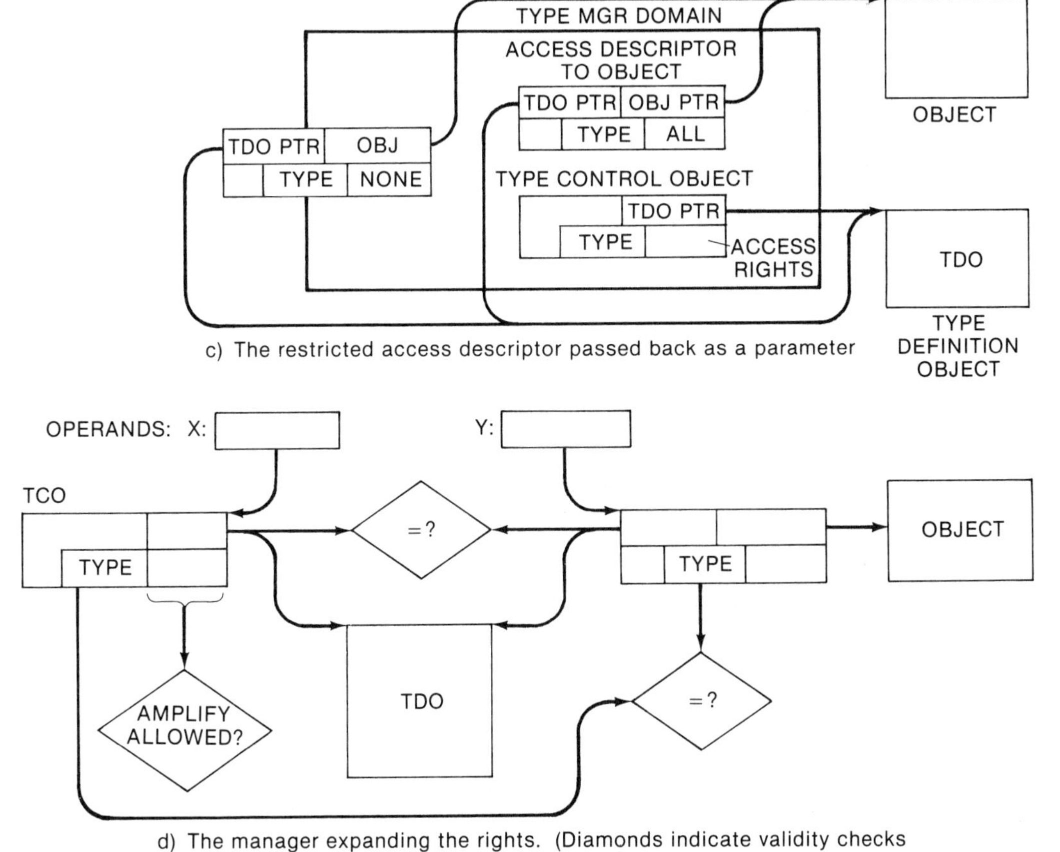

Figure 7-4 (c, d) An Intel iAPX432 type manager creates and uses an object

Thus the type manager can obtain access permissions which were not available outside the package; with these access permissions it can manipulate the representation of the object to perform the requested function.

Example 7-11

The IBM System/38 contains object type information in the ODT (Object Definition Table); all computational operations are memory to memory. Figure 7-5 illustrates the access path to an operand leading through the ODT. Three numeric representations are supported: binary integers, packed decimal strings, and zoned decimal strings. There are two add instructions: ADDLC (unsigned) and ADDN (signed). As the processor executes these instructions, it examines the types of both sources and the destination to determine the appropriate format conversions. The result type determines whether a format conversion has to be performed after the addition and before the store. In this design the object type is indicated along the path to the object in memory.

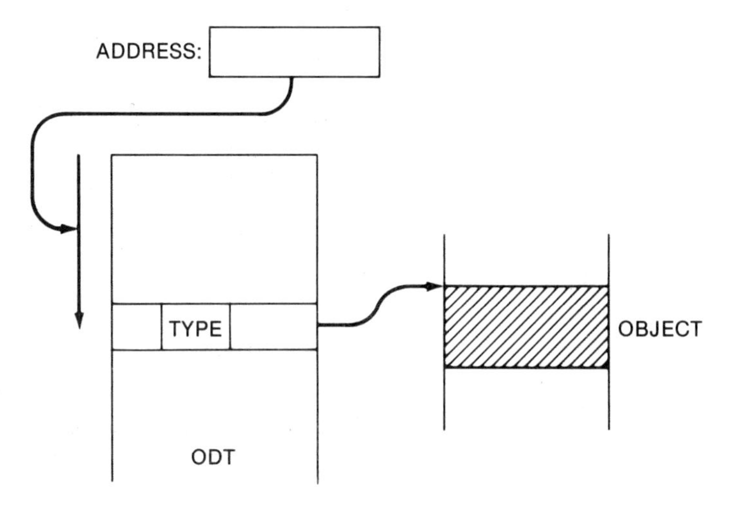

Figure 7-5 IBM System/38 object-type information in the object description table (ODT)

Value tagging is used in the B5700 machines to distinguish numeric values from control objects, and to separate some classes of control objects from each other.

Example 7-12

In the Burroughs B5700 the tag associated with a numeric object indicates whether the associated value is single or double precision.[4] There is one ADD instruction; its implementation determines the operand widths from their tags.[5] This design illustrates the second option, with tags specifying the operand types.

Example 7-13

The CDC 6600 processor [CONT66] has three sets of registers, with different lengths and different primary uses. The A registers hold memory addresses and are 18 bits long. The

[4]The processor does not support integer values; rather, the floating-point representation was chosen so that the mantissa field in the real format is interpreted as an integer with radix point at the right end. Furthermore, the exponent is encoded so that a zero in the exponent field does mean a zero exponent. Thus if an integer value is small enough, its representation as a real is the same as its representation as a sign/magnitude integer, which is the convention chosen for the machine.

[5]A similar statement is true for subtraction, multiplication, and division.

B registers, holding index values, are also 18 bits long, and the X registers, holding numeric operand values, have 60 bits. For any operation, the type of register holding each operand is determined from the function code. The selections of the "basic operation" and the register set are not orthogonal; for example, there is no operation that interprets an index quantity (from a B register) as a real value. One could take two views of this design. Everything is specified by the function code, but the register type (admittedly specified by the function code) places limits on the interpretation of the register contents.

Example 7-14

The CRAY-1 processor [CRAY75] contains five register sets:

1. A: 8 address registers, 24 bits each
2. B: 64 address buffer registers, 24 bits each
3. S: 8 scalar registers, 64 bits each
4. T: 64 scalar buffer registers, 64 bits each
5. V: 8 vector registers, 64 components, 64 bits each

The register holding a CRAY-1 operand is selected by a 3-bit field in the instruction, with the function code determining the register set. The four integer ADD instructions use different register sets, as follows:

$A_i := A_j + A_k;$
$S_i := S_j + S_k;$
$V_i := S_j + V_k;$ --scalar added to vector
$V_i := V_j + V_k;$ --vector added to vector

Here i, j, and k are register numbers taken from instruction fields.

At both the processor and microcode host levels, object type correctness relies on correct programming, and implicit type information is inferred from function codes in most designs.

7.2.4 Host-Level Typing

At the host level most object typing is specified by function code associations. If the processor has tags, the microprogram must check the operand tags and then choose the appropriate sequence of microinstructions to perform the operation for the types presented. We discuss ways to speed this operation sequence in Section 7.6.4.

7.2.5 Comments

A great concern for a structured approach to object typing is characteristic of programming languages. The structured typing is rapidly lost as one moves to lower system levels. At the microprogram level, correct programming can be assumed, so operand types can be implied by the function codes sent to the ALU. At the processor level, objects can be tagged or described by type information along the access path from the operation or address specification. At this particular level, the designer makes a conscious choice regarding the system design philosophy (should it be "everything checked" or "nothing illegal?") when she decides how types are bound to values.

7.3 OPERATOR–OPERAND BINDINGS

A program implementation binds operands to operators using static association rules. In a high-level language program an expression may state a complex sequence of operations, and the compiler determines the corresponding operator–operand associations. At lower levels there are fewer choices, as the number of different operand sources and the complexity of a single operation decreases.

7.3.1 Basic Options

Two issues that affect the operator–operand binding scheme determine (1) how to associate the operator with its operands, and (2) how to interpret each operand specification.

The operator–operand association issue is important at the language level, where many options, including functional notation and relative positions in expressions, are available. Processor and host instructions directly specify both the operation and its operands, so there is no ambiguity concerning which operands and operations go together.

The high-level language options are based on several mathematically equivalent techniques for writing and interpreting expressions. To illustrate the options, consider operator f with two operands denoted by x and y. If f is not commutative, the x and y operands have different effects on the result and their roles must be distinguished by their positions. There are three locations where f could be written (see Table 7-5).

TABLE 7-5 SYMBOL ORDERING OPTIONS WITH TWO OPERANDS

Symbol Order	Option Name
f x y	Prefix
x f y	Infix
x y f	Postfix

In complex expressions, operator precedence rules and parentheses may be used to indicate the evaluation order (which defines which operands go with which operator). The prefix and postfix forms do not require parentheses or precedence rules, as each legal expression is unambiguous if each operator symbol implies the number of its operands. Prefix notation is similar to functional notation, except that the parentheses used in functional notation are not present in the prefix form.

The operand specification interpretation possibilities include:

1. The name specifies a memory location.
2. The name specifies a register number.
3. No name is needed because the operand comes from a stack.

There are few choices in languages, where names specify memory locations, and in microprogrammed hosts, where names specify register numbers; all choices are available in some processor.

7.3.2 High-Level Languages

High-level languages use prefix notation for function and procedure calling. Infix notation is commonly used in forming mathematical expressions. Prefix notation and postfix notation are used in some languages to form expressions.

However they are chosen, the operand–operator association rules fix the execution sequence, which can be expressed as a program fragment. Consider the program fragment

```
y:=f(a, b);
z:=g(y, d);
x:=h(z, e);
```

Suppose that x is the only result. Then each of the following assignment statements in functional, prefix, infix, and postfix notation, respectively, corresponds to the previous program fragment:

```
x:=h(g(f(a, b), d), e);
x:=(h (g (f a b) d) e);
x:=(((a f b) g d) h e);
x:=(((a b f) d g) e h);
```

The order of the operand names is the same in all these representations.

Example 7-15

Infix notation is used in conventional algebraic notation; in contemporary technology, most calculators (excepting HP calculators) handle infix notation with parentheses.

LISP programs use prefix notation; a LISP expression is written as a list, such as (+X Y).

Postfix notation is the basis for the stack evaluation model used in both the B5500 series machines and the HP pocket calculators.

Two groupings in the symbol sequences of Table 7-5 suggest interesting interpretations of the operator and its operands. Conventional functional notation is obtained by adding parentheses to the prefix form, as in f(x, y). A second interesting variation groups the function name and its first parameter in parentheses, as in (f, x)(y); this description suggests that the function (f, x) be applied to the operand y.

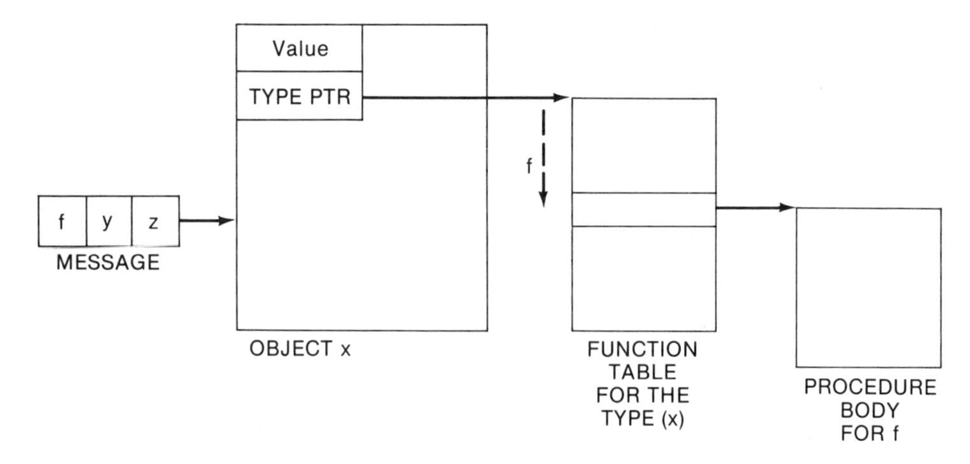

Figure 7-6 The object-oriented (Smalltalk) view of type-based procedures [calling f(x,y,z)]

Example 7-16

In the Smalltalk language [GOLD83], a request to perform a procedure is considered to be a message sent to the object which is the procedure's first parameter; the message contains the function name and the second (and subsequent) operand(s). Figure 7-6 depicts this view, showing how an object "contains" the procedures and functions of which the object can be the first operand. The function bodies appear to exist within x, but in an implementation the function bodies for one object type could be collected together in a separate common space, as shown in the picture. The function bodies are not externally visible because they are accessed only through the type pointers, as shown in the figure. The net effect of this structure is that the name of any procedure is a pair (function_name, first_parameter).

Many of these formats effectively place the operand names and the operator name on an equal footing. Thus we could allow the program to make an assignment (during program execution) to an operator name. The next example illustrates this possibility in a LISP program.

Example 7-17

A LISP expression [WINS84] is a prefix list whose first element, considered as a symbol string, is the symbolic name of the function that performs the operation. Thus the three-element list (+ 3 6) represents the addition of three and six.

The contents of a variable could be interpreted as a program fragment and executed; the APPLY primitive function initiates this activity. APPLY interprets its (single) argument (which is a list) as a program fragment and performs the indicated operations. Table 7-6 shows a few LISP program fragments and the corresponding results. A short introduction to LISP will help explain these examples. The single quotation mark causes LISP to defer the evaluation of the expression following the quotation mark (up to the next unmatched right parenthesis) until program execution. The SETQ operator performs an assignment operation; the value of its second argument is the list to be assigned to the object named as the first argument. Thus the LISP

TABLE 7-6 SOME LISP PROGRAM FRAGMENTS AND THEIR EFFECTS

LISP Fragment	Result
(APPLY '(+3 4))	7
(SETQ A '(+3 4))	(assigns prefix list to A)
(APPLY A)	7
(SETQ A '(+3 4))	(assigns prefix list to A)
(RPLACA A '−)	(replaces "+" with "−" in A)
(APPLY A)	−1

expression (SETQ X Y) is equivalent to the Ada assignment statement X:= Y. Finally, (RPLACA X Y) replaces the first element of the list named in the first argument (X) with the value of the second argument (Y). To support the run-time execution of a variable string as a statement, LISP's run-time support must include a compiler or an interpreter for the language.

We elaborate on the LISP language and the design of a LISP machine in Section 7.7.

In high-level languages, expression formation conventions define the associations of operators with operands. Some representation conventions permit more flexibility or introduce unique viewpoints such as the association of an operator with its first operand—the view espoused in some "object-oriented" languages, such as Smalltalk.

In high-level languages, all operand specifications are interpreted as names of memory locations or values of constant objects; other operand interpretation options do not apply since processor registers and the evaluation stack are encapsulated within the implementation and are not visible at the language level.

7.3.3 Processor-Level Operator–Operand Associations

At this level each operator is an instruction, complete with operand specifications. These specifications may be explicit names or implicit names. The operand location specifications from each instruction specify the source(s) of the operand(s) and the destination(s) of the result(s). At this level many implementation mechanisms are visible, so that registers, the evaluation stack, and addressable memory can be specified as operand or result locations. The processor design may be oriented toward one of these viewpoints. In a traditional design, the role of each named operand is determined by its location within the instruction.

7.3.3.1 Operand location options. Some processor designs make the operator–operand choice simple. If a design emphasizes stack operands, there is no choice because all operands come from the stack! Exceptions may be made for operands so large that one would not want to copy them to the stack just to use them once or twice: vectors and strings fall in this category. For these operand types, a descriptor of the operand's memory space (rather than the operand's value) is taken from the stack.

Table 7-7 summarizes (and labels) 12 ways that an operand's location might be specified. Under the options in the first row the function code fixes the location, much as the MIN instruction always used the register called the accumulator. Under the options in the second row, a fixed field in the instruction contains the selection. Options G through L all describe operands in memory; they differ with respect to the placement and form of the address information. In options J, K, and L, the operand site is a set of memory locations described by a descriptor found in the indicated location. This writer is not aware of any machine using option K; brief examples of some other options follow.

TABLE 7-7 SUMMARY OF OPERAND SPECIFICATION OPTIONS

How Particular Location Is Found	Type of Operand Location		
	Register	Memory	Stack
Implied (fixed) location	A	B	C
Location in instruction	D	E	F
Memory location found indirectly from:	G	H	I
Descriptor of memory space found indirectly from:	J	K	L

Example 7-18

The MC6800 Decimal Adjust (DAA) instruction always adjusts register A, so it falls under case A.

Example 7-19

Case A appears in the VAX architecture; the polynomial evaluation operation, one of several operations that use fixed registers, is discussed in Example 7-32.

Example 7-20

Case B, an implied memory location, can be used to specify an immediate operand value found either in the instruction itself or immediately following the instruction in memory.

The MC68020 ADD QUICK instruction is a single (16-bit) word; bits 11, 10, and 9 of the instruction contain the value to be added.[6] Figure 7-7 illustrates this operation when the destination is a processor D-register.

[6]For maximum utility, the value in these 3 bits is interpreted as a positive integer (since there is a subtract quick instruction, this choice does not limit the programmer's options); when the field contains 000, the value is taken to be eight.

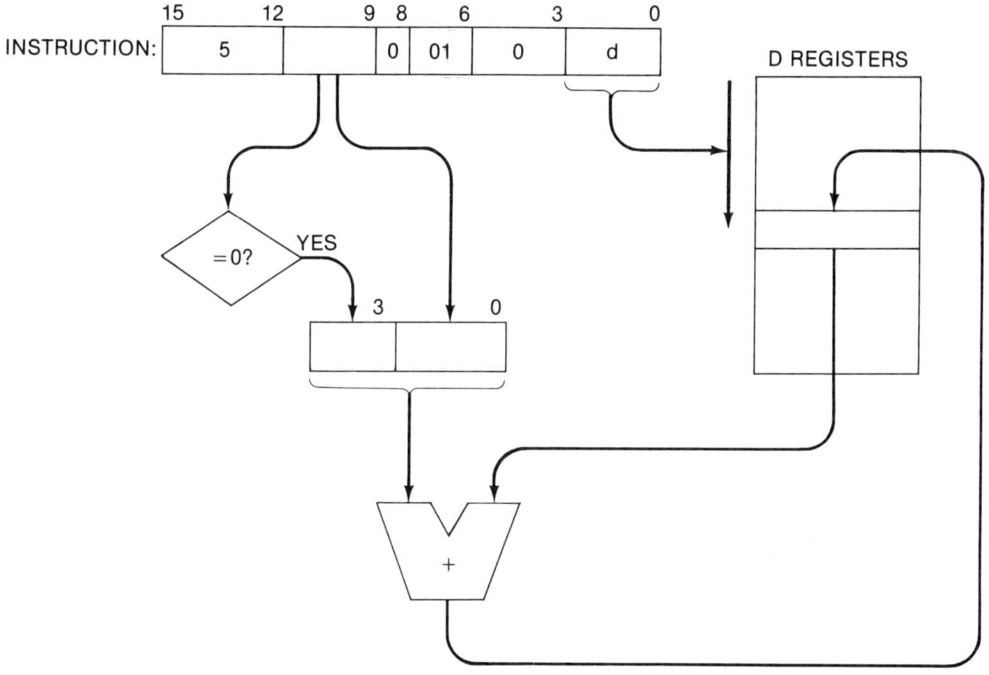

Figure 7-7 The MC68020 ADD QUICK instruction with a D-register destination

Example 7-21

Case C, an implied stack location, is used in arithmetic operations in the B5700 machines. These instructions occupy a single byte since no operand specification is needed (because the top two stack entries are popped and used as operands; then the result is pushed). Figure 7-8 illustrates this flow.

Example 7-22

Case F, a numbered stack location, is uncommon, but this addressing mode is available in the HP3000 processor, whose S-relative addressing mode addresses objects within 63 locations of the top of the stack (see Example 5-22 and Table 5-5).

Example 7-23

The B5700 STORE operations have two operands at the top of the stack containing the value to be stored and the address at which the value is to be stored. The address from the stack is a case I operand specification.

Example 7-24

Case J, a memory region described by a descriptor in a numbered processor register, is used in the Cyber 205 processor to describe a vector operand.[7] This mode is used to specify operands for vector arithmetic operations, among others.

[7]We discuss vector operations and the Cyber 205 in Chapter 1 of Volume 2.

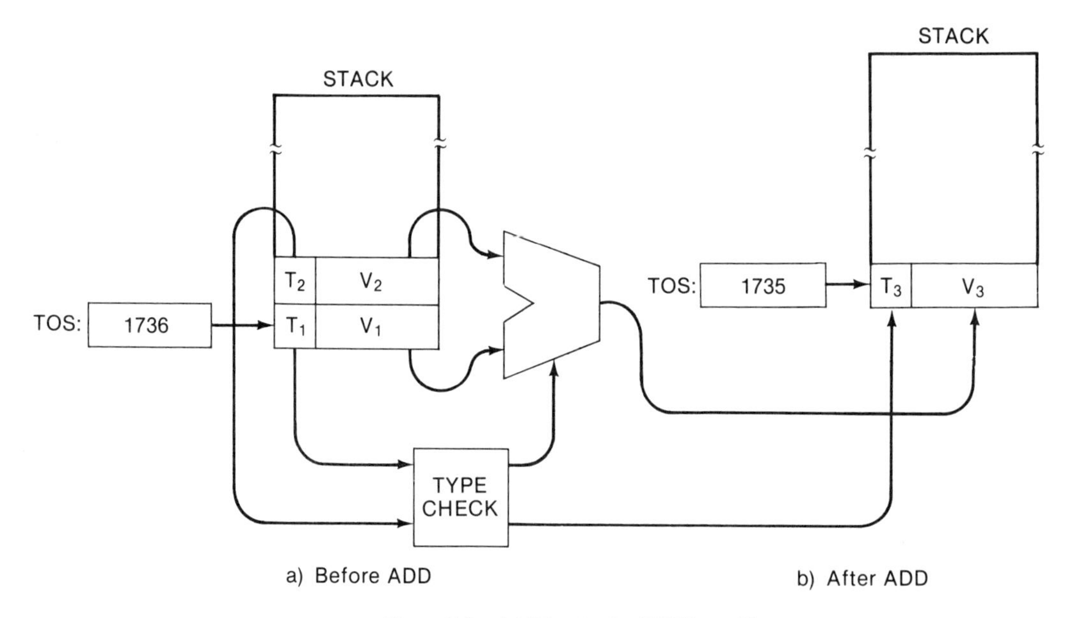

Figure 7-8 Addition in the B5700 machines

Example 7-25

Case L, a memory space described by a descriptor found at a location in the stack, is used in the B5700 system for character string operations. The locations at the top of the stack contain the origin and the byte count describing an operand string.

7.3.3.2 Operand role options. What is the correspondence between the location of an operand's specification and the operand's role in the operation? In many designs these roles are fixed, as in MIN, where every arithmetic result goes to a processor register. A processor design may allow a destination change, as specified by the direction bit in some MC68020 instructions (see Table 2-8). Some instruction sets include "reverse" versions of noncommutative operations, such as subtraction; the BRISC design illustrates this option (see Table 2-5). A more elaborate scheme allowing great flexibility in this regard is provided in the Intel iAPX432.

Example 7-26

In each iAPX432 instruction [TYNE81] the format field specifies which operands are accessed on the stack or through an operand addressing specification, and which operand specifications assume which roles (as both an operand and a result location).[8] With one operand/result there are two possibilities (stack or addressed memory). With two operand/results, there are five combinations (see Table 7-8). Note the special case with both references made to the same memory address; this is useful for replacing an operand with the result (as in x:= −x;). The number of combinations for three operands/results is left as an exercise.

[8]There are no register options because this processor does not have any programmer-visible registers.

TABLE 7-8 OPERAND SPECIFICATION POSSIBILITIES IN THE INTEL iAPX432 FOR AN INSTRUCTION WITH TWO OPERANDS/RESULTS

First Operand/Result	Second Operand/Result
Stack	Stack
Stack	Memory
Memory	Stack
Memory	Same memory location
Memory	Memory

7.3.3.3 Comments. The spectrum of options is very broad at the processor level with respect to both operand location specifications and their modes of use; this breadth occurs because the implementation details including processor registers and the evaluation stack are all visible at the processor level.

7.3.4 Operator–Operand Associations in the Host Machine

At the host architecture level each operation is simple and its operands and results are the contents of registers. Operations that transfer data between registers and memory may be distinct from operations that manipulate values. In this model the implementation of a processor instruction whose operands or results are in memory locations must encompass several microinstructions. The microinstruction that actually performs an operation by passing data through a functional unit specifies which host register contains each operand and which register should receive the result. Elaborate operand selection options are not realistic at this level.

It is not feasible to support flexible operand role changes at this low level, due to the logic delays that would increase the instruction execution time. Furthermore, since all operand locations are registers, a role change entails a simple register number exchange in some microinstructions; this change could be made during program development.

7.3.5 Comments

The flexibility of specifying the operand–operator associations in high-level languages is absorbed by compilation and processor instruction operand specifications. At the processor level many operand specification options have been chosen, but at the microprogrammed host level the operands and results of each operation must be host machine registers, and there is no benefit from adding any flexibility.

Some viewpoints from high-level languages affect the programmer's view of how an operation is performed, but do not affect the operation's representation. For example, under the Smalltalk viewpoint, an operation is performed by sending a message containing a request to perform the operation, along with the specifications of the other operands, to the object that is the operation's first operand. This viewpoint suggests certain implementation possibilities.

7.4 VALUE REPRESENTATIONS

The value representation choice affects the ease of object manipulation. At high levels a convenient representation may shorten programs; at the host machine level a convenient representation may save logic gates (thereby reducing complexity) or reduce the delay through the computational logic (thereby speeding operations). A wise representation selection can also simplify a serial implementation of the processing steps in a design that saves hardware cost and complexity.

7.4.1 Basics

We study these five techniques for defining the value representation scheme to be used for a new type N:

1. Parameter setting
2. Restricting the range
3. By construction
4. By enumeration
5. By encoding

The list order is selected so that the first options require less detail than the last option.

A specific representation can be defined from a previously defined parameterized representation technique by choosing a specific set of parameter values. In Ada, this option can be specified by a "pragma" defining the widths of numeric values or by a generic package instantiated with specific parameter values.

A range restriction definition of N's representation combines a representation technique previously defined for type P with value restrictions that must be satisfied by each object of type N. There is no logical reason why the system can not represent type N objects just like type P objects, with the values within type N objects satisfying the range constraints. Range limits are usually restricted to a contiguous set of P values. With this representation technique type N can inherit all operations from type P, and can use the same operation implementations.[9]

Under the construction representation technique user-defined combinations of **record** and **array** structures specify the representation of an object of type N. The interpretation of the values included therein is defined by the operations that manipulate the objects.

[9]A result range check might be tacked on at the end.

An enumerated type's value set is a (finite) list of constant values. The implementation can assign arbitrary codes for the enumerated values; integers are sufficient. In effect, the representation specification states the possible values that must be distinguished, and how the values are ordered (according to their positions in the value list, with the smallest values first). Pascal and Ada permit enumerated types.

In the final representation technique an object's value is denoted by a bit pattern which can be algorithmically interpreted to determine the value. Hopefully, the representation is a simple encoding of the value. Such encodings are usually based on binary integer representations. The encoding details are of little consequence at the language level, but very important at the hardware level; most programming languages do not permit specification at this level of detail. Even if they did, there would be little reason to change the encodings since all processing algorithms would have to be modified, which would slow the processor.

7.4.2 High-Level Languages

Every language that allows a programmer to define a new type permits the programmer to specify the representation of an object of the new type. In some languages, such as Pascal, type definitions are limited to representation specifications. In a strict sense, this is true in Ada, but an Ada program can hide the representation by declaring it **private** to a **package**. To encapsulate the chosen representation completely, operations must be defined; this is possible in Ada and most languages permitting programmer-specified type definitions. An Ada package that specifies an externally visible private declaration (of type N) containing functions and procedures that manipulate objects of type N does encapsulate the representation of type N objects. Value encoding details are usually not significant at the language level; high-level representations are constructed on a base type set having prespecified representations. The base type set includes integers, reals, and booleans.

Ada permits all the representation techniques except encoding. Ada allows parameter settings that affect value encoding, but this feature is buried in pragmas and is infrequently used because any program that demands a representation incompatible with the ones directly supported by the processor will pay a high price in degraded system performance.

When specifying a new object type, it is wise to choose a representation that directly incorporates the elements expected by programmers thinking about manipulating the objects that will have that type.

Example 7-27

This Ada program fragment includes each of the type representation techniques:

```
generic
  type T is range < >;
              --declaration specifies integer base type
  size : integer;
package stack_with_flag is
  type stack is private;
```

```
  procedure push(s : stack, v : value);
  ..
private
  subtype stk_index is integer range 1 .. size;
              --declaration by value limitations
  type stk_status is (empty, ok, full);
              --declaration by enumeration
  type stack is
    record
              --beginning of declaration by construction
      space : array(1 .. size) of T;
      top : stk_index;
      status: stk_status;
    end record;
end stack_with_flag;
package stack1 is new stack_with_flag(integer, 100);
              --declaration by integer parameter setting
```

Note that in Ada a representation declaration using parameter setting can appear only within generic program elements, which must be either procedures or packages.

The reader has undoubtedly noticed the close relationship between the act of defining a type (Section 7.1) and the act of defining a representation. This similarity is a direct consequence of the common interpretation under which a type definition is merely a way of specifying an object representation; the addition of procedures and functions to complete an abstract type declaration simply adds features to type declarations, without changing the representation definition portion of the type declaration.

7.4.3 Processor-Level Object Representations

At this level most value representation schemes amount to separating each object into fields containing integers; within each field a value encoding representation such as two's complement is specified. An occasional design permits some control over integer widths.

A designer's choices are limited by compatibility, both with previous designs and internally among the various types. In fact, the desire for compatibility with several representations leads to an interesting conjecture, based on the following argument. Take the character as the lowest common denominator. Now we choose the word length to be a multiple of the character length to eliminate waste when packing characters into words. Three common character widths are: 4 bits, sufficient to represent decimal integers; 6 bits, sufficient to distinguish among the keys on a typewriter keyboard, and 8 bits, for an ASCII coding. Thus the word length should be a multiple of 4, 6, or 8. The conjecture is that in any "interesting" machine the word length can be expressed as $2^n 3^m$, for n an integer, and m an integer in the range 0 .. 2. The multiplier is a power of 2 so that every character can be given an easily interpreted address at a character granularity. To illustrate the conjecture, examine Table 7-9, which lists the word and character sizes of several machines.

TABLE 7-9 WORD AND CHARACTER SIZES FOR SOME INTERESTING MACHINES

Machine	Sizes (bits)	
	Word	Character[a]
Z80	8	8
8080	8	8
PDP8	12	6
PDP11, VAX	16	8
MC68020	16	8
PDP-1	18	6
B1700	24	4, 6, 8
SDS 940	24	6
MC68020	32	8
iAPX432	32	8
IBM 370	32	8
IBM 704, 7094	36	6
UNIVAC 1108	36	6
B5500	48	6, 8
CDC 6600	60	6
CYBER 205	32/64	—
CRAY-1	64	—

[a]A dash indicates lack of character support.

The representation selection is completed by choosing value encodings for each data type. With respect to integers, the decision chooses an encoding for signed values. The options include sign/magnitude, one's complement, two's complement, and biased encodings. Two's complement is used in most machines, partly because two's-complement addition and subtraction can be performed in one pass of byte-serial processing. A biased encoding is often used for the exponent part in representations of real numbers. Sign/magnitude encoding is used for real number mantissas.

Real numbers are represented by two fields—a mantissa containing the numeric coefficient, and an exponent, containing information about the location of the radix point. The design issues concern:

1. Location of the radix point within the mantissa
2. Radix value
3. Encoding of the exponent value
4. Encoding of the mantissa value

The first two choices together determine the formula that gives the overall value in terms of the values in the fields of the representation of a real quantity. The last two decisions define how the bit patterns in the mantissa and exponent are interpreted as numeric values. We use the following variable names in the formulas:

r = radix value

e = exponent value

m = mantissa value

f = width of the mantissa field (measured in bit positions)

Table 7-10 shows the value expressions for three common representation schemes.

Figure 7-9 shows the field positions in some real formats; the formats are labeled for reference in Table 7-11, which shows the representations used in selected systems for "single-precision" values.

The IEEE floating-point representation standard [IEEE85] specifies three widths for different accuracies and representation ranges. The standard specifies

TABLE 7-10 REAL NUMBER REPRESENTATIONS AND THEIR VALUE FORMULAS

Mnemonic Name	Scheme	Value
frac	Fractional	$r^e 2^{-f} m$
msbo	Most significant bit one	$r^e(1/2 + 2^{-f-1} m)$
int	Integer	$r^e m$

TABLE 7-11 THE IEEE STANDARD AND THE REPRESENTATIONS OF NUMERIC VALUES USED IN SEVERAL COMPUTER SYSTEMS

	Integer		Real						
				Mantissa			Exponent		
Machine	Size	Encoding	Format	Size	Encoding	Interp.	Size	Encoding	Radix
IBM 370	32	2c	A	25	2comp	frac	7	bias	16
iAPX432	32	2c	A	24	s/m	msbo	8	bias	2
Univac1108	36	1c	A	28	2comp	frac	8	bias	2
B5500	48	s/m	B	40	s/m	int	7	s/m	8
CYBER 205	64	2c	C	48	2comp	int	16	bias	2
CRAY-1	64	2c	A	49	s/m	frac	15	bias	2
HP3000	32	2c	A	23	s/m	msbo	9	bias	2
DG Eclipse	32	2c	A	25	s/m	frac	7	bias	16
PDP11	16	2c	A	24	s/m	msbo	8	bias	2
MC68020	16	2c	A	24	s/m	msbo	8	bias	2
IEEE Std.	—	—	A	24	s/m	msbo	8	bias	2

FORMAT A: | MS | EV | MV |

FORMAT B: | ▨ | MS | ES | EV | MV |

FORMAT C: | EV | MS | MV |

Figure 7-9 Some real number formats. (Key: MS = mantissa sign; MV = mantissa value; ES = exponent sign; EV = exponent value.)

representations for the three special values listed in Table 7-12. The "not a number" (NaN) case can be used in various ways; it could denote an uninitialized operand or the result of meaningless arithmetic operations, such as $\infty - \infty$. Every zero is taken to be a positive number. Infinity can have either sign, indicated by the sign bit.

TABLE 7-12 REPRESENTATIONS OF NONSTANDARD "VALUES" IN THE IEEE STANDARD REAL FORMAT

	Representation Value	
Type	Exponent	Fraction
infinity	maximum	0
NaN	maximum	$\neq 0$
zero	0	0

Character representations usually follow standards, such as the ASCII coding standard. Some manufacturers have defined their own character coding standards; IBM uses EBCDIC (Extended Binary-Coded Decimal Interchange Code).

A decimal integer could be represented by a binary integer or by a sequence of ASCII characters. This coding is extremely inefficient, because it uses 8 bits to distinguish among 12 characters (including the sign). It is quite efficient to use a packed (BCD) decimal representation, in which each digit value is represented by a 4-bit binary integer corresponding to the value of the decimal digit; the sign appears like a digit in the least significant position of the complete number. Figure 7-10 illustrates

1 2
6 7
3 C

+12673

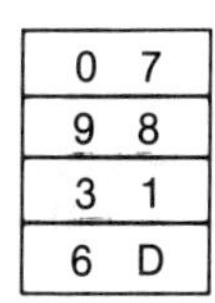

−798316

Figure 7-10 Packed decimal representations (IBMS/370 sign encodings; hexadecimal values)

some decimal integer values encoded in packed format. The packed BCD format is efficient of space and arithmetic operations can be performed easily.

The processor's value representation choice is also used at the host level.

7.4.4 Comments

All value representation schemes reduce to simple, basic elements, but at high levels of abstraction we want the ability to build structured representations, with the representation matching the way we think about the objects in the problem domain. Several methods for building structured representations are available; all methods reduce to using record and array constructs to build up from simpler objects. At both the processor and host levels we need to deal with integers and with representations constructed from sets of integers. At both levels, simple encodings are used to represent integer values.

7.5 OPERATION SELECTION AND SPECIFICATION

Having bound types with operands, operands with operators, and values with representations, we are ready to bind operators with specific implementations. In this context it is appropriate to discuss briefly the choice of operations to be made available. Techniques for specifying the proper performance of an operation are also presented in this section; in the next section we complete the discussion by covering the implementations of the operations.

7.5.1 Basics

Choosing an operation set is an art; the author knows of no systematic method for selecting a good operation set. We face a trivial logical requirement—that we have a functionally complete operation set to cover the operations used in the task at hand.

Definition. Operation set S is *complete for operation set V on data type T* if one can combine operations from S to implement any operation in V for operands of type T.

Achieving completeness is trivial, since subtraction over integers is complete for any operation set on any data type. The difficulty is that using only subtraction to do something interesting is, at best, tedious and difficult. The difficulty arises because the "distance" between subtraction and useful operations is too great. Thus we raise our goal: We aim for a complete operation set that is close to the operations that are useful for the task.

One approach is to choose operator/operand combinations that provide wide-ranging support for basic object types and include an expansion interface. Then a user can either configure[10] or program the extensions she desires. As this approach

[10]By adding either hardware or firmware modules to expand the system.

is attractive, in this section we assume the existence of useful operations for standard operand types and emphasize techniques for expanding the basic operation set.

The second topic of this section concerns how a designer specifies the effect of each chosen operation. Two essentially different approaches toward specifications are specification by example and specification by declaring the changes caused by performing the operation. Each approach has its advantages. A specification by example gives one implementation, which could be used as the implementation. On the other hand, a specification by effects states what the operation should do without biasing the implementation in any way; this form may be more useful when reasoning about program properties. As we discuss operation specifications, we digress and illustrate techniques for specifying the properties of and reasoning about general programs.

7.5.2 High-Level Languages

Our major topic at the high-level language level is operation and program specification; the basic operations were selected by the language designers and, by writing procedures or functions, any programmer is free to add operations as her heart desires.

The program specifying a new procedure or function could be treated as a specification by example, but this viewpoint is hardly useful—using the specification as the implementation makes it trivially true that the implementation does meet the specification.

Specification by effect is a useful specification technique, since it decouples the specification from any implementation. Effects can be expressed in terms of an *observed space*. A specification by effect relates the state of the observed space after the operation has been completed to the state of the observed space before the operation was performed. One observation space choice includes the values of the variables that represent the state of the object. Under this view, the effects of push on a stack object can be written as

$$(s, t) = [push(st, v)](s', t') = (s'\&v, t' + 1)$$

The apostrophes mark values existing before the operation; unmarked symbols denote their values after the operation has been completed. The ampersand operator concatenates the second (scalar) operand to the end of the first (vector) operand. This statement could be read as though it were a function call: "The function push(st, v) applied to stack st (whose state is denoted by (s, t)) leaves a state whose value is s' concatenated with v and t' = t + 1." The close relationship between this statement and the internal representation should be clear.

Another way to describe operations by their effects describes the externally visible results of applying one or more functions to one or more objects. For a stack we might start with these descriptions of the effects of the pop and push operations:

```
pop(newstack) = error;
pop(push(stack, x)) = x;
```

A little thought leads one to the conclusion that this start cannot be completed if one does not include a description of the internal state of the object along with the outputs; here the dilemma is that one seeks to encapsulate the representation details, but one needs to expose the internal representation to express correctness conditions.

The preceding development is based on the notion of tracking an object's state through the operations performed on the object. This approach is an extension of Hoare's use of predicate logic to reason from rules describing the effects of each program step to obtain conclusions about overall program behavior [HOAR69]. The reader interested in techniques for reasoning about program behavior is referred to recent literature to find current efforts in this important evolving field.

As with hierarchical program development, working with program specifications is much simpler when each logical step remains "close" to its neighbors in the hierarchy.

7.5.3 Processor Operation Selection

The selection of processor operations is often dominated by compatibility requirements. For this reason alone, the operation selection process may be downplayed. An important decision concerns the instruction set's complexity. Raising this issue places one in the middle of the debate between the RISC (Reduced Instruction Set Computer) and CISC (Complex Instruction Set Computer) camps. A basic claim of RISC proponents is that the implementation of the simple instruction set can be made very efficient and that the time penalty exacted for a soft implementation of more complex instructions is justified in view of the overall gain in processing speed. Since the majority of the most frequently executed instructions are quite simple, an infrequent digression into an inefficient procedural implementation of an operation may not be too harmful. However, in this connection it is interesting to observe that some RISC designers admit that the performance of their system would be improved by adding a floating-point processor.

For reference, the basic classes of MC68020 operations handling data values are listed in Table 7-13, where they are grouped by operand types.

The final processor-level topic concerns semantic specifications. One specification method uses a register-transfer program to describe an implementation of the operation, but often (especially in programmer's reference manuals) the necessary checks for erroneous conditions are omitted from the description.

7.5.4 Host Level

At this level the designer choosing operations has many options, since discrepancies between the host level and the processor level can be handled by firmware emulation. A minimum host design supports byte addition and subtraction plus shifting. Such a minimum host will be cheaper and will execute programs more slowly than a host with more built-in functions. Thus the operation set selection affects system speed and some optimization strategies discussed in Section 7.6.

Operation specifications at the host level use state-machine descriptions or logic

TABLE 7-13 SUMMARY OF MC68020 OPERAND MANIPULATION OPERATIONS

Operand Type	Mnemonic Representative of Operation Class	Description of Operation Class
Boolean	AND	Logical operations
	NOT	Complement
	BCHG	Test bit and toggle/set/clear it
Bit field	BFINS	Insert/set a bit field
	BFEXTS	Extract a bit field (signed/unsigned)
	BFCHG	Test a bit field and toggle/set/clear it
	BFFFO	Find first one in a bit field
Integer	ADD	Binary arithmetic
	NEG	Negate
	EXT	Extend sign bit
	ASL	Arithmetic shift
	CHK	Check register contents against bounds
	CMP	Compare (and set condition codes)
Multiple precision integer	ADDX	Add/subtract with extend
	NEGX	Negate with extend
Decimal	ABCD	Add/subtract decimal with extend
	NBCD	Negate decimal with extend

equations along with timing diagrams. These techniques are discussed thoroughly in logic design texts and thus are not repeated here.

7.5.5 Comments

Some major architectural issues arise from the choices of operation sets and the method(s) that can be used to expand the sets. The effects of an operation can be specified by giving relations between system state before and after the operation has been performed. This technique is valuable for reasoning about program properties, but it is not too helpful when the operation has to be implemented. If the implementation and the specification are close, the transitions between the two are easily made and it is easier to reason about the system's properties.

7.6 OPERATION EXECUTION

Now that we have discussed operand–operation bindings, operand–type bindings, and operation-(argument types) bindings, and all operations are defined, we are ready to discuss how the indicated operations are performed. Even though the implementation of the operation itself may be simple, we still need to think about two important aspects: the selection of the implementation in case the operand type information was not bound earlier, and modifications of the operation sequence or the hardware to reduce the execution time.

Thinking about the act of executing the operation moves our focus down one level in the hierarchy. To perform the calculations denoted by an Ada expression, the compiler generates a sequence of processor instructions, each being executed by a sequence of host operations, each of these being executed by a hardwired sequence of actions in the host machine's hardware.

7.6.1 Basics

Three aspects of operation execution will be covered:

1. Operation selection
2. Operation execution
3. Performance improvement

The basic operation selection question is: Which operation implementation should be used? The question arises if the operation might be overloaded. However, if there is only one version of the operator, the selection question reduces to the question: Do the actual operand types correspond to the required (ordered) set of operand types? With operation overloading, each operation name can stand for any member of a set of operations. Three different approaches to the type-based selection of the proper version of an overloaded procedure are:

1. There is a table with entries containing (f_name, operand_type_vector, entry).
2. There is one procedure implementing the operation; it tests the actual operand types to select one version of the operation.
3. There is a different procedure for each (f_name, first operand type) pair.

Under the first view, the procedure name and the operand type vector together serve as the key for an associative search whose result is the entry to the desired procedure (see Figure 7-11). There is a separate table entry for each different operand type vector. Performing this search during program execution could be inefficient if the operand types were static and known at compile time. With static type information there is no logical disadvantage to binding with the correct operation during compilation.

Under the second view, each function has an implied operand whose value is a list[11] containing the actual argument types. Within the function body the argument type vector is examined and appropriate operation sequences are selected. A distinct disadvantage of this approach is that the common procedure body must be augmented whenever a new definition overloads the operation for a new operand type

[11]The type list could be a list of operands, each denoting one type, or one operand whose type is "list_of_types" and whose value is the vector of operand types.

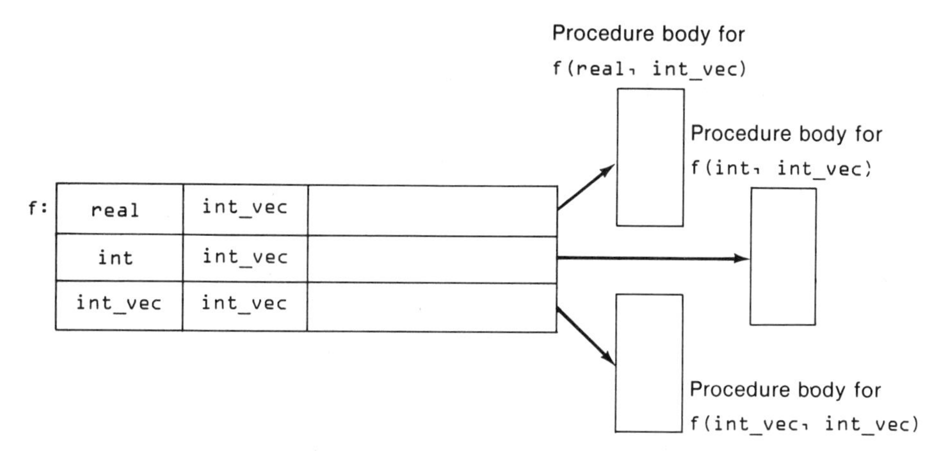

Figure 7-11 Entry table for an overloaded operation

vector. To permit this augmentation, the implementation must be publicly visible, contrary to our encapsulation goal.

Under the third view there is a separate procedure for each possible type of the procedure's first operand. This option shares attributes with the previous one: Decisions must be made internal to each procedure based on the actual types of the second and succeeding arguments, and encapsulation will be violated when a new object type is introduced. However, if the new object type never appears attached to an operand in a list whose first operand has an old type, encapsulation could be honored.

The second operation performance issue concerns the invocation of the algorithm chosen above. This "little" step actually activates the next lower level of the system to perform the steps that accomplish the desired operation. There are not any interesting design options here, except for reducing the execution time.

The final operation performance issue concerns techniques for reducing the execution time. Here are four basically different approaches to this issue:

1. Change the basic algorithm.
2. Execute steps in parallel.
3. Overlap steps.
4. Reorder steps to produce more parallelism possibilities.

We explore these options as we discuss operation speedup at each level of the system.

7.6.2 High-Level Languages

Most of these design issues arise in Ada and its implementation because Ada permits operation overloading.

7.6.2.1 Selecting the operation. If the language supports strong typing, with each object bound to its type during compilation, the compiler can choose the appropriate implementation of each operator and place the corresponding particular instruction or function calling sequence into the object program. However, if the language allows a programmer to defer type-object binding until run time, the operation must be selected during program execution. Certainly, there will be a performance penalty for dynamic operator-type binding, since the operator selection process takes time.

One advantage of deferring the object-type binding is that it permits the reuse of generic programs for common functions. To illustrate this point, consider a sorting algorithm that takes a list of objects of a generic type and rearranges it into sorted order. Clearly, the choice of sorting strategy (bubble sort, quicksort, or radix sort) is not affected by the object type of the list entries. Within the algorithm the basic compare and copy operations are the only things that depend on the object type of the list entries.

When constructing a type definition one may want to build upon a subroutine which has been shown to be correct. For example, if the new type has an ordering relation (such as "<"), one might construct a sorting procedure for vectors whose elements are of the new type using a generic sort routine whose parameters are the dimension of the vector and the type of the vector's components. A vector sort procedure for an element type could then be instantiated by using **new** with the appropriate parameter values. Consider the program structure illustrated in the next example.

Example 7-28

```
generic
  type T;
  type vector is array(size) of T;
  with function "<"(a, b : T) return boolean;
procedure sort(list : vector) is
  index : integer:=1;
  temp : T; --temporary for swapping
  more : boolean:=false;
begin
  while more loop
    more:=false;
    for index in 1 .. size-1 loop
      if list(index) < list(index+1) then
        temp:=list(index);
        list(index):=list(index+1);
        list(index+1):=temp;
        more:=true;
      end if;
    end loop;
  end loop;
end sort;
```

```
generic
  element : type;
  size : integer;
package thing_vector is
  type thing_vec is private;
  function read(a : thing_vec; b : integer) return element;
  procedure write(a : out thing_vec; b : integer; c : element);
  procedure sort(a : in out thing_vec);
private
  type thing_vec is array(1 .. size) of element;
end thing_vec;

package body thing_vector is
  function read(a : thing_vec; b : integer) return element is
  begin
    return a(b);
  end;

  procedure write(a : out thing_vec; b : integer; c : element) is
  begin
    a(b) := c;
  return;

  procedure sort is new sort(element, thing_vec);
end thing_vector;
```

To build upon an existing generic algorithm in Ada, the specific type must be given and a complete copy of the algorithm made to handle that type. The personalization of the sorting algorithm to the object type involves placing calls to the comparison and copying procedures in the appropriate places within the sorting algorithm.[12] Thus to sort both integers and reals in the same program, two personalized copies of sort are required (See Figure 7-12a). If we could leave type binding until run time, a single generic sort routine could be used for the major part of the sorting algorithm for any object type; to customize it, general compare and copy routines that take the object type as a parameter would be included. These routines would just dispatch to the specific routine that handles the actual object type. With this design, the type-dependent elements are confined to the specific compare and copy routines (see Figure 7-12b), plus entries in the dispatch tables. By using this technique, we achieve space saving at the cost of some run-time decisions. Furthermore, compilation is simplified.

7.6.2.2 Performing the operation. The actual operation implementation is simple from the high-level view; with static object typing the compiler simply inserts calls to the appropriate functions and procedures and the correct things will

[12]Even if one of these routines reduces to a single machine instruction for a user-defined type, most compilers will still insert a function call. Alternatively, the compiler could be designed with special rules for operations on built-in types so that it would insert a single instruction where appropriate.

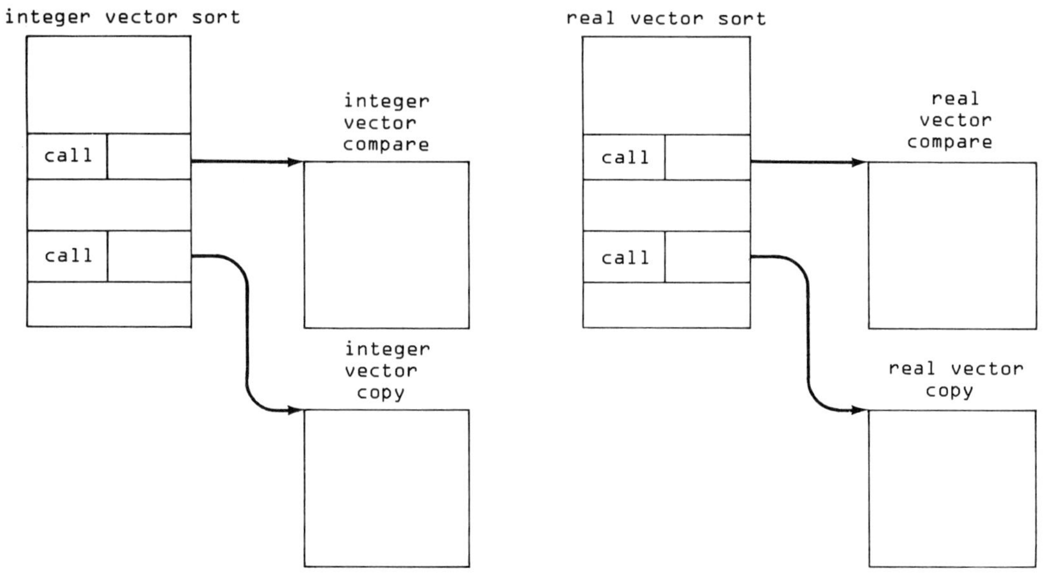

a) Static-type binding—a sort routine for each operand type

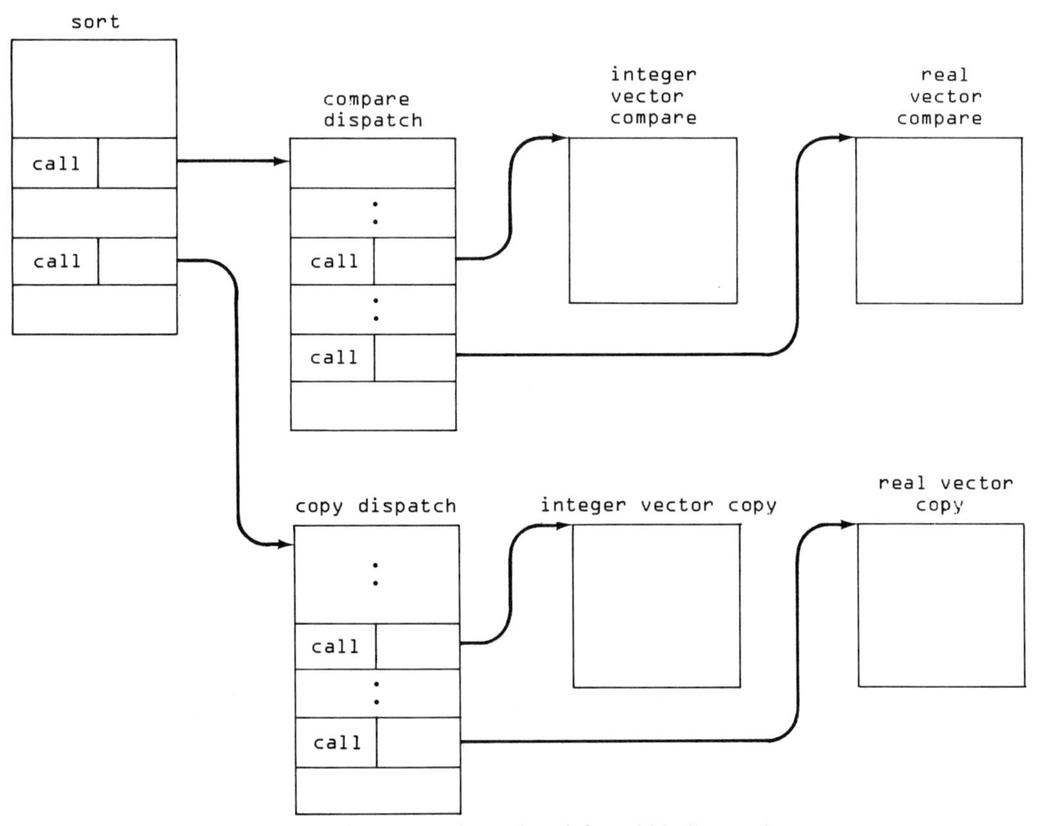

b) A generic sort routine using deferred binding and type-based dispatch routines

Figure 7-12 List sorting

happen when the program executes. With dynamic object typing the correct steps must be selected dynamically based on the actual operand types. The conceptual associative table containing the type-function mapping information could be implemented within the software.

7.6.2.3 Speedup. The third design issue concerns execution speedup. Certain naive approaches to speed a system can introduce erroneous behavior. Of the four general approaches for achieving speedup, only step reordering is used at this level. Step reordering can speed execution if the processor can overlap instruction execution. The basic optimization strategy is to rearrange the order of operation execution in such a way that the processor can execute the complete program more quickly and still obtain the correct results. The optimizer uses the associative, commutative, and distributive properties of the operators, plus an analysis of logical interdependencies based on the source/destination roles of operands to uncover opportunities for reordering among source language statements.[13]

A reordering that appears to be functionally proper may change the result values if the actual operators have side effects or do not satisfy the assumed mathematical properties (associativity, commutativity, and distributivity). These mathematical properties may be violated if an operation is overloaded with a function that does not satisfy the properties of the base operator (without overloading). In addition, if the problem values are such that intermediate results may lie outside the representation range, the operators that mathematically commute may not commute in the implementation. We illustrate these problems with examples.

Example 7-29

Operators f and g in this program fragment return boolean results. Each operator has a side effect: It writes a new value into the location named "side." Suppose that f(x) and g(y) are both true for the values in x and y. Then the expression

f(x) **or** g(y)

evaluates to "true." To save execution time, an optimizing compiler might produce a program that evaluates the general form

a **or** b

as follows:

if a **then** true **else** b

This is an example of the "short-circuit" evaluation strategy: The evaluation proceeds only as long as necessary to determine the expression's value. In this example, if a is true, the expression's value is known to be true and b's value is irrelevant. Therefore, b is not evaluated in the short-circuit version. This omission is acceptable if b has no side effects. But if f(x) were true the second write from b to location side would not occur because the evaluation of g(y) would be bypassed in the short-circuit evaluation.

[13]Analyses based on such object-based interactions are discussed further in Chapter 3 of Volume 2.

To underscore the importance of side effects, recall that in Prolog all database changes occur as a result of side effects. On the other hand, structured programming advocates abhor side effects and would claim that our example was a flagrant example of poor programming. We note the controversy and continue to the other difficulties.

The second problem situation involves violation of the assumed associative, commutative, and distributive properties by overloaded operator definitions. It is easy to construct an example illustrating this point—one simply overloads an associative arithmetic operator with one that is not associative. We leave such a construction to the reader.

Finally, the operator rearrangement for optimization may introduce problems if the arithmetic operations actually implemented within the computer system do not obey their mathematically ideal properties. For example, an operator might not commute or associate as a consequence of limitations imposed by the number representation conventions.

Example 7-30

In the following program fragment, suppose that all objects are reals, which are limited to the value range 10^{-40} .. 10^{40}.

$$a := 10^{12};$$
$$b := 10^{-25};$$
$$c := 10^{-25};$$
$$d := a * b * c;$$

Mathematically, the product could be evaluated in any order, since multiplication is both commutative and associative. With the values in this example, evaluation in the order (a * b) * c gives the correct result. However, in an evaluation corresponding to a * (b * c), the first multiplication causes underflow and the final result will be incorrect. Thus the arithmetic operators do not associate when an intermediate value does not lie within the range of values encoded by the representation conventions.

Notice that reversing the values of a and c reverses the consequences: The first ordering produces underflow and the second gives the correct result. Without foreknowledge of the approximate values assumed by the operands, the optimizer cannot choose an evaluation order that will give the correct results.

In conclusion, the compiler may inadvertently introduce problems as it tries to reduce the program's execution time by rearranging the evaluation order. This effect, which may occur if program procedures have side effects or if the assumed mathematical properties are not satisfied, can be eliminated only by eliminating optimization.

7.6.3 Processor Level

At the processor level, operation selection is quite simple—the function code in combination with the operand tags selects the action. Also, its execution is easily handled. Thus the important logical requirement that the processor correctly execute the algorithm specified in the program is easily met. Speeding execution, the third design issue, is an important topic. Four techniques can be used:

1. Change the implementation of a frequently executed operation.
2. Speed up the execution of a frequently executed operation sequence.
3. Dynamically detect overlapped execution opportunities.
4. Add operators that replace or shorten useful instruction sequences.

Techniques for changing an arithmetic operation's implementation have been covered in other books, so we will not dwell on this topic here.

The second option, speeding instruction sequences, is attractive. Usually a compiler generates a specific instruction pattern every time it detects a particular language construct. Procedure calling, for example, translates into a fixed pattern, including standard algorithms for parameter evaluation, state saving, and stack management. A computation that determines effective addresses follows another template. These patterns may occur so frequently that it may be worthwhile to detect the occurrence of the pattern within the processor and perform the whole pattern more quickly by using a special sequence designed to match the pattern's semantics. The following example illustrates this technique.

Example 7-31

In the B5700 processor, accessing a subscripted component (as for the name A(X)) is handled by a sequence of processor operations. For loading the component's value, the sequence is

```
LOADNAME A
INDEX
LOAD VALUE
```

This fragment assumes that the index value was pushed on the top of the stack before the operation sequence is initiated. The B7700 processor's control unit detects this common instruction sequence, executing it using a single indexed load sequence. Time is saved thereby in several ways, partly because the single indexed load avoids many top-of-stack manipulations that would be performed during a literal interpretation of the program fragment as a sequence of separate instructions.

Couldn't the previous example be speeded up by introducing a new processor instruction? Certainly, the new instruction would do the job. But introducing an instruction makes the new processor incompatible with the previous models.

The third technique for speeding operations uses a control unit designed to detect when the execution of consecutive operations can be overlapped without modifying the results. The control unit determines the usage of registers and functional units, which may be considered as resources shared between different instructions. We discuss this viewpoint and the dynamic detection of such parallelism in Chapter 3 of Volume 2.

The fourth speedup technique adds processor operations to handle common situations with dispatch. New operations can be added during system design or during program execution. To add operations during execution one uses processor instructions that change the control program or that connect procedures to the microprogram. We return to dynamic instruction changes after we study the addition of instructions during processor design.

Instructions may be added during system design with an eye toward particular data types. These changes are not an attempt to encapsulate the data type; in particular, the instructions added to support data type T may not form a complete operation set for type T. We are aiming for speed here; we seek a performance improvement from implementing a frequently executed function as a single processor instruction. Table 7-14 summarizes some representative instruction set expansions, grouped by data type.

TABLE 7-14 SOME OPERATIONS FOR SPECIAL DATA TYPES AND SOME SPECIAL OPERATIONS FOR ORDINARY DATA TYPES

Data Type	Processor	Operations
Doubly linked list	VAX 11-780	Insert, delete
	MC68020	Store double links
Queue	iAPX432	Insert/remove
	S/38	Insert/remove
Character string	Most mainframes	Edit
List	Symbolics 3600	(many)
	TI Explorer	
Decimal integers	Most mainframes	Add, subtract, multiply
	MC68020	Byte add/subtract
Sorted list	B5500	Lookup
	HP3000	Lookup
Reals	VAX 11-780	Polynomial evaluation
Integers/ character strings	System/370	Binary–decimal conversion

Example 7-32

The VAX 11-780 includes single- and double-precision polynomial evaluation operations. The operands are an argument value, the degree of the polynomial, and a pointer to a memory-resident table containing the polynomial's coefficients.[14] The operations utilize processor registers R0 .. R3 (or R0 .. R5 if the instruction specifies double-precision values) and returns the result in register R0 (or the pair R0, R1). The implementation performs this algorithm (for single-precision evaluation):

```
1. R0:=0; R2:=degree; R3:=coef_origin;
2. R1:=R0 * arg;
3. R0:=R1+memory[R3];
4. R3:=R3+4;  --4 bytes per coefficient
5. R2:=R2-1;
6. If R2 ≠ 0, goto step 2;
7. R1:=0;
```

[14]The coefficients are stored in order, with the coefficient of the highest power first and the constant term last.

Example 7-33

The MC68020 provides partial support for linked list insertion and deletion through its CAS2 instruction. The program reads and computes the proper values for the new bead before the processor executes CAS2. In Figure 7-13a we see these values in the new bead

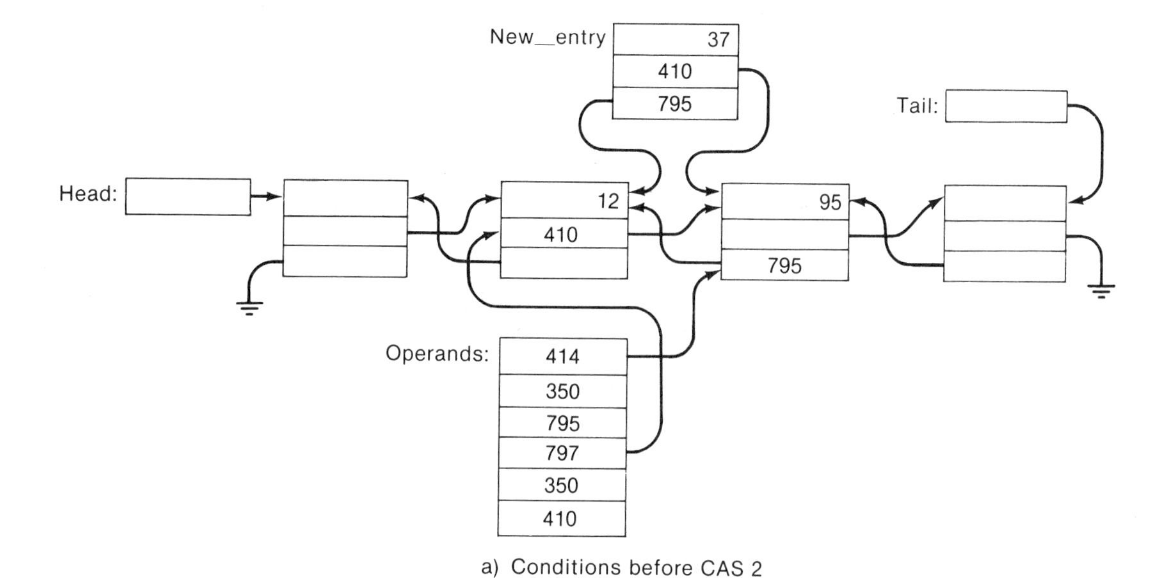

a) Conditions before CAS 2

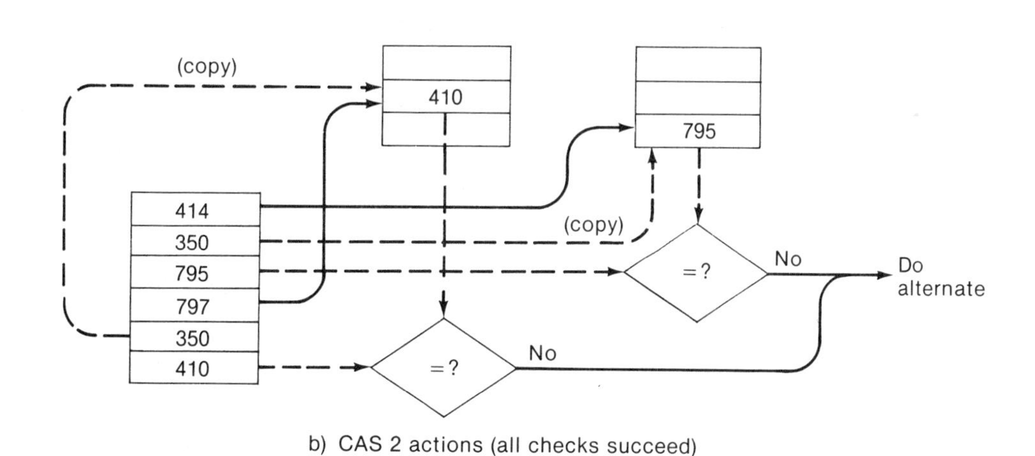

b) CAS 2 actions (all checks succeed)

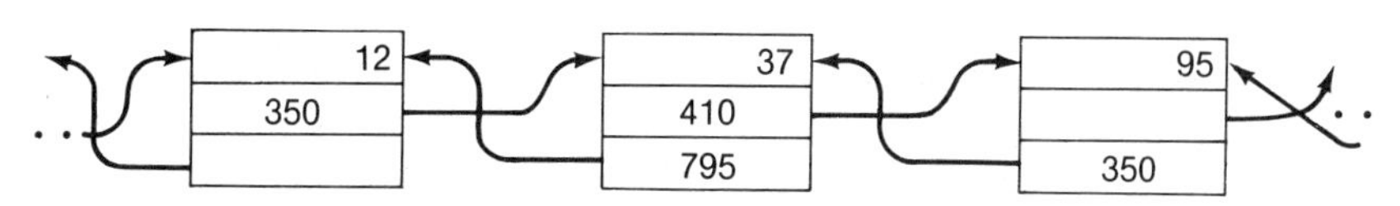

c) Conditions after CAS 2 (checks succeeded)

Figure 7-13 The MC68020 CAS2 instruction updates a doubly linked list (word width version)

about to be inserted into the queue. Figure 7-13b shows the actions of CAS2 that update the doubly linked queue. The final state of the queue is shown in Figure 7-13c. Since CAS2's actions do not depend on the queue's format, CAS2 actually does not support queues as formatted objects. The instruction is valuable because it encapsulates all substitutions required to update a doubly linked list into a single uninterruptible operation sequence. Because this instruction is uninterruptible, it supports queues describing shared resources; this use of CAS2 is described in Section 3.7 of Volume 2.

Contrast the MC68020's list and queue support with the VAX, the S/38, and the iAPX432: The VAX has queue manipulation operations that both construct proper linkages and insert them. The iAPX432 and the S/38 queue insertion instructions even search the queue and find the proper place for the insertion, according to the discipline specified for the queue and the queue's current contents.

Example 7-34

The VAX 11-780 has "queue" insertion and deletion instructions.[15] A queue is represented by a doubly linked list; the first bead entry contains the forward pointer, and the second entry, the backward pointer. While the processor performs either queue operation, it turns the interrupts off; if there is only one processor in the system, proper synchronization can be achieved between processes that share the same queue.[16]

While making a queue insertion, the IBM System/38 processor finds the proper location within the queue based on the queueing discipline (FIFO, priority, etc.) specified in the queue's description.

Example 7-35

In the IBM System/38 five processor operations support queue objects:

CREATE
DESTROY
ENQUEUE
DEQUEUE
COPY QUEUE DESCRIPTION

This operation list encompasses all the basic queue operations that one would include in a package encapsulating the queue data type. Each queue specification in the system includes information regarding the format of the entries in the queue, including their sizes and types. Each queue can be managed using a LIFO or FIFO discipline, even with a priority ordering. The queue's descriptor specifies its discipline.

Now we turn to the final technique for speeding execution—dynamically adding or modifying processor instructions by changing microprograms or by adding

[15]We place the word "queue" in quotes because whereas DEC says that these operations support queues, in fact they support doubly linked lists. We make the distinction because some expect that a queue instruction would use the queue discipline to find the spot for inserting a new entry, but here the program is charged with that task; the insert operation will do the right thing with the pointers, given the proper pointer as an operand.

[16]We will discuss synchronization of this variety further in Chapter 3 of Volume 2.

a software routine that can be invoked like an instruction. We illustrate these options as they appear in the Data General Eclipse processor.

Example 7-36

The Data General Eclipse architecture includes a WCS (Writable Control Store) option that allows the user to specify up to 16 new instructions by adding microinstructions to the control store [DATA74]. The processor instructions that write into the control store also establish the connection between the microprogram that defines an operation and the subfunction code that invokes the operation. The microinstruction word has 56 bits, wider than the machine's 16-bit word, so four load microcode instructions must be executed to store one microinstruction; three store a 16-bit piece of the microinstruction word and one stores an 8-bit piece.

One of these new instructions can be invoked by executing the special instruction XOP1. The "subfunction" bits (9 .. 6) in the XOP1 instruction are used as an index in a "decode" table. The selected entry contains the control store address of the first microinstruction to be executed during the execute phase for the added operation. Figure 7-14 illustrates this use of the decode table. The interpretation of the two register numbers appearing as operand specifiers in the XOP1 instruction is determined by the user-written microcode.

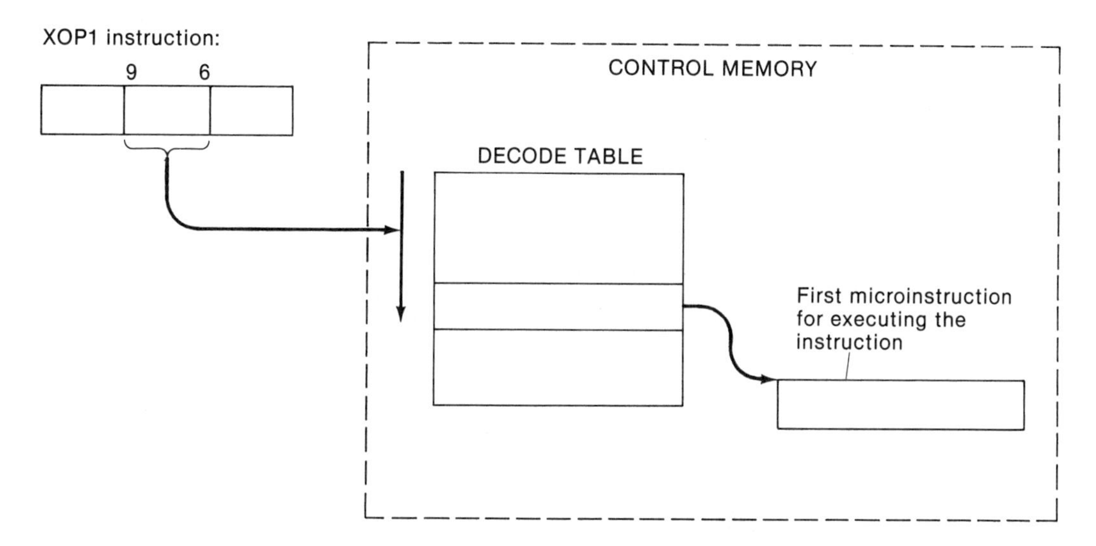

Figure 7-14 The decode table for interpreting Data General Eclipse XOP1 instructions

The writable control store contents become part of the process state that must be saved if the process happens to be interrupted and rescheduled for continued execution. The latter requirement discourages the use of writable microcode if the processor will be shared among different user programs.

Another way to expand the processor's operation set is to build a routine within user memory that can be invoked quickly based on the function code value in a processor instruction. Logically, this scheme is identical to adding microprogram extensions, but the execution speed will be slower than that of a system that has been expanded in a logically equivalent manner by adding microinstructions. The special state-saving requirement does not exist under this design because the personalizing information is located within user memory, which is saved in the normal course of multiprogram memory management.

Example 7-37

The Data General Eclipse architecture supports user-defined operations called XOPs (eXtended OPerators), implemented by software routines residing in user memory. During the invocation of one of the XOP operations, the following steps are performed:

1. The processor state is saved as if for procedure call;
2. The two effective operand addresses replace the stack locations where AC_2 and AC_3 were saved;
3. Bits 10 .. 6 from the XOP instruction (which specify the software routine to be invoked) are added to 24_{16}; call the sum S;
4. Transfer control to the location specified in memory location S;

After the routine has completed execution, it executes a POP BLOCK instruction which removes the saved processor state from the stack, restores the stack pointer, and returns control to the calling context. Up to 32 new user-defined operations can be added in this manner, in addition to the 16 WCS operations that can be initiated by the XOP1 instruction.

An XOP implementation will be faster than a procedure call because the XOP parameter fetching process uses the built-in address evaluation mechanisms.

Processor performance can be enhanced by adding a coprocessor to the system. This amounts to adding special hardware to execute special instructions; this method for speeding processor execution is discussed in Section 2.5.1 of Volume 2.

7.6.4 Host Level

At the host level, operation execution entails performing manipulations in response to microinstruction commands. There are few options that affect correctness or operation selection. One key design decision chooses the host complexity; it determines the distance between the processor's instruction set and the primitive host operations. Within a family of compatible processors, the fast machines will have a host structure close to the processor's functionality, while the slow machines will have a single simple ALU. Designing a fast host to be close to the processor's structure allows many machine instructions to be executed in one (wide) microinstruction.

In this section we cover some techniques that speed a host system. We start with a basic host architecture that has one ALU with two inputs and one output. Each of the inputs and the output are connected to separate internal buses connecting the ALU with its sources and destinations. Figure 7-15 illustrates this basic three-bus design, with a shifter connected between the ALU's output and its output bus; it is a common design practice to include this shift function.

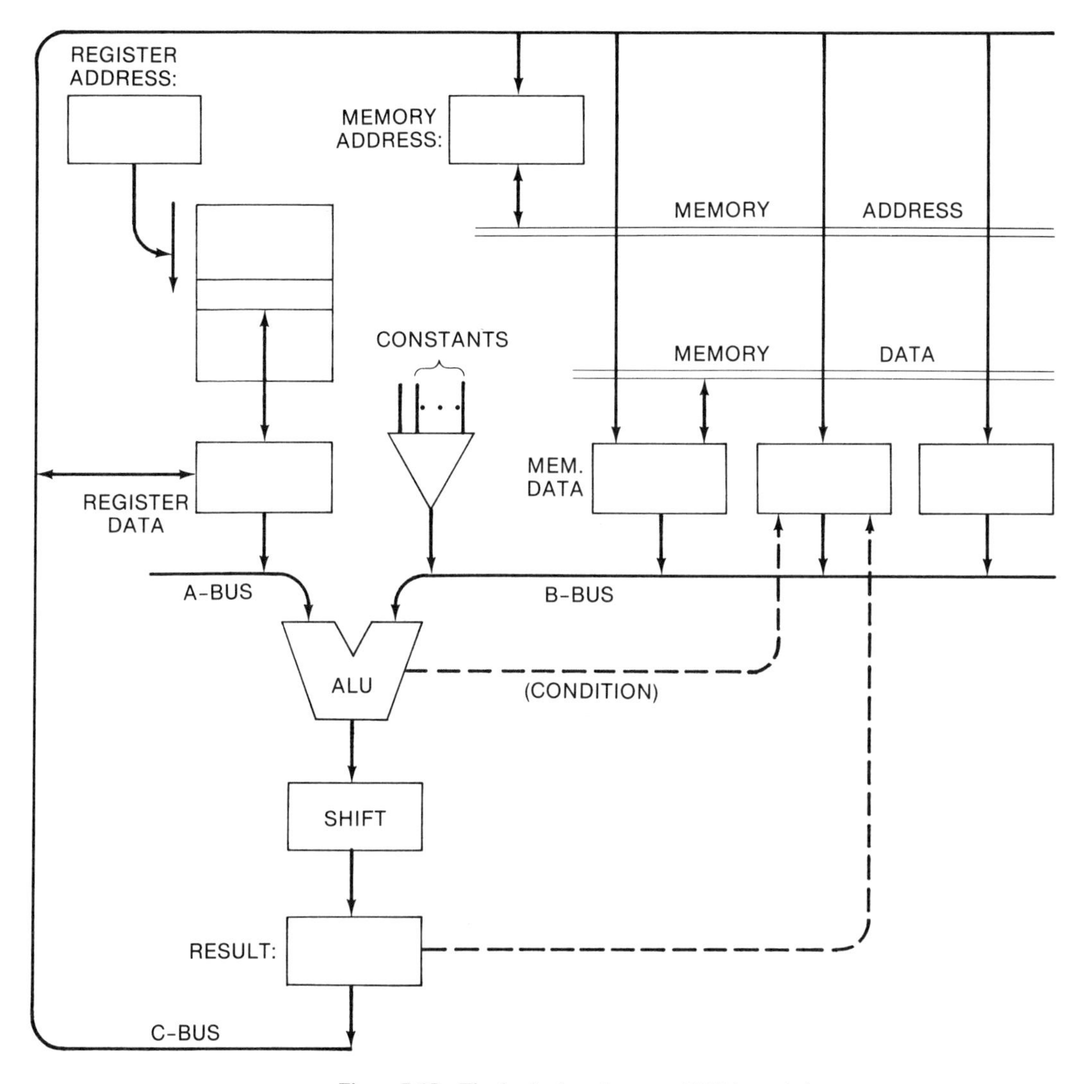

Figure 7-15 The basic three-bus one-ALU host design.

The basic three-bus ALU-based host design can be enhanced in several interesting ways:

1. Widen the data paths.
2. Add ALUs.
3. Add data paths between modules.
4. Add access paths to the registers and register memories.
5. Expand the ALU to handle other operations.
6. Overlap the execution of operations within the system.

All of these techniques improve system performance because more useful work can be accomplished in the same time intervals.

Enlarging the host data paths will improve performance if fewer passes through the ALU are required to complete an operation. If the data path is wide enough to pass common operands, further width increases will give little performance improvement. In a very flexible design the ALU width can be changed dynamically to match the widths of the operands being handled at the moment.

Example 7-38

The B1700 designers built a variable-width ALU. Its width for arithmetic operations was an additional ALU input [BURR72]. The flexibility was inserted partly because when the ALU was designed the language implementers had not chosen the structures of the virtual processors they would use to emulate each language. The flexible-width ALU design has a certain aesthetic appeal, even if its additional logic does slow the execution of certain operations.

Since an ALU module can perform at most one operation at a time, adding ALUs to the host system can increase the amount of work that could be accomplished in parallel. Separate data paths should be provided for the operands and results for each ALU. In addition, the modules that hold register contents may be redesigned to add independent parallel access paths to each module.

Adding functionality to ALU modules increases their complexity but makes the execution of complex instructions simpler. For example, a real adder provides great speedup for operations on real operands compared to a field-serial implementation using integer ALUs. One simple modular approach to providing added ALU functionality adds separate modules tailored for particular object types. In this vein, modules supporting real and string data types would speed scientific and business programs, respectively.

Example 7-39:

The Honeywell DPS6 minicomputers have two optional modules that support real operations and character string operations. All these operations are included in the basic machine instruction set; if the accelerative module that would perform an instruction is absent, the processor will cause a trap to invoke a software trap handler that will implement the instruction. With the appropriate trap handlers, the processor is functionally identical to, but slower than, a processor having the accelerative module.

By adding coprocessors a designer can provide a similar benefit in a different manner (since each coprocessor's connection is external to the processor); coprocessors are discussed further in Section 2.5.1 of Volume 2.

The processor might be speeded a bit by reordering operation execution and operator decoding. In particular, its controller might be designed to pass operands and to initiate execution simultaneously in several different ALUs, and (in parallel) determine whether (one of) the result(s) that is(are) produced is in fact the desired result. By using this design, the desired result can be obtained more quickly than by waiting to decode the instruction before initiating the operation. The structure of an ALU using this initiate-select strategy is contrasted with the conventional decode-initiate strategy in Figure 7-16. To study the speed, let t_t denote the logic delay in the

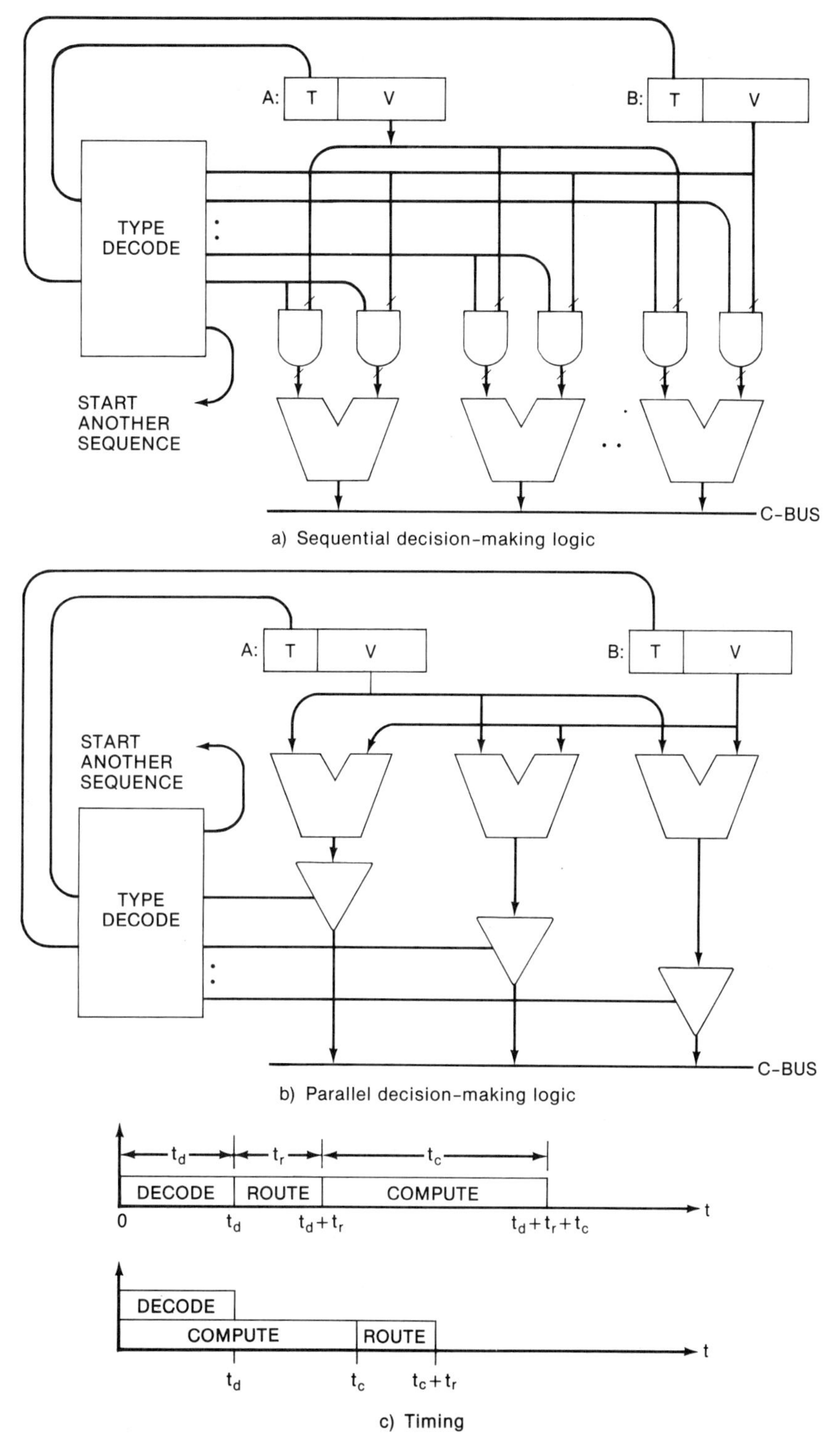

Figure 7-16 Sequential versus parallel type-decode-compute logic ($C = A + B$)

type decoder, t_c the compute delay in the ALU, and t_r the routing logic delay. Since $t_r < t_d < t_c$, the total delay is $t_d + t_r + t_c$ for the decode-initiate design and $t_c + t_r$ for the initiate-select design, and the latter design is really faster. Under the initiate-select design, what happens if the desired result will not be produced by any hardware present? Clearly another implementation of the operation must be activated. This strategy is used in the Symbolics 3600, described in Section 7.7.

7.6.5 Comments

While instruction set selection does not affect functional completeness, it can be important in easing understanding and speeding operations. It can also pay to define new operations at the processor level by changing the microprogram.

Our discussion reinforces the fact that it can be useful to keep neighboring implementation levels logically close. A close implementation is easily shown to be correct. A close processor instruction set reduces program length and improves the processing rate. A host design close to the processor's structure reduces the number of microinstructions needed for each processor instruction, reducing the execution time for individual processor instructions.

Several operation reordering techniques, with static or dynamic detection of parallelism opportunities, introduce parallelism, but they could change program semantics and must be used with care. Most of these parallelism issues will reappear in Volume 2.

7.7 LISP MACHINE ARCHITECTURES

In this section we present some features of the LISP programming language [WINS84] and a machine designed for efficient execution of LISP programs. Information in this section related to operand types and operations applies to both the programming language and machine implementation levels.

7.7.1 The LISP Programming Language

You will not become a proficient LISP programmer from reading this summary of LISP object types, data structures, and elementary operations, but you should get the flavor of the language and see why its implementation presents an interesting challenge.

7.7.1.1 LISP object types. Three important LISP data types are:

1. Lists
2. Structures
3. Association lists

We discuss structures and association lists after we present some LISP operations in the next section.

The *list* is the primary LISP object type. A LISP list is structurally equivalent to a binary tree; each internal node has two successors, which themselves may be either subtrees or atomic elements. From a logical viewpoint, a list contains two elements, each one possibly being a list itself. This logical view can be used as the basis for constructing a (linear) parenthesized representation of the list. A two-element list is represented by the parenthesized expression (A B), where A and B are the first element and the second element of the list, respectively. The linear representation of a complete list is constructed by repeated applications of the representation rule for each internal node of the tree. It is easy to see that the linear representation will contain a parenthesis pair for each internal node. Linear list representations are used to express LISP objects and programs.

Example 7-40

Figure 7-17 contains several lists represented as trees along with their corresponding linear parenthesized representations.

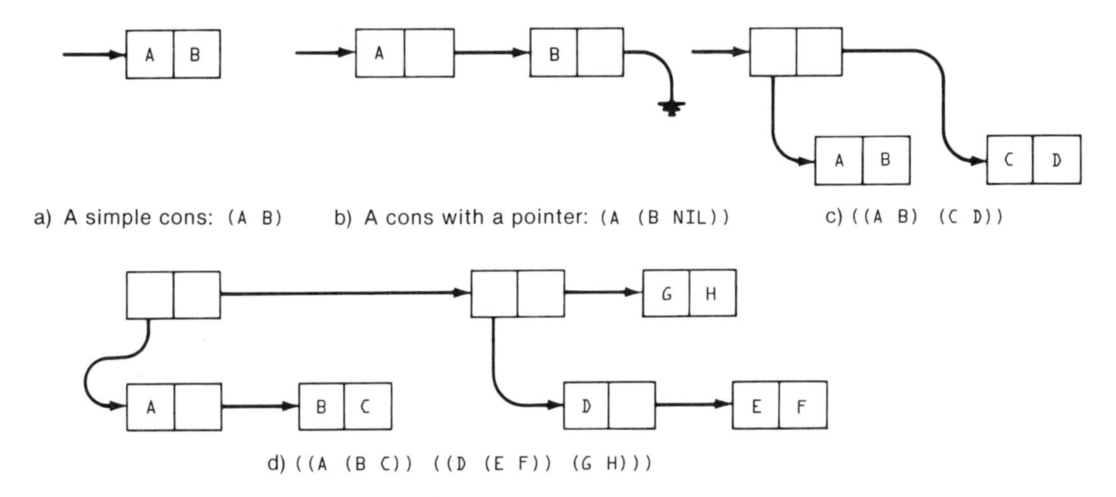

Figure 7-17 Representations of LISP lists

Small LISP data objects that are not lists are called atoms. The data types for atoms include character string, integer, and real.

The pointer type is basic to a LISP list's representation. In particular, a two-element list can be represented by a two-component record containing a pointer to each of the list's components. In LISP such records are called "cons"es. There is one cons for each internal list node. Some pointers in conses locate other cons objects, while others locate atomic objects.[17] A little thought reveals a problem—we need to distinguish pointers from atom values. For the moment, assume that this detail has been handled within the representation. We will return to representation details when we discuss LISP machine design.

[17]One may save space by substituting a short atom for the pointer that otherwise would locate it; this refinement is not important in this discussion, which focuses on LISP's logical properties.

A common list configuration is a linear list of n elements. In a LISP program this structure can be represented by a single list within a single pair of parentheses, such as

(A B C D E)

This list is really represented in the system as a chain of lists:

(A (B (C (D (E)))))

or

(A (B (C (D (E NIL)))))

The second form is a more accurate reflection of the structure, since in the representation each atom in the list is the first element of some cons. A LISP list will end with a lot of right parentheses when written in this form. Figure 7-18 depicts the representation of this list structure. In a structure NIL denotes a special pointer value which indicates that the pointer object does not point to anything. In a diagram a null pointer terminates at the symbol for electrical ground.

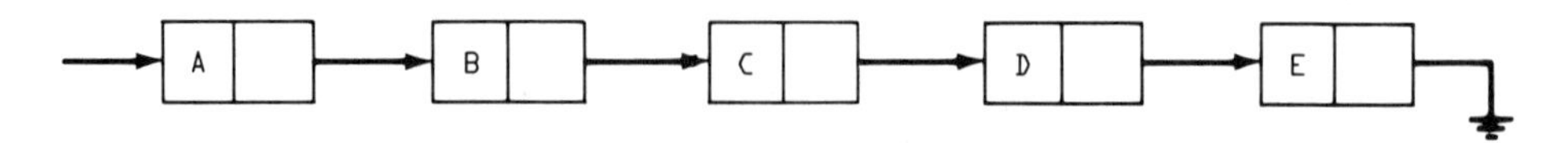

Figure 7-18 The representation of the linear list (A B C D E)

7.7.1.2 LISP operations. Like Prolog, LISP is an interactive language. The user can type a name, to which LISP will respond by presenting the value stored in the object whose name was given. The user can also type in an expression which will be evaluated and its value presented to the user. Every expression has a value. A LISP expression may be expressed in terms of operations performed on LISP objects; we discuss the syntax and semantics of LISP expressions in this section.

Since LISP uses prefix notation, the first member of a LISP object treated as an expression is interpreted as a function (or operation) name. The remaining list elements are the function's actual parameters, passed by value.[18] The manner of handling function parameters is affected by the function name. If the function is user defined, all its parameters will be evaluated before the function is called.[19] If the function is a LISP primitive, it may be specified that one or more of its arguments must not be evaluated before calling the function.

The programmer may use a single quote mark to defer the evaluation of the expression that follows the quote. The scope of the single quote extends to the next

[18]But lists are passed by copying only the pointer to the root of the list, not by copying the entire list.

[19]Numbers, of course, do not need to be evaluated. If you insist that there should be no distinction between numbers and other objects, you can adopt the attitude that each number in an expression is a name for a location that always contains the value of the number.

(unmatched) right parenthesis or space. The characters within the scope of the quote are treated as a string, not as an expression to be evaluated. If the object starting with the quote mark is evaluated, the result is the enclosed character string.

Now we are ready to describe simple LISP operations that create and manipulate list objects. Each LISP operation returns a value, so an operation without side effects simply computes one value that it returns. The basic LISP list operations include assembling a list, disassembling a list, and testing whether an object is an atom. Table 7-15 lists some of these operations, with L and M denoting object names.

TABLE 7-15 SOME BASIC LISP OPERATIONS WITHOUT SIDE EFFECTS

Operation	Value Is
(CAR L)	The first element of L
(CDR L)	A list containing the rest of L (its second element expressed as a list)
(CONS L M)	A list whose first element is L and whose second element is M
(ATOM L)	T (true) if L is an atom (i.e., not an internal node); NIL (false) otherwise

A sequence of CAR and CDR operations can be used to "walk around" a list, selecting an element by its position within the list. The CDR operator always returns a list, which will be empty if the list which is its operand has only one entry.[20] The CONS operation obtains a new instance of a cons node (from the global heap) and fills it with pointers to the two arguments of the CONS (which may have been lists themselves). Since the CONS operator does not recopy the list components, any subsequent operation that changes one of these components will also change the composite list created by CONS.

The SETQ operation performs an assignment as a side effect; its value is the value of the expression that was assigned to the named location. Thus (SETQ L M) assigns the value of M to L and returns the value of M. There is a rule stating that the first parameter of SETQ is not evaluated before SETQ is called. This convention saves writing a quote mark in front of the destination name. SETQ can also be called with any number of argument pairs (expressed as a single list); each odd parameter is not evaluated and is taken as the name to which the value of the next parameter will be assigned. These evaluations and assignments are performed sequentially.[21]

The EVAL operator evaluates its single argument. It is the left inverse of the quote operator since the following two expressions are equivalent.

```
(EVAL 'S)
S
```

[20]The empty list is the same as the NIL pointer; this object is considered to be both an atom and a list; it is the only item with this peculiar property.

[21]The built-in operator PSETQ is similar to SETQ, but performs parallel assignments; all expressions are evaluated before any assignments are performed.

A sequence of operations can be written as a list containing those operations in the order of their execution. The value of the sequence is the value of the last operation executed. Thus the "expression"

```
((SETQ C 'B) (SETQ M 'C) (CONS C M))
```

sets C to point to a list having one element whose value is the string "B", sets M to point to another one-element list containing "C", and then constructs a new list from those two. The value of the expression is the list (B C).

One may use the COND (conditional) operator to test whether a predicate is true and, if so, to evaluate a corresponding expression. This is similar to an Ada **if** .. **then** statement; the value returned by COND is the value of the evaluated expression, or NIL, if the predicate is false. A list generalization of COND has several parameters, each consisting of a list of two expressions. The first expression is a condition; if its value is non-NIL, the condition is true. The list CONS is evaluated by sequentially evaluating the conditions until one of them is found to be true. Then the corresponding expression is evaluated. The value of the COND expression is the value of the expression chosen to be evaluated. If all the conditions are false, the value of the COND expression is NIL.

Example 7-41

Consider the following program fragment:

```
((SETQ L '(A (B ((C D) (E (F G))))))
(SETQ M L)
(SETQ N (CONS M M))
(COND ((ATOM M) (SETQ N L))
      ((ATOM (CAR L)) (SETQ M (CONS N L)))
      (T NIL)))
```

The first three lines of this program establish the environment in which the COND expression will be evaluated. The COND states that if M is an atom, then set N to point to L; if the first element of L is an atom, then set M to point to a new list constructed from a copy of N concatenated with L; and otherwise (the predicate T always being true), return NIL as the result. Without looking at the values in L, M, and N, we can state (weakly) that the overall result returned by this program fragment is the value returned by the last function executed (which is the value of L, the value of M, or NIL, depending on the predicate evaluations). What is the program's actual behavior? The result is the same as the final contents of M, which obtained a second value during the CONS evaluation.

Table 7-16 lists a few basic LISP predicates that one can use to write simple LISP programs.

7.7.1.3 More LISP data structures.

With our understanding of some basic LISP operations, we are ready to discuss structures and association lists, two important LISP data types.

TABLE 7-16 SOME LISP PREDICATES

Predicate	True if:
(ATOM M)	M is an atom
(EQL A B)	A and B are structures represented by the same memory objects
(EQUAL A B)	A and B are matching lists[a]
(LISTP A)	A is a list
(NUMBERP A)	A is a number

[a]In particular, A and B represent logically equivalent lists but do not have to be represented by the same memory cells.

The *structure definition* function DEFSTRUCT defines a record structure type. The effect is somewhat analogous to that of a Pascal or Ada record declaration. There are several important differences, however:

1. The LISP DEFSTRUCT operator is an executable function.
2. While executing DEFSTRUCT, LISP creates an instantiation routine which can be called to create an instance of the structure.
3. While executing DEFSTRUCT, LISP creates a set of accessing functions which can be used to access the components of an instance of the structure.

The following example will clarify these differences.

Example 7-42

```
 ((DEFSTRUCT (THIS)
  (NAME NIL)
  (VALUE 3)
  (COMMENT 'Here it is))
(SETQ HERE (MAKE-THIS))
(SETQ M (THIS-VALUE HERE))
(SETF (THIS-NAME HERE) 'thing)
(SETQ TWO (MAKE-THIS :NAME 'SIX :COMMENT '6)))
```

The first statement defines the type THIS; each instance of an object of type THIS will have three components named NAME, VALUE, and COMMENT, with default initial values NIL, 3, and "Here it is", respectively. The second statement creates an object of type THIS and assigns to the object named HERE a pointer to the new instance. Notice how the name of the creation operator was constructed from the type name. The third statement illustrates how a value is read from a named record's field; the statement reads the field named VALUE of the object HERE and assigns it to M. The last statement assigns a new value to the NAME field of HERE. The fourth statement shows how a "function," which obtains a pointer to the field, can be used as a destination specification for an assignment in a SETF operator. (It cannot be used as a destination in a SETQ operation.) Finally, the last statement illustrates how the default initial values can be overridden when an object is created; the value of (THIS-NAME TWO) is "SIX".

The *association list*, which is a list of lists, is the third important LISP data structure. The associative lookup operation ASSOC looks in an association list (which is the value of its second argument) for a list whose first element matches the value of ASSOC's first argument; the result is the entire list of which the specified key is the first element. Observe the behavior in the following simple example.

Example 7-43

```
((SETQ A '((FIRST this) (SECOND thing) (THIRD is)))
(SETQ M (ASSOC 'SECOND A)))
```

The first expression assigns an association list to the object named A. The second expression looks in the value of A for a component list whose first entry is "SECOND" and returns that entire sublist. So the value assigned to M is the list

```
(SECOND thing)
```

7.7.1.4 LISP functions. LISP functions are basic to most LISP operations. A LISP function receives all its parameters by value, as we noted earlier. A list parameter is passed by passing the value of a pointer to the list, not by copying the list itself; this rule saves memory space but has important consequences if one uses operators that change a list internally without copying it.

A LISP programmer can define a new function by executing the DEFUN function. DEFUN has three parameters, which are not evaluated before DEFUN is called. The parameters are the name of the function, a list of its formal parameter names, and a list that is its body. The following example should be obvious:

```
(DEFUN SQUARE (X) (* X X))
```

Notice that function definition is a run-time activity.

LISP utilizes dynamic nesting for name resolution. The set of declarations local[22] to a function f includes f's formal parameters and those names assigned values during f's execution by the LET primitive assignment operator. Recall that one implementation of dynamic nesting uses a stack onto which the old values of all newly declared objects are pushed during procedure call and from which they are popped during procedure return. The LISP system uses this implementation; it will push the old values of the parameters during call, but the old values of objects that become local by execution of the LET operation are not pushed until LET is executed. LET is similar to SETQ, but has four important differences:

1. LET's list parameter is not evaluated before LET is called.
2. LET takes one argument, which is a list of name–value pairs enclosed in parentheses.
3. LET performs parallel assignments if given a list.
4. LET allows a name without a value in an argument pair— a NIL value will be stored in the designated location.

[22]The objects that we call "local" are called "bound" objects in LISP terminology.

The previous (i.e., external) values of all local variables are popped off the stack when the function returns.

A function will be called during the evaluation of an expression if the name of the function is the first entry in the expression that is being evaluated. Also, a function can be called by executing the primitive FUNCALL. This primitive accepts any number of parameters. It evaluates them all and then uses the value of the first one as the name of the function to be called. The values of the remaining list entries are the parameters passed to that call.

Example 7-44

We can use FUNCALL with association list retrieval operations to implement object-oriented programming in the manner of the "message to the first parameter" school. In this implementation, calling sequences to all versions of the overloaded function OFCN are listed in an association list which is searched using the types of the actual parameters passed to the overloaded version of the function. In this model the generic function simply searches the association list and then executes FUNCALL to call the function found there. This program fragment shows the dispatching within the overloaded function definition

```
(DEFUN OFCN (x xtype y ytype)
  ((FUNCALL (CDR (ASSOC FLIST xtype)) x y ytype)))
```

An entry in FLIST would look like (integer first). Notice the use of CDR to remove the parameter type list that served as the search key. The effect of a call

```
(OFCN 6 'integer 8 'integer)
```

is to produce a call (first 6 8 integer) if (integer first) is an entry in FLIST.

7.7.1.5 Comments. The LISP programming language emphasizes lists as both data and program objects. All operations are expressed in prefix notation. Basic LISP functions include those that construct lists, select from them, call functions, and test predicates.

Several aspects of this language make its implementation difficult:

1. Objects are created dynamically from free storage, which has to be managed as a heap.
2. Object types and functions can be defined during program execution.
3. The data structures contain many pointers.
4. The implementation has to distinguish pointers from other values.
5. Many functions will be called during program execution.
6. Object sizes vary.
7. Dynamic nesting is used for name resolution.
8. The set of objects local to a procedure may be changed during program execution (by executing LET).

These aspects introduce requirements that make it difficult to realize an efficient implementation of the language. Now we will see how one design team designed an efficient LISP host.

7.7.2 A LISP Processor Architecture

In the remainder of this section, we discuss the Symbolics 3600 family of machines ([MOON85], [MOON87]), designed to support LISP. We discuss the following aspects of the machine's design, showing the relationship between LISP and the machine's design:

1. Object typing
2. Operator selection
3. Operator implementation
4. Internal processor state
5. Garbage collection

7.7.2.1 Type implementation. In the Symbolics 3600, each word contains 36 bits, of which some may be used for tag information. Every object is either directly tagged or belongs to a structure whose header defines the types of the components within the structure. Directly tagged words have a 2-bit tag called the "cdr code," which occupies bits 35 and 34. We illustrate the important type-coding cases, starting from the bottom with representations of atoms.

7.7.2.1.1 ***Atoms.*** The interpretation of an atom does not depend on the cdr code. Thus all atoms have to be represented in 34 bits, including their type tags. A 34-bit indirect pointer is used to access an atom if its representation will not fit within 34 bits.

Figure 7-19 illustrates three important object types and their representations. Our short tag names for these object types are listed in Table 7-17. Single-precision reals and integers have 32-bit encodings, with reals conforming to the IEEE

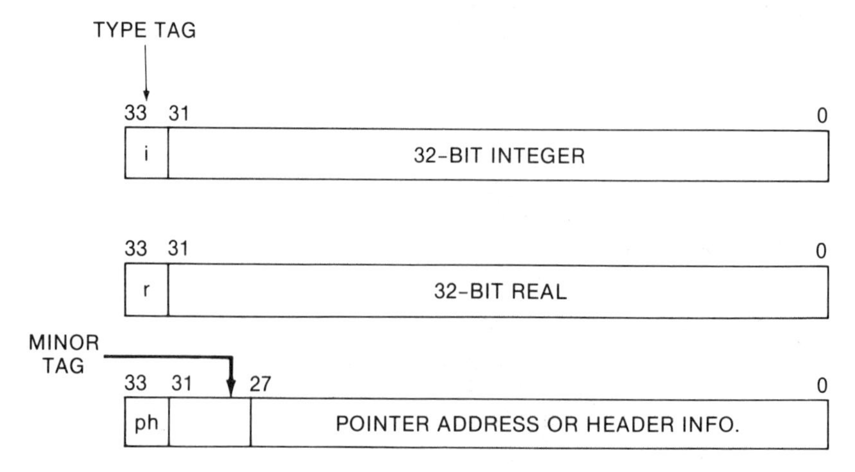

Figure 7-19 Simple object representations in the Symbolics 3600 (after [MOON87], Figure 1; © IEEE 1987)

TABLE 7-17 TYPE TAG INTERPRETATIONS IN THE SYMBOLICS 3600

Short Name	Meaning
r	This word contains a single-precision (32-bit) value
i	This word contains an integer (32-bit) value
ph	The minor tag (bits 31 .. 28) plus one bit from the major tag determine the meaning of the word as a pointer or a header

standard format. Since these data types are used so frequently, the designers sacrificed pointer space so that integers and reals could be accessed quickly. A pointer contains a 6-bit type tag and a 28-bit virtual address. The pointer's type tag specifies the type of object located at the indicated address. Table 7-18 lists some interpretations of the pointer's type tag.

TABLE 7-18 THE SYMBOLICS 3600 MINOR TAG VALUE DEFINES THE INTERPRETATION OF THE OTHER 28 BITS IN THE WORD[a]

Name of Tag Value	Type of Thing in the Remaining 28 Bits
Symbol	Pointer to a "value"
List	Pointer to the next entry in a list
Nil	Pointer to nothing (the pointer is NIL)
Array header	Word contains type and length of the array
Prog header	Word contains the length of the program object
String	Pointer to the string's representation in an array
Array	Pointer to an array header
Type instance	Pointer to an array defining a type (a "flavor")
Compiled program	Pointer to a program header
Single-precision	Pointer to a single-precision value
Double-precision	Pointer to a double-precision value
Rational	Pointer to a pair of locations representing a rational fraction
Indirection	Pointer to the value that logically belongs here

[a]This list is not comprehensive.

One important special case is the indirect[23] pointer used to signify that the object that was expected here actually exists elsewhere (namely, at the location whose address is stored in the pointer). Such indirect pointers are automatically traversed by the processor, so that the processor does properly access the object. Special operators are provided to manipulate indirect pointers.

[23]These are called "forwarding pointers" in Symbolics literature.

7.7.2.1.2 *Lists.* The *list* is a very important object type in LISP. Thus it is important to choose an efficient list representation. One could choose a machine representation of a list that mirrors a literal interpretation of the list as a set of two-element beads linked together by pointers. Such a representation is logically correct, but a machine using this list representation scheme would spend many cycles fetching pointers from memory and using their contents as addresses to direct further fetches. Clearly, we need to seek a better way to represent lists.

We start with the linear list, a common case. In a linear list the cdr of each cons points directly to the next cons in the list (see Figure 7-20a). The general list representation seems particularly inefficient in this case, because the actual list can be compressed easily to a vector. Introducing a special format for this simple case alone might not be effective, since any node in the list could be changed and destroy the simple linear structure. The Symbolics system uses the cdr tag to define the relationship between the word associated with the cdr tag and the remainder of the list of which it is a part. In essence the cdr tag specifies whether a simple case applies, and if so, which case does apply. The cdr tag codes are listed in Table 7-19. The representation of a linear list uses two of the cdr tag codes. The "next" tag indicates that the

TABLE 7-19 INTERPRETATIONS OF THE CDR TAG (BITS 35 AND 34) IN THE SYMBOLICS 3600

Abbreviation Used in Figures	Short Name	Meaning of Appended Tag
n	next	The next word contains the CDR of this entry
c	cons	The next word contains the value of the CDR of this entry
e	end	The next word is not part of this structure
—	other	This word contains something which is not necessarily part of a list entry

next word contains the list element which is the cdr of this word. The "end" tag indicates that the cdr of this word would be null, which means that this element is the last word of this construct. Figure 7-20b illustrates the use of the next and end tags to compress the linear list. In this simple example each integer list entry does fit into the single tagged word provided for each list element in the compressed structure. If a list entry is a character string, the tagged word in the compressed structure contains a pointer to a structure containing the character string (see Figure 7-20c).[24]

To represent a general list node we need two words, the first tagged with the cons cdr code, and the second with the end cdr code. The Symbolics 3600 representation of our simple list using cons nodes is shown in Figure 7-20d. The generalization to other list structures should be obvious.

[24]This indirection is used even if the character string is short and could be stored in the single word.

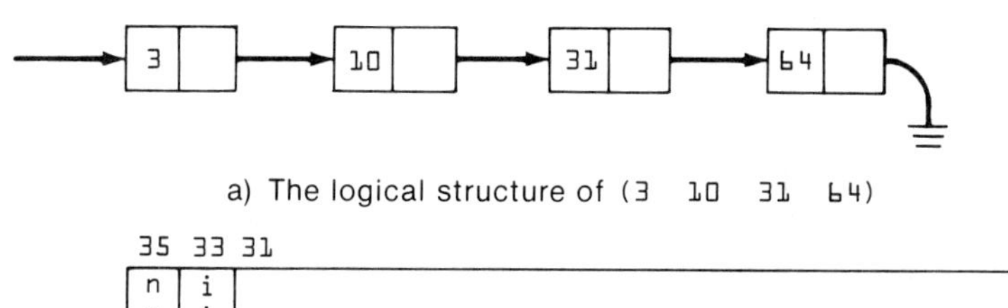

a) The logical structure of (3 10 31 64)

35	33	31 ... 0
n	i	3
n	i	10
n	i	31
e	i	64

b) A compressed representation of (3 10 31 64)

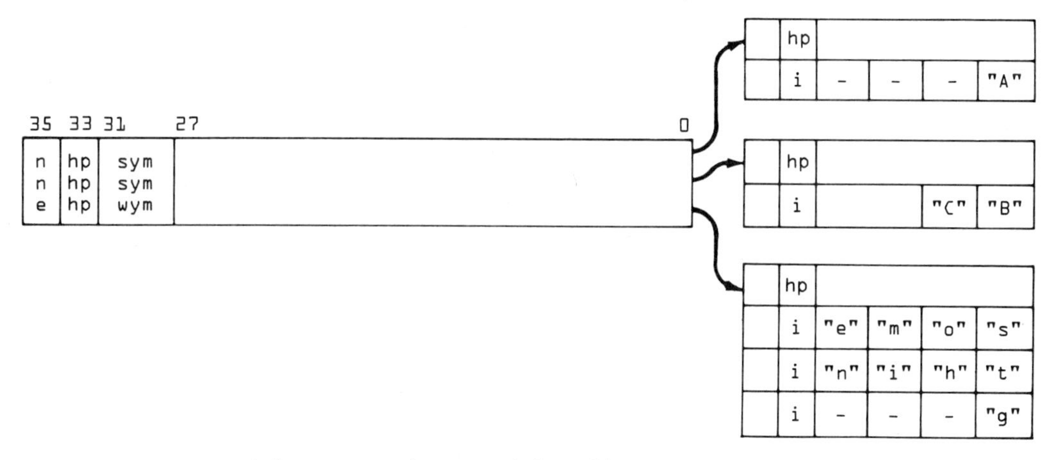

c) A compressed representation of (A BC something).
("Sym" denotes the tag for a pointer to a symbol).

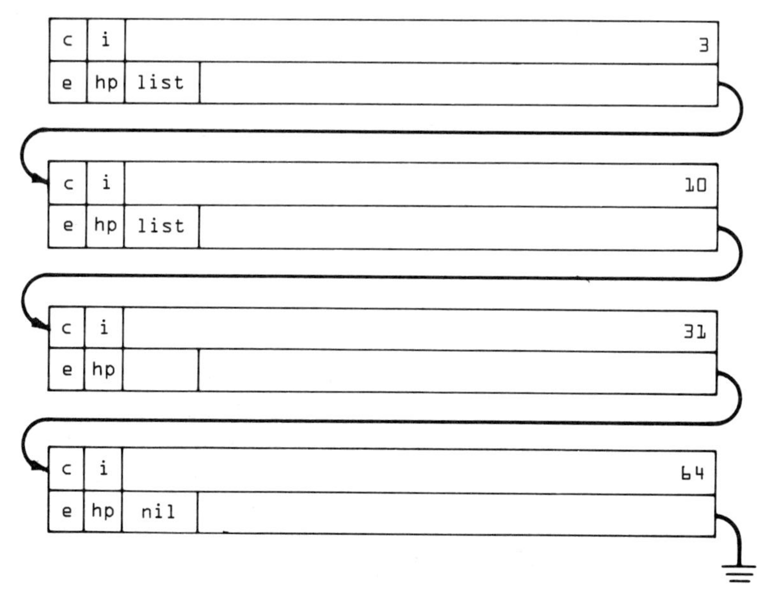

d) A cons representation of (3 10 31 64)

Figure 7-20 Compressed list representations used in the Symbolics 3600 (after [MOON87]; © IEEE 1987)

Now suppose that the entry holding 10 in our list were changed so that its successor becomes an existing list containing (2 -7 13). Figure 7-21a illustrates the logical structures after that change. Logically, the system should replace entry 10 with a general cons structure. Unfortunately, the needed cons structure takes more space than the compressed node representation that it logically replaces. We cannot just overwrite the next entry (containing 31), because it might be accessible through one or more pointers elsewhere in the system. This reasoning shows that the (single word) entry that previously held 10 has to (logically) hold its larger replacement. In the Symbolics 3600 this difficulty is handled by replacing the old entry (10) with an indirect pointer that specifies the location where the new, larger entry is located. Figure 7-21b illustrates the modified list.

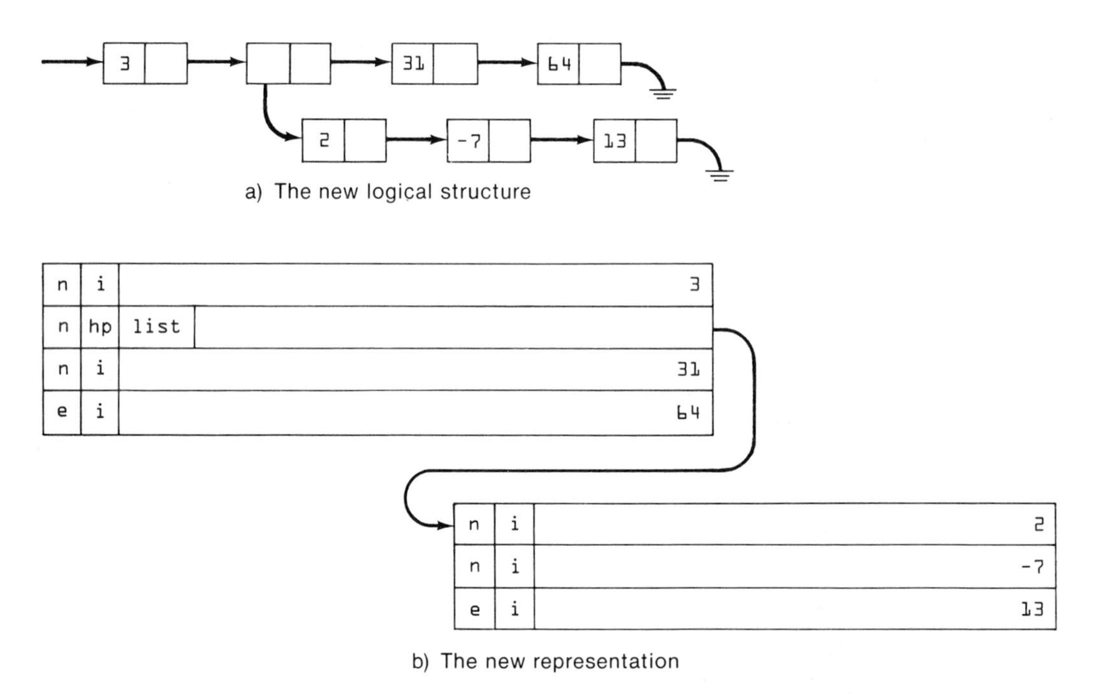

Figure 7-21 Replacing an entry in a compressed list may change its structure

7.7.2.1.3 *Structures.* Recall that a structure, like an Ada record, is a collection of diverse kinds of objects. Structures have a very straightforward representation in the Symbolics 3600 machines. The first word of the structure is typed as an array header; it contains information about the size and type of the structure. Since the header word cannot be a member of a list, its cdr code bits will not be used to decide how to interpret the word as a list member, so the cdr code bits are used to extend its type code field. The consecutive words immediately following the header hold the structure's contents; each is self-describing, thanks to its own tag. None of the components within a structure can serve as an element in the middle of a list. Thus there is no need for the cdr codes associated with the structure's entries. The Symbolics 3600 representation of a structure is illustrated in Figure 7-22.

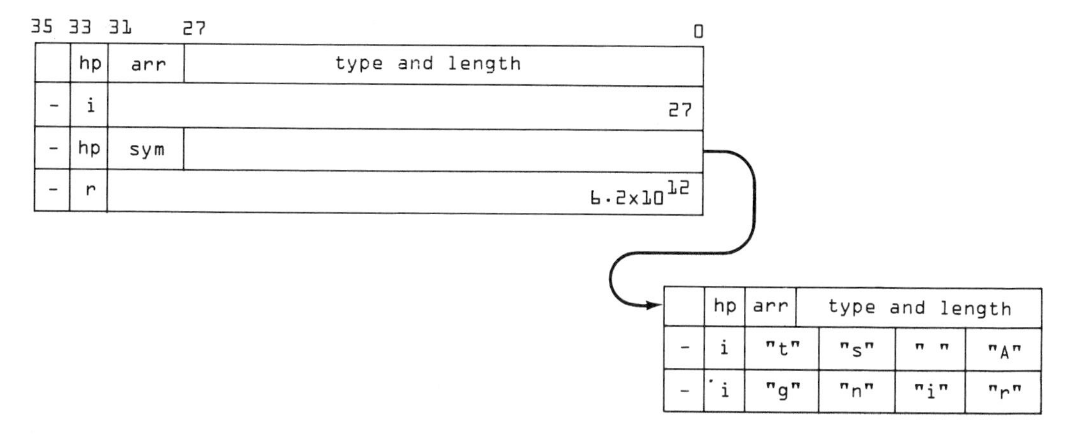

Figure 7-22 The Symbolics 3600 representation of a three-element structure containing (27 "A String" 6.2×10^{12})

Special structure types are used to hold character strings and programs. A character string is stored in an array packed four characters to each word, which is tagged as an integer. The leftmost character code is stored in the rightmost byte.

7.7.2.1.4 ***Program Representation.*** A program will be stored in several arrays because each function occupies an array (see Figure 7-23). The array's header and

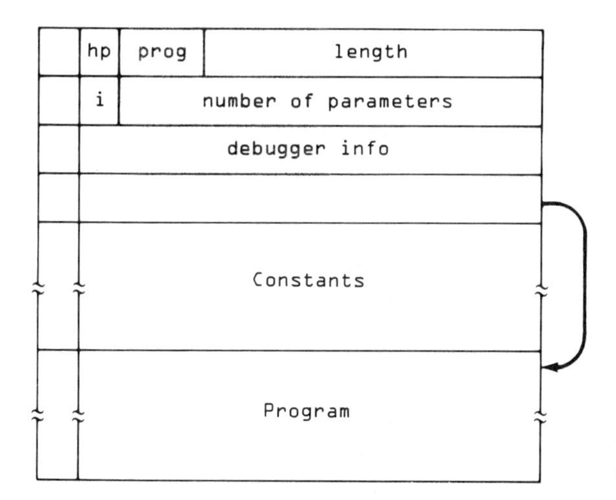

Figure 7-23 The Symbolics 3600 representation of a function body

first word together specify its type, its overall size, the size of its constants region (see below), the number of arguments expected by the function, and the location of the first instruction word within the array. Following this header information, space is reserved for use during debugging; this information is not interpreted during function execution. The debugging information is followed by the constant values used by the function. The instruction words occupy the remainder of the array.

Each instruction word (plus tag) contains two instructions (in 34 bits) and is tagged as an integer; its two cdr tag bits extend the two instructions to 17 bits apiece (see Figure 7-24). There are two instruction formats; one has a 9-bit function code and an 8-bit operand field, whereas the other has only a 7-bit function code and a 10-bit specification of the location of a bit field (i.e., its first bit position and field width). The latter format is used for a few instructions that manipulate bit fields.

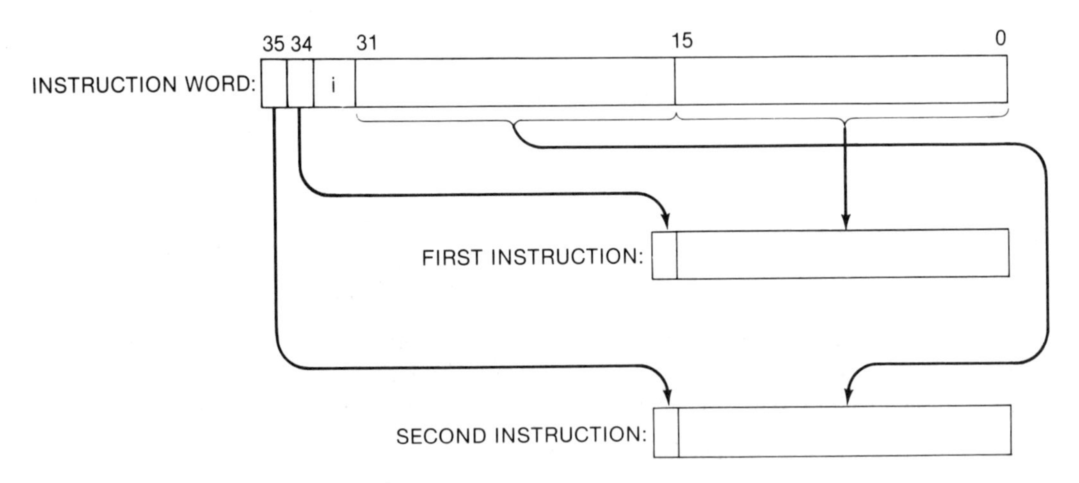

Figure 7-24 A Symbolics 3600 instruction word contains two 17-bit instructions

The function code determines the interpretation of the operand field contents. Table 7-20 lists some of the possible uses of the operand field information. Since the function code determines the use of the operand field information, the operation code and addressing selections are not orthogonal.

TABLE 7-20 POSSIBLE INTERPRETATIONS OF THE OPERAND FIELD IN SYMBOLICS 3600 INSTRUCTIONS

Case	Operand Field Usage
PC-offset address	Offset range -128 .. $+127$
Local operand	Unsigned offset within local stack frame
Temporary result	Unsigned offset back from top of stack
Flavor instance component	Unsigned offset within flavor instance
Indirect FIC	Indirect through the previous
Link operand	Unsigned offset within program's constants
Indirect link operand	Indirect through the previous
Structure component	Offset from structure origin
Global reference	Unsigned offset from link pointer
Immediate unsigned	Value range 0 .. 255
Immediate signed	Value range -128 .. $+127$
Function	Extension of the function code

Source: After [MOON87], Table 1; © 1987 IEEE.

7.7.2.2 Operator selection. The Symbolics instruction set was selected so that its operators would be close to LISP primitives. It contains the usual arithmetic operators, list manipulation operators, several operators to support fast function calling, and many operators that manipulate pointers. The instructions were carefully chosen so that operations occurring most frequently would complete quickly. Tagging reduces the number of different operators, since a function code can be overloaded so that its effects depend upon the types of its operands.

7.7.2.3 Operator implementation. The Symbolics 3600 implementation of frequently executed operators attempts to use parallelism as much as possible. In this spirit, the add instruction implementation uses the initiate-select design, feeding its operands directly to the integer adder (and the optional real adder, if present) and checking their types in parallel. If no result obtained from the hardware can be used for the sum, the controller issues more microinstructions to perform the desired operation.

Other techniques used to speed instruction execution are closely related to the representation of each process's internal state.

7.7.2.4 Process state. The Symbolics 3600 machines do not have any programmer-visible registers; all operations are stack oriented, so operands are popped from the stack and results are pushed on the top of the stack. This "control" stack is cached in a local fast memory that contains four 256-word pages. The (control) stack cache memory is designed so that words near the top of the stack can be accessed quickly. An implementation restriction demands that the local stack block remain small enough that the entire block can be held in the control stack cache.

Each Symbolics 3600 process has three stacks. One stack holds binding information (values pushed to retain the external state of the LET and parameter objects), one holds program-allocated information, and the third (the control stack) holds the usual combination of control information, parameter values, and saved stack pointers plus small local objects. The configuration of the control stack is similar to that of the B5700 stack, except that a complete copy of the parameter values is present in both the old and new stack frames (see Figure 7-25). The procedure calling instructions are analogous to the B5700 set; there is a "start-function-call" instruction, a push instruction (to store parameters at the top of the stack), and a "complete-function-call" instruction which actually transfers control to the new procedure. The Symbolics 3600 versions of these instructions state how many parameters are being passed. During the execution of the call instruction the processor checks the number of actual parameters against the number of formal parameters (obtained from the procedure's header), and inserts default values for any missing parameters.

During function call and return the stack buffer may be changed so that the new block will fit in the stack buffer. During call, the bottommost page may be copied to memory to free a buffer page for the new top of the stack. During return, an old page may be read from memory to the buffer so that the entire block will be present in the buffer.

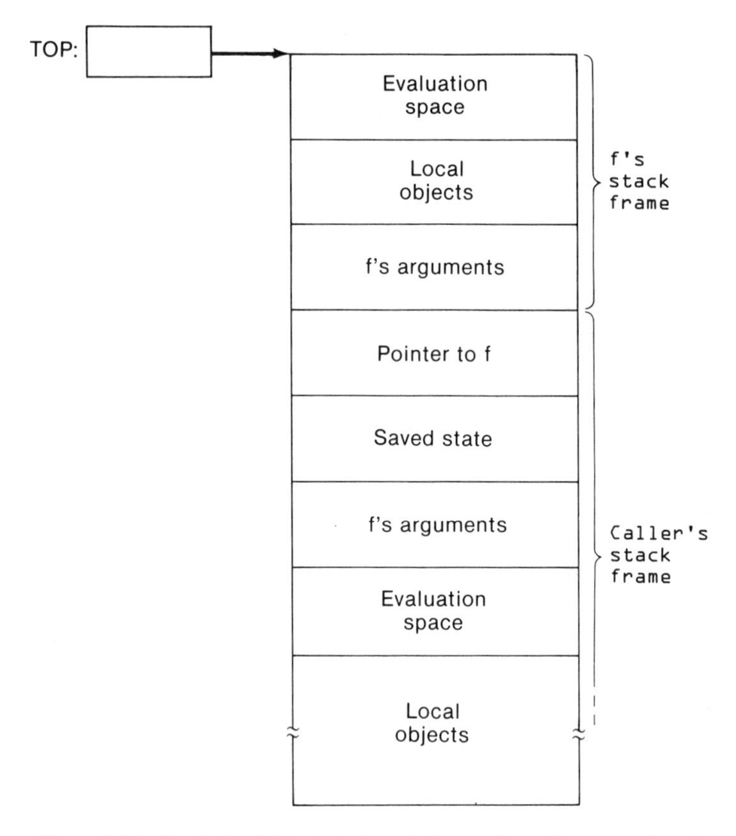

Figure 7-25 Symbolics 3600 control stack format for calling procedure f

7.7.2.5 Garbage collection. LISP uses heap allocations to manage the memory spaces that hold conses and other dynamically created objects. Whenever a new cons is created, space is obtained from the heap. No LISP operations explicitly deallocate any storage. In fact, space becomes free only after all pointers to that space have been deallocated or overwritten. There is a great need for garbage collection in LISP systems due to the need to traverse all "live" pointers within the system to ascertain which space is indeed free.

LISP garbage collection algorithms typically follow these phases:

1. *Scan.* Recursively follow all "live" pointers to find and mark all values currently in use;
2. *Compress.* Compress space by relocating all live objects to a contiguous space at low addresses, changing all pointers accordingly;
3. *Free.* Adjust the free-space descriptors to make the free space at high addresses available to the space allocator.

The Symbolics 3600 architecture includes several low-level mechanisms that assist garbage collection. First, each physical page has an associated tag that is set when a pointer to reclaimable space is written into the page. A scan of these tags during garbage collection uncovers those pages that must be scanned in detail to find pointers. Second, a similar table is kept by the software for all disk-resident pages; this table determines which disk pages must be copied from the disk during the garbage collector's scan phase. Third, it is possible to run programs during the compression phase because objects that have been relocated can still be accessed from their old locations through the indirect pointers that replaced the original entries. Setting this up requires additional work to install the indirect pointers; it may be easier and faster just to permit garbage collection to complete with all user programs suspended. The programmer may control whether garbage collection will complete without interruption. The negative aspect of uninterruptible garbage collection is that the complete garbage collection process could take many minutes.

7.7.3 Comments

The LISP language presents some unique architectural challenges due to dynamic typing, dynamic nesting, garbage generation, and a large number of function calls. The Symbolics 3600 designers devised self-describing data objects, a LISP-oriented instruction set, and operation implementations that perform frequently executed instructions quickly. By these means they produced a machine architecture tuned to LISP program execution.

7.8 SUMMARY

Strong object typing and encapsulated type definitions can enhance program clarity and ease the implementation of operand manipulations. The type definitions themselves can be interrelated in various ways to build type definition structures.

Before an operation can be performed, several bindings must be made: a type to an object, an operation to a combination of operand types, and the operation to its operands. These bindings may all be made during compilation and linking (as in Ada), or deferred until run time. There exist a variety of ways to specify these bindings.

Processor designs can be slanted toward certain languages and related object representations. A careful operand representation choice can save both memory space and processing time; this effect influenced the design of the Symbolics 3600 machines, with, among other features, a special representation for a common list configuration.

There are several ways to speed program execution by changing the order of operations, the object representation technique, or by introducing parallelism. Special attention should be paid to frequently executed operations, since a great performance benefit can be obtained from speeding these operations alone.

Numerous parallelism techniques can further speed processors; they are presented in Volume 2.

7.9 PROBLEMS

7-1. Write the specification of a generic Ada package that generalizes the integer_stack_ package of the text. The general version should describe a stack that can hold objects of type T (T is a parameter of the generic package).

7-2. Draw a picture illustrating two logically different paths reaching to an object x. Designate a place for type information in a location along each path to the object.

(a) How can type consistency be assured if x is a local automatic object?

(b) How can type consistency be checked if x is a component of a local automatic record? What if x is in a statically allocated record?

(c) What part of the system bears the responsibility for correct type checking in each case? Explain.

7-3. In Section 7.2.1 we presented the option that object type information be found along the path to a storage object. Concerning this design, two designers argue about the semantics of the STORE operation in a register-based processor. Designer A argues that object type information should be specified by the type declaration in the high-level language; therefore, the type information along the access path to the object governs the representations that can be stored in the location. As a consequence, during the execution of a STORE operation, the value representation may have to be changed to conform to the destination's type designation. Designer B, on the other hand, argues that the type of the value held in the processor register should govern the type actually stored. After all, she argues, the transformation proposed by designer A could destroy information that might fit into the destination location if the representation did not have to be changed. Therefore, she continues, it is better to change the type information along the access path than to change the representation of the information. Any subsequent operation that needs the specified value can change its representation, if that seems to be necessary, she concludes.

(a) Specify the behavior of the STORE operation under each option.

(b) Discuss these two arguments with respect to compatibility with an Ada program.

(c) Designer C argues that although it might be fine to store the value exactly as it was computed, without type constraints that result may be larger than the operands, and thus performing a sequence of operations on the values without any representation changes just makes the representations longer and longer. Discuss this argument in relation to the points claimed by designers A and B.

(d) Which approach to the STORE operation do you recommend?

7-4. It might be argued that there is little point to making the type tags on values so large that all types could be designated by the tag value alone. Rather, the set of types could be divided into classes, such that a particular operation performed on an object of any type within class A always produces a result having some type in class A. For example, it might make sense to separate arithmetic values from bit strings because the result of performing arithmetic is never typed as a bit string and one never performs logical operations on numeric quantities.[25] The proposal continues with the suggestion that the function code of a processor instruction imply the type classes of its operands and the result; the tag information associated with the individual values would be used to identify a particular type within the type class.

[25]Do not consider logical masking to extract field contents since such operations expose the encoding and representation which we are trying to encapsulate within the operation implementations.

(a) We wish to design an extension of the MC68020 processor that handles tagged values following the encoding scheme proposed above. To this end, divide the object types supported by the MC68020 processor into classes so that the number of object tag bits is reduced by following the separation rules suggested above.

(b) List the arithmetic and logical operations that manipulate object values (not simply copying them). Construct a set of lists with tuples of type classes as list labels. A typical list label might be (arithmetic, arithmetic, arithmetic), where the first two entries represent the two classes of operand types and the last represents the class of the result type. Place each arithmetic and logical MC68020 operation into the list corresponding to the combination of its type classes.

(c) Discuss how lists constructed by following the procedure above could be used to find a smaller instruction set which encompasses all operations of a general machine. (Your answer should not be specific to the MC68020.)

7-5. Discuss the following argument: A processor-level object manipulation architecture with all operands and results located in memory closely resembles the high-level language view of object handling. We also know that processors using operand registers can operate more quickly than those without registers, since memory accesses are not required to access operands or to store results. But caching memory information is just like placing it in registers. Thus caching memory objects is adequate for implementing high-level language functions efficiently with a memory-to-memory model of object processing.

7-6. Discuss the following argument: In a processor that uses the instruction representation scheme in which operand register classes are selected by function code information, one of the following is true:

1. Some function code bits could be reassigned to register designation fields without changing the operation repertoire. (This may require recoding the instructions.)
2. The function set is asymmetric with respect to the registers (i.e., there exist some functions that can be performed on the contents of only some registers).

7-7. Complete the argument which shows that the strongly typed emulator E_L does not really violate the encapsulation of the processor's value representation scheme. (*Hint*: See Example 7-6. Which representation scheme was made visible by the emulator?)

7-8. Try to find at least one example of each of the operand selection techniques (see Table 7-7) in the MC68020. Some techniques might not be available with this processor.

7-9. Repeat Problem 7-8 for a familiar processor.

7-10. What combinations of representation conventions permit an integer compare operation to produce correct results when the operands being compared are actually reals? What combinations of representation conventions are compatible with using an integer compare operation to compare an integer against a real value?

7-11. Design an implementation of integer addition for two 32-bit integers represented in sign/magnitude representation. The host machine has an 8-bit adder. Conditional branching based on the sign bit of the most recent value produced at the output of the ALU unit is available (branch on plus and branch on minus are the tests). Specify how the desired integer addition could be performed using serial manipulation of operand bytes. Contrast the implementation complexity and execution time for sign/magnitude operands with a similar byte-serial implementation for two's-complement operands.

7-12. Define a package for a procedure_table data type to be used in a compiler that supports overloaded procedure definitions. An object of the type of your data structure will be searched to find the appropriate entry point for a call to an overloaded procedure name. It should be structured so that overloaded procedure names with different numbers of arguments and different combinations of argument types will be handled correctly.

(a) Define the interface to a procedure_table package designed to encapsulate the procedure_table data type.

(b) When are entries added to the table?

(c) How is the table used to find the proper program to execute for each call?

(d) Comment on the viability of using this approach in an Ada compiler.

7-13. Write the body of the generic package specified in Problem 7-1.

7-14. Write a generic package that generalizes the integer_stack_package to describe a stack holding objects that are tagged with their types. The set of types of objects permitted to reside on the stack is presented as a list that is a parameter of the package. Make a global definition of an object type whose values can range across this set of types. Then you can design the package so that the same entry point can be called to push a value of any type onto the stack. To maintain strong typing, when your package pops the stack, design it to check the type of the topmost stack entry against the type requested (this type name being a parameter of the pop call). The pop procedure should raise the externally defined type_mismatch exception if the type of the popped object does not match the type requested.

7-15. Modify the design of Problem 7-14 to remove the need for an external data type which lists the types that can appear on the stack. Try to keep all type codes internal to the package. Describe any significant difficulties that you encounter. As in Problem 7-14, record the types of the objects on the stack and raise an exception if a pop request would cause a type mismatch.

7-16. This problem concerns the construction of an Ada package that encapsulates an object which is a region containing records that may be associatively selected. The record structure is globally defined; in other words, all records in the region share the same type declaration. The search key is to be matched against the contents of a field from the record. The particular field to be searched is designated by a parameter of the search request. (This implies that any field named in the record declaration may be used as the key for a particular associative search request.) The following operations should be supported:[26]

1. insert(rec);
2. delete(field_name, key);
3. find(field_name, key) **return** index;
4. next(field_name, key) **return** index;
5. read(field_name, index) **return** ??;
6. replace(index, new_rec);

You may wish to introduce a data type whose values are the field names and then use it as a subscript for accessing record components stored in the area. The key values could be used to find an exact match.

(a) Complete the specification of the read function. Explain your answer.

(b) Write functions that store the records in the order of their arrival and perform the search by a sequential scan.

[26]For brevity, we list only parameter types here.

(c) Write a different implementation that builds a reverse index based on component values and uses a binary search of the index list to locate a record that meets the search criterion.

(d) What information must be stored within the package to properly implement the next function? It is supposed to find the next record (after the one found in a previous find or next operation) whose field_name component matches the given key value.

7-17. Write an effects specification for the integer addition instruction in a familiar machine.

7-18. Write a processor program fragment for a familiar machine to perform the assignment statement

```
w:=w+x*y;
```

where w is real and x and y are integers. Assume that all objects are stored in memory.

7-19. Write effects specifications of floating-point addition for each of the nine combinations of exponent and mantissa representations chosen from this list:

1. Biased
2. Sign/magnitude
3. One's complement

(a) Do this at the processor level.
(b) Do this at the register-transfer level for a host architecture.

7-20. Write a formal specification of the floating-point number representation of "normal" values under the IEEE standard format and then write a formal specification for the normalization process that takes an unnormalized operand with its leading 1 bit present and produces a normalized number represented in the IEEE standard format. Be sure to detect underflow and overflow.

7-21. A processor designer proposes to reduce the number of program bits required to specify a given algorithm by redesigning the instructions so that there is only a single processor instruction. The proposed instruction has four parameters:

r: an integer selecting a processor register;
i, j, k: addresses of words in memory.

Each instruction occupies a single word, which is the granularity of memory addressing. The execution of the instruction (r, i, j, k) has the following effects:

1. Subtract the contents of memory location i from the contents of register r;
2. Place the result of step 1 in both register r and memory location j;
3. If the result computed in step 1 was negative, jump to memory location k;

(a) The designer makes two claims:

1. The design is functionally complete.
2. The design actually does save program bits.

Discuss these claims. Do you expect them to be true? Explain.

(b) Would your answers be changed if the direction of the subtraction in step 1 were reversed?

7-22. A designer wishes to modify the processor instruction set to support objects which are singly linked lists linked in increasing order of a (single) key value. In addition to the linked list lookup instruction (discussed in Example 4-17), she proposes to add bead insertion and deletion operations.

(a) Specify these insertion and deletion operations, based on the B5700 list format used for its linked list lookup instruction.
(b) Discuss the advantages and disadvantages of the proposal.

(c) Another designer proposes to speed linked list insertion and deletion by designing processor control logic to detect sequences of processor instructions that correspond to performing these list operations. The idea is to avoid generating intermediate results. Discuss, but do not implement, this suggestion; just compare this proposal with the proposed instruction set expansion.

7-23. Under the Smalltalk view, a call to an overloaded function generates a message sent to the first operand containing the function name and its parameter list. A designer proposes an alternate design in which function calling is implemented by sending a similar message to the last operand (chosen because it would be on the top of the operand stack). Discuss her proposal, citing any advantages or disadvantages you can find.

7-24. For each of the three approaches listed in Section 7.6.1 write a description of a single add operator that will handle all combinations of integer and real operands. You should have three descriptions in your answer.

7-25. Here are two proposed methods for implementing operations on objects which are represented by Ada variant records. For simplicity, assume that all operands have the same record type (in other words, their type differences are restricted to differences in the values of their discriminant parts—you do not need to worry about verifying this assumption):

1. Use the discriminant value(s) to select the function bodies.
2. Use common operation implementation routines, with conditional execution based on actual discriminant values to vary the basic operations when required.

Compare these options. Consider the specification of the operations, the operand representations, the implementation complexity, and the execution times.

7-26. To speed the determination of the proper implementation of an overloaded operation, a designer proposes adding a cache to the processor. The cache entries would contain entries from the mapping

```
(function, operand_type_vector) -> entry_address
```

(a) Describe the role of the cache in the execution of a high-level function call.
(b) Where in the execution sequence would you use the cache to speed execution of the call?
(c) Are there any benefits of the design that includes the cache? Explain.

7-27. A designer suggests that a system support dynamic register assignments automatically, just like it might support dynamic assignment of items to different levels of the memory hierarchy, including the cache. To complete this design, she must specify:

1. How operands are named in instructions
2. How registers are assigned

Suggest answers to these two design issues and comment on the advantages and disadvantages of the suggested design. Provide an overall evaluation of the suggestion, comparing it against the traditional method of having the compiler assign objects to registers in advance of program execution.

7-28. To save time while evaluating a complex arithmetic expression, an optimizing compiler looks for common subexpressions within the expression being evaluated. If the processor has registers, the compiler may assign a register to hold the value of the common subexpression between the time that it is evaluated and the time that it is last used during the process of evaluating the complete expression. If the processor design has an evaluation stack rather than a set of registers, retaining the subexpression's value between uses and then managing to have it at the top of the stack when it is required for later use may require tricky management of the entries near the top of the stack. To assist in this endeavor, a stack-based processor may have DUPLICATE and EXCHANGE instructions. DUPLICATE pushes a second copy of the top of the stack, whereas EXCHANGE interchanges the top two stack entries.

(a) What expression is evaluated by the following program fragment?

```
LOAD A
LOAD B
MULTIPLY
DUPLICATE
LOAD C
ADD
EXCHANGE
LOAD D
SUBTRACT
MULTIPLY
```

(b) It would be convenient to be able to address the intermediate values near the top of the stack as though they were located in registers. This could be accomplished through addressing relative to the top of the stack. Write a program fragment that evaluates the same expression using this kind of operand addressing.

(c) Did your first attempt to write the program fragment for part (b) leave the stack cleaned up after it completed execution? Explain. Discuss whether the opportunity to access operands within the stack saves instructions. Consider both this example and the general case.

7-29. This problem explores the possibility of shortening a program by redefining the interpretation of the instruction function code field in a context-sensitive manner. The basic idea is that if only a few instruction types are going to be used in a given context, only a few function code bits are really required to specify which instruction should be executed. The resulting reduction in program length would save both memory space and instruction fetch time. The problem develops some alternative means for specifying these changes. While solving this problem, you can assume that the execution context changes only during procedure CALL and procedure RETURN.

(a) In this option the program may redefine any processor operation by changing its microprogram. The claim is made that by overwriting useless operations with useful ones, the total space in the control memory will not have to be increased, yet execution will be speeded because the microinstruction instruction fetch time is short compared to the instruction fetch time. Is this claim valid? Specify a method for an executing program to change the interpretations of the function code field. Does your method achieve any of the claimed savings? Explain.

(b) This variation allows the compiler to add instructions for user-defined types to the processor's instruction set. The declaration section of each program would state which built-in types are not going to appear in the program very frequently. In addition, new type declarations include a usage frequency estimate with each operation specification. The idea is that the compiler can use the frequency estimates to choose which operations to map to microcode.

7-30. Group the instructions of a familiar machine into classes such that all operations in one class can be performed by almost the same execution sequence, with slight variations. Could the microprogram sequences for arithmetic and logic operations be used in common in any class?

7-31. A system that supports string operands has a paged memory. The system must be designed to handle the possibility that one or more string operands might cross a page boundary, and that the next page might be absent, even though the page containing the beginning of the operand is present. Here are four ways that the system might handle the missing page possibility:

1. Execute the operation until a missing page is detected, and then handle the fault.
2. Using the longest possible operand lengths, first determine all pages that might contain the strings and make all those pages present before performing the string operation.
3. Determine the actual operand lengths, checking for page crossings, and make all pages that actually contain the strings present before performing the string operation.
4. Determine all operand bytes that will be accessed through a trial execution of the operation, without storing any results, making all pages present, and then execute the operation from the beginning, storing the results.

Compare these options for a processor designed for efficient Cobol program execution.

7-32. Figure 7-26 shows the LISP data structures in the machine at the start of the execution of some LISP program fragments. Draw a picture of the LISP data structures in the

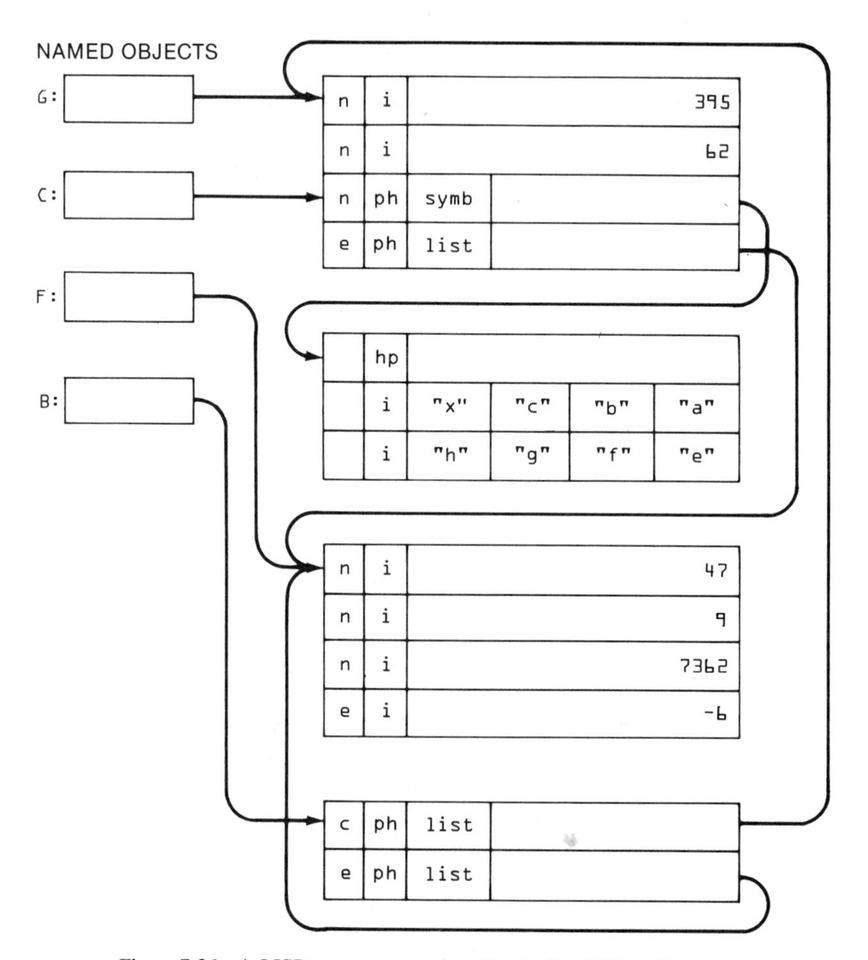

Figure 7-26 A LISP memory snapshot (Symbolics 3600 coding used)

machine after each of the following LISP program fragments completes execution. The conditions of Figure 7-26 pertain at the start of each program fragment.

(a) ((SETQ B (B F)))
(b) ((SETQ G (CAR C)))
(c) ((RPLACD F (CDR (CDR G))))

See Problem 7-35 for an explanation of RPLACD.

(d) ((SETQ G (CAR C))
(RPLACD F (CDR (CDR G))))

7-33. Draw diagrams illustrating the representation of each of the following LISP lists in the Symbolics 3600.

(a) (((A 3 ($ 6 4)) F) (X (Y ((N X) G))))
(b) (((1 2) (3 4)) ((5 6) (7 8)))
(c) (((A B) (C D)) ((E F) (G H)))

7-34. Define a modification of the Symbolics 3600 list element representation rules so that a short character string list element can be stored in a single word. The goals are to save space and memory accesses by avoiding the overhead of an array structure for each short character string. Your solution must conform with the other Symbolics 3600 object representation conventions; this means that you will have to use a new minor tag field value to denote your special case. How long is the longest character string that will fit into your representation?

7-35. The two LISP primitives RPLACA and RPLACD replace the contents of the first (A) or second (D) part of a list cons without changing anything else in the list.

(a) Draw a picture illustrating the transformation that the Symbolics 3600 must make on its internal representation of the target list to perform RPLACA.

(b) Draw a picture illustrating the transformation that the Symbolics 3600 must make on its internal representation of the target list to perform RPLACD when the affected node is a cons memory cell.

(c) Draw a picture illustrating the transformation that the Symbolics 3600 must make on its internal representation of the target list to perform RPLACD when the target list is represented as a compressed list.

(d) Write a series of steps that the Symbolics 3600 could use to perform RPLACD.

7-36. Discuss the following claim: The Symbolics 3600 processor could handle a reference to a component within a LISP structure as an indexed reference to the array holding the structure.

In your answer point out the similarities and differences between accessing a LISP structure component and accessing a component of an Ada or Pascal record.

7-37. This problem is concerned with support for user-defined types within LISP. In particular, we desire processor support for same, so we study the internal representation of objects having user-defined types. We start with the Symbolics 3600 representations for untyped lists and their elements. Each user-defined type is defined by a list of functions that manipulate that type, in the style of an Ada package interface. We propose to list the actual procedure names in a structure. Then the type is described by this structure.

(a) Draw figures representing the data structures and object representations that implement this type package definition scheme. Represent each object as a two-component LISP list of the form (type value).

(b) Draw figures representing the data structures and object representations implementing this type scheme if each object can be represented as a two-component word containing the type and value. Use the compressed format shown in Figure 7-27.

(c) Describe representation and interpretation rules that cover the situation when the value of an object may sometimes be small enough to fit in the compressed word format developed in part (b), but sometimes might need a full word to hold the value alone.

(d) A designer claims that the representation developed in part (c) is both comprehensive (it covers all situations) and efficient in both space and time. Comment on these claims.

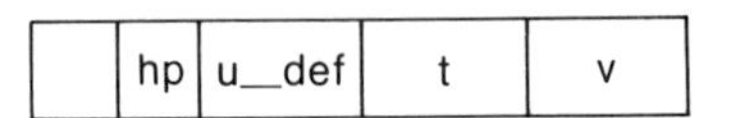

Figure 7-27 A proposed encoding for short objects having user-defined types (u_def is a new minor tag value)

7-38. It has been claimed (with some justification) that memory references are less local when executing a LISP program than when running a program in a "conventional" language like Ada. In view of this situation, a LISP machine designer devises the following schemes to try to localize the reference string in a system using paging for memory management. Discuss each scheme, particularly covering its space and time efficiencies.

(a) Each process is confined to a contiguous partition of (virtual) memory space.

(b) During execution of function f, all space is allocated from a heap for f; each of these heaps is managed using a stack discipline.

(c) Keep a separate heap within each memory page. When space is needed, the new space is allocated (if possible) within the same page where the pointer to the space will be stored. What criteria would you use to decide when to allocate a new object in a different page?

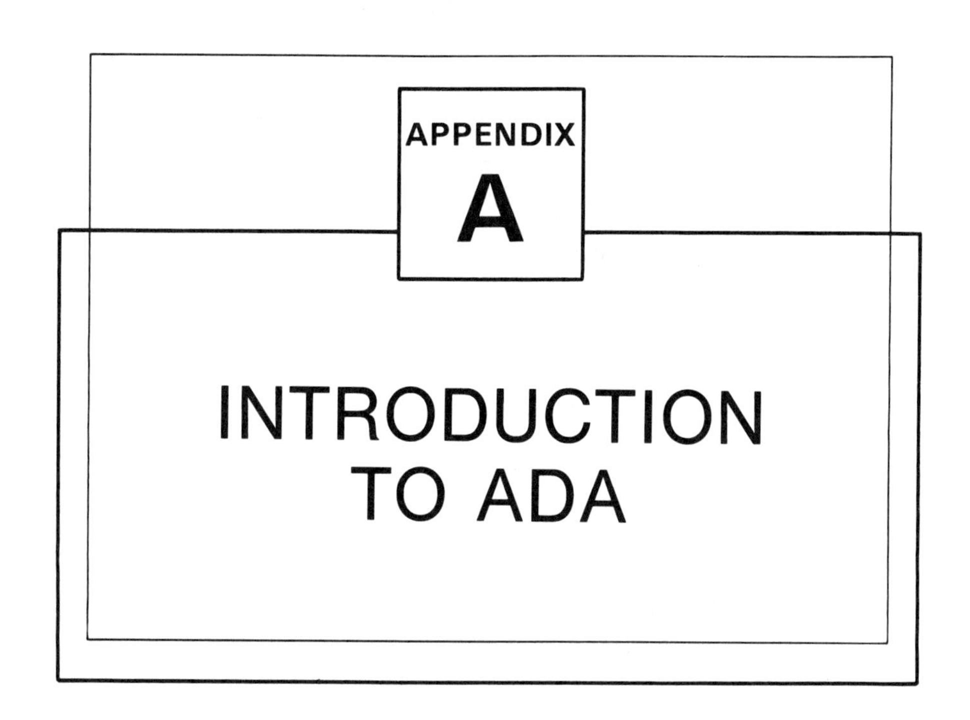

INTRODUCTION TO ADA

The mathematicians are a sort of Frenchmen:
when you talk to them,
they immediately translate it into their own language,
and right away it is something utterly different.

—Goethe

The Ada programming language [ANSI83] was developed to specify programs for computer systems which themselves are components of larger systems. Ada was developed through a long refinement process which honed language specifications until a satisfactory language for the intended purpose was achieved. The final language was developed in France by a group led by Jean Ichbiah. If you think that using Ada makes a program "something utterly different," you must realize that Ada has been adopted as a standard programming language by the U.S. Department of Defense, so, as a consequence, the language will achieve wide use. As Ada contains most features of interesting general-purpose high-level languages, we use it extensively in this book, primarily to illustrate high-level language requirements (which a designer may elect to support with system features).

In this appendix we summarize basic Ada features. We first present modularization techniques, and then object and control structures. We discuss executable statements and modularization features, ending with the package construct, a powerful tool that can be used to hide representation and implementation details. This appendix does not cover all aspects of Ada; to keep the development simple, we present basics, with supplements in the text when desirable. In the appendix we point out where Ada differs from Pascal, a similar language. The syntax of the two languages differs in many details, as you will see in the examples in this appendix and throughout the book.

A.1 MODULAR STRUCTURE

At the highest level of abstraction, an Ada program is constructed from a set of "modules" having very restricted interactions. Details within a module can be "hidden" from outside view, so that one can consider the module as the implementation of a function or a grouping of data that is considered as an "atomic" element at some higher level of description. The module's implementation details, then, are neither available nor of interest at higher levels of description.

A.2 OBJECT IDENTIFIERS

An Ada object identifier (or name) must start with a letter, to distinguish it from a numeric value. Succeeding symbols in the identifier can be letters, numerals, or the underscore character. Underscoring can be used to construct multiword mnemonic identifiers, like "multi_word." The hyphen cannot be used for this purpose because it is the minus sign.

Example A-1

The following are legal Ada object identifiers:

```
thing
number1
an_item_name
this_is_the_first_item
income_tax
program_counter
```

A.2.1 Object Types

The "data type" (such as integer, real, or character string) of an object determines the set of potential values of the object. In addition, the object type specifies how its value is represented and manipulated. Each object, before it is used, must be "declared." An object's declaration states its name (or identifier) and type.

In some languages the same name can denote an object of one type at one time and of another type at another time. Not only is this confusing to people reading the specification or program, but it makes it extremely difficult to reason about program properties. Furthermore, in some languages it is possible to use the same object as though it has one type now and another type later. Thus a value can be stored in the format of an integer representation and that bit pattern read and interpreted as the representation of a real number. If this scenario were possible, it could be used to construct programs whose results depend on internal representations used for object values. Some languages, like Pascal and Ada, prohibit this possibility by requiring that every name always describe an object of a single, constant type. Such a language is called strongly typed.

An Ada object's declaration may state an initial value for the object; such an initialization specification is constructed by placing an assignment operator and an expression after the type declaration, as in

```
thing : integer := 3;
```

Every language supports objects of certain predefined types, often called "basic" or "primitive" data types, usually including integers, booleans, and characters. For each of these types, certain operations and constant values are known to the system. Ada supports the types integer, float, boolean, and character.

Another primitive object type supported by Ada is the access data type. An object of type **access**, called an access variable, contains information about the location of another object. To maintain strong typing, the type of the described object must be declared in the declaration of the access variable; in effect, the type of the described object is part of the type of the access variable that describes it. The operations on access variables are assignment, equality testing, and inequality testing.

Example A-2

The following object types are all different:

```
integer
real
array(1 .. 4) of integer
array(2 .. 5) of integer
access integer
access real
```

A.2.2 Data Structures

A data structure is a collection of objects to be manipulated together. A data structure provides a level of abstraction above that of an elementary object. The set of objects collected within a data structure, such as a vector, can itself be used as a single object. Not only can a programmer declare objects to be data structures, he can also declare new data types. For example, a programmer could define a new data type "vector," along with a set of operators that manipulate vectors. With these definitions made, the programmer could use vector objects directly as operands in vector operations such as dot product.

Two basic data structures, arrays and records, are directly supported in Ada. Arrays, records, and access variables can be used to represent all other data structures.

An array is a compound object containing several instances of "components." All components of an array must have the same type. An individual element of an array can be denoted by the name of the array and a vector of "subscripts." The type of an array includes both the type of the array's components and the range of permissible index values in each dimension. To specify a range of values in Ada one uses two dots, as in "1 .. 100." A declaration of a type which is an array of integers is similar to

```
type integer_matrix is array(1 .. 100, 1 .. 100) of integer;
```

A complete array is denoted by its name. A portion of an array can be named by giving the range of the subscripts which include all selected elements. In one dimension this is simple: v(3 .. 6) specifies four components of the vector v. If an array has several dimensions, Ada allows the range to be applied to the first dimension only.

The record construct is used to collect a set of objects of diverse type into one composite object. Record components are denoted with distinct component names. An Ada record declaration specifies a record type in which the names and types of all components are declared. A record instance is declared in a separate declaration which gives the name of the instance and its (record) type. The following Ada record type and record instance declarations should be obvious:

```
type example_record_type is
  record
    first_part : integer;
    second_part : boolean;
  end record;
example_record : example_record_type;
```

In Ada, unlike Pascal, each record structure must be specified as a separate named type, which is then used in the declaration of the object; such a pair of declarations is required even if the program declares only one object of the type in question.

An individual record component can be denoted by a qualified name, such as example_record.first_part. The name before the period denotes the instance of the record, and the rest of the name selects the appropriate component from the chosen record. It is also possible to denote a record component by its component name alone, if that component name is visible (see Section A.3) and unambiguous.

A.3 OBJECT VISIBILITY

A programmer writing a complex modular program should not have to know all details of all other interacting modules in order to write one specific module. To make this simplification, the names and identities of objects local to the definition of one module should not be visible within another module unless the information is needed to support some intimate interaction between the two modules. In "block-structured" languages such intimate interactions are specified by nesting the module definitions; a "child" module defined within another module can know details of its parent module, but not details about the implementations of its own children, its "brothers," its "cousins," or its more distant relations in the definition tree that mirrors this nested structure.

Both Pascal and Ada are block-structured languages. Within a Pascal module M it is not possible to know the existence of objects declared within modules which are not direct ancestors of M. The contents of more distantly related modules, such as "uncles" and "aunts," are not visible within M. In Ada, on the other hand, under certain conditions an object declared in a module can be named within M by a qualified name that starts with the unambiguous name of a module that is either a direct ancestor of M or the child of a direct ancestor of M. Thus the name q.p could refer to the object p declared in the module named q.

A.4 PROCESSING STATEMENTS

The basic processing statement is the simple assignment statement

```
⟨name⟩ := ⟨expression⟩;
```

When this statement is executed, the expression is evaluated and the result of that evaluation is placed into the named object. The types of the expression's value and the object denoted by the name must match, or the statement is illegal.

A generalized assignment statement (not available in Pascal) assigns a set of values to an array or a portion thereof. The expression must also evaluate to an array or a portion thereof, so that the two sides have compatible types (recall that a specific dimension specification is part of each type declaration).

Example A-3

Here are some Ada assignment statements:

```
x := 3;
y := x / y;
b := x <= y;
m(3 .. 5, 6, 7) := m(6 .. 8, 2, 3);
locator1 := locator2;
locator3.all := locator4.all;
```

If the objects with locator names were declared to be access variables, the pair in an assignment statement must have been declared to access the same object type (if not, there is an error). If these conditions are met, the fifth statement copies locator2 to locator1, and the last statement copies the object described by locator4 into the space described by locator3 (the **.all** qualifier specifies the complete value of the object designated by the access variable to which it is appended).

A.5 ADA CONTROL CONSTRUCTS

Ada provides a flexible set of control constructs allowing specification of both structured and unstructured programs. Most of the structures are specifically included to support modular programs designed following good programming practices. We summarize Ada features supporting these control constructs:

1. Sequences
2. Conditional execution
3. Loops
4. Exits

5. Goto
6. Procedures
7. Exceptions (not in Pascal)

A.5.1 Sequences

In the absence of any explicit sequencing specification, an Ada program is executed in the sequence that the source language statements are written in the program. Sequential execution makes the program's progress clear to the reader and is easily implemented.

A.5.2 Conditional Execution

Conditional execution provides the simplest data-dependent control flow; it can be specified by the **if** and **case** statements. The **if** statement structure is identical to the structure of the **if** statement in Pascal; its structure is

```
if ⟨condition⟩ then ⟨statement_list1⟩;
  [else ⟨statement_list2⟩;]
end if;
```

The square brackets in a syntactic specification enclose an optional element in the structure. Here the **else** clause is optional.

The **case** statement specifies the selection of one out of a set of statement lists, based on the value assumed by an expression. The reserved word **when** separates parts of a **case** statement. The separator = > divides a list of selector values from the corresponding statement list. The following example should make this clear.

Example A-4

Here is an inelegant, inefficient implementation of the body of an integer square root procedure with the argument x restricted to be less than 120; for negative values and for values greater than 120, the result (in y) will be zero.

```
case x is
  when 1 .. 3       => y:=1;
  when 4 .. 8       => y:=2;
  when 9 .. 15      => y:=3;
  when 16 .. 24     => y:=4;
  when 25 .. 35     => y:=5;
  when 36 .. 48     => y:=6;
  when 49 .. 63     => y:=7;
  when 64 .. 80     => y:=8;
  when 81 .. 99     => y:=9;
  when 100 .. 120   => y:=10;
  when others       => y:=0;
end case;
```

Each simple condition in this program fragment specifies one range of values that could match the case expression value. It is also possible to specify a list of matching ranges or values within a single **when** clause; the members of the list are separated by vertical bars, as in

```
when 1 .. 3 | 6 .. 8     => a:=b;
when 0 | 10 | -2 | 13 => b:=c;
```

Here four possible selector values lead to the b:=c assignment in the last line.

A.5.3 Loops

Ada provides general loops and both **for** and **while** loops. An Ada loop is specified by a loop control statement (if appropriate), which specifies how the loop shall be counted and/or terminated, and a loop body, which is enclosed by the reserved words

```
loop .. end loop;
```

The general loop specifies the repeated execution of a list of statements; an **exit** statement is used for termination. A general loop is written with its body enclosed by reserved words, as in

```
loop
  ⟨statement_list⟩;
end loop;
```

Example A-5

```
loop
  x:=x/2;
  if x < 0.2 then exit;
  y:=y + x * x;
end loop;
```

A **for** loop names the loop parameter and specifies the range of values that it should assume during iterations of the loop. The values within the range will be assigned to the loop parameter in order of increasing values (unless the reserved word **reverse** appears before the **in**) on successive iterations. The loop terminates when all values within the range have been used or when an **exit** statement that terminates the loop is executed.

The syntax of a **for** loop is

```
for ⟨parameter_name⟩ in [reverse] ⟨range_specification⟩;
loop
  ⟨statement_list⟩;
end loop;
```

The loop parameter must assume discrete values; this means that it must be an integer or an enumerated type.

Example A-6

```
i, x : integer;
..
for i in reverse 2 .. 5
loop
  x:=x * (i+2);
  if y(x) < 1 then exit;
end loop;
```

This loop will be executed four times, with i assuming the values 5, 4, 3, and 2 on successive iterations. An attempt to write this loop control statement by simply reversing the limits of the range as in

```
for i in 5 .. 2
```

does not work because this range appears to be null, in which case the loop body would not be executed even once.

A **while** loop header specifies a boolean condition which is tested each time before the loop body is executed; the loop body is executed if the condition is true. The loop terminates when the condition becomes false or when an **exit** statement terminates the loop. The syntax of a **while** loop is

```
while <condition> loop
  <statement_list>;
end loop;
```

Example A-7

```
while x <= 7.5 loop
  y:=y+2;
  x:=x-y*y;
end loop;
```

A.5.4 Exits

The **exit** control construct terminates the execution of one or more loop bodies.

A loop can be named by associating a loop name[1] with the loop control statement (or if there is no loop control statement, the loop body), as in

```
lariat: for i in 13 .. n+2
        loop
          <statement_list>;
        end loop lariat;
```

[1]This labeling syntax is different from the syntax for labeling all other types of statements; see Section A.5.5.

If a loop has been named, the corresponding **end loop** statement should contain the name of the loop.

If an **exit** statement does not specify a loop name, it forces an exit from the immediately enclosing loop. If it specifies a loop name, the exit is taken from the designated (enclosing) loop (and all intermediate loops). The syntax for the simple **exit** statement is

```
exit [⟨loop_name⟩];
```

A conditional **exit** statement contains a boolean condition that controls whether the **exit** is performed. Its syntax is

```
exit [⟨loop_name⟩] when ⟨condition⟩;
```

This statement is exactly equivalent to the statement

```
if ⟨condition⟩ then exit [⟨loop_name⟩];
```

Example A-8

This program loop finds the first zero element in a matrix m, by scanning left to right across the rows and then top to bottom:

```
first: for i in 1 .. row_limit
       loop
         for j in 1 .. col_limit
         loop
           exit first when m(i, j) = 0;
         end loop;
       end loop first;
```

A.5.5 Gotos

The **goto** statement specifies an abrupt transfer of control to the statement whose label appears in the **goto** statement. Any Ada statement can be labeled by preceding it with the label name enclosed in double angle brackets,[2] as in

```
⟪a⟫ thing := 3;
```

The syntax of the goto statement is

```
goto ⟨label⟩;
```

One would specify a transfer of control to statement a by the statement "**goto** a;"

[2]This label syntax is different than the label syntax for a loop construct; see Section A.5.4.

A.5.6 Procedures

Three questions related to functions and procedures concern (1) how a procedure is specified, (2) how it is called, and (3) how control returns from the procedure after it has been completed.

A.5.6.1 Procedure specification. A procedure specification (called a "subprogram declaration" in the Ada syntax definition) includes a "subprogram specification" which states the name of the procedure, the names, types, and usage of its parameters, and the type of its result, if any. This is followed by the declarations (including local objects, which may be private, and modules) and then by the body (an executable statement list).

Parameters are listed in the header in the order that they should appear in the call; for each one its type and mode(s) is (are) specified. Types are specified as in object declarations. Parameter modes can be specified explicitly by preceding the type with either **in**, **out**, or **in out**, or implicitly by the absence of a usage specification (this is equivalent to **in**). A contiguous set of formal parameters of the same type and mode can share one type and mode specification. Semicolons separate parameters with explicit associated type declarations, whereas commas separate parameters within a list that shares a type declaration. This punctuation distinction appears only in the subprogram specification and not in invocations of the procedure, where commas are used. The following are legal Ada parameter lists for subprogram specifications:

```
a : integer
b, c : integer; d : real
b, c : out integer; d : in integer
```

A subprogram specification with its body declaration has the form

```
procedure ⟨entry_name⟩[(⟨parameter_list⟩)] is
  ⟨declarations⟩;
begin
  ⟨statement_list⟩;
end;
```

The declarations define "local" objects which are not to be known outside the procedure itself. The statement list constitutes the body of the procedure; execution of the procedure commences with the first statement in the body. Exception handlers may be specified after the procedure's statement list (see Section A.5.7).

A.5.6.2 Functions. A function is a procedure that computes a single result. The function procedure header contains the word **function** (rather than **procedure**) and specifies the type of the result returned in the **return** clause:

```
return ⟨type⟩
```

which appears in the header after the parameter list and before the **is**. All function parameters must be of mode **in**.

The value to be returned is specified in the body by an expression in a **return** statement, as in

```
return &lt;expression&gt;;
```

The function body may contain several **return** statements. If the last statement of a function's body is not a return statement, and control returns by completing that last statement, the program is in error and a predefined exception will be raised.[3]

Example A-9

This function squares an integer:

```
function square(x : integer) return integer is
begin
  return x * x;
end square;
```

A.5.6.3 Procedure calling. A procedure is called, or "invoked," by virtue of the appearance of its name in an expression being evaluated or in a statement by itself. Following the name is a list of the "actual" parameters in parentheses. After the procedure has completed execution, control returns to the place where the call was initiated, for completion of that statement and continuation to following statements.[4] If the procedure was a function, the returned value takes the role of the function name with respect to the evaluation of the expression in which the function call appeared.

A.5.6.4 Procedure return. The execution of a procedure is terminated if it executes a **return** statement, causing control to return to the calling program. An implicit return is executed if processing continues beyond the last statement in the procedure body.[5] A procedure may also return while propagating an exception, as described in Section A.5.7.

The control and management operations supporting procedure calling are summarized in the following steps, which describe all operations performed between the call to a procedure and the return to the calling program:

1. Create space for the parameters;
2. Copy the actual **in** and **in out** parameters into this space;
3. Save the program counter;
4. Create space for the objects local to the called procedure;

[3]Note that this condition, which could have been detected at compile time, is defined to be a run-time error.

[4]This "normal" sequencing rule will be followed unless the called procedure propagated an exception to its caller (see Section A.5.7).

[5]As noted in Section A.5.6.2, this would be an error if the procedure were a function.

5. Initialize the local objects;
6. Execute the procedure (set the program counter to the first statement of the procedure);
7. Procedure (executes and) returns;
8. Copy the values of all **out** and **in out** parameters back to the calling program;
9. Delete the local object and parameter spaces acquired on entry to the procedure;
10. Restore the saved value to the program counter;

Example A-10

Here is a procedure that computes a matrix product (of matrices A and B), leaving the result in the parameter matrix A. The matrices are square and of dimension n (a compile-time constant). The procedure does the multiplication inefficiently by calling a vector dot product function.

```
type narray is array(1 .. n) of integer;
type nnarray is array(1 .. n, 1 .. n) of integer;
procedure matrix_mpy (A : in out nnarray; B : nnarray) is
  i, j : integer;                  --local objects declared
  C : narray;
  function vector_dot(D, E : narray) return integer is
    sum, i : integer;
  begin          --local objects in vector_dot
    sum:=0;            --first action in vector_dot
    for i in 1 .. n
    loop
      sum:=sum+D(i) * E(i);
    end loop;
    return sum;
  end vector_dot;
begin            --first action in matrix_mpy
  for i in 1 .. n
  loop
    for j in 1 .. n
    loop
      C(j):=A(i, j);
    end loop;
    for j in 1 .. n
    loop
      A(i, j):=vector_dot(B(1 .. n, j), C);
    end loop;
  end loop;
end matrix_mpy;
```

Every time the vector_dot procedure is called, a new space to hold the objects sum and i will be allocated, and every time that the procedure exits, that space will be returned to the system for future use.

A procedure may be recursively defined, which means that it may be called while an invocation of it still exists. Some languages, such as Pascal and Ada, support recursion, but others, such as Fortran, do not.

Example A-11

Here is a recursive definition of the factorial function:

```
function factorial(n : integer) return integer is
begin
  if n <= 1 then
    return 1;
  else
    return n * factorial(n-1);
  end if;
end factorial;
```

A.5.7 Exceptions

Exceptions in Ada allow the programmer to specify the handling of unexpected conditions which may preclude correct system operation. They may arise in several ways. First, the system may check the operands and results of an operation to determine whether the operation can correctly be performed; if not, an exception would be "raised." Second, a programming error, such as executing an implicit return from a function subprogram, always raises an exception.[6] Third, the programmer can explicitly cause an exception by executing the **raise** statement. Exceptions are not available in Pascal.

A programmer can declare an identifier to be of type exception. The identifier can then be used as an exception name in a **raise** statement or in a selector in the exception section of a block.

Example A-12

Here is the declaration and use of an Ada exception name:

```
negative : exception;
..
raise negative;
```

An exception handler's body consists of the set of statements executed after the corresponding exception has been raised; it is the program's response to the unexpected condition. All exception responses that are to be handled in one program block are defined at the end of that program block, just before the **end** that delimits the block. One set of exception handler definitions specifies all associations between

[6]The interested reader may consult the Ada reference manual to find the set of errors that always cause exceptions.

exception names and exception handler bodies for the block in which it occurs. The block structure, then, is:

```
begin
  ⟨statement_list⟩;
exception
  ⟨handler_definitions⟩;
end;
```

The format of an exception handler definition is exactly like the format of an option in a **case** statement; exception names are used in the "value lists" to select a handler. The exception section's syntax is

```
exception
  when ⟨exception_list1⟩ =⟩
    ⟨statement_list1⟩;
  when ⟨exception_list2⟩ =⟩
    ⟨statement_list2⟩;
  ..
  [when others =⟩
    ⟨statement_list⟩;]
```

The **others** option is optional; if it is not specified, the exception section may not define a handler for every exception that might be raised. If an unlisted exception occurs and there is no **others** option in the block, the exception propagates to an enclosing block, as described below.

Example A-13

Here is a simple exception section declaring a handler for the negative exception declared in Example A-12:

```
exception
  when negative =⟩
    negcount:=negcount+1;
    flag:=true;
end block_name;
```

When an exception is raised, control immediately transfers to an internal searching process that finds the correct handler to be invoked. First, the search checks the block in which the program was executing when the exception was raised to determine whether it has an exception section and whether the name of the raised exception is listed in one of its **when** clauses. If there is no such explicit specification but an **others** condition is listed, the **others** statement list will be selected.

If the executing block does not specify a handler for the exception that was raised, the exception is propagated to the calling block (not necessarily to the statically enclosing block), as follows. The searching process forces a return from the executing block[7] and then tries to find an appropriate exception handler in the block

[7] The return implies space deallocation, as described previously.

to which control returned. If there is no handler there, the exception propagates again. If the exception propagates out of the program entirely, the program is terminated, and the propagation stops.

After the exception is raised, control passes to the search process that finds the handler, as just described. Then control passes to the first statement of the handler. The handler effectively replaces the remainder of the body of the block in which it appears and must either return on behalf of the block or raise an exception itself. If the execution point passes the end of the handler, an implicit **return** is executed. Note that the handler cannot pass control back to the point where the program was executing when the exception arose.

Example A-14

Here is a program skeleton using exceptions:

```
procedure a is
  alarm : exception;
  ..
  procedure b is
    ..
  begin
    ..
  exception
    when alarm =>
      ..                    --b's handler for the alarm exception
  end b;
  procedure c is
    ..
  begin
    ..
    raise alarm;
  end c;
  procedure d is
    ..
  begin
    ..
  exception
    when alarm =>
      ..                    --d's handler for the alarm exception
  end d;
begin
  ..     --a's body
end a;
```

If the history of calls in executing this program were

```
call a
call b
call c
call d
call c
```

and then the alarm exception were raised, d's handler would be used; the exception was propagated from c to d because no handler for the alarm exception was declared in c. If, on the other hand, the alarm had been raised during the first call of c, b's handler would have been found when the exception propagated out of c. The identity of the handler associated with the exception is dynamically determined.

A.6 MODULES

Ada provides for three types of modules: tasks, procedures, and packages, which can be used in various ways. Generally, a module allows the programmer to collect related implementations and data type definitions for convenience and ease of understanding. Tasks are used in multiprocessing, as discussed in Chapter 2 of Volume 2. A procedure modularizes in an obvious way, collecting the details of the implementation of a function into a single entity. A package collects related data and procedure implementations with visibility restrictions; packages can be used to implement new data types, as described in Section A.7. Constructs analogous to package and task modules are not available in Pascal.

The general structure of a package specification is the following:

```
package ⟨name⟩ is
  ⟨declarations of visible things⟩;
[private
  ⟨declarations of invisible things⟩;]
end ⟨name⟩;
```

The private part is optional but is needed if some of the declarations of visible things are declared "private" by use of the reserved word **private** in the declaration. A **private** declaration signifies that the representation of the declared entity (an object or a type) is to be hidden from the outside, even though the outside knows of the existence of the object or type being declared.

The package specification, like a procedure specification, describes the interface of a package. A separate syntactic structure, the package body, contains the implementation of the package.[8] The format of the package body is similar to a procedure body, as illustrated in the following example:

Example A-15

Here is a package for a random number generator that retains a seed value between calls to the generator:

```
package random_number is
  function random return integer;
  procedure seed(n : integer);    --initialize
end random_number;
```

[8]Making the package body a separate entity permits a programmer to use the package within a program which does not contain the implementation details. The actual body could be compiled separately from the program using the package.

```
package body random_number is
   old_seed : integer;
   procedure seed(n : integer) is
   begin
      old_seed := n;
   end seed;
   function random return integer is
   begin
      ..                     --compute the next random number
   end random;
end random_number;
```

The object old_seed, being declared within the package body, continues to exist as long as the process containing the package exists.

The package specification and the package body are separate syntactic entities and need not be contiguous within the program. By placing the package specification in a public place and placing the package body in a compiled file available for linking with other compiled programs, a programmer can completely hide the package's implementation details.

A.7 NEW TYPES

One powerful modularity feature in some contemporary programming languages is the ability to define new data types, hiding the details of the implementation and the representation of the objects of that type within a separate module. Even without the ability to hide the details, the ability to declare new data types can be useful. Ada provides facilities for both varieties of type definition. We present type definition through enumeration and subtyping before we turn to the general, modular technique using packages.

A.7.1 Enumeration

The possible values of an enumerated data type are listed in the declaration of the type (or of an object of that type), as in the following:

```
type thing is (first, second, last);
```

The only built-in operations on enumerated object types are successor, predecessor (these two based on the order of the entries in the enumeration), assignment and value comparison testing, such as greater than and inequality tests. For comparison purposes, the value ordering is defined by the order of enumeration, with the smallest value first in the list. Other operations on objects of an enumerated type can be defined by declaring functions whose parameters (and results) are of the enumerated type.

A.7.2 Subtypes

An object type can be based upon a previously declared enumerated type (or an intrinsic enumerated type, such as integer) by declaring that an object of the type may assume a value from a given *base*[9] type, such as integer, subject to the condition that the value assumed by the object must lie within a specified range. The following declaration is typical

```
subtype tenonly is integer range 1 .. 10;
```

The objects declared to be of the type of the subtype inherit all operations defined for the base type. Thus an object of type tenonly can participate in integer arithmetic operations and be assigned a value from an integer expression (provided that the range limitation is satisfied).

A.7.3 Modules

An Ada package module can define a type in such a way as to make visible both the existence of the type and the names of the functions manipulating objects of the type. The representations and function implementations remain hidden. This capability is not available in Pascal. The following example illustrates this structure and the corresponding syntactic constructs.

Example A-16

Here is the specification of a module for a data type "vector," including vector operations for addition, dot product, and equality comparison:

```
package vector_values is
  type vector is private;
  function add(a, b : vector) return vector;
  function dot(a, b : vector) return integer;
  function equal(a, b : vector) return boolean;
private
  type vector is array(1 .. 100) of integer;
end vector_values;
```

The **private** appearing in the type declaration hides the vector representation details from the outside. The representation details, however, must be placed at the end of the declaration block so that the translator can know how to allocate space and how to implement the assignment and equality testing operations, which are available automatically outside the package.[10]

[9]The term "base" denotes the relationship established between the new subtype and its parent type by virtue of the subtype declaration. The term does not imply that the base type must be a type built into the Ada language.

[10]The default automatic assignment and equality testing (inequality testing is also included, by complementation) operations can be explicitly excluded by declaring the type to be **limited** in the package specification. (Note that these default operations can be implemented knowing only the size of an object's representation; the details of its contents and their interpretations are not required.)

To complete the specification of the vector data type, we state how the functions are going to be performed in the package body. Here is a package body for the vector data type:

```
package body vector_values is
  function add(a, b : vector) return vector is
    i : integer;
    result : vector;
  begin
    for i in 1 .. 100
    loop
      result(i) := a(i) + b(i);
    end loop;
    return result;
  end add;

  function dot(a, b : vector) return integer is
    i, sum : integer := 0;
  begin
    for i in 1 .. 100
    loop
      sum := sum + a(i) * b(i);
    end loop;
    return sum;
  end dot;

  function equal(a, b : vector) return boolean is
    i : integer;
  begin
    for i in 1 .. 100
    loop
      if a(i) /= b(i) then
        return false;
      end if;
    end loop;
    return true;
  end equal;
end vector_values;
```

The vector package defined in the example defines the type only for vectors of integers of dimension 100. Without a way to declare and use a general specification, a similar package would have to be included in the program text to handle each combination of vector dimension and type of vector component. Ada's generic module construct adds the generality required to save the tedious similar package declaration that otherwise would be needed in the program text.

A.7.4 Generic Modules

It is tedious to have to specify a new data type for every possible vector size, so Ada allows generic module definitions. A generic module parameterizes a defining module. For example, a parameterized vector package could be used to vary both the size of the array and the type of the array entries. The formal module parameters of a generic package may include constant values, type names, and procedure (which includes function) names. The generic module header starts with the reserved word **generic** and an ordered list of declarations specifying the module parameters,[11] as in

```
generic
  size : integer;
  type T is range <>;
package <name> is
  <package_specification>;
end <name>;
```

Note that the syntax for a generic type parameter specification is different than that for a typed procedure parameter. The last part of the type parameter specification indirectly specifies the operations inherited for objects of type T; in this case the built-in integer operations are inherited (the "**range** <>" specifies that the type can be any type or subtype that assumes integer values). Table A-1 lists the generic formal type options.

TABLE A-1 GENERIC FORMAL TYPE OPTIONS FOR ADA PACKAGE DEFINITIONS

Formal Type	Operations
private	assignment, equality, inequality
limited private	none
array	assignment, indexed component selection, qualification, aggregation
limited array	same as **array**, without aggregation
access	from **access** types
<>	from enumerated types
range <>	from the integer type
digits <>	from the floating-point type
delta <>	from the fixed-point type

Example A-17

A generic module with the following heading could specify operations for a vector without knowing its size or the types of its components.

```
generic
  size : integer;
  type T is range <>;
package vector_type is
  ..
```

[11]Unlike formal procedure parameters, the list of formal module parameters is not enclosed within parentheses, even though the actual parameter list is so enclosed in the **new** declaration that creates a specific instance of the generic module.

Within the module, any vector declarations and operations would be specified in terms of the type T, as in the following specification fragments:

```
result : array(1 .. size) of T;
sum : T;
```

Example A-18

Here is a complete version of the generic vector_type package:

```
generic
  size : integer;
  type T is range <>;
package vector_type is
  type vector is private;
  function add(a, b : vector) return vector;
  function dot(a, b : vector) return integer;
  function equal(a, b : vector) return tenonly;
private
  type vector is array(1 .. size) of T;
end vector_type;
package body vector_type is
  function add(a, b : vector) return vector is
    i : integer;
    result : vector;
  begin
    for i in 1 .. size
    loop
      result(i) := a(i) + b(i);
    end loop;
    return result;
  end add;

  function dot(a, b : vector) return T is
    i : integer;
    sum : T := 0;
  begin
    for i in 1 .. size
    loop
      sum := sum + a(i) * b(i);
    end loop;
    return sum;
  end dot;

  function equal(a, b : vector) return boolean is
    i : integer;
  begin
    for i in 1 .. size
    loop
      if a(i) /= b(i) then
        return false;
      end if;
```

```
        end loop;
        return true;
    end equal;
end vector_type;
```

A generic package definition does not create usable packages; rather, one must create instances of the generic package to provide routines and definitions for instances of vectors of various sizes and types. An instantiation is requested in a declaration through the reserved word **new**, which creates a copy of a generic thing with a particular set of parameter values. The parameter values for such an instantiation must be known at translation time, and may include constant values, type names and procedure names. For example, the declaration statement

```
package vector_values is new vector_type(100, integer);
```

coupled with the generic vector_type package from Example A-18 creates a package almost identical to the one created by the program text of Example A-16. The only difference between this declaration and the one in Example A-16 lies in the naming of the type declared in the generic package. In the former example, the type was called vector. Here the type is also called vector, regardless of the parameter values given in the instantiation of the package. The type name is not ambiguous if the preceding created the only instantiation of the vector_type module. In that simple case we could declare a vector object, as in

```
test : vector;
```

On the other hand, if there were several instantiations of the vector_type module, the vector object types would have to be distinguished by using a qualified name for each different type, as in the following example.

Example A-19

Consider this program fragment:

```
generic
  size : integer;
  type T is range <>;
package vector_type is
  type vector is array(1 .. size) of T;
  ..
end vector_type;
package vector1 is new vector_type(25, integer);
package vector2 is new vector_type(25, tenonly);
a : vector1.vector;
c : vector2.vector;
```

The vector a contains integers, while c contains tenonlys; both have 25 components. The package name qualifications in the declarations of a and c are necessary because the name "vector" does not have a unique interpretation.

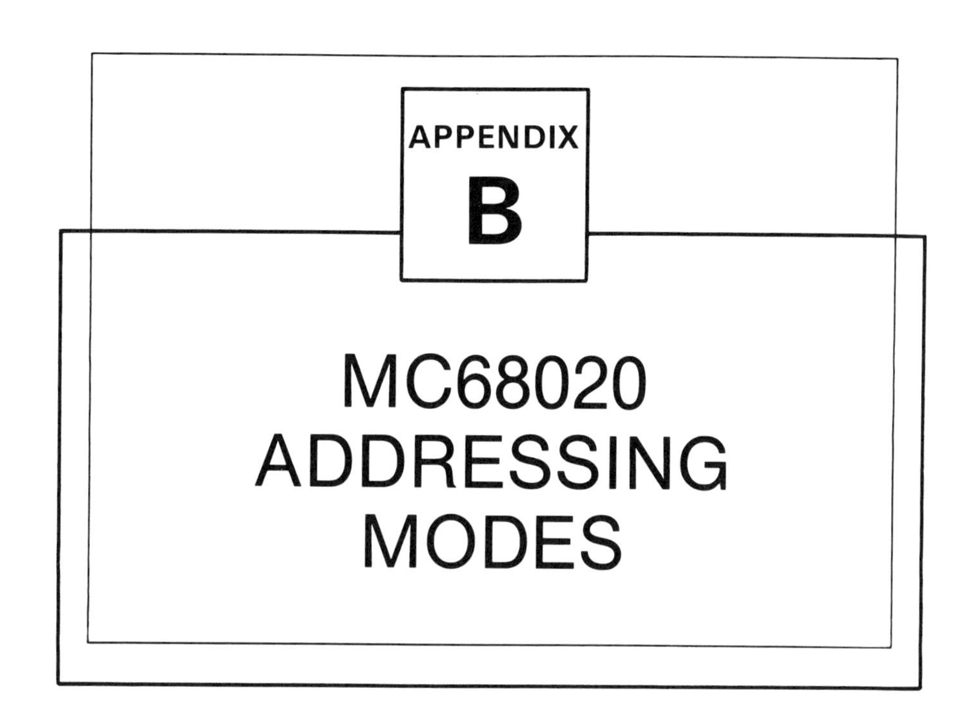

MC68020 ADDRESSING MODES

Table B-1 lists the effective addressing modes for the MC68020 processor; details of the interpretation of the modes can be found in [MOTO84].

TABLE B-1 EFFECTIVE ADDRESSING MODE CATEGORIES

Address Modes	Mode	Register	Data	Memory	Control	Alterable	Assembler Syntax
Data Register Direct	000	reg. no.	×	—	—	×	Dn
Address Register Direct	001	reg. no.	—	—	—	×	An
Address Register Indirect	010	reg. no.	×	×	×	×	(An)
Address Register Indirect with Postincrement	011	reg. no.	×	×	—	×	(An) +
Address Register Indirect with Predecrement	100	reg. no.	×	×	—	×	−(An)
Address Register Indirect with Displacement	101	reg. no.	×	×	×	×	(d_{16},An)
Address Register Indirect with Index (8-Bit Displacement)	110	reg. no.	×	×	×	×	(d_8,An,Xn)
Address Register Indirect with Index (Base Displacement)	110	reg. no.	×	×	×	×	(bd,An,Xn)
Memory Indirect Post-Indexed	110	reg. no.	×	×	×	×	([bd,An],Xn,od)
Memory Indirect Pre-Indexed	110	reg. no.	×	×	×	×	([bd,An,Xn],od)
Absolute Short	111	000	×	×	×	×	(xxx).W
Absolute Long	111	001	×	×	×	×	(xxx).L
Program Counter Indirect with Displacement	111	101	×	×	×	—	(d_{16},PC)
Program Counter Indirect with Index (8-Bit Displacement)	111	011	×	×	×	—	(d_8,PC,Xn)
Program Counter Indirect with Index (Base Displacement)	111	011	×	×	×	—	(bd,PC,Xn)
PC Memory Indirect Post-Indexed	111	011	×	×	×	—	([bd,PC],Xn,od)
PC Memory Indirect Pre-Indexed	111	011	×	×	×	—	([bd,PC,Xn],od)
Immediate	111	100	×	×	—	—	# ⟨data⟩

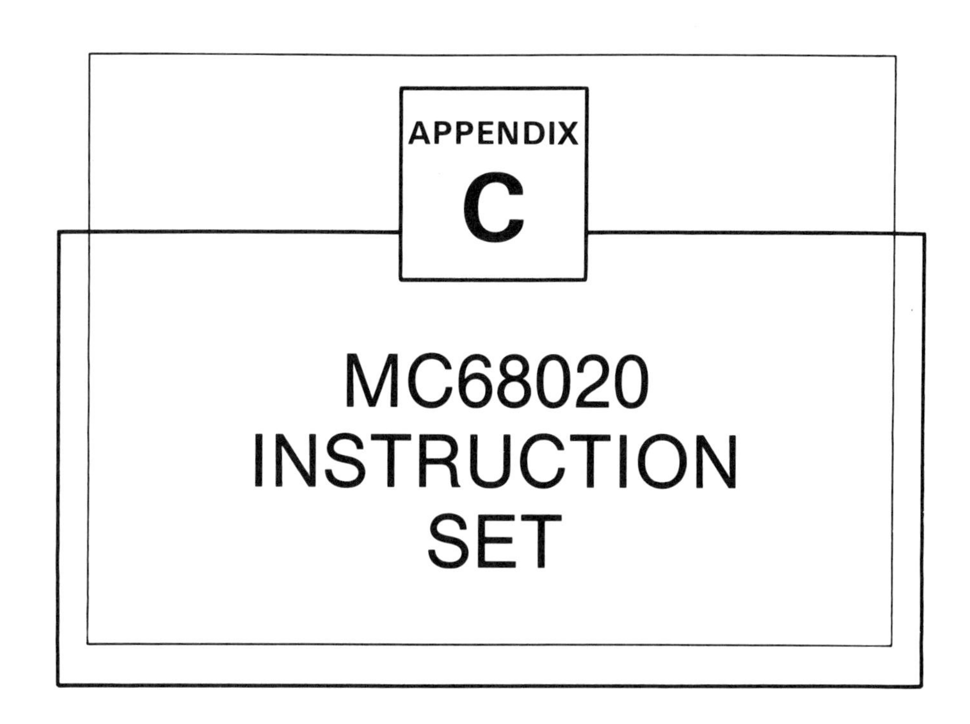

Tables C-1 through C-10 describe all MC68020 processor instructions. All instructions related to the same general function are listed together in a table; the function categories are:

1. Data movement
2. Integer arithmetic
3. Logical operations
4. Shift and rotate
5. Single bit manipulation
6. Bit field manipulation
7. Binary-coded-decimal manipulation
8. Program control
9. System control
10. Multiprocessor support

Details of these operations can be found in [MOTO84].

TABLE C-1 DATA MOVEMENT OPERATIONS

Instruction	Operand Syntax	Operand Size	Operation
EXG	Rn, Rn	32	Rn ↔ Rn
LEA	<ea>,An	32	<ea> → An
LINK	An,#<d>	16, 32	SP−4 → SP; An → (SP); SP → An; SP + d → SP
MOVE MOVEA	<ea>, <ea> <ea>, An	8, 16, 32 16, 32→32	source → destination
MOVEM	list, <ea> <ea>, list	16, 32 16, 32→32	listed registers → destination source → listed registers
MOVEP	Dn, (d_{16},An) (d_{16},An),Dn	16, 32	Dn[31:24] → (An+d); Dn[23:16] → (An+d+2); Dn[15:8] → (An+d+4); Dn[7:0] → (An+d+6) (An+d) → Dn[31:24]; (An+d+2) → Dn[23:16]; (An+d+4) → Dn[15:8]; (An+d+6) → Dn[7:0]
MOVEQ	#<data>,Dn	8→32	immediate data → destination
PEA	<ea>	32	SP−4 → SP; <ea> → (SP)
UNLK	An	32	An → SP; (SP) → An; SP+4 → SP

Source: [MOTO84], courtesy of Motorola, Inc.

TABLE C-2 INTEGER ARITHMETIC OPERATIONS

Instruction	Operand Syntax	Operand Size	Operation
ADD ADDA	Dn, <ea> <ea>, Dn <ea>, An	8, 16, 32 8, 16, 32 16, 32	source + destination → destination
ADDI ADDQ	#<data>,<ea> #<data>,<ea>	8, 16, 32 8, 16, 32	immediate data + destination → destination
ADDX	Dn, Dn −(An), −(An)	8, 16, 32 8, 16, 32	source + destination + X → destination
CLR	<ea>	8, 16, 32	0 → destination
CMP CMPA	<ea>, Dn <ea>, An	8, 16, 32 16, 32	destination − source
CMPI	#<data>,<ea>	8, 16, 32	destination − immediate data
CMPM	(An)+, (An)+	8, 16, 32	destination − source
CMP2	<ea>, Rn	8, 16, 32	lower bound< = Rn< = upper bound
DIVS/DIVU DIVSL/DIVUL	<ea>, Dn <ea>, Dr:Dq <ea>, Dq <ea>, Dr:Dq	32/16→16:16 64/32→32:32 32/32→32 32/32→32:32	destination/source → destination (signed or unsigned)
EXT EXTB	Dn Dn Dn	8→16 16→32 8→32	sign extended destination → destination
MULS/MULU	<ea>, Dn <ea>, Dl <ea>, Dh:Dl	16×16→32 32×32→32 32×32→64	source*destination → destination (signed or unsigned)
NEG	<ea>	8, 16, 32	0 − destination → destination
NEGX	<ea>	8, 16, 32	0 − destination − X → destination
SUB SUBA	<ea>, Dn Dn, <ea> <ea>, An	8, 16, 32 8, 16, 32 16, 32	destination − source → destination
SUBI SUBQ	#<data>,<ea> #<data>,<ea>	8, 16, 32 8, 16, 32	destination − immediate data → destination
SUBX	Dn, Dn −(An), −(An)	8, 16, 32 8, 16, 32	destination − source − X → destination

Source: [MOTO84], courtesy of Motorola, Inc.

TABLE C-3 LOGICAL OPERATIONS

Instruction	Operand Syntax	Operand Size	Operation
AND	<ea>, Dn Dn, <ea>	8, 16, 32 8, 16, 32	source Λ destination → destination
ANDI	#<data>, <ea>	8, 16, 32	immediate data Λ destination → destination
EOR	Dn, <ea>	8, 16, 32	source ⊕ destination → destination
EORI	#<data>, <ea>	8, 16, 32	immediate data ⊕ destination → destination
NOT	<ea>	8, 16, 32	~ destination → destination
OR	<ea>, Dn Dn, <ea>	8, 16, 32 8, 16, 32	source V destination → destination
ORI	#<data>, <ea>	8, 16, 32	immediate data V destination → destination
TST	<ea>	8, 16, 32	source − 0 to set condition codes

Source: [MOTO84], courtesy of Motorola, Inc.

TABLE C-4 SHIFT AND ROTATE OPERATIONS

Instruction	Operand Syntax	Operand Size	Operation
ASL	Dn, Dn #<data>, Dn <ea>	8, 16, 32 8, 16, 32 16	X/C ← [←] ← 0
ASR	Dn, Dn #<data>, Dn <ea>	8, 16, 32 8, 16, 32 16	[→] → X/C
LSL	Dn, Dn #<data>, Dn <ea>	8, 16, 32 8, 16, 32 16	X/C ← [←] ← 0
LSR	Dn, Dn #<data>, Dn <ea>	8, 16, 32 8, 16, 32 16	0 → [→] → X/C
ROL	Dn, Dn #<data>, Dn <ea>	8, 16, 32 8, 16, 32 16	C ← [←]
ROR	Dn, Dn #<data>, Dn <ea>	8, 16, 32 8, 16 32 16	[→] → C
ROXL	Dn, Dn #<data>, Dn <ea>	8, 16, 32 8, 16, 32 16	C ← [←] ← X
ROXR	Dn, Dn #<data>, Dn <ea>	8, 16, 32 8, 16, 32 16	X → [→] → C
SWAP	Dn	32	MSW ⇄ LSW

Source: [MOTO84], courtesy of Motorola, Inc.

TABLE C-5 BIT MANIPULATION OPERATIONS

Instruction	Operand Syntax	Operand Size	Operation
BCHG	Dn, <ea> #<data>,<ea>	8, 32 8, 32	~ (<bit number> of destination) → Z → bit of destination
BCLR	Dn, <ea> #<data>,<ea>	8, 32 8, 32	~ (<bit number> of destination) → Z; 0 → bit of destination
BSET	Dn, <ea> #<data>,<ea>	8, 32 8, 32	~ (<bit number> of destination) → Z; 1 → bit of destination
BTST	Dn, <ea> #<data>,<ea>	8, 32 8, 32	~ (<bit number> of destination) → Z

Source: [MOTO84], courtesy of Motorola, Inc.

TABLE C-6 BIT FIELD OPERATIONS

Instruction	Operand Syntax	Operand Size	Operation
BFCHG	<ea> {offset:width}	1-32	~ Field → Field
BFCLR	<ea> {offset:width}	1-32	0's → Field
BFEXTS	<ea> {offset:width},Dn	1-32	Field → Dn; Sign Extended
BFEXTU	<ea> {offset:width},Dn	1-32	Field → Dn; Zero Extended
BFFFO	<ea> {offset:width},Dn	1-32	Scan for first bit set in Field; offset → Dn
BFINS	Dn,<ea>{offset:width}	1-32	Dn → Field
BFSET	<ea> {offset:width}	1-32	1's → Field
BFTST	<ea>{offset:width}	1-32	Field MSB → N; ~ (OR of all bits in field) → Z

NOTE: All bit field instructions set the N and Z bits as shown for BFTST before performing the specified operation.

Source: [MOTO84], courtesy of Motorola, Inc.

TABLE C-7 BINARY-CODED-DECIMAL OPERATIONS

Instruction	Operand Syntax	Operand Size	Operation
ABCD	Dn, Dn −(An), −(An)	8 8	source$_{10}$ + destination$_{10}$ + X → destination
NBCD	<ea>	8	0 − destination$_{10}$ − X → destination
PACK	−(An), −(An), #<data> Dn, Dn, #<data>	16→8 16→8	unpacked source + immediate data → packed destination
SBCD	Dn, Dn −(An), −(An)	8 8	destination$_{10}$ − source$_{10}$ − X → destination
UNPK	−(An), −(An), #<data> Dn, Dn,#<data>	8→16 8→16	packed source → unpacked source unpacked source + immediate data → unpacked destination

Source: [MOTO84], courtesy of Motorola, Inc.

TABLE C-8 PROGRAM CONTROL OPERATIONS

Instruction	Operand Syntax	Operand Size	Operation
			Conditional
Bcc	<label>	8, 16, 32	if condition true, then PC + d → PC
DBcc	Dn, <label>	16	if condition false, then Dn − 1 → Dn if Dn ≠ − 1, then PC + d → PC
Scc	<ea>	8	if condition true, then 1's → destination; else 0's → destination
			Unconditional
BRA	<label>	8, 16, 32	PC + d → PC
BSR	<label>	8, 16, 32	SP − 4 → SP; PC → (SP); PC + d → PC
CALLM	#<data>,<ea>	none	Save module state in stack frame; load new module state from destination
JMP	<ea>	none	destination → PC
JSR	<ea>	none	SP − 4 → SP; PC → (SP); destination → PC
NOP	none	none	PC + 2 → PC
			Returns
RTD	#<d>	16	(SP) → PC; SP + 4 + d → SP
RTM	Rn	none	Reload saved module state from stack frame: place module data area pointer in Rn
RTR	none	none	(SP) → CCR; SP + 2 → SP; (SP) → PC; SP + 4 → SP
RTS	none	none	(SP) → PC; SP + 4 → SP

Source: [MOTO84], courtesy of Motorola, Inc.

TABLE C-9 SYSTEM CONTROL OPERATIONS

Instruction	Operand Syntax	Operand Size	Operation
			Privileged
ANDI	#<data>, SR	16	immediate data ∧ SR → SR
EORI	#<data>, SR	16	immediate data ⊕ SR → SR
MOVE	<ea>, SR SR, <ea>	16 16	source → SR SR → destination
MOVE	USP, An An, USP	32 32	USP → An An → USP
MOVEC	Rc, Rn Rn, Rc	32 32	Rc → Rn Rn → Rc
MOVES	Rn, <ea> <ea>, Rn	8, 16, 32	Rn → destination using DFC source using SFC → Rn
ORI	#<data>, SR	16	immediate data ∨ SR → SR
RESET	none	none	assert $\overline{RESET}$ line
RTE	none	none	(SP) → SR; SP + 2 → SP; (SP) → PC; SP + 4 → SP; Restore stack according to format
STOP	#<data>	16	immediate data → SR; STOP
			Trap Generating
BKPT	#<data>	none	if breakpoint cycle acknowledged, then execute returned operation word, else trap as illegal instruction
CHK	<ea>, Dn	16, 32	if Dn<0 or Dn>(ea), then CHK exception
CHK2	<ea>, Rn	8, 16, 32	if Rn<lower bound or Rn>upper bound, then CHK exception
ILLEGAL	none	none	SSP − 2 → SSP; Vector Offset → (SSP); SSP − 4 → SSP; PC → (SSP); SSP − 2 → SSP; SR → (SSP); Illegal Instruction Vector Address → PC
TRAP	#<data>	none	SSP − 2 → SSP; Format and Vector Offset → (SSP); SSP − 4 → SSP; PC → (SSP); SSP − 2 → SSP; SR → (SSP); Vector Address → PC
TRAPcc	none #<data>	none 16, 32	if cc true, then TRAP exception
TRAPV	none	none	if V then take overflow TRAP exception
			Condition Code Register
ANDI	#<data>, CCR	8	immediate data ∧ CCR → CCR
EORI	#<data>, CCR	8	immediate data ⊕ CCR → CCR
MOVE	<ea>, CCR CCR, <ea>	16 16	source → CCR CCR → destination
ORI	#<data>, CCR	8	immediate data ∨ CCR → CCR

Source: [MOTO84], courtesy of Motorola, Inc.

TABLE C-10 MULTIPROCESSOR OPERATIONS

Instruction	Operand Syntax	Operand Size	Operation
			Read-Modify-Write
CAS	Dc, Du, <ea>	8, 16, 32	destination − Dc → CC; if Z then Du → destination else destination → Dc
CAS2	Dc1:Dc2, Du1:Du2, (Rn):(Rn)	16, 32	dual operand CAS
TAS	<ea>	8	destination − 0; set condition codes; 1 → destination [7]
			Coprocessor
cpBcc	<label>	16, 32	if cpcc true then PC + d → PC
cpDBcc	<label>, Dn	16	if cpcc false then Dn − 1 → Dn if Dn ≠ − 1, then PC + d → PC
cpGEN	User Defined	User Defined	operand → coprocessor
cpRESTORE	<ea>	none	restore coprocessor state from <ea>
cpSAVE	<ea>	none	save coprocessor state at <ea>
cpScc	<ea>	8	if cpcc true, then 1's → destination; else 0's → destination
cpTRAPcc	none #<data>	none 16, 32	if cpcc true then TRAPcc exception

Source: [MOTO84], courtesy of Motorola, Inc.

REFERENCES

[ANSI83] American National Standards Institute, *MILITARY STANDARD: Ada Programming Language*, ANSI/MIL-STD-1815A, American Nat. Stds. Inst., Inc., Washington, DC, 22 January 1983.

[BARN68] Barnes, G. H., Brown, R. M., Kato, M., Kuck, D. J., Slotnick, D. L., and Stokes, R. A., "The Illiac IV Computer," *IEEE Trans. on Computers C-17*, 8, 746–757, August 1968.

[BATC74] Batcher, K. E., "STARAN Parallel Processor System Hardware," *Proc. Nat. Computer Conf.*, 405–410, 1974.

[BELA66] Belady, L. A., "A Study of Replacement Algorithms for a Virtual Storage Computer," *IBM Systems Journal 5*, 2, 78–101, 1966.

[BELL76] Bell, C. G., and Strecker, W. D., "Computer Structures: What Have We Learned from the PDP-11?" *Proc. 3rd Annual Symp. on Computer Architecture*, 1–14, January 1976.

[BERL76] Berlinski, D., *On Systems Analysis*, MIT Press, Cambridge, MA, 1976.

[BOBR86] Bobrow, D. G., Kahn, K., Kiczales, G., Masinter, L., Stefik, M., and Zdybel, F., "Common Loops: Merging Lisp and Object-Oriented Programming," *Proc. OOPSLA86, ACM SIGPLAN Notices 21*, 11, 17–29, November 1986.

[BOUK72] Bouknight, W. J., Denenberg, S. A., McIntyre, D. E., Randall, J. M., Sameh, A. H., and Slotnick, D. L., "The Illiac IV System," *Proc. IEEE 60*, 4, 369–388, April 1972.

[BURR61] Burroughs Corporation, *The Operational Characteristics of the Processors for the Burroughs B5000*, Document 5000-21005–D, Burroughs Corp., Detroit, MI, November 1961.

[BURR69] Burroughs Corporation, *Burroughs B5500 Information Processing Systems Reference Manual*, Document 1021326, Burroughs Corp., Detroit, MI, 1969.

[BURR72] Burroughs Corporation, *Burroughs B1700 Systems Reference Manual*, Publication 1057155, Burroughs Corp., Detroit MI, 1972.

[BURR73] Burroughs Corporation, *Burroughs B7700 Information Processing Systems Reference Manual*, Order 1060233, Burroughs Corp., Detroit MI, 1973.

[CAVA84] Cavanagh, J. J. F., *Digital Computer Arithmetic: Design and Implementation*, McGraw-Hill, New York, 1984.

[CICH80] Cichelli, R. J., "Minimal Perfect Hash Functions Made Simple," *Commun. ACM 23*, 1, 17–19, January 1980.

[CLOC87] Clocksim, W. F., and Mellish, C. S., *Programming in Prolog*, 3rd ed., Springer-Verlag, Berlin, 1987.

[COHE85] Cohen, J., "Describing Prolog by Its Interpretation and Computation," *Commun. ACM 28*, 12, 1311–1324, December 1985.

[CONT66] Control Data Corporation, *Control Data 6400/6600 Computer Systems Reference Manual*, Publication 60100000, Control Data Corp., St. Paul, MN, 1966.

[CONT70] Control Data Corporation, *Control Data STAR-Computer System, Hardware Reference Manual*, Publication 60256000, Arden Hills, MN, 1970.

[CRAY75] Cray Research, *The CRAY-1 Computer; Preliminary Reference Manual*, Cray Research, Inc., Chippewa Falls, WI, 1975.

[DATA74] Data General Corporation, *Programmer's Reference Manual: ECLIPSE Computer*, Order 015–000024–00, Data General, Westboro, MA, September 1974.

[DENN70] Denning, P. J., "Virtual Memory," *ACM Computing Surveys 2*, 3, 153–189, September 1970.

[DIGI70] Digital Equipment Corporation, *PDP8/e Small Computer Handbook* 1971, Digital Equipment Corp., Maynard, MA, 1970.

[DIGI75] Digital Equipment Corporation, *PDP-11/70 Processor Handbook*, Digital Equipment Corp., Maynard, MA, 1975.

[DIGI77] Digital Equipment Corporation, *VAX11–780 Architecture Handbook*, vol. 1, Digital Equipment Corp., Maynard, MA, 1977.

[DIJK68] Dijkstra, E. W., "Go To Statement Considered Harmful," *Commun. ACM 11*, 3, 147–148, March 1968.

[FAIR75] Fairchild Semiconductor, *F8 Preliminary Microprocessor User's Manual*, Fairchild Semiconductor, Palo Alto, CA, January 1975.

[FAIR85] Fairchild Camera and Instrument Corporation, *CLIPPER Module Product Description*, Fairchild Corp., Palo Alto, CA, October 1985.

[FUKU86] Fukunaga, K., and Hirose, S., "An Experience with a Prolog-Based Object-Oriented Language," *Proc. OOPSLA86, SIGPLAN Notices 21*, 11, 224–231, November 1986.

[GEHR86] Gehringer, E. F., and Colwell, R. P., "Fast Object-Oriented Procedure Calls: Lessons from the Intel i432," *Proc. 13th Annual Symp. on Computer Architecture*, 92–101, June 1986.

[GOLD83] Goldberg, A., and Robson, D., *Smalltalk-80; The Language and Its Implementation*, Addison-Wesley, Reading, MA, 1983.

[HAFT72] Hatfield, D. J., "Experiments on Page Size, Program Access Patterns, and Virtual Memory Performance," *IBM Journal of Research and Development 16*, 1, 58–66, January 1972.

[HAUC68] Hauck, E. A., and Dent, B. A., "Burroughs B6500/B7500 Stack Mechanism," *Proc. 1968 Spring Joint Computer Conf.* 32, 245–251, 1968.

[HENN82] Hennessy, J., Jouppi, N., Baskett, F., Gross, T., and Gill, J., "Hardware/Software Tradeoffs for Increased Performance," *ACM Computer Architecture News 10*, 2, 2–11, March 1982.

[HEWL73] Hewlett-Packard, Inc., *HP3000 Computer System Reference Manual*, HP Manual Part 030000-90019, Hewlett-Packard, Inc., Palo Alto, CA, September 1973.

[HOAR69] Hoare, C. A. R., "An Axiomatic Basis for Computer Programming," *Commun. ACM 12*, 10, 576–580, October 1969.

[HONE80] Honeywell, Inc., *Honeywell Level 6 Minicomputer Systems Handbook*, order no. CC71a, Honeywell, Inc., Billerica, MA, June 1980.

[HUFF52] Huffman, D. A., "A Method for the Construction of Minimum-Redundancy Codes," *Proc. IRE 40*, 9, 1098–1101, September 1952.

[IBM55] IBM Corporation, 704 *Electronic Data-Processing Machine Manual of Operation*, Form 24–6661–2, IBM Corp., New York, 1955.

[IBM80] IBM Corporation, *IBM System/38 Functional Concepts Manual*, Document GA21–9330-0, IBM Corp., New York, June 1980.

[IBM81a] IBM Corporation, *IBM System/38 Functional Reference Manual*, Document GA21–9331–1, File S38–01, IBM Corp., February 1981.

[IBM81b] IBM Corporation, *System/370 Principles of Operation*, Document GA22–7000-7, File S370-01, IBM Corp., New York, March 1981.

[IEEE85] Institute of Electrical and Electronic Engineers, *Binary Floating-Point Arithmetic*, IEEE Standard 754–1985, IEEE, New York, 1985.

[INTE83] Intel Corporation, *iAPX 286 Hardware Reference Manual*, Publication 210760, Intel Corp., Santa Clara, CA, 1983.

[KAUF84] Kaufman, A., "Tailored-List and Recombination-Delaying Buddy Systems," *ACM Trans. on Programming Languages and Systems 6*, 1, 118–125, January 1984.

[KLAP86] Klapp, O. E., *Overload and Boredom: Essays on the Quality of Life in the Information Society*, Greenwood Press, Westport, CT, 1986.

[KNUT73] Knuth, D. E., *The Art of Computer Programming*, vol. 3, *Sorting and Searching*, Addison-Wesley, Reading MA, 1973.

[KUCK82] Kuck, D. J., and Stokes, R. A., "The Burroughs Scientific Processor (BSP)," *IEEE Trans. on Computers C-31*, 5, 363–376, May 1982.

[LAWR75] Lawrie, D. H., "Access and Alignment of Data in An Array Processor," *IEEE Trans. on Computers C-24*, 12, 1145–1155, December 1975.

[LAWR82] Lawrie, D. H., and Vora, C. R., "The Prime Memory System for Array Access," *IEEE Trans. on Computers C-31*, 5, 435–442, October 1982.

[MEYE86] Meyer, B., "Genericity versus Inheritance," *Proc. OOPSLA86, SIGPLAN Notices 21*, 11, 391–405, November 1986.

[MOON85] Moon, D. A., "Architecture of the Symbolics 3600," *Proc. 12th Annual Symp. on Computer Architecture*, 76–83, June 1985.

[MOON86] Moon, D. A., "Object-Oriented Programming with Flavors," *Proc. OOPSLA86, ACM SIGPLAN Notices 21*, 11, 1–8, November, 1986.

[MOON87] Moon, D. A., "Symbolics Architecture," *Computer 20*, 1, 43–52, January 1987.

[MOTO84] Motorola, Inc., *MC68020 32–Bit Microprocessor User's Manual*, Prentice-Hall, Englewood Cliffs, NJ, 1984.

[NANO72] Nanodata Corporation, *QM-1 Hardware Level User's Manual*, Nanodata Corp., Williamsville, NY, 1972.

[ORGA72] Organick, E. I., *The MULTICS System*, MIT Press, Cambridge, MA, 1972.

[ORGA73] Organick, E. I., *Computer System Organization: The B5700/B6700 Series*, Academic Press, New York, 1973.

[ORGA83] Organick, E. I., *A Programmer's View of the Intel 432 System*, McGraw-Hill, New York, 1983.

[OSEC84] Osecky, B. D., Georg, D. D., and Bucy, R. J., "The Design of a General-Purpose Multiple-Processor System," *HP Journal 35*, 3, 34–38, March 1984.

[PATT82] Patterson, D. A., and Sequin, C. H., "A VLSI RISC," *Computer 15*, 9, 8–21, September 1982.

[RADI82] Radin, G., "The 801 Minicomputer," *ACM Computer Architecture News 10*, 2, 39–47, March 1982; also in *IBM Journal of Research and Development 27*, 3, 237–246, May 1983.

[RAND64] Randell, B., and Russell, L., *Algol60 Implementation*, Academic Press, London, 1964.

[SDS66] Scientific Data Systems, *SDS 940 Computer Reference Manual*, Publication 900640A, Scientific Data Systems, Santa Monica, CA, August 1966.

[SHER84] Sherburne, R. W., Jr., Katevenis, M. G. H., Patterson, D. A., and Sequin, C. H., "A 32-Bit NMOS Processor with a Large Register File," *IEEE Journal of Solid-State Circuits SC-19*, 5, 682–689, October 1984.

[SEBE85] Sebesta, R. W., and Taylor, M. A., "Minimal Perfect Hash Functions for Reserved Word Lists," *ACM SIGPLAN Notices 20*, 12, 47–53, December 1985.

[SIEW82] Siewiorek, D. P., Bell, C. G., and Newell, A., *Computer Structures: Principles and Examples*, McGraw-Hill, New York, 1982.

[SLEA85] Sleator, D. D., and Tarjan, R. E., "Amortized Efficiency of List Update and Paging Rules," *Commun. ACM 28*, 2, 202–208, February 1985.

[SMIT82] Smith, A. J., "Cache Memories," *ACM Computing Surveys 14*, 3, 473–530, September 1982.

[SMIT83] Smith, J. E., and Goodman, J. R., "A Study of Instruction Cache Organizations and Replacement Policies," *Proc. 10th Annual Symp. on Computer Architecture*, June 1983.

[SNYD86] Snyder, A., "Encapsulation and Inheritance in Object-Oriented Programming Languages," *Proc. OOPSLA86, SIGPLAN Notices 21*, 11, 38–45, November 1986.

[SUPN84] Supnik, R. M., "MicroVAX 32, a 32 Bit Microprocessor," *IEEE Jour. of Solid-State Circuits SC-19*, 5, 675–681, October 1984.

[SYMB86] Symbolics, Inc., *Internals, Processes, and Storage Management*, Document 999008, Symbolics, Inc., Cambridge, MA, July 1986.

[TENG83] Teng, M.-H., "Comments on the Prime Memory Systems [sic] for Array Access," *IEEE Trans. on Computers C-32*, 11, 1072, November 1983.

[TIME83] "A New World Dawns," (Machine of the Year), *Time Magazine*, January 3, 1983

[TYNE81] Tyner, P. *iAPX432 General Data Processor Architecture Reference Manual*, Order Number 171860-001, Intel Corp., Aloha, OR, 1981.

[UNIV65] Univac, *1108 Multi-processor System System Description*, Order UP-4046, UNIVAC Data Processing Division, St. Paul, MN, (no date—approx. 1965).

[WILK53] Wilkes, M. V., and Stringer, J. B., "Microprogramming and the Design of the Control Circuits in an Electronic Digital Computer," *Proc. of the Cambridge Philosophical Society 49*, 230-238, 1953; reprinted in [SIEW82].

[WILK56] Wilkes, M. V., "The Best Way to Design an Automatic Calculating Machine," *Report of Manchester University Computer Inaugural Conference*, 16–18, Ferranti, Ltd., London, 1956.

[WILN72] Wilner, W. T., "Design of the Burroughs B1700," *Proc. American Federation of Information Processing Societies, Fall Joint Computer Conference 41*, 489–497, 1972.

[WINS84] Winston, P. H., and Horn, B. K. P., *LISP* (2nd ed.), Addison-Wesley, Reading, MA, 1983.

INDEX